DIRECTIONS

Slum Upgrading and Participation

Lessons from Latin America

Ivo Imparato
Jeff Ruster

THE WORLD BANK
WASHINGTON, D.C.

© 2003 The International Bank for Reconstruction and Development/The World Bank
1818 H Street, NW
Washington, DC 20433
Telephone 202-473-1000
Internet www.worldbank.org
E-mail feedback@worldbank.org

All rights reserved
1 2 3 4 06 05 04 03

The findings, interpretations, and conclusions expressed herein are those of the authors and do not necessarily reflect the views of the Board of Executive Directors of the World Bank or the governments they represent.

The World Bank does not guarantee the accuracy of the data included in this work. The boundaries, colors, denominations, and other information shown on any map in this work do not imply any judgment on the part of the World Bank concerning the legal status of any territory or the endorsement or acceptance of such boundaries.

Rights and Permissions
The material in this work is copyrighted. Copying and/or transmitting portions or all of this work without permission may be a violation of applicable law. The World Bank encourages dissemination of its work and will normally grant permission promptly.

For permission to photocopy or reprint any part of this work, please send a request with complete information to the Copyright Clearance Center, Inc., 222 Rosewood Drive, Danvers, MA 01923, USA, telephone 978-750-8400, fax 978-750-4470, www.copyright.com.

All other queries on rights and licenses, including subsidiary rights, should be addressed to the Office of the Publisher, World Bank, 1818 H Street, NW, Washington, DC 20433, USA, fax 202-522-2422, e-mail pubrights@worldbank.org.

Cover photo: Rincón Grande de Pavas, San José, Costa Rica. Photo by José Antonio Venegas. Cover design by Grammarians.

Library of Congress Cataloging-in-Publication Data
Imparato, Ivo, 1959–
  Slum upgrading and participation: lessons from Latin America / Ivo Imparato, Jeff Ruster.
    p. cm. – (Directions in development)
  Includes bibliographical references.
  ISBN 0-8213-5370-5
  1. Urban poor—Housing—Latin America. 2. Community development, Urban—Latin America. 3. Slums—Latin America. 4. Urban poor—Housing—Latin America—Case studies. 5. Community development, Urban—Latin America—Case studies. 6. Slums—Latin America—Case studies. I. Ruster, Jeff. II. Title. III. Series.

HD7287.96.L29I46 2003
307.3'44'098—dc21

2003050072

Contents

Foreword	vii
Preface	ix
Acknowledgments	xiii
Authors and Task Team	xvii
Acronyms and Abbreviations	xix
Introduction	1
PART I: LESSONS FROM THE FIELD	**13**
1. **Facets of Participation**	**15**
The Impact of Participation	18
What Is Participation and Who Benefits from It?	19
Levels and Degrees of Participation	22
Motivations for Urban Upgrading and Housing Programs	28
Some Considerations Regarding Poverty and Social Capital	36
Sustainability and Local Initiative	42
2. **Case Summaries**	
Statistical Comparisons	47
Case Study #1. Bolivia: The People's Participation Law	56
Case Study #2. Brazil: The Guarapiranga Program, São Paulo	61

	Case Study #3. Costa Rica: FUPROVI's Habitat Popular Urbano Program, San José	65
	Case Study #4. Mexico: Community Upgrading Programs, Tijuana	69
	Case Study #5. Peru: The Self-Managed Urban Community of Villa El Salvador, Lima	73
	Other Relevant Cases	76
3.	**Organizing Participation: The Project Level**	**95**
	Development Projects and the Social Process	95
	The Significance of a Strong Social Intermediary	97
	Community Organization and Level of Participation	118
	Community Organization: Area-Based, Interest Group-Based, or Some Combination Thereof?	128
	The Issue of Gender	133
	Looking out for Vulnerable Groups	136
	Mobilizing Local Knowledge and Resources	138
	Information and Communication: Social Marketing Strategies	142
	Participatory Area Development Planning	146
	Creating Incentives for Landlords and Tenants	150
	Privatized Utilities and the Urban Poor	152
4.	**Focusing on Process: Program Design and Rollout Strategies**	**155**
	Stage 1. Preidentification and Consensus-Building	157
	Stage 2. Prefeasibility Studies and Program Identification	163
	Stage 3. Feasibility Studies and Program Design	193
	Stage 4. Establishing a Program Monitoring and Evaluation System	200
	Stage 5. Rolling out the Program	208
5.	**Scaling Up: The Policy Level**	**227**
	Political Will	227
	Policy Environment and a Citywide Upgrading Strategy	230
	Area-Based Needs Assessment, Planning, and Implementation	232
	Subsidy Structures and Cost Recovery Strategies	236
	Legal and Regulatory Framework	243
	Ensuring Land Availability and Security of Land Tenure	248
	Strategic Alliances	253
	Institutional Arrangements and Decentralization	266
	Development of a Critical Mass of Local Capabilities	276
	The Role of Microfinance in Community Infrastructure	279

PART II. VOICES FROM THE FIELD

6. Bolivia: The People's Participation Law — 289
   The Importance of the Bolivian Experience — 290
   Background — 292
   Participatory Process: Law 1551 — 294
   Legal and Regulatory Framework — 313
   Resource Mobilization and Financial Sustainability — 316
   Actors, Alliances, and Institutional Arrangements — 318
   Organization and Implementation — 325
   Scale and Sustainability — 326
   Conclusions — 327

7. Brazil: The Guarapiranga Program, São Paulo — 329
   The Importance of the Guarapiranga Experience — 331
   Background — 332
   Participatory Process — 335
   Legal and Regulatory Framework — 342
   Resource Mobilization and Financial Sustainability — 346
   Actors, Alliances, and Institutional Arrangements — 350
   Organization and Implementation — 354
   Scale and Sustainability — 358
   Conclusions — 361

8. Costa Rica: FUPROVI's Habitat Popular Urbano Program, San José — 365
   The Importance of the FUPROVI Experience — 365
   Background — 366
   Participatory Process — 372
   Legal and Regulatory Framework — 379
   Resource Mobilization and Financial Sustainability — 381
   Actors, Alliances, and Institutional Arrangements — 385
   Design and Technology — 386
   Scale and Sustainability — 388
   Conclusions — 393

9. Mexico: Community Upgrading Programs, Tijuana — 397
   The Importance of the Tijuana Experience — 398
   Background — 398
   Participatory Process — 407
   Legal and Regulatory Framework — 411
   Resource Mobilization and Financial Sustainability — 414
   Actors, Alliances, and Institutional Arrangements — 417

Organization and Implementation	420
Scale and Sustainability	423
Conclusions	427

10. Peru: The Self-Managed Urban Community of Villa El Salvador, Lima — 431

The Importance of the VES Experience	432
Background	436
Participatory Process	439
Legal and Regulatory Framework	441
Resource Mobilization and Financial Sustainability	445
Actors, Alliances, and Institutional Arrangements	450
Design and Technology	458
Scale and Sustainability	466
Conclusions	468

Appendix A. Sample Strategic Plan Outline — 471

Appendix B. Sample Operating Manual Outline — 475

References — 479

Foreword

Oscar Arias

Decent shelter is a basic human need and a basic human right. But as Latin America's urban population continues to grow at a rapid rate, providing safe, sanitary, affordable housing and basic infrastructure for all city-dwellers will become an increasingly serious challenge for the region's policymakers. Already, tens of millions of Latin Americans live precariously in informal settlements, often lacking access to basic social services. In the years ahead, the demand for housing will rise further as Latin America's children reach adulthood and start families of their own. While today 60 percent of the region's population is between 15 and 65 years of age, it is estimated that that figure will rise to 70 percent within the next 20 years. Unless the increasing demand for housing is met, the slums and shantytowns of our region will continue to expand, contributing to the rise of such social problems as crime, violence, poverty, unemployment, and disease. Moreover, unless Latin America's slums are replaced by improved settlements, another generation of our children will grow up without the education that they will need to be productive contributors to the global economy, without faith in democratic institutions, and without hope for the future.

As president of Costa Rica from 1986 to 1990, I made the provision of housing a top priority of my administration. At a time when our urban population was expanding rapidly, I pledged to oversee the construction of 20,000 housing units per year. In a small country like Costa Rica, which had just over 500,000 units of housing in the mid-1980s, such a program was truly ambitious. In the end, we were able to provide many more than the promised 80,000 housing units during the four years of my presidency. Indeed, on a per capita basis, we built more houses than any other country in Latin America. The energy that was invested in the provision of housing and basic infrastructure during those years gave rise to several innovative initiatives, including one that is described in this book. These efforts reflected a desire on the part of my government to meet the most pressing needs of the Costa Rican people, but these programs also reflected my conviction that the availability of decent shelter is an essential precondition for social stability and economic growth. As I said when I received the Nobel Peace Prize in 1987, "We are convinced that a land free of slums will be a land free of hatred."

This publication is intended to help Latin American leaders confront the growing need for housing and basic infrastructure in the cities of our region. Recognizing that traditional public housing policies are unlikely to meet the needs of the urban poor, the authors of this work have sought out successful examples of "participatory urban upgrading." This approach to the provision of shelter calls for the improvement of the built environment within existing settlements, and it calls for the active involvement of members of the community in the enhancement of their neighborhoods. To be sure, implementing participatory urban upgrading on a scale large enough to transform all the slums of our region will be a major challenge, but the case studies included in this book provide a useful "road map" for policymakers interested in this promising approach.

This book also shows, through some remarkable Latin American examples, that it is possible to make a difference in the lives of hundreds of thousands of people through large-scale slum upgrading. This idea is one of the conceptual underpinnings of the "Cities Alliance for Cities Without Slums" action plan, launched by the United Nations and the World Bank in December 1999, under the patronage of President Nelson Mandela. This initiative is the most ambitious attempt to date to face up to the challenge of scaling up slum upgrading and fighting urban poverty worldwide. In his report to the Millennium Assembly of the United Nations, Secretary-General Kofi Annan urged all UN member states to endorse the Cities Without Slums initiative. The world leaders who gathered together in New York for the Millennium Assembly in September 2000 heeded his call and integrated the central aim of the Cities Without Slums action plan—to have achieved a significant improvement in the lives of at least 100 million slum dwellers by 2020—into the United Nations' Millennium Development Goals. It is a pleasure for me to add my own voice to President Mandela's and Secretary-General Annan's rallying cry to the international community for a world free of slums. I hope that this book will prove to be a useful tool in this crucially important endeavor.

Preface

This book talks about participation, from the first to the last page. And that is its strength, for participation is a road leading to democracy. The true participation it talks about does not rely on hours of compulsory labor or imposed levies; there is nothing forced about it. Rather, it is a process in which men and women engage their will, their sense of responsibility, their abilities, their dignity. It is a vital participation, because it affects much of what makes for a better life in a poor neighborhood: water supplies, sanitation, electricity, roads, drainage, public spaces, housing.

For some, participation creates risks, whether of popular protests, mismanaged conflicts of interest, or mounting expectations that are difficult to meet. But, in reality and above all, participation creates opportunity. It favors civic learning and people's empowerment. It opens the way to alternatives. It enhances the quality of projects and the continuity of development. It enables an escape from rigid control or populist clientelism into a practice of strategies of negotiation. And it does this without naïveté, because it does not address ideal communities of 21st century *bons sauvages*. Instead, it creates informed and responsible citizens. Therefore, the participation of the urban poor and disadvantaged should be seen as evidence of a new path to development.

Equally important, this book is the testimony of voices from the field—a direct product of participation. The field is Latin America, the most urbanized developing continent, today experimenting with decentralization, democratization, and participation. Among numerous and diverse experiences, this book zeroes in on five cases, examining in detail their weaknesses, constraints, and successes. This analysis is undertaken with a deep understanding of the local contexts, relations among social actors, institutional arrangements, and financial mechanisms that make up the complexity of an urban upgrading program. The result is a set of rich, interesting, living lessons that may be transposed to other continents when adapted to their particular local contexts.

Above all, these voices from the field come also from the poor and the excluded. They tell us that the poor are active, dynamic, creative. Instead of seeing themselves as victims of some societal ill, they want to fill roles as responsible and committed partners. It is time to drop our negative stereotypes surrounding poverty and social exclusion. The poor need social justice, democratic legitimacy, respect, and dignity. Moreover, as strongly expressed in the Recife Declaration of 1996 on urban poverty: "Each one of us wants to be considered by what he is and what he can do, and not for what he lacks." The inhabitants of Guarapiranga's *favelas*, in São Paulo, Brazil, confirm this idea. As described in chapter 7 of this book, they began to feel like ordinary citizens once they had an address, with a postman coming to their home and bringing them bills for water and electricity.

Among the poor, women are often on the frontlines. Because they are concerned with the survival of their home and of their neighborhood, they prove themselves to be innovative and committed. These voices from the field are calling forth a new culture of rights and responsibilities to be shared among all social actors—from the poor themselves to local political leaders—so that they may all coexist and interact in more democratic cities.

Furthermore, this book is a road map indicating the route ahead. Through hundreds of lessons learned in communities, municipalities, and favelas, it gives us the rules of the road, complete with road signs—"no entry," "danger," "one-way street," "speed limit." A slum upgrading program is not a collection of technical actions to be performed independently of each other. It is an integrated and comprehensive intervention aimed at improving the physical characteristics of a neighborhood and its inhabitants' quality of life. This is very clearly stated and described. What is more, the book offers many tools—multidisciplinary tools—presented with the precautions to be taken and the variety of paths that can be followed.

Social tools are presented first; these range from identifying key conditions to strengthening community organization, building strategic alliances, and communication strategies. Next, institutional arrangements to be invented to meet local conditions and expectations through—as demonstrated by the FUPROVI experience in Costa Rica—a combination of political will and social vision on the part of civil society actors. Financial tools are presented and discussed at length. But in spite of the innovations applied in some programs, the importance of cost recovery and payment for services is still little understood in a paternalistic political culture where hidden subsidies prevail over transparent ones. As to political tools, participation and decentralization trends create room for negotiation and encourage new approaches, such as tenure regularization, which is considered a precondition for infrastructure investments in Mexico and for housing subsidies in Costa Rica.

All these tools may be scaled up to have a significant impact citywide. The great diversity of projects to be implemented demands an equally diverse set of tools; these will be created by drawing lessons from the past and innovating on them. And all of this without utopian naïveté—we know that some local people may oppose an upgrading project, blocking the streets or refusing to pay their bills—but with the social conviction of helping the disadvantaged and building a project with them.

Finally, this book is a future-building tool. Participation is a long trip with many obstacles, but, as a famous Chinese philosopher said, "A journey of a thousand miles begins with one step." So many pilot projects and urban programs have taken this first step, but most of them have not gone farther. Participation, undertaken as a continuous process, should lead to the continuity and sustainability of initiatives—to social, institutional, technical, and financial sustainability. Too often still, visible public works are favored to the detriment of social components or environmental education essential to sustainability. Also too often, interventions are designed for the short life span of a project and not for a continuous long-term process of development after the project.

Development needs innovative mentalities and new forces. A new generation of community leaders is emerging with high ideals of democratic participation. A new generation of politicians, too, is aligning itself against traditional paternalism and for a culture of responsibility and transparency. As observed by a neighborhood committee president in Tijuana, Mexico, "It means that this is a government that believes in its people."

New forces are also emerging in civil society. Participation is no longer seen simply as a tool, but rather as a philosophical approach benefiting all concerned. Such participation is built upon social responsibility, and is reinforced by the sense of belonging created through a participatory project. As Bolivia's Carlos Hugo Molina says of his country's People's Participation Law, "An essential objective of the people's participation process was to create the possibility of the exercise of citizenship." As states redefine their roles, a greater civic awareness together with a greater sharing of responsibilities and access to rights give shape to a true urban governance. The young mayor of Villa El Salvador, Peru, confirms this: "True participation and democracy demand transparency."

This book gives us lessons for life and hope for the future. I visited Villa El Salvador. Like the inhabitants who made this place, I believe in the construction of a real city with its schools, an industrial park, and its Internet café, called Tinkuy. They had a vision of this city, and they turned it into a sustainable project. The numerous lessons of this kind throughout Latin America send out some key messages:

- A participatory partnership between all public, private, and community stakeholders, as a new model to jointly manage the interests of the citizenry
- Shared democratic rights, in particular for the excluded, creating citizen responsibility
- New forms of "social contract" allowing citizens to better plan their neighborhoodneighborhoods and live better lives in their cities.

To believe in a democratic culture is to oppose a mentality of submission or dependency. To rethink social solidarity is to leave behind the pessimism of poverty, defending the dignity of the poorest in partnership with an active citizenry in multicultural, tolerant 21st century cities. To build these cities is a courageous challenge. It is also our human duty.

FRANÇOISE LIEBERHERR-GARDIOL
Senior Advisor and Head, Urban Section
Swiss Agency for Development and Cooperation

Acknowledgments

This book is the result of a study of community participation in urban upgrading and low-income housing in Latin America which was undertaken and funded by the Private Sector Advisory Services Department of the World Bank and the Swiss Agency for Development and Cooperation, with additional support from the Government of Japan. The study was carried out by the Brazilian consultancy Diagonal Urbana, under a contract with the World Bank. The book is being published with support from the Cities Alliance and Diagonal Urbana.

In developing the book, the task team benefited greatly from the assistance of many people and institutions. First of all, we would like to thank the many residents of *favelas* and *barrios* who gave freely of their time and told us their stories with enthusiasm and candor. Their names are given and their stories told in the case studies in part II of this book. The voices transcribed here are representative of entire communities; each interview has been a valuable testimony for which we are grateful.

We are especially thankful to Magdi Iskander, formerly the Director of the Private Sector Advisory Services Department, who supported the concept from the start and provided unfailing support to the development of the study, as did Françoise Lieberherr-Gardiol, of the Swiss Agency for Development and Cooperation. We are also indebted to those who made the publication of the book possible: Mark Hildebrand, Manager of the Cities Alliance, and Kevin Milroy, of the Cities Alliance Secretariat; Kátia Mello and Álvaro Jucá, partners of Diagonal Urbana; and Valentina Kalk, Paul McClure, and Thaisa Tiglao, of the Office of the Publisher of the World Bank.

The comments and guidance received from fellow practitioners throughout the development process have been a vital resource. We are especially thankful to Dean Cira (World Bank), Robert Daughters (Inter-American Development Bank), George Gattoni (World Bank), Eduardo Perez (CDM International and Environmental Health Project, USAID), Omar Razzaz (World Bank), M. Vitor Serra (World Bank), Teresa Serra (World Bank), Tova Maria Solo (World Bank), Kevin Tayler (formerly with GHK International, UK), and Victor Vergara (World Bank), who gave much of their time to help this project take shape.

John Abbott (University of Cape Town), Alex Abiko (University of São Paulo), Fernando Ávila Cortes (PRIMED program, Medellín), Marcello Balbo (University of Venice), Denise Bennett (World Bank), José Brakarz (Inter-American Development Bank), Chanya Charles (Program on Participation, USAID), Rafael Del Cid (ESA Consultores, Honduras), Richard Clifford (World Bank), Maria Correia (World Bank), Ilias Dirie (DfID–UK), Alain Durand-Lasserve (CNRS–Interurba, France), Ingrid Faulhaber (Ford Foundation), Elisabete França (formerly with the municipality of São Paulo, now with Diagonal Urbana), Maria Emilia Freire (World Bank), Pietro Garau (formerly with UN-Habitat, now with the University of Rome), Alan Gilbert (University College, London), Reinhard Goethert (Massachussetts Institute of Technology, School of Architecture and Planning), Germán Gómez Vásquez (PRIMED program, Medellín), Cármen González (FUPROVI, Costa Rica), Camilo Granada (World Bank), Fabrice Henry (Inter-American Development Bank), Lane Hoffman (WASTE International, The Netherlands), Giuseppe Imbesi (University of Rome), Priscila Izar (formerly at the Sanford School of Public Policy, Duke University), Audra Jones (Inter-American Foundation, USA), Christine Kessides (World Bank), Arnold van de Klundert (WASTE International, The Netherlands), Kristin Little (Massachusetts Institute of Technology, School of Architecture and Planning), Peter Loach (Cooperative Housing Foundation, El Salvador), Joyce Malombe (World Bank), Meera Mehta (World Bank), Abel Mejía (World Bank), Roberto Mingucci (University of Bologna), Josefina Ocanto (formerly FUNDACOMUN, Venezuela, now with Diagonal Urbana), Laura Petrella (UN-Habitat), Paula Pini (World Bank), Martín de la Rosa (formerly with the municipality of Tijuana, now with SEDESOL, Mexico), Anne Scheinberg (WASTE International, Eastern Europe office, Sofia), Gabriel Schor (Frontier Finance International), Hernando de Soto (Instituto Libertad y Democracia, Peru), Loredana Stalteri (Ministry of Foreign Affairs of Italy), Eloisa Ulibarri (FUPROVI, Costa Rica), Keshav Varma (World Bank), Erik Vittrup (UN–Habitat), Eric de Vries (International Labor Organization), Ian Walker (ESA Consultores, Honduras), and Anna Wellenstein (World Bank) also provided valuable input.

While the present document owes much to the comments and insights of this distinguished group, it goes without saying that any errors and omissions the reader may find in the book are the sole responsibility of the authors.

The study also owes a great deal to the institutions that provided us with information, suggestions, and logistical support during our field work. Among the many institutions that helped us along the way, we would like to single out the Vice Ministry of People's Participation of Bolivia; the municipality of São Paulo, Brazil; the Fundación Promotora de Vivienda (FUPROVI) in San José, Costa Rica; the municipality of Tijuana, Mexico; and the municipality of Villa El Salvador, the Escuela Mayor de Administración Municipal, and Desco, in Lima, Peru.

Last but by no means least, the authors would like to dedicate this book to their families: to Vania, Vasco, and Tomás, and to Claudia, Jeffrey, and Sofia, with great love and appreciation.

IVO IMPARATO and JEFF RUSTER
São Paulo, Brazil, and Washington, D.C.
May 2003

Authors and Task Team

Ivo Imparato coordinated this study at Diagonal Urbana. He is an engineer and planner who has worked in local government, housing, slum upgrading, provision of services for the urban poor, and their linkages to social policy in most of Latin America and the Caribbean, as well as sub-Saharan Africa. He has worked in municipal and state governments in Brazil, with the Italian Ministry of Foreign Affairs' development aid program (based in Rome), with the United Nations Habitat program (based in Nairobi), and was Director for International Operations of Diagonal Urbana Consultants. He currently is the Cities Alliance Regional Advisor for Latin America and the Caribbean, and a Senior Urban Specialist with the World Bank's Regional Urban and Housing Group. He is based in São Paulo.

Jeff Ruster was the Task Manager for this study at the World Bank. He is Lead Specialist – Private Provision of Social Services for the Private Sector Advisory Services Department of the World Bank. He has worked in over 25 countries on a wide variety of slum upgrading, infrastructure, social services, and economic and workforce development projects. He has worked with the U.S. Department of Housing and Urban Development, where he oversaw a $5.5 billion low-income housing and economic development loan and grant portfolio. He has served as Director of Project Finance for Sumitomo Bank and Banco Nacional de Mexico and has an M.B.A. from UCLA and a B.A. in economics and political science from Stanford University. He is based in Washington, D.C

Kátia Mello, Álvaro Jucá, Vilma Dourado, Lúcia Cavendish, José Geraldo Simões, João Jaime Almeida, Maurício Vieira, Elza Braga, Eliana Cruz, and Djanyse Mendonça, directors and field managers of Diagonal Urbana Consultants, provided essential support and inputs. The field experience of Diagonal Urbana in socio-technical support to participatory slum upgrading and housing projects provided an understanding of the key issues involved and the basis for many of the study's recommendations.

Anna Conigliaro Michelini and Enrico Novara of Associazione Volontari per il Servizio Internazionale (AVSI), Italy, helped develop the approach and methodology of the study, contributed initial drafts of analytical material, and worked as lead consultants for the Brazil and Costa Rica case studies, respectively. Through them, the study drew freely on the knowledge and experience of AVSI, which has been responsible for some of the most innovative and successful approaches to participatory social development and slum upgrading in the region.

Each of the case studies required extensive field work, which involved site visits, focus groups, and interviews. Studies typically took about six months, including field work and preparation of the field report that was the basis for the book's case study chapters. The organization of our study of Bolivia's People's Participation Law reflected the complexity of a national-level process that affects every municipality in the country. We studied the mechanisms of the law's implementation in the four largest urban areas in Bolivia: La Paz, El Alto, Cochabamba, and Santa Cruz. Bolivian consultants Luis Ramírez and Guillermo Bazoberry worked with Ivo Imparato in the four cities. For the study of Brazil's Guarapiranga program, AVSI's Anna Conigliaro Michelini and Brazilian consultant Ana Lúcia Carneiro Leão were responsible for the field work in São Paulo, with supervision from Ivo Imparato. In Costa Rica, field work in San José and surrounding areas was conducted by AVSI's Enrico Novara, with Costa Rican consultants Zaritza Cavallini and Roy Umaña, and supervision from Ivo Imparato. For the Mexican case, Ivo Imparato worked in Tijuana with Mexican consultants Sheila Delhumeau and Germán Vega. In Villa El Salvador, field work was organized and conducted by Peruvian consultant Gustavo Riofrío, who was joined in Lima by Ivo Imparato.

The authors are particularly indebted to Gustavo Riofrío and Luis Ramírez, who, beyond acting as lead consultants in Peru and Bolivia, offered the study unique insights deriving from their experience of many years in participatory urban development.

Gabriele Quinti, of CERFE, Italy, contributed the initial drafts of the sections on vulnerability, social initiative and social capital, decentralization, and monitoring and evaluation. Lupita González of *Asesorias Organizacionales*, San José, Costa Rica, provided editing services for the Spanish originals of case studies. Nita Congress, as the editor of the successive versions of the study report and of this book, contributed greatly to its structure and presentation. Violeta Vidal (World Bank, Washington) provided logistical support, and Miriam Calland (Diagonal Urbana, Recife) assisted in many ways, including travel organization, contracting of needed services, document storage, and version control.

Acronyms and Abbreviations

ABCO	Area-based community organization
ACAT	Asesoramiento, capacitación, y asistencia técnica (support, training, y technical assistance), Costa Rica
AOISPEM	AutoConstrucción de Obras de Infraestructura de Servicios Públicos con Entrega de Materiales (Self-Construction of Public Service Infrastructure Works with Delivery of Materials), Colombia
AOP	Annual operating plan
APEMIVES	Asociación de Pequeños y Medianos Industriales de Villa El Salvador (Small and Medium-Sized Industry Association of Villa El Salvador), Peru
AVSI	Associazione Volontari per il Servizio Internazionale (Association of Volunteers for International Cooperation)
CAMEBA	Caracas Mejoramiento de Barrios (Caracas Slum Upgrading), Venezuala
CDHU	Companhia de Desenvolvimento Habitacional e Urbano (Housing and Urban Development Company), Brazil
CECOPRODE-VES	Centro de Comunicación Popular de Villa El Salvador (Center for Popular Communication of Villa El Salvador), Peru
CEDURE	Centro de Desarrollo Urbano y Regional (Center for Urban and Regional Development), Bolivia
CESPT	Comisión Estatal de Servicios Públicos de Tijuana (State Commission for Public Services of Tijuana), Mexico

CFIA	Colegio Federado de Ingenieros y Arquitectos (Federation of Engineers and Architects), Costa Rica
CIF	Community infrastructure fund, Mexico
CIPRODEC	Centro de Investigación y Promoción del Desarrollo Economico y Comunal (Research Center for the Promotion of Economic and Community Development), Bolivia
CNR	National Committee for Reconstruction
COELBA	Companhia de Eletricidade do Estado da Bahia (Bahia Light and Power Company), Brazil
COFOPRI	Comisión de Formalización de la Propiedad (Commission for the Formalization of Informal Property), Peru
CONALJUVE	Confederación Nacional de Juntas de Vecinos (National Confederation of Neighborhood Associations), Bolivia
COPLADEM	Comité de Planeación Para el Desarrollo Municipal (Planning Committee for Municipal Development), Mexico
CORETTE	Comisión para la Regularización de la Tenencia de la Tierra en el Estado (State Commission for the Regularization of Land Tenure), Mexico
CUAVES	Comunidad Urbana Autogestionaria de Villa El Salvador (Self-Managed Urban Community of Villa El Salvador), Peru
Desco	Centro de Estudios y Promoción del Desarrollo (Center for Development Studies and Promotion), Peru
DESOM	Desarrollo Social Municipal (Municipal Administration of Social Development), Mexico
EMCALI	Municipal Public Works Company of Cali, Colombia
EXPOPYME	Exposición de Pequeñas y Medias Empresas (Exposition of Small and Medium-Sized Businesses), Peru
FEJUVE	Federación de juntas de vecinos (neighborhood association federation), Bolivia
FEPOMUVES	Federación Popular de Mujeres de Villa El Salvador (Women's Federation of Villa El Salvador), Peru
FUNAPS	Fundo de Apoio à Participação Social (Social Participation Support Fund), Brazil
FUNDACOMUN	Fundación para el Desarrollo Comunitario y Municipal (Municipal and Community Development Foundation), Venezuela
FUNHAVI	Fundación Habitat y Vivienda (Habitat and Housing Foundation), Mexico

FUPROVI	Fundación Promorora de Vivienda (Foundation for the Promotion of Housing), Costa Rica
GDP	Gross domestic product
GNP	Gross national product
GTZ	Gesellschaft für Technische Zusammenarbeit (German Technical Cooperation)
HDI	Human Development Index
IDB	Inter-American Development Bank
IFAD	International Fund for Agricultural Development
IFFI	Instituto de Fomento y Formación Femenina (Institute of Integrated Training for Women), Bolivia
IIPLAM	Instituto de Investigaciones y Planificación (Municipal Research and Planning Institute), Bolivia
IMAS	Instituto de Asistencia Social (National Social Welfare Institute), Costa Rica
INETT	Inmobiliaria del Estado (State Real Estate Board), Mexico
INVERMET	Fondo Metropolitano de Inversiones (Metropolitan Investment Fund), Peru
INVU	Instituto Nacional de Vivienda y Urbanismo (National Housing and Urban Development Institute), Costa Rica
MDP	Municipal development plan, Bolivia
MFI	Microfinance institution
MIS	Management information system
NGO	Nongovernmental organization
OSC	Obra Social Comunitaria (Social Community Works), Mexico
PAN	Partido Acción Nacional (National Action Party), Mexico
PAP	Participatory Action Planning
PLN	Partido de Libertación Nacional (National Liberation Party), Costa Rica
PREZEIS	Projeto de Interesse de Zonas Especiais (Plan for the Regularization and Urbanization of Special Zones of Social Interest), Brazil
PRI	Partido Revolucionario Institucional (Institutional Revolutionary Party), Mexico
PRIMED	Programa Integral de Mejoramiento de Barrios Subnormales en Medellín (Medellín Integrated Informal Settlement Upgrading Program), Colombia

PROSANEAR	Programa de Saneamento em Áreas Urbanas de Baixa Renda (Low-Income Urban Areas Water and Sanitation Program)
PUSC	Partido de Unidad Social Cristiana (Social Christian Unity Party), Costa Rica
PYME	Pequeñas y Medias Empresas (Small and Medium-Sized Businesses), Peru
RFP	Request for proposals
SABESP	Companhia de Saneamento Básico do Estado de São Paulo (Water and Sanitation Company of São Paulo), Brazil
SFNV	Sistema Financiero Nacional para la Vivienda (National Housing Finance System), Costa Rica
SINAMOS	Sistema Nacional de Apoyo a la Movilización Social (National Support System for Mobilization), Peru
SPCO	Specific-purpose community organization
UMU	Unidad Municipal de Urbanización (Municipal Urbanization Unit), Mexico
U.N.	United Nations
UNCHS	United Nations Centre for Human Settlements
UNDP	United Nations Development Programme
URBEL	Companhia Urbanizadora de Belo Horizonte (Urbanizing Company of Belo Horizonte), Brazil
UTP	União dos Trabalhadores da Periferia (Union of Peri-Urban Workers)
VES	Villa El Salvador
VPPFM	Viceministerio de Participación Popular y Fortalecimiento Municipal (Vice Ministry of People's Participation and Municipal Strengthening), Bolivia
ZEIS	Zonas especiais de interesse social (special social interest zones), Brazil

Introduction

A growing body of analytical work undertaken in recent years by academia and development aid institutions has quantitatively explored and documented the link between community participation in development projects, overall quality of project implementation, and project impact. Although this literature has also made some attempt to outline methodologies for projects incorporating direct beneficiary involvement, it has not provided a full range of project design options and operational strategies to address key issues or to form partnerships with the private sector and other local stakeholders. This gap is partly due to the fact that most of these studies have looked at various programs in different sectors (e.g., health, education, water and sanitation, rural development, housing and urban upgrading) in an effort to understand and quantify the impact and cost of participation rather than study each process in detail.

In the urban development field, however, going into process details is particularly necessary and worthwhile, since it is well known that the development of low-income settlements is based to a great extent on a process led by the urban poor themselves. It is also well established that the cost-effectiveness of the process and the quality of its results leave much to be desired in the absence of external support. What is not always recognized, however, in upgrading an existing settlement is that the residents usually have been building their homes and the settlement itself over the years, and that therefore they already have a "project" of sorts under way. Such a project is composed of repeated requests to the authorities for improvements and many small, incremental steps of the residents' own making. Residents have priorities and visions for the future, but usually these have not been conjoined with those of other residents and other stakeholders in an organized way and coalesced into a coherent plan. The external project promoter needs to be able to understand the process and interact with the residents when exploring ways to support them, helping the community sharpen the focus of its vision.

Participation Improves Project Implementation and Impact

The strong link between community participation and project impact and sustainability in urban upgrading and housing,[1] coupled with the need for operational strategies for participation based on a better understanding of process, led the Private Sector Development Division of the World Bank to undertake the present study. Its objective is to help local policymakers, officials, and practitioners identify policies, procedures, and program investment strategies that are appropriate to the local context as they design and manage urban upgrading and shelter projects at the local level. The value that this book intends to add to the body of existing literature on urban upgrading and low-income housing is therefore to facilitate the promotion of participatory projects by helping those responsible for their formulation and management address significant social, institutional, financial, and procedural issues.

The book is particularly relevant for people and organizations attempting to answer the following questions:

- How can we increase service provision to low-income areas?
- How can we increase the impact of projects and the continuity of the improvements they bring about?
- How can we increase private sector participation in this kind of initiative?
- How can we enhance projects' financial sustainability?
- What are the key issues this kind of initiative needs to address?

The book aims to provide local decisionmakers with options for setting up a successful project by focusing on the key features of the supply structure and enabling framework and by describing the strategic alliances that lead to their establishment. A major part of the business—and the challenge—of upgrading programs or projects is to set up just such a supply structure, but relatively few have succeeded in doing so. Many urban upgrading projects have faced severe sustainability problems or have not been able to reach significant scale.

---

[1]The terms *shelter* and *housing* are used interchangeably throughout this book to mean both the housing unit and the related basic infrastructure. Also, for simplicity, we here use the term *project* to refer to both *program* and *project*. See chapter 1 for a discussion of the use of these terms in the remainder of this book.

The book also clarifies key concepts, establishes a nomenclature, and draws from recent examples to illustrate key process issues, such as partnership strategies for working with civil society and the private business sector, the importance of participatory information gathering and area-based planning, and the need for competent social intermediaries. The underlying premises of the study are as follows:

- On the demand side, there exists a strong desire and powerful potential within low-income communities to take care of their own affairs, manage financial matters, and create sustainable assets in infrastructure and shelter.
- On the supply side, with the appropriate enabling environment created by a strong and demand-responsive supply structure, this potential can be realized,[2] deeply influencing the impact and sustainability of development initiatives and allowing upgrading and housing programs to go to scale.

This book illustrates and details the above premises by:

- Providing direct project participant feedback from recent Latin American experience through detailed investigations in five countries
- Identifying the key components of a supply structure and enabling environment
- Identifying key process issues and questions that need to be asked at each stage of a project
- Exploring key process issues to provide policy options and operational guidance to both the program cycle and the project cycle.

The literature shows that participation is beneficial to a project—and that its benefits extend well beyond the project. But costs and risks are also involved. Our goal is to help the reader negotiate a complex subject and understand the many alternatives that are available in developing a tailor-made participatory strategy. The ultimate objective is not to achieve the maximum possible level of participation or to replace the state, but to *achieve the level of participation that is appropriate to the circumstances*, taking into account project objectives and local constraints and opportu-

---

[2]One of the fundamental lessons of our study is that major progress can be made in urban upgrading and shelter for the poor through a strong, demand-responsive supply structure and enabling framework to aid community participation, which will allow a program to reap the benefits associated with participation. These benefits include the development of demand-responsive solutions, efficient use of benefits, a sense of ownership, and development of a culture of rights and responsibilities conducive to durable, long-lasting project benefits and to future development initiatives.

nities.[3] Using a qualitative and process-oriented approach, we have tried to provide information and examples that will help project designers identify the level and modalities of participation that will work for them and the components of the environment that they will need to set in place to do so.

Since the study's primary objective was to provide practical, hands-on guidance to local officials and policymakers, the perspective taken here is not tied to the requirements or procedures of any particular donor agency, development aid institution, or government.

A Qualitative Approach

We have used a qualitative approach to gather information on how key issues were addressed—and with what results—in five geographically and institutionally diverse Latin American cases with a wide variety of funding and donor involvement arrangements:

- *The People's Participation Law*, Bolivia, which links, in a national legal framework, participation to decentralization and resource allocation through local level participatory budgeting
- *The Guarapiranga Program*, in São Paulo, Brazil, a large-scale upgrading initiative with an area-based horizontal institutional arrangement and innovative participation mechanisms
- FUPROVI's *Habitat Popular Urbano Program* (Urban Low-Income Housing Program), in San José, Costa Rica, where community management of mutual-help construction is made possible by intense capacity-building and socio-technical support
- *Community upgrading programs*, in Tijuana, Mexico, where communities operate at a very high level of cost consciousness and cost control, with transparent subsidies and an upfront financial contribution from the community
- *The Self-Managed Urban Community of Villa El Salvador*, in Lima, Peru, where participation with state support and an area development plan has permitted the gradual development of a new town of 350,000, which is still in process, with remarkable advances.

---

[3]Meaningful participation is not restricted to community management approaches. Even at a consultation or negotiation level, participation will have a profound impact on a project and can produce good results, if the job of organizing it is well done. According to the United Nations Development Programme (as cited in IDB 1997b), "People may, in some cases, have a high degree of control over the project. In other cases, control may be partial or indirect. The important thing is that people have constant access to decisionmaking and power. Participation in this sense is an essential element of human development."

Each of these locations was visited by a team of experienced international and local consultants who have been involved in significant urban upgrading and low-income housing projects in Latin America and elsewhere, including urban planners, local government specialists, municipal engineers, housing specialists, and sociologists. Information was also collected on several other participatory shelter and urban development projects elsewhere in Latin America to illuminate specific aspects of key issues.[4]

To uncover the reasons behind the success or failure of various project design approaches, we needed to gain an understanding of the relationships among stakeholders and the key process issues entailed in designing and implementing a successful participatory project. Because project success often hinges on the perceptions of the local people and other key stakeholders involved—and their decision to buy into the project or not—we adopted a qualitative, first-hand approach for collecting information. The team gathered information through in-depth interviews and focus group sessions with all stakeholders, and especially with field technicians and residents of the study areas, compiling anecdotal evidence on matters that seemed particularly germane and significant to the people who took part in each local upgrading and shelter process. People interviewed also included central government officials, local authorities, politicians at various levels, neighborhood associations and their federations, nongovernmental organization (NGO) staff, private sector representatives, donor country representatives, local staff of aid programs, and academics. This method has yielded a vast reservoir of anecdotal evidence and local insights from which to draw broad and informed lessons. The basic raw materials of the study consequently consist of personal statements, which has provided us with a better understanding of the interaction between people and groups at the local level.

The material was collated and analyzed to produce the field reports and analytical chapters that make up this book, which were then read by a peer review group comprised of professionals from donor agencies, local governments, local and international NGOs, research institutions, and consultant groups. Their feedback was then incorporated; thus, many of the

---

[4]Chapter 2 presents brief descriptions of the following programs and projects: PROFAVELA program, Belo Horizonte, Brazil; AQISPEM program, Cali, Colombia; Catuche Social Consortium, Caracas, Venezuela; community upgrading programs, Ciudad Juárez, Mexico; El Mezquital project, Guatemala City, Guatemala; PRIMED program, Medellín, Colombia; PREZEIS program, Recife, Brazil; Favela-Bairro program, Rio de Janeiro, Brazil; Novos Alagados project, Salvador, Bahia, Brazil; and the *mutirão* programs in São Paulo, Brazil.

insights and recommendations in this book derive from first-hand experience of consultants and peer reviewers as well as of our study subjects.

A Broad Range of Projects

Because the present analysis is based on the qualitative elements that arose from interviews and work with focus groups, it is not our intention here to compare quantitative data in a statistically representative way. We therefore did not choose projects of comparable dimensions or with similar institutional arrangements. Even though all the cases studied are slum upgrading and/or shelter programs or projects in low-income areas in large cities in Latin America, their dimensions, intervening agents, and institutional arrangements vary widely. In this way, we hope to give the reader an idea of the range of different approaches and arrangements being used in Latin America in participatory urban development and housing.

Latin America was chosen for several reasons, most notably for its high rates of urbanization, its changing demographics, its move toward decentralization, and the broad range of participatory urban development processes that are taking place in the region. Although the cases chosen are very diverse, studying five cases in the same region allowed us to detect issues influenced by common trends—such as democratization and decentralization—and to compare process issues in a more meaningful way.

A Tool for Project Design

Throughout this book, we have tried to identify the most significant areas of concern involving impact and sustainability and to provide:

- An analysis of the pros and cons of different project options and approaches, since awareness of these options may enhance flexibility and the ability to adjust a project to changing needs and circumstances
- Strategies to increase financial sustainability through enhanced cost recovery and linkages with the private sector, including an exploration of the potential of innovative arrangements such as partnerships between local governments, microfinance institutions, local businesses, private utilities, and urban upgrading funds
- An overview of the policy environment, the legal and regulatory framework, and other requirements for scaling up a project
- An overview of the need for, and the implications of, area-based urban planning and management, including the preparation of participatory diagnoses and participatory area development plans

- Strategies for the provision of social intermediation (also known as socio-technical support) services[5]
- Options for monitoring and evaluation and for adjusting a project to changing circumstances.

For the purposes of this study, the physical assets generated by urban upgrading and low-income shelter projects include, among others:

- Provision or improvement of access roads, stormwater drainage, water supply and sanitation, and electrification and public lighting
- Improved physical planning (i.e., settlement layout improvements, improvement of access to individual plots and vehicle access, provision of open spaces and space for public facilities)
- Establishment of cadastral registers and land tenure regularization
- The building of new housing and/or the gradual improvement of existing structures.

In dealing with project costs, we have chosen to convert most cost figures into U.S. dollars at the exchange rates that prevailed at the time the costs were incurred. Thus, dollar figures throughout the book refer to U.S. dollars. This was done to give readers—especially those unfamiliar with the ups and downs of Latin American currencies in recent years—a better idea of the order of magnitude of project costs. These figures, however, should be treated with caution, since all costs were incurred in local currencies, and significant exchange rate movements have taken place in some of the countries studied. Since these movements were not necessarily matched by an alignment of each economy's internal prices, it could be misleading to try to estimate current project costs in local currency by simply converting at the current rate the dollar figures herein presented.

Our Perspective and Basic Assumptions

We now attempt to clarify some of the basic assumptions of this study.

- **Intrinsic value of participation.** Our study does *not* seek to prove that participation improves project performance—rather, for reasons that are explored in the first chapter, that is our point of depar-

---

[5]We use the terms *social intermediation* and *socio-technical support* to refer to the set of services that provide intermediation between the community and other project actors and provide technical assistance to communities, establishing a link between community social processes and the technical and administrative requirements of a project. *Social engineering* is another term used in the literature that covers this concept.

ture. We instead seek to explore different options for the organization of participation in urban upgrading and shelter projects to enhance their long-term impact.
- **External support perspective.** Our perspective is that of the external project promoter operating from local government, who is concerned with the identification, formulation, and implementation of urban infrastructure and housing policies, programs, and projects with a focus on the poor. Although our primary audience is composed of such local operators, this book should also prove useful to others, such as consultants and professionals operating at various levels from within development aid organizations, NGOs, central or provincial governments, academia, and the for-profit private sector.
- **Participatory, area-based planning.** A broad long-term vision of the development of the settlement or area of intervention, rather than the particular requirements of any single type of infrastructure, needs to be the axis for the planning of an urban upgrading project, especially in the context of squatter settlements. A participatory, integrated, and area-based approach to planning supported by participatory information gathering and analysis is critical.
- **Appropriate level of participation.** We do not agree with the idea that "the more participation the better" is true in every case. Low-income communities do not have unlimited time, and the circumstances of project formulation and implementation vary so much that aiming for the highest level of participation may not be beneficial, or even practical or feasible. Our goal is thus not to achieve maximum participation, or replace the state or the private sector in their roles. Participation may be limited in some cases to information and consultation in decisionmaking; in others, to consultation on some aspects of the project and shared control over other aspects. There is also the possibility of full control of some aspects of a project by the target group.
- **Focus on support to participation.** We of course recognize that participatory processes are often spontaneously generated and exist independently of any externally initiated project. Experience shows, however, that participatory initiatives face an uphill battle in the absence of external support and find it difficult to attain meaningful results or scale. The subject of this book is thus not "spontaneous" participation as such, but rather how development programs and projects may strengthen and interact with it, or help bring participation about when it is not already there. Cases in which there is full community control over every aspect of a process, without any external assistance, are not covered by this study.

- **A role for the for-profit private sector.** Community actors, government, and the not-for-profit private sector have traditionally dominated the scene in slum upgrading, whereas for-profit private actors have almost always been absent. Innovative arrangements are opening new avenues for for-profit private sector participation in upgrading. Examples like Guarapiranga and the new project structure that was proposed for Tijuana (see chapters 7 and 9) show that the right incentive structure may favor for-profit private sector participation, with gains in service quality, efficiency, and effectiveness.
- **The focus is not on emergency situations or the destitute poor.** We have not dealt with the direct support required by the destitute poor or with emergency situations, such as those requiring emergency shelter and food relief. Our focus is on improvements in infrastructure and housing that depend on functioning institutions and a capacity to organize and participate—a capacity that is often absent in emergencies or among the poorest residents. The projects under consideration have taken place in countries with functioning institutions; in many of them, there has been direct support and even direct financial contribution by the beneficiaries. Although some project beneficiaries (e.g., some of those of the Guarapiranga program) are certainly destitute, they are a minority.
- **An opportunity to overcome paternalism.** The process of participation offers an opportunity for the community and public institutions to interact in a new way and to overcome the paternalism in their relationships in favor of a culture of rights and responsibilities on both sides. An important part of this is the improvement of cost consciousness, leading to clear subsidy structures and socially sustainable cost recovery mechanisms that improve the financial sustainability of upgrading and housing projects.
- **Recommendations, not prescriptions.** Our recommendations throughout are not prescriptions. They are based on good practice and are meant to be used with discernment according to local needs and conditions, which obviously vary a great deal. Sometimes a suboptimal solution is the best possible one under the circumstances, given time, resource, and monetary constraints.
- **Stakeholder participation.** Stakeholder participation entails much more than just the relationship between the agency promoting the project and its beneficiaries—a point emphasized in *The World Bank Participation Sourcebook* (World Bank 1996). In the complex urban realities we are studying, there exists a multiplicity of actors and stakeholders, all with important roles. Therefore, although our main

focus is community participation, we acknowledge the importance, and explore the role, of the participation of all stakeholders.[6]

Structure of This Book

This book is comprised of two parts: Lessons from the Field and Voices from the Field. The first part contains the main lessons from the experience of participatory urban upgrading and shelter programs in Latin America. Our focus, as explained above, is on the workings and organization of participation, and on how it relates to the other spheres of a program or project. Part I begins with a conceptual framework (chapter 1) that defines and discusses the key terms and concepts used and drawn upon throughout this book. Chapter 2 provides concise versions of the five main case studies, including essential information about each case as well as key conclusions and recommendations.

The subsequent chapters in part I deal with the key issues of process in participatory urban upgrading and housing, starting at the project level (chapter 3), and moving up to the program design and rollout strategy level (chapter 4), and the policy and general framework level (chapter 5). This is not a typical order of presentation; information is usually presented in a top-down fashion, beginning at the policy level and moving down to first the program and then the project level. Our order of presentation reflects the domain and aim of this study, in which the primary idea is to move from the bottom up.

Chapter 3 thus begins with a discussion of the project level, covering its operational requirements, key project roles, and ways of fulfilling them. The chapter explores the project cycle, providing alternatives for designing and organizing participation at the various project stages—i.e., information gathering and analysis, planning, implementation, and post-implementation. Requirements for socio-technical support activities and issues of sustainability and scale are discussed.

Discussion of the program formulation level follows, exploring ways to set up a program structure that is conducive to participation and able to deal with its requirements. Chapter 4 looks at the program design

---

[6]In addition to local residents and other target groups, stakeholders in an urban development process may include public authorities with jurisdiction over the area, public or private utility companies, formal landowners, formal and informal land developers, owners and managers of area businesses, managers and staff of public or nongovernmental facilities in the area (such as health centers, schools, daycare centers), politicians and political party activists, development NGOs, religious groups, and private firms providing services in the context of a program or project.

cycle, providing alternatives for designing and organizing key program features, consensus-building among stakeholders, prefeasibility and feasibility studies, project identification, and monitoring and evaluation. It also discusses and provides alternatives for program rollout strategies. The discussion in chapter 4 of program features (type, scope, format, and structure) and how they relate to the challenges posed by each particular local situation is of particular relevance to program design.

Chapter 5, the last chapter in part I, deals with the factors that are required for ensuring the success of an urban upgrading and shelter initiative and for scaling it up; this includes the policy, legal, and regulatory frameworks as well as institutional and technical factors. The information presented is based on the cases studied and on previous experiences of the study team members.

Part II presents the five cases in detail. Each field report is based on edited transcripts of interview responses and is structured to provide an analysis of key issues in program and project formulation, implementation, and results. Chapters 6 to 10 each present a qualitative assessment based on the views of actual project participants and aim to provide an understanding of the relationships among stakeholders and the ways in which participation mechanisms and institutional arrangements influence project implementation and outcomes.

The wealth of material collected and the complexity of the subject matter have turned this into a lengthy volume. We have tried to organize the material in such a way that readers may locate specific information quickly and easily.

This book offers a panorama of participation in urban upgrading and low-income housing projects in Latin America based on field experience and a wide range of proven approaches. We hope that this material may contribute to the design of effective participatory initiatives to provide basic infrastructure, services, and shelter for the urban poor in Latin America and elsewhere in the years to come.

Part I
Lessons from the Field

1
Facets of Participation

> PARTICIPATION IS ESSENTIAL FOR SUSTAINABLE DEVELOPMENT. IF STAKEHOLDERS HELP MAKE DECISIONS AT ALL STAGES OF THE PROJECT CYCLE, THEN DEVELOPMENT PROBLEMS ARE MORE LIKELY TO BE UNDERSTOOD IN THEIR ENTIRETY AND SOLUTIONS ARE LIKELY TO BE MORE EFFECTIVE. HOWEVER, PARTICIPATION IS NOT A PANACEA; IT CANNOT SUBSTITUTE FOR SOUND TECHNICAL AND FINANCIAL PROJECT DESIGN.
> —Inter-American Development Bank, "Why Is Participation Important?," Resource Book on Participation (1997)

In this chapter, we analyze concepts related to the importance of participation and what it can do in urban upgrading and housing projects, and briefly examine the current debate on the subject. We discuss various definitions of participation, the levels and degrees of intensity of participation, and the entry points for participation—always in the context of slum upgrading and low-income housing development. We also briefly discuss key concepts such as social exclusion, poverty, vulnerability, civil society, and social capital.

The debate about participation has been so intense and partisan in the last decade or so that it will be helpful to clearly state here the conceptual underpinnings of our analysis. What kind of participation are we talking about? Why is it so important? How does it fit in with the other dimensions of a program or project? What are the key factors at work?

The *benefits* of participation that are repeatedly mentioned in the literature can be summed up as follows:

- It improves project design and effectiveness through (1) organized expression of demand, which allows a project to provide what people want at a price people are willing to pay; and (2) access to local knowledge, which helps take all relevant factors into account in the solutions proposed by a project.
- It enhances the impact and sustainability of projects through (1) demand-responsiveness, which is key in enhancing financial sustainability; (2) local ownership of projects, which is crucial to impact and social sustainability; and (3) an enhanced sense of responsibility toward facilities and services on the part of local people.
- It contributes to overarching goals such as good governance, democratization, and poverty reduction by (1) building local capacity to interact with authorities and other stakeholders to further common goals, (2) establishing clear channels for community participation in decisionmaking, and (3) giving people the opportunity to influence the actions that shape their lives.

The *cost* of participation is associated with the time and expense entailed in setting up participatory mechanisms, the procurement of specialized services such as socio-technical support, and the additional staff time required in the program formulation and preparation phases. On the other hand, although there certainly is a cost associated with participation, the evidence so far shows it to be compensated—beyond all the benefits cited above—by more cost-effective project implementation, higher accountability of project promoters, and even faster disbursement.

The *risks* of participation are basically associated with poorly conceived or poorly managed participatory initiatives. Without competent intermediation, for example, the conflicts of interest that arise during a project may paralyze it. Poor intermediation and poor management of the project cycle may mean that stakeholders' expectations are first raised and then frustrated by long delays or changes of approach, compounded by lack of information on their cause or discussion of alternative remedies to the situation with the stakeholders. This situation is unfortunately all too common and leads to a severe loss of credibility. Another risk is loss of focus, which happens when a project becomes bogged down by discussions about issues that are outside its scope. Yet another risk is that a project may be hijacked by political parties or special interest groups. Most of these risks are associated with undue interference in the program or project, or the lack of one or more of the key conditions for success discussed in chapter 5. Suffice it to say that if a conducive environment for participation is competently created by a program or project (see box 1-1), most of the risks are minimized.

Box 1-1. What Do We Mean by *Program* and *Project*?

A sometimes confusing question of terminology is the distinction between *program*, *project*, and *subproject*. In the development field, all of these terms denote an initiative to reach a series of predetermined development goals through an organized series of actions undertaken by an appropriate institutional structure. The difference between program, project, and subproject lies principally in the initiative's scope and scale. Although the word *project* is usually employed for an initiative that is smaller, shorter term, and more narrowly focused than a *program*, different institutions use different terminology which is largely a matter of the convention each adopts. We thus find it necessary to clarify here what we mean by program and project.

For example, the Guarapiranga program is often referred to in English as a project, although it is a complex undertaking that involves many quite different types of actions, such as the building of primary and secondary infrastructure for wastewater collection and treatment, informal settlement upgrading, the development of a legal and institutional model for the management of a metropolitan water catchment, and the preparation of a long-term physical and economic development plan for the area. We prefer to follow local usage and see Guarapiranga as a *program*, i.e., as a number of diverse but coordinated sets of actions that all support a common goal. We see each of these sets of actions that deal with a particular problem as a *project*. Therefore, the convention we have adopted is that the settlement upgrading component of the Guarapiranga program is called a project, and an upgrading intervention in a particular settlement in Guarapiranga is called a subproject.

In Tijuana, Manos a la Obra (Let's Roll up Our Sleeves) and its successors are referred to as programs. Each separate intervention in a low-income area is a project. We agree with this terminology, since we find that Tijuana's community upgrading programs define broad general goals and a framework for action—funding mechanisms, project identification procedures, requirements for project management—to be followed by component projects.

In sum, then, what we refer to as a *program* may be called a *project* in other contexts; similarly, what we refer to as a *project* may be called a *subproject* elsewhere. The terms are often used interchangeably; we have tried to maintain the distinction where it is necessary for reader understanding to do so.

The Impact of Participation

Participation, arguably the most powerful idea and trend currently shaping development cooperation thinking and practice, has been the subject of intense international debate in recent years.

Between 1991 and 1994, an institution-wide learning process was undertaken by the World Bank, with support from the Swedish International Development Agency, in which the experience of the Bank itself and other agencies in supporting participation was investigated. In this context, 45 studies were commissioned to investigate participation-related issues, drawing lessons from participatory projects in many fields. The costs and benefits of participation, as well as the factors enhancing participation or limiting its implementation, were studied. Options open to donor agencies and client governments for supporting participation were outlined.

Overall, the studies found that participation improves project performance and increases project impact and sustainability. There are also risks and costs of participation (touched on above) that, although normally outweighed by the benefits, do need to be addressed. This is illustrated by the studies of Hentschel (1994) and Schmidt (1996), among others. In separate empirical studies undertaken during the Bank-wide learning process, these authors came to a number of important conclusions, among which we can single out the following (Reitbergen-McCracken 1996).

- Beneficiary participation is the single most important factor in determining overall quality of project implementation. Quality of project implementation refers to the efficiency, effectiveness, timeliness, responsiveness, and accountability of the mechanisms set up to implement a project.
- Apart from better project performance, there are clear examples of participation leading to strengthened capacity of community-level groups and empowerment of beneficiaries, as witnessed by their capacity to undertake development initiatives on their own in a project's aftermath (see the examples of Costa Rica and Peru in chapters 8 and 10, respectively).
- Overall, the elapsed time from identification to the start of disbursements was not significantly longer for participatory projects than for nonparticipatory ones. In some cases, in fact, the participatory projects were actually quicker to disburse, due to increased stakeholder commitment and better project performance.
- Participatory projects cost the World Bank 10 to 15 percent more, on average, than nonparticipatory projects in terms of staff time spent in preparation and appraisal. This is because these projects need to devote time and effort to the involvement of more stake-

holders and to the development of a project structure that incorporates the necessary channels and support services for participation. Although Hentschel (1994) does not mention any impact on supervisory costs, it could be inferred from better project performance that they may actually be reduced relative to conventional projects.

Participation costs incurred by beneficiaries and borrowers related to lost wages and transaction costs, as well as the costs of the support services needed for participation, can be considerable. Moreover, they can severely hamper the successful implementation of a participatory initiative if not adequately addressed. In this context, it is important to be able to quantify the cost of participation, an issue covered in more detail in chapter 3. In cases such as São Paulo's Guarapiranga program in which slum upgrading projects are part of a broader program, participation costs may be significant in the context of each upgrading project but limited in the context of the program as a whole.

What Is Participation and Who Benefits from It?

The development literature offers several definitions for participation, notably—and representatively—the following:

- Paul, in a World Bank paper on *Community Participation in Development Projects* (1987), calls community participation "an active process whereby beneficiaries influence the direction and execution of development projects rather than merely receiving a share of the project benefits." The key concept is that beneficiaries influence the project.
- In *Participation in Practice*, Reitbergen-McCracken (1996) defines the term as "a process through which stakeholders influence and share control over development initiatives, decisions, and resources that affect them." The key concept is that stakeholders influence and share control over development initiatives. The Inter-American Development Bank's *Resource Book on Participation* echoes this definition almost verbatim.
- Schmidt, in "Popular Participation and the World Bank: Lessons from 48 Case Studies" (1996), cites "a process by which people, especially disadvantaged people, influence policy formulation and control design alternatives, investment choices, management and monitoring of development interventions in their communities." The key concept is that disadvantaged people influence policy and control the project.
- The Canadian International Development Agency refers to the participatory approach in many of its policy statements as "a self-help approach characterized by the involvement of target groups in

project design, implementation and evaluation, which aims to build the capacity of the poor to maintain structures created during project implementation and continue their own development." The key concept is the involvement of target groups in the project cycle with a view to sustainability (IDB 1997a).
- The International Fund for Agricultural Development (IFAD) defines a participatory process as "a democratic process in which people, particularly the weak and the poor, are not passive receivers of a development project at the end of a top-down approach, but are requested to identify their needs, voice their demands, and organize themselves so as to improve their livelihood with the help of the financial, technical, and human resources offered by the development project, as well as their own" (IDB 1997a).
- The United Nations Development Programme (UNDP) takes a broader view, seeing participation "as an overall development strategy—not just as people's involvement in certain projects or programs. Participation means that people are closely involved in the economic, social, cultural, and political processes that affect their lives. People may, in some cases, have complete and direct control over these processes—in other cases, the control may be partial or indirect" (IDB 1997a).
- In his preface to the evaluation of the first three years of implementation of Bolivia's People's Participation Law, René Mostajo Deheza, formerly Bolivia's deputy minister for people's participation and municipal strengthening, wrote that "participation is not only an instrument for the creation and modification of reality, but also a philosophical approach that is destined to all people. It is a mode of thinking that should touch everyone, but which takes on different forms according to each person's level of awareness and knowledge" (our translation; Deheza 1998).

Our Definition

Drawing on the above, we now attempt to formulate our own working definition of participation for the purposes of this book: *Participation is a process in which people, and especially disadvantaged people, influence resource allocation and policy and program formulation and implementation, and are involved at different levels and degrees of intensity in the identification, timing, planning, design, implementation, evaluation, and post-implementation stages of development projects.*

In our definition, we owe something to each of the preceding ones. We favor a dynamic definition of the process of participation, since the features of a participatory process, and the level of development of the participatory potential of a community, will depend on local circumstances and program objectives and may change over time. To the UNDP definition, we owe the idea that participation is an involvement in processes, not just projects, and that the level of people's control may vary according to circumstances. To the IFAD definition, we owe the idea that the development project offers resources and an enabling environment for disadvantaged people to attain development goals through an organized expression of needs and demands. From all of them, we derive the ideas of involvement, influence, and control.

Our definition also incorporates the idea of influencing policy and resource allocation, which, as we will see, is a very important dimension of many participatory projects and one that enhances cost consciousness and responsibility all around. Finally, we stress the need for people's involvement at all stages in the project cycle.

People, Beneficiaries, Community, or Target Group?

The different definitions of participation suggest that there are different kinds of actors in a participatory process, including people in general, the community, the poor, target groups, beneficiaries, stakeholders, and the disadvantaged. The differences in terminology reveal very real differences in perception that influence the formulation and implementation of projects. *Beneficiary* or *target group*, for instance, has a very passive connotation; the *stakeholders* in a project are more than just the local residents.

Throughout this book, we use the terms *people*, *local residents*, *user* or *client group*, and *community*. We have tried to avoid *beneficiaries* and *target group* because of their passive connotations, but we have used the other terms freely when we felt they were appropriate. For instance, it makes sense to talk about *local residents* in the case of settlement upgrading; whereas in the case of a housing project involving people who originally came from different areas, it makes more sense to talk about the *client group*.

Use of the word *community* requires a caveat, since it so often accompanies the idea of participation and is perhaps the single most ideologically charged word in the development literature. It is common to see it used with a sort of romantic aura attached to it, as if local communities were the 21st century *bons sauvages*. In fact, communities, in the traditional sense, are becoming rare in today's world. Even in its most remote corners, the world is experiencing a process of "cognitive revolution" (CERFE 1995). Radio and television have sprouted up across the globe, as have cellular and conventional telephones and computers, faxes, and Internet access. Educational levels and technical capacity have increased everywhere.

These factors, among many others, have generated sharp social and cultural differences all around the world. Nowhere on earth—not in a rural village, much less in an urban slum—can local people any longer be considered homogenous in their interests, values, motivations, or culture.

Even when we refer to a rural village or a *favela*, it is becoming increasingly difficult to talk about community. More often than not, when we say "community," what we really are referring to is a group of people who happen to live in a certain place, each with different points of view, interests, and goals. Any specific place, therefore, is not really home to a community, but to a multiplicity of actors, be they collective bodies or individuals. Some are stronger and some weaker; each has different needs, views, and political ideals. There is normally a degree of conflict, and sometimes even violent opposition, among them. Rather than looking for a nonexistent community, it is therefore crucial to identify who these individual and collective actors are—to determine their culture, interests, views, potentials, constraints, and opportunities.

The word *community* as used here should be taken to mean the group of residents of a particular settlement or the membership of a housing association and not, as the word usually implies, a body of people who constitute a homogeneous whole with shared traditions and outlook.

Levels and Degrees of Participation

The definitions of participation suggest that it comes in different *levels*. Here again the terminology is revealing: people *influence, share control* over, or *control* the process or project. To influence is not the same thing as to share control or to exercise full control. These differences in perception translate into different approaches, and the idea of different levels of participation comes to the fore, as shown by Goethert (1998). As well as having different levels, participation may also have different degrees of intensity, as we will see below.

Levels of Participation

Goethert sees five different levels of participation (figure 1-1):

- None
- Information, or indirect
- Consultation
- Shared control
- Full control.

The first level of participation in the figure (none) corresponds to the absence of all three dimensions of a participation strategy described be-

Figure 1-1. Levels of Participation

Level of Participation	Community Role			Outsider Role	Levels of the Matrix
NONE	–			SURROGATE	• Levels indicate relationship of community to outsiders
INDIRECT	👥	<			
CONSULT	INTEREST GROUP 👥	<		ADVOCATE	
SHARED CONTROL	STAKEHOLDER 👥	=		STAKEHOLDER	• Levels range from no community control to full community control
FULL CONTROL	PRINCIPAL 👥	>		RESOURCE	

Source: Goethert (1998).

low (absence of participation). The second and third levels (indirect/consult) correspond to communication and negotiation strategies. The fourth and fifth levels (shared control/full control) correspond to community management strategies.

In Goethert's scheme, the importance and control exerted over the process by external support agencies[1] and their representatives (technicians) decrease with each step; and community information, ownership, and control increase. At the level of shared control, the community and external actors interact as equals.

Goethert's matrix is a useful instrument for examining the phases of the project in which community inputs are introduced, with what degree of community control, and with what kind of relationship between the main parties involved (public sector organizations and the local residents or client group).

---

[1] External support agencies are institutions or organizations that promote development initiatives in an area. They may be any of the following or any combination or partnership thereof:
- Public sector agencies at the national, provincial, or local level
- Not-for-profit private organizations such as foundations, development nongovernmental organizations (NGOs) or institutions providing social services such as education and health
- Private for-profit organizations such as those providing services in the context of an upgrading project (e.g., planning and engineering firms, contractors, providers of socio-technical support)
- International development aid agencies such as development banks, agencies of the U.N. system, bilateral aid agencies, and international NGOs.

As will be seen in discussing our case studies (summarized in chapter 2 and individually detailed in chapters 6 to 10),[2] there are three levels of participation in the examples we have studied:

1. Information and communication, which are present in all the cases
2. Debate and negotiation of options, which are also present in all the cases
3. Partnership—in management, as in the San José case, and in management and financing, as in the Tijuana case.

We found no cases in which there is no participation or in which the community exercises full control (the lowest and highest levels of Goethert's matrix). The very first level we have seen is information; participation in decisionmaking follows; at the highest level, the community manages project resources, but control is shared with the institution promoting the program or project. All the cases we have studied include the first two levels listed above; in Bolivia and Brazil, participation is limited to these two dimensions. In Costa Rica and Mexico, the element of partnership in management is also present, as in some of the initiatives that make up the development of Lima's Villa El Salvador in our Peruvian case.

The three levels can apply together or separately in different combinations to various activities in the scope of a project. For instance, the design of a program may be done at level 1, participatory planning of projects at level 2, and implementation of works at level 3. As will be seen, this is roughly the distribution adopted by the Foundation for the Promotion of Housing (FUPROVI) in our San José case.

The three levels are also the three dimensions, or components, of a participatory strategy. Overall, a project has a higher *level* of participation when the community and external actors are involved in each of the three components, though in most cases participatory strategies are limited to levels 1 and 2. It is evident that in a project where strategies are not developed for any of the three aspects mentioned above, there is no participation.

This idea accounts for the variety of approaches found in practice and for the possibility of a project's gradual development toward a more participatory approach, an outcome often seen in the field.

---

[2]These case studies examine Bolivia's People's Participation Law (chapter 6); the Guarapiranga Program in São Paulo, Brazil (chapter 7); the Habitat Popular Urbano Program conducted by the nonprofit foundation FUPROVI in San José, Costa Rica (chapter 8); community upgrading programs in Tijuana, Mexico (chapter 9); and Villa El Salvador, Lima, Peru (chapter 10).

Degrees of Intensity of Participation

There are two elements that we can add to Goethert's scheme to complete our conceptual framework of participation:

- Highlighting the role of other actors, besides the public sector and the community, such as nongovernmental and for-profit private organizations, in the design, planning, implementation, and maintenance of projects
- Refining the concept of levels of participation to include the idea of degrees of intensity of participation within each level.

All levels, except that at which there is no participation, may favor the establishment of significant partnerships. The quality of participation depends not only on the *level* but also on the *degree of intensity* of participation. Even though it is true that the majority of development projects do not reach the highest levels of participation, sometimes the levels of communication and negotiation already imply a great intensity of participation and deeply influence projects' progress, impact, and sustainability.

If we were to apply Goethert's classification to the Guarapiranga program, for example, it would not reach the fourth level, since at no time was the community directly responsible for the management and control of project resources. However, participation in Guarapiranga influenced urban design decisions more than in the San José example, for instance, where the community had an important role in resource management but not in urban design. In San José, participation is intense through community management and mutual-help construction, but decisions on urban and building design are made within a rather rigid framework set by FUPROVI. Therefore, it may be said that participation in Guarapiranga in terms of urban design is more *intense*, although the all-around *level* of participation of FUPROVI's projects is higher.

Another interesting comparison is that between the San José and Tijuana cases. Although both are cases of community management, similar in terms of the high level of responsibility assumed by the community and the high levels of cost consciousness and cost recovery that prevail, they differ markedly in terms of intensity of participation. In San José, people are directly involved in a complex set of activities over an extended length of time (typically 18 to 24 months). In Tijuana, there is only a small works committee that takes active part in the process, which is much shorter (6 to 8 months) and less complex, and most residents limit themselves to paying their share of the community contribution. This difference of intensity leads to different levels of local initiative and resident motivation to promote improvements in the aftermath of the project. Whereas in the Mexican case the paving of a road is usually not followed by any other community-led improvements, in the Costa Rican case housing associations, following an initial period of downtime upon project completion, usually become a vehicle for further improvements over the years.

One of the key features of the development of Villa El Salvador has been a high intensity of participation throughout the process. In some areas, such as infrastructure development, it was the intense and organized pressure of the residents that led to gradual service extension over the years. The *level* of local resident participation in such service extension, however, was relatively low, since decisions and investments were made by government and utilities, and there were no instances of community management. In the area of economic development, however, the Villa El Salvador case combined a high level of participation with the usual high degree of intensity, leading to one of the settlement's biggest success stories: the development of its industrial park. The participation of local microentrepreneurs and their associations in the design and execution of a bold and innovative plan, in partnership with government and with international technical assistance and financial aid, has resulted in a thriving industrial and commercial hub that has changed the local economic scene.

These examples and comparisons show us that participation may take many forms, and that not only are there different levels of participation, but also different degrees of intensity within each level (see table 1-1). Each particular combination has different results and different operational implications. Broadly speaking, increases in either the level or degree of participation require that more resources be devoted to the design of a participatory strategy, to social intermediation services, and to supervision and monitoring of the process of participation. For example, in Tijuana and San José, where the levels of participation are similar, the higher degree of intensity of participation in San José is reflected in a much stronger supply structure in terms of technical assistance, supervision, and monitoring.

Different Levels of Capacity to Participate

Different communities have different opportunities and different levels of capacity to participate. Communities vary greatly in their degree of organization and capacity, which is usually witnessed by the extent of their achievements over the years in advancing such matters as land tenure regularization and access to infrastructure and services. They also vary in terms of their:

- Size
- Wealth

Table 1-1. Levels and Degrees of Participation in the Cases Studied

Case	Stage in project cycle	Level of participation	Degree of intensity
Bolivia	Identification	Consultation	High
	Planning	Consultation	Medium
	Implementation	Shared control	Medium
	Conservation of benefits	Indirect	Low
Brazil	Identification	None	—
	Planning	Consultation	High
	Implementation	Consultation	High
	Conservation of benefits	Indirect	Low
Costa Rica	Identification	Consultation	High
	Planning	Consultation	Medium
	Implementation	Shared control	High
	Conservation of benefits	Consultation	Medium
Mexico	Identification	Consultation	Medium
	Planning	Consultation	Medium
	Implementation	Shared control	High
	Conservation of benefits	Consultation	Low
Peru	Identification	Consultation	High
	Planning	Shared control	High
	Implementation	Consultation	Medium
	Conservation of benefits	Consultation	Medium

Source: Authors' construction from field study data.

- Distribution of wealth
- Willingness and ability to pay for services
- Age of settlement
- Degree of informality and consolidation
- Composition in terms of gender, age groups, income levels, and vulnerable segments
- Degree of information
- Access to education
- Existence of skilled resource persons within the community
- Patterns of representation and leadership
- Political Influence
- Access to credit and savings schemes and business services
- Job opportunities.

Participation does not depend only on the initial degree of organization and/or other characteristics of a community. Organization and participation can be *developed*, as shown by the Tijuana and San José examples. With the appropriate enabling environment, the potential that exists within low-income communities to take care of their own affairs may be mobilized. Anecdotal evidence shows that initiatives that may entail an improvement in people's lives have a mobilizing potential. Encouraging participation is therefore a matter of creating the appropriate channels and an overall enabling environment, and allocating the needed resources to promote participation. In this context, a development project may be seen as an externally generated enabling framework for harnessing and building people's capacity and resources. This can be summed up in one phrase: *a demand-driven project needs a strong and specialized supply structure*. Generating an enabling environment for participation requires technical assistance and specialized services such as socio-technical support, as well as a sound management framework and seed money to leverage local resources. These are the essential components of the required supply structure.

Level of participation thus depends greatly on the will of external project promoters[3] to plan and budget for the capacity-building and technical assistance required for the intended level of participation. This issue is explored in detail in chapter 3.

Motivations for Urban Upgrading and Housing Programs

In all five of the cases covered in our field reports, the original motivating force for the program, project, or process was found in a government response to specific problems such as:

- Demand for housing
- Lack of sanitation
- Environmental/health risks
- Demand for consolidation of infrastructure (road paving, etc.)
- Response to a force majeure situation (e.g., Tijuana's 1993 flood)
- Demand for land tenure regularization.

Government response is generated and shaped by the political context and, as we will see, can be heavily influenced by competition among

---

[3]The degree of control exerted by outsiders over the process may give rise to certain negative outcomes, such as political manipulation of participation, but it is not necessarily a bad thing in itself. We have seen that the resources, technical assistance, and coordination provided by outsiders create an essential enabling framework for participation. In the cases studied, the supply structure set up by external support agencies has ensured that the level of participation would at least reach a certain minimum defined by the project design. In many cases, the level and degree of participation have exceeded what was originally envisaged by project promoters.

political parties and larger processes such as democratization and decentralization.

The problems that initiate a project may be located inside or outside the project area. We have seen that government action originates either from (1) local demands/local problems or (2) problems outside the community (e.g., Guarapiranga, which originated from a metropolitan environmental sanitation issue).

Government response may vary greatly in nature, from comprehensive upgrading projects to sectoral or piecemeal interventions, from projects aimed at solving the most urgent problems of an area with an emergency perspective, to projects that generate a long-term vision for the settlement and initiate a gradual process of development. As we will see in the following chapters, partnerships with community-based organizations and for-profit or other private sector actors such as nongovernmental organizations (NGOs) and foundations may be involved in various ways.

In Latin America, as in other regions, there are many upgrading projects that do not result from government response but are initiated by NGOs or other civil society organizations. Such projects often achieve positive results and represent methodological advances. However, unless they succeed in attracting government support in the long run, they seldom reach an appreciable scale and tend to remain in the category of pilot projects, with varying degrees of success. An example of a project that was initiated by an NGO, in alliance with local residents' organizations, and succeeded in attracting government and development bank support is Novos Alagados, in Salvador, Bahia, Brazil. Government and development bank support has given the project the critical mass it needed. Another example of an upgrading project generated by an alliance of civil society and community-based organizations is the Catuche Social Consortium in Caracas, Venezuela. Both of these examples are discussed in chapter 2.

Types of Upgrading and Low-Income Housing Projects

The main types of programs and projects in urban upgrading and low-income housing are given in table 1-2; box 1-2 discusses related terminology.

Other Approaches to Participation

Two authors, Peter Schuebeler and John Abbott, working from Asian and African experiences respectively, have in recent years proposed typologies of approaches to participation that are related both to the idea of levels and degrees of participation and to the different types of urban upgrading and low-income housing initiatives explored in the last sec-

Table 1-2. Main Types of Urban Upgrading and Low-Income Housing Initiatives

Type	Main features	Examples
Sites plus development plan (and gradual implementation of services)	Settlements are planned and surveyed, lots allocated and occupied, infrastructure gradually implemented	• Villa El Salvador, Lima • INETT land subdivision program, Tijuana[a]
Sites and services	Mass production of serviced sites in large schemes for resettlement of urban squatters, usually in peripheral land in city outskirts; variant: sites and services with basic starter housing units	• Integrated Serviced Land Project, South Africa[b] • Seaview Gardens, Kingston, Jamaica[c]
Comprehensive upgrading of existing settlements	Wide range of improvements involving different types of infrastructure according to predefined area plan; this is integrated upgrading but undertaken in one go, usually in a two-year time frame	• Guarapiranga, São Paulo • Favela-Bairro, Rio • Alvorada, Belo Horizonte, Brazil • Novos Alagados, Salvador, Brazil
Piecemeal upgrading of existing settlements	Improvements gradually added over long-term process but without an integrated area development plan	• Community upgrading programs, Tijuana • People's Participation Law, Bolivia
Technical assistance and credit for home expansion and improvement	Organized support to self-help housing efforts; may be combined with upgrading programs	• Cooperative Housing Foundation, Ciudad Juárez, Mexico[d] • Desco Densification Program, Villa El Salvador
Development of new housing in new settlement	New infrastructure and housing units are built on empty land; variant: new housing on available land in existing serviced areas	• FUPROVI's Habitat Popular Urbano, San José • *Mutirão* programs, Brazil

Type	Main features	Examples
Redevelopment of degraded existing structures	Agreement reached with landlords for building renovation	• Don't Move, Improve program, the Bronx, New York[e]

[a] INETT is Baja California's State Real Estate Board, which pursues an active policy of land delivery to the poor through subdivision of land located in the desert around Tijuana, Rosarito, Tecate, and other major cities. The plots are sold below market prices, the urban layout is well-defined, and infrastructure provision is gradual.

[b] An ambitious undertaking to deliver serviced plots at scale on the outskirts of the country's major cities in post-Apartheid South Africa, this initiative faced some of the same dilemmas as similar projects in other developing countries. Driven by the availability of inexpensive land, these projects have delivered serviced plots in locations that are generally not very desirable in terms of access to services and jobs. Their impact on poverty reduction is therefore questionable.

[c] This is a large 1970s project built in Kingston's western outskirts, close to the city's main industrial area. Like some of its contemporary projects, it included starter housing units.

[d] The U.S.-based Cooperative Housing Foundation, which is present in many Latin American and African countries, supports the local NGO Habitat and Housing Foundation (FUNHAVI) in Ciudad Juárez in implementing the foundation's trademark approach to home improvement in developing countries based on a combination of lending, technical assistance, and deals with materials suppliers to lower construction costs.

[e] This type of program is common in industrialized countries, many of which have degraded inner cities with crumbling tenements (examples of the many developing country versions are the *cortiços* of São Paulo, the *conventillos* of Buenos Aires, and the *casas de vecindad* of Mexico City).

Source: Authors' construction from field study data.

> **Box 1-2. The Many Names of Informal Settlements**
>
> "Informal settlement" is a generic and technical term that seeks to capture the many different features of those settlements that house many of the urban poor in developing countries. The name implies that the dominant feature of such settlements is their informality—the fact that they develop outside the existing legal and regulatory framework. They are sometimes called "unplanned" or "spontaneous" settlements, which is misleading, since many informal settlements are planned, albeit not in a conventional way, and are not at all spontaneous.
>
> Two main types of informal settlements exist: squatter settlements and informal subdivisions. Typically, a squatter settlement is a chaotic, unplanned, "spontaneous" occupation; an informal subdivision is an informal commercial operation in which the entrepreneur—the informal sector land developer—provides a surveyed plot and proof of purchase, but usually no infrastructure and no common space for public uses. Informal settlements have different names in different countries. Here is a small selection from Latin America:
>
> - Argentina—*villas miserias*
> - Brazil—*favelas* or *invasões* (squatter settlements) and *vilas* (informal subdivisions)
> - Chile—*poblaciones callampas* (squatter settlements)
> - Colombia—*barrios piratas* (informal subdivisions) and *invasiones* (squatter settlements)
> - Costa Rica—*precarios* (squatter settlements)
> - El Salvador—*tugurios* (squatter settlements) and *colonias ilegales* (informal subdivisions)
> - Mexico—*colonias populares* (informal subdivisions)
> - Paraguay—*rancheríos pobres* (squatter settlements)
> - Peru—*barriadas* or *pueblos jovenes* (informal subdivisions)
> - Venezuela—*barrios de ranchos* (squatter settlements).

tion. Schuebeler (1996) suggests the following typology of four participatory approaches:

- **Community-based support strategies.** These are appropriate for community-based strategies in which the main objective of participatory activities is to enhance the community's capacity to manage the development and operation of local infrastructure services. The orientation of the public-private partnership is from the government toward the community, and support normally takes the form of organizational and technical support to community groups. The initiatives involved are usually fairly small-scale and relatively simple. The Tijuana community upgrading programs are an example.

- **Area-based involvement strategies.** These are normally government-led; the aim is to mobilize the community to make specific inputs into government-managed activities. This approach is fairly common in externally funded integrated upgrading projects. The Guarapiranga program is a good example.
- **Functionally based collaboration strategies.** These occur when responsibilities are "unbundled," with each stakeholder taking responsibility for a particular aspect of service provision. The division of responsibilities is linked to on-plot or household facilities, local or tertiary facilities, secondary or secondary level facilities, and trunk facilities. A functionally oriented NGO is a common participant organization, and building community management capacity is normally an important objective of the approach. Pakistan's Orangi Pilot Project is an example.
- **Process-based decentralization strategies.** Suggested by the author as the ideal, these aim to bring infrastructure management closer to users and to increase responsiveness and accountability. Schuebeler sees this as going beyond individual projects to operate at a citywide scale. He also sees public-private partnerships as important components of decentralization strategies.

John Abbott (1996) cites two main approaches to participation: community development approaches, which he links to modernization theory; and empowerment approaches, which he links to dependency theory. He suggests the need to go beyond both, to what he calls negotiated development, when the issues to be addressed are anything other than fairly simple.

The State: Different Roles and Levels of Involvement

Although the state is behind almost all urban upgrading and shelter initiatives, its role and level of involvement vary significantly. For instance, we will see examples in the following chapters in which the state generates and coordinates a program (e.g., Brazil, Mexico, and Bolivia) with local community participation and varying degrees of involvement of external donors and other actors. We will also see a case (Costa Rica) in which the state created favorable conditions for a private organization to become an effective tool for shelter delivery to the urban poor. This was done both through the establishment of a national housing subsidy program and by targeting the organization—FUPROVI—as the recipient of a foreign grant and technical assistance. In the case of Villa El Salvador, the state, using the Peruvian formula of sites plus a development plan to cater to a burgeoning housing demand, created the conditions for a long-term development process. In this context, community organizations, the state itself, and other organizations have interacted for almost 30 years in the improvement of shelter and the provision of services, in a process that is still ongoing.

Motivations for Participation

The rationale or opportunity for participation in urban upgrading and shelter projects varies significantly according to the situation. Broadly speaking, the participatory approach is directly linked to the very nature of urban upgrading and shelter projects, and to the reason for undertaking such projects in the first place. Projects stem from needs and demands to be fulfilled through state intervention and/or collective action, and such needs and demands must be organized. Problems must be clearly identified and understood; priorities established; and the groundwork for sustainability laid by securing stakeholder ownership, responding to effective demand, and clearly defining stakeholder roles and responsibilities.

Motivations for designing participation into a project may stem from any combination of the following reasons:

- Enhancing project feasibility by ensuring stakeholder collaboration through demand-responsiveness and open channels for communication of grievances
- Overcoming resource constraints through community labor or financial contributions
- Making use of local information and know-how to ensure that the project management unit makes better informed decisions
- Improving targeting by knowing more about beneficiary communities and the needs of the various groups that comprise them
- Improving the odds for future cost recovery by promoting stakeholders' cost consciousness and fostering in them a responsible relationship to urban services and infrastructure
- Enhancing sustainability by ensuring stakeholder ownership, making information available, and developing local capacities, which will strengthen the odds for further development initiatives in the aftermath of the project
- Enhancing transparency and accountability in the management of public funds
- Promoting democratization and decentralization of resource allocation.

In practice, as shown in table 1-3, the perspectives of external support agencies vary greatly. As we will see in our case studies, participation is sometimes introduced in response to specific problems in a reactive man-

Table 1-3. Approaches and Motivations for Participation

Case	Approach	Motivation
Bolivia	Proactive (policy and methodology focus)	Democratization and decentralization by establishing resource flows to the local level and community participation in resource allocation and expenditure control
Brazil	Reactive (project focus)	Feasibility of project implementation (i.e., ensuring project achieves collaboration of local residents by catering to their needs and demands)
Brazil	Proactive (policy and methodology focus)	Community input in subproject formulation ensured through participatory information gathering and area development planning
Costa Rica, Mexico	Proactive (policy and methodology focus)	Overcoming resource constraints (i.e., achieving cost reduction through community labor or upfront community contribution)
Costa Rica	Proactive (policy and methodology focus)	Targeting of program (self-help construction as a targeting filter)
Costa Rica, Mexico	Proactive (policy and methodology focus)	Ensuring ownership and sustainability through community management and related capacity-building
Mexico	Reactive (project focus)	Political pressure by communities and competition between rival political parties
Mexico, Costa Rica	Proactive (policy and methodology focus)	More effective and transparent management of public funds
Peru	Reactive (project focus)	As a result of organized political pressure, community participates in decisionmaking
Peru	Proactive (policy and methodology focus)	Participation in planning is seen as key to achieving sustainable development (participatory area development planning is a tradition and a key development tool)

Source: Authors' construction from field study data.

ner; sometimes, it is incorporated into project design proactively to make use of local information and resources, ensure stakeholder ownership, develop local capacity, and—ultimately—enhance impact and sustainability. The reactive approach tends to have a narrow project focus, while the proactive approach usually has a broader policy and methodology focus.

The Guarapiranga program shows us that usually in urban upgrading, when a project is not built around participation from the start, elements of participation need to be introduced at a later stage to ensure feasibility of project implementation. Indeed, especially in the case of squatter settlements, the specific requirements of urban upgrading make it difficult to imagine implementing a project without participation. This is explored in more detail in box 1-3.

Although participation can have many motivations and many entry points, as will be seen in the following chapters, it is always a very important force in a program or project, even when it is introduced in a reactive manner. Furthermore, the effects of participation usually go beyond its immediate motivation to an extent determined by its level and degree of intensity.

Some Considerations Regarding Poverty and Social Capital[4]

The strong links between urban upgrading and low-income housing on the one side and the enhancement of social capital and poverty reduction on the other mean that concepts such as poverty, vulnerability, social risk, social exclusion, and social capital recur throughout this book. This section defines and briefly discusses these concepts, exploring the policy implications of each.

Social Exclusion, Poverty, and Vulnerability

Social exclusion may be defined as a process of impoverishment brought about by the simultaneous action, in relation to a person or group or to the area where they live, of various factors of *social risk* such as the following:

- Inadequate shelter and a degraded living environment due to the lack of basic infrastructure and/or exposure to waste loads generated by nearby traffic or industry
- Lack of access to adequate health care facilities
- Lack of access to adequate educational opportunities
- Lack of access to adequate work opportunities
- Presence of criminal activity in the area and a consequent lack of security

---

[4]This section is based on CERFE (1998).

> **Box 1-3. Why Squatter Settlement Upgrading Cannot Be Done without Participation**
>
> The "spontaneous" or "unplanned" pattern of land occupation of squatter settlements is characterized by narrow and tortuous access routes, occupation of areas of risk (e.g., landslide or flood-prone areas) and, perhaps most of all, by the lack of a precise definition of public and private spaces. In a typical squatter settlement, such as those in Rio's Favela-Bairro or São Paulo's Guarapiranga, many plots lack direct access to a street or lane, forcing people to cross other plots to get to their own.
>
> The first task to be contemplated in upgrading a squatter settlement is therefore a physical planning task. This entails improvement of settlement layout to define public and private spaces, provide a means of access to all plots and open roads to improve circulation, find routes for storm drainage, provide pathways for infrastructure, and connect the settlement to the surrounding urban fabric. It is also necessary to remove the structures occupying risk areas and give these areas over to a socially defined use. Both Guarapiranga and Favela-Bairro have contributed important methodological advances in these physical planning tasks.
>
> Even though the first duty of the planner of in-situ upgrading is to preserve the existing stock of shelter and infrastructure as much as possible, the conditions outlined above mean that a certain number of structures will need to be removed and relocated. Depending on the extent of such removals, some families will need to be resettled in other areas. During the implementation of the works, some structures need to be partially demolished and rebuilt; and some kinds of infrastructure, like condominial sewers, need to be built inside private plots. These are complex operations requiring technical skill, ingenuity, and patience. All this is next to impossible to do in an effective way if the people concerned—the people whose lives will be disrupted by removal, relocation, and partial demolition of their homes—do not take part in the discussion of alternatives and do not agree that the goals to be reached justify the disruption they will suffer, and, ultimately, that the end result will benefit them as well. This sort of consensus and collaboration is essential for the successful implementation of such a complex operation and can only be achieved through participation. The municipality of São Paulo realized this during the pilot phase of the Guarapiranga upgrading project, which caused it to adopt a much more participatory approach in its subsequent phases.

- Lack of mobility through lack of access to affordable and efficient modes of transportation
- Gender imbalance, characterized by a lack of opportunities for women and a lack of specific measures to address this imbalance

- Lack of family stability, leading to deteriorated conditions for the care and socialization of children
- Lack or low quality of services provided by the state in the area
- Lack of access to communication and information
- Situations of conflict or violations of basic political and human rights
- Lack of social sector policies that may translate into appropriate assistance from the state or civil society organizations to help mitigate the above factors of social risk.

The combined action of these social risk factors, characterizing a situation of social exclusion, pushes the excluded toward a condition of poverty. The excluded, in some cases, are not yet poor, but they will become poor in the near future if the situation of exclusion does not change. Poverty, therefore, is a condition or situation that results from a combination of factors and not only from lack of income. When poverty is not extreme, it leads to a lack of opportunities for personal, family, and social development, but it does not destroy the capacity to organize, to exert political pressure, or to interact with public and private sector bodies in development initiatives. In many situations, as will be seen in the examples in chapter 2, the poor display a remarkable capacity for self-help and great resourcefulness.

In the cases we have studied, as in most low-income settlements in Latin America, all or almost all the factors of social risk mentioned above were present in varying measures. The only factor that was absent in all cases was the existence of a conflict situation or serious violation of political rights, since all the countries we visited are democracies or have made progress toward a democratic form of government in recent years. In the Peruvian case, the serious conflict situation of the early 1990s was a major factor of social risk and a major obstacle to progress. The removal of such an obstacle has meant that the difficult journey to progress could be resumed.

Extreme poverty, or indigence, is a different matter. It entails a total lack of access to opportunities over an extended length of time, and it brings about severe psychological and social damage, frequently leading to the desocialization of the persons or groups involved. This involves not only a lack of capacity for organization or self-help, but also means that significant and long-term assistance must first be given to mitigate the situation before these groups may be expected to develop capabilities for self-help. The cases we have studied have dealt with people living in poverty, but seldom with those in extreme poverty.

Vulnerable groups are those that not only find themselves in a situation of poverty, but that face particularly serious social risk factors that they cannot overcome without outside help. They may not be in a condition of indigence yet, but they will be relentlessly pushed toward it if they do not receive specific attention and assistance. Vulnerable groups usually include:

- Women who are heads of households and their families
- Youths who are unemployed or employed in low-productivity sectors
- Working children and adolescents
- People with handicaps or illnesses
- Elderly people.

In the cases we have studied, one of the recurring shortcomings was the lack of specific attention to the needs of vulnerable groups. Programs and projects tended to lump them together with the rest of the poor, putting them at further disadvantage.

Civil Society, Social Initiative, and Social Capital

Current definitions of social capital often have a problem when it comes to specifying the locus to which the concept of social capital refers. They usually consider it as an expression or dimension of society or of a community in general. Society (or even a specific community), when taken as a whole, is too broad and vague a concept; thus, the notion of social capital runs the risk of remaining vague, ambiguous, and of little utility.

It is therefore better to consider, not society as a whole, but only *civil society*, the segment thereof that is empirically detectable and that can be mobilized to assume social responsibility. Civil society may be defined as the set of collective and organized actors that exhibit the intention to enter the public arena to tackle the problems that afflict society. It is this entity that can be taken as the empirical reference or locus for the notion of social capital.

To find a stable linkage between social capital and civil society, we must focus on the *composition* of civil society. There is a tendency to identify civil society with a very small number of collective actors, usually citizens' groups, at times businesses, and—on rare occasions—government agencies. In reality, the kinds of actors that enter the public arena are much more numerous. Moreover, the types of actors that exhibit an orientation toward social responsibility vary considerably over time and with the changing social context. Civil society is thus richer and more articulated than had been assumed. It is a dynamic element of society, the features of which must be discerned empirically. This is the way to avoid an abstract or rhetorical view of civil society and instead view it as a circumscribed, quantifiable social reality.

It may be argued that the concept of civil society thus defined includes government agencies, since they are organized actors that play a very important role in the public arena, and the state is after all an expression of society. However, for didactic reasons, it is important for us to be able to distinguish between public and private actors in this book; we therefore use the expression *civil society* to refer only to nonstate actors.

The study of low-income areas shows that there is a link between civil society and social protection. Different kinds of collective actors seek to protect people from existing social and environmental risks (which, obviously, are exacerbated by the difficult conditions of low-income settlements). The ability to produce significant effects in terms of providing people with social protection seems to be an attribute of civil society, and one that is gaining increasing recognition in planning public policies. For example, the Glass of Milk organization and the community-run soup kitchens in Villa El Salvador have played an essential social safety net role during Peru's structural adjustment. The term we have used to describe this function is *social initiative*, which conveys the idea of a concretely measurable quality specific to civil society that involves taking an active attitude to controlling risks (and thus a tendency to operate in the welfare sense). Sometimes, as in the case of Peru, civil society is found to be particularly active, due to the limited action of the state. In other cases, as in Costa Rica, the existence of well-structured public institutions that tend to be adverse to grassroots mobilization reduces civil society activity. Several factors are usually involved when there is a high level of social initiative:

- The quality of the collective actors in terms of culture, orientation to change, and ability to mobilize resources
- The tendency of civil society actors to work in partnership and form networks of mutual cooperation
- The substantial involvement of public administration in forging partnerships with civil society actors to implement systems to control social risks.

Now the issue becomes the relationship between this quality in civil society and social capital. There is a strong tendency to identify or superimpose these two elements, on the notion that a society that can effectively control the risks to which it is exposed must have substantial social capital.

We see the matter slightly differently. Social initiative seems in fact to be a self-defense mechanism of civil society, pertaining mainly to the domain of social reproduction when threatened by social and environmental risks (health crises, illiteracy, unemployment, no access to higher education, geographical isolation, conflicts, etc.). Conversely, social capital, at least by current definitions (and the one adopted in this study is no exception), is aimed at *growth and expansion* rather than the control of risks. In this context, again in the example of Villa El Salvador, the ability of microentrepreneurs to create trade associations and negotiate with the state—a key feature of the creation of the area's industrial park—should be seen as a feature of social capital.

Social initiative and social capital thus appear to be two autonomous dimensions of civil society. To be sure, a high level of social initiative in civil society fosters the production of social capital, but it does not produce it directly. There are in fact groups (rural communities, for example) that have a great capacity for managing risks but exhibit little capacity for development. Therefore, social initiative is not in itself sufficient to produce social capital; there are other factors. But what are they?

Social Capital as the Measure of Civil Society

The question we have just posed leads us to consider how to define and use the concept of social capital. If civil society is the referent of any discussion of social capital, then the latter can be considered a measure of civil society. Yet, having clarified that social capital does not measure civil society's inclination toward social protection (nor, as some suggest, the generic "good functioning" of a group), we must then ask what exactly it does measure.

For the purposes of our study, social capital can be usefully viewed as the measure of the capacity of civil society (using the definition provided, including those economic actors showing a tendency to assume social responsibility) to bring about economic growth. Thus, while social initiative describes the reproductive function of civil society, social capital has to do with another of its functions, namely, the productive function.

Social capital represents an interaction between civil society (and thus its social initiative) and certain elements external to it—in particular three important local factors that can favor its action (confidence in social relations, opportunity, and the existence of cognitive capital) and a number of obstacles (legal, regulatory, social, cultural, and organizational) that can reduce its impact.

All things being equal, the higher the social initiative levels, the greater the probability of the implementation of social protection measures. Similarly, the higher the social capital index, the greater the probability of economic growth. When both indices are high, as in the Villa El Salvador case in Peru, there is more likelihood that we will see greater overall social and economic development.

The above definitions may be encapsulated in the following points:

- *Civil society* does not comprise all collective actors, but only those characterized by an orientation toward social responsibility.
- Civil society is the *locus of both social initiative and social capital* (both are attributes of the former).

- *Social initiative* is the measure of a civil society's capacity to control social risks and thus foster social development.
- *Social capital* is the measure of a civil society's capacity to contribute to economic development.
- The overall *quality of a civil society* will be higher the greater the degree of social initiative and the quantity of social capital it possesses.

Figure 1-2 illustrates these points.

Sustainability and Local Initiative

A program or project is sustainable when it generates a permanent improvement in the quality of life of the people involved. A sustainable project is one that permanently augments a community's resources—and hence its social initiative and social capital—and thus reduces its vulnerability. As in the case of FUPROVI's work with the housing associations in Costa Rica, sustainable efforts permanently improve living conditions; perhaps more importantly, however, they start a long-term development process.

Therefore, sustainability is the most adequate measure of the final success of a program or project. A successful project builds physical assets and capacity that endure after the external assistance is no longer

Figure 1-2. Civil Society, Social Initiative, and Social Capital

```
                    ┌─────────────────────┐
                    │  SOCIAL INITIATIVE  │
                    │                     │
                    │ Measures a civil    │
                    │ society's capacity  │
                    │ to control          │
                    │ social risks        │
                    └─────────────────────┘
                              ▲
                              │
┌──────────────────────┐      │
│   CIVIL SOCIETY      │──────┤
│                      │      │              QUALITY OF A
│ Set of collective    │      │              CIVIL SOCIETY
│ actors characterized │      │                   ▲
│ by an orientation    │──────┤                   │
│ toward social        │      │
│ responsibility       │      ▼
└──────────────────────┘
                    ┌─────────────────────┐
                    │   SOCIAL CAPITAL    │
                    │                     │
                    │ Measures a civil    │
                    │ society's capacity  │
                    │ to contribute       │
                    │ to society's        │
                    │ economic development│
                    └─────────────────────┘
```

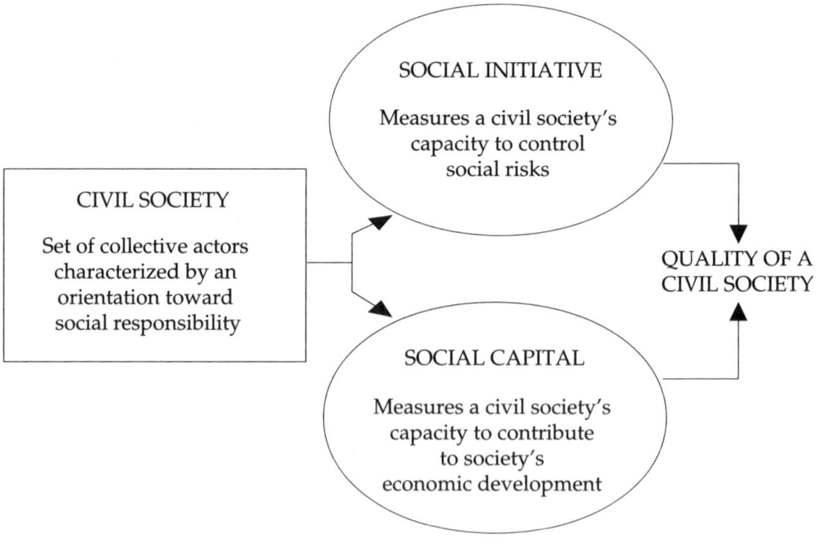

Source: CERFE (1998).

there. Designing for sustainability is an important part of the formulation of an urban upgrading or low-income housing program or project.

Two Dimensions of Sustainability

Sustainability has the following key dimensions:
- Conservation of the benefits that derive from the project
- Continuity of the development process after the project.

Both dimensions depend on the community's motivation and technical, organizational, and financial capacity. Following are some components of the two dimensions, which may be seen as stages of growth and change within the community:

- **Conservation of the benefits that derive from the project**
  - Security of land tenure, which has important practical and psychological dimensions, as will be seen in the case studies
  - Clear definition of public and private spaces, which is one of the foundations defining the relationship of local residents to the city and to each other
  - Availability of basic infrastructure and services that perform well over time
  - Permanence of most residents in the settlement in the project's aftermath
  - Community knowledge of the nature and characteristics of the local infrastructure
  - Consciousness of the investment and operation and maintenance costs of infrastructure
  - The community's willingness and ability to pay taxes, service fees, and consumption tariffs and to repay contracted debt.

- **Continuity of the development process after project completion**
  - Increased interest in achieving further benefits and in organizing in order to obtain them
  - Capacity to improve and gradually expand shelter units
  - Increased entrepreneurship and economic activities stimulated by the upgrading process
  - Increased social mobility
  - Improved access to social services, a stronger solidarity network, and strengthened connections within and among households.

Ultimately, the conservation of the project's benefits and the continuity of the development process lead to a reduction of the social risk factors at work in a settlement and to the reduction of poverty.

Stakeholder Participation and Sustainability

Stakeholder participation in planning and decisionmaking related to the program or project has a positive impact on the conservation of project benefits. In this context, the following aspects may be highlighted:

- Participation in information gathering and analysis raises the awareness level in relation to the area's problems and resources.
- Participation in the analysis of alternatives for intervention and in area development planning allows the project to make better, more informed decisions and enables local people to get acquainted with the key concepts of planning and development in relation to their area.
- Participation in the analysis of alternatives and in the decisionmaking related to the organization of construction activities offers opportunities for community members to know and understand relevant details of the infrastructure being implemented.
- Participation in the discussion of project costs and alternatives for cost recovery and operations and maintenance enhances cost consciousness and acquaints local people with the key issues involved in the conservation of the benefits generated by a project, laying the groundwork for a successful post-implementation phase.

One way to help guarantee the continuity of the development process is the involvement—from the initial phases of the project—of private institutions and services, such as childcare, health centers, and schools that are run by churches or NGOs in the area. Such private intermediary structures constitute a social support network that can exert pressure to ensure the continuity of a development initiative.

Especially in long-term projects, we have verified that private intermediary structures (and also public sector service units such as schools and clinics) represent a stable reference point and a series of stimuli for participation to the families that live in the area, even though they provide specific services not directly related to the upgrading project. Furthermore, the staff of such organizations usually includes some of the most qualified human resources present in a low-income area; these personnel can help in organizing and implementing participation in information gathering, planning, and other project activities.

To stimulate continuity of development efforts, projects should:

- Promote participation in information gathering and analysis, in the analysis of alternatives for intervention, and in area development planning

- Promote participation in the analysis of alternatives and in the decisionmaking related to the organization of construction activities (the same applies to public sector units such as local schools and clinics)
- Promote the participation of private and public actors in the discussion of project costs and alternatives for cost recovery and operations and maintenance
- Contribute to the strengthening of local private social service structures that represent a resource in the network of community relations
- Promote the involvement of these private actors in project development, even when their principal mission or mandate is not directly related to upgrading or shelter.

It is necessary to pay attention to the time requirements of each action. The distinct nature of each component often imposes a distinct schedule for completion. We have verified on several occasions that the completion time of a project in an often fragmented and unstructured context is insufficient to ensure the blossoming of subsequent development initiatives. These efforts can and should, whenever possible, be made to move faster by incentives. But they need a longer growth period and should not be constrained by the time frame of an infrastructure project. These issues are explored in detail in the following chapters.

Finally, it is worth noting, with regard to the relation between participation and the continuity of the development process, that participation can generate significant political power. In a participatory process, new leaders emerge and make their political connections and often pursue a political career. Old leaders may have their power enlarged or eclipsed. Politicians who have their roots in community-based organizations, or in external support agencies that take part in upgrading projects, often build their political base through upgrading-related actions—which may have a positive impact on the continuity of the development process. On the other hand, the close relationship between participation and politics can divert the process from its original aims and make it less representative, for instance when politicians try to strengthen their political allies by excluding opposition groups from participating. In our case studies, we have learned of examples of populist politicians creating this kind of situation in Mexico and Bolivia.[5] In the same countries, however, there are also examples of a new political ethos that is more respectful of democratic principles.

---

[5]Populism, in Latin American politics, refers to a way of governing that is characterized by high-blown rhetoric about poverty and inequality, while government actions often take the form of fiscally irresponsible handouts that are nominally targeted at the poor, but in reality most often end up being captured by the lower middle class and middle class. Populism is normally also characterized by clientelism or patronage, i.e., the allocation of public resources to groups that constitute a politician's power base.

2

Case Summaries

This chapter begins with presentations of key statistics on the countries and cities we have studied, and goes on to provide a brief description and main conclusions of each of our case studies. Table 2-1 is an overview of key characteristics of these cases. A full-length version of each case, with extensive excerpts from interviews with project participants, is contained in part II of this book (chapters 6–10). Other relevant upgrading and housing programs and projects are presented at the end of this chapter.

Statistical Comparisons

Table 2-2 presents statistical comparisons among the countries of our study. We have chosen indicators that portray the respective demographic and social situations to provide some background to the reading of the case summaries.

The statistics reveal that all the countries in our study are undergoing a process of fast urban growth. In all of the countries, the urban population far outnumbers the rural. Costa Rica is the only country in the study where the rural population is still growing at an appreciable rate—although at half the growth rate of the urban population. Peru, which is already over 70 percent urban, has similar relative rural-urban growth rates. The other countries—Bolivia, Brazil, and Mexico—have negative growth rates for rural population and high growth rates for urban population. In Bolivia, where 37 percent of the population still lives in rural areas, city populations are growing at an astonishing 4.5 percent per year.

The poverty and income distribution data show that poverty is more extreme, and income distribution worse, in rural areas than in urban in all five countries. In Costa Rica, most of the poor still live in rural areas;

Table 2-1. Main Features of the Cases Studied

Feature	Bolivia	Brazil	Costa Rica	Mexico	Peru
Type of action (i.e., physical assets built)	Urban upgrading; social investment (schools, clinics, community centers); rural infrastructure	Urban upgrading; environmental sanitation	Low-income housing; urban upgrading	Urban upgrading	Urban upgrading; social investment (schools, clinics, community centers)
Scope	Nationwide	One water catchment in a metro area (pop. 600,000)	Metropolitan	Citywide	One district of a metro area (pop. 360,000)
Innovations	National legal framework; mandatory participatory budgeting at local level; transparent subsidies	Horizontal institutional arrangement; private sector provides socio-technical support; large-scale	Community management of mutual-help construction made possible by intense capacity-building and socio-technical support; transparent subsidies	Communities operate at a very high level of cost-consciousness and control; community contribution; parent subsidies	State support and an area development plan have made a great difference; participation has let community make the most of limited resources
Duration	1994–present	1993–2000	1988–present	1991–present	1971–present
Investment	$100 million (yearly)	$190 million	$14 million (1987–98)	$57 million (1991–98)	$330 million
Promoting agency	National government	Local government; state government	National government; NGO	Local government	National government; local government; community-based organizations

Feature	Bolivia	Brazil	Costa Rica	Mexico	Peru
Funding sources	National government	Local government; state government; multilateral donor	National government; bilateral donor	Federal government; state government; local government; community	National government; local government; donor agencies
Participatory strategies	Participatory budgeting; community control of local government spending	Information; consultation; negotiation; organized community pressure on policymaking	Community management of mutual-help construction	Participatory budgeting; community management	Participatory planning; organized community pressure on policymaking; community control of local government
Cost recovery strategies	High level of cost consciousness	No explicit strategy	High level of cost consciousness; community management of resources	High level of cost consciousness; community management of resources; upfront community financial contribution	Innovative strategies for land tax and service fee collection; metering and consumption-based tariffs for water, sanitation, and electricity
Gender strategies	Design included explicit gender strategy, but little evidence of its application	No explicit strategy; women normally take the lead in community organization	Support to women-headed households through World Food Program packages, National Social Welfare Institute subsidies, and group solidarity	No explicit strategy; women normally take lead in community organization	Very active, increasingly influential women's movement has a major role in addressing issues such as nutrition and basic education

(Table continues on the following page.)

Table 2-1 (*continued*)

Feature	Bolivia	Brazil	Costa Rica	Mexico	Peru
Resettlement strategies	Very little impact on housing or resettlement; need for resettlement is limited for reasons similar to Mexican case	Very elaborate strategy, including temporary lodgings, building of new units within settlement and housing schemes outside settlement	Not applicable (FUPROVI helps associations build new housing)	Very little need for resettlement since the *colonias* are planned informal subdivisions with a regular grid pattern and access to all plots	VES was a major initiative to provide a resettlement alternative for families occupying other areas; planned as, and became, a city
For-profit private sector involvement	Limited (public works contractors)	Socio-technical support providers; project management services; public works contractors	Limited involvement (providers of building materials and specialized building services)	Currently, only public works contractors; potential for partnership between local businesses, *maquiladora* firms, microfinance institutions	Public works contractors and providers of building materials; private electricity utility

Note: Data are current as of field study conduct.
Source: Authors' construction from field study data.

Table 2-2 *(continued)*

Indicator	Bolivia	Brazil	Costa Rica	Mexico	Peru
Urban households					
Children in urban households w/ low-education environment					
0–5	25.0	47.5	17.9	—	—
6–14	24.3	48.7	15.1	—	—
Female-headed households in urban area (%)					
Total	21	24	27	18	—
Indigent	24	24	51	17	—
Nonindigent poor	22	22	36	15	—
Nonpoor	19	24	24	19	—
Access to basic services					
Population using improved water sources (%), total	79	87	98	86	77
Urban	93	95	98	94	87
Rural	55	54	98	63	51
Population using adequate sanitation facilities (%), total	66	77	77	73	76
Urban	82	85	85	87	90
Rural	33	40	40	32	40
Access to electric lighting, 1999 (%)	67	95	—	95	69
Labor market					
Participation rate, 1999 (%), total	62.3	65.5	60.9	60.8	72.0
Men	65.1	79.8	79.0	80.6	82.9
Women	50.8	52.6	44.9	42.8	62.1
Open unemployment rate 1999 (%), men and women	3.6	11.4	6.1	3.3	10.7
Men	3.7	9.4	5.3	3.7	8.1
Women	3.6	14.1	7.4	2.7	13.8

Indicator	Bolivia	Brazil	Costa Rica	Mexico	Peru
Poverty and income distribution					
Participation in household income distribution (total)					
40–	11.7	8.4	13.5	10.2	13.4
10+	42.1	47.0	34.2	44.4	35.4
GINI coefficient	0.53	0.59	0.46	0.56	0.46
Participation in household income distribution (urban)					
40–	13.6	10.5	17.3	17.6	—
10+	37.0	44.3	26.8	33.7	—
GINI coefficient	0.455	0.538	0.357	0.392	—
Health					
Undernourished people (% of total population), 1997–99	22.0	10.0	5.0	5.0	13.0
Life expectancy at birth	62.6	68.1	77.5	73.0	69.3
Mortality rate for under age 5 (per 1,000 live births)	79.0	39.0	13.4	35.8	41.4
Probability of not surviving to age 40 (% of cohort), 1995–2000	18.4	11.3	4.0	8.3	11.6
Education					
Literacy rate, 2000					
Adult (age 15 and above)	85.5	85.2	95.6	91.4	82.7
Youth (15–24)	95.9	92.5	98.3	97.0	89.9
Educational profile, 1995					
No schooling	34.3	18.1	3.4	18.8	9.2
Primary	40.6	67.6	67.3	60.3	47.1
Secondary	16.1	5.6	15.2	12.5	28.2

(Table continues on the following page.)

Table 2-2. Key Statistics of Countries Studied

Indicator	Bolivia	Brazil	Costa Rica	Mexico	Peru
Population and demography					
Total population, 2001 (in millions)	8.5	172.6	3.9	99.4	26.1
Percent urban, 2001	62.9	81.7	59.0	74.4	72.8
Average annual rate of growth, 2000–15	2.0	1.1	1.8	1.2	1.4
Urban	4.5	2.7	3.3	2.7	2.1
Rural	-0.2	-3.1	1.6	-0.6	1.0
Human Development Index (HDI)					
HDI ranking, 2000	0.653	0.757	0.820	0.796	0.747
	114	73	43	54	82
GDP per capita (PPP$, thousands), 2000	2.42	7.63	8.65	9.02	4.80
GDP per capita minus HDI ranking	6	-13	14	1	6
Poverty and income distribution					
Human poverty index, 2000					
Rank	28	17	2	11	19
Value (%)	16.3	12.2	4.0	9.4	12.8
Population below the income poverty line (%)					
$1 a day (1993 PPP $), 1983–2000	14.4	11.6	12.6	15.9	15.5
$2 a day (1993 PPP $), 1983–2000	34.3	26.5	26.0	37.7	41.4
National poverty line, 1987–2000	—	17.4	22.0	10.1	49.0
Poor households (% of total)					
Total	—	29	20	38	37
Urban	47	25	17	31	25
Indigent households (% of total)					
Total	—	11	5	13	18
Urban	19	8	5	7	7

in Brazil and Mexico, poverty has already become a prevalently urban phenomenon. This is about to happen in Bolivia and Peru as well, due to rapid urban growth. The fast growth of cities in Costa Rica means that it is only a matter of time before a similar phenomenon occurs there as well.

Of the five countries in our study, Costa Rica presents the most favorable social picture. It has the highest life expectancy, the highest literacy rate, the lowest infant and maternal mortality rates, the lowest percentage of households without access to basic services, the lowest disparity of income between men and women, and the highest Human Development Index (HDI). Costa Rica also tops the list in social expenditure as a proportion of gross domestic product (GDP). Highlighted characteristics for the other countries in our study follow:

- Bolivia has the highest percentage of people with no schooling. Its income distribution is not as good as Costa Rica's or Peru's, but is much better than Brazil's or Mexico's. Its poverty levels are the highest in the sample, but social expenditure levels have improved significantly following reforms.
- Brazil has the second lowest indicators of schooling and the worst income distribution, but it is second lowest in both overall poverty and extreme poverty rates. Its social expenditure is high; a large proportion of this, however, is spent regressively on social security. Brazil is also the only country in the list whose HDI ranking is worse than its per capita GDP ranking.
- Mexico has the second highest overall and urban poverty levels, and its overall income distribution and schooling indicators are almost on a par with Brazil's sobering figures. The country's urban income distribution is much better, though; it is second only to Costa Rica's. Expenditure in human capital (education and health) as a proportion of gross national product (GNP) is higher than Brazil's and Peru's, but lower than Bolivia's and Costa Rica's.
- Peru's income distribution is on a par with Costa Rica's, the best in the sample. Its social expenditure and human capital expenditure as a percentage of GDP and GNP, respectively, are the lowest in the sample. Its poverty and absolute poverty indicators are in the lower range of the sample.

Social indicators for the cities in our study are consistently above their respective country's national average. Although these cities have a high percentage of their population living in poverty, they are clearly beacons of progress in their respective countries, not only in relation to economic dynamism but also in terms of social development.

Indicator	Bolivia	Brazil	Costa Rica	Mexico	Peru
Labor market					
Disparity of men/women (%)	-40	-38	-22	-41	—
Urban pop. working in low-productivity sectors (%), total	65.5	46.5	39.6	43.6	—
Men	57.1	41.9	37.5	40.4	—
Women	74.1	51.9	40.4	46.0	—
Social expenditure					
Public expenditure per capita, 1997 (US$)	119	951	550	352	189
Education	59	164	153	153	—
Health and nutrition	14	138	193	—	—
Social security	27	487	146	—	—
Housing, water, and sanitation	20	162	52	—	—
Public expenditure per capita as % of GDP, 1997, total	12.0	19.8	20.8	7.8	5.8
Education	5.9	3.4	5.8	3.4	—
Health and nutrition	1.4	2.5	7.3	—	—
Social security	2.7	10.1	5.5	—	—
Housing, water, and sanitation	2.0	3.4	2.0	—	—
Human capital expenditure/GNP (%), total	9.4	7.1	11.3	7.7	5.1
Education	5.6	5.2	5.3	4.9	2.9
Health	3.8	1.9	6.0	2.8	2.2

Note: PPP$ means that GDP per capita is calculated at purchasing power parity; i.e., it is adjusted to reflect differences in purchasing power across countries, so as to allow direct comparisons among the various countries' income figures.

Sources: ECLAC (1998, 2001), IDB (1998), Morley (2001), UNDP (2000), and World Bank (2002).

Case Study 1. Bolivia: The People's Participation Law

> IT IS TRUE THAT WHEN LOCAL PEOPLE HAVE THE OPPORTUNITY TO MAKE DECISIONS, THEY SOMETIMES MAKE MISTAKES AND CHOOSE APPLES INSTEAD OF ORANGES, EVEN THOUGH IT IS ORANGES THEY NEED THE MOST. OFTEN THEY WILL DECIDE TO GET THEIR ROADS PAVED, INSTEAD OF THINGS THAT ARE MORE IMPORTANT BUT LESS APPARENT. BUT IF THEY HAVE THE OPPORTUNITY TO DECIDE AND TO MAKE MISTAKES, IN TIME THEY LEARN AND BEGIN TO FIGHT FOR IMPROVEMENTS IN SCHOOLS AND OTHER THINGS THAT LEAD TO HUMAN DEVELOPMENT.
> —German Marañón, President, Surveillance Committee, Cochabamba

A Major Legal and Institutional Reform

In April 1994, Bolivia went through a major reform in its institutional structure. Up to that year, there were only 61 municipalities in the country, which were confined to the major cities and towns. Municipal jurisdictions were limited to the urban areas. Most of the country's territory and population were directly administered by the central government. Law 1551, known as the People's Participation Law, changed the situation radically by:

- Creating 250 new municipalities, encompassing both urban and rural areas and putting the entire national territory of Bolivia under municipal jurisdiction
- Establishing mandatory budget transfers, known as co-participation, of 20 percent of the central government budget to municipalities—each municipality's share is proportional to its share of the country's population
- Establishing participatory budgeting at the local level, whereby area-based community organizations (ABCOs) are involved in priority setting, as the mandatory mechanism for the allocation of co-participation resources, through annual and five-year investment plans
- Establishing simple procedures for the legal recognition of ABCOs, known as *juntas de vecinos* (neighborhood associations) in urban areas and *sindicatos rurales* (village committees) in rural areas
- Establishing a surveillance committee, a watchdog body composed of representatives of ABCOs, for the control of the allocation and expenditure of the co-participation resources in each municipality.

ABCOs have a long history in Bolivia. In rural areas, area-based organizations and forms of mutual help date back to the Inca *ayllus*. In urban areas, the neighborhood associations, their local federations, and their national confederation have long been important political players. However, both in rural and urban areas, organizations based on special interests, such as professional associations and trade or industry groups, have traditionally been the main interlocutors of government. Before the advent of the People's Participation Law, few area-based organizations had legal recognition, and none had a specified legal role assigned to it. The emphasis placed by the People's Participation Law on the recognition of area-based organizations and the role assigned to them was part of a specific intent to decentralize an important part of resource allocation and decisionmaking to the lowest appropriate level.

In urban areas, co-participation resources are used for urban upgrading and building of social equipment (schools, clinics, community centers) in low-income neighborhoods. The yearly expenditure on these items in urban areas through the mechanisms of Law 1551 is roughly $100 million nationwide.

Immediate and Far-Reaching Impacts

The main achievement of Law 1551 was linking decentralization, budget transfers, and participation in a national legal framework. The impacts were far reaching and immediate in terms of the legal recognition of community organizations, the number of municipalities receiving budget transfers, the municipal share of public investment, and the amount invested in the social sector. This is clearly shown in table 2-3.

A New Dimension for Participatory Budgeting: The Carrot and the Stick

Establishing a national legal framework that associates decentralization to the establishment of a regular, predictable resource flow to municipalities would have already had a major impact on the institutional and governance structure of the country. But Law 1551 went beyond that to mandate participatory budgeting and control of resource allocation and expenditure by community representatives. (See box 2-1.) These instruments are not new, but Bolivia, by adopting a nationwide legal framework for participatory budgeting and community control of expenditure, gave these instruments an entirely new dimension.

By institutionalizing it at the national level, Bolivia has taken local level participatory budgeting one step farther. The limitations of the Brazilian model of participatory budgeting derive in great part from the fact that the initiative was taken by the municipalities, which makes it

Table 2-3. The Impact of the People's Participation Law

Impact	Before the law (1993)	After the law (1995)
Number of legally recognized ABCOs has increased dramatically	Less than 100	15,000
Number of municipalities has increased fivefold	61	311
Budget transfers to municipalities have doubled	10% of central government budget	20% of central government budget
Mechanism for allocation of transfers to municipalities has been changed	Legal residency of taxpayers	Municipality's share of national population
Distribution of transfers has been made more equitable	Three largest municipalities received 90% of the total	Rural areas receive 50% of the total
Municipal share in total public investment has more than trebled	11% in 1993	39% in 1995
Social investment has doubled	1.72% of GNP in 1993 ($90 million)	3.62% of GNP in 1995 ($180 million)
Investment in basic education has trebled	$10 million in 1993	$30 million in 1995

Source: Authors' construction from field study data.

vulnerable to the ups and downs of local politics. As in Tijuana, in Brazil it is the municipality that decides the amount of resources to be allocated via participatory budgeting in a given year. By contrast, the Bolivian model mandates participatory budgeting at the local level through a national law which also establishes the level of transfers to be allocated by participatory budgeting. In doing so, the Bolivian state has launched a process that is nationwide and has built-in continuity and predictability. These are essential conditions for the development of methodologies and of a critical mass of qualified local actors to assume political and technical responsibilities within the process.

While many feared that Law 1551 would be changed following General Hugo Banzer's victory in the 1997 general elections, it has actually endured due to the incentive structure built into the law. At the local level, mayors are delighted to have new powers and resources (the carrot), but they have to live with the fact that the community has a say in

Box 2-1. Bolivia's Six Steps of Municipal Participatory Planning

Step 1: Preparation and Organization. Social and institutional actors are identified and their roles and responsibilities defined. Basic agreements are reached. The surveillance committee has a key liaison role vis-à-vis local authorities and community-based organizations.

Step 2: Participatory Diagnosis. This step is divided into two activities. *Community diagnosis*, which identifies the needs, constraints, and opportunities of the communities and lists their demands, is carried out in all communities. *In-depth diagnosis*, which is used to check the information in the community diagnosis, is carried out in at least 10 percent of the communities in each municipality. The information from all communities is organized in a consolidated municipal diagnosis.

Step 3: Preparation and Approval of the Municipal Development Plan (MDP). The MDP, which has a five-year horizon, is prepared through a series of local and district workshops on the basis of the priorities identified in step 2. Each community is represented by two delegates, one male and one female.

Step 4: Preparation and Approval of the Annual Operations Plan for the Coming Fiscal Year. The AOP is prepared every year by each municipality. It is based on the MDP, but adjusted in light of new demands that may have surfaced in the interim. The surveillance committee is charged with ensuring that communities have a say in operations plan preparation and are informed about its contents so that they may monitor its implementation.

Step 5: Participatory Implementation of the MDP. The MDP is implemented through five successive annual operations plans. Its implementation is the responsibility of the municipality under the auspices of the surveillance committee. Although Law 1551 envisages the possibility of community management of projects, most municipalities prefer to use their conventional investment and procurement procedures, working through contractors.

Step 6: Evaluation and Adjustment of the MDP. At the end of each fiscal year, the municipality prepares a report on MDP implementation, identifying achievements and obstacles. The surveillance committee examines the report and presents comments and suggestions. The report is also submitted for approval to the town council, and the MDP is amended following the debate to provide solutions to problems that have been raised.

resource allocation (the stick). Communities, on the other hand, complain about flaws in the law's application, as we will see below, but uphold their new rights with resolve.

More Capacity-Building Is Needed to Support the Process

In urban areas, mayors have sought to co-opt neighborhood associations and surveillance committees in an effort to adapt the mechanisms of Law 1551 to established political practices and assert their political patronage over the process. By all accounts, the process has worked better in rural than urban areas. New municipalities in rural areas have relied on traditional forms of community organization to set in motion the mechanisms established by Law 1551, with good results.

This was only to be expected. It would certainly be naive to imagine that a long tradition of populist politics and flawed governance could change overnight. However, analysis of the situation in Bolivia's four largest cities—Cochabamba, El Alto, La Paz, and Santa Cruz de la Sierra—shows that, although the application of the law is influenced by the prevailing political culture, awareness of the new subjective rights that have been granted by Law 1551 is contributing to changes in that same political culture. The nationwide character of the process contributes to this. There have already been three national meetings of surveillance committee presidents since 1994, for example, and a community of practice is beginning to take shape.

This will certainly be a long-term process, but there are clear reasons for hope. Some communities are better informed than others about Law 1551. Some municipalities have done a better job than others at setting up information campaigns about the law's application; the central government has organized training activities in some areas; and, in some places, there are particularly active nongovernmental organizations (NGOs) or donor-funded projects spreading the message. We have seen remarkable instances among community representatives of a high level of information about the provisions of the law, the cost and technical features of works, and the mechanics of resource allocation and expenditure. The high level of cost consciousness among some community leaders has struck us as a particularly favorable sign, but we have also seen cases in which the level of information about Law 1551 and its mechanisms was low.

Private sector participation in the application of Law 1551 has so far been limited. The participation of NGOs, by providing technical assistance to community groups, is not institutionalized—and is even resented by some municipalities. As to the for-profit private sector, its participation has not gone beyond the traditional roles of contractor and building materials supplier. Much more must be done to involve the private sector, inform and build capacity of communities and municipalities, and disseminate good practices and methodologies for community involvement in order to strengthen the process and allow people's participation in Bolivia to realize its full potential.

Case Study 2. Brazil: The Guarapiranga Program, São Paulo

> WE HAD AN ENGINEER WHOSE ONLY DUTY WAS THE COORDINATION OF THE WORK WITH THE SOCIAL SUPPORT TEAM AND THE MUNICIPALITY. WE ARE FULLY CONSCIOUS OF THE FACT THAT, IF THE POPULATION DOESN'T PARTICIPATE AND COLLABORATE, THE WORK MAY BECOME UNFEASIBLE. THE SOCIAL SIDE IS FUNDAMENTAL... THIS KIND OF WORK INVOLVES A RADICAL CHANGE FROM ALL POINTS OF VIEW: THE TECHNICAL AND MANAGEMENT ASPECTS OF THE WORK ARE VERY DIFFERENT FROM WHAT WE DO IN THE FORMAL CITY.
> —*Construction Firm Engineer*

Environmental Sanitation as an Entry Point for Urban Upgrading

The Guarapiranga program is a large-scale attempt to deal with the pollution of the Guarapiranga reservoir, one of the key water sources of the sprawling metropolitan area of São Paulo. Uncontrolled informal settlement development in the water catchment area, which gained momentum in the 1970s and 1980s, was one of the key reasons for the deterioration of the quality of this reservoir which provides water for over 3 million people. By the mid-1980s, the water quality problems had become so serious that the São Paulo water utility, SABESP, sought the assistance of the World Bank in implementing a cleanup program. The program, which started in 1993 and was completed at the end of 2000, was comprised of a number of different projects, including the building of major primary and secondary infrastructure for wastewater collection and treatment, comprehensive upgrading of squatter settlements and illegal land subdivisions, and the development of a new legal and regulatory framework to manage the water catchment.

Upgrading was thus part of a regional development plan for a considerable part of a metropolitan area, involving the state and municipal levels. A large part of the Guarapiranga basin is in the municipality of São Paulo, but some small municipalities in the metropolitan area were also involved. The institutional arrangement adopted for the program was a horizontal one, in which each of the main actors was responsible for a component or project, under a general coordination unit established at the state level. This horizontal arrangement was crucial to the program's successful tackling of a wide range of issues at scale.

Recognition of Informal Settlements and an Integrated Upgrading Approach

The urban upgrading component of Guarapiranga in the municipality of São Paulo, which was run by the municipality itself, was the object of our study. The scale of this project was impressive; investment made from 1993 to 2000 totaled approximately $190 million, benefiting almost 200,000 people in squatter settlements and informal land subdivisions.

The entry point for urban upgrading in the case of Guarapiranga was environmental sanitation. It was recognized that the informal settlements of the Guarapiranga basin are a part of the city that is not going to be removed, and therefore needs sanitation infrastructure for social and environmental reasons. Recognition of the importance of interactions between wastewater collection and other branches of infrastructure, such as roads, storm drainage, and water supply, led to the adoption of an integrated upgrading approach rather than a sectoral approach.

Although it increased per capita cost, this integrated approach was necessary to enhance the sustainability of the intervention, since the negative impacts that lack of storm drainage and road paving would have had on the sewerage network, among other problems, were thereby avoided. It also provided an opportunity to boost demand-responsiveness and community ownership of projects by involving local residents in participatory information gathering and area development planning. In spite of uneven implementation, this has represented a significant methodological advance over earlier upgrading projects in São Paulo.

Insufficient Concern for Sustainability

Although its integrated approach was based on a concern for sustainability, there were other aspects of the Guarapiranga program that did not contribute to this goal as much as they could have:

- **Legal obstacles to tenure regularization.** Security of land tenure, although recognized as a key issue, could not be addressed because of the legal situation of the Guarapiranga basin. Severe restrictions on land use and occupation in water catchment areas were enacted by the state of São Paulo in the 1970s, which ironically caused the price of land in the Guarapiranga area to fall, stimulating low-income informal occupation. The same restrictions that prevented legal land development and infrastructure provision also prevented the upgrading project from tackling the issue of land tenure regularization. One of the outcomes of the Guarapiranga program was a sweeping change in the legal and regulatory framework for water catchment management for the entire state of São Paulo, which took place in 1997 and should open the way for land tenure regularization in our study area and elsewhere.

- **Low level of cost consciousness and lack of an explicit cost recovery and subsidy strategy.** Urban upgrading interventions in Brazil have generally not had a good track record with regard to the level of cost consciousness and the adoption of an explicit, demand-based cost recovery strategy. Guarapiranga is no exception to this. The long-time exclusion of the inhabitants of the area from the provision of services, their low level of income, and the desirability of ensuring a minimum level of consumption of certain goods and services (e.g., roads, water, and sanitation) to the population of the area justified a high level of subsidy. This was further reinforced by the relevance of the program to the entire metropolitan area. The problem was thus not the level of the subsidies, but the fact that subsidies were not transparent; there was no attempt to target the poorest, most vulnerable groups, and there was no explicit cost recovery strategy. In our interviews, local residents expressed a wish to regularize their relationships with the municipality and with utilities, and there is a clear window of opportunity for water and electricity metering and land tax collection. The launching of a cost recovery drive, coupled with a transparent subsidy structure, would greatly contribute to the financial sustainability of the intervention.
- **Exclusive focus on feasibility of implementation.** The motivation for community participation for Guarapiranga's sponsoring agencies was to ensure the feasibility of the project's implementation. In the initial formulation of the urban upgrading component, there was no explicit socio-technical support strategy. Although the municipality's small group of social workers did provide some support to the communities, it fell far short of real needs. The problems in the implementation of the project's pilot phase were so many that the municipality decided to resort to the private sector to provide socio-technical support services during implementation. This made a crucial difference in allowing the project to be implemented, but the feasibility focus prevented the project from going one step farther and ensuring socio-technical support to communities in the aftermath of the implementation of the works. Assisting communities with organizational support and environmental education in the post-implementation phase would have contributed greatly to the conservation of the benefits and the continuity of the develop-

ment process. Box 2-2 provides a commentary on the reasons for this, concluding that the problem was a focus on project, rather than policy. For all its accomplishments, focus on feasibility of implementation, rather than sustainability, has kept the project from realizing the full potential of participation.

An Agile Implementation Strategy Helps the Municipality Get the Job Done

The municipality was the institutional motor of the project, which was coordinated by a small, highly qualified unit at the Department of Housing. It was decided to contract out all the specialized services needed. Competitive bidding was used to select planning, engineering, subproject management, construction quality control, and building firms. Sociotechnical support was included in the construction contracts and was also provided by a private firm, which was selected and hired directly by the construction firms involved. The active involvement of the for-profit private sector in the provision of most of the services required by the urban upgrading component enhanced the efficiency, timeliness, and flexibility of the project; it also created relevant capacity in a number of firms. The level of private sector participation and influence in the Guarapiranga upgrading project surpasses anything seen before in Brazil. It may be considered to be, along with the horizontal institutional arrangement, one of the reasons for Guarapiranga's achievements.

Box 2-2. Socio-Technical Support in Guarapiranga: A Typical Project Cycle Issue

The municipality:

- Acknowledges the need to involve communities
- Acknowledges its limitations to carry out some tasks directly
- Has the capacity to coordinate the process
- Has the capacity to hire the needed expertise.

However, the municipality:

- Doesn't go the whole way (it stops short of post-implementation socio-technical support)
- Is more interested in feasibility of implementation than in sustainability
- Takes this approach because its focus is on project, not policy.

Case Study 3. Costa Rica: FUPROVI's Habitat Popular Urbano Program, San José

> FUPROVI COMPLEMENTS STATE ACTIVITY THROUGH A CLOSE RELATION TO THE STATE...BECAUSE THE STATE IS SLOW AND INEFFICIENT IN THE RESOLUTION OF URGENT PROBLEMS SUCH AS HOUSING, THE IDEA IS TO CREATE NONGOVERNMENTAL TOOLS THAT CAN PROVIDE A MORE FLEXIBLE AND EFFICIENT RESPONSE TO THE DEMANDS OF THE MOMENT.
> —*José Manuel Valverde, Applied Research Coordinator with CERCA, a UNCHS (Habitat) Program for Central America*

An Ambitious Housing Subsidy Policy

Costa Rica's burgeoning shelter deficit and the appearance of large numbers of urban squatter settlements in the 1980s led to the adoption of an ambitious housing subsidy policy. In 1986, during the administration of President Oscar Arias, a national housing finance system was created, channeling public funds into subsidies that were targeted to low-income households and complemented, for households in all but the lowest income brackets, by private institutions such as commercial banks, savings and loan institutions, and cooperatives.

This was matched by an intense movement within civil society, which led to the establishment of myriad housing associations among low-income people. These were groups comprised of families from different locations, usually formed on the basis of political or work connections, and with a very clear goal in mind: obtaining a house. Housing associations immediately set about finding suitable plots of land, often aided by political connections. Since Costa Rica's Central Valley, where the capital city's metropolitan area is located, is not as densely populated as many other Latin American urban areas, many groups did succeed in finding suitable land with reasonable access to infrastructure for an affordable price. There was usually an element of subsidy involved, since many plots were on public land that was released for sale, at a low price, due to the housing association's political connections. In many instances, the land could be bought for a low price because it lacked a legal title deed.

A New Kind of Actor Is Needed to Reach the Poor

Although households in the lowest income bracket—up to two minimum wages, or roughly $350 per month—were entitled to a full subsidy (up to $4,000, depending on the prevailing exchange rate), they tended to be excluded from the benefits of the subsidy program. This fits a pattern seen in the national housing finance systems established by most Latin American countries. Although theoretically targeted at the poor, these systems were hijacked by the middle and lower middle classes, while the poor continued to resort—in ever-increasing numbers—to squatting or informal land subdivisions. In Costa Rica, it quickly became apparent that regularizing land tenure, lowering building costs, and providing credit and technical assistance to households in the informal sector were the keys to allowing poor families to gain access to the housing subsidy program.

The Foundation for the Promotion of Housing (FUPROVI) was founded in 1987 as a not-for-profit independent institution with this aim in mind. The institution was singled out by the Costa Rican government to be the recipient, in the following year, of a development aid package from the Swedish International Development Agency. FUPROVI received $14 million in Swedish grants over the following years; it used these to establish its longest running and most successful program, Habitat Popular Urbano. This program aims to systematically tackle each bottleneck of the housing subsidy program that prohibits access by the poor.

Specifically, Habitat Popular Urbano provides assistance to housing associations and single families in planning and implementing housing projects. FUPROVI provides planning, engineering, and land tenure regularization services; socio-technical support to project implementation through the application of its assisted mutual-help construction methodology; and a bridge loan to allow households to implement their projects while their housing subsidy applications are being processed. Assisted mutual-help construction lowers costs significantly so that the subsidy often covers the full cost of a house and related infrastructure. When it does not, FUPROVI prequalifies project participants for a loan from a private institution to cover the difference.

Mutual-help construction also serves as a targeting filter. Only poor families that could not have access to a house by any other means subject themselves to FUPROVI's requirement of 30 hours of labor a week for an average of 18 to 24 months. By any measure, this is a tough regimen, which places a particular burden on households that have only one adult. This also ensures the demand-driven nature of the projects, since the communities only make a commitment after a thorough analysis of all the implications, and, when they do, they are required to sign a formal contract with the institution.

In the FUPROVI system, the institution provides intensive assistance and supervision in technical, organizational, and administrative matters. The community manages funds, procurement of materials and specialized services, warehousing and stock administration; organizes and keeps track of the contributions of community members; sets up support services such as soup kitchens and daycare; and—last but not least—performs the building. These functions mostly cover project implementation rather than planning. FUPROVI, in order to optimize the use of available land and lower the cost of construction, does most of the planning itself. As a result, compared to the other cases we have seen, there is not much community participation in area development planning or discussion of urban and architectural design options in the FUPROVI model.

A Demand-Driven Approach Needs a Strong, Sustainable Supply Mechanism

FUPROVI's approach is demand driven and based on community management. Its assisted mutual-help methodology represents the meeting point between supply and demand. The technical assistance and capacity-building activities required by FUPROVI's system are intense, showing that a demand-driven program needs a strong and well-organized supply mechanism to succeed. In this context, continuity is essential, and FUPROVI has sought to ensure from the start that it would be a viable and sustainable institution that would not be perpetually dependent on donor grants. FUPROVI charges between 16 and 23 percent of the cost of a project for its services; these services include preparation of all necessary contracts and documentation; intermediation between housing associations and the national housing finance system; assistance in land tenure regularization; urban planning, architecture, and engineering services, including obtaining all necessary permits; training activities required by the assisted mutual-help construction system; and technical assistance and supervision of the building process from technical, organizational, and administrative points of view. FUPROVI makes a point of negotiating the services package and its price with its clients before embarking on a project. This contributes to the institution's financial sustainability and its ability to attract and retain qualified personnel without having to rely on grant funds alone. Close to full cost recovery is thus one of the pillars of the FUPROVI system. The rationale for this is that FUPROVI provides a mechanism to allow the poor to access the government housing subsidy scheme, but FUPROVI's services themselves cannot be provided on a grant basis, since the institution is not likely to receive any grant funding beyond the original Swedish grants.

FUPROVI has sought to preserve as much as possible of its seed capital of $14 million, which has been kept in a rotating fund, part of which is loaned out to project participants and part of which is invested. The institution has thereby helped families build 15,000 houses over 10 years with a high degree of cost recovery and client satisfaction. (See box 2-3.)

> **Box 2-3. The Four Pillars of the FUPROVI Model**
>
> FUPROVI has demonstrated the important role the private sector may play in delivering housing to the poorest groups. Currently, there are no other institutions in Costa Rica capable of providing similar services in urban areas. Replication of the FUPROVI model elsewhere would probably require building the capacity of a number of institutions, especially considering the much larger scale that would be necessary in other Latin American countries. This is an issue of concern in analyzing the FUPROVI model, particularly since the Costa Rican government has strongly reduced the scale of its housing subsidy program in recent years, reducing the incentives for the creation of new FUPROVIs.
>
> The four pillars of the FUPROVI model are as follows:
>
> - A generous housing subsidy program, which covers up to 50 percent of the market cost of a house and related infrastructure, and frequently—because FUPROVI manages to cut market cost roughly in half thanks to its assisted mutual-help system—ends up covering the full cost of the house for the lowest income bracket
> - Availability of suitably located land—which in Costa Rica is an important requirement, given the country's tradition of detached or semi-detached houses and strong cultural resistance to densification
> - A motivated and relatively well-educated clientele
> - Intensive assistance and capacity-building provided by a strong, motivated, well-organized, and sustainable institution.

Operating at Scale Is Difficult without the Subsidy

With the woes of the housing subsidy system in recent years,[1] a critical pillar of the FUPROVI model is at stake. Without the subsidy scheme, the bridge finance FUPROVI provides needs to be transformed into a long-term loan, with the consequence that the institution's resources remain tied up, and the rotating fund mechanism has a much slower cycle (15 years instead of 2, on average). FUPROVI's ability to leverage funds, one of its key assets, is thus jeopardized. FUPROVI has been able to survive the impact, but it has had to reduce its output strongly, dropping from the 4,000 units per year it had reached in 1996 to about 1,500 units per year in 1999. It has also had to trim its workforce, which has meant a loss of qualified and specialized staff.

---

[1] The administration that took office in 1997 halted the subsidy scheme at first, due to Costa Rica's difficult fiscal situation, and later resumed it under roughly the same rules and procedures as before but at a far smaller scale.

FUPROVI is managing to cope with the situation, however, and to survive. Perhaps most importantly, it is exploring new alternatives to increase the scale of its operations. It is launching a savings and loan scheme in partnership with a private commercial bank which could provide the key to both sustainability and scale in the long term, building on the tradition of on-time repayment of its client base and moving toward market-based interest rates.

Capacity-Building Is Good for Sustainability

Another key aspect of sustainability is communities' ability to undertake further development initiatives on their own. The sustained commitment FUPROVI requires of communities takes its toll; normally, there are no further community initiatives for the first two or three years following completion of the works, during which time people focus on improving their homes. After that, community organization slowly resumes to deal with issues such as street paving and bus routes.

Such long-term participation seems to benefit greatly from skills acquired during the construction process. However, the lack of socially meaningful post-implementation community development activities such as soup kitchens and daycare facilities seems a missed opportunity to work on area-based development and ensure continuity of participation in the mid-term. The exclusive focus on housing of FUPROVI's projects, while it helps people concentrate their energies, also has its disadvantages.

Case Study 4. Mexico: Community Upgrading Programs, Tijuana

> I BEGAN TO WORK ON THE PROJECT ALONE, AND MY NEIGHBORS THOUGHT I WAS CRAZY. THEN I WAS JOINED BY ONE OF THE NEIGHBORS, AND THEY SAID THAT WE WERE TWO LUNATICS. GRADUALLY, ALL THE NEIGHBORS JOINED IN: NOW WE ARE ALL CRAZY.
> —*Lucio Quiñones, President, Works Committee of Huejotzingo Street*

Political Competition as an Entry Point for Participatory Upgrading

The 1990s have seen significant reforms in Tijuana's municipal government. An overhaul of the municipal cadastre, the enhancement of local revenue generation, and the involvement of civil society and the private sector in the city's strategic planning have been some of the advances made. Further, in the area of informal settlement upgrading, Tijuana has pioneered an approach that couples participatory budgeting with community management of small local works projects (most frequently, street paving; improvement of sidewalks, public places, and school buildings; and sports facility construction), to which the community makes an upfront cash contribution averaging 30 percent of the cost. The government subsidy, averaging the remaining 70 percent of the cost, is paid directly to a community works committee that manages the resources, hires the contractors, and oversees the work.

Tijuana's community upgrading programs have made significant progress in the city's *colonias populares* (informal settlements) between 1991 and 1998, during which time the municipality spent $40 million in small-scale local infrastructure works to an upfront contribution of roughly $17 million on the part of the local communities themselves. These programs have successfully challenged conventional assumptions about what poor urban communities are willing and able to do.

Community upgrading initiatives, which had already been in place for some time, were intensified in Tijuana by the Solidaridad program, a federal social investment fund launched by the Salinas administration in 1989. Solidaridad was initially managed by local social development department offices, which, as delegates of the federal government, bypassed the municipalities. The program was a key political instrument for the ruling Institutional Revolutionary Party. When the rival National Action Party was voted into office at the Tijuana municipality later that year, the program was modified to reflect the principle that the state is not particularly effective at delivering certain types of infrastructure and services and should consequently move away from direct service provision and toward an enabling role.

Methodology Has Improved over the Years

As decentralization has taken root in Mexico, the management of community upgrading programs has increasingly shifted to the purview of local municipalities. One of the results of this trend has been the decentralization to municipalities by the Zedillo administration of the management of Solidaridad itself. Additionally, while participatory budgeting in Tijuana was initially conducted through large community gatherings, over the years, delegations and subdelegations—decentralized offices of the municipality—have become the preferred channels for presentation of community requests. An institutional structure for participatory budgeting has been established whereby delegational committees analyze community requests, select projects for the coming year, and present a project list to a citywide committee for approval. The Tijuana program has also introduced community management of project resources, community procurement, and the requirement of an upfront community contribution to the cost of works as well as adoption of more stringent technical standards and project supervision routines. Decentralization of program management, technical assistance, and outreach to the delegations and subdelegations were introduced in 1998. A new, direct relationship with the community has taken shape through the mechanism of participatory budgeting. This participation has ushered in a new generation of active community leaders, although some residents have continued to plead for projects in the old "handout" tradition.

The improvements in methodology introduced by the Tijuana program are related to Mexico's ongoing process of democratization and decentralization.

A Response to the Infrastructure Deficit

Tijuana is home to 711 *maquiladora* factories which employ 147,000 people. Unemployment is very low here, and the city's proximity to the United States and its booming economy have made it an attractive destination for migrants. Migrants who arrive in Tijuana usually settle in one of the colonias in the eastern part of the city. These colonias are usually informal land subdivisions where public and private spaces are clearly defined but basic infrastructure and services are lacking. Over a period of years, these are gradually installed in response to community pressure, with electricity provided first, since it has fewer constraints than other types of infrastructure and lower cost, followed by water and sanitation.

Tijuana's community upgrading programs have been an attempt to respond to the needs that arose as a result of such large-scale informal subdivision of land. To the uncontrolled dynamics of urban development were added the city's irregular topography, the great number of inhabited areas of risk, and the fact that 46 percent of the land area was dedicated to low-density residential use. These factors all exacerbate the infrastructure deficit and make it expensive to reduce.

The community upgrading programs aimed to construct basic works that are in the municipality's sphere of competence to respond to the direct demand of the sectors of the population living in colonias populares. In general, these requests have primarily involved the paving of streets (48 percent), the improvement or construction of schools (16 percent), and the introduction of storm drainage infrastructure (15 percent). (See box 2-4.)

The Project Cycle Orientation Prevails

This perhaps excessive emphasis on one type of infrastructure—paving—reflects a lack of structured, area-based participatory planning

> ### 2-4. Street Paving Projects Predominate in Tijuana
>
> According to the operating manual for Tijuana's community upgrading programs, program funds may be applied to paving, sewers, electricity, storm drainage, earthworks, foot and vehicle bridges, containment walls, perimeter fencing, stairways, ramps, stream fords, sports fields, educational infrastructure, maintenance and restructuring of pathways, basic health infrastructure, and community centers.
>
> In the face of all these options, why does street paving predominate in Tijuana? For one thing, since many colonias already have land tenure regularization, electricity, water, and sanitation, it is logical for them to request the paving of their streets as a next step in infrastructure extension. Also, paving works are simple and not very expensive, and they are a municipal responsibility. Street paving is also a solution to unfavorable soil and terrain conditions (clayey soil and steep slopes) and the consequent difficulties of access during the rainy season and presence of dust during the dry season. Street paving has symbolic value as well. The status of an area changes overnight with street paving, since it is thenceforth perceived as part of the "formal" or developed portion of the city.
>
> Finally, though, the prevalence of street paving reflects another, more negative, circumstance: a lack of a concerted, coherent, and comprehensive approach to community upgrading. In short, the process sees the trees very well, but not the forest: it lacks a systemic vision.

which has in turn led to a piecemeal approach to upgrading, and has meant that the significant mobilization generated by the programs has not been channeled into a long-term development process for Tijuana's colonias populares.

In Tijuana, as in Guarapiranga, a project cycle orientation prevails over a long-term policy vision, and the opportunity to ensure sustainability is missed. The municipality, which is responsible for street paving, has not coordinated with the state and federal levels to include other types of infrastructure in the community upgrading programs. Moreover, parallel state programs, such as the one for water and sanitation service extension, are still run in a populist manner and do not benefit from the innovative and effective mechanisms the municipality has developed.

In Tijuana, civil society organizations are very active in the traditional social sector fields (health, education, assistance to vulnerable groups), but have so far been absent from the housing and urban development field. Although some in the for-profit private sector have started to think about ways of improving their employees' quality of life, the potential for cooperation with the maquiladoras and other private sector firms in community upgrading and shelter improvement projects has not been tapped. The current community upgrading programs lack a channel for civil society and private sector involvement.

Case Study 5. Peru: The Self-Managed Urban Community of Villa El Salvador, Lima

> LAST NIGHT, I WAS TALKING TO SOME OF THE FOUNDERS OF VILLA EL SALVADOR. THEY FEEL THAT THE MOST IMPORTANT THING IS THAT THE TOWNSPEOPLE MAY DECIDE WHAT TO DO. IT DOESN'T MATTER IF THEY MAKE MISTAKES. EVEN IF THEY DO, THEY WILL LEARN FROM THEIR MISTAKES.
> —Juan Arbañil, Villa El Salvador Leader

A Different Paradigm: State-Assisted Barriada Development

Since the end of World War II, the urban share of Peru's population has gone from 30 to over 70 percent. The bulk of this phenomenal growth has taken place in Greater Lima. The capital's share of Peru's population, which was 5 percent in 1905, is now about 30 percent. Lima is 10 times bigger than the country's second largest city, Arequipa.

The informal settlements known as *pueblos jovenes* or *barriadas*, where 30 percent of the capital's population now lives, have accounted for much of Lima's growth in the postwar years. Peru's informal settlements have developed against a backdrop quite different from the circumstances existing in the rest of Latin America. For one thing, the desert surrounding Lima represents a vast amount of unused available public land. For another, the region has a long tradition of mutual help, dating back to the original Andean migrants. Further, as early as 1961, legislation (Law 13517, the Law of the Barriadas) has been in place that sets forth guidelines and procedures for orderly informal settlement development, with the state taking a key role in guiding this development.

Villa El Salvador (VES), founded in 1971, is the epitome of state-assisted barriada development. (See box 2-5.) The development of VES was initiated to accommodate 4,000 families that had begun to occupy land in one of the southern suburbs of Lima; the government soon came to see this as an opportunity to provide land to more migrants who wanted it. The reformist military regime of General Velasco Alvarado, which was in power at the time, adopted a collaborative stance vis-à-vis the grassroots organizations that were demanding a solution to the housing problem in Lima. With the mediation of the National Support System for

> **Box 2-5. Villa El Salvador in the Context of Lima's Barriadas**
>
> Villa El Salvador (population 350,000), with more than 50,000 lots, is part of the vast area of barriadas known as Lima's Southern Cone, occupied in all by some 900,000 people. As of the late 1990s, throughout Lima:
>
> - There were about 370,000 plots in barriadas.
> - Of these plots, some 220,000 had been in existence for more than 20 years.
> - An additional 90,000 had been in existence for at least 10 years.
> - Only 50,000 plots lacked a property title, thanks to Peru's innovative approach to land tenure legalization.
>
> *Source:* Desco (1998).

Mobilization (SINAMOS), the central government social development agency, the government and grassroots organizations worked together on an ambitious plan to develop VES. The government chose a relatively flat area of desert near the southern exit to the Pan American Highway in Lima's Southern Cone, and, in a process organized by SINAMOS, laid out a city plan in a neat grid pattern and began allocating plots to settlers.

At first, infrastructure and services were nonexistent. The first settlers received a demarcated plot, built straw huts, and moved in as community leaders began the long process of negotiating with the government to obtain improvements. Under the Velasco administration, the government was very responsive and took it upon itself to provide access routes for tank trucks to deliver water, to bring in electricity, and to build the first elementary schools. One year after its foundation, the population of VES was already 70,000. Over the following years, infrastructure and services were extended to most of the settlement. People improved their homes, and many started businesses. Children went to school, and a thriving industrial district developed. In light of this development, VES was made a district with its own municipality. Today, Villa El Salvador is a bustling city, despite the fact that most of its residents are still in the low-income bracket.

VES: Planned Informal Development

VES is very similar to all the other barriadas in Lima in terms of the makeup of its population, its level of organization, and in the fact that it started out as demarcated plots in the desert. Yet VES has been able to go much farther in its three decades of existence than most other barriadas, primarily for the following reasons:

- The central government provided strong support from the very start; the settlement was planned and built as a partnership between the community and the state. Although state support decreased with the fall of the Velasco regime in 1976, VES leadership by then had a knowledge of the workings of government and a command of political mechanisms that allowed it to lobby every subsequent administration very effectively.
- The street layout adopted for VES had a city, not a slum, in mind, and, in terms of street width, plot size, and space reserved for public uses, it was conducive to quality development and densification. It also defined a basic neighborhood unit, the residential grouping, whose configuration and size make it a natural unit for area-based community organization. The residential grouping is a neighborhood complete with its own square and space for local sports and elementary school facilities.
- Along with its layout, VES had from the beginning an area development plan developed with the participation of ABCOs. The plan was such a powerful instrument that the land it reserved for the industrial park was successfully defended by the community for 15 years from occupation by squatters, until the industrial park was finally implemented. The VES development plan was revised in the mid-1980s and went through an extensive revision in 1999, with support from, among other NGOs, Desco (the Center for Development Studies and Promotion), a Lima-based NGO that has provided support to the VES leadership since the early days.

The new VES development plan is an effort to understand the problems and potential of the area in a systematic way and establish a common vision for the future. The process of its preparation, through thematic working groups and general meetings at certain milestones, generated intense community interest and participation, and built on the many participatory initiatives under way in VES. As discussed in chapter 10, these include a scheme to improve property tax collection, a street paving scheme very similar to Tijuana's, and an Internet café that provides a range of online services and is attracting many of VES's youth.

Meaningless Alone: Participation and Initiative

While it is true that urban upgrading projects do not work without participation, the VES experience over the last 30 years proves the reverse to be true as well. Participation does not often produce meaningful results without the support structure provided by a project. For example, as will be seen in chapter 10, although some of the microenterprises for solid waste collection that were set up in the early 1990s managed to survive the municipality's withdrawal from the program, many did not. On the other hand, sustained state support to the development of the industrial park allowed community hard work and resourcefulness to produce impressive results in a short span of time. Villa El Salvador is a testimony to what communities can achieve when they are given a long-term enabling framework. Further, the area's remarkable history allows us to understand the components and nature of the kind of enabling framework that needs to be in place for participation to produce results.

Other Relevant Cases

Throughout this book, we make reference to examples from other programs and projects in Latin America that have used important methodological innovations or reached appreciable scale. Information on these initiatives was obtained through desk research, our peer reviewers, and our own previous experience. Brief descriptions of the following programs and projects are presented below:

- The PROFAVELA program, Belo Horizonte, Brazil
- The AOISPEM program, Cali, Colombia
- The Catuche Social Consortium, Caracas, Venezuela
- Community upgrading programs, Ciudad Juárez, Mexico
- The El Mezquital project, Guatemala City, Guatemala
- The PRIMED program, Medellín, Colombia
- The PREZEIS program, Recife, Brazil
- The Favela-Bairro program, Rio de Janeiro, Brazil
- The Novos Alagados project, Salvador, Bahia, Brazil
- The *mutirão* programs in São Paulo, Brazil.

PROFAVELA Program, Belo Horizonte, Brazil[2]

Belo Horizonte, the capital city of the state of Minas Gerais, has a population of 2.5 million. Of these, it is estimated that 400,000 people live in roughly 200 squatter settlements known as *favelas* which occupy public and private lands in many parts of the city—sometimes quite near the city center. Generally, the land that has been occupied by the favelas is less suited to urbanization than the rest of the city, since it tends to be situated in flood-prone or high-slope, landslide-prone areas. The favelas may therefore be considered high-risk areas.

---

[2]This section is based on information provided by the Association of Volunteers for International Cooperation (AVSI) and the Urbanizing Company of Belo Horizonte (URBEL).

Until 1974, the government followed a repressive policy aimed at the removal of favelas from urban and suburban areas. From 1974 on, however, as the military regime began to weaken, community organizations began to be formed within the favelas with the aim of obtaining security of land tenure and improvements in infrastructure and services. This community movement was particularly well-organized in Belo Horizonte.

With the gradual return of democracy, the proposals of the community movements began to be taken into serious consideration. A new expression, *planejamento participativo* (participatory planning), was coined to describe a method of intervention in low-income areas that involved their inhabitants in the choices to be made and entailed the contribution of their labor. After the first free elections were held at the state level in 1982, the new government began studies aimed at changing the existing legislation in recognition of squatter settlements and to lay out procedures for land tenure regularization. The debate was intense, for the new PROFAVELA law was very innovative. Recognizing the favelas was a profound and far-reaching change, not only in the existing legislation, but also in the very conception of the city and its development that was behind the legislation that had prevailed until then.

The Belo Horizonte PROFAVELA law was passed in 1983 and was widely hailed as a major breakthrough, the first legal instrument of its kind in Brazil. The law changed the zoning status of the 120 favela areas that were then identified, creating the concept of special social interest zones (SE4). Designation as SE4 was a precondition for land tenure regularization, which was given a set of well-defined rules. The PROFAVELA law also set forth planning criteria for SE4s, eliminating the unrealistic standards (plot sizes, width and slope of streets, etc.) that had for so long helped keep favelas illegal.

Even with the necessary legislation and political will in place, municipal inexperience in dealing with the regulatory, administrative, institutional, financial, and technical problems of informal settlements impede implementation of a land tenure regularization and settlement upgrading policy. Belo Horizonte therefore initiated a PROFAVELA program to foster institutional capacity-building.

Soon after the PROFAVELA law was enacted, two international development partners—the German governmental development aid agency GTZ and the Association of Volunteers for International Cooperation (AVSI), an Italian NGO—signed agreements with the municipal government and initiated upgrading projects in the favelas. These partners structured their projects around the idea of participatory planning, contributing 50 percent of the cost of the projects and asking the municipality for the remaining share. While GTZ concentrated its interventions on infrastructure upgrading of the informal settlements, AVSI additionally focused on the recognition and legalization of land tenure in favelas and settlement layout improvements.

Contemporaneously, the Urbanizing Company of Belo Horizonte (URBEL) was established to tackle the various technical problems involved in settlement upgrading. In this capacity, it coordinates with the various municipal departments and public utilities involved, and works with the community in defining priorities, choosing alternatives, and mediating conflicts. Capacity-building was a feature of URBEL's work from the start. It addressed the main issues arising from the participatory process, such as the integration of the operational units and the community associations, which was made possible by the creation of joint working teams. Other activities undertaken by URBEL and its development partners were joint preparation of instruments for data collection and project management, periodic joint evaluation seminars, and specialized courses in the use of computer mapping and planning tools.

In the 1980s, the achievements of the PROFAVELA program included legalization of land tenure and issuance of title deeds to 120,000 *favelados* in 22 settlements; infrastructure upgrading and establishment of basic social services in five favelas with a population of 30,000; implementation of a pilot project for solid waste disposal, reaching 25 percent of Belo Horizonte's favelas; and the establishment of various initiatives for poverty reduction and promotion of the socioeconomic and cultural development of favelados.

These results were so encouraging that the Brazilian federal government requested the support of the government of Italy for a second project phase implemented in the mid- to late 1990s. It replicated previous AVSI interventions in 10 favelas with a population of roughly 50,000. The funding that was made available for upgrading in the Belo Horizonte metropolitan area in the 1990s totaled about $30 million, about 25 percent of which came from the Italian government, with the rest from municipal and state sources. A significant portion of the funding package came from Belo Horizonte's participatory budgeting scheme.

Today, settlement upgrading and land tenure regularization are part of Belo Horizonte's planning process and the object of a specific investment policy and methodologies for intervention. Although an explicit strategy for subsidy targeting and cost recovery has been lacking, as in other Brazilian cases, much has been achieved. Notably, one of the innovative features of the PROFAVELA legislation and the municipal programs that derived from it has been the special attention paid to the rights and needs of women. PROFAVELA gives preference to women in the issuance of property title deeds and removes all previous legal, regulatory, and customary obstacles to the issuance of title deeds to women.

This was a way of recognizing the role of women as organizers and mobilizers in upgrading projects, as well as their role as the mainstay of a high proportion of favela households.

Unfortunately, budgetary constraints have so far prevented the PROFAVELA program from fully living up to the expectations it generated at the time of its inception and operating at the large scale that would be needed by the city's favelas.

AOISPEM Program, Cali, Colombia[3]

Santiago de Cali, in the southwestern part of Colombia, is a city of roughly 1.8 million people. One of the four largest cities in the country, it is an industrial center which, since the 1940s, has been a magnet for Colombians seeking to escape the violence and backwardness of rural areas. As in many Latin American cities, rapid growth outstripped the municipality's capacity to provide infrastructure and services, and the lack of affordable serviced land resulted in the emergence of informal settlements with a severe infrastructure deficit. In Cali, the highest concentration of these is in the Aguablanca district, where 140,000 people lived in such settlements in 1996.

The AOISPEM program (Self-Construction of Public Service Infrastructure Works with Delivery of Materials) is an attempt to answer to this problem. Initiated in 1990, the project relies on partnership, which enables both operational efficiency and successful cost recovery. In the project, a nonprofit foundation (Carvajal Foundation) provides management skills, community contacts, and credibility; a municipal public works company (EMCALI) provides technical skills and financial resources; the community provides engagement, labor, and monitoring; and building materials companies provide materials at a reduced cost. The communities pay EMCALI for the cost of a construction foreman and materials. The cost of the materials for mutual-help construction of the water supply and/or sewer systems is initially covered by EMCALI and charged to the beneficiary community over a 48-month period, with a 24 percent annual financing rate on the debt and a 36 percent annual interest rate on arrears. Because the participants involved in the project are willing to keep their costs low enough to enable full repayment of the loans provided, it is estimated that costs are some 60 percent lower than those for private contractors.

The initiative came from EMCALI, which approached the Carvajal Foundation for an estimate of the costs of meeting the demand of local residents for water supply and sewerage services. Carvajal's budget was

---

[3]This section is based on World Bank (n.d.).

some 25 percent below that of the municipality because of its long experience in the field and its well-established contacts with private construction firms that were willing to offer significant discounts to support social projects. AOISPEM benefited some 5,000 families from 1990 to 1997. The cost recovery mechanism worked well. Despite its small scale, AOISPEM's demand-responsive formula, promoting affordability, cost consciousness, and cost recovery, is a promising alternative for small community upgrading works.

Catuche Social Consortium, Caracas, Venezuela[4]

Catuche is one of 115 squatter settlement units that were identified and delimited by the Plan Sectorial, a study of the Caracas metropolitan area's informal settlements undertaken in 1993–94 by a team from the Central University of Venezuela. In addition to delimiting the informal settlement areas, the plan also undertook to propose an integrated upgrading methodology. It addressed the issue of access routes as well as all types of infrastructure, and provided preliminary cost calculations to upgrade all the *barrios* in Caracas. Catuche was selected as the site for a pilot project to test the plan's upgrading methodology. The Catuche settlement is composed of 11 barrios that occupy high-slope areas along a ravine near the old city center. Its total land area is 28.3 hectares, almost all of which belongs to the municipality. Its population is about 9,000 and consists of some 2,100 households.

The cost of the upgrade was estimated at an average of $3,500 per household, for a total cost of $7.35 million. Factoring in the high slopes and need to create access routes resulted in a cost breakdown of 31 percent for roads and storm drainage, 29 percent for other infrastructure (water supply, sanitation, and electricity), 28 percent for resettlement and relocation, and 12 percent for community facilities and urban equipment.

The municipality accepted the proposal and funded the preparation of a detailed, integrated, and participatory area development plan for Catuche, taking the work of the Plan Sectorial one step farther. The next steps were then spearheaded by a social consortium made up of an NGO, a local ABCO, and a group of engineering and planning professionals. Operationally, the consortium is structured in three units: a technical unit, an administrative and management unit, and a community organization unit. The consortium's governing body is the community's general assembly. Between 1993 and 1997, this consortium succeeded in raising a total of about $2 million from the municipality, the central gov-

---

[4]The information in this section is based on Brandt and Ayala (1996).

ernment, and the United Nations Development Programme and undertaking a series of works envisaged by the area plan. Although it was concluded that the cost savings secured by the consortium and its efficient coordination arrangements would have allowed it to complete the upgrading works in three years, the consortium's limited fundraising capacity has meant that in reality the project will take a much longer time frame—seriously compromising the momentum that is an important feature of successful projects.

Besides providing essential social support, social intermediation, and administrative and technical assistance services, the consortium coordinates and manages the upgrading project and is responsible for raising the necessary funds. In many ways, it replicates an organization like FUPROVI at the settlement level. Several other consortia have since been organized in Caracas along the Catuche model at the initiative of various NGOs. Each has its own built-in *assessoria*, as in the Brazilian *mutirão* model (see below), plus an NGO for social and political intermediation. The community is one of the partners in the consortium, which contributes to a high level of participation. Naturally, the number of consortia that is feasible to implement depends on the critical mass of available local capacity. If the organization of consortia could be stimulated and promoted by a program with the adequate resources to subsequently fund upgrading projects, this model could yet prove to be a good alternative for large-scale urban upgrading.

Community Upgrading Programs in Ciudad Juárez, Mexico[5]

Like Tijuana, Ciudad Juárez, in the state of Chihuahua, looked to implement community upgrading programs through participation and cash contributions from the beneficiaries. In the period 1995–98, the municipality's Let's Pull Together program completed 580 works, 70 percent of which are in the Zona Poniente, the city's most backward and marginal area. About $4 million was invested, with approximately equal contributions (of 33 percent each) coming from the municipality, the state, and the community. The program was managed by the Social Development Department. Its priority works included paving, water supply, sewerage, and electrification. As in Tijuana, paving is the type of work most requested by the communities; unlike Tijuana, the water and sewer works in the colonias are built by the municipality's community upgrading programs, although the water board participates in a technical assistance and regulatory capacity.

---

[5]This section is based on information provided by the municipality of Ciudad Juárez and on-site interviews.

A parallel program managed by the Social Development Department executes works with federal funds from a local government transfer mechanism known as Ramo 33. An average cash contribution from the communities of 33 percent is also applied to these works, which address electrification, school improvements, and housing improvements. From 1995 to 1998, 64 low-income settlements were electrified, with an investment of about $1.8 million. The relationship between the municipality's Social Development Department and the Federal Commission of Electricity is not as good as with the water board; the commission selects contractors and manages contracts, and some conflicts have arisen.

In 1992, the first properly constituted neighborhood committees were formed, according to the regulations on neighborhood committees that were adopted by the municipality. At that time, there were 120 committees; six years later, in 1998, there were already 276. The municipality has 23 community development workers, each of whom covers about 13 committees (each committee represents between 35 and 500 families). There are still many areas in which there are no neighborhood committees.

Concurrently, the Social Development Department launched a successful credit program for the purchase of construction materials for housing improvement using a revolving fund mechanism. In the 1995–98 period, $360,000 was invested, and 1,824 loans were granted. The recovery rate was 85 percent; the loans were paid off in 6 to 48 months, without interest, and were adjusted according to variations in minimum wage.

The methodology followed in Juárez is similar to that in Tijuana, with some important differences. The municipal Social Development Department has the mission of assisting local people in identifying priority works. For each work, a specific file is opened. The municipality handles design, prepares the budget, selects the contractor, supervises the work, and makes payments. In the case of water and sewer works, it is the water board that handles design and supervises the work. The community contribution is received by the municipal treasury, into which each community's members make direct payments. All residents affected by a given project must deposit their individual contributions in the treasury; those who do not pay do not receive water or sewer connections. Residents who have not made their deposits by the due date are forced to pay their entire share of the cost of the work when they pay their debt—including the government contribution. Those communities that pay on time are rewarded; for example, the municipality often begins follow-up works before the community puts together all its share of the funding.

The most evident differences from the Tijuana model are the following:

- The lack of an institutionalized structure of participatory budgeting

- The fact that the community doesn't manage the selection of the contractor or the resources
- The individualized relationship established between each resident and the municipality for the payment of the contribution and the consequent qualification to receive benefits
- The centralized management of the entire program, since the municipality of Juárez is not decentralized into delegations.

According to a municipal official, it is very difficult to convince communities to dedicate funds to less immediate problems. This official also notes, however, that, civic participation is higher in Juárez than for the community upgrading programs in Tijuana, and that committees here receive more support. Although he is happy with the progress that has been made in Juárez, he acknowledges that there is still much to do: "How good it would be if the entire city was organized in committees, if no works were made without going through a participatory process, and if there were more activities that go beyond infrastructure provision, such as environmental and health education."

El Mezquital Project, Guatemala City, Guatemala[6]

Exploiting a newly opened window of opportunity for municipal reform in the mid-1980s, a team of World Bank and Guatemalan officials began to design a municipal development project, components of which addressed urban upgrading and road maintenance. Unfortunately, although the project was approved by the World Bank in 1988, the country's situation, undermined by decades of civil strife, was a major obstacle. The Guatemalan government's serious difficulties in financing project counterpart funds and the suspension of all World Bank disbursements to the country from 1989 to 1992 led to a long delay in project start-up. Moreover, when the project finally could begin, the Guatemala City administration then in office did not favor municipal reform.

The World Bank and the Guatemalan government considered canceling the loan altogether, but a Bank mission in 1993 saved the situation by deciding to refocus the project entirely on the urban upgrading component. This decision was reached through a careful and insightful reading of the local situation and the opportunities it offered. In particular, it was the level of organized demand for improvements in low-income urban areas that caught the mission's eye.

In the interim, the UNICEF Urban Basic Services Program had been working with low-income communities in and around Guatemala City

---

[6]This section is based on World Bank (1998) and Bravo et al. (1997).

to develop participatory approaches to urban upgrading and housing development building on previous NGO experiences. The National Committee for Reconstruction (CNR) had already envisaged funding urban upgrading in the El Mezquital district through the World Bank loan, and when the 1993 Bank mission visited the area and learned about the existing plans and level of community organization, a partnership began to take shape.

Subsequently, local community groups—under the supervision of CNR, representing the Guatemalan government, and with UNICEF-provided technical support and financial management—launched an innovative upgrading project in El Mezquital, which coincided with the main objectives of the peace process.[7] The project included land tenure regularization, new settlement layouts and street and footpath networks, storm drainage, street paving, new water supplies, sewerage networks and wastewater treatment, paving of access roads, new housing construction, home improvement, and new community facilities such as schools and clinics. The total project cost was about $14 million, with 37,600 beneficiaries, for a rough per capita cost of $370. The project was implemented between 1993 and 1997. Some of the most interesting features of the El Mezquital experience were as follows:

- **Community participation.** The project's beneficiaries participated intensively in planning and executing upgrading works in their areas. The project had a high level and degree of intensity of participation.
- **Community organization.** The project provided the necessary support and incentives for communities to organize, which bodes well for its sustainability.
- **Complementarity between the World Bank and UNICEF.** While the Bank provided resources and overall supervision, UNICEF provided technical assistance and day-to-day project coordination and management on the ground, compensating for the weaknesses of Guatemalan institutions.
- **Importance of intensive supervision and socio-technical support.** The intensive support of UNICEF and some NGOs, working closely with local community groups, was a key success factor.
- **Dedication of key individuals.** Some highly qualified and experienced personnel from UNICEF, CNR, and some NGOs worked zealously to organize the process and support communities; their efforts had a major impact on the process and its results.

---

[7] Guatemala's civil war ended with a cease-fire in March 1996, followed by a peace accord in December of the same year.

- **Emphasis on cost recovery.** From the start, the project has promoted the principle of cost recovery and has established various mechanisms for cost recovery, such as metering and billing service consumption. For example, all the water connections provided by the project are metered. Community acceptance has been good: residents pay their community-based organizations a monthly water bill, and delinquency is practically nonexistent.
- **Wastewater treatment.** Unlike many other projects in poor and nonpoor areas alike, the El Mezquital project included both wastewater collection and wastewater treatment. As with paving and drainage, low-cost solutions were adopted for wastewater treatment.

El Mezquital's is a success story that began in very unfavorable circumstances but went on to become a practical lesson on the importance of flexibility, a good eye for local demand, and the ability to set up meaningful partnerships in which each partner's comparative advantages are fully put to use.

PRIMED Program, Medellín, Colombia[8]

Medellín has gone through a process of rapid urban growth similar to Cali's. The city's population jumped from 170,000 in 1940 to almost 2 million by the end of the 1990s. Growth rates went down to about 2 percent per year in the 1990s, down from a 1960s high of almost 6 percent, but the rapid population growth has left its mark. The city has 104 officially recognized informal settlements, with an additional 25 settlements appearing after 1990. The total population of Medellín's informal settlements is 250,000, or roughly 13 percent of the city's population. The violence and lawlessness that have plagued Colombia in recent decades are present in the city to a high degree. Armed groups control many of the informal settlement areas, and Medellín's homicide rate, which hovers around 200 per 100,000, is one of the highest in the world.

The Medellín Integrated Informal Settlement Upgrading Program (PRIMED) is working to improve the situation in the city's informal settlements through an integrated approach. The program's key components are the following:

- Land tenure legalization
- Home improvement
- Removal and resettlement of families occupying areas of geological risk

---

[8]This section is based on information provided by PRIMED management and on Medellín Municipality (n.d.).

- Settlement upgrading, including improvements in the road system, storm drainage, consolidation of slopes and earthworks, water supply and sanitation, and community facilities such as schools, health centers, and leisure areas
- Support for community development and participation.

The program's first phase began in 1993 and was completed in mid-1999; the second phase is planned for completion by 2004. PRIMED has intervened in 15 settlements in its first phase and will reach 15 more in its second. During the program's first phase, about 11,000 families benefited. The total invested was $15 million, and the average cost per family was approximately $1,400. The sources of funding were the GTZ (31 percent), the municipality of Medellín (30 percent), the national government (27 percent), and community contributions (12 percent). The program also received technical assistance from the United Nations.

During the program's second phase, it is expected to invest roughly $82 million, benefiting 25,000 households. The municipality intends to contribute 55 percent of that amount and sees PRIMED as a long-term effort, with a clear mission and conceptual basis. The principles underpinning the PRIMED methodology are as follows:

- **Area-based, integrated planning and execution.** A horizontal institutional arrangement and the use of integrated and area-based, rather than sectoral, planning and execution have been adopted. This has allowed PRIMED to lower the cost of its interventions by 15 to 25 percent, mostly by consolidating project management, instead of having different parallel projects in the various infrastructure sectors.
- **Stimulating community ownership of the new infrastructure and services.** PRIMED conducted an interesting comparative study that shows that the degree of deterioration of public works undertaken in other poor settlements of Medellín, as well as their maintenance costs, is much higher than in PRIMED areas. This is attributed to the intensive community development and social support provided by the program.
- **Participatory planning of urban development.** The program seeks to enhance the effectiveness of its investments by promoting participatory area-based development planning in its areas of intervention and making sure that every initiative it funds is included in the settlement's area plan. As we will see in later chapters, this is the best way to avoid spending a program's resources on ephemeral, poorly planned works.
- **Focus on governance and governability.** The program has sought to revert the situation of lack of governability generated by the decades-long absence of the state from the informal settlement areas of Medellín. This was achieved through mutual recognition of the

local government and local residents, and a program design that encourages shared power and responsibility.

The PRIMED literature stresses that these four principles enhance the impact of the program's interventions, which is not measured solely in terms of physical improvements, but rather as a broader transformation that affects relationships within communities, between communities and government, and between the different branches of government, all of which have had to learn to work together in an integrated program.

PREZEIS Program, Recife, Brazil[9]

Recife's PREZEIS program ranks with Belo Horizonte's PROFAVELA as one of Brazil's first and most important attempts at creating a citywide framework for urban upgrading. In 1983, a key year for the country's transition from military to civilian rule, Recife's new zoning law instituted special social interest zones (ZEIS), thereby legally recognizing the existence of the city's favelas for the first time. The new law called for the establishment of special planning standards to promote legal regularization and physical integration of the informal settlement areas.

This was accomplished in 1987, when, at the initiative of local community organizations and NGOs, a proposal was presented for a new law to institute the Plan for the Regularization and Urbanization of Special Zones of Social Interest (PREZEIS); this was a comprehensive framework for informal settlement regularization and upgrading in Recife. PREZEIS was explicitly recognized as a key urban policy instrument by the Lei Orgânica Municipal, a kind of municipal constitution, in 1990, and by Recife's 1991 Master Plan. In 1993, a new law instituted the Municipal PREZEIS Fund, a dedicated vehicle for settlement upgrading investment. In 1995 and 1996, respectively, a new PREZEIS law and a new land use zoning law were enacted, updating the delimitation of the favela areas and improving the mechanisms for community representation and participatory planning.

The PREZEIS law contains several innovative and ingenious instruments. Its merit resides in establishing a well-defined institutional structure for resource allocation and decisionmaking regarding settlement regularization and upgrading. One of the principles of the PREZEIS law is to respect and build upon the characteristic features of each settlement and preserve what has been built by the community, limiting removals and resettlement to the minimum required to open access routes and deal with risk situations.

---

[9]This section is based on information from the Recife Municipal Urban Development Company.

Although the law defines the areas to be considered ZEIS, it also establishes procedures for the creation of new ZEIS, so that the municipality may keep up with the growth of the informal city. Once it is officially created, the first step for each ZEIS is to establish a five-member legalization and upgrading committee, composed of two community representatives, two municipal representatives, and one representative of the organization providing socio-technical support (usually an NGO). This last is called an assessoria, as in the São Paulo mutirão projects (see below). Committee meetings take place every two weeks. The community representatives are chosen in a democratic election.

Representatives of all the ZEIS legalization and upgrading committees, plus government and civil society representatives, congregate in the PREZEIS Forum, the program's steering committee, which has real decisionmaking power and legal responsibility over the management of the Municipal PREZEIS Fund. The forum has a five-member coordinating group composed of three community representatives, one municipal representative, and one representative of the assessorias. One of the community representatives is the general coordinator of the forum, which operates through three thematic committees: an upgrading committee, a legalization committee, and a budget and finance committee. Overall technical assistance and supervision of the program are provided by the Recife Municipal Urban Development Company.

As in the PROFAVELA program, PREZEIS has set up a comprehensive and participatory legal, regulatory, and institutional framework for settlement upgrading. This is a remarkable achievement. However, weak political will and inadequate funding—about $2 million per year in recent years—have kept the program from fulfilling its promise of promoting citywide settlement upgrading. It is estimated that at least 30 percent of the Recife municipality's 1.2 million population—or around 360,000 people—live in squatter settlements. At the current rate of investment, it could take almost a century for PREZEIS to cater to them all.[10]

Favela-Bairro Program, Rio de Janeiro, Brazil[11]

Favela-Bairro is one of the largest and most ambitious urban upgrading programs ever undertaken. The program's first phase was implemented from 1994 to 1999, at a total cost of $380 million. Of that amount, the Inter-American Development Bank (IDB) provided a loan for $180 million, and the rest was provided by the municipality of Rio itself.

---

[10] At an average per capita cost of $500, it would take $180 million to upgrade all of Recife's existing informal settlements. At $2 million a year, this would take 90 years.

[11] This section is based on IDB (1997a), IPLANRIO (1996), and Sekles (2000).

Rio's landscape is dotted with over 500 favelas which house almost a million people, one-sixth of the city's population. Favela-Bairro set out in 1994 to upgrade 105 settlements which are home to about 400,000 people. The cost limit per household was set at $4,000. The favelas chosen for upgrading were consolidated settlements, ranging from 500 to 2,500 households in size. The services included in the projects were access roads, storm drainage, consolidation of slopes, water and sanitation, and electricity.

In 1993, the mayor of Rio created a committee to develop a new housing policy. The committee concluded that the city needed to focus attention and resources on the favelas, acknowledging and complementing the effort and investment already made by their inhabitants. The city lost no time in approaching the IDB, which at first thought the plan too ambitious. Urban planner José Brakarz, the IDB team leader for Favela-Bairro, said that this impression soon changed:

> Once in Rio, however, we found that the concept of transforming favelas into neighborhoods was indeed viable. We met with the local technicians, very motivated people who had been put down by their colleagues as the "engineers of the poor." Together we developed a plan to upgrade not only the favelas but also the low-income, "irregular" subdivisions. Working together, we learned a great deal, such as the need for a very capable executing agency to manage this kind of project. We helped them to organize their unit and develop a methodology, an important part of which was a system of indicators for selecting the favelas to be upgraded. We set very strict cost control measures...to keep the project within budget. We also required that all the improvements for a given favela be carried out by a single contractor. At first the bigger contractors didn't want to work in the favelas. But now that the program has proven itself, they are eager for the business (IDB 1997a).

The program was launched in 1994 with a public competition among Rio's architects to select the best proposals for upgrading. Compared to other upgrading initiatives, Favela-Bairro pays particular attention to urban design and urban form, and to the quality of public spaces and urban equipment. Contrary to what was done in São Paulo for Guarapiranga, the municipality of Rio decided to use its in-house capacity to manage the program and provide socio-technical support.

According to Sérgio Magalhães, Rio's secretary of housing, the program's cost limit of $4,000 per household is about a fifth of the cost of building new housing on the city's outskirts, not including indirect costs. He notes, "Relocating them to another site where everything has to be built costs about five times more just for construction. If we add the indirect costs such as expanding public transportation, water and sewerage services, health and education, who knows how much it would cost" (IDB 1997a).

The improvements have encouraged favela residents to invest in home improvement in their turn, as Maria Lúcia Petersen, manager of the Favela-Bairro program, explains. "The project is founded on the premise that the city pays for the common services, and the residents are responsible for improving their own houses. We are seeing that when we put in the services, the residents lose their fear of being uprooted from the favela, and they begin making improvements with their own money" (IDB 1997a).

Phase II of the program, which is now under way, has almost the same amount of funding as the first phase. By the end of 2004, it is expected that 70 to 75 percent of Rio's favela population will have benefited from the program. Favela-Bairro suffers from some sustainability-threatening problems—problems it shares with other Brazilian initiatives including Guarapiranga—such as a lack of emphasis on cost recovery and weak social support after project implementation. At the same time, Favela-Bairro and its impacts reveal the promise of urban upgrading and show that it can be done at a scale that makes it possible to think of improved living conditions for all slum dwellers in a large developing country city in the foreseeable future.

Novos Alagados Project, Salvador, Bahia, Brazil[12]

Salvador, the capital city of the state of Bahia, is, with a population of 2.4 million, the fifth largest city in Brazil. It has 357 favelas, where almost 29 percent of the total population lives. It is a dynamic economic and cultural hub, located on the scenic Baía de Todos os Santos, on the country's northeastern coast. Novos Alagados is a settlement of pile-dwellings situated in an inlet of the Baía de Todos os Santos. At the beginning of the upgrading operation, 13,100 people lived in this settlement, in subhuman conditions. To mitigate the problems of living on water, the families tried to fill the area underneath their dwellings using mud and solid waste. In this manner, some of the shacks came to rest on dry ground, while the settlement kept expanding toward the bay with the addition of new pile-dwellings. The average family income was $87 per month in the pile-dwellings and $184 per month among the inhabitants of the huts on dry ground.

In July 1989, an initial memorandum of understanding was signed between the Italian NGO AVSI and the government of the state of Bahia, through which the parties committed themselves to seek funding for an upgrading project in Novos Alagados. The project began in 1992 and

---

[12]This section is based on information provided by AVSI.

was completed at the end of 2000. The total cost was set at $10.8 million. Funding was provided by the government of Bahia, the World Bank, the government of Italy, the European Union, Swiss Caritas, and AVSI itself, from its private sponsors. A second phase of the Novos Alagados project is now under way in a neighboring area.

The project originated from an alliance between AVSI, the local Roman Catholic archdiocese, and the local community. It is a good example of how civil society and community-based organizations can organize to promote a project idea and get local and provincial authorities and international aid agencies to buy into the project and provide funding and technical assistance, while still maintaining a strong role in project planning and execution. The main actions promoted by the project were the following:

- Urban upgrading of the zone on dry ground, with the provision of basic services and creation of a road system combined with the existing urban road network
- Creation of a coastal scenic pathway which delimits the settlement and makes new pile-dwelling occupations very difficult, by giving a socially recognized use to the coastal strip in terms of access, public spaces, and services
- Building of three council housing complexes in an adjoining area on dry ground for the residents of the pile-dwellings who cannot be accommodated in the new coastal strip and for the residents of the dry ground zone who had to be resettled
- Environmental education activities
- Training on building techniques to support home improvement efforts
- Creation of a housing, production, and services cooperative that generates jobs for its members, provides microenterprise loans, and develops business to build homes and provide services in the external market
- Incentives to income generation and job creation through the creation of a job search office and the provision of training aimed at young people involved in micro-units of manufacturing and trade
- Establishment of basic social services such as daycare centers, preschools, and health clinics
- Development of social organizations centered on the artistic and cultural traditions of the population, particularly in music, dance, and the martial arts.

Community participation in the Novos Alagados project was intense, although mostly confined to the information and negotiation level, except for some initiatives (such as social service and cultural activities) that were managed by the community. The project's integrated methodology and horizontal institutional arrangement made it possible for the various public and private participants to cooperate. The participation of the NGO was key to speeding up the bureaucratic process and increasing accountability in resource management.

A geographic information system was used to plan and control project activities; this encouraged communication between experts and area residents, making it easier to share an overall vision of the area's problems and reducing the time needed for planning while improving project quality.

Mutirão Program, São Paulo, Brazil[13]

One alternative that has been used in São Paulo in the last two decades to step up housing delivery for the poor has been the provision of funding and technical assistance to mutual-help housing construction. Mutirão, as mutual-help construction is known in Brazil, is a traditional practice in rural areas and in urban informal settlements. Typically, it is used for small-scale expansion or improvement of individual homes. The idea of organizing and focusing this traditional practice to mass produce new units, providing technical assistance and financial support, came from the experience of the housing cooperatives in Uruguay. In 1982, the mutirão-based Vila Nova Cachoeirinha housing project in São Paulo was launched. Starting that same year, several other Brazilian municipalities—São João da Boa Vista, Penápolis, Bauru, Americana, Goiania, Angra dos Reis, Lages, Vila Velha—began their own mutirão projects.

São Paulo's mutirão program of the 1990s evolved from these experiences, and has moved toward a format similar to that used by FUPROVI. As in Costa Rica, organized community groups deal with an organization that provides them with technical and financial assistance, while the actual building is done by the communities themselves, with support from contractors for some specialized services. In Brazil, however, the housing associations approach the government and apply for its subsidies directly, instead of using the intermediation services of an NGO, as in Costa Rica. Another difference is that in Brazil the land is included in the subsidy package, whereas in Costa Rica the housing associations usually approach FUPROVI after they have secured a suitable plot. Technical and administrative assistance is provided in much the same way in both cases—that is, by an organization outside the government that

---

[13]This section is based on information provided by Prof. Alex Kenya Abiko, Department of Urban Engineering and Civil Construction, Polytechnic School, University of São Paulo.

possesses the necessary technical capabilities. In Costa Rica this organization (FUPROVI) is also the external support agency responsible for the project as a whole; in Brazil, there is a roster of qualified organizations (called assessorias) from which communities may choose. The units produced by the Brazilian system tend to be more sophisticated than the very simple units produced by FUPROVI projects. Many of the Brazilian projects produce apartment buildings, while FUPROVI's are always horizontal.

One of the most innovative and promising features of São Paulo's mutirão programs is the role of the assessorias. They are basically groups of professionals—architects, planners, engineers, social workers—that are organized as NGOs but operate more like small consulting firms. They have to go through a screening process to be included in the rosters maintained by the municipality and the Housing and Urban Development Company of the State of São Paulo (CDHU). Once they are part of the roster, they may start to compete for business. The key feature of the process is that the decision on which assessoria to hire is made by the housing associations, not by the project sponsors. Therefore, although they are also accountable to CDHU or municipality technical supervisors, the assessorias' clients are actually the community groups.

This demand-based and commercially oriented system has led to the acquisition of a critical mass of socio-technical support capacity, outside the public sector, that can be mobilized for urban upgrading and low-income housing initiatives in São Paulo. It has also provided the incentives for lowering costs, increasing efficiency and effectiveness, and enhancing client orientation in the provision of services. Although they operate commercially, the NGO roots and legal status of the assessorias provide flexibility and community contacts. The fact that the capacity exists outside the public sector means that the assessorias suffer less of an impact in times of political transition. The municipality of São Paulo practically discontinued its mutirão program when a new administration took office in 1993, but the assessorias continued to exist and were there to help CDHU when it started its own program in 1995. The existence of the assessorias in São Paulo can be seen as a key enabling factor for future large-scale urban upgrading and low-income housing initiatives.

The two main mutirão initiatives of the 1990s were the Municipal Community-Managed Social Housing Fund (FUNAPS Comunitário) program of the municipality of São Paulo and the state's CDHU Mutirão program. The municipality's program had great momentum from 1989 to 1993, when a new municipal administration's housing policy veered away from mutirão and toward favela upgrading and new housing construction. The state program, which started in 1995, is partly based on the municipality's experiences.

The key features of the FUNAPS Comunitário program were the following:

- Housing units had a cost cap of $6,000 for houses or apartments of up to 60 square meters.
- Of the program's costs, 4 percent goes for technical assistance, 4 percent for setting up the building site and buying tools, 10 percent for specialized building services, and 82 percent for building materials.
- The program's funding source is a municipal fund called FUNAPS, which is specifically targeted to informal settlement residents.
- The program has about 15 assessorias in its roster.

The key features of the CDHU program are the following:

- The program basically produces apartment blocks.
- The amount financed for a 48-square-meter apartment is about $7,600, not including the cost of land and infrastructure. This is 30 to 45 percent less than the cost of building through conventional methods.
- Of the program's costs, about 3 percent goes for the building site, 6 percent for technical assistance, 24 to 40 percent for specialized services, and the remainder for materials.
- The program is funded through a state tax.
- The program has 30 assessorias in its roster.

Recent research has shown that the cost of units built through São Paulo's mutirão program is about 30 percent lower than current market costs (as a point of comparison, the cost of units produced through FUPROVI's mutual-help system is 50 percent lower than market cost). The program's lower costs are partly due to the use of community labor, but lower indirect costs are a factor as well. Some items, such as contractors' profit margins and financial costs, simply do not exist in mutirão; others, such as central administration costs, do exist but are much lower.

One disadvantage of mutirão is the longer time frame of projects, which take at least 24 months to be completed. This is due to the lower level of training and lower productivity of mutirão workers, and to the fact that they generally work on weekends or after hours, during what would normally be their free time. On the other hand, initial concerns about working conditions and worker safety have proven unfounded.

Overall, assisted mutual-help housing construction is a methodology that requires great dedication from the communities involved and high quality socio-technical assistance and supervision to succeed. It does lower cost and helps ensure project feasibility, though, and the effort required and learning opportunities created during construction are a definite plus for project sustainability.

3
Organizing Participation: The Project Level

This chapter discusses some of the key issues involved in designing and implementing a participatory initiative from the specific point of view of the organization of participation. Issues such as the different levels and degrees of participation, what to do when the community is not organized, and the need for good intermediaries between different stakeholders involved in the project are discussed. The key role of women in infrastructure and shelter projects is highlighted, as is direct community participation in project management—a feature of some very successful projects. The chapter is organized according to the order in which these, and related issues, typically present themselves in actual projects.

Development Projects and the Social Process

Recognizing the benefits of participatory approaches, local governments and development aid institutions are faced with the challenge of designing development programs and projects that are built to encourage participation. To do this, they need to provide an environment that is conducive to the articulate expression of community demand and to active community participation in decisionmaking. They also must design for efficiency and effectiveness, and avoid the risks and excessive costs sometimes associated with poorly conceived participatory initiatives.

At the heart of these challenges is the need to match two very different things: *a development project or program* and *a social process*. The difficulties involved in such a match may be part of the reason why relatively few projects can be considered truly participatory, in spite of the widespread recognition of the advantages of participatory projects. A program's funding, technical assistance, operations, and procedures must be able to interact with a community and its complex demands, expectations, levels of understanding of the project and its requirements, willingness to participate, trust in the process, vested interests, and internal power disputes—in short, all that constitutes the *social process of participation*.

Projects, the usual instrument of development initiatives, create an environment with a variety of *external actors*, each with its own priorities and hidden and/or explicit agendas, rules and regulations, knowledge base, management styles, and so on. Projects also have their *funding mechanisms*, with the different conditions that may apply. They have a *time frame*, which is influenced by fiscal years, elections, and other political and institutional constraints and events; and a *system for measuring success*, whose indicators are often based on easier-to-measure means rather than ends. Rates of disbursement or lengths of pipe are therefore the most common yardsticks, rather than such items as improvement of health indicators, time and cost savings accrued to households due to more efficient infrastructure services, or the level of a community's social capital. Subjective, hard-to-measure improvements, such as added convenience, self-esteem, or better quality of life, are included even more rarely in performance ratings. This serves to divert resources from anything that is not directly part of the physical works. Moreover, such aspects of the project environment often deflect attention from the real objectives of a project and serve as justification for introducing approaches and management styles that are focused on the short term—and which are often not conducive to participation.

The key elements needed to bridge the gap between a program or project and the social process, all of which are linked to the structure of the organization, may be summed up as follows (see figure 3-1):

- Information on the process needs to be available to the community, disseminated by a good communication strategy.
- Adequate participatory planning tools need to be used, based on participatory information gathering and analysis, so that the community may influence the process and planning may benefit from local knowledge.
- A strong intermediation structure must exist, capable of establishing links across disciplinary areas and between the community and other stakeholders.
- A change of attitude on the part of the staff of the agencies promoting projects needs to be actively sought and promoted by project organizers by creating an appropriate incentive structure. Such an incentive structure should include the provision of adequate resources, time, and recognition to socio-technical support tasks. It also requires appropriate rewards for performance and career ad-

vancement possibilities to staff who work directly with the community.
- The quality of the participatory process becomes as important a success criterion as the rate of disbursement. To provide incentives for demand-responsiveness, project promoters need to demonstrate through their actions that they value participation.
- An institutional arrangement (project coordinating unit, its links to its parent institution, and coordination arrangements with other institutions involved) must exist that is integrated, flexible, and demand-responsive; this again requires the correct incentives.
- The appropriate skills and capacity to establish links between the social and technical spheres must be available.

The Significance of a Strong Social Intermediary

In the absence of a tradition of participation, what mechanisms need to be set up for local people to participate actively in a project? And how is it possible to reconcile the timing and rhythm of longer term community participation processes with the—often very different and shorter term—project objectives and time frame? The answers to these questions can-

Figure 3-1. The Seven Pillars of Participation

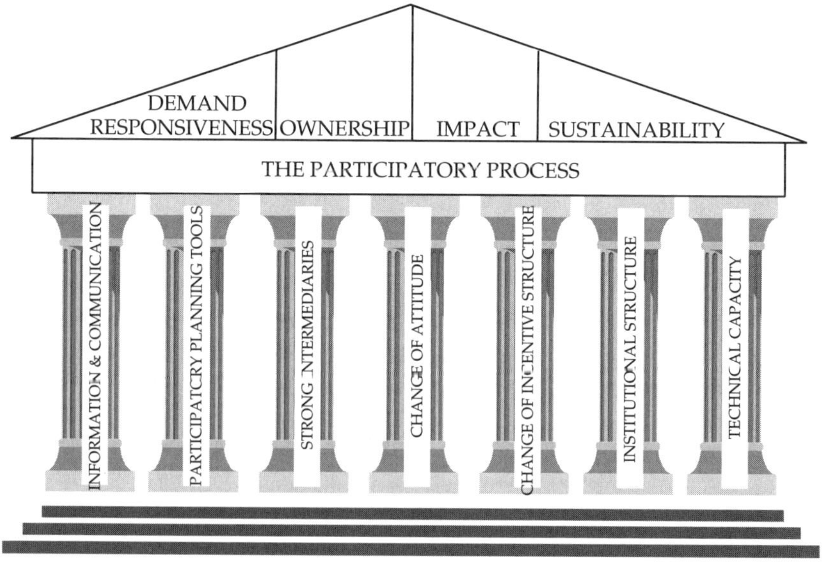

[Figure: A temple-like diagram with a pediment labeled "DEMAND RESPONSIVENESS | OWNERSHIP | IMPACT | SUSTAINABILITY" above an entablature labeled "THE PARTICIPATORY PROCESS", supported by seven pillars labeled: INFORMATION & COMMUNICATION, PARTICIPATORY PLANNING TOOLS, STRONG INTERMEDIARIES, CHANGE OF ATTITUDE, CHANGE OF INCENTIVE STRUCTURE, INSTITUTIONAL STRUCTURE, TECHNICAL CAPACITY.]

Source: Authors' construction from field study data.

not be left to chance. They depend on the crucial function of intermediation, which is intrinsically linked to the relationship between the project and the social process described above.

Encouraging participation in a project is a matter of creating an enabling environment and appropriate channels for participation, and allocating the needed resources to its promotion. Intermediary organizations,[1] as will be seen in the course of this chapter, may belong to the public or private sector and may take various forms. The important thing is that they have an appropriate set of procedures—a methodology—and the skills and knowledge to apply it.

Appropriate intermediaries between project promoters and beneficiaries are one of the critical components for the success of a project involving community participation. From an operational point of view, the key factors that influence the effectiveness of these intermediaries are:

- The existence of organizations qualified and willing to act as intermediaries
- The allocation of sufficient resources to cover the cost of such intermediation.

Intermediaries are particularly critical where community-based organizations are weak or not sufficiently representative at the outset of a project, or where there is a high potential for conflict within the community or between the community and the project promoters.

Intermediaries in Action: Case Study Actors

In all of the cases we studied, we found at least one actor among the project participants that carried out the strategic function of articulating and mediating between the requirements of the project's promoters and those of the community. Table 3-1 identifies this social intermediary organization and summarizes its key features for each of the cases studied; the following provides a more in-depth examination of the social intermediary role in each case.

- In Bolivia, this function is partially carried out by the municipalities themselves through the staff of their own social development departments. Since municipalities often try to co-opt community

---

[1]Although in reality, intermediary organizations offer much more than social intermediation, it is common to see the terms *social intermediation* and *socio-technical support* as equivalents. Although the latter term is certainly more exact, we use both interchangeably in this text. We prefer not to use the term *social engineering*, since some feel that it has overtones of social manipulation.

Table 3-1. Identification and Key Features of Social Intermediary Organizations in Cases Studied

Case	Organization	Key features
Bolivia	Municipality social development departments	Technically weak and vulnerable to political manipulation; attempts by national government to build capacity of intermediaries and ABCOs
Brazil	Private contractor providing socio-technical support services	Rapid mobilization for recruitment, training, and placement of social workers, engineers, architects, and administrative staff; ability to meet stringent performance requirements; flexibility (ability to increase or reduce numbers of staff according to pace of works)
Costa Rica	Specialized NGO promoting low-income housing	Offers social, technical, and administrative assistance services to community groups in exchange for a fee; ability to provide and coordinate full range of services efficiently and effectively; emphasis on training and capacity-building for own staff and client groups
Mexico	Decentralized governmental agencies operating from municipal offices	Effective mechanism to support yearly works programs; insufficient staff to support a long-term development process; decentralization has brought the process closer to communities but has weakened coordination and peer review process
Peru	Various NGOs, municipality, ABCOs, and SPCOs	Lack of adequate socio-technical support for many initiatives has been a key limiting factor leading to varying degrees of intensity of participation in relation to the amount and quality of external support provided

Source: Authors' construction from field study data.

leadership and manipulate participation, the quality of the intermediary is often poor. Improving the quality of intermediation, perhaps by entrusting it to organizations like the Participatory Ac-

tion Planning (PAP) project,[2] would do much for the quality of the entire process in Bolivia.
- In Brazil's Guarapiranga program, the intermediary role was performed by Diagonal Urbana, a private company hired to provide this service, mobilizing a team of specialists.
- In the San José case, the Foundation for the Promotion of Housing (FUPROVI), the nongovernmental organization (NGO) that promoted the projects mobilized social workers as well as technical advisors.
- In Tijuana, the social workers and engineers mobilized by the municipality were indispensable intermediaries, bridging the gaps between the demands and schedules of the project and those of the population—so much so, that when their numbers and availability began to be reduced, this resulted in complaints from the community members about the inconveniences and delays.
- The case of Villa El Salvador (VES) is a very special one in this regard. The quality of the community organization in VES and the dynamics of the relationship between the VES-wide area-based community organization (ABCO)—the Self-Managed Urban Community of Villa El Salvador (CUAVES)—the local specific-purpose community organizations (SPCOs), the local government, the various central government bodies involved, and support organizations such as NGOs have produced different arrangements for different projects.[3] Sometimes ABCO leaders have acted as organizers and mediators; on other occasions, NGOs or the local government have done so. The strength of community organization has allowed for a sharing of responsibilities.

Other Functions of Intermediaries: Socio-Technical Support

Intermediation is just one of the dimensions of the activity of intermediary organizations. The ACAT concept—*asesoramiento, capacitación, asistencia técnica* (support, training, technical assistance)—practiced by San José's FUPROVI nicely sums up the functions of such organizations. A wide array of skills needs to be mobilized in order to fulfill this role,

---

[2] Funded by Dutch development aid, PAP promotes participatory action planning in Bolivia in low-income urban areas of Santa Cruz and El Alto. As discussed in chapter 6, PAP provides important skills and capacity-building for participation, but unfortunately does not enjoy sufficient support from its partner municipalities.

[3] Throughout this book, the term ABCO is used to mean a variety of area-based community organizations, including neighborhood associations; SPCO refers to a variety of specific-purpose community organizations, including special interest groups.

which is described by some as *socio-technical support* and by others as *social engineering*. The key areas of competence of intermediary organizations are the following:

- **Coordination and project management.** The complex processes we are talking about involve many stakeholders both at the community and institutional levels, and the ability to coordinate diverse inputs (e.g., technical, administrative, financial) and different time frames is crucial. Project management skills are needed to keep track of planned and actual resource use, time frame, and results achieved.
- **Social intermediation and community mobilization.** The complexity of the social process of participation requires that organizations know how to talk to community organizations and individual local residents to obtain their organized cooperation. Consensus building, negotiation, conflict resolution, and grievance management are all important skills in this regard.
- **Planning, engineering, and architecture.** These skills are required to provide technical assistance to the participatory planning process and to be able to interact productively with the various line agencies and public sector entities involved.
- **Training and capacity-building.** Social intermediary organizations need to be good at providing training and other capacity-building activities—a very important dimension of the participatory process.

Socio-technical support provides information and interfaces between the community and the authorities and between the community and the technical and administrative functions of the project. Such support ensures that information flows smoothly and creates a channel for discussion and negotiation of alternatives, organizing and clearly expressing demand. It provides a guaranteed source of information for the community, dissipates rumors, and reduces the level of confusion. It plays a fundamental role in mediation and conflict resolution and constitutes a vehicle to facilitate the community's access to the different actors involved in the project. In fact, one of the most important functions of social intermediaries is providing local residents with a single, clearly identified, and easily available access channel to the project and all its partner organizations (note the "on-call" socio-technical support provided in the Brazil and Costa Rica cases).

In some projects, socio-technical support is provided by the same organization that provides engineering, planning, project management, and construction management services. When this is the case, all of what is usually considered project *software*—i.e., all of the nonphysical components of a project, as opposed to its physical works components, or *hardware*—is provided by the same organization, which enhances coordination, ensuring that all project design and management functions are responsive to participation. (See box 3-1 for an example of the power this arrangement can wield.) However, while this would be a desirable situation, there are few organizations that can cover the full range of project software services; thus, the key focus from the point of view of project sponsors should be coordination.

Nowadays, acknowledgment of the importance of socio-technical support is widespread, and it comes even from some unexpected corners. The traditionally minded management of the construction firms that were involved in *favela* upgrading works in the Guarapiranga program were initially reluctant to accept the need for this function—and loath to pay for it—but are now the first to admit that nothing could have been done without it. According to the coordinator of the Guarapiranga program, Dirceu Yamazaki, "Social support and technical assistance to communities in projects such as these is fundamental before, during, and after the physical intervention. To meet these demands, which had not initially been taken into account, we found a way of including a clause in the contract with the construction companies that required them to hire support services for the population. They must have found the demand strange in the beginning, but I am sure that they now understand the importance it has."

When the initial project budget does not provide for the necessary socio-technical support, a makeshift solution is necessary. As we saw in Guarapiranga, the social intermediation provider was hired by each construction firm, and, from the point of view of the project, the cost was

---

Box 3-1. Introducing Participation into Project Design and Management: The FUPROVI Program in San José

Socio-technical support and a conducive environment with the right incentives help stimulate participation. In FUPROVI's projects, for example, individual homes are not assigned until after construction. This means that all participants work on many different homes and have an incentive for doing quality work, since each home they are working on might turn out to be their own. This system of house assignment adds further incentives to participation. Points are awarded to participating households on the basis of transparent criteria such as their punctuality, number of hours contributed, etc. Households are ranked according to the sum of their points, and their turn to choose their home only comes after all the better ranked households have chosen theirs. The fact that in any project some homes are better finished or better located than others turns this into a powerful incentive to do a good job.

considered part of the construction costs. In this way, provision of socio-technical support was included in the program budget under the "construction" heading. In spite of this, socio-technical support is a clearly identified cost item of the project, since it is provided by a private company under market conditions.

The Cost of Socio-Technical Support

This brings us to the issue of cost. Such delicate and complex tasks as the ones described here require time, specialized personnel, and money. The cost of socio-technical support is part of what may be called "the cost of participation." This may represent a significant portion of project cost.

In Tijuana, socio-technical support was provided by the municipality, partly by its own permanent staff and partly by professionals hired specifically for this purpose. In practice, the cost is added to the subsidy the municipality gives each project. Although the subsidy given for the works is totally transparent—the community manages those funds and has to account for them—the part of the subsidy given as technical assistance is not made clear to the community. In fact, it is not even clear to the municipality itself, since most of the staff, who are on the municipal payroll, are also involved in other activities, and the costs that accrue to each activity are not tallied. The same thing goes for other costs such as the use of equipment, office space, etc. Roughly the same situation prevails in the cases of Bolivia and Peru.

We will here try to clarify the cost implications of socio-technical support and project software, using the case studies from Costa Rica and Brazil as these are the only ones in which the full costs of project software were provided.

Cost of Project Software in the San José Case. In San José, FUPROVI's approach to cost recovery has changed with experience. The institution used to assess the cost of its services (i.e., the full range of project software services, including socio-technical support) for each project, and charged the client group for them. This approach had several disadvantages. Notably, communities did not know, at the outset of a project, how much socio-technical support would cost. Additionally, there was much bickering over the cost attached to specific services, and even more regarding indirect costs related to FUPROVI's general management and administration.

Therefore, the institution changed the system to apply a flat rate to all its projects. FUPROVI now charges its client—the group known as a housing association—a price for its services equal to 12 percent of the estimated cost of the housing units as assessed by the Costa Rican Federation of Engineers and Architects (CFIA), including basic finishings and infrastructure. The use of the CFIA parameters, which are somewhat lower than actual market costs, provides the community with a clear benchmark before a project even starts. The price of socio-technical support is made clear to the client group, which recognizes its value and agrees to pay for it. This is part of FUPROVI's policy of maintaining clear contractual relations with its clients and ensuring the financial sustainability of its operations.

With the new system, FUPROVI may incur losses on some projects that are particularly complex, but to compensate for these losses, it makes a "profit" on projects that require comparatively less input. Through practical experience, FUPROVI found that 12 percent of CFIA-assessed cost was an adequate margin for ensuring its continued economic sustainability. As a percentage of the *actual* cost of the houses it helps people build, however, the cost of FUPROVI's services ranges between 16 and 23 percent (see table 3-2).[4] This variation is linked to the location and complexity of each project. The easier the project, the higher the percentage, since the CFIA estimated cost—and FUPROVI's 12 percent of it—are the same per square meter, if the type of building is the same, anywhere in the country. In reality, prices are lower outside of San José, and the characteristics of the building site and available infrastructure have a big impact on the cost.

Cost of Project Software in the Guarapiranga Upgrading Project. Table 3-3 presents the cost of project software for seven favelas of the Guarapiranga upgrading project. The project software package considered includes:

- Engineering and planning
- Project coordination and management
- Information gathering and diagnosis
- Construction management and quality control
- Socio-technical support
- Technical assistance for land tenure regularization.

The figures in table 3-3 are almost all actual figures, drawn from actual project expenditures and provided by the Coordination of the Guarapiranga Upgrading Project at the Municipality of São Paulo. Calculations were made by Diagonal Urbana to establish average values and to add an important item that was missing from the Guarapiranga

---

[4] Even when the price of FUPROVI services is added to the other cost items—land, materials, specialized workmanship—the total cost of its housing units is significantly lower than either the CFIA estimated cost or market cost. Indeed, table 3-2 shows that it is usually less than half the cost of a similar unit built by a private company at market cost.

Table 3-2. House Cost Comparison: FUPROVI versus Private Companies

	Project				
Comparison item	21 de Noviembre	Nueva Primavera	Lomas de Parrita	Valle Escondido	Los Parques
Plot surface (m²)	154	164	333,250	120	182
House surface (m²)	45	45	42	42	60
FUPROVI					
Cost per m²	139	113	118	95	102
Total cost of house[a]	6,260	5,068	4,947	3,983	6,099
Cost of FUPROVI services	985	928	1,050	913	1,114
Services as % of total cost	16	18	21	23	18
Private companies					
Cost per m²	228	231	304	205	211
Total cost of house[a]	10,275	10,390	12,772	8,626	12,638
Margin[b]	3,550	3,609	4,551	2,958	4,318
Margin as % of total cost	35	35	36	34	34

Notes: This cost comparison regards the total cost of identical homes with basic finishings and infrastructure. FUPROVI costs are those for houses built with the FUPROVI assisted mutual-help construction system. Private company costs are FUPROVI estimates of the cost of houses built by a private company at market prices and conditions in the same locations.

[a] These costs include the cost of FUPROVI's services and the private company's margin, respectively.

[b] Margin includes indirect costs (6 percent), pretax profit (15 percent), and discounts obtained from contractors and materials suppliers (10 percent).

Source: FUPROVI, 1999.

project, namely technical assistance to land tenure regularization. The original calculations were made in Brazilian currency (*reals*), and the results were converted into dollars at the November 1999 rate of R$2 per US$1. The figures in table 3-3 are all in U.S. dollars for comparison purposes. However, it should be borne in mind that the Brazilian real was worth significantly more against the U.S. dollar at the time the expenditures were actually made.

The sample selected for table 3-3 includes favelas representing a range of sizes, degrees of consolidation, levels of organization, population densities, and geomorphological features—all factors that influence the cost of project software. The selected favelas and their key features at the start of the project were the following:

- **Nova Guarapiranga I and II.** These are small favelas, located in low-lying, flat areas on the banks of the Guarapiranga reservoir.

Table 3-3. Cost of Project Software in the Guarapiranga Project

Favela	Area (hectares)	No. of households	Density (households/hectare)	Total project cost ($)	Project cost/household ($)	Project software cost ($)	Software as % of project cost	Software cost/household ($)
Nova Guarapiranga I & II	1.90	261	137.4	671,754	2,574	142,341	21.2	545
Jardim Manacás	1.27	288	226.8	1,066,667	3,704	170,644	16.0	593
Jardim Floresta	1.60	234	146.3	586,646	2,507	129,735	22.1	554
Parque Amélia	5.89	736	125.0	1,684,402	2,289	365,632	21.7	497
Santa Tereza	0.60	101	168.3	256,699	2,542	51,304	19.9	508
Jardim Dionísio	5.00	549	109.8	1,145,653	2,087	242,601	21.2	442
Jardim Iporanga/ Jardim Esmeralda	17.60	2,074	117.8	8,342,468	4,022	1,267,864	15.2	611
Total		4,243	137.5	13,754,289	3,242		19.2	589

Note: The totals for columns 3 (density), 5 (project cost/household), 7 (software as % of project cost), and 8 (software cost/household) are weighted averages per household; weights used are number of households per favela.
Source: Diagonal Urbana from data supplied by the Coordination of the Guarapiranga Urban Upgrading Project.

There was a high degree of consolidation (i.e., most homes were built of durable materials) and partial water and sanitation network coverage. The works consisted of minor layout changes, water and sanitation network repairs, extension building of infrastructure networks, and paving of main roads. The main cost item was soil replacement for the main roads.
- **Jardim Manacás.** This is a small favela on a high-slope area, very densely occupied, with a medium level of consolidation. The project included the opening and paving of streets and pathways, and the building of infrastructure networks, storm drainage and protection, and consolidation of slopes. The high cost per household is due to this last item, a very costly one in a high-slope area.
- **Jardim Floresta.** This is a small favela, very dense, with a medium level of consolidation. A small risk area required removal and resettlement, as did significant layout changes and the opening of new roads and footpaths. Infrastructure networks had to be built from scratch.
- **Parque Amélia.** This is a mid-sized favela, densely occupied and not very consolidated, with shacks interfering with the area's main drainage. The project had a major storm drainage component and included the building of infrastructure networks, the reduction of density through removal and resettlement, and the opening and paving of streets and footpaths.
- **Santa Tereza.** This very small and highly consolidated favela required the building of infrastructure networks and the paving of streets and footpaths.
- **Jardim Dionísio.** This is a mid-sized favela, densely settled and highly consolidated, with interferences between the settlement and the area's main drainage. The intervention included, besides the usual infrastructure networks, a major storm drainage component, with the building of a covered drain along the valley's floor, which also serves as the new main access.
- **Jardim Iporanga/Jardim Esmeralda.** This is a large, dense, and highly consolidated favela, with major interferences between existing structures and drainage. The works here were the costliest in our sample, since they included the building of major drainage works and the removal and resettlement of almost 25 percent of the households, mostly to new units built within the area itself.

Table 3-4 gives suggested parameters for the various software components, expressed as percentages of total project cost. These are based partly on the weighted average costs of the different services in our sample and partly on the broader experience of Diagonal Urbana. Note

Table 3-4. Structure and Cost of Project Software by Type of Service
(As percentage of total project cost)

Type of service	Weighted average cost	Suggested parameter
Engineering and planning	3.33	3.25
Project coordination and management	4.08	3.75
Information gathering and analysis	0.44	0.50
Construction management	3.18	3.00
Socio-technical support	2.43	4.50
Land tenure regularization	5.77	5.00
Total	19.24	20.00

Note: Weights used are number of households per favela.
Source: Diagonal Urbana from data supplied by the Coordination of the Guarapiranga Urban Upgrading Project.

that the average cost of socio-technical support in the Guarapiranga project was lower than Diagonal's experience in other projects, partly because some activities normally carried out by socio-technical support providers were distributed among other items in Guarapiranga.

Figure 3-2 provides a curve that relates the cost of project software, as a percentage of total project cost, to total project cost per household. The curve is based on the Guarapiranga figures, and we feel that it provides a reasonable first guess, or ball park figure, in the range that goes from $2,000 to $7,500 of total project cost per household. In plotting the curve, we needed a point corresponding to a higher total cost, since in the Guarapiranga data, the cost only ranges from approximately $2,000 to $4,000. Therefore, point A in the curve was drawn from a project of São Paulo's Housing and Urban Development Company, in which the degree of removals and resettlement is very high, the cost per household is $7,500, and project software cost is just over 11 percent of total project cost. The curve loses practical significance beyond that point, since it is not realistic to expect the cost of project software to move to under 10 percent of the total project cost per household. Another caveat is that these figures were drawn from a project that included simultaneous interventions in many areas, which generated economies of scale. Experience shows that economies of scale lower the relative cost of project software as the total project cost per household goes up; it also shows, however, that the cost of project software rises significantly in isolated interventions, especially in small areas.

Figure 3-2. Cost of Project Software as Percentage of Total Project Cost and Total Project Cost per Household

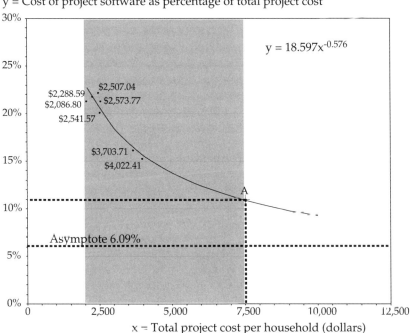

Source: Authors' construction from field study data.

Alternatives for Organizing Socio-Technical Support

There are many effective alternatives for organizing the provision of socio-technical support. Table 3-5 highlights some examples from the projects covered in chapter 2. Let us explore for a moment the pros and cons of the different arrangements cited in this table and summarized in figure 3-3.

In Tijuana, socio-technical support is organized and provided by the decentralized offices of the municipality. In Ciudad Juárez, in the Mexican state of Chihuahua, it is also organized and provided by the municipality, but by a centralized social development department. Tijuana's decentralization brought the program closer to the communities, but it also had a negative impact on coordination and professional exchange among the technicians. The centralized model in Juárez has avoided these problems, but in neither city has the municipality given due importance to the nonphysical aspects of the community upgrading programs. This is at once a missed opportunity and a risk to sustainability. In the Boliv-

Table 3-5. Types of Providers, Contractual Arrangements, and Compensation Structures for Socio-Technical Support

Project	Provider	Contractual arrangements	Compensation structure
Tijuana	Decentralized offices of the municipality	Contract between a community works committee and the municipality	Service provided by municipality as (hidden) subsidy; staff are employees of or work under contract with the municipality
Ciudad Juárez	Central social devel. dept. of municipality	Same as above	Same as above
San José	FUPROVI (local NGO)	Contract between a housing association and FUPROVI	All staff are permanent employees of FUPROVI; housing associations pay for services a percentage of estimated construction cost
Guarapiranga	Diagonal Urbana (private consulting firm)	Contract between construction contractors and Diagonal	Diagonal is paid a fixed percentage of construction costs; all staff are Diagonal employees
Cingapura	Diagonal Urbana	Contract between municipality and Diagonal	Diagonal is paid according to staff time employed and expenses incurred; all staff are Diagonal employees
Mutirão, São Paulo	Assessorias, hybrid structures (consulting firms/NGOs)	Contracts between housing associations and assessorias	Assessorias are paid according to staff time employed and expenses incurred; all staff are assessoria employees

ian case, some cities are organized along decentralized lines similar to Tijuana's (e.g., Cochabamba), while others follow a centralized model similar to that of Ciudad Juárez (e.g., Santa Cruz).

In San José, socio-technical support is organized and provided by a private nonprofit organization; in Guarapiranga, it is organized and provided by a private consulting firm.

In the *mutirão* projects in São Paulo,[5] which are based on successful experiences in Uruguay, socio-technical support is organized and pro-

---
[5] The mutirão is a tradition of mutual-help housing construction which is common in rural areas in Brazil and was brought to low-income areas in Brazilian cities by migrants. Two examples of mutirão-based housing projects in São Paulo are described in chapter 2.

Project	Provider	Contractual arrangements	Compensation structure
Novos Alagados	AVSI (international NGO)	Contract between state government and AVSI	AVSI is paid for services at cost, partly with resources it helped raise; subsidy element, since AVSI's indirect costs are not covered; all staff are AVSI employees
Cochabamba, Bolivia	Decentralized offices of the municipality	No contract as such; relations between communities and socio-technical support providers conform to rules laid out by Law 1551	All staff are employees of or work under contract with the municipality
Santa Cruz, Bolivia	Central social devel. dept. of the municipality	Same as above	Same as above
Catuche Social Consortium	Fé y Alegria (local NGO) and technicians' co-op	Contract between Fé y Alegria, co-op, and ABCO	NGO is funded by other sources and recovers only part of its cost from the project; the rest is provided as a subsidy; technicians charge modest fees

Source: Authors' construction from field study data.

vided by *assessorias* (advisors); these are hybrid structures (NGOs organized as consulting firms) hired by the communities to provide technical assistance and intermediation services for mutual-help construction. In Caracas, the Catuche Social Consortium—which is both a project promoter and service provider—is made up of three partners: the community; an NGO that provides administrative support, handles public relations, and raises funds; and a group of engineers, architects, and planners who provide technical assistance. The Catuche structure is like that of Costa Rica's FUPROVI, only set up at the level of one settlement.

A common characteristic of the above formulas is the interdisciplinary nature of the socio-technical support teams. These teams are nor-

Figure 3-3. Various Scenarios for Provision of Socio-Technical Support

1. Project promoter is provider of socio-technical support (e.g., San José, Tijuana), and community has a direct contractual relationship with other service providers.

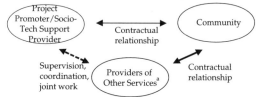

2. Socio-technical support is hired by construction contractors (e.g., Guarapiranga)

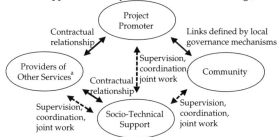

3. Socio-technical support is hired by the project promoter (e.g., Cingapura)

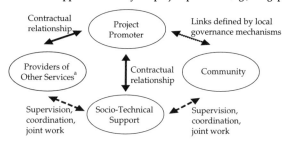

4. Socio-technical support is hired by community (e.g., Mutirão project, São Paulo)[b]

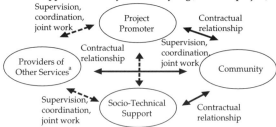

[a] May include engineering, urban planning, project management, construction contractors, quality control, microfinance, etc.

[b] Another possibility is for the community to enter into an agreement with an NGO to prepare and present a proposal that is later supported by a project promoter.

Source: Authors' construction from field study data.

mally made up of sociologists, social workers, engineers, architects, planners, communication experts, and administrative and technical support staff. When community management is utilized, these last two groups are responsible for providing training to community members in administrative and technical areas.

As the cases we have studied show, economists are conspicuously absent from many socio-technical support teams, which is probably part of the reason why cost recovery and economic sustainability issues and the targeting of subsidies are often not given the attention they deserve.

Despite the variety of models developed by the above institutions, the socio-technical teams have the common task of untangling difficult situations and problems in their daily work in the field. They play a natural coordination role and end up serving as the interface among all the different actors involved, not just between the community and each actor. The different types of organizations involved in socio-technical support have different incentives, and a profit motive may or may not be present, but most share a commitment to local development and a belief in the potential of low-income communities. We have seen that it is easier to find distortions in their role when they are part of the municipal administration. Outside organizations, although often working under a contract with the municipality, usually manage to retain a greater degree of autonomy and independence from political pressure.

Selecting a Social Intermediation Organization. Socio-technical support is a crucial project component, but it takes an organization that is capable and has the right kind of motivation to do it well. Results therefore depend primarily on who does it. The nature of the organization is not the deciding factor: we have seen that NGOs, for-profit private operators, municipal departments, public sector line agencies, statutory bodies, utility companies, and even university groups can be effective at it. The overall approach, the level of capacity, the motivation, the resources available, and the methodologies used are what make the difference.

The examples we have seen are very eloquent in this regard. In Mexico, the Solidaridad program did have a socio-technical support strategy, but its underpinnings and results were very different from what the municipality of Tijuana set in motion with the Manos a la Obra program. The institutional reforms Tijuana undertook included the creation of mechanisms to allow the citizenry to participate in the definition of priorities, as well as a measure of democratization of community representation. A specific innovative feature of Manos a la Obra is a show of confidence in the community by directly handing over to it the resources for project execution. All these features of the project had repercussions on the nature and organization of socio-technical support.

In the early stages of São Paulo's Guarapiranga project, the municipality had a unit charged with social support, but means, methods, and results changed overnight when adequate resources were allocated and a private firm was hired for the job. The municipality's social workers were too few and thinly spread, and they had been working with scarce resources and limited recognition of their efforts. Once it became clear that this situation was jeopardizing the very feasibility of implementation of the works, the project promoters exercised their creativity to find adequate resources to devote to socio-technical support. Hiring a private firm allowed the municipality to address the problem without having to hire and train staff directly.

In sum, the organizations that are qualified to do this job may be of several different kinds, but must meet the following criteria:

- Background and attitude of genuine interest in the urban poor, demonstrated by a track record of development activities in low-income urban areas permitting them to understand and adjust to community dynamics
- A strong professional team with all the necessary skills: social workers, social scientists, engineers, architects, planners, economists, project managers, and communication experts
- Strong conflict resolution and negotiation skills on the part of all team members, regardless of their professional background
- A culture of interdisciplinary teamwork
- Specific experience in and access to the necessary methodology and tools (or willingness to hire specialists with the requisite know-how and experience)
- Knowledge of the local cultural and political context and ability to partner effectively with its key actors
- A proactive, problem-solving attitude and mental and organizational openness and flexibility to accommodate changing needs and circumstances.

Another option in organizing social intermediation is to have separate organizations provide different parts of the socio-technical support package. In the social consortium model of Caracas, for example, social support is provided by an NGO, while technical support is provided by a cooperative of engineers and architects. The Caracas model works well, because the NGO and technicians have close links and are jointly answerable to the community. There are, however, certain inherent risks in awarding separate contracts for tasks that are so intimately connected. Contracts with separate organizations may lead to coordination difficulties and finger pointing. Therefore, although separate organizations may very well team up to provide socio-technical support, separate contracts should be avoided.

Can the Community Itself Provide or Hire Socio-Technical Support?

In Tijuana, one of the ideas under discussion for the future of the Obra Social Comunitaria (Social Community Works) program is hiring social workers who are local residents themselves. This has been done in the past in certain instances, but as a rule the social workers have been outsiders.[6] The proponents of this idea believe this brings the program closer to the people and to their needs and aspirations. The social workers who took part in the workshop we organized in Tijuana opposed the idea because they think that the role of the social worker is to represent the agency and channel its support to the community. Experience seems to confirm this view; the case for the outsider seems indeed stronger than that for the local in the intermediation role. The outsider stands a better chance of being recognized as a reliable intermediary, a recognition that is often an important asset. The ability to have a broader outlook—to see the forest and not just the trees—may be one reason; another may be the advantage of a trained professional who is less personally involved, less prone to political interference, and better able to evaluate a situation. In fact, there is much to be said for a professional organization with a professional team in this role. A compromise solution offering the best of both worlds would be to hire outsiders as social intermediaries, but to have them work in two-person teams with local individuals. This solution would allow an unbiased and objective outsider to work closely with someone who is local and therefore able to provide an insider's knowledge and insights.

Another approach is for a community itself to hire an external socio-technical support provider; this bottom-up approach was successfully taken by FUPROVI, the social consortium in Caracas, and São Paulo's mutirão. In these three examples, the social intermediary is chosen and hired by the community—a bottom-up approach. The community's choice may sometimes be guided to some extent by the agency promoting the project. In São Paulo's mutirão, for example, the community may choose from a roster of competing assessorias, or socio-technical support providers. This method promotes healthy competition, providing an incentive for competing firms to keep their costs down, be innovative in their approaches, improve their services, and develop a true client orientation. Obviously, for a number of providers to exist in a market, there needs to be a steady flow of work opportunities, a point discussed in more detail in chapter 5.

Competition and a direct contractual relationship between a community and a socio-technical support provider can combine to create a truly demand-driven approach. Since technical assistance to community

---

[6]In this context, we use the term *social workers* because of the role that is played, even though many of Tijuana's *promotores sociales* are not trained social workers.

groups is often funded through grants, the situation would typically lend itself to the establishment of some sort of voucher system, in which vouchers issued by the project are exchanged for services from any one of a list of authorized providers.

Another possibility is that an NGO may initiate a project upon the direct invitation of a community group. In this case, the NGO would operate under a direct agreement with the community. Local government may at first be indifferent to—or, in some cases, even oppose—the project. Experience has shown, however, that after a project has been planned through an open, participatory process, local administrations often become involved—and with good results. The NGO in this scenario fulfills an intermediary role, but its primary client is the community, not the municipality; an example of this approach is the Novos Alagados project in Bahia, Brazil.

In the community infrastructure funds (CIFs) that were proposed as a promising way forward in the northern border of Mexico (see chapter 9), the idea is that intermediary organizations would receive technical assistance in project proposal preparation from the CIF, and subsequently compete for community contracts. In this format, only intermediary organizations that succeeded in helping their client communities prepare a good proposal that was subsequently approved by the CIF would actually have contracts. In this scenario, a project would set up a framework to create private capacity and would also create a market for such capacity, complete with bidding and contracting procedures. Organizations that would receive technical assistance would be prequalified to compete for a share of the market, and communities would have access to a number of competing social intermediation organizations from which to choose.

Should Community Organizers Be Paid a Salary? Participation is hard work, both for outsiders providing socio-technical support (who are normally paid for their efforts) and for community organizers, the people in the community who are most actively involved in meetings and other activities of the project. Should community organizers be paid for their efforts as well?

In the FUPROVI example, organizers have their work contribution assessed and recognized—just like the labor contributions of other members of the community. The catch is that organizers need to work more than anybody else. In cases where no community labor is present, it is more difficult to ensure equity, since community organizers work hard while others work very little or not at all.

In the San José case, the organizational work of the leaders is computed as time dedicated to mutual-help construction. The problem is that those in this role tend to dedicate up to 50 hours a week to their tasks, rather than the agreed 30 hours, without any extra compensation. Furthermore, they incur extra expenses for which they do not receive any reimbursement. In Tijuana, there is neither compensation nor reimbursement, and community organizers have to pay telephone expenses and transportation to city government or bank offices. This all-too-common situation results in negative incentives for community organizers and is part of the reason why so many people play this role for a limited period—and why those who do stay on often do so to further their political ambitions or for illicit personal gain. The usual situation, in which organizers are not paid, tempts them to secure undue advantages as compensation for their work. And they are suspected to act in this way even when they don't, which creates a lasting credibility issue.

Rather than paying a fixed monthly salary to a leader or organizer, the equitable and transparent solution to this dilemma is to identify, with the assistance of the socio-technical support provider, tasks and specific activities that can be quantified in terms of time. The idea would be to pay the organizers an agreed flat rate or an hourly or daily fee for those activities. They should also be reimbursed for any expenses not included in the general obligations of all participating households under the project. For example, local residents involved in the collection of data might be paid an agreed fee per questionnaire. In addition, they might also be reimbursed for the food and allowances that they need to provide during these activities.

The problem of the remuneration of community leaders was discussed in our community focus groups in São Paulo. All agreed that their work often requires an enormous amount of time and energy over an extended period. The majority of those present believed that paid leaders could be constrained in their role by those who paid them, but also that the benefits of fairness and transparency are considerable. A clear and reasonable structure of compensation and reimbursement, paid for by the project, is a big step forward in avoiding corruption and the enlistment of community organizers by vested interests.

As in the case of socio-technical support, compensation and reimbursement for community organizers are part of what may be called the cost of participation. As such, this is a cost that should be funded by the project and considered a legitimate project expense that needs to be budgeted for and whose expenditure needs to be monitored and accounted for.

Influence of Participatory Strategies and Project Stages on Socio-Technical Support Services. Socio-technical support services vary according to the participatory strategy chosen and the ongoing project stage. At each stage, in fact, participation has specific objectives, involves different groups within the community to various degrees of intensity, and makes use of different instruments (see table 3-6). Different strategies, in terms of the choice of level and degree of participation, will also mean differences in services.

Our field reports demonstrate the importance of continuing socio-technical support work after construction in order to produce a more profound and lasting impact on the development process. It is wrong to believe that this process ends with the completion of the physical works, or that local communities can achieve sustainability of project outputs on their own. Approaches and strategies are needed for the provision of socio-technical support to communities for an extended period of time after project completion. Parameters in this regard are hard to come by, since this is a relatively new idea, and examples are few. São Paulo's Cingapura project is one example where up to 36 months of socio-technical support are provided following completion of the works to assist communities in the organization and management of building maintenance, collection of residents' contributions, etc. In this context, FUPROVI's experience with *sustainable development promoters* is very interesting. FUPROVI does not provide post-implementation socio-technical support, but it has set up a program to train people who have taken part in its projects to provide consultant services related to the sustainability of investments made in an area and its long-term development. These people go on to provide services to neighborhood associations or institutions such as Costa Rica's National Directorate of Roads, which recently hired a group of FUPROVI-trained sustainable development promoters to set up a system for the upgrading and conservation of landscaped areas along national highways.

Socio-technical support is one of the few instruments available to help overcome the limitations of the sectoral approach of most infrastructure and housing projects. Their proximity to social processes gives social intermediaries the opportunity to interact and exchange information with public and private institutions that can contribute solutions to other issues associated with poverty, such as education, work opportunities, and health.

Community Organization and Level of Participation

A weak community organization is not in itself an obstacle that cannot be overcome. Rather, the real problem is to create a participation strategy that can, on the one hand, make the project respond to the expectations and needs of local people and, on the other, match operational solutions to the community's degree of organization. This latter does not always allow for the delegation of complex functions, under penalty of failing the project's objectives.

Table 3-6. Socio-Technical Support and the Project Cycle

Stage	Focus
Identification	• Setting up participatory strategy, i.e., gathering basic information to define entry points for participation • Analyzing alternatives; developing participatory strategy
Planning	• Eliciting and organizing participation in planning, i.e., communication strategy • Participatory information gathering and analysis • Participatory evaluation of needs and demands • Discussing and negotiating alternatives • Participatory planning of proposed intervention • *For community management strategies:* intense training activities

Implementation	• Handling problems related to construction work, e.g.:
	  – organization of information flow
	  – coordination with contractors and community to plan work phases
	  – information and support to households affected by specific work fronts
	  – support services to households affected by resettlement
	  – arrangements for moving families to temporary shelter and later into their own homes
	  – accident prevention and general troubleshooting
	• *For community management strategies:* technical and administrative assistance to works development

Post-Implementation	• Handling critical issues regarding sustainability:
	  – monitoring use of project benefits and operation/maintenance of infrastructure
	  – health and environmental education
	  – promotion of correct use of new infrastructure
	  – awareness-raising regarding rights and access to appropriate authorities
	  – promotion of responsible attitude toward consumption of water and energy, disposal of solid waste, and payment of bills and taxes
	  – prevention and control of new informal land occupations in area, especially risk areas and land set aside for community uses
	  – care and maintenance of public spaces and urban equipment
	  – microcredit schemes and technical assistance for home improvement and generation of employment and income

Source: Authors' construction from field study data.

Matching Level of Participation to Community Organization

In defining the level of participation that will be attempted by a project, it is necessary to consider the requirements of difficult tasks—such as, for example, the management of financial resources—which demand more complex forms of organization. Next, it is necessary to verify if the capacity for undertaking these tasks already exists or if it can only be reached via a training effort to be undertaken by the project (as in the examples of Tijuana and San José). Otherwise, it is better to choose less ambitious solutions. This does not necessarily mean that participation will be less intense—the *degree* of participation may still be very high—but that its *level* will be more appropriate to the realities of the relevant community.

Although it certainly has much to do with operational considerations, level of participation is also influenced by a fundamental political decision by project promoters regarding their willingness to share decision-making powers and management responsibilities. What experience seems to indicate is that the conditions for community management in general are not given; it is necessary to build them. A clear decision must be made and resources allocated, as was done in Tijuana and even more in San José. In fact, one can observe from our field reports and other experiences that the practical solutions in terms of level and degree of participation are the fruit, not so much of what the sponsoring agency *could* do, but mainly of what it thought appropriate to the circumstances and *wanted* to do. This is clear from the cases we have studied:

- In Bolivia, the level of capacity of the ABCOs varies greatly. Although some were capable of undertaking community management with a small amount of training, most required intensive training for them to be able to do so. The legislators who developed Law 1551 therefore decided to aim for a less ambitious level of participation, in which organized communities take part in participatory budgeting and exercise control over project execution. With the experience that has accumulated since 1994, it has become clear that while the better organized ABCOs are capable of playing an informed and critical role in the process, many others still require significant capacity-building. The situation is bound to evolve, but for now the level of participation that was determined by the legislators seems to be in keeping with the circumstances.
- In Guarapiranga, the level of community organization was very uneven in the 180 informal settlements involved. With some significant exceptions, associations dedicated to specific social programs—e.g., the distribution of milk tickets—prevail. These are

obviously not prepared to give support to a vast infrastructure program. Since the infrastructure to be built in Guarapiranga included large works that have metropolitan relevance, it was not thought possible to resort to community management, not even for part of the works—even though there is in Brazil a certain community management tradition, an expression of which is the mutirão. Therefore, the preparatory work for community management that was carried out in Tijuana and San José had no parallel in Guarapiranga.

- In Costa Rica, the groups that contacted FUPROVI had already been mobilized around the problem of housing construction, but initially did not have the capacity to manage the construction process. Since the assisted mutual-help methodology is central to FUPROVI's objectives, the foundation set up an intense—and successful—training program to reinforce the groups' organization and skill base. In the case of FUPROVI, the housing associations are representative of the group that constitutes them, and their leadership is democratically elected. It is clearly perceived that the role of the leaders in organizing the community is critical to the successful implementation and completion of the project. The limits of their representativeness are clearly defined, and the contract the association signs with the foundation, being within those limits, is recognized by all parties.
- In Tijuana, area-based community associations are almost nonexistent. It was thus decided to create a new and specific organization to manage each project (the *obra social* committees). These were based on a specific short-term task that coincided with one of the community's main aspirations. Obra social committees are not particularly strong or durable, yet they are recognized by the small group that they represent for the clearly defined objective of road paving or construction of a sports facility. These organizations are thus recognized by their members as being able to establish contracts with the municipality. The committees were provided with very focused training by the municipality, and people showed remarkable capacity for initiative and management. The high rate of literacy and low rate of unemployment in Tijuana also played a role in this favorable situation.
- The community of Villa El Salvador has shown a particularly strong predisposition toward participation. Here, community management could have been adopted more often, since community organizations have given proof of a high level of capacity on many occasions. Few places would have a better opportunity than VES for the successful application of community management models, due to the quality of its organizations. However, the level of participation has seldom reached that of community management since the

organizations promoting the projects have not been willing to provide the necessary training and the intensity of socio-technical support needed to promote the necessary enabling environment required for the higher levels of participation.

In Guarapiranga, a conscious decision was made not to pursue a community management strategy, due to the size and complexity of the infrastructure. Although São Paulo does have experience in community management through the mutirão programs, it was thought that the approach was not appropriate for Guarapiranga. In the Bolivian case, it was probably believed that participation in participatory budgeting and expenditure control was already a sufficiently ambitious objective for a nationwide program in a country with a limited tradition of participation. The cases of Tijuana and San José show that a high level of participation may also be the object of a conscious choice by project organizers. In both experiences, advanced forms of community management were arrived at—although initially it was not possible to count on particularly strong and structured community organizations. The objective of community management was pursued through an appropriate participation strategy, including training and socio-technical support. In our Peruvian example, the degree of participation was always high due to the predisposition of the community of Villa El Salvador, but the level of participation varied greatly according to the decisions of the organizations promoting the various projects.

When a more consolidated organization exists, there is a need to find adequate channels for the interaction between this organization and the project. The existence of a strong organization does not guarantee success: there are cases in which the participatory process doesn't work, because the project encounters constant conflict and opposition from a strong community organization that, for any reason, has not bought into the project. The Cingapura project in São Paulo is an example. When the program began, the umbrella organizations of the favelas were hostile, since the project's initial formulation had very limited room for dialogue and consultation with the communities and was seen merely as a repackaging of the old mass housing formulas of the 1970s. The initial confrontation was followed by dialogue between the favela organizations and the municipality and by the creation of avenues for consultation and negotiation of options, along with a carefully designed socio-technical support component. These developments have reduced the obstacles to what has subsequently become a relatively popular, if still problematic, program.

Although the level of participation of a project or program is normally defined by the promoter's strategy, this is a dynamic process and often evolves over time. The gradual change in methodology promoted by FUPROVI, delegating ever-widening tasks to the community, is a clear example of this. The level and degree of participation a project starts out with may be very different from what exists two or three years down the road. As a FUPROVI engineer notes, "In the beginning, we were worried that the communities would not be able to do certain things...We managed the supplies and the procurement, and the community did the construction work. Later, the management of the warehouses was passed on to the communities. They started to do all the handling, custody, and reception of materials. Then we saw that the communities had more capacities than we had thought, and now they manage the procurement and all those tasks." The organization found it possible to match the level of socio-technical support it was able to give to a higher level of participation than had been originally envisaged—a clear gain for the program.

The FUPROVI example shows that, although one cannot expect the community to participate beyond the limits set by the project, the group may sometimes push these limits and show project promoters it is capable of and willing to operate at a higher level.

Community Management

Community management usually means shared control over the management of a project between external actors and local residents. Full control, less common in practice, would mean placing control of the project entirely in the hands of local residents. Whether shared or full control, community management represents the highest level of participation. Through community management, the poor are themselves participants in a poverty reduction strategy.

Community management is feasible when:

- **There is a community organization that is recognized** both within and outside the community, with representative leadership, that is able to negotiate in the community's name, to represent the community as a party to contracts, and to help organize the community's inputs.
- **The community organization has the adequate level of training** to be able to select and interact with service providers, understand design and construction issues, purchase and store building materials, collect payments, keep accounts, etc.
- **The level of effort that will be required of the community is reasonable.** Community management takes a great deal of time and energy. Poor people who need to earn a living in difficult circum-

stances may not have the time and energy required, depending on project complexity and size.
- **The relationship is based on a clear contract** to allocate rights and responsibilities, define resource flows, facilitate accountability and transparency, define recourse mechanisms, etc.

Reducing the vulnerability of a group may be seen as the product of interaction between a set of positive external actions and the group's existing set of assets, with a view to reinforcing the assets. The definition of the needed external actions depends, then, on a careful reading of a community's assets.

Before the implementation of shelter and infrastructure improvements in a community management mode, it is usually necessary to improve the community's assets, in terms of organization and know-how, through training activities. Training is thus the usual starting point of community participation in project management.

There are various possible entry points for community management. For example, in the FUPROVI case, the need to lower cost and to target the project to the poor were entry points for community management. Before committing to community management, however, the cost and time involved in preparing for it, the complexity of project tasks, and the level of effort required of the community need to be evaluated by project promoters and discussed with the community. Both sides need to be fully aware of the implications. Especially in large-scale or technically more complex projects, it may be risky to attempt community management, especially if there is no prior local experience to guide project participants. One formula that may be attempted is to entrust certain parts of a project to community management and expand the scope for it gradually, based on a careful reading of the results.

Community management is not attempted just to improve the quality of project implementation. The experiences of Tijuana and San José show that the practice of community management strengthens very tangible elements of a community's set of assets, with a special impact on project sustainability. Other positive effects of community management include:

- High level of ownership of the project by local people, leading to better use of project benefits, better care of the new infrastructure, and an appreciation of the benefits of community initiative
- The development within the community of a group of people who know the project down to its technical details and who thus may become a key resource for operation and maintenance
- Enhanced trust between the community and the agency promoting the project

- Significant development of capabilities at the community level (social capital), as well as at the level of the promoting agency and providers of socio-technical support.

All the above benefits point to the two key dimensions of operational sustainability after closure of a project as mentioned previously in chapter 1. Specifically, these relate to the maintenance of the assets acquired through the project and the ability to generate further development initiatives.

Figure 3-4, taken from Goethert (1998), explores the different levels of community participation that may apply to the different stages of projects and programs.

Contract-Based Relationships

The decision to formalize community participation in a written contract is an interesting indicator of the level of participation chosen in the

Figure 3-4. A Model for Participation

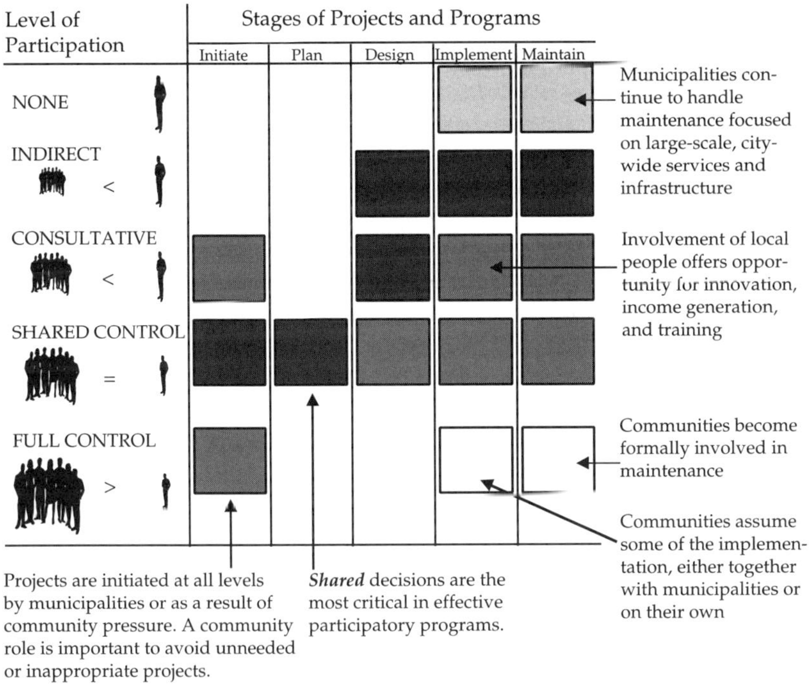

Source: Adapted from Goethert (1998).

project's strategy. The higher the level of participation, the stronger the motivation to put into writing the responsibilities and obligations that sustain the relations between the parties. When participation reaches the level of community management, formalized contractual relations are particularly needed, especially with regard to the management of a project's financial resources.

Legal recognition of the community organization is an essential requirement for it to be able to enter into a contract with the agency promoting the project. In the case of Costa Rica, this aspect is so important that FUPROVI routinely helps housing associations obtain legal recognition as a prerequisite for signing the formal agreement that is a cornerstone of the foundation's methodology. In Bolivia, one of the key achievements of the People's Participation Law is making it simple and straightforward to give a community organization legal recognition.

Different approaches towards defining the legal agreement between the community organization and the agency promoting the project are observed in the different cases.

- **Bolivia.** Law 1551 recognizes ABCOs or neighborhood associations and establishes the rights and responsibilities of all parties. In many respects, the procedures defined by the law play the part of a contract, but there is no contract as such between municipalities and neighborhood organizations.
- **São Paulo.** The community has not signed contracts with promoting agencies.
- **San José.** A legally constituted housing association signs a contract with FUPROVI.
- **Tijuana.** The neighborhood obra social committee signs an agreement with the municipality.
- **Peru.** There is a recognized ABCO structure with a clear institutional base. These organizations frequently enter into contracts with the municipality or other service providers.

Programs such as the ones in San José and Tijuana normally create standard templates for a limited number of contract types as needed. This is made possible by having one standard type of community organization and just a few types of interventions. Complex and large-scale projects like Guarapiranga present greater difficulties in this regard. It is certainly more difficult to define and administer contracts with a large number of counterparts that have different structures and levels of organization. However, the many benefits of a contract-based relationship make it worth trying to overcome such obstacles.

Not having just one clearly defined project goal and one clearly recognized organization that can sign for the community is another obstacle to establishing a contract-based relationship. The Guarapiranga case is a clear example in this regard. In each settlement of Guarapiranga, there usually is an ABCO with broad developmental goals. This might be the natural vehicle for a contractual relationship with the community, but the degree of legitimacy and representativeness of such organizations is very uneven; also, in each area, there are special interest groups or SPCOs that carry as much or more weight than the area-based organization. This makes it difficult to sign a contract with any one organization that the community at large would recognize. And if the majority of local residents do not feel bound by a contract, it will not serve its purpose.

A related issue is ensuring a straightforward distribution of tasks and responsibilities in a contract when project plans are complex and diversified and there is no clear community counterpart. Our suggestion is to use the preparation of the participatory area development plan (discussed later in this chapter) as an opportunity to identify tasks that might be matched to the broader area-based organization and to specific special interest groups, and to enter into different contractual agreements with each of them. The process of participatory information gathering and analysis and the subsequent area development planning process offer good opportunities for identifying specific development initiatives and their constituencies in a community. This may seem a rather complex route to follow, but the benefits of establishing clear contractual relationships for subsets of activities of a development plan are well worth the trouble in terms of transparency, accountability, and capacity-building. See box 3-2 for items to consider in designing a contract.

Box 3-2. Key Specifications for a Well-Designed Contract

- Goods and/or services to be delivered
- Calendar of activities
- Effective and termination dates
- Rights and responsibilities of the parties
- Reporting requirements and performance indicators
- Price of goods and/or services and links between deliverables and payments
- Payment and surety mechanisms
- Dispute resolution mechanisms
- Appropriate representatives of the parties

Community Organization: Area-Based, Interest Group-Based, or Some Combination Thereof?

Nature of the Collective Actors in a Settlement

The collective actors in a settlement can be subdivided into those that have a broad development agenda for the area (ABCOs) and those that focus on a special issue or interest (SPCOs).[7] The design of a participatory strategy needs to consider the diverse characteristics of such actors in relation to the objectives of the project.

ABCOs:

- Are generally larger organizations than SPCOs, with a wider membership base
- Are formed with a view to the development of the neighborhood, with a wide range of purposes, and concern themselves with problems that have a large constituency within the community
- Have a longer term, and more broadly developmental, perspective
- Have greater access to the authorities and greater political representativeness and legitimacy.

SPCOs:

- Generally are smaller and more agile than ABCOs
- Are formed to act on a specific problem
- Are normally more compact and have fewer internal conflicts, because their sphere of action and interest is more limited.

ABCOs, when they do exist, are important partners, since they are often legitimized by their previous history and are usually the main vehicle for wider community demands. At the same time, social cohesion tends to weaken when a community is large or dispersed, and the monitoring of individual behavior becomes more difficult. For this reason, it is preferable to formalize rules to delegate decisionmaking or to create smaller working groups.

SPCOs are effective partners for many specific matters within a project and are often easier to work with from an operational standpoint. The most interesting results are obtained when a project has the capacity to involve both types of organizations at different levels.

---

[7]Collective actors often are informal groups, which sometimes carry much more weight than formal groups, such as neighborhood organizations and associations of various kinds. Not all of these actors have a positive impact. Groups of petty criminals or drug traffickers are also collective actors that have to be reckoned with, as in the case of Guarapiranga.

The examples we have seen work in different ways (see table 3-7). In the Bolivian case, all the mechanisms of the People's Participation Law entrust community representation to area-based organizations. This was done to encourage the emergence of area-based players, which had a limited tradition in the country's previous highly centralized system. One of the drawbacks of the new system has been that the contributions of the country's strong SPCOs, many of which could play an important role, are thereby foregone entirely. Reflecting on possible changes or improvements to the legal framework for participation, Carlos Hugo Molina, one of the law's main architects, says that "There ought to be room in the surveillance committees for special purpose organizations, whose members are usually more politically aware and would be more difficult to corrupt. Plus, the middle classes have remained outside the law's framework, and they could become involved if we had people from professional associations, for example, in the committees."

In Guarapiranga, a working partnership was established with the area-based organizations (neighborhood associations), while smaller working groups were formed in parallel, founded on homogeneous needs or interests. They included families in temporary housing, representatives of each lane, mothers' groups, parents' school support groups, and groups for environmental education (a pilot project in this latter field was implemented in some areas of Guarapiranga).

In Tijuana, the process began with general interest neighborhood development committees; later, smaller community upgrading committees were created, each based on a specific project. The neighborhood development committees were in reality superseded by the upgrading committees, which served only a limited purpose. As a result, the long-term vision of development and wider range of activities that usually characterize neighborhood associations are missing from the *colonias populares*

Table 3-7. Types of Community-Based Organizations in the Cases Studied

Case	Type of community-based organization
Bolivia	ABCO only
Brazil	ABCO and SPCO
Costa Rica	SPCO only
Mexico	SPCO only
Peru	ABCO (initially very important but declining in importance over the years) and SPCO (increasing in importance over the years)

Source: Authors' construction from field study data.

(the low-income settlements of Tijuana). In this context, Tijuana social workers note that the program has worked well with the upgrading committees, but that, since it didn't succeed in involving and strengthening the neighborhood committees, "it lost social energy."

In San José, FUPROVI works with housing associations, 80 percent of which are already constituted before they contact the foundation. These associations are in fact special interest groups, since families associate themselves with a clear goal in mind, that of getting a house. Such housing associations often have no real local basis, since they may gather groups from different places.

In Villa El Salvador, the participatory ethos that led to a strong area-based development organization—CUAVES—in the early years, later fueled development of many strong special interest organizations, such as Vaso de Leche (Glass of Milk), which seem to have used up most of the available participatory energy, vast as it is. Through CUAVES, the settlers of Villa El Salvador had given themselves their own local government, as it were. With the establishment of the District of VES, the municipality became the main political player, and CUAVES lost most of its weight. Area-based organization has survived, but at a level of mobilization that is not sufficient to ensure that it can fulfill its basic role of organizing demand at the grassroots level and negotiate with other public and private actors.

The Dynamics of Leadership

In order to choose between several options in the design of a participation strategy, it is necessary, before anything else, to know the communities and their forms of organization. As discussed below ("Participatory Information Gathering and Analysis"), some projects have developed innovative methods for this task, based on the simultaneous use of quantitative and qualitative data, obtained with a mixture of techniques from traditional structured interviews to nonformal techniques of rapid valuation.

When outlining a community's organizational profile, one of the essential points is to evaluate the quality and representativeness of its leaders. In fact, analysis of the communication flows and decisionmaking processes of our field reports clearly shows that almost everything passes through the mediation of community leaders. The behavior and motivating factors of the leaders condition, at least in part, the collective behavior.

Certain leaders are political influence peddlers. In the north of Mexico, the very word "leader" has that connotation. In programs that encompass large urban areas, as in Guarapiranga, we face diversified situations. Some leaders, in the populist tradition, induce the community to wait for the government's favors. Others, more outspoken and politically active, sometimes exert almost dictatorial control and get people accustomed to depending completely on their personal initiative. Yet others take advantage of their position to cater to the interests of strong pressure groups (for example, those involved in drug trafficking). Finally, there are those who are able to distribute responsibilities, train others, and create incentives for local people to play active roles in the development process.

In attempting to enter into a productive relationship with the community, a project cannot either choose new leaders or fail to reckon with existing leaders. Thus, systematic procedures are needed to identify leadership and verify their representativeness, modus operandi, and legitimacy—in short, to know what to expect and how to deal with the different types of leaders.

Such procedures will help avoid an all-too-common mistake, that of automatically and exclusively working with the people who are identified by an external actor, such as local government, as the community leaders. It very often happens that such "leaders" are simply the most vocal, or the ones who make themselves most visible to outsiders, but who are not really legitimate and representative. There often are rival leaderships with a considerable following, as well as a significant number of people who do not recognize any leaders at all. A project that associates itself exclusively with the leader who is most visible from the outside may risk attracting hostility and creating conflicts even before it starts. Few things can be as damaging to a project as working exclusively through a discredited leader or ignoring or slighting a leader with a large following who may then react in a hostile manner.

Interesting examples of trying to address these issues are found in several Brazilian cases. The Guarapiranga and Cingapura projects in São Paulo, the Alvorada project in Belo Horizonte, and the Novos Alagados project in Bahia included structured questions about the leaders in the very first stage of information gathering, which aimed to find out:

- Which persons among the local residents are known, respected, and recognized as leaders by their fellow citizens and what are their respective areas of influence
- The institutions or groups to which the leaders are connected
- The degree of correspondence that exists between the demands voiced by the leaders and the needs and aspirations of the community.

The main features of quantitative socioeconomic surveys and instruments for defining the organization and leadership profiles, which have been developed in Brazil, are outlined in chapter 4. The output of such organization and leadership profiles is a short history of community organization in the settlement, with a description and evaluation of the local organizations and of the local leaders, in terms of legitimacy and following, strengths and weaknesses, and capabilities and interests. Some leaders are influential in a specific sector of activity only, while others have a broader role.

The territorial distribution and nature of leadership may be represented in thematic maps of the settlement. This will orient the participation strategy by identifying the main local brokers for participation who need to be encouraged to buy into the project, whose opinions need to be heard, and whose roles need to be clearly defined. Sections of the community that do not take part in any organization and that recognize no one as their leader will be identified in the thematic maps. These people will need to be brought into the project through direct participation mechanisms such as open meetings, or through participation in new bodies to be created for the purposes of the project.

Defining the correct mix of participation mechanisms is directly dependent on a careful reading of the organization and leadership profile. The roles and responsibilities to be ascribed to the various leaders and organizations, the new area-based and special interest groups to be created, and the frequency of open meetings all vary according to the specific nature of organization and leadership in a given community; they also vary over time.

In this context, one of the primary functions of intermediary organizations is to monitor the implementation of the participatory strategy and adapt it to the changing nature of the project and its relationship with the community. The stage at which leadership problems are most intense is the implementation phase of the project. This is because the more the community has taken an active part in planning decisions, the more it will feel the need to reformulate its organizational structure to take an active part in the implementation process.

Participatory information gathering and planning present many opportunities for the emergence of latent leadership. New representation mechanisms arise, and delicate situations and conflicts can come up because new leaders often emerge. Throughout this process, it is necessary to clarify the decisionmaking mechanisms as well as the functions and responsibilities of the various actors.

Old leaders are not always willing to join forces with new ones, nor are the technicians of public bodies necessarily very enthusiastic about having to go beyond their comfortable relationship with established leaders and form new relationships with more residents and with different points of view. Also, many factors external to the project influence community dynamics and the relationships between the various executing bodies that are often present in the field. Among these factors is the problem of manipulation by political parties, and the problems derived from the fragility of the social structure (for example, the groups involved in organized crime which wield considerable power and are often contrary to the integration of the informal settlement into the formal city). This is, therefore, a process of accommodation, rearrangement, and negotiation, the dynamics and results of which change depending on the situation and forces involved.

Helping this process along and moving the parties toward an understanding is one of the primary functions of social intermediary organizations. Experience shows that the dialogue between groups in the community and between the community and public bodies and other stakeholders does not flow in an entirely spontaneous way. It normally requires the presence of facilitators and intermediaries that can competently execute a socio-technical support strategy. Such articulation and mediation efforts are needed to get the community and the institutions involved fully engaged in a participatory strategy, transforming conflicts and mistakes into opportunities for growth and change.

This process of accommodation, rearrangement, and negotiation through articulation and mediation requires a lot of listening and the active creation of opportunities for listening—and influencing—through separate meetings with conflicting parties. These should be followed by joint meetings with the mediator in which differences are ironed out. Usually, opportunities are given to old and new leaders to help organize different parts of the upgrading process, and the mediation efforts succeed in improving the situation and allowing the project to move forward.

Obviously, projects that involve a smaller group and/or a more limited goal require a less elaborate organization and leadership profile and participatory strategy. The Bolivian cases, San José, and Tijuana exemplify this; while Guarapiranga and Villa El Salvador are examples of cases where a wide range of actors and a large number of initiatives over a longer time frame make it essential to know the organization and leadership patterns in detail.

The Issue of Gender

Beyond "Gender Focus"

Our field research and experience have shown that women play by far the most important role in infrastructure and shelter projects. This is a fact that merits recognition, and that should have a far greater impact on project design than it does at present. Among the cases we studied, only the Costa Rica one had an explicit gender strategy. This is a sobering realization, especially since we selected programs and projects for our study that are considered to have an above-average success rating.

Shelter and infrastructure projects have a direct impact on the quality of life of the whole population, but they have a particular impact on the lives of women. These projects reduce the female workload, as well as the material penury and health risks to which women are subjected to a greater extent than men. Also, an improvement in infrastructure and shelter usually reduces the incidence of psychological and social problems tied to poverty that hit women particularly hard: marital separations, domestic violence, school abandonment. For all these reasons, women's level of interest in urban upgrading and housing projects is very high, as shown by their key role and high degree of participation.

However, to insist on a "gender focus" approach that sees women exclusively as the main victims of urban poverty and discrimination overlooks the enormous contribution that they make to the urban economy and the life of the informal city. In fact, they take charge, to a much greater extent than men, of essential functions such as the provision of food and water; the care of the home; and the care of children, the sick, and the old. Moreover, women are the head of household, solely responsible for maintaining the family nucleus, in a proportion that approaches and even surpasses 30 percent of households in many cases.

The female population is, in fact, the main human resource in the development of low-income settlements (see box 3-3) and plays the main role in all aspects of a project: community mobilization, project management, monitoring and evaluation, and financial contributions. Women's contribution in terms of time and even labor is greater than that of men, as documented by numerous examples in the cases we have studied. However, in none of these has any specific attention been given or specific channels created in project design to harness the potential of women's participation. In reality, participation happened naturally and the challenge for the project promoters was to accommodate and harness the participation during project implementation.

Making Projects More Responsive to Women's Needs

The examples we have studied show that there is need for more than the rhetoric of "gender focus" (which in any case very rarely surpasses the level of declarations of principle), because women are not just a special interest group to deal with typically "feminine" topics. The examples point to the need to change the approach to the problem, recognizing in women the key interlocutor that projects have among the beneficiaries, and drawing appropriate methodological and operational conclusions from this fact.

> **Box 3-3. Positive Discrimination of Women in the San José Low-Income Housing Program**
>
> In San José, construction technology had to be partially modified because most of the available labor for mutual-help construction was female, and the prefab panels initially envisaged were too heavy for the women to lift. But the same filter that was designed to target the projects to the poor by demanding that each household put in 30 weekly hours of labor had the disadvantage of making it more difficult for women-headed households to participate. FUPROVI has taken specific measures to address this problem. The institution helps women-headed households receive a three- to six-month subsidy from the National Social Welfare Institute. Until recently, they also received food packages from the World Food Program. Housing associations frequently offer special terms and conditions to female-headed households, giving them less strenuous tasks, e.g., in daycare centers and soup kitchens rather than in construction. Finally, working women normally try to put in as many as possible of their 30 hours over weekends. Although the burden on women-headed households is still particularly heavy, these "positive discrimination" measures have good outcomes. Between 25 and 40 percent of the participants in FUPROVI projects are women-headed households, a figure consistent with FUPROVI's target group.

Projects must be specifically designed to meet women's needs. There are three key dimensions that projects need to address in order to achieve this goal:

- One of the problems that came up in our field interviews is of a cultural and family nature: the difficulties faced by women in overcoming the obstacles put up by men to their participation. The toughest challenges that many women leaders have to face is within the home. As we heard from one of the female organizers in San José, "There are things that they [FUPROVI] could help us more with; they lend us the money and provide the technical assistance, but they don't get involved in the fights." Certainly, the *macho* culture is an inheritance difficult to overcome in Latin America, but socio-technical support strategies can address the issue as a theme within communities, as is done with many other issues that require a change of mentality and collective behavior.
- Generally, women are left on their own to face the problem of reconciling the extra activity brought about by the project with their jobs, their role as mothers, and their responsibilities in the home. In the case of mothers who are heads of households, juggling all these

roles can be very difficult; the risk is the exclusion of families headed by women from participation in the projects, which would have happened in the San José case were it not for the specific mechanisms put in place. Ways need to be found around this problem, since this is one of the key mechanisms in the vicious cycle of poverty. The availability of support services (cooking, nursery, laundry, etc.) is a crucial contribution to women's participation that can be set up by a project, as is clearly shown by the example of FUPROVI.

- Finally, in defining all project features, the specific needs of women must be considered. From meeting times and technologies to the distribution of project tasks and workloads, the planning of a project must specifically address women and their special needs. Women will usually be the ones carrying the greater proportion of the load, accepting most of the responsibility, and doing most of the work; this must be acknowledged and planned for.

Looking out for Vulnerable Groups

The internal differences of each community have important consequences in the identification of the project and its design, planning, and implementation. The complexity of the phenomenon of poverty, which does not have the same impact on all people, needs to be taken into account.

In general, as we saw in relation to gender, projects give little specific attention to the most vulnerable groups, and they distribute benefits and obligations with little differentiation. The absence of any differentiation in the subsidy policy, for example, is a striking feature of all the cases covered by our field reports.

In the cases studied, projects and programs seem to be based on the assumption that the groups involved are homogeneous, which in reality is far from the truth. In Guarapiranga, for example, the same benefits of upgrading accrue equally to all residents, and no attempt is made to recover at least part of the cost of the intervention from the better-off among them. It is obvious, from a cursory look at any of Guarapiranga's favelas, that there are great differences in income and living standards among the residents. Although almost all of them are indeed poor, a great many households are not in extreme poverty and could contribute to cost recovery through betterment levies or the property tax. On the other hand, in the projects we have studied, when the community does make a financial contribution, it is expected from all participating households to the same degree, regardless of their capacity to pay.

Urban upgrading interventions thus reproduce the Latin American tradition of disregarding the needs of the poorest by aiming development interventions at the not-so-poor. Frequently, it is the unemployed, the women who are heads of households, and those subject to the worst social conditions who end up having to give up more in relation to their socioeconomic status. In upgrading projects, it is often mentioned that the poorest families are those that abandon the improved areas with greater frequency, cashing in on their houses and being replaced by people with higher incomes.

In programs like FUPROVI's Habitat Popular Urbano, there is obviously no intention to exclude the poorest. These programs often do so unwittingly, through perverse mechanisms that are set in motion by aspects of their formulation. In San José, the demand for 30 hours a week of community labor is made in an attempt to target the program to the poorest groups. The reasoning behind it is that if someone is willing to contribute 30 hours of hard work each week toward the construction of the house, then he or she must be truly committed to the project. The majority of people would not be prepared to undertake this commitment if they had sufficient sources of income to be able to afford a house by any other means.

Families who sign up for the project often have a tough time making ends meet during construction, and the man usually has to continue to work to earn the family's keep while the woman takes part in the construction. This is necessary if they are to achieve their dream of becoming homeowners as well as make ends meet in the short term.

For vulnerable groups, things are considerably more difficult. If FUPROVI and the housing associations themselves had not taken specific measures to aid women-headed households, the elderly, and people with handicaps, these groups would have been excluded from the program. In most mass low-income housing of the 1960s and 1970s in Latin America, the exclusion of the poorest—although unwitting—occurred through a less sophisticated mechanism. The units built according to middle-class technicians' ideas of what a house for the poor should be like were simply too expensive for the real poor, and were thus bought by the not-so-poor, who also needed houses and usually have better political connections than the very poor.

Careful program monitoring allows identification of such perverse mechanisms and enables program promoters to take corrective measures, seeking to identify and protect vulnerable groups. Poverty indicators are important in this regard. Some of the information gathered by the socioeconomic quantitative survey discussed in chapter 4 can offer pointers. For example, structures built with nondurable building materials, especially if the time of occupation is long, tend to house the poorest families. Structures built in high-risk areas, such as along the banks of streams or in areas with difficult access, also usually house the poorest families.

Identifying the poorest is important in defining an equitable subsidy structure for a project. All the cases we studied tend to consider "the poor" as a homogeneous group—which is far from true—and to distribute subsidies with no differentiation. Targeting subsidies is a great challenge, and most traditional methods are seriously flawed. The Costa Rican policy of adjusting the housing subsidy to income brackets, for instance, has similarities to many others around the world and presents the same problems. It is usually not easy to ascertain a poor family's income, since so many of the poor work in the informal sector, their income fluctuates, and there are no reliable records. A household's actual standard of living, in terms of the location, size, building materials, access to services, and whether the family owns, shares rooms, or rents, is a far more reliable indicator of household income and ability to pay. A rapid assessment of levels of poverty in a settlement is not a particularly complex task (see chapter 4 for more information about undertaking quantitative surveys); and, unless it is carried out, projects will continue targeting poor *areas*, and not poor *people*.

A significant example of a project that changed its approach and began to look out for a vulnerable group is the Cingapura project in São Paulo. Initially, people with handicaps had wanted to stay on in the informal settlement and not move to the new apartments built by the project. The situation changed when specific resources were provided, including priority for housing on the lower floors of the buildings, construction of ramps, special fittings in apartments, etc.

Another important dimension in paying heed to the needs of the most vulnerable is communication, since information does not arrive in the same way to every group in a community. In this aspect also, the poorest are the most difficult to reach. In most field situations, it is evident that there is a large gap between the level of information of the leaders and community organizers and that of the other residents; in the case of the poorest, that gap is even larger. A careful information strategy, with particular attention to the communication instruments to be used, could reduce the problem. In the case of the poorest, numerous examples show that the most effective communication vehicle is that based on interpersonal relationships (via home visits and participation in cultural events, local festivals, and open meetings). It is also the most time-consuming and personnel intensive—but without it, the risk of not reaching the poorest is great.

Mobilizing Local Knowledge and Resources

Local Insights and Problem Solving

People who live in a community know its needs and ways better than anyone, since they internalize its culture. Many local people also have enormous common sense and, consequently, are often capable of finding creative solutions to problems that are apparently technically insoluble. In a community of the Florido-Mariano district, Tijuana, one of the key problems in securing the community contribution for an upgrading project was finding the owners of the vacant lots. They were supposed to pay their share like the rest of the area's plot owners, but, contrary to the lot owners who live in the area, were extremely difficult to find. The municipality's technicians went to the cadastral and property registers, which were outdated and often either gave the contact details of a previous owner or an old address of the current owner. Everyone was at a loss as to how to proceed but anxious to find a solution, since the contribution of vacant lot owners would make a significant difference to project finances.

The obra social committee had a simple and excellent idea. They put up "For Sale" signs on all the vacant lots. The contact phone on the signs was actually that of one of the committee members. The owners immediately began to appear—sometimes, even, more than one owner for the same lot.

In Novos Alagados, a favela of pile-dwellings in the Enseada do Cabrito in Salvador de Bahia, Brazil, a cooperative had been formed for mutual-help construction of new housing. In defining the rules for loan repayment for residents' purchase of construction materials, discussion had become bogged down in a prolonged consideration of the indices that should be applied to compensate for inflation. On one side, the technicians were divided, because several different types of indicators were in use in the country, each with its own pros and cons. On the other side, the residents' distrust was increasing, as they were afraid of some entanglement or speculation behind the matter of indices. After several meetings, an old woman stood up at the end of the room and said that, in her opinion, since the money was used for the purchase of materials, it would suffice to calculate the amount of money that could buy the same number of cement bags. Everyone immediately agreed.

Projects need to create communication channels to ensure that mechanisms are in place for receiving such feedback both initially and over time.

Transforming Technician Attitudes and Methods

When socio-technical support providers need to compete for contracts and operate in a professional manner, there is a strong incentive for technicians to abandon a top-down, paternalistic attitude in favor of an attitude of respect for their ultimate client and for this client's potential to contribute to the process. Other service providers, such as construction contractors, are also subject to this change. This is especially true when the decision to award socio-technical support or construction contracts is made by community groups, as in the case of São Paulo's mutirão projects (in the case of socio-technical support), or Tijuana (in the case of construction contracts). However, even if the contracts are awarded by a municipality or other institution, the accountability that is part of a professional relationship with local people leads to a change of attitude—which in turn often leads to the development of a new and more appropriate set of methods that incorporate local knowledge as a key input.

The population has knowledge, insights, and problem-solving skills that are nonsystematically acquired, heterogeneous, and very down-to-earth, since they are based on daily experience. The knowledge of the technician is the result of a systematic approach of long years of study and is based on content, interests, and work experience that are defined and delimited by academia and the work environment of public or private institutions. Knowledge and attitudes are, in each case, based on a wholly different sort of logic.

Opening up to the knowledge and insights of the community can produce a new and very useful synthesis between technical knowledge and local knowledge. Through their role as intermediaries, social workers and other technicians providing socio-technical support are often the agents of this synthesis and cooperate in bringing about change in the approaches and methods of other technicians working on the project.

Very significant, as we have seen, was the change in the mentality of the professionals of the construction companies involved in the large-scale infrastructure works in the informal settlements of Guarapiranga. They state that this experience has transformed their view of the city. Their unprecedented interaction with the reality of the informal city has made them revise project management and technical approaches, and to develop new solutions. It has also helped them question deeply ingrained social prejudices and develop a genuine professional interest in this new field.

To a great extent, it was day-to-day contact with the community that produced the transformations that have occurred in technician perception and methods. A Guarapiranga architect says, for example, that her initial perception in designing the project was "romantic." But she then had to take into account "the down-to-earth perceptions of the inhabitants, who don't have a macro vision, because of the material limitations in their daily lives"; this helped her to be realistic in the solutions she proposed.

It is interesting to look briefly at the incentive structure that allowed this to happen. As we have seen, practically all the work of the Guarapiranga upgrading component was done by private companies, under the coordination of a small and highly qualified unit in the municipality. Technicians working for private companies in the field in such tasks as project management, construction, and socio-technical support need to achieve a high level of productivity and to find creative solutions to everyday problems. They want to advance in their company, and they are under constant pressure from their management to produce results. And it is not just a matter of getting the job done in a quick-and-dirty way either, since these companies face tough competition, and the works at Guarapiranga have so many social implications that they are under constant scrutiny by the press and opposition parties.

Identifying and Developing Community Capacity

A fundamental consideration that begins to penetrate (although with difficulty) the culture of development projects is a concept expressed in the 1996 Recife Declaration (Habitat II Conference 1996): "Each one of us wants to be considered by what he is and what he can do, and not for what he lacks."

Trying to see the resources as well as the problems allows one to perceive the endogenous factors of development—the resources and strategies that people use to cope with difficult circumstances and improve their quality of life. Important aspects of these strategies, however, escape traditional methods of analysis because they are contributions that cannot be easily quantified.

The business of every development project is, to a great extent, to identify, strengthen, and mobilize a community's assets and resources. Moser (1996) defines five constituent elements of the "asset base of the poor":

- The ability to work
- Human capital
- Shelter (used with great imagination as a productive resource)
- Family relationships
- Social capital.

These elements are described as the assets that individuals, households, or communities can mobilize to face deprivation. Moser notes that "The possibilities of households to reduce their vulnerability and increase their economic productivity depend not only on the above assets, but on their capacity to transform those assets into income, food, and other basic necessities."

Ignoring these aspects, it would not be possible to explain the survival of families with an average income of approximately $200 per month in urban areas with rather high costs of living, as in the cases studied in our field reports. And it would be even more difficult to understand the mechanisms that make it possible for the resources invested in improving infrastructure to be more than matched by private investments in shelter improvements in informal areas, a phenomenon that is particularly evident in Guarapiranga, Tijuana, and Villa El Salvador.

Mobilizing the community's knowledge and resources is a key to success. This is partly due to psychological and cognitive factors. The power of some projects lies in knowing how to create in the local people the belief that, through the project, the sacrifices the community has gone through to obtain a piece of land, a house, and access to services will finally bear fruit. External intervention is perceived as something that gives the community a decisive hand in its daily struggle in hostile circumstances to improve living conditions. This identification of values and goals gives impulse to participation, reinforcing the identity of the local residents and their self-confidence.

Identifying the endogenous factors of development and devoting attention to their strengthening in program formulation is possible only if a careful process of participatory information gathering and analysis is carried out, and a participatory area development plan is prepared with adequate socio-technical support. One of the missed opportunities of the Tijuana case, for example, is that there was no real process of information gathering, which could have given the municipality invaluable input for the formulation of its social programs. Much more time, attention, and resources than are commonly employed need to be invested in knowing more about one's partner communities. In this way, we will be able to target subsidies to real needs and to benefit from and strengthen existing resources.

Information and Communication: Social Marketing Strategies

Two questions arise with regard to social marketing strategies:
- How does the population learn about the project?
- By what mechanisms of information and communication does the participatory process first get under way?

Given the importance of infrastructure and shelter problems in informal urban areas, projects really do not need to invest a great deal in sophisticated promotion strategies for news of their existence to reach the communities. In fact, person-to-person contact and word of mouth tend to work better in local communities than other, more sophisticated instruments of dissemination. Sometimes the problem is just the opposite. There is a need to control the many rumors that circulate about the project among local people. Socio-technical support providers play an important role in this objective, achieving much through personal contacts.

During project implementation, there is a particular need for social marketing strategies to ensure that critical information about the project reaches all local people. For this, it is important to differentiate among the various beneficiaries (e.g., disadvantaged or vulnerable groups, or special interest groups). Especially in the case of the most disadvantaged, it is necessary to work consciously to counteract the tendency many projects have of unwittingly leaving them out of the information loop—a situation that often excludes them from participating and reaping a fair share of project benefits.

An important aspect that needs to be stressed is that communication, which is such a large part of social marketing, works both ways. When communication channels are established, they are not just a means of conveying information *to* the community, but also a means of gathering comments, suggestions, and information *from* the community, to identify potential conflicts brewing within the community and allow the early activation of conflict resolution mechanisms. Usually, it is the socio-technical support team that is in charge of social marketing and communication in a program or project, and interpersonal contact is a key part of two-way communication channels, which makes it easier to act quickly on information received from the community.

Social marketing has another important dimension: garnering the interest and support of society at large to urban upgrading initiatives. We have seen the key role political will has played in the cases studied for the adoption of upgrading policies. Political will, although it certainly has to do with organized pressure from poor communities, also depends greatly on public opinion in general and on the views and leanings of the middle classes. It is therefore crucial to create a favorable climate of opinion by making clear to society as a whole the advantages and importance of urban upgrading for the attainment of poverty reduction, public health, and environmental improvement goals that benefit the entire city, rather than just a program's target beneficiaries.

The development of a favorable climate of opinion with regard to upgrading may also serve another important function. By depicting the informal city and its future possibilities in a more favorable light, the private business sector may be influenced to recognize the market potential of these areas and begin to target its investments to them. This result is already visible in many areas, such as Tijuana's Florido-Mariano district, but it needs to be strengthened considerably for true integration of the informal city.

Social Marketing in the Case Studies

Table 3-8 summarizes the wide range of social marketing strategies that were adopted in the different urban upgrading programs and projects described in the case studies.

Table 3-8. Social Marketing Strategies in the Cases Studied

Strategy	Bolivia	Brazil	Costa Rica	Mexico	Peru
Word of mouth	✓	✓	✓	✓	✓
Community radio	✓				✓
Community TV				✓	✓
Radio ads		✓		✓	
Leaflets	✓	✓		✓	
Booklets			✓		
Short courses		✓	✓		
Meetings w/ ABCOs and SPCOs		✓		✓	✓
Meetings w/ housing association managing committees			✓		
Meetings organized by municipality					✓
Community assemblies	✓			✓	
Placards and billboards		✓			
Press ads		✓			
On-call socio-technical support		✓	✓		
Distribution of text of the People's Participation Law	✓				
Special events (barbecues, etc.)	✓				
Raffles and sweepstakes for model taxpayers					✓
On-line communications					✓

Source: Authors' construction from field study data.

In Guarapiranga, social marketing, like information and communication, is handled by the socio-technical support provider. A great variety of communication and dissemination materials have been prepared for diverse themes and occasions (posters, folders, audiovisuals, murals, comic strips, jingles, and radio advertisements). These have been used in a variety of contexts, including meetings and social and theatrical events. These instruments were not utilized during the program formulation phase or during the selection of areas of intervention, which were driven principally by technical criteria. Rather, they were used to mobilize people for the implementation phase, through information campaigns on specific themes such as health and environmental education. They were also used to promote the project in neighboring areas and in the city at large.

In the case of Costa Rica, an organized group (a housing association) contacts FUPROVI on its own. FUPROVI does not advertise, since it has more business than it can handle. Housing associations learn about its services by word of mouth. These organizations visit the foundation's projects and receive information on the mutual-help construction process and its costs, financing mechanisms, and obligations. This is the beginning of a process of information exchange and negotiations that may take a great deal of time—four years in the case of the Lagos de Lindora project. Because the FUPROVI system demands great dedication and initiative on the part of the participants, an association usually looks at other options as well. While these other options may look simpler and more attractive, the community comes to realize that there are no other viable options catering to those at the income level of the FUPROVI clientele. The agreement with the foundation is preceded by a long and thorough consultation and information process. Even so, many of the participants claim that they accepted the proposal because they would have agreed to sign anything in order to obtain access to housing, even without having a clear notion of what mutual-help construction would entail.

Social marketing and information/communication in Tijuana depend principally on direct contact among the decentralized offices of the municipality and the community groups. Radio has been efficiently used to publicize community upgrading programs, but other forms of communication are not very developed, in part due to the fear of increasing the expectations of unserved communities and lengthening the list of literally a few thousand projects already awaiting realization.

Women and Leaders Should Receive Special Attention

Leaders carry out the important task of informing their constituencies and, at the same time, they filter information according to their own vision and agenda. They have an essential function in the flow of communication, which is part of the reason why they profoundly influence the reaction and behavior of other inhabitants. Many of these leaders are women; and even when the leader is a man, women play a central role in improving infrastructure and shelter. It therefore follows that a project's communication strategy should focus above all on how to garner the attention of both leaders and women.

Participatory Information Gathering and Analysis

One of the key aspects of organizing participation in urban upgrading is setting up a truly participatory process of information gathering and analysis. The benefits of a participatory approach in this process are manifold:

- The process leads to a vision of the problems that includes, in addition to technical aspects, the knowledge, views, and expectations of the community.

- It transforms the local residents involved into communicators and resource persons, strengthening the link between the population and the project.
- It creates trust and establishes a working relationship between sociotechnical support providers and local residents.
- It helps create a core group of community organizers with attitudes and skills that will be necessary throughout the project's life.
- It contributes to the building of an interdisciplinary vision that takes into account the community's diversity and contributes to the compatibility of the proposed solutions.

Urban development projects that aim for the improvement of shelter and infrastructure require—as a first step—the *description* of the settlements under consideration and a *diagnosis* of their problems.

The lack of organized information on practically any subject is a defining feature of the informal city. Information gathering is thus essential in planning an upgrading intervention. By gathering and analyzing information with the active participation of local residents, not only is the quality of the information improved, but also the community is involved in identifying the area's problems, assessing their causes, and defining priorities. This is essential for eliciting and organizing local demand—a precondition for developing adequate, demand-responsive solutions.

Information gathering and analysis is also the first process in a project in which the community participates in a big way. It is the point at which the relationship between the community, the project promoters, and the intermediary organization takes shape. In particular, active leaderships emerge, organizational capabilities and community resources are revealed, preliminary impressions on organization and leadership are tested, and the participatory strategy takes its final form.

Some interesting methodologies to accomplish this goal were developed in Guarapiranga and in other Brazilian cases. Based on these examples, it is possible to outline the principal elements and stages of participatory information gathering and analysis, as described in chapter 4.

Participatory Area Development Planning

Quality Information Is Key to Effective Participation

Despite the consensus on the need for community participation, many projects still cannot be considered participatory. And, for their part, communities cannot be expected to participate effectively in the key decisions involving urban upgrading if the resources and constraints involved, as well as the implications of the various alternative solutions, are not clear to community members. For a project to be truly participatory, management of the information needed for infrastructure development should take into account the need to allow the local community to understand the community infrastructure and shelter upgrading process and to influence it.

Lack of an Overall Vision Leads to Piecemeal Interventions

In many cases, community movements and an increased public and political awareness have prompted local authorities to undertake projects that have been confined to tackling a few urgent issues such as the drainage of particular trouble spots or the creation of an all-weather access route. This kind of "scattered showers" approach is attributable at least in part to the lack of an *overall vision* of problems and solutions. By focusing on specific situations and introducing new physical constraints (such as the location and width of a paved road or an open drain), such attempts have often created obstacles to the design of a wider ranging intervention, and thus to the adoption of an integrated planning approach. We will see more of the drawbacks of piecemeal upgrading in chapter 4.

An integrated planning approach to upgrading requires that opportunities for *synergy* among local government authorities and service agencies be actively sought and fully exploited. The planning of settlement layout changes, for instance, requires the input of sector line agencies, since the location of pipes and other technical requirements for infrastructure have to be taken into account. On the other hand, the exchange of cadastral information among different utilities and local government agencies would have positive implications for the establishment of a framework for operations and maintenance and even for cost recovery.[8]

Participatory Area Development Planning

A participatory area development plan is an instrument that provides a long-term overall vision of the development of an area and allows for the identification and use of such synergies. The process of preparation of such a plan is as important as the product, since it provides a forum for negotiation and comparison of different views involving local resi-

---

[8]The lack of accurate cadastral information is one of the reasons why collection of property taxes, user fees, and consumption tariffs is often erratic. Typically, electricity utilities have the best records, and municipalities and water utilities lag behind. An established mechanism of information exchange would help improve the latter's cadastral databases and facilitate the cost recovery process.

dents and other key project stakeholders. This is both a consensus-building and partnership-forming process.

The plan is developed by a committee of local residents with support from planners, engineers, and social workers. It is based on the participatory process of information gathering and analysis as described above and involves a survey of the situation of the settlement and its inhabitants, covering physical aspects, existence and state of repair of infrastructure, service availability, environmental aspects, land tenure status, and socioeconomic situation. The information is organized and analyzed by an interdisciplinary team and presented to the community in a series of meetings with area-based and special interest groups. Based on analysis of the information and discussion in the community meetings, a coherent pattern of problems and priorities emerges. It is then possible to begin to propose and discuss alternatives for intervention in an interactive process in which the community, through established representation mechanisms, eventually reaches decisions that reflect real demand. The technicians' support is there to ensure that the chosen alternatives are affordable and technically sound. The final product of the exercise is a logical long-term sequence of activities and an agreed blueprint for the improvement of the area.

Participatory area development planning was undertaken in various ways in the cases we studied. In San José, we found that, in striking contrast to the high level and degree of participation in the building process, participation in planning is weak. In the FUPROVI model, planning is seen as something the institution brings to the table, and FUPROVI's client groups seem to accept this as a given. In Guarapiranga, although reference to participatory and area-based planning was made in the terms of reference of the firms that carried out the planning and design work, the concept was not fully spelled out. As a result, although all the subsequent plans are area-based and integrate the various branches of infrastructure, not all can be termed fully participatory. Nonetheless, there is a clear trend toward a participatory area-based and integrated approach—this is a significant step forward in relation to previous practice in São Paulo.

In Tijuana's community upgrading Obra Social Comunitaria projects, priority setting is based on a simple list of desirable public works, not on a participatory planning process. The process of priority setting may be deemed participatory; but the planning element is missing. Community requests to *delegaciones* (decentralized municipal offices) or to the municipal department of social development, which are often made during well-publicized public gatherings, are lumped together in a laundry list. Following a preliminary feasibility check, the list is presented to a committee, with community representation, at the level of the delegación.

This latter establishes priorities, seeking, among other things, to spread the benefits of the project to the various parts of the delegación. The decisions of the delegación committees are submitted to a citywide committee for ratification.

In Tijuana, the lack of a planning element has meant that community requests have focused heavily on road paving; among infrastructure types, this is the most visible, easiest to identify, and one of the least expensive to address. In addition, road paving falls within the sphere of competence of the municipality, requiring minimal coordination and a moderate amount of supervision. Road paving is undoubtedly very much needed and in great public demand in the colonias populares of Tijuana, but so are many other things that could have been identified by a participatory planning process. In Ciudad Juárez, a very similar priority-setting process has taken place, and road paving has also dominated the local version of Obra Social Comunitaria.

These Mexican examples are very similar to the local planning process established in Bolivia by the People's Participation Law. In this process, as discussed in chapter 2, a series of logical steps are followed to set priorities in each of the city's low-income areas. As in Tijuana and Ciudad Juárez, however, a true planning element is missing since there is no participatory information gathering and analysis to inform the process, and decisions are made without proper study of the alternatives. In Santa Cruz and El Alto, Bolivia, the PAP project, funded by Dutch development aid, seeks to build the planning capacity of local communities and enhance their participation in the planning process established by Law 1551. The fact that PAP relations with the municipalities are tense in both cities, however, indicates the resistance large municipalities feel toward participation.

The Mexican and Bolivian examples are similar to the *orçamento participativo* (participatory local government budget) procedure used in Porto Alegre, Belo Horizonte, and other cities in Brazil. In Belo Horizonte, the drawbacks of defining priority works in the absence of a coherent plan led to the development of the concept of a sort of broad-stroke participatory area development plan, which is called Plano Global. Indeed, participatory area development planning may be undertaken at different levels of detail, according to local needs and conditions. In a case like Guarapiranga, where the plan will be used to execute an ambitious program of works in the short term, a very detailed development plan, coupled with detailed engineering plans, is vital. In a case like Belo Horizonte's, in which the participatory area development plan is meant to guide a long-term process, much less detail is needed upfront.

In Peru, participatory planning has been a key element of the development of Villa El Salvador from the very beginning. It has also been one of the reasons why VES has outpaced all similar settlements in Lima in terms of what it has achieved. The example of the VES industrial park shows what a development plan can do when it is known, shared, and fully backed by a community. In VES, the land for the industrial park was successfully withheld from residential development for 15 years pending the creation, after much debate and many false starts, of a public-private partnership. Protecting the land from invasion for all those years was no easy feat, particularly given the area's demand for residential land. In 1999, 28 years after the first VES plan, a third participatory VES plan was prepared after hundreds of meetings and was approved by a citywide referendum, with an impressive voter turnout. Participatory area development planning is alive and well in Villa El Salvador.

Creating Incentives for Landlords and Tenants

The landlord-tenant relationship can be a powerful deterrent to urban upgrading projects in many situations. We have observed this in some parts of Latin America, but especially in Africa, where renters usually are the majority—and sometimes the vast majority—of the population of low-income urban settlements. In many of these situations, many informal settlement residents are not stable urban dwellers and are only interested in paying as low a rent as possible during their brief foray into the urban cash economy. Their intention is not to stay in the city for long: rather, when they feel they have made enough money, or when harvest time comes, they rejoin their families to work in subsistence agriculture.

Such people feel no incentive to take part in initiatives to improve the quality of the settlements in which they live. Here we will use an African example: the case of the regularization and upgrading of the Ronda informal subdivision in Nakuru, Kenya, where a technical assistance project took place in 1994–96. Local landlords, many of whom live in the area, were interested in land tenure regularization, but not really in the improvement of infrastructure. They were also wealthier and had far more political clout than their tenants, and strongly opposed the participation of tenants in any initiative concerning the settlement. Therefore, "community" participation was restricted to landlords and to land tenure regularization—a situation that was fully accepted and even abetted by the municipality. We had found at the time that many in the city's professional class, including high-ranking municipal officials, owned shacks for rent in Ronda that were managed on their behalf by resident landlords. It therefore was no surprise that no one seemed to think that tenant participation was called for—not even the tenants themselves, who did their best to keep out of harm's way by not participating. In contrast to the enthusiastic participation of the landlords, many of whom lived in the area, it was virtually impossible to enlist the participation of tenants in information gathering. Again in contrast to the landlords, their interest would have been service improvement (as long as rents stayed low); since the landlords' only interest was tenure regularization, tenants had all the more reason to stay away.

Although such a situation is certainly to be regretted and constitutes a major obstacle to development, it is easy to understand how it arises. When informal developers are providing low-cost and low-quality mass housing to migrant workers in collective structures—as they were in Ronda—landlords and tenants have different, and frequently opposite, interests. In the Latin American cases we studied, a large majority of settlement residents own the plots and structures where they live, a fact that undoubtedly makes a great deal of difference in terms of the incentive structure. And even where people are building extra units for rent within their plots, tenants are a minority, and most of them are in the city to stay, which is not the case in Kenya.

In situations like the ones we have studied, the incentives for participation are clear, and the project's business is to create an appropriate enabling environment. In Belo Horizonte, for example, tenants were so scarce at the time of the promulgation of the PROFAVELA law that the law's controversial provision of ignoring landlord-tenant relations and legalizing tenure for any occupant of a favela shack, whether owner or tenant, went virtually unchallenged.

When tenants are a majority, however, things are considerably more complex. Any attempt at addressing this problem needs to give careful consideration to the often conflicting interests of landlords and tenants, and create an appropriate incentive structure for both. In a case such as Ronda's, for example, tenure regularization, which appeals to landlords, might be pursued independently of service improvement. The latter could be pursued through demand-side subsidies and technical support and start-up finance for small-scale entrepreneurs who, through water vending, latrine emptying, etc., could provide a minimum of the required services. In Ronda, water supplies are built and operated by local landlords, who tap existing mains in the formal city and bring water to their compounds through rickety piped systems. Their incentive is to provide a minimum level of service to their tenants and to charge for the water. Nakuru's chronic water supply problems, however, coupled with the precarious nature of the systems installed, make it difficult to reach an acceptable level of service.

What would be an acceptable level of service at an acceptable cost to households? Although it certainly is not the intermittent and unreliable service at high unit cost that is provided to Ronda residents, it is difficult to determine exactly what would be a good alternative. Careful analysis of the spending and consumption patterns of local households would need to be undertaken to determine affordable service standards and willingness and ability to pay consumption tariffs; this in turn would help determine the needed levels of subsidy.

Privatized Utilities and the Urban Poor

Even in cases where owners occupy most of the structures and urban services are provided by large utility companies, service standards and levels of subsidy must be examined and a new relationship built with the urban poor. Electricity is usually the first service to be provided in a low-income settlement, due to its comparatively low cost and ease of installation. Electricity companies are also proving to be leaders in developing this new relationship with the poor.

As we see in the case of Villa El Salvador, many marketing studies ignore the areas in which the urban poor live, dismissing them as homogeneous lower class settlements with no purchasing power or specific requirements. In most Latin American cities, informal settlements house between 30 and 50 percent of the population and represent a market that cannot be ignored by utilities. On the one hand, universal access to services is a political imperative and a cornerstone of most concession agreements; on the other hand, the present situation, characterized by illegal connections and lack of cost recovery, undermines the viability of private sector service provision and the profitability of privatized utilities. The first step in overcoming this situation is trying to learn more about the needs, preferences, consumption patterns, and purchasing power of the urban poor. This information will allow utilities to:

- Base extension of coverage and service upgrading on an accurate perception of demand
- Identify needs for subsidies and negotiate their management with the state
- Devise a marketing strategy that takes the reality of the poor as a consumer group into account
- Extend service coverage in a financially sustainable way, by matching investment and cost recovery strategies.

Utilities need to couple this information-gathering exercise with an effective outreach strategy. Most utilities have weak consumer relations strategies across the board, and many have launched efforts to improve the situation. Such efforts have seldom targeted the poor, however, and utilities generally do not have a track record of success in sustainable extension of coverage to the urban poor. In this context, some of the recently privatized electricity utility companies in Brazil, such as Rio's Light and Bahia's Light and Power Company (COELBA), have come to realize that there is a gap that needs to be bridged in establishing new relations with the urban poor and that they are ill-equipped to bridge this gap on their own. This gap consists of a lack of knowledge about the poor and their settlements as well as of:

- Social and cultural differences
- Lack of a culture of consumer rights and responsibilities
- A heritage of paternalistic relations with the state that perpetuates a low-level equilibrium between low-quality services and lack of cost recovery.

Bridging this gap takes an array of social intermediation techniques and specialized personnel.

Accordingly, utilities are forming partnerships with social intermediaries to provide socio-technical support. These partnerships might be the embryo of specialized units within the utility that deal with this large market segment. Privatized water utilities in Argentina and Bolivia are also developing specific strategies in this regard.

There appears to be a significant need, and a significant scope, for the training of consulting firms and NGOs to fill the role of intermediaries in those parts of Latin America where utility privatization is advancing, but specific marketing and client relations strategies targeting the poor have yet to be developed.

4

Focusing on Process: Program Design and Rollout Strategies

To establish the participatory process—particularly in the face of any resistance by entrenched interests—requires a well-thought-out plan. For instance, in Bolivia, participation was tied to resource flows to the municipalities, thus taking the various conflicting interests into account and creating incentives for stakeholders to participate in a process that is the result of a of conscious *design*. Although the specifics of this plan will vary with location and circumstance, the common denominator for success is that sufficient thought and attention are given to *process*. This chapter analyzes key issues of process in settlement upgrading initiatives with regard to program planning and design. It also deals, at its conclusion, with the program rollout stage; here we discuss some of the project-level process issues identified and outlined in chapter 3 from an operational standpoint. (See box 4-1.)

The presentation is based on lessons learned from the formulation and implementation of participatory urban upgrading and shelter programs. It draws on the experiences of the five case studies as well as those of the study's authors, consultants, and peer reviewers. Because program circumstances vary greatly, we do not—indeed, we cannot—offer a recipe to be followed. Rather, we call attention to important and recurring process issues, following the chronological sequence of the major stages of program design and rollout.

The objectives of this chapter are to:

- Facilitate an optimal use of resources in program design and implementation
- Ensure that the key issues related to a project's social and financial sustainability are appropriately addressed during program formulation

> **Box 4-1. How to Use the Information in This Chapter**
>
> **Who Should Take the Actions Outlined Here?** Program design efforts are usually initiated and led by the organizations sponsoring the program (e.g., a municipality in partnership with an international development bank or central government agency). Due to the multidisciplinary nature of urban upgrading, it is a good idea to set up a small unit led by an experienced professional and staffed with representatives of the sponsoring organizations and people with backgrounds in urban planning, municipal engineering, economics, and the social sciences. For example, the unit that formulated the CAMEBA program, the first large-scale slum upgrading effort for the *barrios* of Caracas, was housed in the Municipal and Community Development Foundation (FUNDACOMUN), the Venezuelan government agency promoting the program, and had two co-directors: a social scientist and a civil engineer with municipal management experience. A few other professionals, with backgrounds in urban planning, public administration, and economics, completed the unit. The program design process was supported by a steering committee comprised of representatives from FUNDACOMUN, the World Bank, other government agencies, the municipalities of the Caracas metropolitan area, and the general public. Such an organizational structure will go a long way toward ensuring that the key disciplines for upgrading are adequately represented in the program design process. This small unit coordinates all and conducts some of the work, recruiting specialized consultants as needed.
>
> **What Time and Money Requirements Are Associated with These Actions?** Some readers may feel that the procedures outlined in this chapter are too costly and time-consuming. In reality, although it is true that adequate program preparation does have resource implications, a great deal of time and money may be saved over the life span of the program by adequate preparation. Nevertheless, we admit that it is not always possible to follow these procedures exactly. The presentation that follows is therefore what we believe a sponsoring organization should aim for, although we realize that it will sometimes be necessary to settle for suboptimal solutions on some points.

- Build on previous experience so as not to "reinvent the wheel" each time
- Be a tool in designing programs that lend themselves to scaling up.

The program design and rollout cycle is subdivided into five stages:

1. Preidentification and consensus-building
2. Prefeasibility studies and program identification
3. Feasibility studies and program design
4. Establishing a program monitoring and evaluation system
5. Rolling out the program

For each of the stages in program design (stages 1 to 4), information is provided on objectives, key process issues, typical sequence of activities, as well as considerations before moving on to the next stage of the process. Discussion of the final stage of the process—the program rollout stage—is organized by major issue areas.

Stage 1. Preidentification and Consensus-Building

Designation of a consensus-building stage, which may also be called the *preidentification* stage, is an attempt to transform the development of initial contacts with stakeholders and potential program partners[1]—an activity that occurs at the start-up of every program—into a less hurried and superficial exercise. We propose making these initial contacts with key stakeholders and potential program partners into an opportunity to establish strategic alliances and ensure that the program receives the necessary measure of support.

During the consensus-building stage, the program design unit identifies potential program partners and begins to formalize their role in the project and contractualize their contribution. This initiative is conducted proactively by deliberately organizing an inclusive and open consensus-building stage in which:

- Key stakeholders and potential program partners are identified
- Information about the basic aims and outlook of the program is provided
- The views of key stakeholders and potential partners are expressed
- Channels for negotiation and conflict resolution are established at the outset
- Local rivalries that may stand in the way of a program are identified and dealt with
- Tentative basic agreements regarding the roles to be played by potential program partners are reached.

The first stage of a participatory urban upgrading program entails building consensus among the likely key stakeholders in the program. This of course begins with a preliminary identification of these stakeholders, usually via informal networking with planning officials; infra-

---

[1]*Stakeholders* are people and organizations whose mandate, field of activity, or interests are related to or affected by the program; this relationship entitles them to a say in its design and execution, which may benefit from their information, insights, and collaboration. *Program partners* are people and organizations that will actually carry out specific program tasks and enter into contractual arrangements with the program.

structure line agencies or ministries; community-based organizations, nonprofits, or federations of such organizations; representative offices of donor agencies; large private firms that hire from or work within targeted communities; and related industry organizations. Ultimately, the stakeholders in an urban development process may include public authorities with jurisdiction over the area, public or private utility companies, formal landowners, formal and informal land developers, owners and managers of area businesses, owners and managers of businesses that hire or are patronized by people from the area, managers and staff of public or nongovernmental facilities in the area (such as health centers, schools, and daycare centers), politicians and political party activists, development nongovernmental organizations (NGOs), religious groups, private firms providing services in the context of a program or project, and local residents and other target groups.

The consensus-building stage lets government agencies and other key stakeholders deal with common concerns and uncertainties regarding a process that introduces many novel elements. Many entities fear that participation, area-based development, and a multidisciplinary approach may lead to loss of control, long lead times, and inefficient disbursements, among other problems.

To allay these fears, it may be useful to present and analyze successful examples from other cities to the stakeholders. Organizing study tours of successful projects can be particularly useful in this regard.[2] Studying successful examples is also useful in involving potential stakeholders in discussions about institutional and funding arrangements and for providing an opportunity to begin conceptualizing possible roles for each partner in the program. It is also important to inform stakeholders and program partners that the program will only operate at its intended scale after a successful pilot stage.[3] This information will reassure these key decisionmakers that there will be sufficient opportunity to test out the approaches and methodologies to be used in participatory upgrading.

A well-organized consensus-building stage is particularly important when communities and other stakeholders are deeply divided by politics. As demonstrated by the Tijuana case study, there are many situations in which affiliation with a political party has traditionally been the passport to obtaining government support, while affiliation with a rival political party has meant foregoing that support—at least until the po-

---

[2]Chapter 2 provides a summary overview of participatory upgrading and housing projects in Latin America which could serve as possible study tour destinations.

[3]The importance of a successful pilot stage is emphasized in the discussion of Stage 5 later in this chapter.

litical tide has turned. While local politics will continue to be an important factor in urban upgrading, the trend toward democratization and decentralization in Latin America has created new opportunities for participation, negotiation, and mediation. A thoughtful program design process must acknowledge political rivalry and provide the necessary opportunities for conflict resolution, beginning with a well-organized consensus-building stage.

Similarly, the consensus-building stage is an opportunity to identify and deal constructively with rivalries among organizations and individuals at the local level and other human nature issues that too often stand in the way of a program. Skepticism and turf issues must be addressed early on, or they will certainly materialize later to the program's detriment. Box 4-2 provides a list of questions which are frequently raised during the consensus-building stage. Suggestions as to how to deal with these questions are provided throughout the book, especially in chapters 3 and 5.

Box 4-2. Questions Frequently Asked during the Consensus-Building Stage

- How is it possible to deal with some stakeholders' notions about participation being too complicated and time-consuming, and thus negatively influencing the attainment of project goals?
- How is it possible to organize a successful participatory project if, at the start of the project, we do not have strong community organizations as counterparts?
- How does one reconcile a participatory and area-based approach with existing practices—and the existing knowledge base—in planning, design, funding, and execution of public works with effective results?
- How is it possible to organize a process that involves different institutional missions and technical disciplines so that coordination is ensured and major turf issues avoided?
- How does one deal with the level of expectations and initial assumptions regarding project timing that often do not take into account bureaucratic difficulties and other delaying factors (e.g., the need for building first consensus and then capacity)?
- How does one deal with the information gap that frequently exists regarding low-income areas?
- How does one deal with the all-too-common uncertainties that exist regarding funding?
- How can the project survive transitions in political power, e.g., as one mayor's term of office ends and another's begins?

Objectives

- To reach a consensus among key stakeholders regarding the use of a participatory and area-based approach in an initiative to improve the provision of basic infrastructure and services and the shelter conditions of the urban poor. This consensus is required to overcome misunderstandings about what exactly is meant by participation and area-based planning and implementation, as well as misunderstanding of other parties' agendas and mistrust among organizations, and doubts about the cost-effectiveness of participatory initiatives.
- To overcome common fears of government agencies and other community and private sector stakeholders regarding participatory and area-based approaches. Commonly perceived fears include loss of control, lack of established coordination capacity and lack of capacity of local governments and communities to carry out the actions required by a participatory urban upgrading program.
- To reach a basic agreement among key stakeholders as to the steps to be taken for the formulation and launch of an urban upgrading and shelter initiative.
- To ensure that the level of expectations among key stakeholders regarding the program's time frame, cost, and objectives remains realistic.

Key Process Issues

The key process issues that apply to the consensus-building stage are similar to those that apply to any group dynamic in which consensus and collaboration are sought. Thus:

- The process needs to be inclusive, and needs to be perceived as such. When in doubt about including a particular stakeholder, err on the side of inclusion; the process itself will in due course weed out participants who are not really interested or who cannot contribute much. Groups and people who feel that they are entitled to a say in program formulation but are denied the opportunity to do so may turn into enemies of the program.
- Adequate opportunities (e.g., brainstorming sessions, one-on-one interviews, structured workshops) need to be created to permit expression of stakeholders' views and suggestions, and note needs to be taken of the views expressed and the consensus reached. Efforts should be made to use existing—as opposed to ad hoc—forums to foster consensus among stakeholders. Existing discussion venues such as parent-teacher associations or mothers' clubs are

more likely to be culturally acceptable and to pose less of a threat to the way beneficiary communities are organized.
- Every effort must be made to ensure that information flows freely and that people and groups have access to all the information they need to make decisions.
- It is useful to have a mediator who is perceived by all stakeholders as impartial and knowledgeable. This role is often played by the coordinator of the program design unit. It is particularly important when local politics come into play to have an external, politically neutral program design unit coordinator who has no current or past links to the local power structure and who has strong diplomatic and mediation skills.
- The consensus-building stage should aim for an explicit statement of the ground rules: what the forum for discussion of program issues will be, what the expected time schedule is, what the standards/format are to exchange information, and what skills each partner can, in principle, contribute.

Typical Sequence of Activities

1. Perform a preliminary identification of the key stakeholders who will need to be involved in the consensus-building process.
2. Conduct one-on-one interviews with the key stakeholders to get to know their perspective and motivations, understand what they may bring to the program, and identify conflicts and unresolved issues that may hamper the development of the program.
3. Hold a workshop with stakeholders for the presentation and discussion of successful cases from other cities as well as to identify community priorities on a preliminary basis. (A sample program for a consensus-building workshop is provided in box 4-3.)
4. Conduct brainstorming sessions with key stakeholders to begin conceptualizing what a participatory and area-based urban upgrading program might look like in their city, province, or country (depending on the level at which the program is being designed).
5. Consider organizing a study tour of successful programs for a small group of key stakeholders, especially in those situations where there is little similar experience at the local level.
6. Prepare a draft action plan for the program design cycle that reflects the consensus of the key public and private sector stakeholders, and the likely role of each program participant. Note that this document does not constitute a formal agreement.

> **Box 4-3. Sample Program for a Consensus-Building Workshop**
>
> Following is the agenda used in Ciudad Juárez, Mexico, for a first workshop with key stakeholders in an urban upgrading program. The program allowed ample time for questions and answers and for plenary discussion.
>
> 1. Welcome and Objectives
>
> 2. Latin American Experiences
>   - Social Investment Funds in Central America
>   - Bolivia's Social Investment Fund
>   - The Guarapiranga Project, São Paulo, Brazil
>
> 3. The Development Plan for the Western Part of Ciudad Juárez (Zona Poniente), where most of the city's informal settlements are located
>
> 4. The Ciudad Juárez Urban Upgrading Program
>   - Objectives
>   - Methodology
>   - Components
>   - Coordinating Unit
>
> 5. Plenary Discussion
>
> 6. Conclusions and Next Steps

Considerations before Moving On

The consensus-building stage should have produced the following results as a minimum; it is not prudent to proceed to the next stage unless these have been achieved:

- A good level of understanding and agreement on the part of key public and private sector stakeholders regarding the major issues involved in a participatory and area-based upgrading and shelter project has been reached.
- Major misconceptions on participation, including potential benefits, costs, and risks, have been clarified.
- A consensus has been reached on the level and degree of participation that would be feasible/desirable to implement, as well as on the program's objectives and design parameters, and on the expected contributions of each stakeholder.
- The benefits and coordination requirements of area-based development planning and implementation are understood by all stakeholders.

- Key stakeholders have bought into the idea and have agreed to take an active part in program design and—hopefully—implementation.
- A tentative action plan for the program design cycle has been drafted, including objectives and activities and their sequence and key milestones; the observations of the key stakeholders have been incorporated into this plan.

Stage 2. Prefeasibility Studies and Program Identification

The prefeasibility studies carried out for the purpose of program identification include some of the most important work of program design; this may also be the most creative stage of the program's formulation. At this stage in the process, the following activities are undertaken:

- Essential information on local conditions is collected and collated
- Identification of key stakeholders and potential program partners is finalized
- Alternatives regarding the key features (type, scope, format, and structure) of the program are formulated and discussed (see box 4-4)
- An evaluation of the different alternatives regarding program features, according to local constraints and opportunities, is carried out.

The activities outlined above allow for the development of a proposal regarding program features including institutional arrangement and implementation strategy, to be tested and refined during the next stage of the process—the feasibility studies and detailed program design.

Objectives

- To reach a good level of understanding about local conditions and to identify key constraints (e.g., social, economic, technical, institutional, legal, regulatory, and financial).
- To finalize identification of program stakeholders and partnership opportunities with civil society, the private sector, other tiers of government, infrastructure line agencies, and the donor community.
- To develop and evaluate different possibilities in terms of program features (type, scope, format, and structure) according to local needs, priorities, constraints, and opportunities; and to discuss these possibilities with key stakeholders.
- To learn stakeholders' views on different options regarding program features and facilitate a consensus among key stakeholders regarding the main aspects of program structure.

> **Box 4-4. Program Features: Type, Scope, Format, and Structure**
>
> **Program type** is defined by the type of action undertaken by the program to improve access to infrastructure and shelter by the urban poor. Following are the main types of programs found in practice, each of which has two main subtypes:
>
> - Upgrading of an existing settlement: (1) piecemeal upgrading, in which infrastructure improvements are undertaken without the benefit of an area-based upgrading plan; (2) integrated upgrading, in which an area-based upgrading plan that considers the requirements of the various types of infrastructure is the basis for a coherent set of infrastructure improvements
> - Land delivery: (1) sites and services, in which land is subdivided according to a plan, and basic infrastructure is put in place before the plots are sold or distributed; (2) beaconed sites with a plan, in which a settlement is laid out and surveyed according to a plan, and plots are sold or distributed before the basic infrastructure is in place; infrastructure is then built gradually, according to resource availability, to the specifications of the original plan, as in Peru's *lotes con tiza* strategy
> - Housing programs: (1) home improvement programs, in which technical assistance and credit are extended to low-income households for the expansion and improvement of existing homes; (2) new housing in new settlements, in which new infrastructure and housing units are built simultaneously in an empty or "greenfield" site; this type of program has been the object of most conventional public housing projects in industrialized and developing countries alike
>
> **Program scope** refers to the range of types of improvements undertaken by the program. Some programs focus only on water supply and sanitation; others also include, for instance, storm drainage, road paving, public lighting, and land tenure regularization. Some programs include

Key Process Issues

Several critical process issues must be addressed at this stage; these involve:

- Collecting available information regarding the infrastructure and shelter needs of low-income communities and the relevant constraints and opportunities at the local level
- Finalizing identification of the program's key stakeholders and potential partners, and outlining the key strategic alliances that will be the backbone of the program's structure

technical assistance and credit for home improvement, while others focus on infrastructure only.

Program format refers to the kind of system and procedures adopted for project selection, resource flows, and the relationship between beneficiaries and implementing agencies. Approaches to targeting and cost recovery are also part of program format. The main program formats found in practice are:

- Social investment fund, or programmatic, in which municipalities or organized communities present project requests to a central facility which evaluates them, and later funds and supervises the execution of the approved requests
- Participatory budgeting, a variant on the programmatic format, in which part of the budget of a municipality is allocated through a participatory and transparent process in which requests are presented by community groups and ranked by priority at public meetings organized by the municipality
- Comprehensive upgrading, in which certain informal settlement areas in a city are chosen, according to predetermined criteria, to receive a wide range of upgrading investments over a relatively short period of time (usually two to three years).

Program structure refers to the institutional arrangements and implementation strategy adopted by a program, in terms of its participating institutions and their roles and relationships.

Note that any initiative in upgrading and low-income housing needs to create channels for the involvement of the community or client group in the project's planning, design, and implementation to ensure responsiveness to demand and to plant the seeds of sustainability. The support services needed for effective participation are very similar regardless of program type, scope, format, or structure.

- Understanding and developing a proposal on the type, scope, format, and structure of program required.

Collecting Available Information. Although some information is gleaned during the consensus-building stage, information collection begins in earnest at this stage, when the program design unit identifies sources and seeks to gather all available information regarding the infrastructure and shelter needs of low-income communities and the existing social, technical, environmental, institutional, economic, and financial constraints and opportunities at the local level.

This information, especially that relating to the informal settlements themselves, is often hard to come by, and a special effort will need to be made to gather information based entirely upon secondary sources. This exercise will allow the program design unit to identify information gaps and propose ways to overcome them through direct information gathering in the field, which will be undertaken in the next stage.

Finalizing Identification of Program Stakeholders and Potential Partners. Building on the preliminary identification carried out in the consensus-building stage, the program design unit will now be able to finalize identification of the program's key stakeholders and potential partners, and outline the key strategic alliances that form the backbone of the program's structure. Partners need to be identified within the communities, in the public sector, and in civil society. Willing and able partners from the for-profit private sector (specialized service providers, microfinance institutions or commercial banks, small and medium-sized providers of infrastructure, private utilities, materials and equipment providers, private landowners, etc.) should also be identified at this stage.

Features of Urban Upgrading and Shelter Programs. All urban upgrading and shelter programs have common features, but it is important to bear in mind that there are as many different types of programs in this field as there are cities, each with its own distinctive circumstances and requirements. As discussed in box 4-4, a basic distinction can be made between programs that aim to:

- Improve existing settlements—whether squatter settlements (e.g., São Paulo's Guarapiranga program) or informal land subdivisions (e.g., Tijuana's community upgrading programs)—and deliver serviced sites or sites plus a plan (e.g., Villa El Salvador)
- Produce housing, whether under the form of new housing and new urban settlements—e.g., the Foundation for the Promotion of Housing (FUPROVI) in Costa Rica—or improvement of existing homes— e.g., the Desco (Center for Development Studies and Promotion) Densification Program in Villa El Salvador.

Not surprisingly, these different types of programs have different requirements in terms of participatory strategies. Specifically, each program type poses different challenges in terms of urban form and structure, forms of participation, and expression of community demand.

Urban Form and Structure. Existing informal settlements are part of the structure and history of a city, and have acquired, over time, their own specific features with respect both to urban form and content and to social constraints and opportunities. There are significant differences between the upgrading of squatter settlements and that of informal subdivisions. In the case of squatter settlements, upgrading usually requires extensive layout changes and partial removal of the structures to deal with risk situations, provide space for public uses, and create access routes as well as ensure access to each plot. Depending on the site's physical features, the above may entail the need for significant removal of existing structures and resettlement of local residents.

With informal land subdivisions, public and private spaces are usually already defined, and there is far less need for removal and resettlement. In this case, the need for removal and resettlement is dictated by the need for public use areas (e.g., parks, schools, clinics), which are usually not provided for by informal developers, and the existence of situations of risk (e.g., plots on unstable slopes or flood-prone areas).[4]

As a rule of thumb, the complexity of informal settlement upgrading is directly proportional to the need for layout changes and removal and resettlement, which are usually the costliest items in upgrading projects. This is why upgrading a squatter settlement is usually costlier and more complex than upgrading an informal subdivision.

Another difference between upgrading squatter settlements and informal subdivisions regards the need for a plan. In many cases, upgrading interventions take place without a plan, in what is called *piecemeal* upgrading. Piecemeal upgrading is not as harmful in the case of informal subdivisions, since they already have a layout. Piecemeal upgrading of squatter settlements, on the other hand, is definitely to be avoided, since it creates technical problems and unnecessary physical constraints to future layout improvements (see box 4-5). In the case of squatter settlements, a plan is not only important, it is essential.

In most countries, there is some flexibility in terms of technical standards when it comes to upgrading, but *housing and sites and services projects* are subject to a wide variety of strict rules and procedures involving, e.g., admissible land uses, population densities, minimum plot sizes, requirements on land to be set aside for public uses, minimum width and maximum slope of roads, etc. One of the reasons why informal settlements develop in the first place is the unduly high cost of developing land imposed by such standards.

In this context, a community infrastructure or housing program must ensure that the existing planning standards and real estate market rules

---

[4]Resettlement may well be considered the Achilles' heel of community infrastructure projects, since it causes social disruption and entails the need to find suitably located and affordable land for substitution housing as well as the resources for the construction of such housing and related infrastructure.

> **Box 4-5. Problems Caused by Piecemeal Upgrading**
>
> In Belo Horizonte, Brazil, a change in land use laws took place in 1983 that acknowledged the existence of *favela* areas and created the concept of special social interest zones, opening the way to their regularization and upgrading (see PROFAVELA program description in chapter 2). The new law was a valuable instrument, but the level of local experience with integrated upgrading projects was practically nil. The result was that many settlements were surveyed as they stood, and land tenure regularization processes were undertaken without any change in settlement layout. As a result, plots were regularized that lay on unstable slopes or in the middle of natural drainage paths. In other cases, political pressure from the communities led to piecemeal improvements in many settlements, such as the paving of a main access route or the building of a concrete drainage gully. Regularization without layout improvements, coupled with piecemeal upgrading works, had the effect of consolidating situations that were often undesirable and unsustainable and that had to be modified further on, wasting valuable resources and effort. Such experiences led, in the early 1990s, to the postulation of *integrated* regularization and upgrading by the organizations sponsoring the Alvorada upgrading program—an Italian-funded program which was executed by the NGO AVSI in the context of PROFAVELA—as the correct methodology to be followed.
>
> Integrated upgrading means that any action—upgrading or regularization—undertaken in a particular settlement needs to follow a participatory area development plan of the settlement, which considers all the needed layout changes, relocation and resettlement needs, and require-

and regulations do not conflict with real needs or pose affordability problems for municipalities and target groups. In actuality, however, affordability and standards usually do conflict, making it necessary to promote a study of existing standards and their impact on land and housing costs. This exercise will be important in order to identify specific areas of conflict and to explore ways to resolve them, which may involve the preparation and promotion of appropriate legal and regulatory changes or the obtainment of waivers as needed. It is also necessary to undertake this exercise in order to identify the ways in which the same standards that have pushed so many people into informality in the first place become one more obstacle to improvement of the situation and a key factor in the creation of new slums.[5]

---

[5]Another reason why it is important to study the impact of standards and approvals procedures on land and housing cost is that agencies often try to lower low-income hous-

> ments of the various types of infrastructure. In this manner, even if the actual actions that are undertaken are discrete and upgrading takes place through a gradual, long-term process, every action is a contribution to the achievement of a well-defined goal. Upgrading is thus no longer piecemeal, although it may still be partial and gradual. In reality, most integrated upgrading programs take the form of *comprehensive* upgrading, a particular type of integrated upgrading that transforms an area typically over a span of about two years, with simultaneous investments in all the different branches of infrastructure.
>
> In the case of informal subdivisions, piecemeal upgrading does not do as much harm as in the case of squatter settlements, because informal subdivisions generally have a much better layout. This is shown in the Tijuana case, which also shows, however, that even in the case of informal subdivisions, a long-term plan is important in guiding a community's development efforts and public and private investment over the years.
>
> Piecemeal upgrading is sometimes undertaken due to a lack of experience in undertaking a wide range of sectoral interventions. The short-term perspective that often dominates local politics is another leading factor. There is often a temptation, on the part of mayors, other local authorities, and even community leaders, to generate a large number of small works that can be inaugurated with fanfare. Part of the advocacy work of an upgrading program is showing politicians that the same political impact can be achieved *with* planning, which has the added benefits of a much better quality end result, sustainability, and overall good use of resources.

Forms of Participation. In the case of *existing settlements*, participation needs to operate within the framework of a methodology for improvement that has the existing settlement and its physical and social reality, including the residents' vision for the future, as its point of departure. The upgrading of existing settlements also has as a key constraint the need to preserve the existing stock of housing and infrastructure. The fact that people already live in the area and share its problems, however, represents a key cohesion factor and incentive to participation for diverse groups in the community.

In the case of *new housing/new settlements and sites and services schemes*, the challenge is to bring dispersed and heterogeneous individuals to-

---

ing costs by using less expensive construction techniques, rather than addressing more relevant cost issues. A rule of thumb derived from the authors' experience is that local regulations on land development may account for as much as 40 percent of low-income housing costs.

gether to collaborate in a common venture, with no prior history of joint work, differing visions of what the new settlement should be like, and often few personal connections within the group.[6]

Expression of Community Demand. In the case of *existing settlements*, demands are usually complex and clearly articulated, and there is already a history of attempts to cater to them. There may be an existing plan for the development of the settlement, or at least some form of shared vision among the residents. Spatial and behavioral constraints are usually very challenging, however.

In the case of *new settlements*, community demand usually focuses narrowly either on the plot or on the house itself, to the exclusion of almost everything else. Since sufficient land is usually available, spatial constraints are much less severe, but economic and financial constraints condition everything, since the time frame is usually much shorter than that of the gradual, step-by-step growth and improvement of an informal settlement.

Choosing the Appropriate Program Type. Local needs and circumstances will normally dictate the choice of program type. Key factors in this regard are:

- The relative frequency of squatter settlements versus informal land subdivisions versus tenement housing as the shelter alternative most used by the poor in the program area
- Density of existing settlements, existing infrastructure and service levels, materials, quality and crowding of existing structures, and risk factors
- The need for resettlement that an urban upgrading intervention is likely to generate, which is usually a function of the presence of existing structures in risk areas, of excessive horizontal density,[7] and/or of the need to open access routes
- The land tenure situation in existing settlements and the legal and political viability of land tenure regularization

---

[6]One way to foster involvement in such programs is to "contractualize" or formalize involvement. When people are selected to move into a new community, they can be asked to attend a community development class, understand what their participatory obligations are, and sign a community charter.

[7]The density of squatter settlements in the Guarapiranga basin, for example, sometimes exceeds 1,000 persons per hectare, which is extremely high for a horizontal (one- to two-story) settlement pattern. It is often not possible to create a minimal road network and provide infrastructure without reducing this density, thereby creating a need for resettlement.

- Land and trunk infrastructure availability near the program area or in locations that may be attractive to the client group, which is a precondition for effective resettlement
- The overall policy environment and existing legal and regulatory constraints and opportunities
- The socioeconomic situation of the residents of the target areas, subdivided by their different income levels and living conditions, and the indications thus gleaned regarding ability to pay and needed subsidy levels
- Residents' willingness and ability to pay for basic infrastructure and services
- The existing subsidy structure and the political viability of reforming it
- The mix of available funding sources and their conditions and relative advantages
- Particular problems faced by women in the program area and specific requirements the program would need to address through an appropriate gender strategy
- Prevailing perceptions and political will regarding priority low-income communities to be tackled and types of initiatives to be included in the program.

Table 4-1 provides an overview of the variables influencing the choice of program, and box 4-6 describes how these may be applied in practice using specific cases studies. Note that integrated upgrading, which in theory allows gradual implementation (as we have seen in box 4-5), normally takes the form of comprehensive upgrading in practice.

In the gradual implementation of integrated upgrading, a negotiated area development plan would be used as a blueprint for upgrading over a number of years, with gradual improvements following a logical sequence and negotiated cost recovery targets. In actuality, gradual approaches tend to be piecemeal, following no particular plan. Projects that do follow a negotiated plan are usually comprehensive upgrading projects. The sizable investments required by comprehensive upgrading are usually made by a government. Usually, as in the case of Guarapiranga and Favela-Bairro, limited attention is paid to cost recovery, and the large subsidies that are provided are not well-targeted or transparent.

Choosing People and Organizations to Work with the Program. Determining the applicability of community-based shelter and infrastructure development in a given situation, and the options for its implementation, requires an assessment of the local situation in terms of the local expertise, resources, and capacity.

Table 4-1. Key Variables Influencing Choice of Program Type

Variable	Program type and examples
• Settlements are regularized informal subdivisions with a grid layout • Lack of vacant affordable land • Public subsidy mechanism allocates small sum to each settlement each year	**Piecemeal upgrading** (improvements are added gradually over a long-term process, but without a negotiated plan) *Examples:* Tijuana, Ciudad Juárez, Bolivia
• Squatter settlements with a chaotic settlement pattern but no insoluble tenure problems • Scarce availability of vacant affordable land • Large infrastructure deficit • Availability of significant amount of resources "in one go" and political decision to subsidize	**Comprehensive upgrading** (a wide range of improvements according to a predefined area plan, as in integrated upgrading, but undertaken in one go, usually in a time frame of about two years) *Examples:* Guarapiranga, Novos Alagados, Alvorada, Favela-Bairro
• Vacant affordable land • Finance for servicing this land • Political decision to deliver serviced land at scale	**Sites and services** (mass production of serviced sites in large schemes for resettlement of urban squatters; variant: sites and services with basic starter housing units) *Example:* Integrated Serviced Land Project, South Africa
• Vacant affordable land • Lack of finance for servicing this land • Political decision to deliver land at scale in a disciplined manner, laying groundwork for gradual installation of infrastructure	**Sites with a plan** (the Peruvian strategy of lotes con tiza—surveyed and beaconed lots—defined by the 1961 Law of the Barriadas) *Example:* Villa El Salvador
• Vacant affordable land • Small number of existing informal settlements • Demand-side subsidy within established housing finance system	**New housing in new settlements** (new infrastructure and housing units are built on empty land; variant: new housing in available land in existing serviced areas) *Example:* FUPROVI

Variable	Program type and examples
• Degraded structures in serviced areas housing significant numbers of urban poor • Potential for negotiation with owners of existing structures • Availability of significant resources and political decision to subsidize	**Redevelopment of degraded existing structures** such as tenement buildings *Example:* Don't Move, Improve, the Bronx, New York
• Significant self-help efforts in low-income areas that lack technical guidance and access to credit • Demand for credit and technical assistance that can be stimulated through well-targeted financial instruments (including savings products) and adequate social marketing strategies • Possible alliances with banks, microfinance institutions, and institutions able to provide technical assistance	**Technical assistance and credit for home expansion and improvement** (form of organized support to self-help housing efforts that may be combined with upgrading programs) *Examples:* FUNHAVI-Cooperative Housing Foundation, Ciudad Juárez; Desco Densification Program, Villa El Salvador
• Dense informal settlements that need de-densification to deal with risk situations and improve access • Severe lack of vacant affordable land • Large infrastructure deficit • Availability of significant resources and political decision to subsidize • Groups in settlements that can afford to move to apartment blocks	**Comprehensive upgrading with partial verticalization on site** (horizontal density lowered through partial removal of squatter settlement and building of apartment blocks on site; remainder of original *favela* is upgraded) *Example:* Cingapura

Source: Authors' construction from field study data.

> **Box 4-6. Choosing the Program Type**
>
> The Brazil, Costa Rica, and Peru cases provide good examples of how different circumstances make for different choices regarding the type of program that is eventually selected. These three cases demonstrate the importance of land availability, demographic pressure, the existence of squatter settlements, and the availability of housing subsidies as factors shaping the choice of program type.
>
> In the case of Guarapiranga, the high frequency of squatter settlements and the scarce availability of suitably located land practically imposed the alternative of the comprehensive upgrading program. There were serious legal constraints, but these were overcome through strong political will—specifically through a combination of environmental activism and pressure from local community-based organizations, leading to an unprecedented alliance between the *favela* residents and middle-class environmentalists. The cost constraints of comprehensive upgrading of such a densely populated area were as serious as the legal constraints, but a political decision was made to mobilize the necessary resources with World Bank support. In the case of informal subdivisions, the problem of cost was not as serious, and the decision to upgrade was easier to make.
>
> In San José, where squatter settlements are not so predominant, the availability of suitably located land and the existence of a housing subsidy scheme make it possible to think of building new housing as a mass solution. The members of Costa Rica's housing associations are usually people who live in formal sector rental housing, and their first task upon establishing an association is looking for a suitable empty plot. The fact that they usually succeed in finding one, through a combination of their own efforts and political patronage, is testimony to the relatively ample availability of suitably located land in the San José metropolitan area.
>
> In Peru, where even more land was available than in San José (albeit without a housing subsidy) and where a specific legal framework for orderly land occupation by low-income people—the 1961 Law of the Barriadas—was in place, the alternative chosen was the creation of a new town in the desert. Villa El Salvador began with a layout and a development plan, and basic infrastructure and services were provided gradually over a span of more than two decades.

The preliminary identification of program stakeholders and *potential* partners was carried out in Stage 1. What happens at this next stage is identification of the *actual* partners who will be involved in the design and rollout of the program, i.e., the people and organizations that will be directly involved in program activities. Many of them will be program stakeholders, while others may be selected and brought in from elsewhere based upon their specific expertise. But from where are the program's partners to be drawn, and what do we expect them to do for us?

In this regard, the agency promoting the program must do four things at this stage:

1. Get to know, and assess the potential to develop strategic alliances with, likely local partners, including those based in the targeted communities, in the private sector (both nonprofit and for-profit entities), and in other tiers of government.
2. Assess the type and level of contribution each partner may be able to provide to the program, such as concessional or commercial-based funding, technical assistance, or in-kind support.[8]
3. Assess the legal and regulatory environment regarding the mandates of existing institutions as it relates to their authorized sectors of intervention, ability to effectively set and regulate tariffs and impose fines for noncompliance, procurement and contracting constraints, as well as potential constraints regarding long-term funding commitments for specific physical works in the targeted communities. Box 4-7 provides an example of the difficulties caused by existing institutional structures.
4. Assess the comparative advantages of existing institutions as a home for the program, and the constraints and advantages of the creation of a new agency to coordinate the program.

Assessing Local Capacity and the Legal and Regulatory Environment. Assessing local capacity, the legal and regulatory environment, and the comparative advantages of local institutions is important in identifying people and organizations to work with; specifically in identifying and comparing the relative advantages of agencies to provide program coordination and management services. The coordinating agency would need to be able to coordinate internal actors, such as the different departments of the municipality promoting the program; and external actors, such as participating community-based organizations, government agencies, utility companies, private foundations, NGOs, and for-profit private firms.

The key questions to be asked in performing these assessments fall into several categories, as they relate to aspects of the specific program environment.

On the *social front*:

---

[8] A proposal made in Tijuana for an in-kind contribution provided by a for-profit private sector partner would entail use of the *maquiladora* payroll for disbursing and collecting payments on microcredit loans provided by a private financial institution.

> **Box 4-7. Coordinating Different Sectors of Intervention**
>
> In the Guarapiranga upgrading project, one of the key challenges in implementing an integrated approach was coordinating the authorized sectors of intervention of the several agencies involved. In Brazil, responsibility for public thoroughfares, storm drainage, and solid waste collection and disposal rests with municipalities. Water and sanitation and electricity services are provided by utility companies; these are usually linked to the state level, and many are being privatized. In Guarapiranga, the coordinating role of the São Paulo municipality was recognized by all parties. Although this helped a great deal, the technical and procedural problems were still daunting. The intersections among the various types of infrastructure constituted the main technical problem to be faced.
>
> The routing of electricity cables through a settlement does not have to correspond with the road layout, and does not interferes much with the provision of other types of service infrastructure. On the other hand, streets and lanes provide the path for a large part of water supply and sewerage networks. Good storm drainage is important for the conservation of road and sewerage infrastructure, and an effective solid waste management system is required to ensure that the sewers do not become choked with refuse and other solid wastes.
>
> Each of the agencies involved has its own technical standards and approvals procedures, and engineering design for each type of infrastructure also had to take into account the requirements of all the other infrastructure types. This explains why, in the Guarapiranga project, the coordination of engineering services was a major cost item—comparable, in fact, to the cost of the engineering services themselves. Fortunately, the municipality's recognized coordination role allowed it to hire a single contractor for each area to carry out all the different works under the supervision of the different line agencies. This arrangement simplified matters considerably.

- Who are the actors that work with communities in the program area? How well organized is each of them, and what is their level and record of achievement?[9]

---

[9]These questions refer to all social sectors, not just infrastructure and shelter. We are trying here to identify, beyond existing local actors with specific experience in upgrading and shelter, those who work with communities in other social sectors such as health and education and might have an interest in receiving training and thereby widening the scope of their activities. The reasoning is that organizations with community development know-how and experience, albeit in other sectors of activity, should be seen as potential resources for an upgrading program.

- Are there any previous experiences with participatory mechanisms in shelter and infrastructure projects? If so, what was the rationale behind the approach utilized? What was the degree of participation in these past projects? What institutions and organizations (governmental, community-based, nongovernmental, private for-profit) have that experience?
- Which of the existing local actors would be interested in and capable of providing social intermediation services? Who is familiar with the concept of socio-technical support? Are there agents whose credentials and record of achievement indicate that they could become good socio-technical support providers if they were to receive appropriate training? Basic credentials might include a proven track record working with the targeted communities (albeit in other sectors of intervention such as health or education). Such experiences usually provide an organization with an understanding of community needs, capacities, priorities, leadership structure, and willingness and capacity to pay for certain services.
- Is there any experience in contracting with these providers? If so, what was the experience (e.g., with the Ministry of Health, Ministry of Education, etc.)? What was the selection procedure? What were the contractual arrangements? What was the structure of compensation?

On the *technical front*:

- Is there core competence, at the local level, in the required technical areas (e.g. urban planning, engineering, urban economics, sociology, information and communication, social work)? Where is that competence located?
- Beyond the people at the local level with academic knowledge of the core technical subjects, are there technicians with hands-on experience in the application of such knowledge to urban upgrading and low-income housing projects?

On the *institutional front*:

- Is there any experience with area-based planning and management, as opposed to sector-based? If so, what was the rationale behind this approach? What lessons may be drawn from the experience?
- Which of the existing agencies would be a likely coordinating agency? Would it be necessary to create a new body or agency for the purposes of the program?
- Are political decisionmakers open to the idea of the creation of a new body or agency for the program, and are they willing to give it operational capacity and autonomy? Would the new agency have an adequate resource base?

- What is the position of the line agencies? Would they be interested in and willing to work in a new format, under the coordination of a different entity? Is any one of the line agencies well-placed to be the coordinating agency, or is it better to propose a different entity altogether?

On the *financial front*:

- What is the experience regarding cost recovery, taxation, subsidy administration, and loan recovery? What are the prevailing attitudes and political climate regarding these issues?
- What kind of access does the community have to credit and savings services, whether informally or formally provided, for microenterprise development, home improvement, new housing, or other purposes?
- On the basis of existing practice, what are the likely paths that financial flows to and from the program would follow? What are the key bureaucratic obstacles? What are the main pitfalls to avoid in managing program resources?
- On the basis of the above concerns—management of program resources, cost recovery, subsidy administration—which of the existing institutions (public bodies or private institutions such as foundations) would be best placed to coordinate financial matters?
- Does it make better sense to devolve financial management to a new body specifically created for the purposes of the program?

No matter what entity is charged with managing program resources, two factors need to be taken into account:

- Competing sources offer funding under different terms and conditions, and with different *conditionalities* or policy requirements attached to a loan or grant by the funding agency. These will influence both the choice of funding source and the entire program approach. The choice of funding source, with its specific features and requirements, may in turn influence the choice of entity to manage program resources.
- Direct management of program resources by a government bureaucracy, even at the local level, is usually cumbersome and time-consuming, due to the existence of many onerous controls. Experience in Latin America has shown that it is often difficult to match the bureaucratic requirements of external funding agencies, whether bilateral or multilateral, and those of local administrations. This mismatch often results in long delays and even stalemate situations. Many programs have thus opted to create or use independent structures such as NGOs or foundations that have government and civil society participation. Since these entities are legally outside the

government sphere, they are free to utilize private sector-like procurement, accounting, and auditing procedures, thereby enhancing efficiency, effectiveness, and transparency.

Key Features of a Coordinating Agency. In light of the above, the key characteristics to look for when selecting an agency to coordinate and manage a participatory urban upgrading program are the following:

- An *institutional mission and mandate* that legally allows the agency to play the coordinating role
- *Core technical capacity* in at least some of the disciplines involved and willingness to procure any elements that may be missing
- A good track record of *experience in area-based urban planning* and management
- *Authoritativeness* that makes it likely that other agencies will agree to work under its coordination
- A *good image and reputation* for past achievements that make it a strong advocate and catalyst of resource mobilization for the program
- *Internal motivation and incentives* to seek a coordinating role and play it effectively.

Assigning Program Tasks. Answering the questions formulated in the previous section will help the program promoter visualize the different possible scenarios regarding program structure. For each of the key functions—such as construction management, engineering, social intermediation, technical coordination among line agencies, and financial coordination—the program promoter will need to identify appropriate actors and explore various options.

For instance, for each key function the promoting agency will need to decide whether to:

- Create in-house capacity (as in Bolivia and Tijuana)
- Work through an alliance of different government agencies and/or infrastructure line agencies (as in São Paulo)
- Work through NGOs, universities, or research institutions (as in Costa Rica and Peru)
- Establish contractual arrangements or strategic alliances with for-profit private sector parties, such as providers of specialized services, utilities, financial institutions, building materials providers, etc. (as has happened in some measure in all the cases studied).

Box 4-8 illustrates the variety of approaches to the division of labor found in the cases we have studied.

Among the important decisions that will need to be made are:

Box 4-8. Approaches to Program Management

- **Bolivia.** Municipalities have opted to create in-house capacity, creating and staffing social development departments to handle the mechanisms of the People's Participation Law.
- **Brazil.** At the program level, Guarapiranga was based on an alliance between municipalities and sector line agencies. Under the coordination of a program management unit at the state government level, each of the projects that composed the Guarapiranga program was run by a municipality (e.g., São Paulo, which took care of the urban upgrading project) or line agency (e.g., SABESP, the water utility, which built trunk infrastructure for wastewater collection and treatment). At the project level, in the case of the upgrading project, the municipality of São Paulo established a small high-level coordinating unit and hired for-profit private sector firms for all the necessary expertise and services.
- **Costa Rica.** The government housing policy for the lowest income bracket is implemented by FUPROVI, an NGO. FUPROVI decided to build in-house capacity in all the sectoral disciplines (surveying, planning, engineering, social intermediation, legal and financial services, project management, construction management). This improves the coordination and interdisciplinarity of FUPROVI's work. FUPROVI occasionally hires outside professionals as private consultants when necessary.
- **Mexico.** The municipality of Tijuana decided to create in-house capacity, at first at the central level and more recently at the level of delegations and subdelegations, for all tasks related to social intermediation and technical supervision. For future community infrastructure programs in Tijuana, the municipality has considered setting up a new organization—a foundation—as the coordinating agency and focal point of a public-private partnership, interacting with the delegations and subdelegations and organizing technical assistance, capacity-building, and resource flows. The foundation would not carry out all necessary tasks directly but would define procurement rules, ensure that all the participating agencies played their agreed roles, and provide overall supervision.
- **Villa El Salvador.** A variety of approaches have been used in Villa El Salvador for the distribution of different project tasks. The most frequently used has been alliances of different public entities, each with a clearly defined role or set of roles, as in São Paulo. Unlike São Paulo, however, Villa El Salvador has not made extensive use of for-profit private sector expertise; NGOs, though, have been extensively involved and have been instrumental in providing badly needed technical assistance to community organizations and local government.

- Whether to create a new, independent agency or to manage the program under an existing structure
- The extent to which it will be possible to rely on local actors for each of the key functions or necessary to bring in outside expertise.

The answers to the above questions will depend on institutional, legal, regulatory, financial, and social constraints as well as on the availability of qualified and motivated local actors. Program promoters will select their options based on their knowledge of local conditions, their assessment of the feasible level and degree of participation, and their estimation of capacity-building and technical assistance requirements.

Institutional Options for the Program Management Unit

A key institutional issue is choosing an agency to lead the program and to ensure that the appropriate linkages to local government structures and other line agencies are in place. This issue is resolved in different ways in different situations. In many instances, the managing agency is an existing local government department; in other cases, a specific unit with special powers and resources is created within a local government agency. Yet another approach is the creation of an independent agency.

Regardless of the option selected, the key function of the program management unit should be that of project promotion, coordinating agency, and clearinghouse, and not necessarily an agency that controls and executes everything.

The diagrams in figures 4-1 through 4-5 illustrate the different flows of funds and program management arrangements that have been adopted in the cases we have studied. (Note that figure 4-5 reflects the complex relationships of the Villa El Salvador process over several decades and cannot really be considered a replicable program management arrangement.)

Institutional Affiliation and Degree of Decentralization of the Program Management Unit

Several options exist regarding the program management unit's institutional affiliation and degree of decentralization. For example, although the unit is usually located within the municipality, it can alternatively be managed by a line agency or NGO. Similarly, in terms of the extent of decentralization, it can operate from a central office, town hall, or a series of smaller local offices close to the project areas. The choice among these alternatives should be based on the relations between the program

Figure 4-1. Options for Flow of Funds, Contractual Relationships, and Program Management: Bolivia

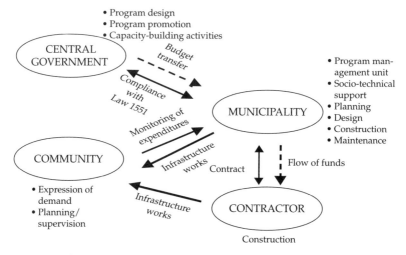

Source: Authors' construction from field study data.

Figure 4-2. Options for Flow of Funds, Contractual Relationships, and Program Management: Brazil

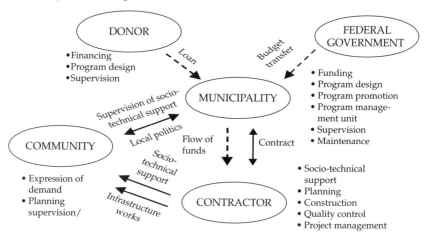

Source: Authors' construction from field study data.

Focusing on Process: Program Design and Rollout Strategies

Figure 4-3. Options for Flow of Funds, Contractual Relationships, and Program Management: Costa Rica

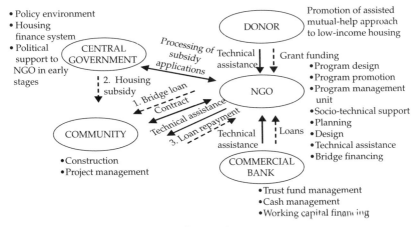

Source: Authors' construction from field study data.

Figure 4-4. Options for Flow of Funds, Contractual Relationships, and Program Management: Mexico

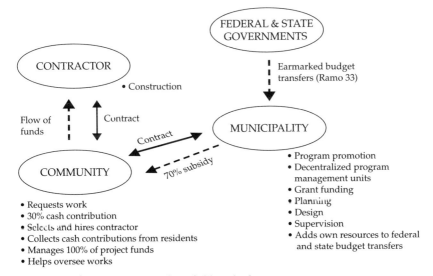

Source: Authors' construction from field study data.

Figure 4-5. Options for Flow of Funds, Contractual Relationships, and Program Management: Peru

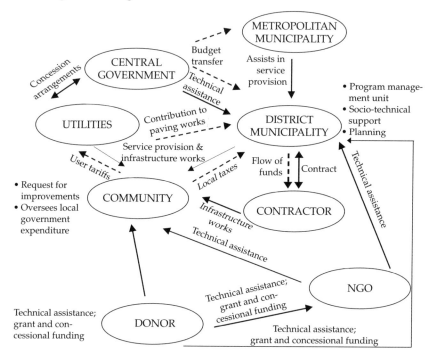

Source: Authors' construction from field study data.

partners and the political, technical, organizational, and intermediation capacities of the parties involved.

It is important to realize that the differences among the various options are also related to different levels of participation. A program management unit that operates centrally within a governmental organization will probably work with lower levels of participation. As shared responsibility and the delegation of tasks and roles increase, the program's management must move closer to the private sector, civil society in general, and in particular the communities where projects are envisaged or proposed.

This will invariably require decentralization, and there is a strong argument for the delegation of program management to a new, autonomous, ad hoc agency. Table 4-2 summarizes the position of the program management unit in each of the cases we have studied in terms of institutional affiliation and degree of decentralization.

Table 4-2. Position of the Program Management Unit in the Cases Studied

Case	Location of unit	Centralized/decentralized
Bolivia	Municipalities	Centralized (Santa Cruz) Decentralized (Cochabamba)
Brazil	Municipalities	Centralized
Costa Rica	NGO	Centralized
Mexico	Municipality	Centralized until recently, now decentralized[a]
Peru	1971–84: ABCO[b] 1984 onwards: Municipality	Centralized until recently, now decentralized

[a]The management of Tijuana's community upgrading programs is now decentralized to the city's neighborhood administrative units: delegations and subdelegations. The management of a similar program in Ciudad Juárez is centralized.

[b]The Self-Managed Urban Community of Villa El Salvador (CUAVES) is an ABCO which was so strong in the 1970s and early 1980s that it practically constituted a community-based local government entity.

Source: Authors' construction from field study data.

Advantages and Disadvantages of an Independent Program Management Unit

The case for an independent agency, or at least one endowed with considerable operational autonomy, is a strong one. The FUPROVI example from Costa Rica (as described in chapter 8) shows that an NGO can be an effective coordinator and mediator, combining technical expertise and diplomatic and political skills. In the Guarapiranga case, an autonomous unit within the Department of Housing and Urban Development of the São Paulo municipality ensured the coordination of the urban upgrading component. The unit has awarded and managed contracts to private sector firms for the provision of all necessary services.

In Tijuana, the delegations have seen their degree of autonomy in managing community upgrading programs increase steadily over the years. The delegates and subdelegates play a central role in securing resources for their area, selecting and hiring social workers and engineers for socio-technical support teams, and managing individual projects.

The main disadvantage of independent agencies and specific project management units endowed with special powers is that the acquired capacity may be lost once the project is over and the unit dismantled. In addition, staff members who are recruited to the unit usually command higher salaries during the project, which causes jealousy and friction with their colleagues who remain in low-paying public service jobs. These people often have key roles to play in ensuring the flow of resources or other inputs to the project. But, since they are jealous of their better-paid colleagues in the program management unit, they may feel they have good reason to sabotage the program.

For these reasons, this is one of the toughest choices in setting up a program's institutional structure. An independent program management unit may seem to be the only way to get the job done, but its drawbacks in terms of sustainability and capacity-building are apparent and very real, as summarized in table 4-3.

Selecting a Program Format. The term *program format* refers to the kind of system and procedures adopted for project selection, resource flows, and the relationship between beneficiaries and implementing agencies. In our research, we identified three basic formats used in urban upgrading programs throughout Latin America:

Table 4-3. Advantages and Disadvantages of Independent Program Management Units

Advantages	Disadvantages
• Significant operational advantages, making them faster and more efficient	• Better salaries and working conditions generate jealousy and lack of cooperation
• Less (or not at all) constrained by the bureaucratic obstacles typical of the public sector	• Tend to operate in isolation and thus add no capacity to the public entities involved
• Less subject to political interference	• Risk to sustainability and a negative impact in the post-project phase: once the independent unit is dismantled, nothing takes its place, creating an institutional void
• Less affected by changes in political administrations and therefore better able to ensure continuity	
• Unconstrained by public sector salary and career structures; are thus able to attract and retain high-quality staff	
• For the above reasons, have more external credibility	

Source: Authors' construction from field study data.

- The social investment fund, or programmatic, format
- The participatory budgeting format, a variant on the above in which resource allocation takes place at the local level
- The comprehensive upgrading program format.

A brief explanation of these formats follows.

The Social Investment Fund, or Programmatic, Format. In the wake of the many social investment funds that have been organized in Latin America in recent years, some urban upgrading projects have set up a facility to receive and evaluate project proposals according to a set of predefined criteria, and fund and monitor the selected projects. This social investment fund format is generally used for nationwide programs, such as PROSANEAR in Brazil, with municipalities, utility companies, and NGOs presenting proposals to a central or provincial-level facility (see box 4-9). This approach has been called the *programmatic* format by Kessides (1997), who has analyzed its application to water and sanitation programs. Another example of this format is the FUPROVI program in Costa Rica (see box 4-10).

A problem with this program format arises when funding eligibility is restricted to municipalities and utility companies. In such cases, program performance is often marred by two factors:

- Lack of experience or incentives for local governments and utilities to work with low-income settlements, which often translates into a lack of willingness to apply for funds earmarked for low-income settlement regularization and upgrading
- Lack of capacity for proposal preparation and/or lack of creditworthiness on the part of municipalities and utilities, which leads to the rejection of many proposals.

The advantages of the social fund format are linked to its clear application process and streamlined project approval and funding procedure. Because a single agency is ultimately responsible for a program that is often nationwide or statewide, it can compare the quality and performance of many projects and establish benchmarks. Arguments against this format include the fact that the creation of a national-level independent agency to manage social funds and similar programs may be used as an attempt to "re-centralize" processes that had already been decentralized to the local level, and that it may detract from the development of public sector capacity by establishing a unit that functions under separate rules and conditions from the rest of the public sector.

A variant on this format in which project proposals are presented by *community organizations* to municipalities is the participatory budgeting mechanism, which is presented below.

> **Box 4-9. Social Investment Fund Format: The PROSANEAR Facility**
>
> The Low-Income Urban Areas Water and Sanitation Program (PROSANEAR) is one of the examples of programmatic water and sanitation programs mentioned by Kessides (1997) which are set up along the lines of social investment funds. The PROSANEAR facility was organized in the mid-1990s following the success of the PROSANEAR program, which had pioneered the use of low-cost technology in almost 100 locations in different parts of Brazil. The PROSANEAR facility provided access to soft loans to municipalities and water utilities for water supply and sanitation interventions in low-income urban areas. The Brazilian federal government, by making consistent funding available and delegating outreach to municipalities and utilities and credit approval to the state level, had hoped to boost the levels of investment in urban upgrading projects in low-income urban areas. The impact of the new facility was lower than expected due to a combination of factors. In many cases, interested municipalities did not meet creditworthiness criteria or their proposals were not up to the standards established by the Federal Savings Bank. In other cases, the facility did not succeed in attracting the interest of large water utilities, which do not have a track record of working in low-income areas. The fact that this initiative fell short of expectations shows that the establishment of such a facility must be supported by capacity-building measures and stimulation of demand. Institutions and organizations that are likely project promoters must be made aware of the positive impacts such projects may produce and of the existence of methods that favor long-term sustainability. They must also be supported and trained in the preparation of proposals that follow participatory area-based planning methods.

Participatory Budgeting Format. In participatory budgeting, government resources are allocated with the participation of organized communities, through a structured series of meetings in each administrative area of a city. With few exceptions, it is used for the allocation of resources owned or managed by local government. This program format is based on the belief that a direct, rather than representative, democracy approach is more effective in ensuring that municipal resource allocation responds to community demands and aspirations.

The way this format usually works is that local government first decides on the sum to be allocated to public works via participatory budgeting—usually a set percentage of a municipality's investment budget for a given year. A certain sum is then allocated to each of the city's different administrative zones. The local government makes these

> **Box 4-10. Social Investment Fund Format: FUPROVI**
>
> Costa Rica's FUPROVI acts in a manner analogous to social fund facilities, but its clients, rather than being municipalities or utilities, are housing associations. A candidate association contacts the organization, whereupon it receives a full briefing on the FUPROVI-assisted mutual-help system. Candidate associations are required to visit FUPROVI projects and have discussions with other associations that are currently working with FUPROVI. After this introduction, the candidate goes through a "dating" stage with FUPROVI, which usually takes a long—sometimes a very long—time (four years in the case of the Lagos de Lindora project). During this time, associations explore other, potentially easier, routes before opting for the rigorous FUPROVI regime. Once they decide to work with FUPROVI and the contract with it is signed, the foundation provides associations with a full spectrum of capacity-building activities; social, technical, and administrative support; bridge financing; and legal assistance. The successful FUPROVI example shows that a funding facility for urban upgrading and shelter must be able to stimulate and organize demand and to offer (directly or through subcontracts) a whole gamut of capacity-building and technical assistance services.

allocative decisions based on resource availability, demands, and opportunities to invest in different parts of the city.

Next, a series of public gatherings by zone is organized; at these, local citizens and organizations present requests and proposals, usually regarding necessary public works such as stormwater drainage, access roads, road paving, or social facilities such as schools and clinics. At this stage, community requests are little more than indications of location and type of works required. They have not yet been the object of a technical assessment or any design work. The proposals are priority ranked at the meetings. Next, the municipality's technical departments screen proposals for technical feasibility and establish preliminary cost estimates. Based upon this screening process, a list of priority public works is defined according to resource availability. This process, pioneered in the early 1990s by the city of Porto Alegre in southern Brazil, has been adopted by several other Brazilian cities, such as Belo Horizonte.

Variations on participatory budgeting have been used in programs in Brazil, Bolivia, and Mexico. In Brazil, participatory budgeting is based on collection of requests and suggestions from the public, but lacks a true participatory area development planning process. Instead, public gatherings are held for each of the administrative regions of a city. These are of course much larger than a single settlement, which is the ideal unit for participatory area planning. Nevertheless, the process of priority setting may be deemed participatory, and is certainly a step forward from the conventional top-down approach, especially for works that are important for single neighborhoods but do not have citywide relevance. The area planning element is missing, however, and therefore priorities are set without a long-term vision of the development of each area.

The example of Belo Horizonte, however, shows that participatory budgeting can be combined with participatory area development planning. In Belo Horizonte, the drawbacks of selecting priority works in the absence of a coherent plan led to the adoption of a sort of participatory area development plan in broad strokes called Plano Global.

Comprehensive Upgrading Program Format. This last program format entails definition of areas of intervention in advance in accordance with a predefined set of criteria and creating the needed conditions for a participatory area-based planning process to take place in each of them. In this format, the community infrastructure and shelter program takes the form of a comprehensive upgrading program[10] for a predetermined part of a city, and each of its component projects is an upgrading project for a particular settlement.

This format was used by the Guarapiranga program's settlement upgrading project, in which the *favelas* and illegal subdivisions that were thought to be the main cause of pollution by household wastes in the area of influence of a large-scale area-based environmental cleanup plan were selected for intervention. At a later stage, as discussed in chapter 7, more communities were included in the upgrading component, due to public pressure.

In the formulation of the World Bank-funded CAMEBA informal settlement upgrading program in Caracas, Venezuela, where a large proportion of the population lives in dense squatter settlements, a set of criteria for project selection was developed to facilitate identification and prioritization of communities whose features corresponded to the program's objectives. It was decided to start with the *barrios* with the highest probability of success, so the program would establish credibility and build capacity to tackle more difficult cases at a later stage. The criteria were aimed at ensuring that the program had sufficient time for

---

[10]The idea of *integrated upgrading* is that a negotiated area development plan taking all the different types of infrastructure into consideration becomes the blueprint for gradual upgrading, but does not necessarily mean that all related works will be undertaken at one time. When they are, this is usually referred to as *comprehensive upgrading*, which is therefore a particular kind of integrated upgrading.

its learning curve and did not begin its activities by tackling the most difficult settlements, which would be an unnecessarily risky proposition. The objective was to evaluate and score each settlement according to the criteria (see box 4-11), and, by attributing weights to each criterion, attribute to each settlement an overall score. The contiguous informal settlement areas that had a higher proportion of higher scoring settlements were selected, since it was thought more advisable to intervene in all the settlements in a given zone, rather than intervening in isolated settlements throughout the city.

Typical Sequence of Activities.

1. Collect existing information regarding the infrastructure and shelter needs of low-income communities and the existing social, technical, environmental, institutional, economic, and financial constraints and opportunities at the local level. At this stage, the program design unit works basically with information made available by the program's participating institutions. Such information, especially that relating specifically to the informal settlements themselves, is often hard to come by, and a special information-gathering effort needs to be made to support program formulation, with assistance from the participating institutions.[11]
2. Finalize identification of the program's key stakeholders and potential partners, and outline the key strategic alliances that will be the backbone of the program's structure. Partners need to be identified within the communities, in the public sector, and in civil society. Also identify willing and able partners from the for-profit private sector (specialized service providers, microfinance institutions or commercial banks, small and medium-sized providers of infrastructure, private utilities, materials and equipment providers, private landowners, etc.).
3. Identify potential financing sources and mechanisms for urban upgrading and shelter initiatives, along with their applicable terms and conditions.

---

[11] One of the few cities where adequate information was available for program design from the outset is Caracas, where a major effort to gather and organize information on the city's barrios—the Plan Sectoral—was undertaken in 1993 and 1994 by a team from the Central University of Venezuela. The availability of this study was a major contribution to the design of the CAMEBA program. The investment made in Caracas by the university to collect and organize the information paid off handsomely in terms of public benefits. Unfortunately, in most cases, no such information is available.

Box 4-11. CAMEBA Program in Caracas, Venezuela: Subproject Selection Criteria

- **Socioeconomic situation.** The prevalence of waterborne diseases and critical poverty, as evaluated by appropriate socioeconomic indicators, were considered criteria for settlement selection.
- **Level of community organization.** Since the existence of a strong network of community-based organizations facilitates the adoption of a participatory approach, it is a good reason for selecting a settlement.
- **Land tenure situation.** It was thought advisable to avoid settlements located on invaded private land due to legal obstacles to land tenure regularization, and instead to focus on settlements located on land belonging to the state, public statutory bodies, or companies, which offer better conditions for tenure regularization.
- **Risk situations and need for resettlement.** It was decided to avoid settlements that, due to occupation of high-risk areas or the need to open new access routes in high-slope areas, would require the removal and resettlement of a large proportion of the residents.
- **Land use constraints.** Some informal settlements are located in areas set aside by law for a specific use. In many instances, it is possible to change land use laws or regulations, but in other cases, it is very difficult or undesirable to do so. An example of a situation in which it is difficult to justify a change in legislation is the case of the barrios that lie inside the El Avila National Park in Caracas. This park is the one nature reserve available to *caraqueños*, and it is unlikely that legislators would agree to compromise its integrity.
- **Overriding public interest.** Some informal settlements are located in areas earmarked for large infrastructure of citywide, or even metropolitan, interest. Unless an alternative location can be found for the infrastructure, it is unwise to upgrade such settlements, since they will almost certainly have to be removed at a future date. A case in point is the linkage between the Cota 1000 freeway and the La Guaira highway in Caracas, which will almost certainly require the removal of a large portion of the barrios that exist along the projected location of the new road. For this reason, it would not be appropriate to select those barrios for upgrading.
- **Existence of trunk infrastructure.** It was thought that settlements located near existing spare capacity in terms of trunk infrastructure should receive priority, since investments will be more cost effective.

4. Identify opportunities and constraints for developing participatory urban upgrading initiatives through analysis of the information gathered and through interviews with key local stakeholders.
5. Assess the existence, interest, and availability of appropriate local expertise through analysis of the information and interviews with key local stakeholders.
6. Develop alternative program features (type, scope, format, and structure) and implementation strategies based on the above.
7. Conduct a workshop with key stakeholders to examine the pros and cons of the various proposed institutional arrangements and implementation strategies and choose one to be explored in detail in Stage 3.

Considerations before Moving On

By the end of this stage and before undertaking the feasibility studies and program formulation stage, key stakeholders should have reached a consensus on the following:

- The most advisable type and format of program to implement and a basic program outline, including types of actions to be undertaken and targeting criteria
- Strategic alliances and institutional roles and responsibilities
- The needed expertise and support services for subsequent phases of the program design cycle and how these would be recruited
- Cost recovery strategies and subsidy design
- Likely sources and uses of program funds.

Stage 3. Feasibility Studies and Program Design

In the prefeasibility stage described above, the program's main features were defined through data gathering, analysis, and discussions with key stakeholders. Next, feasibility studies need to be undertaken in each of the key areas of program design. This allows the program design unit to test the assumptions defined during the prefeasibility stage as well as the proposed program features, and to move on to detailed program design in collaboration with program stakeholders.

Discussion of the results of the feasibility studies with key stakeholders leads to further definition of program features and procedures through the preparation of a preliminary version of a strategic plan and operating manual. Program design is then finalized through a last round of discussions with key stakeholders, which leads to the final version of these two important documents.[12]

- The *strategic plan* provides the general program framework and strategic context; outlines the program rationale; defines program features, design options, and institutional arrangements including roles and responsibilities of key stakeholders, sources and uses of funding, and flow of funds arrangements. The program's major activities are described, including project formulation, evaluation, and approval; procurement policies; and financial and administrative aspects. The strategic plan also spells out technical assistance and training requirements, cost recovery strategies, targeting criteria, monitoring arrangements and impact indicators, and administrative and logistical requirements.
- The operating manual presents, in a clear and concise manner, the program's operating rules and procedures. It usually has annexes presenting terms of reference and templates for frequently used documentation. It presents technical standards and requirements for contractors and service providers, and describes the program's procurement procedures. In the case of programs based on the social investment fund or participatory budgeting formats, it also spells out the specific procedures for receiving, evaluating, approving, funding, contracting, and monitoring the implementation of project proposals presented by the community on the basis of a participatory area planning exercise.

Objectives

To define parameters and procedures for:

- Program institutional and flow of funds arrangements, defining roles and responsibilities of participating institutions, and arrangements for program resource management
- Targeting criteria (e.g., geographic, gender, income, sector)
- Detailed criteria for project identification, building on the preliminary criteria developed during the preceding prefeasibility stage and on the targeting criteria
- Technology options to be used based on previous local experience and careful testing of any new technologies for compatibility with local conditions

---

[12]The contents of a typical strategic plan for an upgrading program and a typical operating manual are in appendices A and B, respectively.

- Expected environmental impacts and the mitigating measures that will be needed
- Involuntary resettlement strategies, including the definition of delivery mechanisms for land and housing to cater to resettlement needs
- Sources and uses of funding for the various program components
- Subsidy structures and cost recovery strategies
- Participatory strategies
- Partnering with civil society and the for-profit private sector.

Key Process Issues

- Availability of baseline data, and especially of information on informal settlements, is a key issue in undertaking the appropriate range of feasibility studies. The information available on informal settlements—such as their delimitation, needs profile, willingness and capacity to pay, or social composition—is normally very limited. To collect and organize such information will have a cost impact, and this needs to be taken into account when deciding on the level of resources to devote to the program design effort.
- The existence of a strong core team operating at the local level is a key requirement for the feasibility studies and program formulation stage. If there is no appreciable local expertise on urban upgrading, it will need to be secured elsewhere. Such specific expertise, regardless of whether it is local, will have to be integrated into a local team whose members know the area, people, institutions, history of institutional relations, and other local information relevant to the process.
- Adequate resources and time need to be devoted at this stage if it is to lay a sound foundation for the program. Involving key stakeholders, for example, takes some time and requires the organization of workshops or similar public forums for the discussion and debate of specific issues. The process also needs to be made transparent and understandable to all stakeholders, which in turn requires the preparation of user-friendly documentation. All of this has a cost, but the investment made in careful formulation will certainly add to the program's chances of success and help in avoiding costly mistakes.
- Detailed feasibility studies are a major contribution to sound program design. In certain cases, however, local circumstances or resource availability may make it impractical to undertake all the studies needed or desired. The program design unit must then make do with an analysis of indirect data so as to infer the necessary in-

formation.[13] As elsewhere, our recommendations in this section are based on good practice and are meant to be used with discernment, according to local needs and conditions.

Typical Sequence of Activities

Feasibility Studies.
1. Collect and systematically present baseline data for each component.[14]
2. Conduct individual feasibility studies:
   - **Legal and regulatory analysis**, in which the legal and regulatory framework is studied, obstacles to program implementation are identified, and recommendations are made as to the appropriate course of action to deal with each obstacle (e.g., promoting settlement regularization and upgrading within the existing framework or promoting the introduction of new legislation or procedures as appropriate). Legal and regulatory provisions to be studied include those that apply to land tenure, land subdivision, urban upgrading, and housing—e.g., the legal status of community-based organizations, building codes (and especially the relationship between existing engineering standards and those of any innovative technologies the program intends to use), local physical planning bylaws and regulations, land rights and land registration systems, and regulations for financial institutions which constrain the implementation of housing and infrastructure catering to the poor.
   - **Social analysis**, which looks at key features of the target communities, their history and level of organization, leadership structure, presence of support organizations, area-based community organizations and special interest groups, the participation and

---

[13]For instance, a study on willingness and ability to pay for infrastructure and services is a valuable input when defining the subsidy structure and cost recovery strategy of a program. If local circumstances or resource availability make it impractical to undertake a full contingent valuation-based willingness to pay study, the program design unit may use an analysis of indirect data, such as current patterns of payment to water vendors, to infer the necessary information. This would certainly be a suboptimal solution, but probably the best one available under the circumstances.

[14]In the prefeasibility stage, the program design unit works basically with information that is made available by the program's participating institutions. This allows the unit to identify information gaps and plan the information-gathering exercise that will be necessary in the later feasibility stage.

overall situation and requirements of women, and the community's main demands and expectations in relation to the program, with recommendations regarding the participatory strategy to be followed, in relation to the level and degree of participation to be pursued and the support structure that will be necessary.
- **Technical/environmental analysis**, in which existing levels and main technological alternatives for infrastructure provision and their cost, suitability, labor requirements,[15] and environmental impacts are analyzed and discussed with technicians from participating institutions and with local residents; recommendations are made as to the use of technological alternatives for each type of infrastructure; and the resettlement needs of the program are analyzed in relation to the presence of risk areas, removals related to the need for new access routes or reduction of density in very crowded areas, etc. At this stage, the program design unit also needs to look into the availability of suitable land in or near the area to absorb the resettled population.
- **Institutional capacity analysis**, in which the structure, functions, and levels of capacity of each institution in terms of equipment, human resources, technical and management experience, and knowledge and experience of participatory approaches are studied in depth, and proposals are made regarding the impact of existing capacity on alternative institutional arrangements and required capacity-building activities. One of the key outputs of the institutional capacity analysis is the recommended institutional arrangement for the program, including the location and degree of decentralization of program management activities.
- **Economic analysis**, including a profile of demand, a cost-benefit analysis (with sensitivity analysis), a least-cost analysis, and an analysis of the distribution of program benefits. Whenever possible, a willingness-to-pay and affordability study should also be undertaken. The scenarios developed by the economic analysis should be used to make recommendations regarding the subsidy structure and cost recovery strategy of the program.[16]

---

[15]The use of labor-intensive construction techniques allows urban upgrading and housing programs to provide significant employment opportunities and should be pursued whenever possible.

[16]For a thorough treatment of economic analysis, see World Bank, Learning and Leadership Center and Operations Policy Department (1996).

- **Financial analysis** of the participating institutions, looking at their sources of revenue, financing mechanisms, and level and structure of debt to gauge the potential contributions each institution will be able to make and recommend a financing structure and resource management arrangement for the program.

3. Develop a feasibility report, containing drafts of the strategic plan and operating manual. At a minimum, the feasibility report should include:

    - A summary of baseline information for the distinct program components
    - Identification of constraints and opportunities for the development of a participatory urban upgrading program
    - Measures to address specific constraints and make use of specific opportunities
    - Institutional and flow of funds arrangements, including an outline of the strategic alliances and commitments of each party
    - Preliminary identification of the technological options to be used and their cost implications
    - Preliminary list of geographic areas of intervention, with an outline of the needed interventions both within and outside informal settlement areas[17]
    - Evaluation of involuntary resettlement needs and strategy to address these needs
    - List and proposed roles of key community-based, government, civil society, and for-profit private sector participants
    - Outline of a socio-technical support strategy, with a cost estimate
    - Outline of a technical assistance and capacity-building strategy, with a cost estimate
    - Cost estimate of investment requirements (within ±10 percent accuracy)
    - Funding and cost recovery arrangements
    - Rollout strategy for the program
    - Terms of reference for the development of more detailed versions of any of the documents prepared during the feasibility studies, when needed
    - Terms of reference for developing contractual arrangements between and among stakeholders

---

[17]Informal settlement upgrading normally requires interventions outside the settlements themselves for the construction or renewal of the trunk infrastructure—roads, water and sewer mains, etc.—that connects settlements to the rest of the city.

- Terms of reference to hire the needed expertise for the subsequent stages.

Participatory Program Formulation. Stakeholder participation in program formulation contributes to the enhancement of stakeholder ownership of the program, demand-responsiveness of the arrangements, and the establishment of the strategic alliances that are the engine of many a successful program. For example, it is difficult to imagine that, if the municipality of São Paulo had not been involved in the design of the Guarapiranga program from the start, it would have assumed such a leading role in the program's settlement upgrading component. The typical sequence of activities in participatory program formulation is as follows:

1. Finalize selection of key program stakeholders and partners from government, community, the for-profit private sector, and civil society.
2. Define and implement a strategy to disseminate and discuss feasibility study findings and impacts on program structure with potential governmental, community, civil society, for-profit private sector, and donor stakeholders and partners.
3. Establish working groups with key stakeholders and program partners to work on specific aspects of program formulation.
4. In collaboration with the key stakeholders and program partners, refine the preliminary version of the strategic plan.
5. Develop proposals for contractual arrangements with program partners from government, community, the for-profit private sector, civil society, and the general public.
6. In collaboration with the key stakeholders and program partners, refine the preliminary version of the operating manual.
7. In collaboration with the program partners, develop a rollout strategy for the program (see Stage 5).

Considerations before Moving On

- The results of the feasibility studies and of the participatory program formulation exercise should be sufficient for a final decision to be reached by funding and implementing agencies on moving ahead with the program. The information thus gathered should allow for the preparation and adoption of all the formal agreements that will be required in the specific circumstances of the program. It should also be sufficient to guide the program's start-up phase.
- As soon as all formal approvals are obtained and a loan agreement (or other applicable document) is signed, the agencies concerned may move toward setting up the project management unit. It is

often the case that the existing program design unit responsible for program formulation is expanded and given additional capacity at this stage and converted into the program management unit.

Stage 4. Establishing a Program Monitoring and Evaluation System

Monitoring and evaluation, including measurement of program impact, provide essential feedback for the successful implementation of an urban upgrading policy. In fact, one of the main reasons for the partial failure of many upgrading initiatives is the lack of a reliable monitoring and evaluation system that may sound an alarm when things are going less than well. On the other hand, the lack of emphasis on monitoring and evaluation makes it difficult to gauge the real impact of many projects that seem successful. It also makes them difficult to replicate, since there is rarely an audit trail or record of how decisions were made or actions that were taken, what the situation was before the project started, and what changes were brought about by the project.

In this section, we provide a brief outline of the monitoring and evaluation system that needs to be established as an essential component of the design of an upgrading program. In so doing, we differentiate between *project* monitoring and *program* monitoring. Monitoring and evaluation need to be undertaken as a regular feature of the projects that make up a program. Information from project monitoring and evaluation, coupled with that drawn from program-wide monitoring, will make up the program's monitoring and evaluation system.

Objectives

- To monitor the development of the program as a whole and of its component projects with regard to goals, time lines, and any unforeseen circumstances that may occur.
- To measure the impact of the program and of its component projects.
- To implement a rapid problem identification system as well as a system for internal communications to the various stakeholders.
- To facilitate evaluation procedures during and after activities through the definition of specific indicators.
- To be able to correct the course of the program or of its component projects during their implementation according to reliable feedback.
- To establish parameters in relation to cost, time requirements, performance of implementation arrangements and technological alternatives, etc., as a contribution to future upgrading activities in the same city and elsewhere.

Key Process Issues

In addition to daily control over project operations, deadlines, and any problems that may arise, the institution promoting a development program, or an administration responsible for policy implementation, should also perform periodic evaluations of the program or policy as a whole. Such evaluations are needed to gauge the results obtained by each stage of implementation of the program or policy within its economic, social, cultural, institutional, and environmental context.

In this regard, the key process issues relate to different types of performance indicators. Specifically, they relate to indicators for:

- Program monitoring in terms of input and output
- Evaluating program outcomes, i.e., the impact of upgrading programs on living conditions
- Project monitoring through effectiveness, efficiency, and pertinence indicators—which relate to input and output—and "reality monitoring"—which relates to impact.

Gauging the changes brought about by the project and its long-term impact is essential. One of the functions of monitoring and evaluation is to ensure that the resources devoted to a program are put to good use and that the program is competently managed, which is done by tracking input and output. Monitoring and evaluation, however, must go beyond that to assess development impact. This is an assessment that can only be made long after the completion of each project, however. Programs that have a long-term perspective must go back to evaluate projects undertaken in their earlier years, and the time and resources needed to do so must be considered from the start in program design.

Indicators for Program Monitoring. Angel (1999) defines 10 indicators for monitoring the progress of upgrading programs:

- **Program coverage structure:** the proportion of households living in unauthorized settlements where the upgrading program has been fully implemented, partially implemented, planned, surveyed, and untouched.
- **Program coverage potential:** the proportion of households living in unauthorized settlements where the program can be legally implemented.
- **Tenure registration structure:** the proportion of housing units in unauthorized settlements with fully registered ownership documents, partial registration in some approved form, and no registration at all.

- **Program cost-to-income ratio:** the ratio of the median cost per household of implementing the upgrading program and the median household income in the city during the past year.
- **Program cost structure:** the proportion of total program cost to date spent on overhead, surveying and planning, infrastructure, titling, social services, compensation to landowners, and resettlement.
- **Program time horizon:** the time required to fully implement the program to serve all the population living in existing and anticipated unauthorized housing, given the program implementation rate during the latest year.
- **Housing subsidy structure:** the proportion of the total government subsidy to the housing sector (both on the books and off the books) allocated to urban upgrading, housing allowances, public and public-assisted housing, interest-rate subsidies, and tax credits.
- **Cost recovery rate:** the percentage of the total cost of the program to date that has been recovered during the latest year.
- **Program decentralization structure:** the proportion of total program cost to date spent by central government, transferred and spent by local government, transferred and spent by voluntary organizations, and transferred and spent by communities.
- **Program privatization structure:** the proportion of total program cost to date spent by government agencies, nongovernment agencies, the private sector, and as self-help work by members of the community.

Indicators of Impact of Upgrading Programs on Housing Conditions. Angel (1999) notes that the impact of upgrading programs on housing conditions can be gauged, for example, through a before-and-after comparison of housing conditions in a group of communities that underwent an upgrading process. He continues:

> A second form of linkage is a control-group comparison of housing conditions between communities which underwent an upgrading program and a control group of communities in similar circumstances which did not undergo such a program. A third, more analytical, form of linkage is econometric modeling, where variations in housing conditions—in different communities, cities or countries—are explained statistically through variations in a number of other variables that describe the upgrading program.

Typical indicators of housing conditions mentioned by Angel include the land price-to-income ratio, house value-to-income ratio, rent-to-income ratio, owner occupancy, credit-to-value ratio, indices of quality of construction and infrastructure, floor area per person, residential economic activity, and residential mobility.

Indicators for Project Monitoring. A system of appropriate indicators must be developed for use in project monitoring. This system should comprise two types of indicators:

- Those that allow a sort of "reality monitoring," which are the basis for an evaluation of impact
- Those that look at effectiveness, efficiency, and pertinence, which relate to input and output.

An appropriate balance should be sought between *input indicators* (e.g., the length of pipe installed in a sewerage project), *output indicators* (e.g., the number of sewer connections installed), and *impact indicators* (e.g., a measurable reduction in the incidence of waterborne disease). Impact indicators are harder to measure, but essential in ensuring that a program or project gets its real job done. Statistics about road paving, for example, tell us nothing about access and mobility improvements for the poor if mentioned in isolation. As Angel (1999) notes, "monitoring the progress of upgrading programs tells us little about their impact."

Reality Monitoring. All development programs or policies (and particularly those that aim to improve informal settlements) can be seen as initiatives for fighting poverty and social exclusion as well as for strengthening social capital (CERFE 1998). Indicators relative to reality monitoring should therefore be focused on three orders of macro-phenomena: poverty, social exclusion, and social capital.

If we define poverty as a continued deprivation of the means of well-being over time, we could consider the following six points as poverty indicators, as a proportion of the target population:

- Homes built with nonpermanent materials
- Households that do not have access to safe water supplies
- Households that do not have access to sanitation facilities
- Economically active individuals with annual incomes lower than the income poverty line of the country in question
- Children between the ages of 5 and 14 who do not attend school
- Children who are malnourished.

Obviously, not all changes recorded over time with regard to the conditions of poverty, social exclusion, and social capital can be considered solely as effects of the project being monitored. For example, if a project implements environmental sanitation activities and a clear improvement of health indicators is recorded, there will probably be a connection between the two. In this situation, the variation of health indicators would measure, even if indirectly, the effects of the project. This first subsystem of indicators should make it possible to monitor the evolution of the economic, social, cultural, institutional, and environmental contexts and thereby gauge project impact, although it is well known that development impacts often take time to materialize.

Effectiveness, Efficiency, and Pertinence Indicators. The second subsystem should be formed by specific indicators pertaining to the activities undertaken and their expected results. Obviously, these indicators can be conceived only in conjunction with the formulation of their corresponding activities. They should include:

- Effectiveness indicators to (1) measure the level of execution of the various activities within a program or project (for example, in the case of constructing a sewerage system, one can measure the length of pipes installed in relation to the total to be installed; in a training activity, one can analyze the number of people who participated in specific activities in relation to the anticipated beneficiaries; etc.) and (2) measure the satisfaction of participants (or beneficiaries) regarding specific activities.
- Efficiency indicators, which can be determined by comparing actual costs with those budgeted for specific activities, actual time of implementation with the time frame originally proposed, and actual costs with those incurred by analogous projects.
- Pertinence indicators, which can be determined by linking the specific outputs of the project to the variations in the related indicators in the first subsystem (for example, changes in the youth unemployment rate—an impact—would be related to the number of jobs created for youths by specific project activities—an output).

By linking the various outputs produced by the program with social exclusion factors on the one hand and social capital factors on the other, it is possible to gauge the extent to which the activities of the program produce the kind of improvement in social indicators that was intended.

Typical Sequence of Activities

The development of the appropriate indicators needs to be an integral part of the program formulation exercise. The establishment of procedures for the regular collection of the information needed to measure these indicators needs to be envisaged and spelled out during the preparation of the operating manual and taken into account by the program's management information system (see box 4-12).

During the implementation period of each project, the system of indicators described above could be used as follows:

> **Box 4-12. Management Information Systems**
>
> An appropriate management information system (MIS) is a key requirement for effective monitoring and evaluation of program implementation. One of the key tasks in the program formulation stage is to design an MIS that will allow program managers to act on sufficient and reliable information. A typical MIS would be composed of two main subsystems: a process subsystem and a management information subsystem.
>
> The process subsystem is comprised of eight modules that allow the program coordination unit to manage and process information from the full project cycle, from project identification to operations and maintenance:
>
> - Record and manage project requests
> - Request prioritization module
> - Request evaluation module
> - Project approval module
> - Procurement and contracting module
> - Supervision module
> - Accounting module
> - Ex-post evaluation module.
>
> The management information subsystem consists of six modules that allow the program coordination unit to manage and process general information:
>
> - Targeting and programming module
> - Baseline information module
> - Program promotion module
> - Program budgeting module
> - Work assignment planning and workload control module
> - Performance and impact indicators module.

- The reality monitoring indicators would be measured once a year. Secondary information sources would be tapped most of the time, although rapid on-site research would be conducted on an ad hoc basis. As mentioned above, the variations of the indicators would be evaluated. In this manner, indirect information on the development of the project can be obtained.
- The efficiency, effectiveness, and pertinence indicators would be measured frequently based on the internal documentation of the project and through rapid on-site appraisal techniques.

Special attention needs to be paid to the timely execution of monitoring activities. Delays can lead to a loss of control during project implementation, with negative economic consequences and loss of impact.

Program monitoring—gathering and processing project implementation data and monitoring a set of indicators such as the ones suggested above—is one of the core functions of the program management unit. If indicators are well-designed and consistently monitored, stakeholders can be kept abreast of the program's development, and participatory evaluation techniques (see box 4-13) can be used to gauge the results obtained during each stage of implementation, to correct shortcomings in its operating strategy, and to adapt the program to changes in the circumstances in which it operates.

Considerations before Moving On

Before moving on to the program rollout and project implementation stage, it is essential to have a reliable monitoring and evaluation system firmly in place. The definition of responsibilities for data collection, pro-

---

Box 4-13. Participatory Evaluation

Participatory evaluation provides essential feedback on project implementation and impact; it also increases community involvement and sense of ownership. The opinion of the residents about the progress and impacts of the project is invaluable, since they are both key actors and subject to the change processes that upgrading sets in motion.

Technicians and residents should be open to each individual's point of view. They also need to understand the importance of critical assessment of their own actions as well as those of others. In participatory evaluation, both the evaluators and the evaluated are subjects of the same common work, although in different roles and conditions.

The evaluation will conclude a phase in the work, but will not conclude the process. Findings should be used as input for planning the next phase, as a basis for interventions in other areas, and as indicators of the residents' progress toward autonomy and self-reliance. Some issues to be considered in participatory evaluation are highlighted below.

In relation to the project
- Objectives
- Activities
- Expected and achieved results
- Positive and negative impacts
- Aspects enhancing or obstructing community mobilization.

In relation to the residents
- **Community identity:** evaluation of people's investment in the project and perception of internal community dynamics, relationship to their surroundings, and level of solidarity

cessing, and storage is as important as the definition of good indicators. It is also important to estimate the cost of monitoring and evaluation activities and to include this in the program budget. Before moving on to the program rollout stage, the organizations promoting the program should have reached an agreement on the definition of responsibilities and on the sources of funding for monitoring and evaluation activities. Proper monitoring and evaluation are as important for the success of upgrading and housing programs as are physical investments, and it is essential to ensure that the appropriate resources and capacity are in place. If monitoring and evaluation are an integral part of program activities from the start, it is easier to overcome the resistance of staff who often fear the threat posed by monitoring as a judgment on their performance. Finally, care should be taken not to waste resources by "overshooting the mark" by generating an excessive amount of data that will not be used.

- **Interpersonal relationships:** dealing with differences of opinion and conflicts between residents and leaders and with external agents, as well as conflicts among the residents themselves
- **Social and political awareness:** notions about rights and responsibilities
- **Critical ability:** perceptions about the actions and services offered by the external agents and the role of the socio-technical support providers
- **Autonomy:** identification of attitudes of self-reliance and initiative, and of attitudes of passivity and submission on the part of the community
- **Self-reliance of community organizations:** movements toward financial and administrative autonomy of the representative bodies
- **Capability for self-criticism:** perception of residents' own weaknesses and willingness to overcome them.

In relation to the services provided by external agents
- **Technicians' knowledge** about the object of their work and ability to clarify residents' doubts concerning ongoing work
- **Coordination of groups by the technicians:** ability to facilitate group activities and type of relationship established with the community
- **Critical ability of the technicians:** perception of the dynamics within the community and in terms of relations with the other agents, and quality of services rendered
- **Capability for self-criticism:** perception of the weaknesses of their technical actions and willingness to correct their course
- **Pertinence of the work:** services that meet the real needs of the population
- **Quality of services:** level of satisfaction with the services rendered.

Stage 5. Rolling out the Program

A good rollout strategy is essential for a successful program. The first year or so of operations usually needs to be devoted to setting up and testing the institutional and administrative machinery of the program. This should not be seen as a waste of time, but rather as an insurance policy on future performance.

This section deals with the key issues to be addressed during program rollout, namely:

- **Administrative/operational issues**, which have to do with building central implementation capacity at the program level, by organizing the program management unit, starting out small, and setting up a pool of service providers
- **Project/process issues**, which have to do with building capacity in areas that are essential for the implementation of each of the projects that make up the program, i.e., setting up a social marketing strategy, participatory information gathering and analysis, participatory area development planning, and engineering and design.

Organizing the Program Management Unit

The first key issue to be addressed during the program rollout stage is to organize the program management unit—the agency that will direct and coordinate the process, and the relations between the different partners.

As we have seen, the decision as to the institutional affiliation, location and degree of autonomy, and decentralization of program management functions is taken in the feasibility and program design stage, following the analysis and discussion of alternatives that takes place in the prefeasibility stage.

In the program rollout stage, the agencies promoting the program need to recruit the necessary staff for the program management unit and prepare adequate facilities and logistics for its operation. The options in this regard are many and are directly influenced by the decisions made in regard to the institutional affiliation, location, and degree of autonomy and decentralization of the unit. A new, independent agency created solely for the purposes of the program will probably be located outside of the participating institutions and will have the opportunity to hire staff from the outside. On the other hand, when a program management unit is established within an existing agency, existing facilities and staff are normally utilized. Between these two extremes, many possible permutations and combinations are possible. The most common one combines new staff with existing staff, with some degree of use of existing facilities and logistics.

An option that is often followed is to strengthen the existing program design unit, giving it the needed resources along with new management responsibilities. This approach has obvious advantages, shortening the program management unit's learning curve considerably, since the group that leads the program design effort is already familiar with all the stakeholders and program partners, and with the arrangements and procedures chosen and the reasons behind them.

Starting out Small: The Importance of Pilot Projects

At the start-up phase of an upgrading program, it is wise to devote the first year of operations to setting up and oiling the institutional machinery and to building capacity. This usually includes undertaking one or more pilot projects meant to test out the proposed methodology for project identification, planning, design, implementation, and monitoring.

Urban upgrading is always complex, and it is a good practice to achieve scale through a series of incremental steps, which involves learning by doing, rather than trying to start a program already at scale.

As noted previously, low-income communities usually have already been building their settlement for years, and some form of informal community upgrading project already exists. By giving itself a little time to learn how best to relate to its target communities and coordinate the actions of its stakeholders, a program increases its own chances of success.

The number and location of pilot projects that are undertaken will depend upon the overall scale of the program. Efforts should therefore be made to undertake a number of pilots that are representative of the different types of areas in which the intervention is proposed, but care should be taken to ensure that the scale of the pilot project activities does not overwhelm a fledgling program management unit.

Note that these pilot projects should be just that—test runs taken within the framework of a larger initiative. Too often, pilot projects are conducted as small projects intended to test out an approach or prove a point and are funded, staffed, and managed on a one-off basis. Although there is usually reference in pilot project proposals to future replication and scaling up, even successful pilot projects often find it difficult to generate sufficient interest and funding for follow up initiatives. The frustrating result is that pilot projects are seldom scaled up and seldom reach critical mass. Furthermore, whatever good results they may achieve are ascribed by skeptics to particular circumstances that would not work at a larger scale. Therefore, when we refer to a pilot project, we mean an initiative undertaken by a program management unit that is consciously testing project methodologies for a larger initiative whose funding is already ensured.

Setting up a Pool of Service Providers

One of the key concerns of the program rollout stage is to ensure that an adequate pool of service providers is available locally for the various tasks to be performed. The identification of these providers is relatively easy with regard to conventional tasks such as those related to construction, but more difficult when it comes to project "software" aspects such as socio-technical support.

Activities at this stage should therefore focus upon building local capacity, either within the program management unit or in the local nonprofit and for-profit private sector, ensuring the emergence of a sufficient number of organizations and practitioners with the necessary skills. The program can then hire the necessary expertise and operational support from this pool.

The provider of socio-technical support may be the municipality (as in Tijuana), a private contractor (as in Guarapiranga), a nonprofit private contractor (like FUPROVI, in its work for the National Housing and Urban Development Institute in San Juan de Pavas), or an NGO that is itself the project promoter (as is the case for FUPROVI in its usual work).

In the cases studied, we found that the existence of competing private organizations in service provision can make a program more accountable and demand-responsive. It can also enhance its efficiency and effectiveness by letting the program management unit focus on strategy and coordination. If there is a clear and consistent procurement policy to ensure a level playing field and a steady flow of contracts, the work opportunities generated by a program are a strong factor in encouraging the establishment and development of a range of for-profit and nonprofit private actors. However, it is usually necessary to "prime the pump" by publicizing the existence and key features of the program, as well as the specific opportunities it offers, and providing opportunities for capacity-building. A prime opportunity for capacity-building is offered by the implementation of pilot projects as described above.

Who should be offered capacity-building opportunities? Normally, there are individuals and organizations that are identified during the program design phase as having qualifications, a background, and interest in community work that make them natural candidates. In addition, it is advisable to seek and screen applications from other interested individuals and organizations both at the local level and farther afield. Successful service providers operating in other cities in the same country, or even internationally if the size of the program justifies it, may also be brought into the project. This approach may contribute to faster development of the local capacity pool if they are required to operate with a local partner.

Once this initial screening process is completed, it will be possible to establish a list of prequalified service providers that can compete for the contracts generated by the program. The program management unit will need to establish and publicize a clear procurement policy and accompanying procedures to ensure equal opportunities. It will also need to periodically revise and update the list of prequalified providers to add new providers and to disqualify existing providers with a poor performance record.

As is seen from the experiences in the case studies, socio-technical support contracts may be awarded either by the program management unit or directly by community-based organizations. Direct community contracts enhance the demand-driven nature, the accountability, and the client orientation of the whole exercise. However, these will require a similar set of conditions, in terms of local capacity and representative structure, that apply to community management (as described in chapter 3). It may therefore be necessary to build capacity at the community level prior to pursuing a strategy of community-based contracts.

In programs that adopt a social investment fund or participatory budgeting format, the community will need to hire an intermediary organization to help it design project proposals, which will be evaluated by the program management unit. This methodology has the advantage of "conditioning" the contract for socio-technical support during project implementation to the success of the initial project proposal. It also provides the community with an opportunity to test the intermediary organization before a longer term commitment is made and provides an obvious incentive to the organization in terms of client orientation and level of performance.

In programs that adopt the upgrading program format, the community would hire an intermediary organization to assist it throughout the project cycle.

Setting up a Social Marketing Strategy

The main steps in devising and establishing a social marketing strategy are outlined and discussed below. We begin with a discussion of social campaigns, one of the main instruments of social marketing, and move on to a discussion of communication planning, control and evaluation, and communication tools.

Social Campaigns. The social marketing strategy of a program is normally carried out through one or more social campaigns—organized communication efforts carried out by a program or project promoter. Social campaigns are aimed at stimulating participation and/or producing changes in the ideas, practices, and behavior of the target population. Such changes can be classified as cognitive changes, changes of behavior, and changes of values as described below.

- *Cognitive changes* provide new information to people and raise their awareness level. They are brought about through campaigns to inform or educate the target population, such as environmental education and adult literacy efforts.
- *Behavioral changes* are more difficult to achieve than cognitive changes, because they involve changing deep-rooted personal and collective habits, learning new ones, and sustaining the new behavior. Campaigns dealing with habits related to solid waste disposal, correct use of sanitation facilities, and personal hygiene are examples of campaigns aimed at behavioral changes.
- The last category of changes refers to the *change of deeply rooted values* and beliefs. Examples would be campaigns about family planning or the importance of schooling.

Social marketing uses segmentation, research, and direct communication concepts to maximize the response of the various groups in a community to social communication campaigns. These campaigns must be structured and oriented to the needs of each specific audience, including its socio-demographic characteristics, sociological profile, and behavioral characteristics. They should also identify and target influential groups that may affect the success of the program or project.

The objective of social marketing is more than simply transferring information—it should also concern itself with the meaning and quality of its messages to be an effective tool for forging consensus among the community and promoting desirable changes in perceptions and behavior. For example, if a project wants to stimulate participation—in addition to offering information about the possibilities and benefits available through the project—the content of the messages should be based on the factors that are known to motivate participation.

Communication Planning. Communication planning is the foundation for the formulation of social marketing strategy and tactics. The development of the scope of communication work will be based on the results of participatory information gathering and analysis, particularly the information on key variables of the program; what it controls and is responsible for, its strengths and weaknesses, and an analysis of the external environment in which it operates.

The information on which communication planning will be based should be organized as follows:

- Specific aims of the program and its processes
- Social objectives and goals of the program
- Dimension and coverage
- Service criteria
- Limitations of the program
- Comparable experiences
- Alternative methods for execution of an information and communication campaign
- Training requirements for social and technical teams to disseminate information
- The participatory strategy envisaged.

The focus of a communication strategy can be the individual, groups in the community, or the target population as a whole. Success in disseminating new ideas and social practices and getting the target groups involved will be based on the knowledge of their objectives and aspirations, and on appropriate segmentation. Nevertheless, as the goals of the various communication campaigns undertaken by a program are different, depending on whether they seek information and mobilization for action, cognitive changes, or changes of behavior and even of values and beliefs, these goals will determine the tactics to be used.

Relatively simple tactics are generally sufficient to bring about cognitive changes. However, to obtain mobilization for action, several cognitive tactics are required, followed by tactics that generate interest, create the willingness to act, and lead individuals to take action. Goals requiring changes of behavior demand, in addition, tactics that encourage the repetition of activity by experimentation (confirmation) and tactics that provide follow-up (to ensure continuity).

Monitoring and Evaluation of the Communication Plan. Monitoring of the main indicators of means employed and results achieved is an essential mechanism that allows feedback and the reorientation of actions toward the objectives of the program's social marketing strategy. The main aspects that are normally monitored are the following:

- **Performance and effectiveness of the strategy and the sequence of tactics:** appropriateness of message, language, and medium; adequacy of contents and strategies regarding population profile and preferences
- **Performance of the agents of social marketing:** flow of messages and mobility, dissemination of messages, uniformity of the messages transmitted; engagement and motivation of the population
- **Responses of target population:** assimilation of information, increased capacity to take initiatives, increased demand for information, engagement and motivation.

Communication Tools.

- **Personal contact.** Often the most effective means of communication, personal contact (e.g., word of mouth and house-to-house visits) is a crucial element of any communication strategy in housing and upgrading. Its importance is such that grassroots organizations, working with limited budgets, may achieve better results with it than through elaborate communication campaigns.
- **Signs, banners, placards, posters.** Media of high visual impact, these transmit messages quickly for informative and educational campaigns. These may be placed in the streets, or on the walls of buildings, or in schools and religious and community centers.
- **Scale models, plans, thematic maps.** These visual models can support the dialogue between the technical team and the community in the initial presentation phases of the project and in the stages related to discussion and approval of alternative solutions and a general intervention plan.
- **Community newspaper.** This reflects daily life in the community and reports and comments on local events. It may be a useful mechanism in establishing credibility with the population and transmitting messages rapidly.
- **Community/local radio.** This is a medium of high impact and mass appeal. It transmits messages with great speed, which may be quickly passed on to other members of the community.
- **Loudspeakers.** These are important for speed of communication, wide coverage, and flexibility in announcing community meetings at short notice. Loudspeakers may be fixed or mounted on vehicles for wide-ranging dissemination of messages.
- **Video and slide presentations.** These types of media may be used for presentations for educational purposes, as a complement to other technical information for training, or as a means for stimulating discussion in focus groups.
- **Brochures, folders, leaflets, primers, manuals.** These various tools provide different formats according to the type of message to be delivered to the public. They allow for accurate dissemination of a specific message and concepts.
- **Workshops.** A workshop is an important mechanism for information exchange, discussion, and feedback, as well as interactive training to promote capacity-building. The format of a workshop is highly flexible and may be adapted to suit the participants.
- **Direct mailing.** Although this is a relatively expensive form of communication, it may be useful to send customized material by post to a specific audience that has been previously selected and targeted.

- **Didactic games.** There is a wide range of games or group activities that can serve to stimulate learning and promote interaction and participation among community members.

Participatory Information Gathering and Analysis

As discussed in chapter 3, community-based information gathering and analysis is one of the key activities for participatory planning. The main steps in participatory information gathering and analysis are outlined and discussed below.

Note that this section refers to information gathering and analysis at the *project* level, which is different and separate from the information-gathering exercise undertaken during *program* design. During the program rollout stage, the concern is to establish capacity for the participatory information gathering and analysis that will be an important activity for each of the program's component projects.

The importance of this exercise should not be underestimated, so it is necessary to consider the capacity available for undertaking these activities. In particular, the availability of socio-technical support will be a crucial factor for a number of reasons, in particular to:

- Clarify residents' queries
- Represent the project and serve as a conduit for complaints and suggestions, referring the questioner to the appropriate authority where necessary
- Respond and intervene rapidly to any internal or external conflicts.

The availability throughout the project of on-call socio-technical support to local residents from a social worker or technician is also important. This support must be available at easily accessible locations within or near the area and at specified times.

Preliminary Information Gathering and Community Mobilization. First of all, a preliminary picture of the level of community organization and the community's priorities and aspirations needs to be drawn. This can be done in the following way:

1. A rapid investigation can be carried out by conducting interviews with key informants, such as those who lead neighborhood development organizations, religious groups, sports clubs, or commercial organizations.
2. Once the interviews are completed, the participants are invited to evaluate the results together with the outside experts. In this manner, a more realistic picture of the situation, its opportunities and constraints, and the community's interest in the project emerges.

3. The next step is to inform and mobilize the community so as to coordinate the specific tasks associated with the formal collection of information through conduct of a diagnostic survey (see below for more information). This survey consists of qualitative interviews and assessments plus a quantitative social and physical census of the area, involving all residents.

The objective during this phase is to communicate directly with as wide a range as possible of local residents, and not only with the leaders. This may be achieved by calling large meetings of specific social sectors and by announcing them through a variety of media (radio, mobile loudspeakers, posters, newspaper advertisements).

The first general assembly is an important occasion to present the general goals of the project, its promoters, and the technical team with which the community will be dealing throughout the project.

Participatory Diagnostic Survey. Data collection for the diagnostic survey entails the use of several survey methods and sources to study the area's infrastructure and shelter problems while outlining its socioeconomic characteristics. Besides gathering information about the physical, economic, and social infrastructure, the survey also aims to document the community's development history, organization, and leadership profile as well as the availability of economic and human resources that may be used during the project.

The first task is to organize the information that is already available to the different organizations and entities promoting the project. Immediately thereafter, the following instruments may be used.

Quantitative Survey of the Physical and Socioeconomic Environment. If the project envisages a wide-ranging intervention, the quantitative survey is usually conducted in a census format in which all households are interviewed. This survey is preceded or done in tandem with an all-important operation called *enrollment*.[18] Each of the structures in the area of intervention receives a numbered identification tag that records the household or households inhabiting the structure. This identification tag is important, as it is the document that ensures participation in the upgrading project, and a copy is given to the head of each household. Any opportunists settling in the area after this time to take advantage of the upgrading project will not be eligible to participate; in this manner, the scope of the project is defined at the outset and remains constant long enough to enable the planning process to take root.

---

[18]Note that an information campaign about the enrollment initiative and the quantitative survey's objectives and mechanisms needs to be conducted prior to their undertaking. See the previous section, "Setting up a Social Marketing Strategy."

The quantitative survey of the physical environment usually begins by collecting data regarding housing and infrastructure, including:

- Type of use and occupation of structure (e.g., commercial, residential, owner-occupied, rented)
- Duration of residential or commercial use
- Access to footpath or road
- Building materials and state of repair of structures
- Existence and state of indoor plumbing, electricity outlets, and other facilities
- Existence and state of repair of latrines or other means of sanitation
- Existence and state of repair of legal or clandestine hookups to water supplies, sewers, and electricity
- Existence of trunk infrastructure in or near the area
- Risk situations.

Physical survey data is complemented by the collection of socioeconomic data, which generally includes:

- Age and sex of household members
- Marital status of the head of the household
- Literacy, level of instruction, profession, and employment of the members of the household
- Sources and level of income, and household patterns of consumption and expenditure.

A complete list of the information collected by the quantitative socioeconomic survey is shown in box 4-14. Box 4-15 describes the tools that may be used during a participatory diagnostic survey for understanding the organization and profiles of community leaders.

Data collection may be conducted either by community members or by interviewers from outside the community. In both cases, the key to success relates to the ability of interviewers to engage community members in the exercise and obtain access to local information and knowledge. The need to train community members to become interviewers may mean that it makes more sense to use trained and experienced outsiders for this task, but there are a number of advantages in using trained neighborhood interviewers, which include the following:

- They can more easily establish trust and make themselves understood.
- They can use the evenings for the interviews, when the majority of the heads of households are at home.
- The interviewers become communicators/multipliers and resource persons for the project.

Box 4-14. Quantitative Socioeconomic Surveys

Quantitative socioeconomic surveys can provide data that help clarify organization and leadership patterns and power relationships within an area, indicating the presence and influence of area leaders and community organizations. By mapping sectors using geographic information systems, areas under the influence of particular leaderships—as well as the presence and significance of community-based organizations—can be identified and analyzed. Examples of data collected by these surveys include the following:

- **Enrollment:** enrollment numbers, by address and by head of household; households and cohabiting households
- **Local organizations and leadership:** institutions that provide assistance to the community, institutions through which local residents voice their demands, institutions attended by settlers, membership in local area-based organizations, membership in local specific-purpose community groups, membership of religious groups, attendance of community meetings, list of leaders by sector
- **Household socioeconomic features:** household size and income, head of household marital status, households by household composition, households by household income, households by per capita income, settlers' sex by age group, total households by sector, number of people by years of schooling, number of people by profession, number of people by occupational status
- **Access to basic services:** structures by modality of water supply, structures by means of water storage, structures by means of garbage disposal, structures by electric power use, structures by type of sanitation alternative
- **Housing quality:** structures by predominant wall and floor materials, structures by number of rooms, structures by number of floors, structures by existence and type of bathroom
- **Occupancy patterns:** structures by number of cohabiting families, structures by type of tenure (owned, ceded, rented), structures by time of occupation, structures by type of risk, structures and lots by type of use
- **Correlated indicators:** predominant materials by duration of occupation, family income by family composition, predominant materials and risk situation by family income, income of head of household by sex, income of settlers by occupancy status and sex, per capita income by sex of head of household, per capita income by duration of occupation
- **Other:** formal or informal providers of services (e.g., tanker trucks), businesses that work inside the community or hire from the community, absentee landlords, vacant plots.

> **Box 4-15. Tools for Understanding Organization and Leadership Profiles**
>
> The organization and leadership profile tries, with the assistance of formal and informal leaders and veteran residents, individually and/or in groups, to record the history of the community, recalling their main demands, movements, and struggles. This information provides insights into the process of land occupation, the most important stages of community development, and the main features of the dynamics of social relations—including the power structure—over time.
>
> The main tools for creating these profiles are an interview outline and a set of observation criteria and techniques for focus groups. Unlike the quantitative survey based on questionnaires, the interview outline is semi-structured and serves as a tool to guide communication so that the point of view of the different social actors can be understood. Although the outline is open-ended, each question must fit within the general theoretical and methodological framework of the investigation. Therefore, these interviews should be carried out by trained interviewers. The outline covers the following basic topics:
>
> - History of the settlement
> - Community organizations: demands and struggles
> - Participation in popular movements and committees
> - Main community demands
> - Internal and external power structures and forces at play.
>
> During the interviews, the technical team takes note of respondents' comments, attitudes, and reactions to the interviewer's questions. It is important to capture spontaneous and informal reactions in order to complement the information about leadership.

Because the quantitative survey process involves all households, it serves as an important opportunity to build social cohesion, which will influence mobilization. The act of counting and identifying each household makes all residents responsible for the delimitation and care of the area covered by the project. This is the only real insurance against opportunistic invasions into the area once news of the project spreads.

Qualitative Interviews. These interviews provide information about the daily life of the neighborhood, the survival strategies adopted by the residents, cultural factors and cultural change, behavior and consumption and expenditure patterns, and expectations with regard to the project. This information is necessary for formulation of the project itself, as well as the development of its socio-technical support and communications strategy. The qualitative survey allows project promoters to have a better grasp of the "assets of the poor." This kind of knowledge is crucial, since, as mentioned above, the main business of a development project is precisely to strengthen the poor's asset base and their potential to contribute to the development process.

Several methods may be used to conduct the qualitative survey, such as open or semi-structured interviews and various rapid assessment methods—e.g., focus groups, collective interviews, interviews with key informants, and direct observation through field visits.

Survey respondents should be selected based on the following criteria:

- They should be *representative*, not in the sense of political representation (community organization or political party leaders), but in the sense of representing the types and categories that make up the community (such as heads of households, young men and women, workers in the trades or activities that are prevalent in the area).
- They should have *lived in the community for at least the last five years*.
- They should *live in different parts of the area* (spatial distribution of the informants is especially important in large, heterogeneous settlements).
- They should *represent different perspectives*, preferably in equal numbers, especially where there are antagonistic groups or conflicts (for example, between different political factions or different religious or ethnic groups).

It is also useful to include people with a broad network of relations and who are widely known in the community because of their role or profession. These may be organizers of community or sporting activities, religious leaders, political activists, trade union leaders, educators, or owners or managers of widely patronized collective services and stores. These participants can vary according to the type of information required and the activities envisaged for the project.

Qualitative investigation permits us to fill in the rough outlines sketched by statistics, which tend to circumscribe and limit the analysis of the most entrenched causes of poverty. Examples of themes that may be examined qualitatively include:

- History of the community
- Migration patterns
- Actions and behaviors in relation to the environment
- Values and family relations
- Family planning and health
- Education, causes of failure at school, and school abandonment

- Domestic routines and division of labor
- Consumption patterns and distribution of family expenses
- Access to systems of formal and informal credit
- Economic activities and home-based businesses (use of the home as a productive resource)
- Forms of participation and community organization
- Resource institutions such as community-based organizations, NGOs, charities, and public sector bodies operating in or near the area
- Presence of the for-profit private sector in or near the area
- Profile, legitimacy, and representativeness of the leadership
- Aspirations and expectations of individuals and groups.

This type of research requires experienced interviewers who know how to gather information through informal communication and can lead a group discussion or focus group.

Geographic Information Systems (GIS). Information obtained through quantitative and qualitative surveys may be entered into a computer database and associated with a cartographic base of the area using GIS software. GIS permits the creation of thematic maps, which can be used to visualize geographical distribution and diagnose various types of problems related to a wide range of data including:

- Environmental and social risk factors in the settlement
- Availability and state of repair of infrastructure
- Materials used for construction and the state of housing units
- Different patterns of infrastructure availability and state of shelter within the settlement
- Income distribution and social indicators
- Household data and community leaders
- External resource institutions operating within or near the communities
- Private sector actors operating within or near the communities.

These maps can be an extremely useful resource for a wide range of planning and monitoring activities. They can facilitate a readily understandable synthesis of a variety of types of information, while allowing planners to visualize the different degrees of problem intensity across the area. They can also help local residents visualize and understand a range of problems during the presentation and discussion of the surveys with the community.

An important caveat on the use of GIS is that, although these systems are relatively easy to set up in the framework of a development project, experience has shown that they are much more difficult to maintain and update after the project. This is unfortunate, since they are costly to implement and can be an important planning and monitoring tool in the long run. To mitigate these potential problems, it is necessary to find a clear institutional home for the GIS and to make appropriate arrangements for access to the information and definition of the essential program tasks to be undertaken by the program management unit for maintenance of the database.

Restitution of the Survey. A crucial step before the planning phase proper is the restitution of the diagnostic survey to the community. This is a process in which the results of the surveys are shared, discussed, and analyzed with the community. Meetings need to be organized with the community as a whole and with local area and special interest groups. There are a wide range of techniques that may be utilized to facilitate the workshops, which may involve small group discussions and plenary presentations by each group, as well as a wide range of instruments (from chalk and blackboard to thematic maps, murals, and flipcharts) which may help stimulate discussion.

This participatory process allows people to influence and fully understand the diagnostic, so the community actively contributes to the survey's contents and acquires capacity for an educated analysis and approval of proposals in the planning stage. The process also builds awareness and responsibility, and helps overcome the "short-term syndrome" in priority setting (i.e., when all the community wants is road paving or some other immediate and visible results).

Participatory Area Development Planning

The contents of the participatory area development plan were presented in chapter 3. In this section, we provide information on its development. The plan is based on the participatory process of information gathering and analysis described above and is developed by a committee of local residents with support from a social intermediation team usually consisting of planners, engineers, and social workers.

From an operational standpoint, the key steps in preparing a participatory area development plan are the following:

- **Information gathering.** This is a survey of the situation of the settlement and its inhabitants, covering physical aspects, existence and state of repair of infrastructure, service availability, environmental aspects, land tenure status, and socioeconomic situation (as described above).
- **Participatory analysis of the information.** The information is organized and analyzed by an interdisciplinary team and presented

to the community in a series of meetings with area-based and special interest groups (see previous section on Restitution of the Survey).
- **Identification of problems and priorities.** Based upon an analysis of the information and discussions in the community meetings, a coherent pattern of problems and priorities emerges.
- **Identification and discussion of alternatives.** Alternatives for intervention are proposed and discussed in an interactive process in which the community, through established representation mechanisms, eventually reaches decisions that reflect real demand.
- **Choice of recommended alternatives.** The discussion of alternatives leads to the choice of the recommended options. The technicians involved ensure that the chosen alternatives are affordable and appropriate.
- **Final product.** An agreed blueprint for the improvement of the area is developed, defining all relevant physical aspects as well as a logical long-term sequence of activities for the improvement of the area in terms of its physical configuration and infrastructure and also in terms of basic services.

Who Should Direct Participatory Planning? Many alternatives exist regarding coordination of participatory planning. At the project level, planning is normally coordinated by the organization providing sociotechnical support. At the program level, a local urban policy bureau with overall responsibility for the participatory planning process may be a good candidate for managing the planning process as a whole. To facilitate this bureau's task, institutional mechanisms and instruments to create conditions for involving the population in the definition and implementation of urban development strategies need to be developed (e.g., as in the several examples of participatory budgeting set forth in this book, including the Tijuana democratic planning system experience or Bolivia's People's Participation Law).

Where should such a bureau be located? The focal point for area-based development planning is usually the municipality, and less often the water company or an NGO (such as FUPROVI or Red Hábitat). Regardless of where the coordination role is situated, utilities and other line agencies, public or private, must be involved throughout the identification and planning of upgrading projects.

Direct project experience is often the catalyst for changes in public policy. In Belo Horizonte, for example, the concepts of integrated structural intervention and the participatory area development plan pioneered by the PROFAVELA program have been formally adopted by the city in its new master plan. The city has thereby acquired an instrument for the coordination of its sectoral interventions, all of which must make sense when confronted with each area's development plan. In a big city like Belo Horizonte, the management of all the necessary physical and socioeconomic information has required the introduction of GIS, which in turn has led to the development of significant information management capabilities.

Engineering and Physical Design Aspects

The work of planners, engineers, and designers needs to conform to the indications of the participatory planning process, and they must work under close coordination and guidance of the interdisciplinary socio-technical support team. Their work also needs to take into account two key factors for the design of an urban upgrading intervention:

- The need to strengthen existing and create new physical linkages—access routes and connections to urban services—between the informal settlement and the centralized urban infrastructure. This is a crucial factor for integrating the informal settlement into the city as a whole.
- The need to preserve the existing stock of buildings and infrastructure as much as possible. However substandard this stock may be, it represents the effort and investment of local residents over the years and is not easily replaced.

Planners and engineers working in urban upgrading should therefore use the existing settlement as their point of departure for the design process. This requires an appreciation of the specific physical features of informal settlements and an ability to develop creative and innovative solutions.

Professionals involved in urban upgrading must therefore have access to a large repertoire of technological options and know which to use in each situation. The level of skills required for this kind of work is actually higher than that normally required by conventional situations in the formal city, which is compounded by the fact that a basic understanding of informal sector social dynamics is also required.

The degree and quality of community participation in the definition of urban and building design and choice of technology depends on the degree to which the work of engineers and designers is linked to that of the socio-technical support team, and on the degree to which the latter effectively presents the options and promotes discussions with representative groups within the settlement.

It will also depend on the effectiveness of the methodology and techniques used by the socio-technical support provider. Obviously, responsiveness to real and perceived needs and community demand will depend on the degree and quality of participation. More opportunities for discussion, and more open and better informed discussions, will help ensure a better level of understanding on the part of residents and technicians of the linkages between different urban functions and between the settlement and its surroundings.

Participation in the Definition of Standards and Choice of Technology

Definition of standards and choice of technology are directly related to levels of service and also, obviously, to service costs. This is why it is very important to inform local residents about the implications of each technology in terms of cost and level of service and to involve them in technology choice. These discussions will lead to informed decisions about tariffs, user fees, and subsidy levels. A participatory planning process that does not address these issues poses a direct threat to future cost recovery. In general, methodologies that are based on direct beneficiary involvement in managing the construction process, such as in the case of FUPROVI, are more conducive to such discussions from an early stage. If a lower level of participation is envisaged, discussions about choice of technology and cost and service levels must be included in the analysis and negotiation of alternatives during the participatory planning process.

Besides the capital cost, the choice of technology is often influenced by its specific implementation features, as in the case of FUPROVI's Mansiones project, where prefab panels were too heavy to be moved by the women who constituted the majority of the workforce and were replaced by concrete blocks. Another factor to be taken into account is the labor requirements of different technologies, both in the construction stage and for operation and maintenance, since the use of labor-intensive technologies has a proven positive impact in terms of employment and income generation.

The choice of technology requires an iterative process between the community and the technicians to ensure that demand and supply meet.[19]

---

[19]Fabrice Henry, of the Inter-American Development Bank, provided the following example. In a recent low-income water supply project in Haiti, the community and the engineers met three times to look at the project design and see what could be done to ensure that project costs would be more in line with what the community could afford. This required good communication skills on the part of the engineers and a willingness to understand on the part of the community—and patience on both sides. The engineers came up with a simplified cost table explaining how each system component contributed to the costs; the community was presented with several levels of service and a price tag for each level. At the end, a consensus was arrived at, and the service level adopted proved to be both affordable to the community and in line with its aspirations. This iterative process was critical to ensuring that the community understood what it was paying for.

One factor that should be taken into careful consideration by projects that produce shelter units is the variety of uses to which a house is put and the need to add floors and otherwise increase available space in existing units. Some of the prefab technologies in use in Costa Rica, for instance, will not allow the addition of a second floor, which lowers upfront cost but severely limits a family's future options and precludes densification of existing settlements. Densification is often consciously pursued by upgrading or home improvement projects, as it is one of the best alternatives to urban sprawl and burgeoning infrastructure deficits. Although dictated by cost, which is obviously a very real and serious constraint, using construction technologies that preclude densification is a decision that may have negative overall impacts and come to be regretted in the future.

Design That Takes into Account Belonging and Ownership

People participate in activities to the extent that they feel they belong. Participatory projects thus need to transmit messages that strengthen a sense of social ownership, both at the level of primary groups (families, neighbors) and on a secondary level (solidarity, citizenship).

Human beings perceive certain architectural contexts as emotionally stimulating and others as meaningless and anonymous. Thus, the design of people's living spaces—both housing and public spaces—affects their psychological structure and their social relations. The fact that dwellers can recognize references of significance and familiar use in their environment directly influences the quality of the social relations they develop in this space. The resistance they exhibit in the face of relocation, even a relocation to a much better housing option, reflects both the desire to avoid the inconvenience of a move as well as the sense of belonging that they have attached to the functions and meaning of their original environment.

Programs such as Rio's Favela-Bairro and Guarapiranga have attempted to take these considerations into account by devoting attention to the design and quality of public spaces and urban equipment, by creating incentives for people to improve such elements as the external finish of their houses, and by devising creative solutions with viable costs. In this way, the programs have attained a greater identification of the inhabitants with their environment and ultimately have achieved a higher level of participation and sustainability.

5
Scaling Up: The Policy Level

In spite of the many successful examples of participatory urban upgrading in Latin America, most instances have been limited to pilot initiatives or scattered interventions. (The Guarapiranga program in São Paulo and Rio de Janeiro's Favela-Bairro program are notable exceptions.) Though these various initiatives have increased access to essential services and improved living conditions in certain limited areas, they have failed to address the problems of the informal city at a scale that would make any decisive difference. Informal settlements have a significant presence in most Latin American cities. For instance, about 50 percent of Venezuela's urban population lives in *barrios* (1.2 million people in metropolitan Caracas alone). In Brazil's metropolitan areas, the percentage of the population living in *favelas* or illegal subdivisions ranges from roughly 15 percent in Porto Alegre to roughly 50 percent in Recife. Other examples abound throughout the region. Reaching a scale that would make a difference means establishing programs that would cater to hundreds of thousands of people.

In this chapter, we outline the factors needed to scale up current initiatives and set the stage for sustained and successful long-term upgrading efforts across Latin America. These factors are summarized in box 5-1 and detailed in the following subsections.

Political Will

None of the other preconditions, discussed below, for large-scale upgrading can be achieved without political will. Political will, expressed by both the government and society as a whole, is essential for the promotion of large-scale urban upgrading with community participation.

> **Box 5-1. Conditions for Success and Scaling Up**
>
> **What are the criteria for success in an urban upgrading intervention?**
> - Impact in terms of improvements in health, quality of life, and the local environment
> - Ability to go to scale and stay focused on the target population
> - Long-term sustainability of social, environmental, technical, and economic benefits
> - Ability of program participants to fulfill their obligations in a timely and cost-effective manner
> - Ability to leverage government and donor funding while allocating risks to those program participants best able to assess and manage them
> - Ability to minimize transaction costs faced by program stakeholders regarding project design and implementation
>
> **What can be considered meaningful scale?**
> - Program reaches at least 10 percent of the city's low-income population
>
> **What are the key factors that ensure successful urban upgrading and low-income housing at the necessary scale?**
> - Political will, initially and over time, to develop and proactively implement the policies and institutional framework needed to effect change and mobilize the subsidy funding needed for urban upgrading

In Recife, Brazil, for example, the Plan for the Regularization and Urbanization of Special Zones of Social Interest (PREZEIS) program had established a conducive legal, regulatory, and methodological framework for participatory upgrading by the mid-1980s, and the program seemed ready to go to scale. Instead, it went on to languish for more than a decade due to a lack of political will on the part of government and a lack of collective pressure placed on government by local society; these factors in turn resulted in a lack of interest and a lack of funding. Similarly, in the Belo Horizonte case, also in Brazil, the conducive legal, regulatory, and institutional framework that was established in the 1980s was not followed up by a clear political decision to undertake mass upgrading.

A key aspect of political will, at least initially, seems to be the presence of a charismatic champion who is willing to fight the battles and share the power. Clear examples of this in the cases we have studied were General Velasco's role in the beginning stages of Villa El Salvador, Presi-

- A citywide urban upgrading policy, supported by an appropriate national policy environment and a conducive national and local legal and regulatory framework
- Capacity for area-based needs assessment, planning, and implementation
- Subsidy structures and cost recovery strategies that enhance financial sustainability and reduce the need for subsidies, allowing governments to do more with limited resources
- Land release mechanisms and shelter alternatives for resettlement, including systematic land tenure regularization
- Appropriate mechanisms to collect, process, and update information on the informal city
- Careful selection of program format: demand-driven programs, but with a strong supply mechanism and strong coordination
- Strategic alliances with the private sector and civil society to facilitate the affordability of and access to the material, capital, and informational inputs required for community infrastructure and housing development
- Development of appropriate institutional arrangements that facilitate cost-effective interventions, transparent allocation of resources, and ability to respond to varying demands and capacities within different communities initially and over time
- Development of a critical mass of local capabilities to carry out the various specialized tasks involved in urban upgrading and low-income housing

dent Sánchez de Lozada's role in the design and implementation of Bolivia's People's Participation Law, and President Oscar Arias's role in the launching of the housing subsidy scheme in Costa Rica. In all these cases, the personal involvement and enthusiasm of the country's highest political authority was a critical factor in moving upgrading to scale. Over the longer haul, as champions come and go, political will can be maintained and even enhanced via institutional mechanisms that provide incentives for organizations and individuals to stay the course. As one Colombian mayor told us, "By training local leaders in management skills and putting them in charge of local works projects, we were able to execute 120 projects in 18 months. I had the reputation for being the 'super executive mayor'—which is ironic, for had it actually been the administration attempting to do the executing, we certainly would have got nothing like that amount done."

Policy Environment and a Citywide Upgrading Strategy

There is an urgent need to capitalize on successful experiences to set up favorable citywide policy frameworks for upgrading projects in as many cities as possible. In many cities, the constraints experienced for the scaling-up of urban upgrading efforts have been primarily connected to policy as well as legal, institutional, and informational issues rather than financial problems. Experience suggests that such programs can be affordable for both the government and the community, as investment in basic tertiary infrastructure for urban populations currently lacking it is estimated to cost only 0.2 to 0.5 percent of gross domestic product (GDP) over 15 years.[1]

Once the decision is made to pursue informal settlement upgrading as an element in a poverty reduction and social inclusion strategy, a city needs to:

- **Build an appropriate information base on informal settlements.** The example of the 1995 Plan Sectorial by the Central University of Venezuela which delimits, names, and describes the barrios of Caracas, assessing their needs and estimating costs at various levels of intervention, could be followed in this regard. The geographic information system developed by the municipality of Tijuana is another good example of the efforts made by a city to build an appropriate information base on its informal settlements.
- **Eliminate legal, regulatory, and procedural bottlenecks** that impose requirements on buildings and land use that are not appropriate to local conditions and that make it impossible to upgrade existing informal settlements without a high degree of removal and resettlement. Peru pioneered the adoption of barrio-friendly legislation in 1961 with its Law of the Barriadas. The two Brazilian innovations of the early 1980s, the PROFAVELA legislation in Belo Horizonte and the PREZEIS legislation in Recife, are still valid models. There are formal and informal dimensions involved here. The formal elements include the laws, codes, and regulations that structure the interaction among the various program stakeholders, from national constitutions down to contract law and budgeting regulations. The informal dimensions are the uncodified norms and

---

[1]This figure reflects the incremental investment cost of secondary works only; it excludes costs for expanding primary (trunk) and secondary infrastructure networks, which would approximately double the range of expenditures. Operations and maintenance, technical assistance, and community mobilization would also be additional. The range is based on various regional unit investment costs and assumed settlement densities (World Bank 1996a).

attitudes that underpin the formal rules and determine how those rules are actually interpreted. Politics and power structures clearly come to the fore in this context, as do the deeply rooted cultural factors that support such structures: whether there is a culture of public service or citizenship rights, for example; or whether the public and private actors have good, bad, or any experience in working together and the reciprocal attitudes they have shaped. The combination of formal and informal factors provides the basis for the incentive structure for participatory initiatives and creates an environment that can be either helpful or obstructive.
- **Build a *plano y plan* (beaconed sites plus a development plan) strategy for informal settlements,** i.e., promote the preparation of participatory development plans *(plan)* and physical plans *(plano)* for each settlement. This has proved to be a major catalyst for community organization, besides being essential to long-term development and investment planning, as is clearly shown by the Peruvian example of Villa El Salvador. Having a plano y plan is also important in ensuring that isolated works gradually coalesce into a coherent whole.
- **Establish funding arrangements with a built-in long-term perspective.** Upgrading processes are complex and usually take place over extended periods of time. In a citywide strategy, it is necessary to establish a successful track record in a few areas before a program can consider itself to have consolidated a methodology that allows it to go to scale. At the same time, the sheer magnitude of the problem in most Latin American cities requires a long-term sustained effort. Flow of funds arrangements need to take this into account. The adaptable lending approaches emerging from the repertoire of international donors could be an answer to this problem.[2] Another interesting approach is the Bolivian mechanism of the People's Participation Law, through which a steady funding stream to municipalities is established.

---

[2] With adaptable lending, a program framework is set up and finance is provided for the first two years of operation, with the understanding that the success of this initial stage will lead to further funding for program continuation. Any adjustments in program design or procedure may be carried out before the subsequent stage starts. All the lengthy and cumbersome approval procedures that have been carried out for the first stage remain valid, and subsequent stages can be authorized through a much simpler procedure. This approach is ideal for a long-term urban upgrading process since it allows the process to continue for as long a time span as needed, and funding can be channeled according to actual requirements instead of having to conform to a predetermined plan developed and approved years before.

Area-Based Needs Assessment, Planning, and Implementation

An integrated, area-based approach to needs assessment, planning, and implementation is required to ensure an efficient use of financial and technical resources, while maximizing the community's willingness to participate. A broad long-term vision of the development of the settlement or area of intervention, rather than the particular requirements of any single type of infrastructure, needs to be the axis and connecting thread of the planning of an urban upgrading project, especially in the case of squatter settlements.

Municipal infrastructure is usually built and operated by line agencies that specialize in one kind of infrastructure: roads, stormwater drainage, water supply, sanitation, light and power, etc. Such agencies frequently report to different political levels. Roads and stormwater drainage are usually handled by local governments; water, sanitation, and electricity are often under state or provincial responsibility. Water and sanitation are often the responsibility of a sole agency, but in many cases they are handled separately. Land and housing are normally dealt with by different agencies, and often simultaneously at the municipal, provincial, and central levels. In a context of growing private sector involvement in service provision, electricity services are being privatized faster than water and sanitation. The agencies that are being set up for utility regulation report to the provincial, state, or central government level, and less frequently to the local government level.

The line agency model has worked reasonably well in most industrialized country cities and in the formal parts of developing country cities. One of its weak points is that different line agencies usually find it difficult to take coordinated action. In the formal city, this merely leads to various forms of inefficiency; in the informal city, such a lack of coordination causes problems that are much more serious. Especially in the case of squatter settlements, it frequently means that projects simply cannot be implemented, or that project benefits will be very difficult to operate and maintain.

The reason behind this failing is that there are many complex interactions among the different branches of infrastructure. For instance, if sewerage infrastructure is built in an area with stormwater drainage problems, this will jeopardize the operation of the sewerage. Rainwater will penetrate the sewers, often aided by residents who see the sewers as a means of solving the drainage problem. In time, the sewers will be clogged by the sediments carried by rainwater. At the same time, wastewater treatment facilities will become swamped by rainwater, leading to constant operational problems. Moreover, erosion linked to the lack of stormwater drainage may in time result in a loss of the investment in sewers and related infrastructure.

These partnerships thus pose many challenges. Each separate public entity—be it a ministry, a national institute, or a municipal or other subnational department—must be able to function effectively with its own internal procedures. Quite often, however, a mayor will make a decision and send the message down the line, only to have the measure languish unimplemented since there is no capacity at lower levels to translate the meaning of the orders.

When coordination with other parties is required, there emerges a host of problems in adapting internal procedures to those of others. Most government agencies are used to working in isolated, monolithic fashion. Communication among different parties is made difficult by the lack of fluid channels of communication.

Intersectoral collaboration also means, of course, that the public sector must have the capacity to interact with the private sector—both profit-making and nonprofit. Most current laws, however, do not explicitly create incentives or even authorize governments to deal with public-private partnerships. For example, budget, contract, and control rules in most countries in Latin America tend to restrict the capacity of the state to allocate state funds to finance partnerships or their programs, projects, or actions.

The private sector tends to expect shorter time frames than does the public sector for execution of any project phase, which can lead to particularly severe problems. Tensions can also arise out of the dual requirements for control by the state on the one hand and flexibility on the other. A common complaint from nongovernmental organizations (NGOs) is that they are forced to account for the minutiae of their expenditures when working under contract for a state body in a way that public bodies are not required to do, and that they thereby waste time and energy. Compounding these frustrations are issues of slow disbursement—and these are problems that arise when the parties involved are trying their best to work together.

Nonetheless, such obstacles should not be seen as insurmountable. Chapter 2 presents an example of a well-oiled collaboration: that between the Carvajal Foundation and the municipal public works company EMCALI in Cali, Colombia.

Special Features of Squatter Settlements

Among the inherent features of squatter settlements that make infrastructure planning more difficult and impose a higher level of coordination are the following:

- Exclusion from available cartography and databases, on the assumption that such settlements are not part of the city and will eventually be removed
- Steep slopes and tortuous alleyways that make surveying by traditional techniques slower and more difficult
- "Fluidity," i.e., the absence of a set of generally accepted rules for land use and occupation
- Demographic pressure, which, coupled with fluidity, causes rapid change, creating unstable situations that are difficult to manage.

Let us take the example of São Paulo's Guarapiranga project. The intervention in each favela included the following:

- Removal of structures from risk areas and public rights of way
- Opening up of new access roads and improvement of existing ones
- Building of stormwater drainage infrastructure
- Building of water supply and sewerage infrastructure
- Light and power and public lighting infrastructure
- Household hookups to the new infrastructure
- Paving of roads and sidewalks
- Urbanization of public open spaces.

In addition, new housing units had to be built, partly on-site and partly off-site, for those families that had to be removed from risk areas or because of the building of new drainage infrastructure and roads. Temporary shelter needed to be provided to relocated families, as well as storage and removal services. Moreover, these activities took place in areas where gross densities before the project were often close to 1,000 people per hectare, and where people continued to live and work throughout the project.

How could such a complex project possibly work? For it did work, and on a large scale (176 favela areas and over 20,000 households). Let us try to understand how it was done.

Guarapiranga's institutional framework was a horizontal one, in which the different line agencies served as equal partners under the coordination of a project management unit which encouraged the adoption of collaborative arrangements. The project's favela upgrading component was coordinated by the municipality of São Paulo, which is responsible for physical planning, roads, and drainage. Public utility companies owned by the state of São Paulo provide water, sanitation, and electricity, these last under concession arrangements. As the recognized coordinator of the favela upgrading component, the municipality led the process of preparing an area-based development plan that addressed all infrastructure types.[3] The execution of the plan for each favela was contracted out to a technical bureau that had in its terms of reference the obligation to submit the plans to both community scrutiny and technical scrutiny of the utilities responsible for each infrastructure branch. This was especially important since innovative technological solutions were often used, especially for water supply and sanitation; these had to be approved by the utility that would ultimately be responsible for system operation and maintenance.

Execution of the works was coordinated by the municipality, which hired contractors and subproject management and quality assurance services. Socio-technical support services were provided by a private firm hired as a subcontractor by the various construction firms involved.

Three key elements ensured the success of this highly complex operation:

- An *area-based plan* taking into account community demand and technical requirements of the different branches of infrastructure
- A *coordinating agency*, recognized by the community, the various utilities, and the branches of government, with overall command of operations and the authority and resources to hire specialized technical support and executing companies
- *Adequate socio-technical support* to the participation of local residents in the preparation of the area plan and implementation of the works.

In Guarapiranga, the coordinating agency for the preparation of the area development plans (the municipality's Housing and Urban Development Department) was also responsible for coordination of the execution of the works. In addition, works related to the different branches of infrastructure all took place simultaneously, with a single contractor responsible for each area. This simplified matters considerably.

Conflicts with Traditional Line Agency Structures

In cases such as the above, where the works related to each branch of infrastructure are managed by a different line agency over an extended

---

[3]The Guarapiranga program was a large undertaking within which each of the state agencies and the one large municipality involved (São Paulo) had coordinating responsibilities for the component that was closest to its institutional mandate. The only state agency that could conceivably have tried to take the urban upgrading component from the municipality would have been SABESP, the water and sanitation agency. Since SABESP was already the program's main executing agency by virtue of the extensive wastewater infrastructure that was built, there was relatively little resistance to the municipality taking the lead in upgrading.

period of time, a properly negotiated area development plan is critical. Each of the agencies involved must be represented in the planning process to ensure that its particular technical requirements are met. It is also important to ensure that the results of the area-based planning exercise properly feed into each line agency's planning process. Resistance to the coordination of an outside agency may sidetrack the results of participatory planning done by others in favor of a line agency's existing master plans, no matter how inadequate and outdated these may be.

Guarapiranga's innovative area-based and horizontal institutional framework and clear assignment of responsibilities made it possible for one of the agencies to coordinate each of the project's components under the overall coordination of the project management unit. Although conflicts nonetheless arose, they were manageable because the institutional framework and resources made available to the coordinating agency lent sufficient authority to the latter.

Conflicts with the traditional line-based structure and coordination difficulties are the norm, which hampers the implementation of many projects. Also in São Paulo, in an area not far from Guarapiranga, urban upgrading projects initiated by the water utility SABESP outside the Guarapiranga framework met with major coordination difficulties that brought the projects to a standstill. The very actors of Guarapiranga, operating in the same city, find it difficult to produce results in the absence of an enabling program framework such as Guarapiranga's. This proves the importance of a clear institutional arrangement that clarifies responsibilities and establishes a generally accepted coordination mechanism.

Subsidy Structures and Cost Recovery Strategies

Establishing a clear subsidy structure and cost recovery strategy is crucial to making a long-term, citywide upgrading program financially sustainable. The examples we have seen in San José and Tijuana, as well as in Bolivia, indicate that communities are willing and able to work with cost information. In Tijuana, they interact with program promoters to determine levels of community contribution to construction. In San José and Cochabamba, they monitor expenditures and propose ways to cut costs. It is possible to imagine communities taking part in decisions regarding their own financial commitments to pay for operations and maintenance of infrastructure in the long run.

There is a need to develop clear and consistent mechanisms for cost recovery as it relates to connection fees, tariffs, or user charges for utility services, as well as financial contributions to construction by communities and mobilization of local fiscal revenues from increased property or betterment levies. There was a conscious effort to address these issues in the Tijuana and San José cases; while in São Paulo, the community's willingness to pay has not so far been significantly tapped. In Tijuana, we have seen that the municipal community upgrading program is more advanced in establishing a responsible and transparent relationship with the communities than parallel efforts by the state government water utility CESPT, which feature such paternalistic hallmarks as hidden subsidies and a lack of willingness to discourage "free riders" (see below and chapter 9).

Perceived, and sometimes real, capacity to pay constraints act as disincentives to service providers, discouraging them from extending services to low-income communities. To circumvent this constraint, a transparent mechanism for subsidizing lower income segments needs to be developed. An optimal subsidy design should provide clear, predictable, and performance-based incentives to operators to deliver services on a commercial basis; among others, via subcontracting mechanisms with smaller scale providers while also providing clear economic signals to users regarding demand, cost of service, and corresponding out-of-pocket payment obligations. In all the cases we have studied, the targeting of subsidies was a problem, and the special difficulties of the poorest and most vulnerable groups were not fully taken into consideration.

Community Contributions and Cost Recovery

Cost recovery is crucial to the sustainability of project benefits, the establishment of a responsible relationship between user and service provider, and the development of a culture of rights and responsibilities. Progress on this aspect has been very uneven in Latin America: While some highly innovative approaches are being successfully pioneered, the old populist tradition of state handouts still prevails in many cases (see table 5-1). As a result, the significant advances in participatory mechanisms of the last two decades have not produced the improvement in cost recovery that might be expected.

In all its dimensions, cost recovery is a central element in increasing scale. The variety of conventional cost recovery approaches in use include betterment levies, "social" (flat rate) tariffs, consumption-based tariffs, hookup fees, municipal or private fees and charges, and the property tax.

Municipalities throughout Latin America find it difficult to collect the property tax, which is usually their main source of revenue. Many people fail to pay, and municipal mechanisms for debt collection are slow and inefficient. In an attempt to overcome this situation, the Villa El Salvador municipality has introduced a series of innovative mechanisms. These

Table 5-1. Cost Recovery Formats in the Cases Studied

Country	Approaches	Comments
Bolivia	• Water and electricity tariffs • Local property tax • Transparent subsidies	Privatization has enhanced water and electricity metering; on property tax collection, advances are slow in spite of decentralization and participation; high level of cost consciousness
Brazil	• Water and electricity tariffs • "Social" tariffs • Hidden subsidies	Advances in metering of water and electricity are slow: illegal hookups are still common; property tax is not levied due to land tenure situation; low level of cost consciousness
Cost Rica	• Communities meet bridge loan payments and pay back principal when government pays housing subsidy • Water and electricity tariffs • Transparent subsidies	Full cost recovery is a cornerstone of the FUPROVI methodology; level of cost consciousness is very high, and project costs and loan payments are negotiated with the community
Mexico	• Upfront 30% community contribution to cost of works; property tax • Water and electricity tariffs • Transparent subsidies from municipality; hidden subsidies from water company	Community makes upfront contribution and manages resources; high level of cost consciousness; advances in land registration, municipal cadastre, and property tax collection
Peru	• Water and electricity tariffs • Solid waste removal fees • Property tax • Tradition of hidden subsidies, but municipality moving to transparency	Advances in metering of water and electricity due to privatization of electricity and better water management; advances in property tax collection and community collection of solid waste removal fees

Source: Authors' construction from field study data.

include an awareness-raising campaign and the creation of specific incentives. Neighborhoods with a good repayment record are given preference in consideration for infrastructure improvements, and people who have paid the municipality all they owe can take part in raffles.

Although property tax collection in informal settlements is even more of a problem than in the formal city, there seems to be a window of opportunity for property tax-based cost recovery. In Guarapiranga, for example, residents would like to pay the property tax because they feel it would give them some recognition—and added security of tenure. The same pattern can be found in favelas throughout Brazil, but there are many upgrading and land tenure regularization projects that, instead of looking into what would be a feasible level of subsidy, simply exempt project beneficiaries from the property tax. This is usually done for a term of 10 years, as in the case of Belo Horizonte's PROFAVELA law.

The Tijuana and Ciudad Juárez examples introduce a new and very interesting format: direct community contribution to the cost of the works, prior to and during implementation. The Tijuana/Juárez format is made possible by three factors that, taken more generally, seem to condition the possibility of cost recovery:

- The nature of the relationship between the promoting agency and local residents is not paternalistic.
- Both parties are clearly conscious of the cost of the improvements.
- There clearly is high *demand* for the improvements and *motivation* for participation.

Influence of the Promoting Agency's Attitude. Looking at the track record of urban upgrading projects in terms of cost recovery, there is a clear case for cost consciousness and for a mature relationship. In many projects, the cultural and political environment can lead to a paternalistic relationship, which tends to produce a negative result in terms of cost recovery. Willingness and ability to pay are important, but are far from representing the whole picture: the attitude of promoting agencies is just as important. Examples of both attitudes are present in our field reports: a mature relationship in the cases of San José and Tijuana, and a paternalistic one in the case of Guarapiranga.

It is very interesting to note the contrast between the community upgrading Obra Social Comunitaria (OSC) program of the municipality of Tijuana and the *autogestión directa* (direct self-management) water supply and sewerage network extension program of CESPT in the same low-income areas of the city. A different attitude toward cost recovery and a different system for community contributions make for very different results. Although demand for water supply and sanitation is certainly high, "free rider" issues are much more serious for CESPT. The key differences between the two programs are as follows:

- In OSC, residents are asked for an upfront contribution, and only after they come up with 30 percent of the required sum does the municipality deliver the first check.

- In OSC, a local residents' public works committee manages the funds, selects the contractor, and oversees the work. There is full cost consciousness on the part of the community.
- Although there is a free rider problem in OSC, this is limited by the social pressure free riders have to endure. In the CESPT case, there is no social awareness as to who the free riders are; the issue remains between CESPT and each individual free rider.

The CESPT program, which in theory has no subsidy, has a 30 percent default rate on the community contribution on average, and debtors are not pursued. This works in practical terms as a 100 percent subsidy that is not targeted or transparent, since it simply benefits those who do not pay. This is clearly an incentive to the culture of nonpayment and to the permanence of a paternalistic relationship. In OSC, the average level of subsidy is much higher than in the CESPT program—70 percent—but the subsidy is transparent and benefits all residents equally.

Social Pressure Limits Free Rider Issues. The Obra Social Comunitaria program also faces free rider issues, but to a far smaller degree, due to social pressure. This brings up the issue of how to enforce community contributions and what to do about those who do not pay. In Tijuana, since they cannot be legally pursued, free riders eventually get away with not paying. In the Ciudad Juárez OSC program, which promotes many water supply and sewerage projects, each participant is required to deposit his or her contribution directly with the municipal treasury, and free riders are denied hookups to the system. If they relent, they are charged the full nonsubsidized cost. This is of course much more difficult to do in other cases, such as road paving or school improvement.

In the Costa Rican Foundation for the Promotion of Housing (FUPROVI) case, families that fall behind in their in-kind labor contributions of 30 hours a week are charged a heavy fine of as many hours again as the ones they owe. If such episodes are repeated frequently, persistent defaulters are simply struck off the project participant list. Such extreme measures are rarely adopted, since social pressure and the desire for a home provide a powerful incentive and families normally put in their 30 hours every week.

What experience seems to show is that free rider issues can be kept to a minimum with strong community participation. This is illustrated by the experience of Kiwi Street in Tijuana, where the public works committee posted "For Sale" signs in vacant lots in a successful bid to identify absentee lot owners and get them to contribute to the project.

The Issue of Subsidies

Subsidies Are Fair and Necessary... Especially in the case of off-site infrastructure, but also arguably in the case of shelter improvement, urban upgrading projects have a common good nature and benefit society as a whole. This justifies the adoption of subsidies in the common interest and as a measure of equity. From a practical standpoint as well, subsidies are necessary due to limitation in poor residents' ability to pay for improvements.

...But They Must Be Well-Targeted and Transparent. To be effective, subsidies must be correctly targeted, temporary, and transparent. Subsidies that fall outside these tenets place an undue burden on the public purse, often create or worsen social inequities, and contribute to a culture of paternalism.

Consequently, the process of designing and delivering subsidies is very important. Although the cases we have studied show that hidden subsidies are still common, there are also clear signs of hope, especially in relation to transparency. Targeting is still a problem in most cases, as we have seen above. The Bolivian case, for example, is one in which subsidies, although transparent, are targeted to poor areas and not to poor people.

Villa El Salvador: Moving toward Transparency. In the Villa El Salvador home improvement credit project, promoted by the NGO Desco (the Center for Development Studies and Promotion), technical assistance, whose cost is 15 percent of each credit package, is provided as a subsidy. The amount of the subsidy is clear to all parties, as is the fact that technical assistance has a value that can be quantified and that a service worth that much is being provided as a subsidy. Subsidies and financing, although handled by the same organization, are here clearly separate. The Desco project is a clear example of a transparent and temporary subsidy that is targeted to a well-defined group—the borrowers in a home improvement credit project. The process of the development of Villa El Salvador has many examples of hidden subsidies, but the municipality's moves toward fiscal transparency and the public discussion of its accounts indicate a positive trend.

Guarapiranga: No Discussion of the Subsidy Policy. Many factors would justify a high level of subsidy for the favela upgrading component of the Guarapiranga project; the following are among the most important:

- The Guarapiranga reservoir accounts for 20 percent of São Paulo's water supply and is one of that huge city's few open leisure areas. As such, its value to the city is immense.
- Beyond their poverty, the vast majority of the population of the favelas of the Guarapiranga basin live in a state of social exclusion that entails limited access to essential public services such as water supply, sanitation, primary health care, and basic education. Improving their access to infrastructure and services is part of fulfilling the state's essential redistributive function and has a direct poverty-reduction impact that benefits the whole of society.
- Many of the sewerage, stormwater drainage, and roadworks that are implemented within each favela directly benefit other parts of the city that are located upstream, downstream, or in that favela's vicinity.

The above factors would have justified the adoption by the municipality of a high level of subsidies, in a motion that could have been presented to lawmakers and the citizenry and easily carried. In Brazil's political culture, however, there is no tradition of subsidies being made explicit and being discussed, and Guarapiranga was not an exception. The project does not have a clear subsidy policy, and little thought has been given to long-term cost recovery. The result is a lack of transparency, cost consciousness, and targeting—and a missed opportunity to help change the paternalistic political culture.

Costa Rica: Challenge of Accessing Commercial Funding. The FUPROVI model is built around the existence of a generous government housing subsidy scheme. Using the FUPROVI methodology of organized mutual help, housing associations usually succeed in covering the full cost of the units with the housing subsidy that is granted to each of the association's members. This is important, since one of the key recurring obstacles to housing subsidy programs in several countries has been the fact that the subsidy often barely covers the cost of a serviced plot—which at best leaves the very poor living in unsound structures on serviced plots. Furthermore, location of serviced plot schemes in the outskirts of cities, far from services and job opportunities, often means that residents find it difficult to improve their homes over time and have a very limited ability to pay for services.

FUPROVI's success in making the most of the Costa Rican housing subsidy scheme has inevitably meant that the institution's modus operandi has become dependent on the existence of the subsidy. Once the country's macroeconomic problems led to reduction of the scheme, FUPROVI had to look for ways to overcome the cash flow problems it began to experience. FUPROVI is keenly aware of the fact that unless it is able to access commercial funding in the long run to finance its operations, its successful efforts thus far at attaining economic and financial sustainability will be undermined.

Tijuana: Several Coexisting Models. It is interesting to compare the Obra Social Comunitaria and the CESPT water and sanitation extension programs. Both work with the same communities. In the municipality's program, the level of subsidy varies between 50 and 80 percent (70 percent on average); through better targeting, full transparency, and cost consciousness, it seems more sustainable overall. Communities pay what they have agreed to pay. By contrast, in the case of the CESPT subsidy scheme, recovery of what the community is supposed to pay is around 70 percent, and the CESPT policy is to avoid litigation. This leads to a classic "hidden subsidy" situation, with the aggravating factor that the subsidy is neither targeted nor evenly distributed—it simply goes to those who do not pay. This, besides being unfair, sends the wrong kind of message, contributing to the paternalistic political culture.

Another subsidy worth noting in Tijuana is the one built into the *land release mechanism* through the State Real Estate Board (INETT). In INETT subdivisions in the explosive growth areas of the eastern part of Tijuana, plots are sold well below cost, and payments are deferred. INETT plots have full documentation. This has led to a containment of new illegal subdivisions; thus, the policy of land tenure regularization in informal land subdivisions is gradually catching up with the existing backlog.

Legal and Regulatory Framework

For community upgrading and shelter programs to be sustainable, attain scale, maintain a focus on reaching the poor, and optimize environmental and quality of life benefits, a conducive policy environment, supported by an appropriate legal and regulatory framework, needs to be in place. This section provides an overview of key issues in the legal and regulatory environment that may constitute impediments if not adequately addressed.

Building Codes and Land Use and Physical Planning Laws and Regulations

In some countries, these are the responsibility of the local level; in others, of the national level. Peru, Chile, and Costa Rica are examples of countries where a national norm is followed. In the case of Peru's Law of the Barriadas, a national legal framework was established for the occupation and subdivision of land for housing the poor. In Chile and Costa

Rica, standards and regulations for land use and housing construction are national, taking no account of regional differences. In Brazil, these norms are local; this does not mean, however, that they are necessarily well-suited to local conditions since they still tend to copy industrialized country models.

National or local, these laws and regulations are often based on imported models that require, among others, maximum densities, minimum plot sizes, minimum width, and maximum slope of streets that make it very difficult to upgrade informal settlements without de-densification, mass removal, and resettlement. (For example, Brazil's U.S.-inspired norms not only outlaw the informal city but also, in theory at least, the older parts of the formal city as well, with its narrow streets and high slopes.) The Brazilian cities of Belo Horizonte and Recife have created a supportive legal and regulatory framework for upgrading that is based on standards appropriate to local conditions.

Landownership and Land Registration

In this field, most laws and regulations are national. Outdated cadastres and land registries, complex bureaucratic procedures, and an extraordinary resistance to change fueled by entrenched interests conspire to make this one of the most complicated legal and regulatory conundrums in the urban development field. Alternatives for creating a more conducive environment are discussed below.

Technical and Service Standards for Infrastructure

Standards used in the developing world are often borrowed from high-income countries and applied across the board. The result is that formal sector activities are normally guided by such standards, while no standards at all are applied with regard to the informal sector activities that are responsible for most of the housing and infrastructure produced in many developing country cities. Standards must be developed that ensure adequate performance while keeping costs within a range that does not make it impossible to extend services.

Legal Recognition of Community Organizations

One of the key changes wrought by Bolivia's People's Participation Law is the creation of clear and simple rules for the legal recognition of area-based *juntas de vecinos* (neighborhood associations) with jurisdiction over their areas. Having a legally recognized community organization is a key factor for organized participation and for creating channels for dialogue and negotiation. One of the cornerstones of the FUPROVI program in Costa Rica is the ability of a legally recognized association to enter into a formal contract with the supporting organization.

Procurement Rules

Stiff rules and procedures for procurement are often one of the key obstacles to sound management of the program and project cycles. Many programs are characterized by long bureaucratic delays followed by periods of hectic activity in which organizations try to make up for lost time—often overlooking quality in the process. One of the key arguments for setting up autonomous project management units or entrusting project management to a third party (such as an NGO) is the need to bypass the bureaucratic morass of most countries' public sector procurement rules.

Exclusivity Provisions

A significant constraint to community-based and micro- and small enterprise-based provision of infrastructure services often has been the exclusivity or monopolistic rights granted to public and private sector operators. Notwithstanding these legal restrictions, informal sector and community-based operators have found a significant niche. Studies carried out a few years ago by the World Bank Water and Sanitation Program in 16 countries (6 in Latin America and 10 in Africa), coupled with those undertaken by the World Bank Urban Environment Thematic Group on independent providers of solid waste collection and disposal services in Latin America (six countries), reveal the significant promise of these types of investment.

On average in Latin America, private independent operators provide 25 percent of the urban population with water services and 50 percent with sanitation. In Guatemala City alone, over 200 independent entrepreneurs provide over half the population with water and sanitation services. These range from full-service companies serving over 70,000 persons to community enterprises and water tankers. Paraguay, Peru, Colombia, and Bolivia have burgeoning independent water and sanitation services. Over one-third of the growth in urban water service in Paraguay over the past 20 years has been due to independent operators. Currently, these operators provide water to about 600,000 people through more than 100,000 separate connections. Reportedly, the providers have invested $30 million in private capital. Some have multiple networks and assets whose replacement costs are in the range of a few million dollars. Most operate in the formal sector and get their licenses from the municipalities and technical approvals from the Ministry of Health. The investment cost for water supply from a well via pipe distribution to about 300 households can be around $60,000. A surprising number have been flourishing in Colombia, where the Ministry of Economic Development has recently endorsed a water and sanitation strategy based entirely on independent providers. Reportedly more than 1,000 private water vendors operate in the *pueblos jovenes* (informal settlements) of Lima alone, many of which serve 500 households or more—albeit at rates two to three times that charged by the water company. Bolivia has long relied on a special form of independent provider, the water and sanitation cooperative. Despite serious limitations resulting from lack of access to long-term financing and limitations on existing regulatory frameworks, they consistently sell water of high quality and at lower costs than the public (and recently privatized) monopoly companies.

Formal Recognition

Formal recognition through the legal framework of the right of small operators to exist and the establishment of a regulatory mechanism would permit greater competition and encourage investment. This would presumably lead to lower cost services, improve services from a technical and environmental standpoint, and provide access to lower cost and more reliable sources of funding for small-scale enterprises. An interesting example is in Cordoba, Argentina, where the exclusivity provisions attached to the privatization of the water company have thrown the *aguateros*, small private water supply operators, some of which have been operating successfully for decades, into a legal limbo that severely affects their incentives to invest in their operations, thereby restricting their capacity to serve a larger customer base or provide a more efficient/competitive service (Solo et al. 1998).

Legal Ownership of Assets

Although communities and small-scale local operators can operate and maintain assets for which they also take an active role in design, construction, and funding, legal ownership often remains with the relevant local authority or utility. This can be an enormous disincentive for communities and small-scale local operators in mobilizing their scarce resources, given the uncertainty of how the legal owners of such assets may deal with them in the future. Formal mechanisms for granting communities and small-scale local operators continued control of these assets would be important, not only in pursuing demand-driven approaches, but for any strategy over time to facilitate their access to more formal sources of capital to finance working capital and investment needs.

Participatory Planning

The requirements of formal master plans are often an impediment to the adoption of participatory planning mechanisms. In Peru, for example, although families can fund works to connect to the local water system, they are only reimbursed for related expenditures if the proposed projects are contemplated in the utility's master plan. These plans, however, lack flexibility. In response, some communities in Lima have attempted, albeit unsuccessfully, to seek legal recourse against the water utility SEDAPAL for recovery of related costs. A formal requirement that communities be consulted prior to formalization of master plans would provide a clear incentive to participation.

Ex-Post Supervision and Evaluation

An explicit institutional and regulatory strategy needs to be formulated to assess project/program impact vis-à-vis corresponding poverty alleviation and technical, environmental, and financial objectives. Program monitoring responsibilities and corresponding budgets, along with associated capacity-building, should be formally assigned to those parties with the incentives to pursue these activities diligently. The regulatory framework should encourage the incorporation of required modifications on a timely basis. Similarly, transparent channels need to be established to allow communities to have a voice in evaluating project/program impact.

Regulations for Financial Institutions

Private sector initiatives aimed at delivering financial services to low-income populations need a conducive policy and regulatory environment, including interest rate liberalization and development of prudential regulations relating to capital adequacy that foster a more conducive environment for small-scale microcredit programs. It is important to foster an enabling environment to support monitoring/enforcement mechanisms for microfinance institutions (MFIs), including efforts to assist MFIs in improving the quality, consistency, and timeliness of information provided to regulators via their conformance to generally accepted accounting standards, as well as support capacity-building for regulators themselves.

Ensuring Land Availability and Security of Land Tenure

Secure Land Tenure Is Key to Sustainability...

Secure land tenure is one of the most important factors in the sustainability of any intervention in informal settlements. It is arguably the number one aspiration of Latin American informal settlement dwellers. It is also the key that unlocks investment in home improvement and motivates residents to help maintain new infrastructure and engage in further improvements.

...But Full Legalization Should Not Be Considered a Prerequisite

Full legal regularization of land tenure should not be considered a prerequisite for urban upgrading and shelter projects. The Costa Rican and Mexican cases show that this is a requirement that slows projects down and makes it difficult to achieve scale. Rather, it is important to identify the minimum level of legal recognition of settlements that is necessary to ensure security of tenure and to provide services and promote urban upgrading projects. Extension of basic services needs to be based on the mutual recognition of authorities and informal settlement residents. The recognition of the rights of settlers and the gradual upgrading of informal settlements may subsequently lead to an initiative for full tenure regularization.

Tenure Regularization as a Precondition for Infrastructure Investments

In Mexico, full land tenure regularization is a precondition for any investment in infrastructure in a settlement. Consequently, Mexico's federal government has set up a land tenure regularization program that is one of the largest and longest running in the world (it has been in operation since the early 1970s). The program is highly centralized and politically charged, having been considerably strengthened by the Mexican government in the early 1990s. The program has focused until now on *ejido* land. The ejidos, communally held agricultural properties, are the result of the agrarian reform brought about by the Mexican Revolution in the early 20th century. Many of them, located in rural areas that have since become urbanized, have been illegally subdivided into parcels that have been sold to low-income people. The dominant form of informal settlement in Mexico is not the squatter settlement, but the illegal subdivision.

Tenure Regularization as a Precondition for Housing Subsidies

Costa Rica's rigorous legal system—and its law-abiding tradition—makes it unthinkable to provide a housing subsidy to someone who is not the legal owner of a plot. There is no mention of an intermediate form of land tenure security short of full legalization. This means that a subsidy that is intended for the poor requires a precondition that the poor are rarely able to fulfill—and is part of the reason why it was necessary to create FUPROVI as a mechanism to enable poor families to fulfill the subsidy's requirements.

Housing associations usually come to FUPROVI after securing the land they need, usually through a grant or subsidized sale of public land holdings. The land then needs to have its legal situation checked and regularized, after which it needs to be parceled out to the members of the association. A land subdivision scheme needs to be designed, presented to the appropriate authorities and approved, and individual title deeds issued to each of the members of the association. Only then will they have access to the government housing subsidy.

Land tenure regularization is normally carried out in parallel with the construction of the new settlement and is completed by the time families start to move in. FUPROVI must complete regularization as soon as possible, for until then, it is unable to recover its bridging loan from the housing subsidy scheme; because the funds are tied up, FUPROVI is unable to move on to new projects.

A Specialized Authority Makes the Job Easier

Experience shows that governments' establishment of a specialized authority with competence in land use and tenure regularization in informal settlements (to handle permits, property titles, cadastral registers, etc.) is a positive measure. This specialized authority, as in the example given below of Baja California's State Commission for the Regularization of Land Tenure (CORETTE), should be capable of tackling the complex series of interrelated tasks necessary for tenure regularization. It also provides informal settlement residents with a "one-stop shop," instead of requiring them to face the bewildering array of government departments involved in legalization of land tenure.

In Tijuana, for example, land tenure regularization has proceeded at a steady pace since the 1990 creation of CORETTE, which concentrates all needed professional skills under one roof. Client relations, surveying, estimating, conveyance and legal services, and liaison with the land registry office are all provided by CORETTE.

CORETTE's systematic approach led to the delivery of about 38,000 title deeds between 1990 and 1996. CORETTE built on the experience of Mexico's long-standing federal regularization program, whose Tijuana branch delivered about 10,000 title deeds in the same period. Together, the state and federal programs succeeded in regularizing about 48,000 plots between 1990 and 1996—nearly half the existing demand at the time of 100,000 plots in Tijuana's informal *colonias populares* (illegal land subdivisions).

In Costa Rica, FUPROVI has a series of departments involved in ensuring regularization of land tenure. Its structure for this purpose is similar to CORETTE's. FUPROVI staff, who have legalized 15,000 plots between 1988 and 1998, believe that the process, which takes two years on average, is too slow.

Rationalize the Process or Change the Rules of the Game?

The relatively slow pace of CORETTE's and FUPROVI's progress is linked to their implicit acceptance of the status quo rules for land tenure regularization. All necessary tasks are located under a single roof, which streamlines a process that would probably not be feasible otherwise, but there is no attempt to simplify the regularization process per se, with its outdated procedures and unreasonable demands. Peru's Commission for the Formalization of Informal Property (COFOPRI), still an isolated example in Latin America, demonstrates that dramatic results may be achieved through reform of the land registration process itself.

COFOPRI's objective is to create a system that ensures formal and sustainable rights to real property in low-income settlements in larger urban areas. The Law of Promotion of Access to Formal Property that was passed in March 1996 essentially applied the new system to all of Peru's informal urban settlements. The program targets more than 4 million people, or around 25 percent of Peru's total population, including those living from just above to below the poverty line. The National Formalization Plan, supported by the World Bank, covers informal urban settlements in areas where poverty indicators, as measured by the lack of basic necessities (education, health, housing conditions, employment, and infrastructure services), are at their highest. COFOPRI assumed the functions of about 14 separate agencies that previously regulated the titling process and now issues titles on the basis of legal and physical verification in the field. Operating under streamlined verification and registration procedures, the Urban Property Registry works closely with COFOPRI to register titles into a National Formalization Plan. The registry has regularized around 1.2 million properties by 2003 through the new simplified process. COFOPRI titles over 10,000 urban properties each month. Prior to program implementation, titling costs were approximately $25 per square meter. It reportedly now takes one week at a cost of approximately $15 to register a mortgage.

Tenure Regularization Does Not Mean Automatic Access to Credit

Although the COFOPRI program has titled about 1.2 million lots, few associated homeowners have been able to access mortgage financing (only around 4,000 between 1996 and 1999). This is largely due to the various problems that make access to credit difficult for low-income people:

- The formal financial sector's lack of interest in this particular market segment
- The formal financial sector's lack of information and inability to evaluate the credit risk of low-income borrowers
- A lack of financial products specifically designed for the requirements of low-income borrowers
- Language, cultural, and gender differences between bank personnel and low-income communities, which have in turn led to significant social barriers.

Moreover, a title deed does not automatically mean that its owner will seek access to credit in the first place. Once their property is legalized, low-income residents already have 100 percent equity on their home. Their interest in taking out a mortgage to improve their homes or invest in a business may thus be limited.

Regularization of Private Lands Is Always More Difficult

The problem posed by the regularization of invaded private land is always a complex issue in any country, given the implications related to the legal nature of private property and the interests of formal owners. In Costa Rica, invasion of private land is by definition not bona fide, which precludes legalization. In contrast, in Brazil, the 1988 constitution established the social function of private property as a principle and urban usucaption or adverse prescription as a right. Usucaption, from Roman law, is the acquisition of a title or right to property by uninterrupted and undisputed possession for a prescribed term—for private urban land in Brazil, a term of five years.

In Guadalajara and Northern Mexico, some of the new local governments of the National Action Party have begun regularization of private lands through decentralized mechanisms and are cracking down on illegal land subdivision. Informal developers are being given jail sentences for the first time ever. This is certainly a positive development, but it would also be necessary to review the legal and regulatory tangle that, as in many other developing countries, encourages developers to subdivide land illegally. São Paulo's Guarapiranga project is a good example.

Misguided Legislative Zeal and Lack of Enforcement Capability May Lead to Widespread Land Invasions and Illegal Subdivisions

The Guarapiranga project conspicuously lacked a land tenure regularization component. This is understandable, given the complex legal and regulatory situation and because tenure regularization is usually not considered a precondition for infrastructure investment in Brazil. Interviews with local residents and technicians, however, suggest that this has had a negative impact on sustainability, and that much more investment by homeowners in shelter improvement could have been generated if the project had included a land tenure regularization strategy.

The explanation for this apparent gap in Guarapiranga's formulation is the same legal and regulatory tangle that has led to widespread informal occupation of the Guarapiranga basin in the first place. São Paulo's Water Catchment Areas Protection Act of 1975 is a prime example of the misguided zeal that led so many developing country legal codes to mirror colonial and industrialized country models. This has often led to the adoption of a legal and regulatory framework that is at best impossible to enforce, and at worst may have diametrically opposed effects to those desired, as seen in the Guarapiranga case.

The Water Catchment Areas Protection Act, in a bid to protect the reservoir from pollution, imposed low-density residential occupation as the only acceptable land use in the Guarapiranga basin. At the same time, regulations for the approval of land subdivisions were made much more stringent for lands located within a water catchment protection area. The combination of these two legal impediments led to a fall in value of the land around the Guarapiranga reservoir, making it attractive for low-income occupation, and to an incentive for developers to engage in illegal land subdivision. The Guarapiranga basin thus became São Paulo's biggest urban frontier, with hundreds of new occupations and hundreds of thousands of people attracted to the area by the jobs offered by the dynamic economy of the southern part of the metropolis.

Meanwhile, legal restrictions made it impossible for the state government or the municipalities to invest in basic infrastructure in the area, which has led to a huge deficit over the years. The Guarapiranga project required strong political will, for it required placing the reality of deprivation and environmental degradation first, and a flexible interpretation of the law. Fortunately, Brazilian legislation, unlike Mexican, does not impose tenure legalization as a precondition for investment in infrastructure.

Guarapiranga's perverse legal and regulatory tangle is only now beginning to be unraveled. The River Basin Management Act of 1997 repealed the restrictive provisions of the 1975 law and laid the foundations for area-based planning and stakeholder participation in river basin management.

Informal settlements, however, are still at least in theory under threat. Pollutant load limits have been set, and it will be up to municipalities to decide how such limits will have to be met within their territory. Better equipped municipalities will probably act on this faster and with better results. Smaller and poorer municipalities are slow to react to the new law, making it very likely that the legal tangle—or at least a legal void—will persist. Security of tenure will in this case remain elusive for hundreds of thousands of people, and all the uncertainty, social malaise, and disincentive to investment associated with uncertain tenure will continue.

Mechanisms Are Needed for Affordable Land Release

The lack of appropriate mechanisms to release sufficient affordable land into the market is one of the key reasons why the urban poor squat in the first place. As the example of Peru shows, when land is made available in a reasonably orderly way, even though services may be a long way off in coming to an area, the worst long-term layout problems typically found in informal settlements are avoided.[4] Apart from their overall importance, land release mechanisms may be an important element in an urban upgrading strategy, and a crucial one in cases in which there is need for much involuntary resettlement. Resettlement is arguably the most difficult issue to be addressed by upgrading interventions, because of its social impact and cost implications. A range of instruments needs to be deployed to cope with it, including the development of housing for various income brackets and new settlements using sites and services approaches or variants of Peru's *lotes con tiza* (surveyed and beaconed plots) strategy in the vicinity of the original settlement.

Strategic Alliances

Key Actors: Who Are They?

An urban upgrading project is a complex undertaking that requires a common goal and long-term coordinated action by many parties. The capacity to involve key stakeholders in strategic alliances often means the difference between success and failure, and is a key program coordination role. Urban upgrading cuts across disciplinary and institutional boundaries and involves an impressive array of stakeholders, including:

---

[4]These problems include lack of definition of public and private spaces, plots without direct access to a public thoroughfare, lack of an adequate road system, and lack of rights of way for the installation of network infrastructure.

- The local residents or groups that stand to benefit from the program or project
- The various public authorities with jurisdiction over the area
- Public or private utility companies
- Formal and informal landowners
- Formal and informal land developers
- Owners and managers of area businesses
- Managers and staff of public or nongovernmental facilities in the area (such as health centers, schools, daycare centers)
- Politicians and political party activists
- Development NGOs or other private nonprofit organizations and intermediaries that propose to represent the interests of the poor
- Religious groups
- Micro- or small enterprises that provide infrastructure services in such areas as water, sanitation, telephony, road maintenance, etc.
- Technical and professional associations
- Foundations, microfinance institutions, and other private financial entities
- Private businesses whose employees live in the area
- The private firms providing services in the context of a program or project.

Alliances with these parties should not be seen as a substitute for the need to strengthen public sector capacity. All the cases we have studied suggest just the opposite: for the partnerships to achieve their full potential, private actors require effective public partners. The idea of partnerships is clearly still one that is rather alien to a public sector emerging from decades as the sole arbitrator of the common good, but the will to change seems to be emerging, albeit slowly and unevenly.

New Actors on the Urban Relations Scene

Urban planning instruments are becoming less top down and prescriptive as the role of the state is progressively redefined and urban governance relies more and more on participatory mechanisms. The reality of the city is the product of the actions of myriad public, private, and community-based actors. Development activities in complex urban situations thus need to involve a growing number of stakeholders, all with vitally important functions and roles. As we have stressed in the introduction, when we speak of participation, we refer to a broader concept than simply the relationship between promoters and beneficiaries of projects.

The surge of new actors on the urban relations scene implies various changes, many of which open a route to more democratic, participatory, and sustainable development of cities. All urban policies—and all activities realized through urban programs and projects—are influenced by these trends.

Municipalities stand out among these emerging players. Even in countries with a strong centralist tradition, municipalities have taken on a key role in recent years, as in the case of Bolivia. City governments are the ones that frequently take the initiative in housing and infrastructure projects—and, even when they do not, they are always an important actor. Without the municipality's active involvement, even projects that are sponsored by central governments and international donors have serious difficulties, as the Participatory Action Planning projects in Bolivia clearly show.

By contrast, the community-based urban movements that were so strong in Latin America in the 1970s and 1980s have declined, along with the broader networks of neighborhood associations and federations. These have been weakened by their dependence on political parties and difficulties in renewal of leadership. On the other hand, in recent years new forms of partnership with civil society have become increasingly common. Such organizations as development and environmental NGOs and professional associations (of engineers, architects, or lawyers) are showing increasing capacity and a more professional attitude. Groups based on ethnicity, like black or indigenous movements, are also on the rise. Although with different motivations, many of these groups purport to speak for the sectors of the population that stand to benefit from urban upgrading and low-income housing programs.

Finally, phenomena such as the privatization of utility services and the large-scale upgrading projects that involve construction and engineering firms and other for-profit private actors create new roles for private enterprise. These roles include traditional areas such as engineering, planning, and construction as well as new opportunities in project management, quality control, and socio-technical support.

Identifying Key Partners

The variety of actors and stakeholders with potential roles makes it important to manage the choice of partners for a program or project carefully. With distinct interests and priorities, diverse backgrounds, differing institutional and funding capacity, and various levels of power and influence, this choice presents a challenge. It is crucial to achieve a unified and shared vision of the objectives and strategic plan. Once this is resolved, there is the further need to identify a partnership that may make it possible to define a resource base for the project and set up an efficient operation, coordinating the modes and pace of action of the various actors. The process of partnership building should make it possible for each participant to be heard and to be involved in the definition of precise tasks and responsibilities.

Not all parties that have an interest in the project can automatically become associates; one important filtering criterion is their possible contribution (that is, not only what they plan to gain from the project, but also what they can give). We must also ask ourselves what reasons would impede the participation of any actor in the project. The attempt to overlook actors who may appear less directly involved with the objectives of the project for fear of losing time or power, or for fear that the process may become too complex sometimes transforms potential partners into damaging opponents. This process may be reversed if an effort is made to involve these actors (see, for example, the difficult relations of the program management unit with environmental NGOs in Guarapiranga).

Evaluation of Options to Select Public Sector Partners

Public entities are the traditional partners of development aid institutions. They are responsible for repaying loans and are the ultimate decisionmakers regarding the policies, programs, and projects assisted by international organizations. Although the public sector continues to be the first interlocutor, note that, as part of the changes in the role of government over recent years, decisionmaking and power over projects are being shared more and more with other actors.

One positive trend—but one that also presents risks, as we will see below—is the decentralization of the functions of central governments as well as of the provincial level and large municipalities. Decentralization makes it possible for funding to be channeled through local governments, bringing decisionmaking closer to the beneficiaries. This option requires investment in skill development, since the technical capabilities of the local level are often scarce. As far as the applicable laws and situation permit, it is better to avoid a dual command situation and to weigh down a project by involving too many central government organizations. If a municipality or province responds individually for a loan, it is better to involve national structures only at a supervisory and controlling level.

Even though it is necessary to choose a principal stakeholder from among the public entities involved (see box 5-2), it is also important to establish effective channels of consultation with other entities that are directly or indirectly involved in the process. Such channels should be operational throughout the project, from the preparation phase through design through implementation and operation and maintenance of the project, so that their technical requirements and contributions may be taken into account.

> **Box 5-2. Choosing Public Sector Partners**
>
> There is a clear trend toward the management of projects by the lowest appropriate level of government, i.e., a municipality or a subdelegation, *casa municipal*, or *subalcaldía* (administrative subdivision of a municipality) in the case of large municipalities.
>
> The involvement of various line agencies as partners is positive, but it is important that the coordinating role be entrusted to organizations that by nature have a global vision of urban policy.
>
> In most successful projects, the public entities have chosen to delegate functions and responsibilities to private sector groups and to the population. This has modified the management style of the projects, which is now more focused on efficiency gains, cost control, and the achievement of concrete results within a well-defined time frame.
>
> Delegation of tasks has not weakened the capacity of public entities to control a project (if we understand the term "control" to mean the capacity to ensure results and not merely the affirmation of power). Moreover, delegation has enhanced budgeting and cost control methods, and has led to greater cost consciousness of both government and communities. This is a dramatic change from when the functions of planning, implementation, and control resided entirely with the public promoter of the project.

One factor that has made programs and projects more efficient and effective is the delegation of functions and responsibilities to private sector actors. Examples like Guarapiranga, for the for-profit private sector, and FUPROVI, for the nongovernmental sector, show that it is possible for a public entity to delegate functions to the commercial or nonprofit private sector without losing control of the process and with clear gains in efficiency and effectiveness. The Cali partnership example given in chapter 2 is another good illustration of this.

Involving the Private Sector

The examples we have studied show that the participation of both the for-profit and nonprofit private sector and the involvement of civil society can increase the impact and sustainability of urban upgrading and low-income housing programs and projects.

Private organizations intervene in low-income areas for a variety of reasons: with a developmental motive, as in the case of nonprofit organizations; or by necessity, as in the case of the privatized utilities that need to increase market share, develop an image as a good corporate citizen, and/or improve cost recovery in low-income areas. Without overcoming the paternalistic relationship that state-run utilities have traditionally had with low-income people, they will never be able to meet the investment and service expansion targets imposed by regulators while operating within reasonable tariff levels.

Two key elements guarantee the development of private sector participation in urban upgrading and low-income housing:

- **Continuity.** Entry into any new market typically involves considerable upfront investment and opportunity costs in terms of gathering information; developing a business strategy; and mobilizing the required technical, human, and financial resources. One-off transactions rarely justify such investments. Rather, the private sector tends to seek out the elements that can guarantee the continuity of a process—and guarantees its own development in this way. Thus, a "specialized" private sector (which is totally or partially focused on the market segment represented by the urban poor) comes into being. FUPROVI is a good example of a private sector actor that has always focused on creating the necessary conditions for its own continuity in its market segment.
- **Strategic alliances.** The complexity, diversity, and dynamism of informal settlements requires specialization. Emerging specialized organizations tend to develop strategic alliances with other parts of the private sector as well as with the public sector. These alliances in turn strengthen the specialization of each participant. For a privatized water utility, for example, an important benefit relates directly to core business activities and its ability to gain markets. Through a partnership with an NGO, it may be able to fulfill its commitment under the privatization agreement to expand coverage to low-income communities. In addition, its staff can receive training from the NGO and acquire skills in how to work with low-income communities. The company's ability to work with this nontraditional clientele may become a key comparative advantage in international bids for contracts. For the NGO partner, such a partnership may allow it to achieve a much higher level of effectiveness in its work at the neighborhood level, as well as provide the opportunity to expand its influence on local development issues to other neighborhoods and municipalities.

These key elements apply to both for-profit and nonprofit private organizations. If a specialized organization wishes to establish a sustainable process, it must meet the above two conditions. For example, we have seen that FUPROVI has planned for its continuity since the beginning as one of the founding tenets of the organization. FUPROVI did not come into being in order to manage a specific project with a limited budget and time frame. It was formed to confront the problem of low-income housing in Costa Rica in general terms, based on a certain amount of start-up funding that it sought to preserve and leverage. The institution has endowed itself with a structure that is adequate to its specific market sector and has invested in staff development from the beginning. The programs with which it currently works are products created by trained and experienced teams that are able to develop new participatory programs in response to the needs that arise in their daily work.

The Role of the For-Profit Sector

A glance at urban upgrading and low-income housing projects shows that the role of private enterprise has traditionally been limited to the provision of some types of specific services. Architects, engineers, and public works contractors are normally the only private sector actors present in upgrading, while private financial institutions are added to the list in the case of low-income housing in some countries.

Some recent examples suggest that the private for-profit sector has a wider role to play in urban upgrading processes. Some of the innovations that we have observed include the case of private providers of sociotechnical support in Brazil, who are beginning cost recovery programs on behalf of some of the recently privatized electricity companies. Other examples include for-profit microcredit institutions that grant credit for home and community infrastructure improvement projects, such as Caja Popular Mexicana in Mexico, Financiera Calpia in El Salvador, and Caja de los Andes and BancoSol in Bolivia.

The market potential for private for-profit actors in upgrading and low-income housing includes:

- Engineering firms
- Architecture and urban planning firms
- Building contractors
- Project and contract management providers
- Quality control providers
- Financial institutions (commercial banks and microfinance institutions)
- Cooperatives of technicians (like the *assessorias* of São Paulo's *mutirão* programs and the Catuche consortium in Caracas)
- Socio-technical support providers
- Building materials suppliers
- Private landowners
- Privatized utilities
- Small and medium-sized providers of infrastructure services (see box 5-3).

> **Box 5-3. Micro- and Small Enterprises in Solid Waste Management**
>
> One of the infrastructure services that could be delivered via micro- and small enterprises in urban upgrading programs is waste management. A study carried out by the NGOs IPES (Peru), ACEPESA (Costa Rica), and WASTE International (the Netherlands) in 1996 covered a total of 89 micro- and small enterprises involved in street sweeping, collection, recycling, and disposal in seven countries in Latin America. Although there are huge differences in the operations of the enterprises studied, some of the common aspects and main findings can be summarized as follows:
>
> - Some of the enterprises studied started in the early 1950s (Guatemala and Costa Rica). They deliver services mainly in middle- and high-income areas. At the end of the 1980s and beginning of the 1990s, enterprises were set up under different development programs in, among other countries, Bolivia, Peru, and Colombia. They particularly serve low-income areas. Most of the enterprises studied are still operating. However, in Peru, microenterprises had to discontinue their services, because the municipalities where they had previously offered their services had decided not to renew their contracts. The principal reason for this was that the municipalities in the meantime had acquired compactor trucks (basically from donations) and began offering their own services.
> - Costs of the enterprises studied are lower than or equal to the costs of conventional systems within the region. Average collection costs are $15 to $25/tonne in Latin America; costs of the enterprises studied vary between $7.50/tonne in Guatemala and $19.50/tonne in Bolivia. Average street sweeping and cleaning costs vary from $7 to $12 per curb kilometer in Latin America, while costs of the enterprises in Peru are around $4.50.
> - The relationships between the municipalities and the enterprises are very different in the countries investigated. In Guatemala, the relationship is distant because the municipality does not intervene in any way in the functioning of waste collection. There the enter-

Investing in the Informal Sector. For decades, urban policies in many countries have ignored the informal sector and have concentrated all planning and land management functions in the state. The result has been an apartheid-like division between formal and informal sectors, where legal, economic, and social systems have functioned according to separate logics. The private business sector's usual lack of interest in investing in the informal sector reflects this segregation. Yet the new

> prises decide for themselves who they will provide their services to, how much they will charge their clients, when they will attend to them, and so forth. In Peru, on the other hand, the municipality determines in great detail how the enterprises must operate. In general, adequate municipal supervision enhances quality of service.
> - In the majority of the cases, the enterprises operate under contract or concession from the municipality. Contracts vary from a period of four to six months (Colombia) to a period of 10 years (Costa Rica and Guatemala), but are usually for a period of one year. Some enterprises operate without written contracts but have been granted authority to operate by the municipality. Contracts help clarify the tasks both of the enterprises and of the municipality and improve the quality of service. Even when there is no contract, a dependency relationship with the municipality exists; for example, for secondary collection or for access to the final disposal sites.
> - The waste collection enterprises establish close relationships with the communities they serve. They usually offer personalized service and form part of the community. The client's satisfaction with the service offered is a necessary condition for success. In some cases, e.g., in Bolivia, community associations supervise the performance of the enterprises.
> - Waste collection enterprises obtain their revenues either by charging the population directly or by being paid by the municipality. The arrangement depends on what works best in the particular local situation. In Guatemala, the method of direct payment by the residents is very effective. In Peru, where the municipality has granted the enterprises the right to charge the people directly for this service in some areas, this method has had little success, and nonpayment or delayed payment is a frequent result. One of the reasons for nonpayment is that people consider that these services should be provided by the government free of charge. Municipalities also can be bad payers, as is also the case in Peru, where payment may be delayed by several months.
>
> *Source:* Arroyo and Larinois (1999).

supermarkets, building materials suppliers, and automobile service stations that can be seen sprouting up in places like the Florido-Mariano district of Tijuana, or the telecenter operations that offer telephone, fax, and Internet services in Lima, are proof that changes are under way. These investments create job opportunities in low-income areas and can contribute to the start of a cycle of gradual increase in residents' incomes. Urban upgrading projects can contribute decisively to the elimination of some key obstacles to private business investment by improving access to the areas; solving conflicts on landownership; and improving essential infrastructure such as water, sanitation, and electricity.

Private Business as a Project Sponsor. It should be possible to create incentives for various forms of association with the private business sector in undertaking urban upgrading projects. The involvement of the private for-profit sector in sponsoring upgrading projects is a very recent phenomenon, and there is scarcely a track record yet established. Nonetheless, our interviews with private business leaders in Tijuana and Ciudad Juárez have shown that a well-planned and efficiently run initiative could attract considerable business support. The logic for private sector involvement may be one of trying to develop its image as a good corporate citizen; expanding its market share; or that the target settlement may be home to a firm's employees.[5] In the logic of participatory area development planning, private businesses with interests in the area could be consulted to explore possibilities for synergy and collaboration. Through these consultations, partnerships and specific agreements could be reached concerning one or more aspects of the project.

Upgrading Can Create Job Opportunities. Another aspect that should be emphasized is that the public works contracts involved in upgrading can offer job opportunities to the local population. Many projects negotiate specific conditions for the training and hiring of labor with the contractors responsible for the work. An example of such synergy is in Brazil, where an agreement with SENAI (a training entity allied with the Federation of Industries) has allowed the training of the local construction workers who took part in the Novos Alagados project in Bahia. An agreement with the contractor gave hiring priority to area residents, reducing unemployment in the area by 25 percent. In Belo Horizonte, Brazil, upgrading projects in the Nossa Senhora Aparecida and 31 de Março slums have actively encouraged the establishment of small local businesses that performed project-related construction work. These businesses have continued to operate in the external market. Also in Belo Horizonte, collection of construction-related waste was put in the hands of community cooperatives, especially when it required the employment of manual labor due to difficult access to the sites. Public agencies here had shown a certain reluctance to employ large contingents of local residents, since

---

[5]Improving living conditions could contribute to reduction of employee turnover and increase worker productivity, which is extremely high in the *maquiladora* industry of Mexico's northern border.

they feared political pressure to keep people in employment even after the end of the works, which does not seem unjustified. More involvement of private sector actors could modify this scenario and broaden the opportunities for the employment of local people, community cooperatives, and small local businesses in local projects.

Involving the Nonprofit Private Sector. While the private for-profit sector needs incentives to do more in low-income areas, the nonprofit sector appears to face the opposite problem. Despite the considerable growth of nonprofit organizations in both qualitative and quantitative terms, governments are still reluctant to work with NGOs. One example of such reluctance is that consulting and project management assignments for which NGOs could be qualified are often subjected to procurement procedures that make it difficult for them to compete for contracts.

Nonetheless, private nonprofit organizations (NGOs, foundations, and associations that purport to represent the population's interests) more and more frequently act as key project participants for the following reasons:

- Their knowledge of the culture, needs, and aspirations of poor communities makes them effective mediators between the population and the government.
- Their greater flexibility in managing funds than is possessed by public entities makes them attractive channels for more efficient disbursement of project funds.
- There is a growing political acceptance of the social role that such intermediaries can play in development activities.

This has impelled the emergence of new NGOs and the growth of existing ones, and above all, has begun to create a wealth of experience and specialized know-how in the nongovernmental sector. NGOs can play two roles in upgrading and low-income housing: at the program level and at the project level. They also often carry out both functions in a complementary fashion.

1. **At the program level, in association with other actors.** In this scenario, the NGO plays the role of the program management unit and usually also of the program promoting agency. FUPROVI is one such nonprofit organization that performs both roles. Another example of an NGO that both promotes and manages a program, although in this case in association with municipal organizations, is the Association of Volunteers for International Cooperation (AVSI) in Belo Horizonte. This NGO has catalyzed resources and partnerships for the formulation and application of the PROFAVELA law. The result in both cases was the development of approaches and

methodologies that have had a strong impact on public policy. In Bolivia, NGOs such as Red Hábitat and Gregoria Apaza in El Alto (discussed in chapter 6), the Institute of Integrated Training for Women in Cochabamba, and Cidcruz and the Center for Urban and Regional Development in Santa Cruz provide program support both to municipalities and community organizations, especially in participatory long-term planning.

2. **At the project level, working in the project area alongside the community.** This is a very common situation with several variants. FUPROVI, in the case of San Juan de Pavas, executed the project as part of a program that had been promoted by another institution. As we have seen, FUPROVI usually works both at the program and project levels, as does AVSI in Belo Horizonte, where it helps define participatory development plans in each area. The NGO Desco in Villa El Salvador, Peru, similarly provides program support to the municipality and the Self-Managed Urban Community of Villa El Salvador (CUAVES), while also promoting specific projects.

In Guarapiranga and Tijuana, although NGOs are active in the informal settlements, they are not involved in urban development or housing work. NGOs function as social service providers in Tijuana and Ciudad Juárez, and as environmental organizations in Guarapiranga.

The Advantages of NGOs. The participation of NGOs and similar institutions can be particularly fruitful for the development of some project tasks for which public entities are less sensitive and organizationally more rigid. Among these are the capacity to gather information and analyze needs with the cooperation and involvement of the population, social communication and the strengthening of community organization, and attention to the use of local resources and of low-cost appropriate technology. NGOs generally appear to be better at providing socio-technical support, assisting communities in the design and management of their own development projects, than are public entities. In the context of the cases studied, FUPROVI in San José, Desco in Lima, and Red Hábitat and Gregoria Apaza in El Alto are NGOs performing essential development promotion and support functions.

NGOs can also be important fundraising agents. Besides finding resources for a project, they often succeed in obtaining further in-kind or financial support to solve specific problems and broaden the project budget to account for the unforeseen circumstances that are so common in upgrading projects.

Another advantage NGOs often have over the state is the tendency to favor the continuity of upgrading actions. In the Latin American context, there is a strong inclination by new administrations to discontinue their predecessor's programs. NGOs often serve as a connecting link between successive municipal administrations, exerting pressure to complete an initiative that is under way. They are often also the only guardians of the historical and documentary memory of the process of intervention. A good example in this sense is ASVI, which serves as a guarantor of the continuity of the PROFAVELA program in Belo Horizonte.

The Liabilities of NGOs. The problems that have arisen in many situations result from some organizations' lack of technical capacity and from the difficulties and limitations of certain NGOs in working with large institutions and managing financial resources. Some NGOs are very adept at social promotion work among the population, but they dedicate little time and resources to written documentation and systematization of methodology. As a result, their experiences are difficult to reproduce in other situations and on a larger scale.

Moreover, some NGOs focus on the promotion of one particular cause in such an exclusive way that they lose sight of many of the factors at play in a given situation. This can produce a sterile, confrontational relationship with government and impede collaboration, which is the basis for all successful cases of NGO involvement. In successful cases, the all-too-typical lack of trust between government and NGOs is overcome through a conscious effort on both sides.

National and international NGOs often work together, which tends to work well, since their strengths and weaknesses are complementary. National NGOs can be more aware of the needs and preferences of local people, but are subject to the manipulations of local interests; the latter, by contrast, generally possess a certain cultural and economic independence and more advanced levels of organization and resource administration. International NGOs, however, do not always know how to meet local needs and demands. In many successful cases, one sees forms of alliance and collaboration between local and international NGOs. However, the nongovernmental sector is so broad and diversified that it is difficult to generalize about qualities and defects. Some so-called NGOs have self-serving, rather than developmental, goals; some have even served as vehicles for corruption. The very term "nongovernmental organization" has a different meaning in each country. In some countries, any not-for-profit association in the field of civil society can call itself an NGO; while in others there are forms of classification, accreditation, and control that regulate their activities and their possibilities of access to financing.

These points demonstrate the need to establish selection criteria for organizations under consideration as partners or associates of a program or project. Among the possible types of information to be considered in evaluating candidate NGOs are:

- Their documented work experiences with grassroots organizations in urban poverty reduction projects
- The qualifications, experience, availability, and motivation of their technical team
- The specific staffing arrangements, work methodology, and budget they present for the project.

Institutional Arrangements and Decentralization

One of the issues discussed in chapter 4 is the choice of program format. The social investment fund format (and its variant, participatory budgeting) and the comprehensive upgrading program format were identified as the main existing formats. In the former, communities present requests to a facility that selects and funds projects. This format has the advantage of ensuring response to direct demand, and the disadvantage of encouraging a piecemeal approach to upgrading, since community requests are normally not based on any coherent plan. In the comprehensive upgrading program format, investments fit into a coherent overall plan, and the interactions among infrastructure systems are taken into account. However, unless every effort is made to involve the community in the discussion of alternatives and their cost, comprehensive upgrading may select costly solutions that preclude tariff-based cost recovery.

Organizing and creating channels for participation that ensure response to demand does not mean that one can forget the supply side. In fact, participatory upgrading requires a stronger supply mechanism than conventional urban development work, because of the much wider skill set and stronger coordination capacity that is required.

Area-based needs assessment, planning, and implementation has been identified as a key requirement of urban upgrading. The potential for conflict with traditional line agency-based institutional structures has been identified and discussed, and the need for a strong coordination mechanism that is accepted by all parties has been determined. The various possible institutional arrangements have been discussed in an earlier chapter and are further explored in this chapter. Decentralization, with its advantages and pitfalls, is also discussed in detail in this chapter. Decentralization processes are often not as well-thought-out and well-managed as would be desirable, and it is important to identify recurrent problems and possible solutions. Examples drawn from the cases studied are briefly discussed below and summarized in tables 5-2 and 5-3.

The genesis of a program or project usually defines the key actors and their functions. Government is almost always involved from the very beginning, either because it promotes the project directly (as in Guarapiranga or Tijuana), or because a government entity acts as a resource and focal point for a range of partner organizations.

Strong government involvement is the rule rather than the exception. In a few cases, the state plays a more limited role of promoter and regulator—as in the case of FUPROVI's program in Costa Rica—but it tends to play a dominant role in most cases. This does not mean that there have not been changes in the role of government. The key role of partnerships and the abandonment of a sectoral approach in favor of an area-based, integrated approach are two of the most important and far-reaching of these changes. They are also elements of successful large-scale programs such as Guarapiranga or Favela-Bairro.

The viability of undertaking a partnership-based interdisciplinary program or project at scale thus depends a great deal on government's openness to two factors:

- A real participation of the government's partners in the definition of the strategic plan
- An integrated, area-based approach to problems and to the development of alternative solutions involving the different spheres of the administration.

It may thus be said that the project begins with the meeting of its different actors, and its institutional structure is a consequence of the culture and modus operandi of its context. The idea of participatory budgeting arises from the encounter between the political will of the administration (or, in the Bolivian case, the administration's legal obligations) and the demand of the neighborhood groups. In the case of FUPROVI, the point of departure is the basic need for housing, and the decision on the part of the government to meet this need. In addition, the availability of international support (in this case, from the Swedish International Development Agency) played a key role. In the case of the legalization and upgrading of informal settlements in Belo Horizonte, the process began with a coalition of grassroots organizations and local and international civil society which succeeded in pressuring local government to change the rules and in garnering local and international funding.

Table 5-2 gives the general features of the cases we have studied in terms of program type and responsibility for promotion and process coordination. Table 5-3 explores the ways in which key responsibilities were allocated in the institutional arrangement adopted.

Table 5-2. Process Features in the Cases Studied

Feature	Bolivia	Brazil	Costa Rica	Mexico	Peru
Program type	Participatory budgeting at local level based on specific central government transfers; piecemeal upgrading	Upgrading program	Participatory low-income housing development	Participatory budgeting at local level based on central and state government transfers plus local resources; piecemeal upgrading	A process, not a program
Process type	Urban upgrading (isolated works) and social investment	Integrated urban upgrading	New housing and infrastructure	Urban upgrading (isolated works)	Building of a city
Process promotion	State (central)	State (provincial); state (local)	State (central); NGO	State (local)	State (central); state (local); ABCO
Program coordination	State (local)	State (local)	NGO	State (local)	State (central); state (local); ABCO
Methodologies used	Participatory budgeting with community control of expenditure; general meetings of ABCOs; neighborhood associations and surveillance committees are area-based	Participation in definition of upgrading plan and during works implementation, involving both ABCOs and SPCOs	Assisted mutual-help construction; community management of the works (shared control)	Participatory budgeting, community management of the works (shared control) and community financial contribution	Entire city based on community management principle (shared control) local government established on basis of preexisting ABCO; the use of *lotes con plano y plan* strategy;[a] direct democracy mechanisms

Feature	Bolivia	Brazil	Costa Rica	Mexico	Peru
Socio-technical support	Scarce (exception is PAP project)	Intense, but limited time frame; absent in post-implementation period	Intense and long-term (18 to 24 months), but absent in post-implementation period	Limited in intensity and time frame; absent in post-implementation period	Limited outside support, due to high level of community organization, responsibilities can be shared among local government, ABCOs, and SPCOs
Resettlement/ replacement housing	In a few cases	Yes	In a few cases	No	No

[a]Beaconed sites plus a development plan.
Source: Authors' construction from field study data.

Table 5-3. Allocation of Responsibilities among the Partners in the Cases Studied

Responsibility	Bolivia	Brazil	Costa Rica	Mexico	Peru
Project management	S-L	PC	NGO; SPCO	S-L; SPCO	S-C; S-L; ABCO; SPCO
Socio-technical support	S-L	PC	NGO	S-L	S-L: ABCO; SPCO
Construction	PC	PC	SPCO	PC; SPCO	S-C; PC
Engineering, architecture, and urban planning	S-L	PC	NGO	S-L	S-C; S-L
Quality control (works)	S-L	PC	NGO	S-L; SPCO	S-C; S-L
Control of budgetary expenditures	S-L; ABCO	S-L	NGO; SPCO	S-L; SPCO	S-C; S-L; ABCO; SPCO

PC   private contractor
S-C   state (central)
S-L   state (local)
Source: Authors' construction from field study data.

Dealing with Decentralization

Over the past 30 years, the concept of decentralization has gained wide acceptance. It has been translated into policy—and, in turn, into programs and projects—by decisionmakers and policymakers at all levels from international organizations to local governments, although with many different approaches. Decentralization can be considered one of the global trends that characterize economic and social development in the world today (CERFE 1995).

The rationale is that decentralization, by delegating resources and responsibilities to the lowest appropriate level, brings government closer to the people it serves, recognizing that local governments, being closer to the problems, have access to knowledge about local constraints and resources that provincial and central governments will never have, and are likely to be more accountable and use simpler procedures.

Decentralization has been implemented in many contexts. Urban policies in Brazil, the new role of municipalities in Venezuela, the recently enacted Costa Rican local government reform, the decentralization that has accompanied democratization in Mexico and Bolivia, health policy in countries as disparate as Brazil and Burkina Faso, and rural development initiatives in many countries are only a few examples. Nonetheless, while recognizing both the need for decentralization and its highly positive aspects, it is useful to undertake a serious analysis of the limits and negative aspects that decentralization policies have often had.

The Three Missed Opportunities of Decentralization

It is possible to identify at least three missed opportunities that are often evident in decentralization processes:

- **Responsibility.** Theoretically, since decentralization attributes more functions to those who are closer to the problem, it should also increase their administrative, technical, and implementation responsibilities. In practice, however, since these people are often given a weak motivational structure (e.g., inadequate salary ranges, career opportunities, and status), they tend to pass on the responsibility for resolving thorny problems. In addition, a lack of clarity in determining roles and responsibilities at the various levels can weigh down the entire process and can in fact lead to a decrease in responsibility.
- **Bureaucratic simplification**, a goal toward which administrations that want to be closer to the people strive. Decentralization does not mean the elimination of central or provincial actors. In practice, therefore, decentralization increases the number of bureaucratic layers, as each decisionmaking level has its own bureaucratic structure. In particular, in situations of overlapping administrative levels, each level will usually retain some of the responsibility over a given issue, which causes bureaucratic complications and delays.
- **Local knowledge.** A local government is by definition located in the town or city that it administers, and the assumption is that it knows much more about it than the faraway central government. This can only be true, however, if the local government has the will or material conditions to produce that knowledge, which does not happen in many cases. Frequently, for lack of human or financial resources, local decisionmakers fall into the "sorcerer's apprentice" syndrome, and learn about or "know" their area through common sense only—and often through prejudiced eyes. This is particularly true in the case of informal settlements and areas of urban poverty in general. Recently, and with difficulty, local governments have begun to recognize the role of information not as a luxury, but as an indispensable tool of government.

It should be noted that centralized administrations are not necessarily models of responsibility, bureaucratic simplification, and local knowledge either. Better coordination and information exchange among peers, one of the supposed advantages of centralized administrations, often exist only in theory.

Decentralization Policies Are Rarely Financed Adequately

Several points must be noted in this context:

- There are many different forms of decentralization. These can be differentiated by their focus (for example, political, fiscal, or administrative decentralization) or by the degree to which decentralization is implemented.
- The resources needed to implement decentralization policies are often not available. From many of the reports prepared by developing countries for the Habitat II Conference in 1996, it was clear that decentralization policies were proposed and implemented to some degree in most countries through more or less adequate reforms in the political, administrative, and legal arenas. However, decentralization policies were hardly ever adequately financed.
- Given the municipalities' proximity to the local community, their ability to provide a more effective interface in terms of engaging local people in the design, implementation, funding, monitoring, and expansion of local programs is fundamental for program social and financial sustainability. However, most municipalities do not have the needed institutional capacity in areas relating to community mobilization, technical assistance, proposal preparation, and—especially—expenditure management, revenue mobilization, intergovernmental transfers, sound financial management practices, and appropriate frameworks for municipal borrowing.

A Framework for Municipal Finance

The severity of the resource bottleneck means that the success of decentralization policies hinges on the improvement of local government financial and institutional capacity, the development of optimal funding strategies for local infrastructure investments, and increasing the stream of private financing for local governments and other subsovereign entities. Key areas of concern in this regard are the following:

- **Local government institutional capacity,** including improving regulations; strengthening autonomy, accountability, and operating capabilities; and promoting private participation and competition in the provision of local infrastructure

- **Local government financial management and creditworthiness,** including improving intergovernmental fiscal relations, improving municipal tax administration, and enhancing local government budget processes and improving payment, cash management, and financial control systems.
- **Local government investments and access to private capital markets,** including strengthening the review process of local public investment programs and outlining the conditions for mobilizing debt funding and budget-neutral funding schemes
- **Role of financial intermediation for local governments,** including the structural, regulatory, and institutional changes needed to develop market-based financial intermediaries; the elements of public support that might initially be needed to assist such intermediaries; and the steps by which existing financial intermediaries could be transformed into market-based operations
- **Links to the capital markets infrastructure,** including discussing benchmarks for pricing debt obligations of subsovereign entities, outlining measures aimed at bridging the gap between demand for and supply of local government securities, and outlining approaches to building closer financial partnerships between local governments and providers of financial services and capital.

Human Resources Are an Even Worse Problem

Local government finances are no doubt a major problem for the implementation of decentralization policies. However, the lack of qualified human resources is an even more serious problem. Decentralization of any kind necessarily means accepting the challenge of greatly increasing the need for qualified personnel.

Decentralization Can Backfire If Certain Conditions Are Not Met

In brief, decentralization is without a doubt a positive political, institutional, and social process. But if certain conditions are not met (authenticity of the process, adequate financing, availability of motivated and qualified personnel in sufficient numbers, clarity in the distribution of responsibility to the different levels, etc.), decentralization can backfire badly—or, at the very least, become a futile waste of energy.

In the cases we have studied, there are several examples of the positive impacts of decentralization and also of its risks—often in the same case. In Mexico, for example, the highly centralized federal program for land tenure regularization has been successful. But it is the ongoing process of decentralization and democratization that is allowing an important step forward—going beyond the legalization of the subdivision of ejido lands, into legalization of tenure in the case of illegal subdivisions of private lands in Guadalajara and other cities.

Centralization versus Decentralization: Two Mexican Cases

It is useful to analyze the differences between the Obra Social Comunitaria programs in two northern border towns, Tijuana and Ciudad Juárez. Municipal governments in Mexico are free to adopt a centralized or a decentralized structure as they see fit. Tijuana and Juárez, two cities of similar size (about 1.5 million), have gone opposite ways: Tijuana's local government is highly decentralized; Juárez's is centralized. Tijuana's territory is subdivided into delegations, with the larger delegations divided into subdelegations. The delegate and subdelegate are the representatives of the local government in their areas, and they are equipped with staff, office space, and equipment to cater to many needs of local residents. They are also there to transmit requests and suggestions to the municipality's specialized branches and to coordinate their action in the area. The delegation is thus a sort of local government one-stop shop.

In Tijuana, the OSC program has seen increasing delegation of powers and resources to the level of the delegation and subdelegation. At the start of the program with Manos a la Obra in 1995, all social promoters worked for the Municipal Administration of Social Development (DESOM). Similarly, all the technicians who assisted communities and oversaw the works belonged to the Municipal Urbanization Unit (UMU), the public company in charge of urban development projects. More powers were passed on to the delegations and subdelegations each year, and, in the 1998 program, Más por Tijuana, social promoters and technicians worked directly for the delegations and subdelegations.

The advantage of decentralization is that social promoters and technicians are now closer to the people, and more day-to-day decisions may be made locally. In fact, the delegate or subdelegate is far closer to the reach of common people than the faraway authorities at the town hall.

There have been disadvantages as well. When all social promoters worked for DESOM, they had regular coordination meetings at the town hall, which allowed them to discuss difficult cases with their peers and learn from one another's experiences. Technicians similarly met regularly at UMU, where they benefited from standardized and up-to-date information on the cost of materials and workmanship and established technical routines such as producing as-built plans of all completed works. Nowadays, with decentralization, these important learning and coordination roles are no longer being filled. Social promoters and technicians unanimously denounce this as a major drawback.

In Ciudad Juárez, centralized control is the norm. An attempt at establishing local offices failed three years ago because the offices were not adequately staffed and equipped, and all meaningful decisions continued to be made at the central level, making the local offices redundant. In the Juárez OSC program, each participating settler has to deposit his or her contributions directly at the municipal treasury in downtown Juárez. All social promoters work for the central social development department and have their offices in downtown Juárez. Similarly, all technicians work at the public works department downtown. The advantage here again is information exchange and coordination; the disadvantage is that local people have far less access to decisionmaking concerning their project.

The happy medium between the Tijuana and Juárez formats could be the adoption of Tijuana's decentralized system with the establishment of a project coordination unit that would establish and enforce uniform procedures, ensure coordination, and promote information exchange and a continuous learning process.

The Increasing Importance of Local Governments in Costa Rica

In the FUPROVI case in Costa Rica, the small size of the country—60 percent of Costa Rica's 3.5 million in population lives in the capital's metropolitan area, known as the Great Metropolitan Area (GAM)[6]—has allowed the institution to work effectively with local communities while having strong links to the central government. But the winds of change are blowing even in Costa Rica—a new local government law has been approved, enhancing the role and political legitimacy of local authorities. Although decentralization is still in its infancy, FUPROVI has already felt the need to establish area coordinators for the various parts of the GAM. The role and weight of local authorities in FUPROVI programs are bound to increase as decentralization proceeds.

The Gap between Large and Small Municipalities in Brazil

Guarapiranga is a case that illustrates at once the weight carried by Brazil's large municipalities in infrastructure, service provision, and shelter policy, and the relative helplessness of small municipalities in the same fields. Although all municipalities theoretically have the same pow-

---

[6]The GAM is formed by the capital San José and the outlying municipalities of Alajuela, Cartago, and Heredia in Costa Rica's Central Valley.

ers under the constitution, in reality, small municipalities are extremely behind in key resources such as knowledge of their own territory, its problems, and potential; qualified personnel; and capacity to formulate and implement policies, programs, and projects. The ability to prepare funding proposals for projects and handle liaisons with financing agents—one of the key functions of local government—is usually lacking.

It was thus decided that the municipality of São Paulo would run its own informal settlement upgrading component under the Guarapiranga project, while the smaller municipalities in the basin would be assisted by São Paulo State's Housing and Urban Development Company (CDHU). The result was that, while São Paulo was able to mobilize further resources and dramatically increase its counterpart funding, covering more favelas and illegal subdivisions with infrastructure and service improvements, the smaller municipalities had little power over decisions and had to depend on CDHU. The state company moved more slowly than its client municipalities or the Guarapiranga project management unit would have liked. One key component of the upgrading subprojects that was held up by this arrangement was the building of new housing units for families who had to be removed from their original locations as a result of the project. Lack of coordination and the resulting delays in resettlement had a very negative social impact.

Development of a Critical Mass of Local Capabilities

The operation of participatory programs and projects in upgrading and housing requires the availability of a range of specialized services. We have seen in earlier chapters that the range of services needed for participatory low-income housing projects is very similar to that needed for participatory urban upgrading. Developing local capabilities in this field requires not just training, but also the attraction of the appropriate outside expertise and active creation of work opportunities in the upgrading field that will allow the emergence and consolidation of local specialized organizations. In this context, the continuity of the funding stream for upgrading and low-income housing is very important: there needs to be a market for specialized organizations to survive and thrive.

Such specialized organizations should be able to provide one or more of the following:

- Socio-technical support, including support to participatory monitoring and evaluation of program and project impact
- Urban planning through a participatory approach
- Architecture and engineering services and technical guidance in appropriate technologies

- Program coordination services
- Project and contract management services
- Construction skills in tune with the specific needs of informal areas
- Quality control in engineering and construction
- Affordable building materials
- Operations and maintenance of assets
- Market-based financial services.

Creating a critical mass of local actors qualified to support a participatory process is a key issue in scaling up programs and projects. The creation of a critical mass of capacities depends on several elements that need to be taken into consideration and stimulated during project implementation, namely:

- **Sustainability of private actors.** It is crucial to be able to count on qualified and sustainable private actors—that is, actors whose survival and development over time may ensure quality provision of specialized services and operational autonomy.
- **A new organizational culture.** The project should be an opportunity to create a new culture in its public and private partners, incorporating the specific methodologies and approaches needed for participatory upgrading work, as well as the habit of interdisciplinary teamwork. This will create an environment that demands the appropriate skills and stimulates their development. In this context, the project should be seen as an opportunity for a process of training by doing.
- **Continuity of funding for the upgrading policy.** A continuous funding stream for participatory upgrading and low-income housing is needed to create the opportunities that will stimulate local actors to continue to work in this sector and build capacities. This is especially crucial in the case of for-profit private actors, which are very important in this process. There has to be a market for them if they are to be expected to develop and consolidate their capacity.
- **Training opportunities.** The creation of local capacity depends on many other things as well, but training opportunities are essential. Since the skills involved in participatory upgrading projects are specialized, they have to be brought from outside if they do not already exist in a given local context, and a process of transfer of know-how to local actors needs to be organized. Due to the magnitude and complexity of the problems in the field, the need to develop skills concerns all the actors in the process—i.e., public agencies, private providers of goods and services, financial institutions, NGOs, community organizations, and community leaders and local people.

By observing the experiences that we have discussed in this work, some key capacity gaps appear that training efforts should attempt to address:

1. Integrated and interdisciplinary approaches to infrastructure and shelter development
2. Methodologies for work with local groups in developing instruments such as a participatory area development plan
3. Methodologies and appropriate technologies for participatory collection and analysis of information and for monitoring and evaluation
4. Methodologies for socio-technical support
5. Cost recovery mechanisms
6. Innovative finance mechanisms for providing access to savings and loans
7. Appropriate technology and standards for upgrading and low-income housing
8. Promotion of the role of women in projects (moving from mere gender awareness to the choice of women as the key partners of a project)
9. Participatory models founded on the association of various public and private actors (moving from simple consultation to more advanced forms of community management and mutual aid).

Of the cases we studied, the most impressive example of training of local community members was undoubtedly FUPROVI's program in Costa Rica. Members of a housing association, many of whom had no previous experience in the construction field, are trained to build infrastructure and shelter and manage a construction process, including procurement, warehousing, cost accounting, and reporting to the group. FUPROVI also has an intensive training program for its own staff.

Other cases we studied offer additional striking examples of skill development. The management of the construction process by neighborhood works committees in Tijuana—although the works are much less complex than in the Costa Rican case—is one of them. Another is the training of hundreds of social workers whose previous experience was mainly in industrial relations to provide social support to favela dwellers in the Guarapiranga program. The development in Villa El Salvador of a generation of able community and business leaders who have been exposed to the day-to-day practice of community organization but who have also had the opportunity to undertake formal studies is also worthy of note.

The Role of Microfinance in Community Infrastructure

Failure of Public Sector Interventions

Though public sector programs for assisting low-income communities in accessing infrastructure services and housing have varied greatly in size, delivery mechanisms, targeted clientele, and autonomy, they have typically fallen far short of their objectives. This has been due to (1) lack of accountability, resistance, and lack of technical capacity of implementing agencies; (2) top-down approaches which lead to the introduction of solutions that have little in common with the needs, priorities, or capacity of the local communities, thus greatly restraining consumer willingness to pay; (3) legal and regulatory obstacles (e.g., building codes, constraints on property rights); (4) poor targeting; and (5) weak focus on cost recovery.

Limited Private Sector Involvement

Private funding for these works has been practically nonexistent given the banking sector's perception of low-income borrowers as "nonbankable." Even in more progressive environments, bank *credit appraisal procedures* are expensive and slow, especially given the small loan amounts, frequent repayments, and heterogeneous nature of technical solutions. In addition, banks seek *physical collateral* that borrowers cannot provide and/or face legal impediments to the registration and enforcement of their collateral/security rights. Even access to savings products has proven quite difficult as banks impose minimum balances, fees, and documentation requirements which increase the direct and opportunity costs to the poor for these services. Private provision of basic services has similarly been limited due to assumed, and sometimes real, *willingness and capacity to pay limitations* of low-income communities for these services. Finally, language, cultural, and gender differences between the service providers/banks and low-income communities have also led to significant *social barriers* to private sector involvement within low-income communities.

Resulting Inefficiencies and Negative Externalities

In light of these circumstances, private financial institutions have focused on the upper income brackets, quite often to the exclusion of 60 to 85 percent of the population. Consequently, low-income communities are often left to finance their shelter needs through personal savings and informal credit sources, including relatives, suppliers' credits, rotating savings and credit associations, and moneylenders. However, these informal sources are expensive and unreliable, leading families to self-construct their communities incrementally, resulting in diseconomies of scale in construction, foregone discounts on bulk purchases of building materials, and construction of structurally unsound housing. Similarly, families, which have been unable to pay the upfront costs of water and sewerage hookup fees, on-site storage tanks, latrines, or septic tanks, often obtain illegal and technically unstable connections, resulting in community-wide negative public health impacts.

Even when funding is available, incremental improvements can add to overall development costs, especially given the natural evolution of household demand, with water supply typically the first priority, followed by on-site sanitation, block-level sanitation, and eventually the public provision of mains. However, these incremental improvements may add to project costs, for example, by adding a water supply, then drains, and then paved roads. Conversely, if such investments are made at the beginning, the result is that the loan needs to be longer term for monthly repayments to be affordable. This situation is even more nebulous for community-wide infrastructure where obtaining payment from each household for its share of the investment can prove problematic due to free rider issues.

Sustainable Banking Services for the Poor

Breaking through the perception of the poor as nonbankable are a growing number of microfinance institutions, including BancoSol and Caja de Los Andes (Bolivia), Compartamos and Caja Popular Mexicana (Mexico), Genesis Empresarial (Guatemala), K-REP (Kenya), ASA and BRAC (Bangladesh), and Bank Rakyat Indonesia. Charging interest rates often well above those of local commercial banks to cover their operating and funding costs, these MFIs feature on-time repayment rates of 95 percent and higher and have reached tens, and sometimes hundreds of thousands, of low-income clients.[7] Their lending methodologies center upon providing quick and convenient access to small (often below $500), short-term loans, while relying on nontraditional forms of collateral such as joint liability between solidarity group members and providing additional incentives for on-time repayment through the promise of continued access to larger loans. MFI credit officers also often either live or

---

[7]BancoSol, a commercial bank, charges 55 percent annual interest for local currency loans, compared to commercial banking rates of around 22 percent. However, interest rates in the urban *informal* markets are as high as 800 percent.

work in the communities they serve, and thus are familiar and comfortable with the social and economic realities of their client base.

Though these programs seek principally to support microentrepreneurs through working capital financing, many recognize that due to the fungibility of money, 20 to 40 percent of their loans are applied for "consumption" purposes, including home improvement.[8] Indeed, often the microentrepreneur's business is home-based. Thus, loan proceeds invested in paved flooring, improved spacing and ventilation, or obtaining access to water and electricity serve to improve shelter conditions, as well as the productivity of the microenterprise.

Some MFIs, including SEWA Bank, Grameen Bank (Bangladesh), FENACOAC (Guatemala), LPD (Indonesia), Financiera Calpia (El Salvador), Mibanco (Peru), and Caja Popular Mexicana, have developed tailor-made programs for home improvement. Typically, these institutions require borrowers to have participated in a series of shorter term loans to qualify and/or to have saved over a substantial period prior to being eligible for these larger and long-term loans. These MFIs recognize that households want an ongoing relationship with an institution that can provide a range of financial services to match their evolving needs. They also realize that home improvement lending requires individually tailored loan terms and conditions (larger amounts, longer maturities, grace periods, collateral) to conform to household needs and payment capacity. In response, they have adapted their appraisal procedures and asset liability operations to better assess and manage the risks and opportunities associated with this product line.

MFIs as Possible Partners in Urban Upgrading Initiatives

Besides acting as a vehicle to leverage donor resources, the availability of market-based credit plays a key role in ensuring true choice by the communities.[9] For example, true choice may mean that demand is expressed for a higher level of service than what the government or a donor may be able and willing to finance, say for waterborne sewerage instead of on-site sanitation. Hence, alternative funding sources would facilitate the demand-responsiveness of participatory urban upgrading initiatives.

---

[8]For example, Bank Rakyat Indonesia, with over 2.6 million borrowers, does not require loan proceeds to be used for any specific purpose. Similarly, credit unions and savings and loan cooperatives, which in most cases are unregulated, provide a broad range of financial services, and most certainly have extended credit for home improvement.

[9]Microfinance programs providing both credit and savings services can also serve to increase community capacity to pay for infrastructure services and housing loans.

An emerging base of commercially oriented MFIs are supporting small-scale urban upgrading projects, such as water, drainage, sanitation, road paving, electricity, and telecommunications, along with home improvement. These loans, which carry fees and interest rates sufficient to cover operating and funding costs, have been issued under three modalities, which are described below and illustrated in figure 5-1.

- **Microenterprise loans.** The MFI issues a loan to small-scale service providers for investment and/or working capital purposes. The microentrepreneur then charges users for the service provided, with corresponding revenues applied to repay the MFI loan. This model has been applied in Guatemala, Mexico, Kenya, and Paraguay.
- **User group-based loans.** Technical assistance providers, often the MFIs themselves, mobilize and assist user groups in the design, implementation, operation, and maintenance of the urban upgrading project. The MFI then provides a loan to cover part of the subproject investment (between 30 to 70 percent of the total cost), with remaining funding secured via a subsidy provided by a government or donor agency. This model has been successfully applied in Guatemala.
- **Individual household (consumer) loans.** Individual families, based on combined household income, receive a consumer loan from the MFI. The household then applies the loan proceeds to cover its cost-sharing of a community infrastructure asset. Similarly, home improvement loans are provided under commercial terms and conditions to support household service connection fees, addition of on-site water and sanitation facilities, and purchases of lot with basic services. This model has been applied in Indonesia, India, Bolivia, and Mexico.

These community infrastructure lending programs have varied significantly in terms of lender legal status, rural-urban focus, borrower profile, and credit terms and conditions. However, the use of the above-referenced nontraditional forms of collateral and expedited loan appraisal procedures, combined with the expectation of follow-up credit, has proven critical in terms of fostering high loan repayment rates for these small-scale infrastructure assets—many of which are indeed characterized by free rider issues. Given that the MFI is typically the only source of financial services (both credit and savings) available to borrowers, they have an incentive to maintain themselves in good standing.

Possible Roles of the Public Sector in Supporting MFI Programs

Some MFI programs have formed strategic alliances, whether formal or informal, with public sector agencies, including municipal governments,

Figure 5-1. MFI Loan Modalities

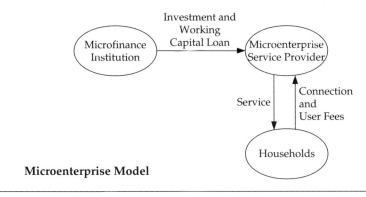

Microenterprise Model

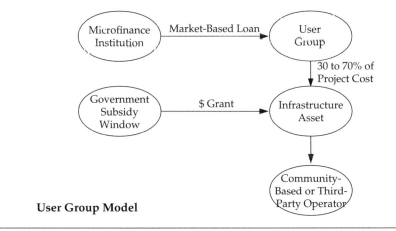

User Group Model

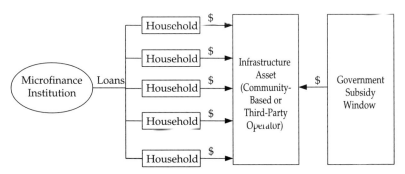

Individual Consumer Loan Model

Source: Authors' construction from field study data.

infrastructure providers, and social investment funds. Government participation has centered upon the following financial, technical, logistical, and legal support:

- Provision of demand-side subsidies to communities approved by the MFI to defray some of the technical assistance and investment costs. Amounts covered have ranged from 30 to 70 percent, with the remainder covered by MFI loans and community/household in-kind contributions.
- Development of secondary and tertiary infrastructure assets, as well as granting of usufruct rights to land required to build, own, and operate the assets.
- Provision of operations and maintenance services for the assets.
- Logistical support in assisting low-income communities in securing, transporting, and warehousing required construction materials.
- Promotion and training in the application of appropriate technologies.
- Legal recognition of the right of community-based groups to own and operate the assets.

Potential Roles of the Private Sector in Partnering with MFIs

Private companies of various sectors have provided support to the work of MFIs and to urban upgrading programs. It is thought that there is much scope for increasing the participation of the for-profit private sector in these initiatives. Some successful examples include:

- Home improvement building material providers that pass on "preferred client" discounts to approved MFI borrowers or social investment fund grant recipients. Such arrangements were employed in the Cali and Tijuana examples.
- Private landowners who agree to solve long-standing disputes over property rights to invaded areas via land swaps.
- Commercial banks, through establishment of commercial lines of credit to the MFI, provision of cash management and trustee services, and application of smart-card technology. In Guatemala, 12 local and private commercial banks have established commercial lines of credit with Genesis Empresarial. Provided under market terms and conditions, these credit lines involve no government or donor guarantees.
- Private infrastructure providers through such mechanisms as subcontracting subproject operations and maintenance to community-based providers; provision of training and technical assistance in the design, implementation, and operation of such assets; and full

or partial funding of upfront investment costs in secondary or tertiary infrastructure assets.

Public-Private Partnerships: Keeping Grants and Loans Separate

Engaging communities as partners serves to increase the technical and social sustainability of urban upgrading programs. However, given these programs' reliance on public sector and donor resources, the issue of *financial* sustainability often presents a significant challenge to program participants. Often it has been the case that strategies to address this matter are not even taken into consideration during project design. Consequently, the opportunity to leverage donor and government funding is lost as private sector or community-based resources are foregone or even crowded out.

Microfinance institutions, on the other hand, though representing a potentially effective mechanism for delivering financial services to low-income communities, confront borrower capacity and willingness-to-pay constraints as they venture down the income scale. Most successful programs typically do not allow borrower monthly loan payments to exceed 25 to 30 percent of combined family income. These limitations usually put the purchase of starter homes or even a housing site with or without basic services outside their purchasing power. Therefore, some level of subsidy will be required for lower income groups, especially since many of the infrastructure-related services to be provided are of a common good nature, with benefits accruing to society in general. Also, in an effort to standardize operations and reduce costs, most successful MFIs have focused exclusively on the delivery of financial services. Consequently, technical assistance and community mobilization activities—centerpieces of successful participatory programs—are excluded from their list of services.

Placing both participatory infrastructure and microcredit programs within a single institution presents clear dangers of mixing a commercial-based initiative with grant-based operations, given the wrong signals the latter might send to MFI borrowers. Thus, although the menu of services offered via participatory community development initiatives, MFIs, social development funds, and the for-profit private sector are highly complementary, the challenge is to develop mechanisms that bring together the community linkages, incentive structures, and services offered by each into a practical, well-coordinated, and sustainable approach without detracting from their respective mandates.

Part II
Voices from the Field

6

Bolivia: The People's Participation Law

In our journey through the four largest cities of Bolivia we found a seed that is blooming and rooting. In a country with an organizational tradition that dates back to the precolonial Inca *ayllu* form of community organization, a country with a long tradition of practical mutual help, the state has legally recognized the existence of legitimate community organizations and their right—indeed, their duty—to participate in local development as both subject and beneficiary. Law 1551, passed in 1994, institutionalizes community participation processes; it also legally recognizes area-based community organizations (ABCOs), granting them the right to participate in local planning and to establish surveillance committees as a mechanism for social control over the actions of the municipal government. Further, it establishes a new concept of municipality in the country, encompassing urban areas and their surrounding countryside; and it mandates budget transfers to municipalities of 20 percent of the national income, which are known as *co-participation resources*.

> BOLIVIA, FREE, INDEPENDENT, SOVEREIGN, MULTIETHNIC, AND MULTICULTURAL, CONSTITUTED IN A UNITARY REPUBLIC, ADOPTS THE DEMOCRATIC REPRESENTATIVE FORM OF GOVERNMENT, BASED ON THE UNION AND SOLIDARITY OF ALL BOLIVIANS.
> —*Article 1 of the State's Political Constitution*

The People's Participation Law is part of a deep institutional change in the country. Before the law's passage, just as in most of Latin America, the state was extremely centralized, and all government activities were managed from the capital city, the presidency, or the ministries. The municipality's power was almost nonexistent except in the largest cities, and most of the country did not even have a local government, since only larger urban areas were under a municipal jurisdiction, while all rural areas were ruled directly by the central government. Under the new law, a participatory planning process is established within all municipalities whereby all communities work with the municipal government to elaborate a five-year municipal development plan (MDP), from which an annual operating plan (AOP) is derived.

The People's Participation Law, together with Law 1654, Administrative Decentralization, is looking to create an environment wherein the country can effectively deal with extreme poverty at the municipal level, since it is here at the municipal level that the actors, potentialities, limitations, and main attributes for addressing poverty exist.

The Importance of the Bolivian Experience

In Bolivia, as in no other Latin American country, the people's participation process has been extended to the whole country and even has a national law effecting its institutionalization. In a short period of time, this institutionalized community participation process has advanced greatly; today, about 15,000 community organizations have legal status throughout the country; there are 311 surveillance committees in full operation, exercising citizen control over the implementation of MDPs; and 311 municipalities are preparing and updating their plans in participatory processes with community organizations. Although the process has advanced much faster in rural areas, municipal activity in the cities uses the People's Participation Law as its framework and is slowly being adapted to national demands.

> POPULAR PARTICIPATION HAS FUNCTIONED VERY WELL IN THE RURAL AREAS; IN THE URBAN AREAS, IT IS JUST BEGINNING TO FUNCTION...THERE IS A CENTRALIZED MANAGEMENT IN THE LARGE MUNICIPALITIES, WITH VERY LITTLE PARTICIPATION FROM THE CIVIL SOCIETY.
> —José Barriga, Vice Minister for People's Participation and Municipal Strengthening

We here discuss and assess the country's experience with popular participation from a macrocosmic perspective—that is, from the national level—placing emphasis on its application in the four largest cities of

Bolivia: La Paz, El Alto, Cochabamba, and Santa Cruz. These metropolitan areas together account for more than half the national population. In these cities, we have tried to see the progress of people's participation through the eyes of the local governments, the nongovernmental organizations (NGOs), and the community organizations involved.

The following may be highlighted as the fundamental points of this experience:

- People's participation is part of the institutional reform of the Bolivian state, which encompasses decentralization to the municipal level, new flows of resources for local development, and organized participation. This reform has had a great impact on the relationship between the population and government institutions, and on the distribution of the government's budget for social programs.
- People's participation in Bolivia—just as in the *orçamento participativo* (participatory local government budget) model used in Porto Alegre, Belo Horizonte, and other cities in Brazil (discussed in chapter 4 under the heading "Advantages and Disadvantages of an Independent Program Management Unit")—involves the population in local development. It differs from the Brazilian case because it is a general norm at the national level and for all the municipalities of the country, rather than the product of a purely local initiative.
- The basis of participation are ABCOs, which are legally recognized as subjects of the development process and as having an important role to play in municipal planning.[1]
- Law 1551 has had an easier application in rural areas due to their traditional social organization. Although progress in the cities has been slower with a weaker organization and a more complex situation to address, there has been a great advance in terms of awareness regarding the new rights, the processes for the law's application, and even the management of relevant technical and accounting concepts.
- Although important strides have been made in terms of local communities' awareness of municipal issues and in participatory planning processes, the concept of popular participation still requires support in the form of technical assistance and training by the central government, prefectures, and NGOs if further progress is to be made.

---

[1] These ABCOs are known in Bolivia as *organizaciones territoriales de base*.

Background

A Tradition of Community Organization

Community organization for the collective satisfaction of basic needs has a long history in Bolivia; there is evidence that such practices existed even before the Incas' conquest of the territory. In Bolivia, people seem to get organized for just about everything, from the *pasanaku* for savings, to the *mink'a* for crops or for building a house, to the bands that dance in the carnivals.[2] This organization has taken several forms and has been subject to local cultural influences—resulting in numerous diverse forms of cooperation corresponding to the country's vast geographic and ethnic diversity.

This tradition of community organization has always been, for many communities, the only way to respond to the constraints imposed by poverty and an absentee state. It has been responsible for most of the infrastructure built in the countryside—schools, roads, and irrigation systems. Frequently, it has played a key role in low-income urban neighborhoods as well. Despite its legitimacy, however, community organization had never before been legally recognized by the state.

Limited Municipal Authority Was the Pattern

Until mid-1994, municipal authority in Bolivia was exclusively urban and confined for all practical purposes to some dozen large and medium cities. Municipal budgets depended on a resource allocation from the nation's general treasury, a transfer of 10 percent of tax revenues, senate-sanctioned funds (in some cases), plus any concession made by bureaucrats appointed by the military dictatorships that governed the country during most of its republican life. Of Bolivia's present 311 municipalities, nine departmental capitals and El Alto spent about 92 percent of the national municipal budget, some provincial capitals shared the remaining 8 percent, and most municipalities did not receive even a cent for their budget. Only the municipalities of the country's three largest cities had achieved an institutional solidity and had the technical capabilities to perform the normal duties of a local government.

When the country returned to the democratic practice of selecting local governments through free elections in January 1988, municipal man-

---

[2]Pasanaku refers to a revolving savings fund, where each member of a group of savers in turn has the right to draw a specified amount from the fund. Mink'a or *minga* is a reciprocal loan of labor for the execution of works, involving the honor-bound participation of men, women, and children among neighbors and relatives.

agement did not, for the most part, change. Rather, decisions on local public investment remained in the hands of a few appointed or elected politicians and civil servants, who together or individually would decide matters without consulting the citizens. Up to this point, Bolivia's few municipal governments were prey in many instances to authoritarian decisionmaking, influence peddling, endemic corruption, and little technical efficiency.

Sucre Was the Forerunner

Between 1987 and 1990, Sucre, capital of the republic, became the site of the country's first formal experience in urban participatory planning when four graduates of Cochabamba's Architecture School undertook as their dissertation work the implementation of four popular planning workshops in Sucre's low-income neighborhoods, in partnership with the local municipality. This experience established the operational and conceptual basis for participatory management in urban local development in Bolivia.

Following Sucre's lead, Cochabamba took a step toward institutionalization of this process by conducting five area workshops between 1991 and 1993. The following year, it created the Department of Neighborhood Management, to be responsible for planning, organizing, directing, and controlling neighborhood development programs executed under the operational plan of each municipal administration. As stated in Cochabamba's 1994–95 operational plan, the department was in charge of eight decentralized local government units known as community houses, "operational units responsible for planning, organizing, directing, and controlling the execution of works for social, cultural, and environmental development, with community participation." In all, Cochabamba's pilot experience reached 66 percent of the city's urban population, and 100 percent of the rural population of the municipality; this accounts for 280,000 inhabitants in almost 90 percent of the municipality's total territory.

With much enthusiasm, technicians—in Sucre through the *juntas de vecinos* (neighborhood associations) and in Cochabamba which put all the neighborhood organizations together—analyzed the situation, the needs and desires of the people, and proposed and carried out identified projects. Oscar Terceros, director of the program in Cochabamba, notes that it became an accepted "custom that all the people working in the urban planning department and in the area workshops worked together with the beneficiaries on Saturdays and Sundays in one or another neighborhood; in this way, the people would see municipal workers performing activities with them." According to Raúl Salvatierra, neighborhood leader in Cochabamba's District VIII, this experience was instrumental in "showing concerned officials that we could decentralize."

Concurrently, the issue of popular participation was being raised in demands and proposals from various community organizations, including the Confederation of Rural Workers and the Confederation of Indigenous People. (See box 6-1 for a summary of popular participation in Bolivia.) Not surprisingly, popular participation became a campaign promise during the election process of 1993—and ultimately resulted in Law 1551.

Participatory Process: Law 1551

Role of ABCOs

Popular participation is based on the state's official recognition of all area-based community organizations, which typically include neighborhood associations in urban areas and community organizations of indigenous people, ethnic groups, or rural workers in rural areas. All of these entities, which are organized according to their local customs and traditions, are granted legal status in the eyes of the state and are granted the full right to participate in the development process of their municipality. To achieve this status, all an ABCO needs to do is register in its

---

Box 6-1. Why People's Participation in Bolivia?

Carlos Hugo Molina, former national secretary of people's participation, and promoter of the People's Participation Law, offers an explanation as to why this movement took hold so dramatically in his country. "First, in 1953 there is a real land reform process in Bolivia...Second, the democratic transition process in Bolivia in 1982 occurs as a submission of the military to civil authority...The third element is that in Bolivia there is such an economic crisis until 1985 that everyone is obliged to accept structural adjustment and the new rules of the economic game, which are critical for the maintenance and conservation of the state...The fourth one is an extraordinary thing that has not taken place in any other Latin American country, and that is the system of pacts and agreements reached by the political parties.

"Finally, the fifth one—which gives context to all the items above—is that the People's Participation Law considers people not only inhabitants, but citizens. It links citizenship with the workings of the state. The municipality is finally recognized as a key state organization and is given territorial jurisdiction. People's participation is the result of the accumulation of all these factors."

municipality; the registration process is both free of charge and very simple. In the first three years of implementation of the People's Participation Law, about 15,000 rural workers', ethnic, and urban organizations obtained their certificate of legal recognition, accounting for an approximate average of 100 families (420 people) each.

Once registered, these organizations can continue to work according to their uses and customs (see box 6-2 for some examples); they also have the right to help identify, prioritize, manage, and supervise the implementation of development projects to be consigned in the municipal plans. This recognition has been instrumental in giving citizens back their right to a participatory and representative democracy in accordance with the state's political constitution. Historically, due to the lack of democracy, the presence of authoritarian governments forced the civil society to get organized by strengthening the associations and not the political parties.

As Carlos Hugo Molina, former national secretary for people's participation, explains, "When you ask who are the members of a civil society, the answer in Bolivia is the labor unions, the federation of private entrepreneurs, the church, universities, civic committees. The reference is to institutions, but the citizen never appears. We are not aware that the citizen is also part of civil society; we have to be an entity or organization to be part of civil society. In Bolivia, if you do not have an organization to support you, you have no chance of being heard."

> THE PARTICIPATORY PLANNING FOCUS IS DIFFERENT FROM THE ONE THAT HAS HISTORICALLY PREVAILED IN OUR COUNTRY; TRADITIONALLY, PLANNING IN BOLIVIA HAS BEEN A VERTICAL AND CENTRALIZED PROCESS. THE PEOPLE'S PARTICIPATION LAW WANTS TO MODIFY THIS UNILATERAL AND BUREAUCRATIC PRACTICE BY GIVING IT A DEMOCRATIC, PARTICIPATORY, AND CONSENSUAL FOCUS. ITS PHILOSOPHIC DIMENSION IS THAT WE INTEND TO DEMOCRATIZE THE COUNTRY; THE PRACTICAL IS THAT CONSULTING WITH SOCIETY MEANS IMPROVING EFFICIENCY AND RECONCILING THE USEFUL WITH THE PLEASANT.
> —*Roberto Barbery, Former Deputy Secretary for People's Participation*

Surveillance Committees

Together with the formal recognition of area-based community organizations, the People's Participation Law created something new—the surveillance committee. A municipality's surveillance committee is comprised of representatives from each district's ABCOs. As set forth in the

> **Box 6-2. Uses and Customs**
>
> An important aspect of the People's Participation Law is that it recognizes the variety of Bolivia's participation mechanisms, which have their roots in the history of this multicultural state.
>
> **Elected by the Dead.** In the community of Coroma, located in Bolivia's highlands, the election of community leaders is done under the inspiration of the dead. When an important decision is to be made, the elders of the community get together in a room where they have deposited the ponchos of the dead. They believe that the spirits inhabit these ponchos and that they will illuminate the decisions that the elders gathered in the assembly have to make. (Note that the elected community leaders are usually middle-aged males, who do not attend this meeting)
>
> **A Woman Decides.** In the Cruceño Chaco, many Guarani indigenous organizations receive the name Capitanía, and their hereditary leader is called the captain. These organizations grew from the structure of the Jesuit missions of colonial times, and they have remained latent during the republic. Recently, they have gained new force and have asked the state to recognize the territory that had been taken away from them. However, what makes this form of representation curious is that, in some of the Capitanías, the chief authorities do not make any decision without first consulting their wife—or, if single, their sister. These women have no voice in the meetings, but, after listening to the men, they whisper the decision to be taken into their ears.
>
> *Source:* Government of Bolivia (1996b).

Procedure Manual for Surveillance Committees of the People's Participation Secretariat, the committee "is the body that organizes the interaction between rural workers' associations, indigenous communities, and neighborhood associations and the municipal council; it also articulates the demands of the population in municipal participatory planning. It represents the population and exercises social control over the municipality." The surveillance committee ensures that municipal participatory planning reflects the various demands from communities, that the municipal government makes the public investments scheduled, and that local participation in the state's tax revenues is used adequately. More specifically, the committee:

- Ensures that resources from central government budget transfers are invested equitably between the urban and rural populations

- Ensures that the municipal government does not devote more than 15 percent of these resources to overhead and that 85 percent is spent in works and services
- Issues binding statements on the budget and reviews accounts on expenses and investments made by the municipal government
- Refers cases of misconduct or disregard of the agreed investment plans to the appropriate judicial authorities.

Roberto Barbery, former deputy secretary for people's participation, adds, "Surveillance committees are organized in all municipal governments, they're seeking to pressure the municipal governments—that is, there's a series of results that we could list which demonstrate that the People's Participation Law is applied in many things, and in those where it's not fulfilled, it grants the right of the individual to complain, to demand compliance."

> DISTRICT DEVELOPMENT PLANS HAVE REALLY BEEN VERY PARTICIPATORY. WE'VE HAD MARATHON SESSIONS IN WHICH WE'VE DEVOTED OURSELVES FULL TIME TO THIS; DIAGNOSIS, VALIDATION HAVE BEEN VERY PARTICIPATORY.
> —*Germán Marañón, President, Surveillance Committee, Cochabamba*

The Bolivian Decentralization Model

As the vice minister for people's participation and municipal strengthening, José Barriga, explains, the People's Participation Law "responds to a decentralization process where the country is betting on municipalization." The new municipality is based on strengthening of municipal management autonomy; expansion of municipal jurisdiction, encompassing both urban and surrounding rural areas; and the transfer of new responsibilities, including infrastructure and maintenance of health services, education, roads and support to production, recreation and sports, and the environment.

By territorializing local management, a great advance has been achieved in terms of the application of public policies—particularly in rural areas, which in theory was a function of the national government, but in reality constituted a sort of "no man's land." Decentralization of responsibilities on a territorial basis has left the central government with very few operational attributions, forcing it to focus on its normative and enabling role, fostering and ensuring compliance with state policies. People's participation is supplemented by the Administrative Decentralization Law, which transfers jurisdiction over all regional ministerial offices to departmental prefectures and mandates departmental administration to support the municipal governments and communities in this new process.[3]

Funding for Participation

For participation to work, the law distributes 20 percent of the national tax revenue across all the municipalities in the country. This distribution of tax revenues in accordance with population size represents an initial exercise in equity. In theory, each resident in the country has an equal opportunity to access public resources for development. The total of participation-earmarked budget transfers is divided by the number of inhabitants in the country; then, the amount that corresponds to each municipality is determined according to the size of its population. The automatic and daily transfer of funds from the nation's general treasury to municipal accounts is complemented and supplemented by the municipalities' own revenues. There is, however, still a historical debt to meet. The older, larger municipalities have received investments over the years at the expense of opportunities being afforded to the remainder of the territory. The constitution of a special fund was envisaged to compensate for this imbalance.

The Impact of People's Participation

Implementation of Law 1551 has had wide-ranging impacts, notably in its "process of citizenship creation," as phrased by former national secretary Molina. Its impacts, like its roots, are based in the nature of Bolivian culture. Roberto Barbery, former deputy secretary for people's participation, points out that "There is a feedback process, a reciprocal influence, between law and culture...the law helps change behaviors, and, in turn, culture intervenes in the application of the law. This means that neither the law will be able to modify the culture, nor will the culture invalidate the law."

This harmony of culture and law is producing solid results. Moreover, the public participation process can be enriched with new tasks. With this new law, Molina notes, "The Bolivian state has created an institutional framework sufficiently functional and sufficiently operational that

---

[3]Like many Latin American countries, Bolivia, although not a federal state, is subdivided into departments with a semi-autonomous departmental government, which in the Bolivian case is called a prefecture.

it can serve as a train engine able to pull new cars. The first cars are control of municipal public investment, efficiency and transparency in budgeting, and participatory planning. If the engine were to pull an additional car, such as housing, there is no reason for it not to work."

The Participatory Process in Urban Areas

In this section we examine the implementation of people's participation in urban areas, based on perspectives from the numerous public and private actors who are contributing to this effort in the country's main cities.

Urban-Rural Differences. In developing and applying the People's Participation Law, the government initially looked more closely at the rural areas—first, because these had traditionally been overlooked, and second, because, for many reasons, it was in the rural areas where participatory processes had always been applied with greater intensity. (See box 6-3.) The cities still have a long way to go in terms of popular participation. "The process is much more rooted in the rural domain and in smaller cities. When the cities acquire an important dimension, like Cochabamba, Santa Cruz, El Alto, La Paz, then the process certainly is weaker: first, because these are old-fashioned municipalities; and second, because of the low degree of consolidation that neighborhood associations have," says Mauricio Lea Plaza, participatory planning director of the Vice Ministry of People's Participation and Municipal Strengthening (VPPFM).

Another difference has to do with the nature of the organizations in the countryside and in the city. In the rural domain, the area-based community organization coincides with the functional organization. The rural workers' union represents all the community that lives in a specific area, but it also represents the functional and productive activities of its population; while in the urban area, people look to the neighborhood association to attend to the broader developmental issues of the neighborhood, but look to other organizations to address their functional problems.

Learning to Do Participatory Planning: A Santa Cruz Example. "In the first moments of people's participation, the mayors would invest in roads near the central square, in the town hall, in ornamentation. They received the first resources ever, they had never handled any money, so at that moment the reaction was to make this type of investments. They bought vehicles, cellular phones. But that is part of a process, it is the beginning of a process," notes vice minister José Barriga.

> **Box 6-3. Voices on Urban-Rural Differences**
>
> "The participation component clearly appears in the rural area, stronger than in the urban area; the reason for this is very simple, since in the rural area there has never been participation in government processes; when the option is opened, people take it immediately..." —*Carlos Hugo Molina, Former National People's Participation Secretary*
>
> "Urban demands are related to the issue of collective consumption, like the sewage system or the water supply, and those demands are the most expensive; therefore, those projects are long-term projects. Rural projects are short-term and punctual, like an irrigation system, which is done fast; the house for the school teacher. These projects are implemented on a yearly cycle." —*Rubén Ardaya, AID Project*
>
> "I think that you work better in rural areas, because the characteristics are different. Since the Bolivian state has historically been centralized, civil society in the rural areas has had a great importance, because the state as a public structure was practically nonexistent. Civil society had to occupy that vacancy...In Bolivia, urbanization is a recent phenomenon; consequently, in the urban areas, civil society has no organizational tradition, which makes some public authorities underestimate the possibility that the citizens, through their organizations, may perform roles of orientation and social control for public administration." —*Roberto Barbery, Former Deputy Secretary of People's Participation*
>
> "Where we have more problems is in the urban municipalities. I have seen that in the department of Santa Cruz, the People's Participation Law has been a great success in the municipalities with a lot of peasant communities, because that was the group that was previously excluded, it was not even part of the municipality. There, the People's Participation Law has been a revelation because it has changed the power relationships in the municipal council; that is, the peasants have come to the town and have taken it in many cases." —*Fernando Prado, President of CEDURE, Santa Cruz.*

> IF YOU ASK A MAYOR RIGHT NOW, DO YOU THINK THE POPULAR PARTICIPATORY LAW IS GOOD? HE OR SHE WILL REPLY "EXCELLENT," BECAUSE, THANKS TO THIS LAW, THERE ARE RESOURCES AVAILABLE...AND HE OR SHE CANNOT BE SO CYNICAL AS TO SAY THAT HE OR SHE DOES NOT LIKE THE LAW WITH REGARD TO THE PARTICIPATION OF THE CIVIL SOCIETY, BECAUSE THE PACKAGE IS COMPLETE, IT'S ALL OR NOTHING.
> —*Roberto Barbery, Former Deputy Secretary for People's Participation*

They began investing in the new municipalities by responding to what seemed to be the needs. Little by little, the municipalities undertook participatory projects. At the beginning, these were heavily influenced by the historical requests each area had. "We've seen that we've been given freedom to identify our needs. In the old days, others used to think for us, they would decide for us and would do works that maybe we didn't even really need, but now we identify in each neighborhood what it is that we really need," explains Raúl Salvatierra, local leader of District VIII in Cochabamba.

In Santa Cruz, participatory planning processes have been developing through Participatory Action Planning (PAP), a poverty relief project financed by the Netherlands that is trying interesting practices that have the potential to be replicated elsewhere. A leader from District VI of the federation of neighborhood associations (FEJUVE) of Santa Cruz, says that "PAP Santa Cruz is carrying out works in different neighborhoods, and there we're really learning, if not everything related to participatory planning, at least what we consider comes close to the ideal. True participatory planning in each neighborhood takes no less than three months, because enough meetings must be scheduled on a sectoral basis." (See box 6-4.) A FEJUVE leader of District VII with the same experience adds, "We have at La Villa true participatory planning. Everyone is participating in planning and summing up his priorities, so that we have a good

---

Box 6-4. Participatory Planning in Santa Cruz

Germán Caballero is sports director within the People's Participation Secretariat of the Santa Cruz municipality. He explains how participatory planning is working in Santa Cruz. "Mayor Johnny Fernández has promoted a series of workshops on Local Participatory Planning, in which the People's Participation Secretariat, with all its structure and technicians, visits the city district by district to hear the requests of each neighborhood. Starting with these local needs assessments, early in the year, the annual operations plan of the People's Participation Secretariat is established. Usually, in December of each year, we do the workshops, and all neighborhood associations participate. I would say that this is the activity that allows the People's Participation Secretariat and the Santa Cruz municipal government to comply with the People's Participation Law. In each workshop, an order of priorities is established by the neighbors themselves. The neighbors request a sports field, health, education, etc., but they also establish an order of priorities; which work is first, which is second, which is third; as a function of this, the resources are distributed neighborhood by neighborhood."

idea of the needs of men, women, adults, youngsters, children. So, I believe we're getting to know a true participatory planning in our local units. The mayor's office should plan that way, too." This last comment refers to the fact that, while PAP dedicates three months to participatory planning in each neighborhood, the municipality tries to do it in three days.

Although there is some friction between PAP and the current administration, the technicians of the Santa Cruz municipality are also enthusiastic about their work with the participatory processes. Notes Germán Caballero of the People's Participation Secretariat in Santa Cruz, "This municipality, like no other in the country, works in a very direct manner, so that the local resident is the one who plans his neighborhood, the one who decides what's going to be done with the AOP. The surveillance committee, which has a representative of that neighborhood, simply has to approve what its neighbors have decided. Observe, for instance, if you, as neighbor, have requested a multifunctional sports court and we have planned a soccer field; there, the surveillance committee says: no sirs, the neighbors requested a multifunctional field and you planned a field only for soccer." Gilberto Bejarano, a colleague of Caballero's, is a technical adviser to the secretariat; he notes solidarity between diverse groups, indicating that "in participatory planning, there has been an unselfish attitude on the part of the neighbors when they requested the works. There, solidarity has existed in the same district when the different local units fought for something: 'I want four classrooms.' 'But, I need three classrooms, you have more, why don't you let them give me one?'…'Well, I give him one because he really needs it.' There, you had solidarity."

The secretariat carries out the annual planning in the months of November and December with three-day meetings for each district, often in sessions lasting until midnight. The president of FEJUVE Santa Cruz, Rodolfo Landivar, says with great enthusiasm that participatory planning is already happening based on the AOP. Nevertheless, there are people who think that the process conducted by the municipal government in Santa Cruz is not completely participatory, since "Planning is indeed done at the end of the year to be approved by the municipal council, but it's not true participatory planning; in other words, leaders make requests, but a true participatory planning coming from the neighborhood doesn't really exist," explains the District VII delegate of FEJUVE Santa Cruz.

"Political practices limit and void effective participation. For instance, the participatory planning that the municipality must do according to the law in order to prepare the annual operations plan only consists of one meeting. The district meeting of participatory planning with the municipality starts at 7 p.m., a request list from the district is prepared, and at 9 o'clock starts the barbecue for the leaders, and there ends the meeting," says Rosario Rosas, director of the NGO Cidcruz.

Fernando Prado, director of the NGO Center for Urban and Regional Development (CEDURE), Santa Cruz, builds on this point. "The municipality says that the participatory planning process is perfect. They send their technicians once a year to each district, they hold a big meeting, and representatives of the local boards make their requests—like in the Middle Ages before the king, a list of good wishes—and in the mayor's office, resources are obviously limited, and they start to define and cut down at their own criterion. That is, priority definitions are not given by the neighbors. And that's what the so-called participatory planning is."

Strategic Planning and Participation. But there are also other problems. Sometimes the population is not aware of other needs that the municipality might attend to, and they ask for what they believe the mayor is most likely to do, as the former national secretary for people's participation points out. "And here we find two things that are almost constant, but not only in Bolivia. When people are asked to set a priority to their demands, they do it based on two things mainly, infrastructure and services. They request the school, they request the health center or post office, and then the teacher, doctor, and medicines. Here we understand why there is no demand for housing, because that's not the municipal government's competence. It's a need of those living there, but it's not a specific responsibility established by law to be addressed by a mayor. If the surveillance committee, districts, and local boards identify a need of this kind, it could be perfectly channeled to a ministry, a fund, an aid institution." The current people's participation vice-minister qualifies the situation in similar terms when he says that "Nobody's going to ask the municipality for something that is not of its competence, that would have to be requested from another institution, so, with the privatization process, they're not going to request either water or electrification."

In spite of the problems, people want to advance toward a new modality of strategic planning; citizens' participation also seeks its place to realistically think of the future. Community organizations and municipal governments both want to launch it, and other sectors would also like to participate. Germán Marañon expands on this point. "We believe that the municipality's strategic plan may not be left out of the participatory process. We want the neighbor to participate in the plan and say what he wants, his opinion in this regard. There, we're making all district representatives go fight for what they want in their district."

Katia Uriona, director of the NGO Institute of Integrated Training for Women (IFFI), Cochabamba, sums up the case. "A strategic planning answer is going to be built from the districts, but also with a summons to the sectors. We believe that, starting from the specificity, for instance, of retailers or private entrepreneurs, there are visions and demands regarding the municipality different from the ones expressed from the territorial ambit. This process will allow us to have sectoral diagnoses; it's going to let us define strategic objectives for the municipality where we can also say, as part of civil society, how we imagine our city and how we want it to be."

Gender Issues

Women's voices are also heard in this process—which is precisely as intended. The *Procedure Manual for Surveillance Committees* of the People's Participation Secretariat mandates that "The mechanisms that enable women's participation must be taken into account. There must be physical presence of women in the assemblies and meetings. Expressly ask women about decisions, expenses, etc. Try to incorporate women into the boards of directors." Moreover, President Sánchez de Lozada created, in 1994, a national Gender, Generational, and Ethnic Issues Secretariat to protect the interests of women, among other focal groups. Several NGOs are working with a gender focus in the development process; among these are Gregoria Apaza in El Alto, IFFI in Cochabamba, and the PAP project in Santa Cruz. (See boxes 6-5 and 6-6.)

The president of the National Confederation of Neighborhood Associations (CONALJUVE), Juan José Diez de Medina, explains that "You will notice that Latin American countries are still backward in their inclusion of women in decisionmaking; at present, CONALJUVE is probably the only popular organization in the continent that has a mandatory quota for women in all its appointments, with equity between men and women: 50-50. That, in our country, is enormous progress, because in congress the fight is still for 30 percent women's representation, and instead, we as an institution have been able to include 50 percent in our bylaws."

International Support

Due to the interest the people's participation venture in Bolivia draws, several international cooperation agencies are supporting it. The process has received support from Danish, Dutch, Swiss, and U.S. bilateral cooperation, as well as from the World Bank and Inter-American Development Bank. The people and institutions involved in setting up people's participation in Bolivia are invited to seminars and workshops or simply to present the Bolivian model throughout Latin America.

> **Box 6-5. Women and Participation in El Alto**
>
> Ana Quiroga, director of the NGO Gregoria Apaza, explains how women are drawn into the participatory process: "In El Alto, Gregoria Apaza applies the methodology of people's participation, but with special attention to women's and youngsters' demands. This process has meant working with women leaders, training them, and supporting them a lot, especially regarding negotiation techniques."
>
> Once women are trained, they take part in the regular cycle of participatory planning "and then negotiate with their associations; they negotiate with the district committee; and, in this process, the board is the one that starts to negotiate women's demands with the surveillance committee, not just the women any more. In other words, the demand generated by women in this process is assumed by the territorial organizations as part of their requests."
>
> "That day, March 8, the agreement with women, youngsters, and neighborhood associations was going to be signed, and there was a standstill here in El Alto. The mayor didn't want to sign because there was no press, no TV. What he wanted was publicity; the international women's day, signing of the agreement. The neighborhood associations—and not just the women—said: 'No! we will not leave, and the mayor will not leave, until he signs.' Then they started to sit down; this is what impressed me the most, the youngsters in the first line, women in the second, and all the local boards, as if protecting them, behind."
>
> In El Alto, there are many female presidents of neighborhood associations, and a woman, Olga Flores, is president of the surveillance committee.

Roberto Barbery points out that "PAP Santa Cruz, which is funded by the Dutch, is possible thanks to the People's Participation Law. Its long-term objective is to link the struggle against poverty with participatory planning." Also with Dutch support, the Housing Ministry is trying to replicate the experience of PAP Santa Cruz in the city of El Alto with interesting results. "Its methodology is participatory from the bottom up, and we have come this far with the FEJUVE organization, which locates the suitable neighborhoods for this plan; then we visit the neighborhoods to collect basic information, because many of these neighborhoods are of recent creation and are not included in the 1992 census. We see how poverty is—just a superficial overview—and how the planning process within the neighborhood is, if they have meetings, who makes the decisions. Then we give training courses on participatory planning, urban planning, and specific topics such as housing, gender, health, and microenterprises. Next we have a workshop on self-diagnosis method-

> **Box 6-6. The Methodology of PAP Santa Cruz: Women's and Men's Participation**
>
> In PAP Santa Cruz, Roberto Barbery, coordinator of the project and former deputy secretary of people's participation, explains that "Women's participation levels in the local units where we work is higher than men's. But what's important here is that men are present: we do not simply have a debate among women; men also participate, and it has been possible to identify many topics related to gender training among the projects they formulate."
>
> Barbery sums up the PAP methodology thus: "Preparation, organization, and execution of differentiated diagnosis by gender and generations. The consolidated diagnosis of each one of the local units is accompanied by gender workshops, activities in the framework of the People's Participation Law, municipality organization, citizen linkages, etc. Finally, formulation of a development plan with four areas: human development, habitat and environment, economy, and community organization.
>
> "This is done in three months, with all territorial and functional organizations organized in a local committee that executes projects worth up to $40,000. For big projects, the municipal counterpart is required. In institutional terms, the municipality's willingness to incorporate PAP mechanisms and methodology has not been declared yet."

ology and how to make a neighborhood development plan. It has four sessions...Each neighborhood has a local workshop. Around 200 neighbors have participated in these workshops, and we work with groups by age and gender—men over and under 25, the same for women, people over 55 years, and children. We try to involve all neighbors. They make their demands," says Héctor Ugarte, Housing Ministry official in charge of the PAP El Alto project.

The U.S. Agency for International Development finances the Democratic Development and Citizen Participation program for municipal strengthening and support to the participatory process, initially in about 20 municipalities. Rubén Ardaya, who is in charge of the program, observes that "For us, the citizen is high up there, organized in surveillance committees, area-based organizations, functional organizations...This scheme of popular participation leads us not only to produce works and services, but also democracy; and this is a characteristic of the people's participation system in this country. Every year we sign an agreement, a plan with all municipalities, mayors, councils, and surveillance committees, and discuss the types of activities to be performed, as well as dates for these activities throughout the year and the results we expect." The project works with surveillance committees and ABCOs, with the executive and legislative branches and all the municipal administration, providing institutional strengthening and training.

Support to Participation: Snapshots of Governmental and Nongovernmental Actors

In Bolivia, there are more than 700 NGOs, many of which support community organization and local development. In fact, they constitute a significant additional resource for these purposes, although most operate at a rural level. In addition, municipal planning institutes and community organizations constitute the support framework for people's participation.

IIPLAM (La Paz). In La Paz municipality, the Municipal Research and Planning Institute (IIPLAM) made a serious citywide effort to apply participatory planning methodology, working by districts and organizing workshops at the district and neighborhood levels. At both levels, neighbors were asked to contribute to a diagnosis of their situation and discuss priorities for development. "During the workshops, people mapped out their reality on paper, which was very effective. A neighborhood's structural elements, roads, major natural and manmade drainage, main buildings, and also its events and important activities, and its problems," says Norman Ramírez, IIPLAM director.

Gregoria Apaza (El Alto). Ana Quiroga, director of the Gregoria Apaza, told us about the participatory planning activities undertaken by her NGO in association with Red Hábitat and other local organizations in order to support local neighborhood associations in the implementation of the People's Participation Law. "We perform the diagnosis with lots of participation from the people, under agreement with local ABCOs...What the law has done is generate conditions to do what Gregoria Apaza wanted to do...then, something that seems like a utopia suddenly happens, and that allows you to accelerate progress, despite the scant willingness of the El Alto municipality."

Red Hábitat (El Alto). Red Hábitat, another NGO of El Alto, has devoted itself since 1993 to microcredit for housing with Dutch support and, more recently, to the fields of environment, local management, and leadership training. Though its housing program had initial grant financing, it has managed the program since 1998 in a self-sustained manner.

"In the city of El Alto, the problems were housing quality, crowding, illegality of land tenure, and regularization of existing constructions. Over

85 percent of the houses have been built through self-help," says David Quezada, director of Red Hábitat.

"For us to enter an area, we need to have a dialogue with the neighborhood association, the signing of an agreement. The housing topic was a pretext to also start supporting diagnosis studies at the local level. We want to make the participation law a concrete reality in El Alto, and specifically in District V. The project is called 'training and strengthening of local organizations'; its objective is to generate management capacities for local development," states Anelise Menéndez of Red Hábitat. Also, technical assistance is offered on topics such as surveying and information and motivating strategies. (See box 6-7.)

CIPRODEC (Cochabamba). The Research Center for the Promotion of Economic and Community Development (CIPRODEC) is an NGO that works in the low-income neighborhoods of Cochabamba in Districts II and VIII. It started with basic infrastructure projects, where it found a great deficiency on the municipality's part, and went on to a more integrated vision. The NGO is very critical of the municipal government and its performance.

Box 6-7. El Alto: Voices from the Leadership of District V

In a meeting with District V leaders, where Red Hábitat works, among the many complaints for the scarce participatory spirit of the municipality, we also heard enthusiastic words. Guillermo Quispe, president of the school committee of Villa Ingavi, notes, "In Villa Ingavi, the school committee is working with the Norwegian Alliance. Currently, we have a water project, we are building a perimeter wall, we're also intending to do part of the patio drainage; but to do that the alliance isn't alone, we also give our contribution."

Others point out the problems they face. Says Victor Paz Quispe about participatory planning, "It almost doesn't exist, even though we've been oriented by the Norwegian agency on this aspect. We lobbied the mayor, demanding participation in the mid-term review of the municipal development plan. We participated through an interview with the technical department, but they had no ears for us...Now, just a few leaders participate in the annual operations plan, but when they showed us a project, it was for another neighborhood!" Local leader Isaac Paredes points out that "The distribution of the popular participation funds is not enough. Besides, the mayor scheduled our annual operations plan for 1998, but the work did not begin until 1999, or later; we don't know when it's going to begin...on the other hand, we would need a little technical support to prepare and propose our own projects."

At its beginning and under a previous administration (1994–95), CIPRODEC coordinated very well with the municipal government. Under the current administration, which has decentralized the application of the People's Participation Law to district offices known as community houses, municipal officials work with the NGO, "I would say, making faces, but they have to invite us; they have no other choice," observes César Virguetti, CIPRODEC's director. "What we have now is a rather authoritarian municipality, a municipality that is corrupting and intimidating the neighborhood associations by creating parallel organizations, accusing leaders, taking them to the courts, and frightening those who think differently."

Mauricio Lea Plaza is both critical and appreciative of the decentralization process in Cochabamba. "Cochabamba has had a very *sui generis* experience, which seems to be the path for large cities, consisting of moving the planning to the district level. But what I have been demanding from the mayor is to know the municipality's vision as a whole. How does A articulate with B, which are the elements that transcend the districts?"

> PEOPLE OFTEN BELIEVE THAT WHEN A LAW IS NOT ABIDED BY EXACTLY [AND] WITH PRECISION, IT NO LONGER WORKS. INSTEAD, THE MERE FACT OF DEMANDING THE FULFILLMENT OF SOMETHING IMPLIES THAT THE LAW HAS MET ITS PURPOSE, BECAUSE IT IS GRANTING THE PEOPLE A SUBJECTIVE RIGHT: THE KNOWLEDGE THAT "I CAN CLAIM SOMETHING."
> —*Roberto Barbery, former Deputy Secretary for People's Participation*

IFFI (Cochabamba). IFFI is an NGO that works in District XIV, especially in Villa Sebastián Pagador. Its main focus is women's support. It manages four programs covering democracy and citizenship, women and economic activities, food security and reproductive health, and preschools and libraries.

Katia Uriona, IFFI director, states that "We believe that we had come to a moment when women recognized their right to participation, the importance of exercising their citizenship; the approval of Law 1551 created a scenario that allows the channeling of this experience by the mechanisms proposed by the People's Participation Law. Women's demands have to do with infrastructure and services, but also with training, economic activities, violence and rights. These demands go hand in hand with another process called sensitization, undertaken along with the leaders, to mixed groups, but especially boys, and the ABCOs, the surveillance committee, and the FEJUVE. We have also had a training workshop with the planning team of the municipal government about gender strategy." She concludes that "The other achievements are having incorporated a significant percentage of women's demands in the district development plans and in the AOPs."

Cochabamba: Community House, District XIV—Villa Sebastián Pagador. Cochabamba municipality is divided into 14 districts, each under the responsibility of a community house, with a district administrator appointed by the mayor. In the community house of District XIV, IFFI has a small office, as well as the surveillance committee, the district council, and the school board. The administrator, Captain Ledezma, explains that when he got there "The district was totally disorganized, and my first task was to visit each one of the leaders and summon them to a meeting for the organization of the ABCOs, as well as the district council and other civic institutions that were still alive."

He is very enthusiastic about the participatory process in his district: "I'm not the one who decides anything for Sebastián Pagador. If something is decided at a meeting, what the majority says is done. If there are three options—some want pavement, others want a multifunctional sports court, others want a bridge—then with these three possibilities, we hold an election, and the votes are counted in the presence of the district director and the surveillance committee. The one with more votes is the priority; if most people say "pavement," then we do it, that's what's taken to the AOP."

Some local leaders told us that "Law 1551 has benefited us, but we do our part. Neighbors supply 50 percent of the counterpart effort for the works." Rufino Huanca, a local leader, is critical, noting, "Nevertheless, help from the mayor's office is very seldom obtained. Most of it is what we, the neighbors, do ourselves. The people who live here work hard to build our city."

Santa Cruz. Municipal administrations are key factors in the popular participation process. In order to have an idea of how they operate, we examined the Santa Cruz People's Participation Secretariat as a sample, which shares the general structure of the large cities' administrations charged with the application of the People's Participation Law, as well as their problems.

In this case, the municipality is in the hands of a political party with populist tendencies, with a mayor who is seen by many as partisan, and of whom many institutions complain regarding the guided participation he practices in their view. The People's Participation Secretariat reports directly to the mayor, and has gender, generational, health, education and sports departments. In the municipality, despite the critics, the staff are very proud of their participatory planning process, which they consider a model for urban municipalities in Bolivia.

Cidcruz (Santa Cruz). The NGO Cidcruz of Santa Cruz started operations before the People's Participation Law, when there was not much of an organization in the neighborhoods, or at least none that had any legal recognition. Initially, promoting committees were created, organizations that, according to Rosario Rosas, Cidcruz director, "quickly became a very masculine space...and became a promoting committee for works in the neighborhood to improve the habitat...There was a very conspicuous absence of women, for, although meetings were mixed, men would make decisions, and it was not possible to get the opinion and concerns of women. So we thought it was important to create an intermediate organization composed only by women, to get to the promoting committee already with more capacity. Mothers' committees were organized. The People's Participation Law arrived just then, so the promoting committee and mothers' committee were deleted from the neighborhood's history, and we started to promote the neighborhood associations."

Regarding the People's Participation Law in Santa Cruz, Rosario notes that "It must be understood as a process...people have to get familiar with it little by little, practice it, understand it, find its gaps and defects." She adds, "From the law's point of view, it has the great virtue of legitimizing the representation space. It's excellent that it has a territorial base; that's why it has men, women, youngsters, children, and the elderly—everyone. This ambit is governable and allows an ordered and coherent work. Upon the achievement of legitimacy through legal representation, there's a faster empowerment, people feel legitimacy before the law."

Where Are the Results?

"An essential objective of the popular participation process," notes Carlos Hugo Molina, "which we can clearly see now, was to create the possibility of the exercise of citizenship, because there was no possibility of citizenship in a country where 42 percent of the population was living in rural areas with no possibility of voting to elect their local authorities. It is as simple as that." (See box 6-8.)

Roberto Barbery notes that "The law is valid in itself; the mere fact that it exists is already a result. Now, we can't say that the law has not been observed—it's observed in some cases, in others a little bit less—but we have to acknowledge that it's sometimes too ambitious. These things take time. For instance, this is an electoral year in Bolivia; therefore, the mayors are more concerned with ensuring a good result in the municipal elections and are not thinking about processes that require long matura-

> **Box 6-8. The Success of the People's Participation Law as Viewed by Cochabamba's District VIII Leadership**
>
> The comments made about the People's Participation Law by local leaders are revealing. They consider it a good law, they express their desire and willingness to participate, and know that they now have a right to do so, but they criticize the nagging problems in the application of the law, especially in the relationship with municipal authorities.
>
> "We, the neighborhood associations, are spreading the word about the People's Participation Law, because we have also seen that out citizenry is not reading-oriented, doesn't like to read, doesn't know how to read. Maybe with the cassettes we are preparing now we're going to help them to know the People's Participation Law. I have a cassette here, for instance, in Quechua," notes Raúl Salvatierra.
>
> Romualdo Pérez, another leader, continues: "What share of the budget transfer resources were we entitled to receive in investments? We didn't know. But slowly, we have been reading the law, we have discerned it, so we already understand the scopes and the spirit of the law. That's why we later requested what is due to our district from the mayor's office."
>
> He adds, his tone somewhere between enthusiasm and disappointment, "This law is wonderful, it even says that the district administrators have to be residents of the district. Nevertheless, that's not observed; it's 'rhetoric,' says Mr. Héctor Vásquez [the district administrator] When we have asked him about it, he says, 'It's rhetoric; who's going to observe that!' This law is wonderful, when I went to Argentina two years ago, I made them read it, and people were amazed. They said: 'You Bolivians are a lucky bunch!' But nobody respects it. What's the use of having good laws if nobody respects them?"
>
> With all the difficulties and setbacks, there have been advances. Verónica Cutipa, a Barrio Universitario leader, points out "Well, my experience would be that, while before the law we knew nothing, we have learned something, at least to complain, to demand the rights that are ours by law. We the neighbors have learned to participate, which we didn't know before. To know my rights! That would be what I have learned."

tion and too much working time." On the other hand, the progress in dealing with concepts and practices that were not known by local people before is palpable. As Vladimir Ameller, the vice ministry's director of economic development explains, "Even the lexicon of the people from rural and poor urban areas has changed. They talk about operational planning, participatory planning, budget, they know what the AOP and MDP are."

> IT'S REMARKABLE HOW THEY HANDLE TECHNICAL TERMS. THEY WILL SAY: "I HAVE BROUGHT A SURVEYOR, HE HAS DONE A TOPOGRAPHIC PLAN." THEY NEVER HAD THE POSSIBILITY TO TREAT THOSE TOPICS AND NOW THEY DO.
> —Ana Quiroga, Director, Gregoria Apaza

According to the president of the Cochabamba Surveillance Committee, local leaders have started to take measurements and even fill their cylinders for concrete resistance tests. He wishes that "Each leader of the local board becomes the supervisor of the work, opens the work book, registers everything in the orders book, starts and concludes the works, and commits him or herself to a project's quality."

Legal and Regulatory Framework

A variety of laws and executive instruments support and institutionalize public participation in Bolivia and make its overturn difficult to effect.

State's Political Constitution

Bolivia's political constitution establishes as a fundamental right of the people the ability to "formulate petitions both individually and collectively" and as a duty the need "to cooperate with state organizations and the community in social service and security, and to safeguard and protect collective goods and interests." The 1994 reform of the constitution included several elements supporting the People's Participation Law, such as the recognition of the rights of indigenous people, legal representation of indigenous and peasant communities and their associations and unions, and the establishment of the new territorial municipalities as autonomous and equal as well as able to form consortia of municipalities, if necessary.

People's Participation Law

This law, which has been in force since July 1, 1994, and was modified and extended in July 1996, recognizes, promotes, and consolidates the popular participation process by incorporating indigenous communities, indigenous towns, peasant communities, and urban neighborhoods into the legal, political, and economic life of the country.

> AT HEART, IT DEALS WITH A DEEP-ROOTED REFORM THAT GOES
> BEYOND THE GOVERNMENT; IT IS A REFORM OF BOLIVIAN SOCIETY,
> OF THE BOLIVIAN STATE TO MAKE IT MORE DEMOCRATIC.
> —*Roberto Barbery, Former Deputy Secretary for People's Participation*

It intends to improve the quality of life for Bolivian men and women through a more egalitarian distribution and better administration of public resources, and it strengthens the political and economic instruments necessary to enhance representative democracy through a participatory democratic process and through equal opportunities in representation levels for women and men. To achieve these objectives, it legally recognizes neighborhood associations and creates surveillance committees that exercise social control over the municipalities.

Administrative Decentralization Law

This law, sanctioned on July 28, 1995, regulates administrative decentralization from the central government to the departmental level within the unitary system of the republic. It consists of the transfer and/or delegation of technical and administrative attributions from the executive branch at the national level, and establishes the organizational structure of the executive branch at the departmental level, as well as the departments' revenue base and budgetary mechanisms. In this way, it improves the efficiency and efficacy of public administration by ensuring the operation of the executive branch at the lowest appropriate level.

Other Related Laws

A new Law of Municipalities has been promulgated in accordance with the provisions of both the Administrative Decentralization and People's Participation Laws. This law establishes, among other items, a constitutional court to determine the constitutionality of laws, decrees, and resolutions; monitor municipal autonomy; and guard against a return of any centralizing or authoritarian trends from the executive branch. It also establishes an ombudsman, whose mission is to avoid citizen abuse and negligence on the part of government and state entities; it controls the operation and compliance of public rights and guarantees regarding administrative activity in all public sectors.[4]

---

[4] In its first year of operation, many of the complaints filed by the ombudsman involved municipal governments.

Pursuant to Law 1551, the Law for Educational Reform adjusted its contents and purposes to incorporate a participatory, multicultural, and multilingual dimension. It also created the school boards as a civil society mechanism related to the neighborhood associations for addressing educational issues. The law also established flexible curricula to be adapted to the needs of each place and designed with the participation of the relevant school boards.

Participatory Planning Manuals

The Vice Ministry for People's Participation has been involved in the development and validation of participatory planning manuals for municipalities that are predominantly urban or predominantly rural and for ethnic and indigenous districts. A manual has also been prepared focusing on gender. Says the vice ministry's participatory planning director, Mauricio Lea Plaza, "At first, I resisted the idea of manuals, but in the end, we have gone for it, because our experience in participatory planning showed us that in some cases, one model of participation was followed, and in some other cases, another one; that the role of neighborhood associations was not always recognized; that the municipal government was not always leading the process, which, for example was sometimes led by an NGO; and that then we had to correct those things. Now we have a procedural instrument that is part of the policy."

The Municipal Development Plan

The MDP integrates strategies, programs, and projects for a five-year period, as prioritized in the participatory planning process. According to the *Procedure Manual for Surveillance Committees*, "The surveillance committee has to exercise its coordinating role between the municipal government and the community organizations, protecting the interests of the latter, and ensuring that municipal action caters to identified demand. For this, it is critical that the surveillance committee participate in the entire process of elaborating the MDP."

The Annual Operating Plan

The AOP can be conceived in a very simplified way, as the result of a process through which a municipality's investment priorities are established for the short term (one year), within the overall framework of the MDP. The *Procedure Manual for Surveillance Committees* notes that "The surveillance committee has to exercise its social control role, assuring that the AOP reflects the demands from the grassroots level, in an equitable balance between urban and rural areas. For this, it has to establish participatory mechanisms that allow for the inclusion of societal demands in the budget; these demands are included in the MDP and are annually reviewed by the communities. Therefore, the AOP becomes a basic instrument for the surveillance committee to perform its social control role, verifying conformity between the local government's actions and the planning contained in the AOPs."

Mechanism for Reporting Mismanagement of People's Participation Funds

The *Procedure Manual for Surveillance Committees* requires that surveillance committees control the proper use of the people's participation funds and that they continually inform their communities and neighborhood associations as to their findings regarding fund usage. To perform this function, a surveillance committee must receive periodic reports from the municipal government. If it detects any irregularity, it can make this observation to the municipal council, which has to reply within 10 days. If the reply is not acceptable, the committee can then report the irregularity to the national treasury, which will investigate the complaint. If it upholds the complaint, the treasury will send it on to the senate within 30 days. The senate can then freeze budget transfers to the violating municipality until the problem is solved.

Resource Mobilization and Financial Sustainability

Municipalities' investment resources originate from various sources: the central government, through mandatory budget transfers; international development aid channeled through the central government; various social investment funds; NGOs; and municipalities' own revenues derived from local taxes, levies, and fees. The MDP, as the instrument that guides investments in local development from whatever source, promotes a clear focus and coherence of effort.

Additionally, because MDPs and AOPs are part of the nationwide General Economic and Social Development Plan, municipalities are allowed to mobilize and leverage resources from other sources. In this way, municipalities can—and many do—multiply the resources they have available for improving the living conditions of their inhabitants. For example, with 5 percent or less of resources from central government transfers, a municipality can take part in a scheme to provide basic health insurance to people who do not have access to medical insurance provided by a trade union; with 20 percent of the cost of a school, joint financing with another entity of the system—e.g. the Ministry of Education—is made possible.

Central Government Transfers (Co-participation)

The importance of co-participation resources for municipalities is highly variable, as table 6-1 and the following discussion illustrate. In general, for larger municipalities, the most important revenues are their own, which are almost five times greater than the transfers known as co-participation.

Table 6-1 illustrates the evolution of revenue from co-participation in five municipalities of the Cochabamba jurisdiction (out of a total of 44 municipalities). As the table shows, the sharp rise in revenues following enactment of the People's Participation Law in 1994 corresponds to the distribution of 20 percent of the national income in accordance with the population of each municipality, which was mandated by the law. Revenues for the Cochabamba jurisdiction overall increased by 6.5 times between 1993 and 1999. This increase was not consistent across the jurisdiction, however. Revenues for the central municipality of Cercado (the capital of Cochabamba) rose only 2.75 times, while those for the important municipality of Sacaba rose some 50 times and those for much smaller Colomi rose 162,000 times. Meanwhile, in Villa Tunari and Tapacarí, revenues went from zero to 9.5 million and 3.8 million *bolivianos*, respectively. This kind of dramatic change happened in municipalities across the country. In Cochabamba, revenues from co-participation in 1996 had increased by 108 percent over 1994 transfers, by 177 percent in 1998, and by 223 percent in 1999. Using the year prior to implementation of the People's Participation Law as a reference, Cochabamba's revenue growth from 1993 to 1999 was 545 percent. In 1994, Cercado, the capital's municipality, received 49 percent of the district's budget; by 1999, this proportion had been reduced to, and stabilized at, 37 percent.

Table 6-1. Co-participation Revenues in Cochabamba, 1993, 1994, 1996, 1998, and 1999

Municipality	Population 1992	Revenues (bolivianos)				
		1993	1994	1996	1998	1999
Total	1,110,205	34,219,378	68,281,988	142,356,727	189,067,766	220,661,402
Cochabamba	414,307	29,811,808	33,542,848	53,143,647	70,581,495	82,327,902
Sacaba	68,127	276,512	3,362,268	8,737,674	11,604,775	13,537,674
Colomi	15,489	19	606,852	1,951,636	2,637,132	3,077,855
Villa Tunari	48,111	0	2,267,053	6,204,078	8,194,766	9,560,248
Tapacarí	19,202	0	867,010	2,461,854	3,269,697	3,815,674

Notes: Revenues for 1993, 1994, 1996, and 1998 are actual; 1999 revenues are projected. 5.80 bolivianos = US$1.00.

Sources: Public Finance Ministry, Internal Tax Department, and State's General Accounting Department.

Social Funds and Prefectures

Besides putting co-participation funds in the hands of municipalities, the People's Participation Law requests that the nation's various social funds—such as the Social Investment Fund and the National Rural Development Fund—support local development plans; these are also supported with resources from the departmental prefecture.

Microcredit

Microcredit has been another important funding resource for development in Bolivia. It has been used to fund commercial, service, and production activities and, to a much lesser extent thus far, for housing and home improvement. The privately run BancoSol of Bolivia is widely known for its success rate and low level of loan delinquency. The association of microfinance institutions operating in Bolivia has the support of the Swiss Agency for Development and Cooperation, whose La Paz representative at the time of the study, Verena Munzenmeier, notes, "Microfinance institutions provide microcredit and are supervised by the same authority that supervises banks. They are allowed to lend money and also take deposits, yet they do not raise that much in savings. Until now, their operations have been based on community resources, with no formal, private banks involved; however, they still are able to finance some home improvement, even though their funding comes from community savings only." Although some other NGOs work with microcredit in the cities, the Red Hábitat example cited above is particularly encouraging for the purposes of this study in its home improvement activities in El Alto. There, it provides loans against the nominal guarantee of the custody of the property title—which is not a mortgage—and solidarity guarantees. Anelise Menéndez, of the NGO, states that "Our building materials credit program has a very low delinquency rate. In the first three years, the average overall delinquency rate was 2 percent." David Quezada adds that "We combined the individual guarantee, the guarantor's collateral, plus a collective guarantee. Each block of 10 neighbors is guaranteed with two property titles, generally those of the leaders."

Actors, Alliances, and Institutional Arrangements

Key actors in implementing the People's Participation Law and its participatory processes are neighborhood associations and their confederate organizations (FEJUVE, CONALJUVE), surveillance committees, and municipal governments. Other actors contribute as well, including the central government, departmental prefectures, NGOs, and international agencies.

Neighborhood Associations

In the case of cities, the recognized organization is the neighborhood association. These boards have been in existence since 1900 and have achieved a certain presence in low-income neighborhoods, making demands and pressing claims in response to community needs; their presence is much less felt in higher income neighborhoods.

Participants in neighborhood associations feel the need for greater state assistance and training in order to be able to operate in a context of frequent political problems and erratic support from municipalities. Explains Victor Paz Quispe, the secretary general of El Alto's Villa Huayna Potosí, "We were sent to the National Regional Development Fund. There we were told that we were not to coordinate directly with them, but that the mayor would be our bridge. We went to the mayor's office, and it took forever for them to process it...We have found many obstacles, and sometimes we just wanted to put our hands up, when we got tired and had nothing. Since we haven't been trained to make project proposals, we, the neighbors, need help."

FEJUVEs

Neighborhood associations join to form a neighborhood association federation (FEJUVE) in each main city, i.e., the nine departmental capitals plus El Alto and Llallagua. These federations were recently restructured to better match the People's Participation Law framework. This restructuring created intermediate entities in large urban districts and promoted the organization of federations in secondary municipalities. Between 1994 and 1999, some 45 FEJUVEs were organized in secondary cities.

The FEJUVEs are somewhat subject to divisiveness. In several capitals, there have been schisms in the federations. Notes a neighborhood association leader in El Alto, Rogelio Challco, "It's as good as having no support at all: there are two parallel FEJUVEs, and this is detrimental."

CONALJUVE represents all the country's FEJUVEs. As a civic organization, it represents neighborhoods in matters of national interest and implements the decisions they make in their congresses, acting as their representative in several sector commissions organized by the government.

The Surveillance Committee

The surveillance committee is the only community body created by the new legislation. As we have seen, it has the task of mediating the relationship between ABCOs and the municipal government and monitoring completion of participatory plans. The committee is made up of one delegate per district, elected by the district's neighborhood associations. Former national secretary of people's participation Carlos Hugo Molina summarizes the duties of the surveillance committee thus: "There are five occasions for which the surveillance committee absolutely must meet: to discuss planning for the subsequent year, to approve the budget at the beginning of the year, to verify what was proposed and incorporated in the budget, to check mid-year on budgetary execution, and to assess the investment made at year-end."

Several of the people we interviewed pointed out that a major problem for surveillance committees was a lack of resources to perform their work. "It is a volunteer organization, and is self-financed," notes Mauricio Lea Plaza, VPPFM participatory planning director. Another problem is lack of training, above all, in large and complex municipalities where the neighborhood leader has to at least know how to interpret a budget and an economic report, as well as a project and its lists of specifications. Information is thus vital to this task.

> YOU KNOW THAT THE FUNDAMENTAL PILLAR FOR A DELEGATE IS INFORMATION. WITHOUT INFORMATION, THE DELEGATE CANNOT DO A THING, HE CANNOT KNOW HOW MUCH IS BEING INVESTED IN HIS DISTRICT, HOW MUCH IS BEING EXECUTED. WITHOUT INFORMATION, HE CAN HARDLY DO HIS JOB.
> —*District VIII Delegate to the Santa Cruz Surveillance Committee*

Despite their problems, the surveillance committees enable numerous positive contributions. Emilio Lobo, of the Santa Cruz Surveillance Committee, sums these up. "We, the representatives of each district, are present in the participatory planning of the AOP and also in all sorts of activities, from the distribution of meals to schoolchildren to a broad range of municipal public works. And we approve all payments."

Municipal Governments

The municipal government is the state body closest to the general population. It is also the entity that is perhaps the most challenged by the new law. Large urban municipalities of long standing must divest themselves of their centralized practices and become accustomed to citizen participation. And newly formed smaller municipalities, for their part, are at the beginning of the learning curve: they have a real capacity problem, and everything must be learned. Moreover, the large urban municipalities must evolve out of their centralist practices and are not accustomed to citizen participation. Mauricio Lea Plaza cites a mayor of Tarija, "Who told me every time I spoke with him: '*I* know what the people need; that is why they elected me mayor!'"

Nonetheless, all municipalities operate under the new legislation and have been taking on, even if only gradually, their principal role in local development. "To conceive of any neighborhood improvement program without the participation of the municipal government is practically unthinkable," observes Vladimir Ameller, VPPFM director of economic development.

Other Actors

Within the central government, the authority in charge of the law's execution is the *Vice Ministry of People's Participation and Municipal Strengthening,* which, in its previous incarnation as a national secretariat, conceived and promoted the law in the first Sánchez de Lozada administration. Although the vice ministry is still highly supportive of the law, people's participation was not a top priority for the Banzer Suárez administration. A high-ranking VPPFM official observes that "The vice ministry had practically disappeared, few people even knew that it existed; I believe that if, a year ago, the vice ministry had been shut down, no one would have noticed." He acknowledges, however, that the vice ministry's importance grew again once the administration realized that the mechanisms established by the People's Participation Law were irreversible and that the central government needed someone to manage the complex central-local relationships these mechanisms entail.

Within the new decentralization framework, the *departmental prefectures* play an important role in supporting local governments and communities with training, technical counseling, and joint financing of municipal projects.

NGOs and *private development institutions* such as universities, the church, and private foundations have played and continue to play a significant support role for communities and municipalities. We have seen the important socio-technical support and resource mobilization provided by Red Hábitat, Gregoria Apaza, CIPRODEC, IFFI, and Cidcruz; there are many more organizations like these that have taken part in the participation process.[5]

The state has promoted the participation of NGOs in training and municipal and community technical assistance, confident of their effectiveness, based on their longevity and the trust they have gained among

---

[5]Most of Bolivia's hundreds of NGOs work in rural areas.

the communities within which they work—often going beyond the specific tasks they have been established to do.

International cooperation has also played a significant role. Most *multilateral cooperation institutions* and many public and private *bilateral cooperation agencies* have been involved in important efforts to support public participation in Bolivia. We have reviewed some cooperation examples from Denmark, the Netherlands, Norway, Switzerland, and the United States; many other cooperation agencies have also helped significantly.

Actors That Are Conspicuously Absent

Although planning guidelines include *other social organizations* besides ABCOs in the process, this participation is still very weak. Participatory planning director Mauricio Lea Plaza notes that "In the cities, the neighborhood associations are not capable of working effectively with trade unions or professional organizations." The disadvantage of this situation is brought home by Fernando Prado, president of CEDURE, Santa Cruz: "In the municipalities that are mostly urban and where there is a power structure and a strong economy, if you only interact with territorial bodies, very localized problems are prioritized, which is appropriate for the neighborhood. But who thinks about the whole? Who considers strategic projects for the city? For this, you need the participation of functional, economic, political, and professional institutions. These currently do not have a participation mechanism."

The former national secretary of people's participation, Carlos Hugo Molina, concurs, noting that this lack of engagement and participation extends to the *middle and upper classes* as well. "Why don't we participate? We should be there; we have opened up this process ourselves. And yet, neither us, nor anyone else of the 'politically conscious' in this country of a certain class has done so; and the neighborhood association continues in the hands of the people who have community problems that they cannot resolve by themselves. Our problems we can resolve by other means, and this is what breaks the solidarity and organization principle. Faced with that reality—and it is neither good or bad; it is a reality—I have suggested that the members of the surveillance committees be increased by 50 percent, with representation originating from functional, professional, civic, and union organizations, and from NGOs."

Problems

Discontinuity in the Institutional Framework. A first issue is the restructuring of the state apparatus between the Sánchez de Lozada (1992–

97) and Banzer Suárez (1997–2002) administrations. The earlier one conceived a cutback in the number of ministries, grouping several of them in secretariats coordinated by three large ministries: Human Development, with "social" secretariats, such as education, health, ethnic issues, sports, housing, and people's participation; Sustainable Development and Planning; and Economic Development, with "economic" secretariats. The Banzer administration returned to the concept of ministries for each sector.

There are also some mismatches between the two forms of government established in the state's political constitution. The new political organization on which the People's Participation and Decentralization Laws are based clashes with the old political subdivision of the country, which has not been totally reformed. The old units, such as the province, provincial section, and canton, serve very little practical purpose nowadays, but they have not been abolished, which creates some confusion.

Relations between Municipal Government/Surveillance Committee/FEJUVE. Frequently, there are evident tensions between these actors. Sometimes the municipal government manipulates the surveillance committee, giving its members advantages that border on the illicit; in other cases, relations remain tense. While the surveillance committee was created by law, the FEJUVE was created autonomously by neighborhood organizations. Between the two, there are tense relations and mistrust, and, until recently, little real understanding of each other's role.

Although normally the surveillance committee and the FEJUVE find it difficult to collaborate, there are some small but hopeful examples such as one presented by Ana Quiroga, of the NGO Gregoria Apaza of El Alto, where the surveillance committee "has achieved what the FEJUVE hasn't. Since the FEJUVE is divided into two factions, the surveillance committee has managed to group together all the social control functions, and now the surveillance committee in El Alto has greater power than either of the two FEJUVEs." Even more so, as CONALJUVE president Juan José Diez de Medina notes, "In Sucre, they have managed to put everything together. The FEJUVE directors who have been elected in the neighborhood association congress have also been appointed members of the surveillance committee. There is no problem there."

Carlos Hugo Molina supports this last solution, explaining that "There must be a fusion of the two bodies into a single one, because both are trying to represent the same people and do the same things."

Politicization Is a Problem in the Process. One of the most frequent concerns in this study has been the topic of the "politicization" of the process, of the co-opting of local leaders by municipal authorities to gain support for their programs. Everyone complains about this, although no one wants to acknowledge having participated in these practices.

> THEY LOOKED HERE IN THE NEIGHBORHOOD FOR PEOPLE TO JOIN THEM, AND OF COURSE, HERE IN BOLIVIA, THERE IS A HIGH RATE OF UNEMPLOYMENT, THERE ARE PEOPLE WHO ARE WILLING TO SELL THEMSELVES, AND THEY ARE TOLD: "LET'S SEE; LET ME GET YOU A JOB."
> —Romualdo Pérez, Neighborhood Leader, Cochabamba

In striking contrast, Oscar Terceros, former director of Cochabamba's area workshops, now muses that maybe the workshops *should* have been politicized, so as to highlight the efforts of the political party that moved that process forward. He observes, "We had said that the area workshops project should not be politicized; this is a project of the people, of the municipality, and should have no political color...I believe now, with hindsight, that if our party had participation as a proposal and put it in motion, why not say it publicly and legitimize its paternity of the process? 'We have promised the following and have fulfilled it,' in an attempt to get a political return." Terceros' main concern is that, since the political returns of the project were small, it lost steam, while it could have continued enjoying political support if the returns had been greater.

Practically all of the interviewees mentioned this topic in one way or another. For example, Fernando Prado of CEDURE, Santa Cruz, notes that "Bribing leaders is easy when there is so much power on one side and such economic precariousness on the other."

Verónica Cutipa, a Barrio Universitario leader, reveals another side of the problem: "They say of these neighborhoods, 'that neighborhood is aligned with the other party, so we won't give them anything,' while of other neighborhoods they say 'that neighborhood is on our side, so we are going to help them.' So there: tractors are taken, even water is distributed, but not to our neighborhood."

Carlos Hugo Molina offers the following thoughts on the matter. "I have another reading, trying to see more into the future. Five years ago there were no possibilities of saying 'it was politicized or not politicized,' because there was nothing...It is impossible to resolve the lack of citizenship of the 170 years of existence of this country in five years; all possible mistakes must be made, because this is the democratic school of the country...it is a long-term process. There will not be enough money for party leaders to buy, to lure, or to bribe everyone, and at some point an expression of the people will surface that will be committed to the future and the country."

When we attempted to discuss this topic with Rommel Porcel of the Santa Cruz Surveillance Committee, he pointed to a small notice in his office, telling us "It says there, 'it is forbidden to talk politics.'"

Organization and Implementation

The implementation of the People's Participation Law was a radical measure, and required—and still requires—the support of all involved institutions and the concrete engagement of many actors. The state established an entity (the People's Participation Secretariat, later the VPPFM) to initiate and monitor the process, with programs for municipal strengthening, community strengthening, and participatory planning, among others. Each ministry and state institution has the specific mandate to support the process in its sector.

> I BELIEVE THAT WHAT MUST BE DONE IS TO STRENGTHEN THE CIVIL SOCIETY AND MUNICIPAL GOVERNMENTS WITH TRAINING PROGRAMS; PROGRAMS THAT ALLOW THE EFFECTIVE LINK BETWEEN THE MANAGED CITIZEN AND THE MANAGER CITIZEN.
> —Roberto Barbery, Former Deputy Secretary of People's Participation

Even though the central government's role is clearly a normative and monitoring one, the departmental level of the prefectures is in charge of providing training and advisory programs to municipal governments as well as to communities, through its popular participation directorates. As vice minister José Barriga states, it is necessary "to seek a single point of entry to the municipalities, to channel training on health, education, housing, and popular participation, in a manner that is accessible to everyone. Otherwise, if you address each of these areas with separate training, there comes a time when the mayor complains about seminar overkill. Seminar followed by seminar, and little remains in the end."

Municipal governments are, in their autonomous framework, in charge of preparing development plans and executing them in coordination with community organizations. Many have established their own people's participation units for this end. In several large cities, they have proceeded with the decentralization of municipal services to the district level—although in this regard, there is still a long way to go to achieve true decentralization. As the main actors in the process, organized communities must strengthen their organizations and improve their capacities, taking advantage of all the available training programs.

Scale and Sustainability

The popular participation experience covers all Bolivian residents, nationals and foreigners—a total of about 8 million multicultural, multiethnic inhabitants. As noted by Vice Minister Barriga, popular participation is both a state priority and a state policy.

However, a state policy does not have the same level of buy-in from all administrations. Vladimir Ameller, director of economic development, explained that the popular participation experience was not, at first, a priority for the Banzer administration. Nonetheless, as participatory planning director Mauricio Lea Plaza points out, "It is a state policy, and this implies that it is on the agenda." Carmen Hada of the Ministry of Housing expands on this point: "Even though the current administration doesn't place as much emphasis on this topic, the mechanisms are clearly established, the roles have been assigned in the municipalities, and the application of the law has also been done at the central level." Further, the technical personnel who were committed to the first phase of implementation are still in place, and they are less sensitive to government changes at either the central or municipal level.

> THIS IS A LONG PROCESS, IT IS A COMPLEX PROCESS, AS WELL AS A VERY DYNAMIC PROCESS OF "MUNICIPALIZATION"; YET, IT IS A STATE PRIORITY, A STATE POLICY. POPULAR PARTICIPATION IS ACKNOWLEDGED AS SOMETHING IRREVERSIBLE, AND EFFORTS HAVE BEEN MADE TO STRENGTHEN THIS POPULAR PARTICIPATION.
> —José Barriga, Vice Minister for People's Participation and Municipal Strengthening

People's participation was not hampered by the Banzer Suárez administration, although it did not get the strong support it will need to continue to be developed. In any event, it has shown great resiliency, and this is what matters. It is only to be expected that in some administrations, this process will move at a slower pace, while in others it will be more dynamic, depending on the level of support it gets.

The automatic transfer of 20 percent of the state's tax revenue to municipalities, coupled with the municipality's new responsibilities vis-à-vis its citizens, are elements that encourage popular participation's sustainability. A mayor can be confident that adequate resources exist to support municipal responsibilities. Moreover, access to public resources for delegated responsibilities is essentially the same across all Bolivian municipalities, ensuring citizen equity and equal opportunities.

Conclusions

The people's participation process in Bolivia can be interpreted as an act of courage on the part of the national government. The innovative Bolivian legislation institutionalizes at a national level what has been suggested so many times throughout Latin America (and elsewhere): a leading role for local communities in their own development.

The key elements of Bolivia's law are legal recognition of organized communities and their prerogative to prioritize development projects in their locality and control local government action, revitalization of municipal power and the promotion of its duties in both urban and rural locales, and assignment of a basic budget to finance local development projects. Implementation of Bolivia's Law 1551 has yielded the following conclusions.

1. **I Participate, You Participate, He/She Participates, We Decide.** Under the People's Participation Law, actors are brought into the political process who have been absent until now and who have different interests than those already on the scene. This situation brings home the necessity of sharing power—a difficult concept to introduce anywhere in the world, since sharing power inevitably means losing some of one's own power. To promote participatory practices means to deal with a set of common and interdependent interests as well as with opposing and contradictory interests; the advocates of these various positions must learn to coexist and coordinate their ends and to achieve strategic or at least ad hoc alliances among themselves. Promotion of participatory practices also implies sharing a stake in the possibilities of development proposals and represents a pooling of wills, resources, and knowledge in processes that will be sustained over time if they become independent from individual action. It means moving toward a solution-oriented perspective, since it is no longer possible simply to demand the granting of a benefit without proposing a feasible solution. Finally, it entails assuming citizen rights and duties in which the attitude of the opposition is infinitely more valuable than the absent one of those who refrain from taking part in the process.

2. **Decentralization or Delegation?** Enactment of the People's Participation Law is resulting in a gradual, unevenly realized transformation. There is much disparity across municipalities as to whether true decentralization with increasing degrees of autonomy is being applied versus a simple delegation of powers from the central to the local governments. In general, the population, its leadership levels, and some politicians tend toward decentralization and are attempting to bring the levels of decisionmaking closer to commu-

nities. The municipal apparatus, on the other hand—particularly in the large ones—persists in promoting delegation without real decentralization. Some traits of the central government also encourage this behavior.

3. **We Move Forward without Going Back—But Not as Fast as We Would Like.** From our review, it is clear that the process has advanced much more in rural areas, although some significant progress can be seen at the urban level as well. Here, we have witnessed both a burgeoning consciousness on the part of the population and authorities that the participatory process must be followed in local development plans and an initial, albeit imperfect, application of participatory planning. As in implementing any innovation, problems have been encountered along the way, from weakness of urban neighborhood organizations to corruption among authorities and community leaders. But the institutionalization of popular participation compels all mayors, regardless of their individual predilections or preferences, to take the population into account. The resources tied to participation oblige mayors to invest in their municipality, and the law allows the population to petition for its rights with a certain amount of clout. This is a powerful tool in community development. In light of much criticism that indicates, "we do not feel represented, the participation mechanisms are not working," Roberto Barbery answers, "This proves that the law helps in itself, because before the law there was not even the possibility of realizing this situation. Now, a need has been created and the people assume that participation is an element that legitimizes the exercise of power. That is a result that in itself justifies the law."

The overall success of the model created in Bolivia proves that this kind of participatory practice can in fact be institutionalized—even though each country will have to adapt it to its own particular characteristics.

> WE HAVE A COMPARATIVE ADVANTAGE WITH REGARD TO OTHER COUNTRIES: HERE, THERE IS AN INSTITUTIONAL FRAMEWORK FOR PARTICIPATION THAT IS BEGINNING TO WORK. I DON'T THINK THAT THERE IS MORE OR LESS CORRUPTION, OR MORE OR LESS EFFECTIVE OR INEFFECTIVE AUTHORITIES THAN A FEW YEARS AGO, YET THERE IS A HIGHER DEGREE OF CONSCIOUSNESS AMONG THE PEOPLE, THERE ARE NOW INSTRUMENTS FOR PEOPLE TO EXPRESS AN OPINION, AND THE CITIZENRY IS STARTING TO ACT, TO DEMAND, TO VOICE ITS NEEDS.
> —Carlos Hugo Molina, *Former National Secretary of People's Participation*

7
Brazil: The Guarapiranga Program, São Paulo

The Guarapiranga program is a large-scale attempt to deal with the pollution of the Guarapiranga reservoir, which provides water for over 3 million people in the sprawling metropolitan area of São Paulo. Uncontrolled informal settlement development in the water catchment area, which gathered momentum in the 1970s and 1980s, was one of the chief reasons behind the deterioration of the reservoir's water quality. By the mid-1980s, these water quality problems had become so serious that the World Bank's help was sought by the São Paulo water utility for a cleanup program. The program, which began in 1993 and was completed in 2000, was comprised of a number of different projects, including the building of major primary and secondary infrastructure for wastewater collection and treatment, comprehensive upgrading of squatter settlements and informal land subdivisions, and the development of a new legal and regulatory framework to manage the water catchment.

Upgrading was thus part of a regional development plan for a considerable part of a metropolitan area involving the state and municipal levels. A large part of the Guarapiranga basin is in the municipality of São Paulo, but some small municipalities in the metropolitan area are also within its borders. As illustrated in figure 7-1, the institutional arrangement adopted for the program was horizontal, in which each of the main actors was responsible for a component or project under a general coordination unit which was established at the state government level.

The urban upgrading component of Guarapiranga in the municipality of São Paulo, which was run by the municipality itself, was the main focus of the study. The scale of the project was impressive; investment in the urban upgrading project alone amounted to around $207 million,

Figure 7-1. Guarapiranga Program's Institutional Arrangements

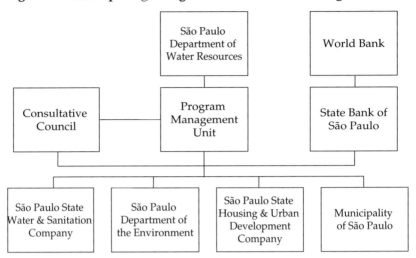

Source: Authors' construction from field study data.

directly benefiting approximately 250,000 people in squatter settlements and informal land subdivisions in the period from 1993 to 2000.

The entry point for urban upgrading in Guarapiranga was environmental sanitation. Planners recognized that the informal settlements of the Guarapiranga basin are a part of the city that is not going to be removed; social and environmental reasons therefore dictated the need for a sanitation infrastructure. An integrated, rather than sectoral, upgrading approach was taken in recognition of the important interactions between wastewater collection and other branches of infrastructure such as roads, storm drainage, and water supply. Since upgrading of all the different types of infrastructure took place simultaneously, Guarapiranga may be considered an example of a *comprehensive* upgrading project.

This comprehensive approach inevitably resulted in increased per capita project costs, but was critical to enhancing the sustainability of the intervention by ensuring that the negative impacts of a lack of storm drainage and road paving on the sewerage network were avoided.

It also provided an opportunity to boost demand-responsiveness and community ownership of projects by involving local residents in participatory information gathering and area development planning. This effort has thus been a methodological advance in relation to earlier upgrading projects in the São Paulo municipality.

Upgrading a dense and highly consolidated *favela* is a feat of planning and engineering, since the settlement layout must be improved and the infrastructure built while preserving the existing permanent structures as much as possible.[1] The constraints planners and engineers must deal with thus far surpass those found in conventional urban development projects. Another difficulty is that local residents continue to live and work in the area while the construction takes place, which presents quite a challenge in terms of construction techniques.

The Importance of the Guarapiranga Experience

Many metropolitan situations present the same challenges found in this program;[2] these include:

- The scale of the program and the complex challenges faced
- The conflict between environmental protection and human settlement needs
- The integration of diverse interests and priorities into a coherent set of actions
- The need to tailor interventions to the expressed needs and priorities of different groups of beneficiaries
- The need to adapt project requirements to the dynamics and pace of a participatory process.

A program this large offers a great potential for learning lessons both from its successes and its mistakes. The most important lessons of the Guarapiranga program relate to:

- Innovative institutional and legal frameworks for administering complex territorial systems
- Changes in the work culture and in the project management methodology, including significant private sector participation

---

[1] Preserving the existing structures as much as possible is important for two main reasons: (1) to preserve the investment made by local people in their homes over the years and (2) to reduce the need for removals and resettlement, which are usually the single biggest cost item in an upgrading project. The need to preserve the existing structures means that planners and engineers literally have to design new roads and infrastructure around them, which poses quite a technical challenge. Some leeway is provided by the possibility of removing and relocating existing structures built of nonpermanent materials.

[2] Although it is sometimes referred to in English as the Guarapiranga *project*, we here follow local usage and call it a *program*, in view of its complexity and the fact that it comprised many large, distinct projects, one of which was the informal settlement upgrading project managed by the municipality of São Paulo. We use the word *program* to refer to the broader Guarapiranga initiative and *project* to refer to its urban upgrading component.

- Definition of a precise function of socio-technical support that uses specific social work and communication methodologies
- The importance of issues such as land tenure and cost recovery, and the price paid for not addressing them.

Background

Rigid Laws and Lack of Enforcement Allow Growth of Informal Settlements

With a population of 16 million people, water consumption in the São Paulo metropolitan area is 60 cubic meters per second. Guarapiranga was one of two great dams built south of São Paulo by the British in the early 1900s for water supply, hydropower generation, and recreational uses. The Guarapiranga reservoir meets 20 percent of São Paulo's water needs: 12 cubic meters per second for 3.2 million people. The water catchment area occupies 639 square kilometers and presently is home to 622,000 people, 170,000 of whom live in more than 180 squatter settlements or favelas, with densities reaching—and sometimes surpassing—500 inhabitants per hectare. In addition, there are 119 informal land subdivisions, which house more than 250,000 people. In 1992, these occupied an area equivalent to the water surface area of the reservoir—approximately 26 square kilometers. For more information, see box 7-1.

Because the Guarapiranga reservoir supplies so much of São Paulo's water, legal measures were taken to preserve the water catchment area. In 1975, the Law of Protection of Water Catchments was enacted by the state of São Paulo, which limited the use of the surrounding land. The law prohibited installation of industrial uses or high-density residential subdivisions in the reservoir's vicinity. Ironically, the prohibition against subdivisions caused the price of land to drop, creating an incentive for informal occupation. Since the laws restricting occupation were rarely enforced, there was nothing to stem the tide of hundreds of thousands of poor people who, attracted by the availability of jobs in São Paulo's dynamic southern zone, settled in the reservoir's vicinity.

Water Contamination Follows

Since the informal settlements had no infrastructure for the collection and disposal of wastewater, untreated sewage discharges into the surface water drainage system flowed directly into the reservoir. The impact on the Guarapiranga reservoir was enormous, and a crisis ensued as the water quality deteriorated. In 1985, the State Water and Sanitation Company of São Paulo (SABESP) performed a number of water quality

Box 7-1. A Snapshot of Greater São Paulo

The metropolitan region of São Paulo, with 16 million inhabitants, is made up of 39 municipalities, including the city of São Paulo itself. Although it occupies just 0.9 percent of the territory of Brazil, it is home to 10 percent of the country's population and contributes 16 percent of the country's gross national product. In spite of the flight of industry toward the state interior and to other states, the São Paulo metropolitan region still accounts for 15 percent of Brazil's industry and 12 percent of its commercial and service establishments. Twenty-eight percent of industrial jobs and 17 percent of tertiary sector jobs are located here. São Paulo is also headquarters for the most important industrial, commercial, and financial concerns controlling the country's private economic activities.

Despite its dynamic economy, the region is characterized by profound inequalities and social imbalances. Even though the median per capita income is relatively high ($4,590), its distribution is unequal. According to a survey of living conditions in the region, 17.3 percent of families were classified as poor or destitute in 1994; the 1990 figure was about 39 percent. Infrastructure is also a problem: 35 percent of housing does not have sewerage, and only 17 percent of the sewage that is collected is treated.

This metropolis is one of the few in developing countries where, contrary to most predictions, population growth rates have actually slowed down. Population projections and census data show that the annual growth rate between 1991 and 1996 was a relatively modest 1.45 percent, yet the expansion of the "clandestine city"—the various shelter alternatives used by the urban poor that are developed in defiance of planning regulations and building codes—in the form of squatter settlements and illegal subdivisions has been enormous. In 1973, just 1.2 percent of the population lived in squatter settlements; in 1993, this proportion was 19.8 percent. The rate of population growth in informal settlements during the 1991–96 period was 16.4 percent per year. Slower population growth has been accompanied by another trend: the dwindling size of households, as progressively fewer people live with extended family.

Growth in the favelas has been the result of increased poverty, and particularly of the following factors:

- The high price of rent and housing units and land in the formal areas of the city makes it impossible for the poor to find formal housing.
- These neighborhoods are characterized by a high concentration of young people in their child-bearing years, which leads to greater population growth in informal areas than in the city as a whole.

Sources: IBGE (1990, 1994, 1996) and PMSP (1992).

studies and determined that a dangerous load of pollutants derived from domestic sewage was being discharged into the reservoir each day. Although the problems in the Guarapiranga reservoir began in the 1970s, the situation became critical during the 1980s when the appearance of algal blooms signaled a high degree of pollution. By the end of the decade, contamination of the reservoir had reached alarming levels and the Department of the Environment and SABESP turned to the World Bank for support for a cleanup program.

The Program Response

Initially, the primary objective of the Guarapiranga program was to ensure the quality of the water supply for metropolitan São Paulo. Without losing sight of this, the range of program actions was considerably expanded during the formulation stage. The program ultimately came to benefit 250,000 inhabitants of the Guarapiranga water catchment, as well as the city as a whole.

Two main courses of action were undertaken by the program. *Corrective action* reduced degradation of the water source; and *institutional capacity-building action* helped develop a legal, regulatory, and management framework to improve and maintain water quality.

To accomplish these goals, five specific objectives were established:

1. Expand and improve water supply, sewerage, and wastewater treatment services.
2. Improve collection and disposal of solid waste.
3. Upgrade informal settlements and provide alternative housing solutions to people living in risk areas.[3]
4. Protect and recover the quality of the environment through the creation of parks and reforestation.
5. Manage the basin through an appropriate legal and regulatory framework, an environmental protection and development plan, an information system, and the development of management capabilities.

Each of these five objectives generated a specific project. The focus of this chapter is on the third of these projects: the upgrading of the Guarapiranga basin's informal settlements.

The Guarapiranga program's primary purpose was to improve the water quality of the reservoir, but the presence of a large, poor popula-

---

[3]Many housing structures have been built in areas that are unfit for human settlement, since they are subject to landslides or floods.

tion in the catchment area made it necessary to shift priorities. In São Paulo, as in other developing country cities, environmental degradation and the lack of basic infrastructure and services in the informal city are intertwined. This issue was addressed squarely by the program so that environmental sanitation became the entry point for catalyzing investments in upgrading and addressing the problems of areas of risk.

The program began in 1991 with an environmental impact analysis. In December 1992, a loan agreement was signed by the government agencies involved in the project and the International Bank for Reconstruction and Development of the World Bank Group; this became effective March 1993. Initially scheduled for completion in December 1997, the program was rescheduled to continue for three additional years. The majority of the program components were successfully completed by the end of 2000, with the exception of some management issues that depend on legislative change.

Participatory Process
Distrust, Apathy, and Submission Undermine Participation

The 100,000 inhabitants of Jardim Iporanga, Vila 7 de Setembro, Jardim Esmeralda, Jardim Pouso Alegre, Vila Eda, and the other 134 favelas learned about the upgrading project by word of mouth from informed neighbors. As community leaders pointed out, promoting new ideas among residents of informal settlements is difficult because the residents have very little trust in government. Politicians' promises are well-known to community leaders, as some of the leaders are themselves on politicians' payrolls. As one project technician says, "There are some good neighborhood associations, but others live off building platforms for politicians."

> AT FIRST WE DOUBTED THE PROJECT BECAUSE HERE IN BRAZIL,
> PEOPLE ARE ACCUSTOMED TO DOUBTING EVERYTHING.
> —*Tereza Neiva Pereira, Community Leader*

All too often, government projects have promised improvements but have been abandoned or have failed to deliver, leaving residents in informal settlements to continue to live under unhealthy conditions, in the stench of wastewater and garbage. To avoid further disappointments, community leaders asked for explanations regarding the upgrading project and demanded conditions to be imposed on the project memorandum of understanding in order to provide reassurance and security to residents on contentious issues such as resettlement and temporary shelter.

Once these reassurances were provided, community leaders became increasingly convinced that they could back the project and encouraged their neighbors to be involved, overcoming residents' initial doubts and lack of interest (see box 7-2). The apathy of many community members was fueled by poverty's "dynamics of submission," as became apparent during the community focus group discussions. During these discussions, it was observed that residents tended to speak little, generally tended to agree with the community leaders, and did not voice their own opinions. There was a pervasive respect for hierarchy and a passive submission to the more dominant community members. One community member explains, "Our culture doesn't allow us to advance, but we are not guilty of ignorance. We just didn't have the opportunity to learn a different way."

In spite of some leaders' attempts to involve local residents, the population remained passive at times. According to the social coordinator of the municipality, Cleusa Mello, "The residents are satisfied by the mere fact that the municipality is doing something in the area…they accept

---

Box 7-2. Tereza Neiva Pereira, President, Jardim Esmeralda Neighborhood Association

Tereza Pereira, 45, directed the Jardim Esmeralda Neighborhood Association for three years, during which time an upgrading project was carried out in her favela. "As soon as I saw that the project was real, I decided to get to know it. My biggest concern was that what would happen with this project was what had happened with some families who were relocated 'provisionally' to a large municipal warehouse. Even today, over 20 years later, they are still living in the warehouse, waiting for a solution. We were not going to allow this to happen here." After she became convinced of the benefits the project would bring to her community, she organized dozens of meetings with families. Afterwards, she began promoting the project house to house.

During construction, Pereira mediated incessantly between the neighbors and the contractor. "When there is a problem, I gather all the parties to discuss it until they find a solution." To live in an informal settlement is difficult enough, she says. "And one day, all the engineers and technicians will leave, and all we will have left is our own capacity to unite for a common purpose." In her opinion, people do not need handouts to improve the conditions of their lives. Referring to calls for consumption-based tariffs for water and electricity, she says, "I am in favor of everyone paying for what they consume. To pay less, people will have to learn to save water and electricity."

almost everything with a patience that, frankly, I find excessive." Nevertheless, as noted by one of the technical support group coordinators, "The apathy does not mean that the people do not want to participate in the project. What I think is happening here is that in many public activities, the policy of 'we give and you receive' is still accepted as the norm."

Drug Trafficking, Another Enemy of Participation

Drug trafficking, and the power of drug lords, is an aspect of the social reality that is prevalent in the favelas of Guarapiranga, and drug traffickers exert a strong influence and control in some communities. As a social worker from Jardim Iporanga explains, "There are places where drug lords own the soccer field, maintain the daycare center, distribute gifts for all the children at Christmas…In short, they do more for the population than the government itself. In this manner, as well as through threats and coercion, they ensure the residents' loyalty, which enables them to continue their illegal activities with immunity from the law."

> I KNOW OF SOME CONTRACTORS THAT HAD TO MAKE PAYMENTS TO THE BANDITS TO BE ABLE TO WORK, BUT THIS WAS NOT GENERALLY THE CASE.
> —*Contractor for the Jardim Esmeralda Works*

On some occasions during the project, contractors had to negotiate with gangs to be able to proceed with the works. Drug gangs often oppose projects, since, for example, installing lighting and opening or fixing streets can be a deterrent to clandestine activity. Fortunately, with only a few exceptions in some communities, drug traffickers did not have decisive power over this project, although there were delicate situations in a few communities.

Women Lead in Participation

Even in Brazil's patriarchal society, women take a lead role in issues related to neighborhood management and are responsible for dealing with refuse disposal, the lack of security in the streets, and other problems in the community. Sueli Esteves Rodrigues, president of the Neighborhood Association of Vila 7 de Setembro states that "It's a fact that, without us, many problems would not be solved. Ours is the work of ants—of suffering and patience. But in the end, it is the only way things get done." The majority of men leave in the morning to go to work and return late in the evening, leaving the women to manage these problems. Among other community projects initiated by Rodrigues are a circus to provide entertainment for the community's children and a variety of training courses for adolescents. As succinctly described by Nair Cerqueira, president of the Neighborhood Association of Jardim Eda, "We, the women, have a bigger heart." Cerqueira's activities are described in box 7-3.

Socio-Technical Support Teams Open New Avenues for Participation

The government's lack of credibility in relation to living up to its promises, combined with residents' apathy and drug trafficking, were not the only deterrents to community participation in the project's early stages. Another deterrent was the lack of sufficient channels for information and communication in the project's original structure. This was corrected in later stages by the work of socio-technical support teams. These teams provided ready access to the project for residents, as well as information on technical and programming issues, and served as an avenue for requests and complaints. They helped organize participation in information gathering and analysis, discussion of project alternatives, and programming of the physical works, staging hundreds of meetings of

---

Box 7-3. Nair Cerqueira, President of the Neighborhood Association of Jardim Eda

Nair Cerqueira is an energetic woman of 60 who made an agreement with her husband so she could become involved in the project and attend meetings both in the daytime and at night. "He doesn't participate, but he doesn't stop me. I do all I need to do in the house; everything is perfectly under control...and then I go to the association to deal with the problems. I don't like to be stuck on myself, only thinking of my own problems." During the project, she offered to solve all types of problems. She campaigned on behalf of the residents and defended their rights. Worried about the lack of play areas for the children, Cerqueira gathered hundreds of signatures for a petition. She also lobbied to modify the upgrading plan of her settlement to include, for example, construction of a park and recreation area.

She also showed that she was willing to act with an iron hand where necessary to ensure that community members were acting for the common good. In one case, she warned a family constructing a new shack during the night in a designated risk area that she would have it demolished if they insisted on building it. She endured various threats, but these people are now her friends and neighbors, living across the street from her in one of the project's new houses.

thematic and area-based groups in each settlement. They also helped negotiate contentious resettlement issues and organized the transfer of families to temporary shelters and, later, to their new homes.

In the project's pilot phase, these social support services were provided by the municipality's own social workers and those of planning and engineering firms. Because there were few of these workers, they quickly became overwhelmed by the task, which subsequently led to delays in the implementation of the project.

The program and project coordinators realized that social support needs had not been adequately reflected in the project's initial resource allocation. They knew they had to move quickly, but found that bureaucratic constraints severely limited their options. The quickest solution found was to amend the existing construction contracts so that the construction firms were required to provide social support services in all subsequent stages of the project. Instead of hiring the necessary personnel directly, these firms decided to enlist a separate private company with the participatory planning and social mobilization skills required for working with communities in slum upgrading projects.

The work of this company, Diagonal Urbana, went beyond what was originally envisaged in terms of social support. Instead, the firm introduced the concept of *socio-technical* support. The technical support group, working in close coordination with the social workers and the construction firms, provided a bridge between the community and the design and construction process, helping find sound technical solutions to cater to community demand and concerns.

Community leaders and construction firm staff soon came to appreciate the importance of socio-technical support services. As one engineer notes, "We had an engineer whose only duty was the coordination of the work with the Diagonal team and the municipality. We are fully conscious of the fact that, if the population doesn't participate and collaborate, the work may become unfeasible. The social side is fundamental... this kind of work involves a radical change from all points of view: the technical and management aspects of the work are very different from what we do in the formal city."

A longer time frame for socio-technical support would have enhanced the project's sustainability. Vilma Dourado, Diagonal's director of social action, observes that "The time allotted was not sufficient to have an impact at the cultural level or to change collective behavior. It was just enough to guarantee the development of the construction work with a minimum of problems." As discussed further below, this statement reflects a larger concern about the lack of environmental education and other community development activities in the post-upgrading phase that would have improved the project's sustainability.

> THESE PEOPLE INVOLVE YOU IN THEIR LIFE; THEY INVITE YOU TO BAPTISM PARTIES AND WEDDINGS, AND AN EXCHANGE OF VALUES TAKES PLACE.
> —Social Worker

The activities of participants in community processes are often permeated with strong feelings. In Guarapiranga, relationships between professionals and community residents became so close that families welcomed technicians into their homes. Although this kind of working relationship may in some situations lead to a dependency relationship between the community and outside professionals, this depends upon the culture of the residents as well as the attitudes of the professionals. During the project, the professionals learned to see the residents of these previously excluded communities with new eyes, and both cultural and behavioral changes were observed in the way they responded to the *favelados*.

A Chain Reaction

"Vila 7 de Setembro was the first favela to be upgraded," according to local leader Sueli Rodrigues. "We spent four years raising awareness in the community to make participation in the project a reality. Our ambition was to set a standard that the other areas could follow." (See box 7-4.)

Vila 7 de Setembro is now, like the other upgraded favelas, a fully serviced part of town, and is a showcase of the urban planning and engineering skills the project helped develop and refine. As the impact of all this work was felt by the communities, a drive to improve homes and their immediate surroundings began. An engineer from one of the contractor firms noticed that "When we began the work, residents started to build sidewalks. They wanted to improve the area in front of their houses. In many places, they began to use the trash containers we put in the area. There was definitely a transformation in their habits." Ney Favela, leader of Nova Guarapiranga (see box 7-5) adds, "The community began to build; it remodeled houses, and people became more concerned with maintenance. Everyone is building; even I am improving my house. The residents themselves bought the trash containers that you see in front of the houses. This is a demonstration of civic consciousness in preserving the new infrastructure. Now, the new works are integrated with the old favela. It's all one."

A chain reaction was unleashed by upgrading. The residents of the informal settlements began to feel like ordinary citizens. They have an address, a postman comes to their house, they receive bills for water and electricity. This normality increased the people's self-esteem and strength-

> **Box 7-4. Sueli Esteves Rodrigues, President of the Neighborhood Association of Vila 7 de Setembro**
>
> Sueli Rodrigues, a 43-year-old woman who acts as president of the Neighborhood Association of Vila 7 de Setembro, has a sweet yet penetrating gaze which is both calm and convincing. The association she directs has made autonomy and independence its motto. After completion of the project, the association continued on its own with educational activities and environmental surveillance. Rodrigues is proud that the association is practically a self-financed microenterprise, thanks to sewing shops, a bakery, typing services, and silk-screening. The equipment for the businesses was acquired little by little by selling crafts or by asking for used furniture and equipment from nearby offices. With support from private companies obtained through the Civil Construction Union and others, it was possible to build a headquarters and promote courses for professional education. According to Rodrigues, the secret to the success of the association's various activities is a capacity to share information and responsibilities. "It's not me the leader. Each resident knows where city hall and where the offices of SABESP are. They know how to talk to those people on the phone and speak out for their rights because this is what we have taught them."

ened their sense of belonging to a physical and social environment. It also clearly stimulated residents' economic investment in their community. In areas with better community organization, these improvements in turn stimulated collective investments in public areas and common facilities.

Demands from other favela areas surfaced as soon as the project started. Residents of areas that had not been included in the project's original plans realized that the project provided unprecedented opportunities for improvement. These demands put pressure on the municipality and led to a broadening of the geographic scope of the project.

> THE ENTRANCE WAS AN UGLY, DARK ALLEY SURROUNDED BY WOODEN SHACKS. PEOPLE WOULDN'T COME TO MY HOUSE; I SEW, I HAVE CLIENTS, AND THEY DIDN'T LIKE TO COME HERE.
> —*Jardim Iporanga Resident*

This political pressure had repercussions even in the Billings Basin (the other great reservoir in the southern zone of São Paulo), where the municipality is planning another large-scale upgrading project. Elisabete

> **Box 7-5. Anselmo José de Almeida, Leader of Nova Guarapiranga and Vice President of the Favela Federation of São Paulo**
>
> The name and personal history of Anselmo José de Almeida (Ney Favela) are identified with São Paulo's favelados (favela dwellers) movement. Twenty years have passed since he was elected leader of the Favela Federation of São Paulo, which in turn created, among other regional organizations, the Coordination of Informal Settlements of Santo Amaro. He took part in the organization of three congresses, in which more than 10,000 favelados participated. The last one, in 1986, called for full land tenure regularization for favelados. Another of the movement's battles was the demand for upgrading, which through the years has become mainstream public policy.
>
> Ney Favela's vision remains relevant today. He recognizes the positive impact of the project on the lives of Guarapiranga residents, and he sees upgrading projects as a way to limit the effects of economic and social injustice. He regrets, however, that upgrading projects do not confront the causes of these social ills. He believes that showy public works are given priority over political and cultural development work and education. He sees the lack of environmental education activities as a major flaw in the Guarapiranga project. He is also a proponent of giving communities more power over decisionmaking and project management.
>
> Ney Favela's strong leadership is due to his innate ability and the political alliances he has built over the years. On some occasions during the Guarapiranga project, his opposition paralyzed construction and unleashed people's protest. For these reasons, the technicians of the different institutions involved in the project show a great deal of respect for this leader.

França, coordinator of the project for the municipality, notes that "Communities are our best allies in broadening the scope of the project."

Legal and Regulatory Framework

The Unresolved Question of Land Tenure

The desire of settlement residents to normalize and legalize their situation is at odds with prejudices held by sectors of government and the general public, to the effect that people living in favelas are natural-born nomads and might abandon their settlement at any time. In reality, many residents have lived more than a dozen years in the same place and feel connected to where they have raised their children. The project sought to strengthen this sense of belonging.

As Elisabete França, the municipal official responsible for the project, explains, "The sewers and drainage infrastructure, as well as the new public spaces, create a sense of affection, belonging, and pride in the residents." Although residents did not know much about the regularization of informal settlements, they said they were ready to pay a fee or levy for legal documents establishing ownership of their houses. "I would like to pay to have a document; I will go into debt if it is for the better. They didn't improve my house, but now that we have the basic infrastructure, I am very happy—and I don't have any desire to leave here," says one resident of Jardim Iporanga, one of the informal settlements urbanized by the project.

The issue of land tenure, which so worries the inhabitants of Guarapiranga, has difficult legal implications. Dirceu Yamazaki, the program management unit coordinator, explains that the Law of Protection of Water Catchments of 1975, which controls the use of the land to preserve water sources, inhibited industrial occupation. He states that it had "exactly the opposite effect with residential occupation." The rigidity of the law, as noted earlier, devalued the land and precipitated informal residential occupation. Yamazaki also observes that "As any occupation was forbidden, the government could not make investments in infrastructure. We have in the Guarapiranga basin the worst level of services in the entire municipality…The road system is chaotic, and, because of the water catchments law, all public infrastructure work is illegal. The result is increased contamination. And the pollution is diffused rather than from a point source, which makes it more difficult to address."

Because the occupation of land took place in a water source area subject to the restrictions of the 1975 Law of Protection of Water Catchments, it was not possible for the project to make progress in regularizing land tenure until the broader legal constraints were removed. Even for the city's apartment buildings, to which about 500 families were transferred, an innovative legal instrument, in the form of a lease giving families permission to use the apartments, was developed. The principle of payment for the housing units was established, but its method of calculation was unclear, and unresolved legal and bureaucratic questions impeded payment for a long time. The problem has only recently been resolved.[4]

---

[4]In addition to the 500 families that went to the municipal apartments, less than 1 percent of the population—the better-off families with stable incomes—were relocated to properties of the Housing and Urban Development Company (CDHU), the state's formal social housing system. It has been difficult to find enough families in the favelas with sufficient income to occupy CDHU units.

The new water sources law of 1997 acknowledges the existence of informal land occupation. However, it does not clearly define legalization rights and delegates everything to regulations the municipalities will adopt later. This adds to an already complex, onerous, and lengthy process.

Land Tenure Issues Compromise Project Results

The legal questions concerning land tenure are a deterrent to external private investment. The Basin Development and Environmental Protection Plan prepared by the program states that if restrictions concerning land use and occupation were loosened and fiscal incentives created, investors would be more interested in the area, which would improve overall conditions. This in turn would increase the sustainability of the project, create employment, and help prevent new land invasions.

Many residents reported that legal status of occupation is a critical issue, since their insecurity of tenure inhibits their participation in the project and has a negative impact on its sustainability.

> IF THE HOUSE IS NOT OURS, THEN ONE DAY IT CAN BE TAKEN AWAY.
> —Community Leader

Resolving these land tenure issues has the potential of alleviating residents' concerns that their houses may be taken away from them. According to the social workers, project beneficiaries need to have a sense of ownership and responsibility; having some form of legal title to their homes would go a long way toward promoting this. In some cases, initiatives taken by community leaders (e.g., providing information on legal rights) compensated for this insecurity and played a decisive role in increasing residents' confidence.

Increased costs and delays in construction resulting from land tenure issues have added to residents' feelings of insecurity. Some contractors said that the ill-defined legal situation of many favelas, especially in cases of invasion of private lands, forced the construction companies to wait for long periods to receive authorization from the legal owners before they could start the works. One contractor notes that "Within the area of the project, you can find a favela located on a piece of land that is public and another that is private. There is no difference between the two physically: it is all the same favela, with the same problems. This is one of the big problems affecting the project. We have to negotiate with landowners, create awareness about the importance of the work, and ask for authorization. We have to take these measures because if we don't, we run the risk of having the work stopped by a legal order. This can sometimes set our work plan back for many months."

Institutional and Legal Advances in Managing Water Catchment Areas

One of the primary results of the Guarapiranga program is the change in the legal instruments governing the management of water catchments in the state of São Paulo. The new legislation embodied by the 1997 State Law of Water Sources is based on a different view of the correlation between water quality and land use, largely due to the Guarapiranga experience.

As general coordinator Yamazaki explains, "It is significant that the philosophy for future management is not based on rigid control of the use and occupation of the land, as the old law was. The state needs a different policy for urban management, based on negotiation and participation, since it doesn't have the capacity to control land use." According to Yamazaki, the old water catchments protection law usurped the right of municipalities to govern their own jurisdictions, especially since some municipalities lie almost entirely inside the perimeter of a protected basin. For that reason, the idea now is that the criterion for evaluation will be the total of existing and potential pollutant loads going into the reservoir. By determining the reservoir's capacity for self-cleansing, the maximum admissible limits of effluent pollutant loads can be determined and fixed by law. Under the new legislation, the load limit translates into reference pollutant loads for each one of the 130 sub-basins of Guarapiranga, and each municipality is able to decide and legislate on land use in such a way that in all sub-basins the defined load limit will be respected.

Other new concepts have been implemented to promote the environmental recovery of the Guarapiranga water catchment. The community's inclusion in the management of the Guarapiranga program gave rise to a committee with representatives from universities, professional organizations, nongovernmental organizations (NGOs), and community entities. This successful effort suggested the basis for the committees organized to manage all water catchments in the new basin management system of the state of São Paulo. The new legal and institutional framework established the State System of Water Resources, which in turn created the Committee of the Alto Tiête Basin (Guarapiranga is a sub-basin of the Tiête River). This committee includes five subcommittees; its executive arm being the Basin Agency, established using the Guarapiranga program's management unit as its foundation.

According to another law, which was passed by the state assembly, revenues collected for water consumption provide the principal source of funds to ensure the Basin Agency's financial autonomy. This complex group of measures took time to discuss and has been slower to mature than originally foreseen, but in principle, the law establishes that river catchments be managed according to principles of integrated water resource management.

Although the structures and procedures for river basin management were to be established within five years of the start of the program, the term was extended in order to create a transition management unit as an interim arrangement between the program's management unit and the formation of the Basin Agency.

Resource Mobilization and Financial Sustainability

Community Pressure Increases Resources

One of the most important conclusions drawn from the study is that, although the low-income residents of Guarapiranga know the value of improving their surroundings, and many inhabitants of the São Paulo metropolitan area value the environmental improvements brought about by the program, they ignore the price required to pay for these improvements. The initial estimate of the cost of the Guarapiranga program was $262 million, 45 percent of which was contributed by the World Bank. Later, additional funding had to be found because the large investment required for urban improvements had not been completely foreseen.

The São Paulo municipality—the most important of the municipalities in the basin—used its influence to draw more attention to urban development in the program design phase. It thus succeeded in increasing the focus on improving informal settlements, which is presently one of the most important aspects of the program. As Dirceu Yamazaki explains, the municipality of São Paulo undertakes this work within its jurisdiction, while the Housing and Urban Development Company of the state of São Paulo (CDHU) is responsible for upgrading in smaller municipalities that lack the capacity for this type of work.

Elisabete França, the municipality's project coordinator, says, "At the beginning of the basin recovery program, there was little concern about the poor settlements. The SABESP initiative was characterized by a focus on sanitation in the basin, with little emphasis on the upgrading of low-income areas. The municipality, however, presented a plan for improving the informal settlements (a cost of $1,800 per lot was foreseen at the time) and for providing environmental education." This initial idea evolved into a comprehensive intervention that included infrastructure for water supply, drainage of wastewater and storm runoff, access roads, paving, and electricity supply as well as socio-technical support during construction, as well as the need for removals and relocation of some families (including temporary lodgings and substitution housing). The average cost per lot for settlement layout and infrastructure improvements, including removals and resettlement, was $5,900, according to França.[5]

The original sources and uses of funding plan has been significantly modified. Matching counterpart funds from the government agencies, which were initially set at about $143 million (see table 7-1), actually reached $293 million, more than double the original figure. SABESP, which was to invest about $40 million, actually contributed a total of $54 million. However, the majority of the increased investment was contributed by the municipality of São Paulo. "The program succeeded in leveraging a lot of funding," notes França. "In the municipality alone, instead of the $38 million initially agreed upon, $174 million has been invested."

Table 7-1. Initial Sources of Funding, 1992

Implementing agency	IBRD		Counterpart funds		Total	
	$ (mil.)	%	$ (mil.)	%	$ (mil.)	%
Program management unit	21.4	8.2	10.2	3.9	31.7	12.1
SABESP	36.7	14.0	39.8	15.2	76.5	29.2
CDHU	17.2	6.6	39.1	14.9	56.3	21.5
São Paulo Dept. of Environment	10.5	4.0	15.5	5.9	26.1	10.0
Municipality of São Paulo	33.1	12.6	38.2	14.6	71.4	27.3
Total	119.0	45.4	142.9	54.6	261.9	100.0

Source: Authors' construction from field study data.

Increased funding was coupled with changes in program design that increased the number of informal settlements to be upgraded, as well as the comprehensiveness of the work. This broadening of the project's philosophy and scope came about as a result of pressures exerted by the community. "There was a lot of pressure from neighborhood organizations for improvements, and the pressure increased with the start of the project. Once construction began, the population could see the results, and the demand increased," França points out.

---

[5]Note that the physical conditions of informal settlements in the Guarapiranga basin, and hence the cost per family of their upgrading, vary widely. Costs for a sample group of favelas are provided in chapter 3 in the discussion on the cost of socio-technical support (see table 3-3).

Finance as a Constraint and a Catalyst

Cash flow difficulties have—not surprisingly—had a negative impact on the project. As funds dried up due to the government's budgetary problems, the pace of work slowed between 1997 and 1998, even coming to a complete halt in some areas.

A construction company representative explains the ramifications: "We had an initial contract to finish the work in 15 months. We made a plan for this, but suddenly the funding stopped. This information shook the community and the professionals involved. The social support work was interrupted. The residents lost confidence. Our company carried on with the work, but very slowly. There were moments of anguish when some residents behaved aggressively, and some leaders hindered our work."

Apart from being the project's lifeline, funding issues had other dimensions as well. Several administrators and technicians, and some leaders, underlined the catalytic effect that World Bank funding had throughout the project. Yamazaki summarizes the situation thus: "The Bank found that the environmental education and housing component should be the entire responsibility of the state. But in our experience, funding from the Bank, even only 10 percent, helps a lot because it convinces the other program partners of the importance of the issue." Many municipal representatives echoed this view, and one of them acknowledges: "If the Bank demands something, everyone complies."

> FOR THE TIME BEING, I CAN'T DO ANYTHING TO THE HOUSE
> BECAUSE I DON'T ALWAYS HAVE MONEY TO EAT.
> —*Jardim Copacabana Resident*

The difficult economic situation caused by increasing unemployment also had at the time a direct impact on the residents' ability to invest in housing and infrastructure improvements. These economic circumstances affected their willingness to participate in the project in the form of financial contributions. The fact that the project was not integrated with employment and income-generation activities made it difficult to overcome this constraint.

Problems with Cost Recovery and Subsidy Policies

The lack of a clear policy concerning subsidies and cost recovery mechanisms posed another obstacle to sustainability. One of the most striking features of Guarapiranga in this regard was the lack of cost consciousness. The project beneficiaries who were interviewed disregarded the cost of the work, as did the technicians, particularly those involved in providing social support, and even the community leaders themselves.

Nevertheless, the potential for more transparent subsidies and enhanced cost recovery seems to be present. Some community members expressed a willingness to pay for services and criticized the flat rate "social" tariff for water and electricity. They favored tariffs based on consumption because, according to them, this would reduce waste and define responsibility for payment.

The Development and Environmental Protection Plan prepared as part of the Guarapiranga program emphasizes financial sustainability and identifies "payment for water use (consumption)" and "payment for scenic landscape potential use (including water activities)" as the two main instruments for cost recovery. However, although the state assembly approved these proposals, these issues are not yet firmly established in the minds of technicians and administrators—and even less so in the minds of residents or the general public.

> NO, I DON'T HAVE THE SLIGHTEST IDEA ABOUT THE COST OF THIS WORK. THIS IS A PROBLEM WITH THE PROJECT. THE CONTRACTOR SHOULD POST A SIGN GIVING THE COST OF THE WORK TO AVOID SPECULATION. OTHERWISE, PEOPLE MIGHT SELL THEIR HOUSE FOR LESS THAN WHAT WAS INVESTED IN IT BY THE PROJECT.
> —*Community Leader*

This lack of concern for financial sustainability led the municipality's social action coordinator, Cleusa Mello, to propose the collection of a special user fee to cover the cost of cleaning and maintenance of the settlements. To her, "Lack of payment implies a lack of commitment," but still municipal officials find it difficult to recover the cost of municipal infrastructure and services such as the road system, storm drainage, and solid waste collection. They believe that the state water company (SABESP) is better positioned than the municipality in terms of financial sustainability, since the utility's costs can be partially recovered through water tariffs. However, this belief is based on the premise that SABESP distributes bills, and communities are willing to pay for the water they consume. One community leader who works with SAPESP notes that "There is confusion about tariffs. There are areas that pay the social tariff, independently of the amount of water consumed; others pay by the meter; and others don't pay anything because nobody charges them."

Actors, Alliances, and Institutional Arrangements

A Broad Horizontal Partnership of Public Sector Actors

Various governmental organizations were involved in implementation and management of the various project components of the complex Guarapiranga program. The institutional arrangement that brought the project to fruition was complicated because the program was complex and incorporated a number of different project components covering a range of sectors. For this reason, the responsibility for project management, which was originally envisaged to be under the control of the water utility (SABESP), was transferred to the Department of Water Resources, where the program management unit was created.

These dynamics resulted in the organizational structure shown earlier in figure 7-1. The chart reflects the complexity of the relationships and the horizontal organization that benefited the project. Elisabete França is convinced that the project's innovative horizontal arrangement brought about good results in comparison to the traditional hierarchical structure commonly associated with government projects. She believes that state and municipality participation contributed to continuity of effort and the creation of joint initiatives.

Conflicts between Environmental Protection and Social Needs

Although community participation was a key element of project implementation, various stakeholders and organizations representing the communities felt that there should have been greater consultation during the course of the development and design of the project itself.

Many groups, including the Favela Federation of São Paulo, acting as the union of informal settlements, and various environmental NGOs, did not feel that they were included in defining the project. Consequently, they pressured the government to create a Tripartite Advisory Council comprised of representatives from the state, municipalities, and civil society, with a total of 42 members. The Guarapiranga/Cotia Subcommittee, a tripartite organization with deliberative power, later replaced this council. This subcommittee consists of representatives from universities, professional organizations (e.g., lawyers, engineers, etc.), NGOs, neighborhood organizations, associations, and clubs. The model is subsequently being used in other river basins of the state.

Yamazaki notes that the confrontation with the NGOs was not limited to requests for greater participation, but also extended to broader criticisms of the program's vision: "Opposing viewpoints have always existed, and they still exist, because some environmental NGOs don't like to see the poor living in this area." Nevertheless, some NGOs work directly with people living in the favelas. For example, one NGO set up by a number of professors at the University of Santo Amaro describes its organization's activities in the informal settlements of the Guarapiranga basin: "We work with the schools and promote some events in which we propose different topics such as public health, conservation, and environmental education. We work for the formation of community leaders and we have also established a community vegetable garden. We are monitoring the concentrations of algae in the reservoir, and the Department of the Environment included us in the Guarapiranga program in the project on environmental education."

As community leader Ney Favela, member of the Guarapiranga subcommittee, states, "There was a time when the government could have slowed the growth of informal settlements, but there was no political interest in doing so. Later on, the environment became a political issue. It was then that the government began to worry and invest in the decontamination of the Tiête River and the Guarapiranga program. The main axis of this program was the environment, because the government saw that it could no longer remove the residents. It wasn't possible to fight the cause anymore, only its effects. And they fought the effects through a program to upgrade the informal settlements."

Participation of Private Sector Organizations

The participation of the private sector was an important innovation in project management in the upgrading component of the Guarapiranga program. A small group of government officials coordinated the program, supported by a variety of private companies in different roles. As described by França, the private sector is no longer viewed as an enemy by civil society and the governmental sector, and it has taken charge of many of the routine operational activities previously carried out by the public sector.

"In the case of the municipality, there are only 16 people in the unit that coordinates the activities in low-income areas: a general coordinator (who is an architect and planner), a contracts and works supervision coordinator (also an architect and planner), a geographic information systems specialist, and a social team comprised of a coordinator and 12 social workers. The result is good; we are much more efficient this way," affirms França.

Under this scheme, subproject management was assigned to a management company; another company was given responsibility for inspection and quality control of the public works. Infrastructure and housing construction was carried out by several contractors.

As described above, socio-technical support was also assigned to a private sector company, which acted as an intermediary between the residents and the various other private sector and government agencies involved in the project. The novelty of this arrangement meant that program and project management had to use some creativity in hiring social support services. That did not detract from the importance of the social work. According to Yamazaki, "Social work, in projects such as these, is fundamental before, during, and after the physical intervention. To meet these demands, we found a way of including a clause in the contract with the construction companies that would require them to hire socio-technical support services for the population. They must have found the demand strange in the beginning, but I am sure that they now understand the importance it has."

The level of participation of the private sector in the Guarapiranga program had some unforeseen cultural impacts, creating opportunities and situations that had not previously existed. For the first time, for example, many middle-class professionals had the opportunity to enter the world of the informal city, which until then had been foreign to them. In addition, companies of diverse sizes and sectors of specialization became involved, exposing them directly to the favelas where they came to understand the lives of the communities living in informal settlements and also appreciate the need for a different approach toward the design and implementation of infrastructure.

> TEN YEARS AGO, NO CONTRACTOR OF IMPORTANCE WOULD HAVE BEEN INTERESTED IN THE UPGRADING OF INFORMAL SETTLEMENTS. BUT NOW, IT IS AN IMPORTANT MARKET NICHE.
> —*Dirceu Yamazaki, Program Management Unit Coordinator*

Professionals who had the opportunity to participate in the project told us about the transformation of their view of informal settlements and their inhabitants. One engineer summarizes his feelings toward the project as follows: "Before this job, I had always worked in the rich areas of São Paulo, constructing luxury buildings in Morumbi and places like that. This experience has profoundly changed my technical, professional, and—I would say—human perspective. My vision of the city is now completely different."

Improving Opportunities for Participation

Not all the actors in the project felt that they had a good opportunity for participation. Some community leaders requested improvements in the channels of participation. They believe that the World Bank could be instrumental in influencing the government in this regard. Ney Favela explains, "I don't think that the Bank should directly finance civil society organizations, but if the Bank wants the project to be a success, it should ensure that certain tasks, such as environmental education and post-implementation socio-technical support, are mandatory components of the project. It is therefore necessary for the government to provide funding to those organizations that are already working closely with the communities, especially because they know how to work with fewer resources. Our proposal is that the World Bank evaluate the program and offer a seminar in which representatives from the government and the community can discuss questions and complaints." Favela's position is similar to that of other participants, such as those in the municipality of São Paulo who regret that, since the state is the loan recipient, the municipality does not have the same influence in decisionmaking as does the state government.

There are also some NGOs critical of the state government for what they consider to be rigid procedures and a lack of opportunities for participation. A representative of the Guarapiranga NGO network cites a specific example: "The government, when it published the request for proposals [RFP] for environmental education services, placed requirements and conditions in the RFP that disqualified NGOs from bidding, in spite of their qualifications to do the work. Not even SOS Mata Atlântica, one of the largest NGOs in Brazil, could participate. At that point, there was a rupture between the NGO network and the coordinators of the Guarapiranga program. As a result, the program was not able to make much progress in environmental education."

The World Bank's procedures and modus operandi also drew some criticism. A municipal representative notes that the Bank team had difficulty understanding the dynamics of the work: "In their first visits, they would request a complete list of the families to be relocated, as if it were possible to determine this before the participatory planning process. In reality, as the project proceeded, we had to invent a thousand mechanisms for adapting the project to the needs of the population. One was called 'chess': a family that had to be removed but didn't want or have the economic means to move to an apartment outside the area could exchange their position with another family whose house was not affected by removal, but who did want to move. This kind of adjustment requires a lot of time and is decided case by case in the field by the social workers with the population."

Yamazaki attempts to sum up the issues of participation that resulted in various difficulties and delays: "These types of programs are very slow to mature and are very different from simple construction programs.

Programs like this require that institutions of diverse cultures, with different levels of organization and autonomy, work together. There are a thousand difficulties, even difficulties in accepting the World Bank's rules for procurement and financial management, which are different from our legal formats and our mentality. All this contributes to delays in the project."

Dynamics That "Greased the Wheels"

Certain dynamics compensated for the above-cited problems, enabling the project to make steady progress. These dynamics included:

- The "human factor" and direct personal relationships
- A sense of belonging to the same team and of a bond between the communities and professionals involved
- The role of private actors in establishing a work style based on efficiency and obtaining results within a specified time frame.

> MANY PROBLEMS COULD HAVE ARISEN THAT WERE AVOIDED IN PRACTICE. WHY? BECAUSE OF PRESSURE FROM THE POPULATION, THE TECHNICIANS, AND EVEN THE WORLD BANK. PROBLEMS WERE JUST NOT LEFT UNSOLVED.
> —*Dirceu Yamazaki, Program Management Unit Coordinator*

And, as stated by an engineer responsible for some of the project areas, "Without a doubt, this project benefited from good relationships among professionals in different areas. Even though we had to solve some problems during the course of the work, people got involved with a lot of goodwill."

Organization and Implementation

Learning the Way

All that occurred in project design and the attention given to problems in specific issue areas gradually gave the project its integrated character. The methodology evolved along the way; this was necessary to achieve sustainability. The technicians acknowledged that the project's initial limitations imposed the introduction of new strategies and new ways of doing things: "Integration among technical actors from different areas of expertise happened naturally, beginning with simple activities and then spreading to more complex ones. Once the various disciplines were integrated, the decisionmaking process became more agile. Integration between the contractors hired by the municipality and the sector of the municipality responsible for project coordination was also built on a day-to-day basis, after the work began. There was no previous planning process or definitions of scope to help us there. The process was a result of good communication and openness between the technical and social work teams."

A Diagonal architect sums up the experiences: "The Guarapiranga project, in terms of life experience, is very rich. The project allowed experimentation with technical, human, and ecological possibilities. In practice, it gave concrete form to ideas about the informal city that were initially very romantic. But as one implements the project, one observes all the variables and the limitations of one's actions, and these ideas become more practical and down to earth. A key role in this is played by the residents, who do not have a macro vision due to the limitations of their daily lives. They are much more concerned about whether the work will take away a piece of their house than they are about the benefit that it might bring to the community; however, that helps us to be realistic in our solutions."

Teamwork and openness on the part of the technicians involved permitted the entire team to exchange perceptions, criteria, and methods. The overarching conclusion of this process was the need to strengthen the social work before, during, and after each upgrading project.

Organization of Socio-Technical Support

The results of socio-technical support work from the second stage of the project onward were made evident by comparison with the pilot stage, which the municipality undertook with minimal social intermediation arrangements. This pilot stage showed the need to intensify socio-technical support and, at the same time, served as a useful baseline in comparing those areas that received an appropriate measure of such support and those that did not. The socio-technical support work also introduced innovations in subproject methodology, opening the way to a participatory process as described in box 7-6.

Upgrading interventions that had already been planned and designed for most areas without participation were submitted to analysis and negotiation with local residents. Diagonal Urbana was hired to provide social intermediation services, under the supervision of the municipality's social workers. The social work addressed the following key areas:

- Identification of community organizations and other stakeholders, key local social features, and leadership patterns

> **Box 7-6. Socio-Technical Support**
>
> The objective of socio-technical support in the project was to open clear channels of information and communication and stimulate greater participation by residents in the project. The steps by which this was accomplished are detailed below.
>
> 1. **Introductory meeting in which the entire population participated.** The municipality presented the project's objectives, criteria, and procedures.
> 2. **Meetings of interdisciplinary technical teams to update project data.** Community representatives were elected to help update existing data and to take part in discussions on alternatives for intervention. After noting all the changes resulting from the new information and discussions, the preliminary projects and work plans were adapted to the new reality through biweekly meetings with contractors, social workers, and officials from the Department of Housing, along with a technician from the company responsible for coordinating engineering work for all Guarapiranga upgrading subprojects. This was called "sweeping" because it "cleared the field," or laid the groundwork for the beginning of the works.
> 3. **Multipurpose meetings with residents.** Participation during the development of the works was ensured by a busy schedule of consultation meetings with community members and special-interest groups, during which information about the development was presented and discussed, and decisions were made regarding work fronts and timing of the needed removals. Prior to resettlement, the problems of life in temporary housing were discussed at specific meetings with groups of families preparing for transfer and relocation. Depending on the works' progress, the relocation or removal of houses affected by the opening of roads and infrastructure development was determined on a case-by-case basis. In such cases, residents were transferred to temporary housing.
> 4. **On-call socio-technical support.** In addition to scheduled meetings with area-based and special-interest groups, the social work-

- Meetings with area-based and special-purpose community organizations to disseminate information and promote the project
- Organization of participatory information gathering and analysis to update existing data and feed into participatory planning exercises
- Support to communities during construction, including discussion of required changes in design which were made possible as long as they did not go against the technical requirements of the construction

ers and support technicians were available at specified times for private, one-on-one meetings with residents. This was needed to ensure that people had an opportunity to discuss topics they would not feel comfortable with in a group meeting.
5. **Special assistance to the population removed to temporary housing.** The most intense work was with the groups most directly affected by the project. Before their removal and while they were in temporary housing, their most common problems were discussed, including garbage disposal, use and cleaning of sanitary facilities, and use and maintenance of laundry facilities. The community shared all these services. Discussions and decisions on alternatives for relocation also took place before removal, so that their final destination was known in advance. Only those with a specified minimum income would be relocated to an apartment; some families refused this because they felt they would not be able to meet the expenses involved. On average, residents stayed four to six months in temporary housing, awaiting transfer to a new house or apartment. When funding was limited, the work slowed down, which meant a lengthened stay and created additional problems for families in temporary housing.
6. **Support to final relocation and handover of the completed works to the community.** As the conclusion of the works drew near, with relocated families beginning to move to their new dwellings and the new infrastructure being put into use, socio-technical support turned its attention to preparing residents for their relationship with a transformed living environment. Although educational activities were carried out throughout the process, they were stepped up at this point. The main topics covered were health and environmental education, preparing for new financial obligations (tariffs, local taxes, user fees), use and care of the new infrastructure and facilities, and water and electricity use with a view to conservation. Promoting educational activities formalizes the handover of the new facilities to the community and helps strengthen community organization to promote new improvements after the project.

- Social communication campaigns
- Minimal follow-up after completion of the works, entailing meetings to encourage community organization and discussion of steps to take to ensure conservation of project benefits.

According to Cleusa Mello, the coordinator of the municipality's social workers, one of the findings of the social work was that it is not up to external actors such as the municipality to determine the best form of community organization. What these external actors can and should do is provide support for community organization in the aftermath of projects—a crucial step toward sustainability.

Scale and Sustainability

The Challenge of an Ambitious Project

Operations in Guarapiranga were multisectoral and on a broad scale, with the goal of righting environmental imbalances in a large area and improving the living conditions of hundreds of thousands of people. Programs of this size face particular challenges where sustainability is concerned.

> WE FEEL THAT LIFE IMPROVED. WITH THE PROJECT, THE QUALITY OF THE ENVIRONMENT IMPROVED. BETTER HYGIENE IMPROVES THE HEALTH OF THE POPULATION. EVEN THOSE THAT DIDN'T GET A NEW HOUSE GIVE THANKS TO GOD BECAUSE IMPROVING THE LEVEL OF THE NEIGHBORHOOD IMPROVES EVERYONE'S LIFE, AND CONSEQUENTLY PROPERTY VALUES ARE RAISED.
> —*Tereza Neiva Pereira, President of the Jardim Esmeralda Neighborhood Association*

Many of the residents stated that the project had a positive impact on their quality of life, but, in order to achieve this, the project required a massive investment in infrastructure works which was disproportionate to the relatively small investments in environment educational activities and the lack of project activities to promote employment and income generation; these are considered to be necessary to ensure sustainability in such a large and complex project.

Even the contractors themselves noted that they were concerned about issues relating to project sustainability. The engineer responsible for the Jardim Iporanga works notes, "I know that the objective is environmental protection and improved hygiene. For that to happen, you would need to work in tandem with the population for a long time to change collective behavior. This is an important factor and should be done starting with the schools, and then with visits to the houses, supervising and informing the residents, especially after the works have been completed."

What was particularly evident from the interviews and focus group sessions undertaken during the project was the agreement among the participating groups for the need to continue social support work and environmental education after the project's completion. They also agreed on the need for a greater emphasis on supervision, provision of technical assistance, control over post-project developments, and credit for home improvement and for the development of income-generating activities.

Obstacles to Sustainability

The following observations from focus group participants are useful in analyzing the obstacles to sustainability, which were observed to relate primarily to a lack of credit facilities, the pervading culture of crime, and a lack of environmental education.

A resident of an upgraded area makes the following observation: "Lack of credit prevents people from making improvements to their houses. People want to invest in their houses; we were only waiting for the completion of the project. Now we will have to wait until we have the money. Besides, people don't receive any orientation on how to improve their homes."

Risks to sustainability also relate to the criminal activities in the favelas. A resident from one of the upgraded areas says, "We have no leaders here. If you complain to the neighbors about their behavior, they might even kill you. If you tell someone they shouldn't throw garbage in the street, the storm drains, or in the canals, they say, 'You don't own anything! Do you rule here?' These violent people invaded the hillside, which we all know is an area of risk, and, next thing you know, they are ordering you about. They're all criminals. We don't know how to defend ourselves, and nobody comes to our help."

Diagonal's director of social action, Vilma Dourado, observes that "There were no provisions for an environmental education campaign as part of the project. Although we always talked a little about this topic in our community meetings, there was not enough time to discuss important issues of maintenance and conservation of the area with the families in sufficient detail." The absence of environmental education after the works were completed proved to be a constraint to the development of a wider social awareness about the importance of environmental protection and conservation.

> THE SPEED OF DETERIORATION OF THE COMPLETED INFRASTRUC-
> TURE IS VERY HIGH; THE ONLY WAY TO STOP IT IS A POST-
> IMPLEMENTATION PACKAGE INCLUDING SOCIO-TECHNICAL
> SUPPORT AND ENVIRONMENTAL EDUCATION.
> —*Dirceu Yamazaki, Program Management Unit Coordinator*

One biologist from the Interdisciplinary Nucleus of Environmental Sciences of the University of Santo Amaro clarifies this when he notes that the project "Created better infrastructure, allowed the entrance of garbage trucks, put in place garbage containers; nevertheless, the population was not made aware of the importance of garbage collection. People aren't aware of the problems they cause because of their behavior, and the garbage dump is seen as a deposit for all types of filth. They throw old sofas, refrigerators, and everything they no longer use into it. The mistake was in not making environmental education part of the process; this inhibits the project's sustainability."

The community leaders believe that more importance was given to the public works than to the problems of education and environmental awareness. "The biggest concern is to show off the works, without involving the population that will be responsible for their maintenance," says a community leader who reiterates the need for socio-technical support and environmental education to continue after the construction of the infrastructure. He attributes this gap to a lack of vision on the part of high-ranking government officials and observes that the funding for social work was insufficient for the scale and complexity of the problems.

This same conclusion was reiterated by the coordinator of the upgrading project at the municipality of São Paulo as well as by the officials responsible for the subprojects, who were insistent in their recommendations. As indicated by the conclusion from one of the focus groups: "There is an urgent need to increase socio-technical support work and environmental education in the post-implementation phase of the upgrading of informal settlements. The lack of such work after subproject completion limits the possibility that residents will participate in any post-project initiatives and affects the environmental, social, and financial sustainability of the subproject."

"Now We Even Want to Plant Flowers"

In the end, the Guarapiranga program has transformed the lives of many people and the life of the city. Not every problem was foreseen, and some aspects of subproject sustainability are at risk, but the reservoir's condition has improved, and many residents reported that they were grateful for what had been done. Tereza Neiva Pereira, president of the Jardim Esmeralda Neighborhood Association, expresses the extent of positive changes in the community: "We have gone through a radical change here. There is a climate of euphoria, and everybody wants to finish their houses, to clean them up. I believe that our lives have improved in several ways. You see children who have started to go to school for the first time, and men who have begun to work again." One of the community women in the Jardim Iporanga adds, "We assemble all the neighbors to take care of the gardens. Now that everything is so pretty, we even want to plant flowers."

Conclusions

Several aspects of the rich experience of the Guarapiranga program, and particularly the process of participation and its effects here, stand out.

1. Although poverty reduction was not an explicit objective of the program, it clearly did have an impact on poverty. In big cities in developing countries, the growth of informal settlements is one of the main causes of environmental degradation. For that reason, environmental sanitation is an excellent starting point for stimulating large investments in settlement upgrading and trunk infrastructure improvements. At the same time, public investment acts as an incentive to private investment in housing improvements, which ultimately enhances the residents' ability to undertake economic initiatives.
2. Communities voiced their concerns and applied pressure on those in power, which resulted in a substantial increase in the level of investment in urban upgrading and improved the quality of the upgrading subprojects. Community participation thus leveraged additional funding, although the channels of participation were not sufficiently fine-tuned to fully exploit the community's ability to contribute to project implementation. In spite of this, dialogue among the various actors often remained difficult, as it was in the process of formulating the subprojects. Reducing the cultural distance between public policymakers and members of poor communities continues to be an uphill battle.
3. The scale of a program of multisectoral intervention such as Guarapiranga is itself an agent for institutional and legal change. The institutional gains of the Guarapiranga program are significant. The program involved a number of institutions that, in spite of some difficulties, created a new type of relationship based on an innovative management model comprised of the state, municipalities, and civil society, interacting in a horizontal and decentralized structure. The following characteristics of the program favor this model:
    - A clear objective—i.e., improving the water quality of the Guarapiranga reservoir
    - A well-defined geographic area of intervention
    - A horizontal institutional arrangement that stimulates interaction between different institutions and civil society.

One lesson learned in this program is that fostering personal, direct relations between technicians of different institutions can allow them to jointly address related activities, speed up the decisionmaking process, and find solutions.

From a legal standpoint, the project is revolutionizing regional planning and management philosophy and is contributing to the definition of a new legal mechanism for river basin management. Perhaps the most crucial issue has been the use of the territory as a unit of planning and management. This regional focus has overcome the sectoral interests that had prevailed earlier.

4. Private sector participation in programs to improve informal settlements is a vehicle for radical changes in perception and contributing to cultural change. Large-scale interventions in the informal city introduce new actors to the process. Due to the large volume of works completed, medium-sized and larger firms have for the first time dealt with the reality of marginalized areas. This encounter has changed the personal and professional view of many middle-class contractors and technicians toward the favelados.

At the same time, the intervention of the private sector has begun to penetrate and influence project management style, which previously was directed by the bureaucracy of public administration. All actions of the Guarapiranga program were coordinated in public institutions by small, high-level technical teams, with most management and implementation tasks delegated to private companies. Integration between public and private sector professionals was good. New workflows and procedures were developed from this interaction on a day-to-day basis, with positive results.

5. The program lacked a clear cost recovery policy, which reflects the paternalism or mentality of dependence that still prevails in Brazil. Guarapiranga was not an exception to this general situation. There was a low level of cost consciousness, and the institutions involved did not shown much interest in developing mechanisms for financial sustainability. This was a missed opportunity, considering that the population appears to be willing to pay user fees, local taxes, and tariffs for water and electricity consumption; and/or to better establish their claim to legal ownership of their homes. The companies providing public utility services seem to think that a system of efficient metering, billing, and collection can only be implemented after completion of the settlement layout and infrastructure upgrading. The rules and criteria for this were not defined during the program cycle.

6. The significant public investment made by the program was not used to help implement a clear policy of subsidies that would have favored the poorest and stimulated mechanisms of social solidar-

ity. As a result, residents ignore the costs of the benefits obtained, and an important incentive for the preservation and maintenance of the new infrastructure and facilities is foregone.

7. The lack of solutions to the problem of insecure land tenure profoundly affected the project. The regularization of land tenure in the Guarapiranga basin was prevented primarily by the 1975 Law of Protection of Water Catchments. The new law of 1997 acknowledges the existence of occupation, but does not clearly define legalization rights and delegates everything to regulations the municipalities will adopt later. This adds to an already complex, onerous, and lengthy process. Meanwhile, the negative impacts are immediate. Residents feel insecure. Internal and external private investors are reluctant to invest. Attitudes of responsibility and participation in maintenance are inhibited.

   The impact of tenure insecurity on cost recovery is a particularly serious problem. On the one hand, there is a negative incentive for residents to do their part in a cost recovery scheme. On the other, informal land tenure poses a legal obstacle to the application of some constitutional cost recovery instruments such as *contribuição de melhoria* (betterment levy).

8. The project's social component was as important as the physical intervention and is essential for sustainability. Socio-technical support work focused on increasing the project's responsiveness to community demands, opening clear lines of communication among diverse public and private sector participants, and involving the population in the project's implementation. In Guarapiranga, innovative methodologies for social action and mechanisms for participation were created.

   Unfortunately, the investment in this area was limited to the implementation phase. Essential issues regarding sustainability—environmental education, methods to prevent and control new land invasions, credit and technical assistance for home improvements, and income and employment generation—were left unaddressed.

9. Without educational activities and structured stimuli to participation following subproject implementation, there will be little impact at the deepest level of individual and collective habits. If behavioral changes do not occur, the benefits achieved will be at risk. A lack of understanding of the essential components of the community development process during the program formulation phase was responsible for this serious gap in project design.

10. All those interviewed, representing the institutions involved in the Guarapiranga program, conveyed a single overarching lesson. The improvement of the physical environment can produce a very posi-

tive impact, but the engine of change is the community, which must be mobilized to continue the development process. Without a strategy for long-term participation, no project will be truly sustainable.

8

Costa Rica: FUPROVI's Habitat Popular Urbano Program, San José

Since 1988, Costa Rica's Foundation for the Promotion of Housing (FUPROVI) has been conducting a program called Habitat Popular Urbano, which can be translated as Urban Popular Habitat, and is based on assisted mutual-help construction. The name of the program refers to a method of developing low-income housing in which a housing association builds homes for all its members as a group, upon consultation and in partnership with an institution (FUPROVI) that offers social, technical, and administrative assistance services in exchange for a fee. Habitat Popular Urbano had, as of the time of our study, helped 15,000 families build their own homes; it employs highly innovative methods within the framework of private sector participation in Costa Rica's social housing policies.

The Importance of the FUPROVI Experience

FUPROVI's experience is relevant outside the Costa Rican and Central American context for the following reasons:

- FUPROVI assists the segment of the population that has little access to the benefits of public policies, such as housing subsidies, by using instruments of these same policies and selling its services in the market. FUPROVI has developed a methodology which not only contributes to its success in assisting the target population, but which may also serve as a guide for formulating appropriate public policy.
- From the start, FUPROVI has made its own continuity a priority. To this end, it caters to Costa Rica's housing association and *precarios* (informal squatter settlements) market sector. Internal staff train-

ing has enabled FUPROVI to better respond to the complex social processes of the poor or informal sector.
- In the FUPROVI program, community members administer and execute the projects, and communities control the project resources. Habitat Popular Urbano uses a formula that reduces the cost of housing construction and that functions as a filter. This formula allows FUPROVI to focus on serving the poorest communities. Moreover, FUPROVI uses clear, easy-to-understand contracts and makes information readily available to its clients.

Background

The Lost Decade and the Challenge of Housing

In the 1980s, the political, economic, and social situation in Latin America became extremely difficult. General instability affected import prices, public finance, inflation, and unemployment—all of which augmented the housing deficit. Not for nothing did statesmen such as Nobel Prize winner and Costa Rica's then-president Oscar Arias Sánchez call this the "lost decade" for Latin America.

The situation was no different for the small Central American country of Costa Rica, where the crisis was compounded by rapid population growth, internal migration, refugee inflow from war-torn neighboring countries, and limited effectiveness of state action. The crisis produced a marked deterioration in housing conditions and a growing tension in the urban development and housing sectors.

Squatter settlements, locally called *precarious,* were a result of the invasion of urban lands carried out by organized groups that hoped to meet their need for housing by collectively demanding public services and the legalization of the lands they occupied. By 1985, the official figures estimated that the housing deficit was at 124,000 units. Taking into account poor sanitation and hygiene in some squatter settlements, however, construction of another 280,000 would in fact be needed.

> AT THE END OF THE 1970S, THERE WERE 11 SQUATTER SETTLEMENTS IN THE GREATER METROPOLITAN AREA. AT THE END OF THE 1980S, THERE WERE 138; OF THESE, 91 WERE LOCATED IN SAN JOSÉ ITSELF.
> —*Lorena Revilla, Social Worker, FUPROVI*

In 1986, the problem of housing and human settlements became one of the fundamental points in Oscar Arias's presidential platform. He promised to build 80,000 houses during his presidency (1986–90). With this promise was born a housing development plan that radically changed the direction of this policy area—and created huge expectations among the people. The chance to acquire one's own home was recognized as a human right, and all succeeding administrations have reinforced this perspective.

An Enviable Level of Human Development

The level of expectation among Costa Ricans has arisen partly because their other vital needs—such as health and education—have been met (box 8-1). For this reason, Costa Rica has been able to concentrate on the problem of housing. It has made the right to proper housing a priority because it promotes family stability and helps raise families' economic level. At the focus group we held at FUPROVI's Villa Maria project, one of the project participants described the situation thus: "Education in Costa Rica is almost mandatory, because the government provides it, almost imposes it. And if we get sick, we go to the social security clinic. It seems that the greatest problem facing us poor people is where to live...Rentals are very expensive, and, if you have to fix anything in your rented house, you have to pay for it yourself...So it is better to have a home."

Box 8-1. Country Overview of Costa Rica

A small Central American country of about 52,000 square kilometers, Costa Rica is considered one of the most durable, stable, and peaceful democracies in Latin America. Sixty percent of the population of 3.4 million reside in the greater metropolitan area of San José, a section in the country's Central Valley that covers about 3.83 percent of the territory. The provincial governments of San José (the capital), Cartago, Heredia, and Alajuela are all located in this metropolitan area.

After many years of consistent investment in the social sectors, Costa Rica ranks high among Latin American countries in terms of its wellbeing. The country is placed at 43 on the world Human Development Index ranking as established by the United Nations Development Programme. A 19th century law that promulgated free and obligatory education in Costa Rica has produced dramatic effects: in 1994, 95 percent of Costa Rican adults could read. The government invests 22.9 percent of the national budget in education each year. Ninety-six percent of Costa Rica's population has access to potable water and electricity, according to data from 1996.

Desire for Housing Translates into Housing Associations

These comments suggest that housing is the top priority for poor Costa Ricans, an observation underscored by the social commitment to housing demonstrated by the large number of housing associations found throughout the country. Housing associations are formed on the basis of a single common interest: the desire on the part of their individual members to obtain housing. Generally, families from different places join together in a housing association. In Costa Rica, these associations are one of the most common ways in which families build a home, and their numbers have grown steadily since 1986, notably among the lower and middle classes.

The rapid growth in the number of housing associations, both formal and informal, occurred in response to the housing deficit and increasing demands from civil society to meet their housing needs. An inhabitant of FUPROVI's Dina project, which serves as a typical example of how a housing association is initiated, explains how this organization began: "The need for housing led us to organize ourselves and form a group. The idea for a collective housing and social infrastructure program arose when we observed the activities in other neighborhoods and the housing programs that other groups had initiated. From this point, we went through the legal paperwork in order to create the association and to identify the institution that offered the best financial deal for us."

By uniting in their search for housing, groups gain government assistance and obtain better prices through their collective purchasing power. A community member from the Villa Maria project explains the situation: "The organization began because of politics; one *compañero* who is involved in politics began to talk to other friends in order to get them involved in housing; in the beginning, in keeping with party politics, we did not allow anyone and everyone to join, but only *calderonistas*.[1] Later though, both liberationists and calderonistas could join, and the leadership was more democratic. From there, the association began to grow: from the 12 original associates, it soon grew to 50 members."

The Birth of FUPROVI: A Private Arm of the State Housing Policy

In 1986, the state introduced a new housing finance system with a strong investment capacity. However, it proved necessary to find new ways of

---

[1] In Costa Rica, two large political parties alternate in power: the National Liberation Party (PLN) and the Social Christian Unity Party (PUSC). Based on the last names of their respective leaders, members of the PLN are referred to as *figueristas*—for José Figueres—and those of the PUSC are referred to as *calderonistas*—for Rafael Angel Calderón.

working with organizations within the private sector that would be capable of producing new responses to the problems of working with low-income people, going beyond the slow pace of state bureaucracies. One of these responses was the establishment of a private sector entity with social goals in the housing sector.

> FUPROVI COMPLEMENTS STATE ACTIVITY...BECAUSE THE STATE IS SLOW AND INEFFICIENT IN RESOLVING URGENT PROBLEMS SUCH AS HOUSING, THE IDEA WAS TO CREATE NONGOVERNMENTAL TOOLS THAT COULD PROVIDE A MORE FLEXIBLE AND EFFICIENT RESPONSE TO THE DEMANDS OF THE MOMENT.
> —José Manuel Valverde, Applied Research Coordinator with CERCA, a UNCHS (Habitat) Program for Central America

FUPROVI was created in 1987 by an independent group of Costa Rican professionals from the public sector, the for-profit private sector, and academia, all of whom shared a desire to develop new and more flexible solutions to low-income housing delivery and urban upgrading. FUPROVI successfully lobbied the government to receive financial assistance from the Swedish government, which offered Costa Rica funding and technical assistance for several development programs.

Subsequently, the Swedish International Development Agency granted a total of $14 million to FUPROVI in three payments. This funding was primarily used for institutional development of the foundation and to set up a rotating fund for bridge loans to participants in FUPROVI's Habitat Popular Urbano program.

In addition to Habitat Popular Urbano—its low-income housing program—FUPROVI works with six smaller programs focusing on housing for the elderly and handicapped, urban upgrading, environmental improvement, community training, and support for income generation.

The Habitat Popular Urbano Program

Habitat Popular Urbano focuses on low-income families in the greater metropolitan area and the province of Limón. This latter was FUPROVI's largest project outside of San José, but there have been four others in different urban areas located near the capital. Table 8-1 presents a sample of FUPROVI's Habitat Popular Urbano projects.

In the Habitat Popular Urbano program, FUPROVI's support to its client families consists of three fundamental components:

Table 8-1. A Sample of FUPROVI's Habitat Popular Urbano Projects

Project	Location	No. of families	Family characteristics	Area of individual lots (m^2)	Construction area (m^2)	Average cost per family ($)
Mansiones	San Rafael de Montes de Oca (east of the capital)	119	38% single-parent families headed by women; 77% have 3–5 members	130	42	3,496
Dina	Patarra de Desamparados (south of the capital)	61		120	42	4,552
Villa Maria	Moravia de Coronado (north of the capital)	140	50% single-parent families headed by women, with an average of 3 members per family	60	42	8,300
Lagos de Lindora	Pozos de Santa Ana (west of the capital)	385	30% single-parent families headed by women, with an average of 4 members per family	120	65	6,960
San Juan	Pavas, San José (west of the capital)	885	50% single-parent families headed by women, with an average of 5 members per family	90	42	2,107

Source: Authors' construction from field study data.

- Bridging loan for the construction, improvement, and expansion of houses
- Bridging loan for building infrastructure
- A package of specialized services such as land tenure regularization, project organization, intermediation with government departments, and technical assistance.

This last comprises training and socio-technical support as well and is collectively referred to as ACAT (*asesoramiento, capacitación, y asistencia técnica*). An important part of the service package is helping families obtain a government housing subsidy voucher.

One of FUPROVI's most important services is legal assistance for land tenure regularization and for formalizing the constitution of housing associations. The need for this assistance is real; as a participant in the Lagos de Lindora project explains: "I belonged to a small association that did not have legal status…After the association was legally established, we had to work even harder…By the time Oscar Arias's government came along with the promise of housing, we were like orphans, knocking on doors all around."

Many of the housing associations that come to FUPROVI for assistance have already obtained land tenancy and a legal construction permit by the time they approach FUPROVI. This provides an indication of the motivation and level of capacity within the associations to develop solutions to their housing problems within the state's policies and legal framework. Notwithstanding, the bureaucratic application and processing procedures can take a considerable time, and funds are usually not available when construction begins. In these cases, FUPROVI offers bridging loans which enable construction to proceed while the transactions for state housing subsidies for each of the families are being prepared and processed.

Even though the FUPROVI methodology lowers costs significantly, the housing subsidy rarely covers the full cost of the house and related infrastructure. Families therefore normally have to take out a small loan from another authorized financial institution in the National Housing Finance System to cover the difference. FUPROVI assists its client families in obtaining this loan.

In exchange for these services, the client families take on a variety of obligations. Each family must contribute 30 hours of work per week to housing construction. "The requirement of 30 hours is a filter: if someone can pay someone else to construct their house, they will not give 30 hours per week. This ensures that the program is directed toward the poorest groups," explains Mario Rodriguez Vargas, FUPROVI's financial director. Thus, mutual-help construction exacts a strict obligation on those who participate.

Participatory Process

Associations Usually Make the Initial Contact

FUPROVI does not initiate the formation of housing associations. Nor does it usually seek out organized groups to offer them its services, as it did in its first years of existence, and still does occasionally when it has a specific interest in a group. Rather, it is FUPROVI that usually receives the requests of those who desire its help.

"In some cases, where we have taken the first step, this action works against us, because they believe that we have come to offer them houses. When we tell them that they have to pay, and that they have to work, they become disappointed because this is, ultimately, exactly what they do not want. For us, it is very important that they take the first step. They must be aware of the need, and they must present this need to us. Now we do it this way: when they come to us, we explain to them what FUPROVI is and say that they should come back when they feel our services are pertinent," explains Fernando Rojas, a FUPROVI engineer.

Once the initial contact between the association and FUPROVI has taken place, a FUPROVI social advisor begins to interface with the group's leadership. "There is a compañero in charge of making the first contact. Through a variety of channels, the groups begin to request information, and this person contacts the group's board of directors. Together, they visit other FUPROVI projects to review the methodology," explains Oscar Mario Garbanzo, a FUPROVI social worker. He adds that in this first meeting they do not enter into details regarding the costs of the construction or the finishings. The leaders then take this information to the association. They are encouraged to make a decision as a group on whether to accept the methodology. Once all members of the housing association group agree, an engineer and a social worker go to the community together to gather more detailed information about the families.

> THERE ARE PEOPLE WHO ARRIVE AND ASK QUESTIONS, BUT WHEN THEY FIND OUT THAT IT IS MUTUAL-HELP CONSTRUCTION, THEY LEAVE BECAUSE THEY DON'T LIKE THE IDEA.
> —Leiner Castillo, Dina Project Leader

Once the process is understood, it generates different kinds of reactions. Some people become involved and view the development of the project as their own, while others of those who go through the experience do not appear to be satisfied. Sonia, a participant of FUPROVI's San Juan project, asserts that she accepted the project because "I wanted a house so badly, but had no idea that it would cost me so much effort." Some do not want to participate at all; others rise to the challenge, as Rose Mary, a leader of the Villa Maria project, explains: "When we went to Lagos de Lindora and I saw the women working alongside the men, I became aware that we were actually going to build the houses, and that I would have to do so much hard work. And then I thought, if they can do it, I can do it." No matter what the initial reaction is, however, it is not until people are actually developing the project that they perceive the full implications of the FUPROVI methodology.

Because of the hard work the system of mutual help poses for the families, the fact that the housing associations are free to search for another alternative that meets their needs means that, in many cases, several years may go by before a group returns to the foundation to sign a contract. The organization behind the Mansiones project was formed in 1986; it did not formalize a relationship with FUPROVI until 1991. (The project was completed in 1993.) Similarly, the Lagos de Lindora housing association began negotiations with FUPROVI in 1991, but did not sign a contract with the foundation until 1995.

The First Step for the Association Is to Obtain Land

Once a contract has been signed with FUPROVI, the first goal for a housing association is to acquire land for construction. No fixed method exists to achieve this objective. In many cases, when associations contact FUPROVI, they already have a lot on which to build and have begun negotiations for its purchase. In some cases, they have obtained the lot through political clientelism or through a donation of land by a state entity. When the association does not already own land, FUPROVI finances the purchase or refers the association to other financing organizations.

Client Expectations versus FUPROVI Offerings

There is usually a mismatch between the initial expectations of client families and the services FUPROVI offers. Realistic expectations are essential, especially if we take into account that FUPROVI's client families have, in 80 percent of the cases, a monthly average income of approximately $180. One of the principal characteristics of these families is that between 30 and 50 percent of them are headed by women. As is often the case where women are heading up households, income is lower.

Both before contract signing and before construction begins, FUPROVI provides extensive information and training on community organization and on the project as a whole. Part of the rationale for these activities is to adjust client expectations to what lies ahead. "The foundation's objective is to transfer resources, knowledge, and technology, but the people want their house right away," says Mario Rodriguez.

As Antonio Benavides, a FUPROVI sociologist, sees it, "The people come for the house, they want to see the four walls...We offer them a package that enables them to build not only the house but also a community." The need for community building is not always perceived by all concerned. In the Mansiones project, for example, the FUPROVI team insisted on building a community soup kitchen and a daycare center to facilitate the work of those involved in the construction. The housing association complied, but only operated these for as long as it took to get the houses built. A member of the project's board of directors, Ana Alfaro, notes: "Those things did not really interest us; what we wanted were the houses."

FUPROVI's ultimate objective of building communities through training and hard work thus contrasts with the client groups' initial expectations, which generally focus solely on house construction. At most, community-building figures only as one of a client group's secondary goals. But unlike many experiences in the private sector—whether for-profit or nonprofit—this apparent conflict has proven to have a positive side effect in FUPROVI's case. It provides a reason for FUPROVI to do an especially thorough information and training job, encouraging its clients to stay grounded and act on realistic expectations.

Socio-Technical Support Is Fundamental to Self-Management

In order to get construction under way, FUPROVI provides a work team to support the community. The team's size and composition depends on the scope of the project, but generally it consists of a project head (with a technical or social background), an administrative instructor, an engineer for technical advice and work supervision, a social worker to consult with the organization, and a master builder who guides the construction step by step. The communities are responsible for all operational tasks, while the team provides needed socio-technical support, reflecting FUPROVI's proven ACAT methodology.

This methodology has changed somewhat over time. "In the beginning, we at FUPROVI were afraid that the associations might not be able to do certain things...We controlled the storage and the purchases, and the community carried out the physical labor. Later, we began to shift storage administration to them as well, and the community began to manage material receiving and custody. Then we saw that they had much more capacity than we had imagined. Now they also manage the procurement and purchase of the materials, negotiations with suppliers, and calendars for payments. This level of responsibility helps communities develop their administrative potential. Moreover, they know where their materials and monies are at all times. At the end of the project, you only see houses, you cannot see everything that has gone into it or that is underground: plumbing, foundations, long hours, machines, and work. The community sees all that, though, and values what it has built," says Mario Peña, a FUPROVI administrative instructor.

The main tasks of a FUPROVI project team focus on consultations and negotiations, intermediation, advisory work, technical assistance, and training. Team members provide technical supervision, guidance, and referrals regarding social, engineering, administrative, and legal questions. The goal is to allow the community group to make its own decisions and undertake the organizational, administrative, financial, and legal actions—not to mention the actual construction—on its own for itself. Through this process, the community learns to negotiate with other institutions, to assign contracts, and to organize and undertake work.

> WHAT WE HAVE SAID TO EACH OTHER IS THAT IF WE ENGINEERS DID NOT HAVE TO DEAL WITH THE PROBLEM OF ORGANIZATION, THE CONSTRUCTION WOULD BE EXTREMELY SIMPLE. BUT THE ORGANIZATIONAL ASPECT IS AN UPHILL BATTLE. IT REQUIRES, ABOVE ALL, THAT THE FAMILIES SEE THAT THEY ARE THE OWNERS OF THE PROJECT, AND THAT THIS OWNERSHIP WILL BECOME CONCRETE IF THEY BECOME INVOLVED AND PARTICIPATE.
> —*Miguel Artavia, FUPROVI Engineer*

So one could say that housing is the means by which FUPROVI achieves its goal: to teach low-income families to be the owners of a development project, something that extends far beyond housing. They begin with a greenfield site. Then they see the idea of the housing project on paper. Later, a tractor comes and begins to move the earth. Slowly, the idea that they are the owners of the project begins to form in people's minds.

In order for them to take hold of this idea, they undergo a lengthy period of training and a tiring process of mutual-help construction, and they need tools, like the technology and methodology that FUPROVI seeks to transfer. The effective appropriation of the project through this complex process is what makes the difference.

The FUPROVI team-provided training improves the aptitude, attitudes, skills, and knowledge of the participants in the above-mentioned areas. Special training is provided to community leaders. Specifically, training is provided to help community members:

- Provide support to the community and participating families through activities such as soup kitchens and daycare centers

- Organize and coordinate the mutual-help program
- Manage and resolve conflicts
- Plan, organize, and administer construction of the projected infrastructure and housing
- Procure and purchase needed materials and equipment
- Handle administration of supplies and storage
- Learn to handle and maintain tools and equipment
- Construct the buildings.

The FUPROVI process of assisted mutual-help construction differs from other mutual-help construction projects, such as those developed by government agencies. The complexity of the organization that is required generates in each of the mutual-help projects a series of subprocesses. Box 8-2 illustrates the complexity of a FUPROVI project and the concomitant need for a wide variety of socio-technical support services.

Training Is Very Important

Training, and the skills acquired through it, has been necessary for project implementation; beyond that, it has been one of the main assets for sustainability and for the continuity of the development process. Training needs are defined through meetings between the FUPROVI team and the board of directors of the housing associations and are ratified at general gatherings of the membership.

Rose Mary, a leader of the Villa Maria project, points out that "The FUPROVI lawyer gave us training and technical advice to legalize our housing association. First the board of directors got together and the lawyer explained the process; then the directors met with everyone else. The whole FUPROVI group—architect, sociologist, social worker, and technical instructor—met with the association leadership and the lawyer. The sociologist visited us on several occasions to prepare us for the process; then we divided into groups and wrote up the statutes."

Ana Lorena, another Villa Maria leader, explains FUPROVI's training in the construction work itself. "In the first training sessions, they showed us how the crowning beams and plates went. Every time we needed it, the advisor showed up at the construction site and told us how to do the things we asked him about."

Training of its own staff is also important. Internal staff training has enabled FUPROVI to better respond to the complex social processes of the poor or informal sector. The process of internal staff development has occupied, from the beginning, a central place in institutional strategy. Eloisa Ulibarri, FUPROVI's executive director, says that the foundation "has 110 professionals on the books and 50 more as consultants.

> **Box 8-2. More Than Just Construction**
>
> A FUPROVI mutual-help construction project encompasses many specialized and diverse tasks, as Rosa Carmona, the leader of the Lagos de Lindora project, explains: "We believed that we could not do it because nobody was specialized, but we learned how. We have housed more than 200 families; we had daycare centers and a soup kitchen; we worked from Sunday to Sunday; we kept track of the hours that people worked. The schedule went from 7:00 a.m. to 5:00 p.m. with 30 hours per week to be done by the husband, the wife, the children older than 15, a friend, a brother...When they did not complete their 30 hours, we sent them a letter of summons, and it was registered in the *libro de actos* [deeds registry] that they either promised to make up the hours or else pay someone else to do them. There was a list in the office with the amount of hours worked by each family. The people who could not manage the physical labor of construction worked in child care or in the kitchen.
>
> "As it was a large project, we divided the work into sections and, from there, into subgroups, for each of which there was a coordinator who oversaw the work. There was a clothing sale and a bakery. The kitchen was in operation for two and a half years." These support activities, which are key to the mutual-help project, arise in consultation with FUPROVI. The activities are generally not permanent, but help to meet needs as they arise. This is how Jorge Rodríguez, coordinator of the Cristo Rey project, explains it: "Other activities such as child care, a soup kitchen, bus services to take people to the project location were needed for the participatory mutual-help labor of construction. Once the construction was finished, these support activities also closed down."
>
> Although understandable, this linkage of the support activities to the project meant a lack of continuity in the development process—with the loss of some achievements, such as child care, that would have continued to be important for the communities. A long-term development perspective that would avoid this loss could perhaps be developed through specific social support work throughout the project.

The institution promotes ongoing education, and, for this reason, many staff members are studying business administration or taking advanced degrees in their areas."

The Key Role of Women's Participation

It is not strange that two women leaders provided us with details regarding construction; the labor for these projects is performed mostly by women, due to the fact that they head up a significant number of households (between 30 and 50 percent). Also, women sometimes dedicate their time to the mutual-help construction while their partners work to maintain the household. This is why so many of the support activities undertaken by housing associations, such as daycare centers and soup kitchens, focus on freeing up women so they can devote time to the project.

> THE MAIN PROBLEM I SEE IS TIME. WE ALREADY WORK A LOT OUTSIDE THE PROJECT. I AM A SINGLE MOTHER, I HAVE A FIVE-AND-A-HALF-YEAR-OLD DAUGHTER, AND I WORK TO MAKE A LIVING AND ALSO HAVE TO COME TO THE CONSTRUCTION SITE. FOR THOSE WHO HAVE A PARTNER IT IS EASIER, BECAUSE THEY COME TO WORK HERE, AND THEIR HUSBANDS PROVIDE FOR THEIR LIVING EXPENSES.
> —Deysi Ribera, Dina Project Participant

Ana Alfaro, a leader at Mansiones, explains that this participation has given particular characteristics to the projects: "We had to overcome the challenge of having men accept that the head of their work team might be a woman, that we women can work, that we know how to make a mix, that we can make solid frames…In the end, the majority came to recognize that we could do it." Certain accommodations were made in deference to the predominantly female composition of the workforce, Alfaro acknowledges. "We decided at the beginning that we would use prefabricated houses, but when we realized that we were mostly women, and that the prefab panels would be too heavy for us, we decided to use cement block and iron rod construction."

The Process Requires Sacrifices

To participate in a project requires other sacrifices for families, such as making payments on the bridge loan. This problem makes itself felt toward the end of projects when families are supposed to start paying back their loans, the subsidy money has not yet arrived, but the houses are not yet ready for the families to move into. "Almost all of us pay rent or live with a family member. We cannot move in nor camp out nearby, because the municipality does not allow it. If they had allowed this, the project would have been finished already," says one woman involved in the Dina project.

Furthermore, the majority of project participants (if not all) claim that mutual-help construction is exhausting, and the laborers become so tired after a certain point that burnout sets in and they want nothing more to do with the project. For this reason, once the project is completed, they generally dedicate themselves to fixing up their own houses and forget about communal life for one to two years. This is one reason why the daycare centers, communal kitchens, bus services, and other community initiatives do not survive the completion of construction.

Community leaders are particularly vulnerable to this burnout. In the opinion of Rosa Carmona of Lagos de Lindora, "As for the management of the construction, we did very well. But there were things they [FUPROVI] could have been more helpful with. Sometimes we felt that we alone were committed to the project. They didn't have to deal with surly families. It would be good for them to support us in this aspect, but I'm not sure they would be willing. They loan us money, so maybe it is not good for them to have problems with the families."

Legal and Regulatory Framework

A Foundation Serving as a Private Arm of State Policy

According to FUPROVI legal advisor Ana Yancy Valverde, "Prior to setting up FUPROVI, we investigated several possible legal structures. We decided that the most appropriate was that of a private foundation, because this format permits smooth resource flow, and its legal framework facilitates many things. For example, a foundation enjoys a series of tax breaks. In a way, in Costa Rica's legal system, the foundation forms part of the state, even though it is private. There is a legal structure that enables the foundation to extend the state's arm; therefore, we concluded that this would be an ideal format."

The Legal Status of Housing Associations

One of the principal characteristics of the groups that are FUPROVI's clients is that they are organized entities and, in the majority of cases, legally registered as associations. To be formally registered is a requirement for an association to sign a contract with FUPROVI. Once the associations decide to work with FUPROVI, they must sign a contract in which both parties' rights and obligations are stipulated; once legal recognition has been gained, an association is ready to negotiate, manage resources, and sign contracts.

FUPROVI does not limit itself to working with formal associations. It also works with groups of families that are not legally organized. In these cases, training is provided, with instruction about the association's leadership and operational structure. The training covers issues related to making collective decisions as an association, how to write statutes, and how to obtain legal recognition.

Legalizing the Land Is a Lot of Work

Upon its founding, one of FUPROVI's first activities was to work with precarios, the groups of squatters who had been awaiting a solution to their housing and infrastructure needs for a long time. Until FUPROVI's arrival on the scene, Costa Rica's public institutions had not created appropriate regulations to regularize squatters' land tenure. One of FUPROVI's first projects, La Floresta, involved the relocation of squatters to a new site, with a very complicated contingent legal situation. Explains Ana Yancy Valverde: "Their land situation seemed to suggest that we could never help them. We had to do a thorough legal diagnosis for each family…and, in some cases, we had to freeze the land titles in the public registry, because the problem was such that we had to suspend any transactions that might affect the properties."

As it did in this very first case, FUPROVI's legal division continues to undertake diagnostic studies to identify if land is suitable for the construction of houses and if it can be legalized. FUPROVI assumes total responsibility for all the tasks that fall in this area. The administrative route for the legalization of the land, which can take two to three years, can be undertaken only when the land is not affected by any lawsuits, which prolong the process of legalization due to judicial procedures.

Valverde notes, "In our Costa Rican reality, much of our juridical statutes derive from the Napoleonic Code, in which one must first demonstrate that one operates in good faith. And when one knows that the land belongs to a third person, one has already lost good faith. The proceedings are very cumbersome; as a result, many people say, 'Better for me to remain illegal.' For the average poor person, the only way to obtain a title is through a government program. If they attempt the legalization as individuals, the land is usually eaten by the lawyers, the experts, and others."

FUPROVI has made an effort to propose alternatives and demand the modification of some Costa Rican norms and procedures. It has promoted change in the legislation and has generated a series of exceptions that permit the approval of this type of project without the need for a special ruling on informal settlements in general.

Resource Mobilization and Financial Sustainability

Subsidies and Soft Credit According to Income Level

Costa Rica's National Housing Finance System (SFNV) plays an essential role in the financing of the Habitat Popular Urbano program by mobilizing financial resources from the government and directing them toward investment in housing projects. With 3 percent of the national budget, SFNV is funded by 33 percent of the Fund for Family Grants and 25 percent of the investment proceeds of the Costa Rican social security. The Housing Subsidy Fund authorizes subsidies and soft loans that can be complemented by authorized credit providers. Public and private institutions such as banks, credit unions, cooperatives, and other providers of housing finance function under the authority of the Housing Mortgage Bank, the government financial entity that regulates housing finance. SFNV's governing body is the Ministry of Housing and Human Settlements.

SFNV operations are based on the classic instruments of subsidies and soft loans. The composition of the state's contribution depends on a family's income. At one extreme, those who receive the minimum wage are granted a full subsidy; at the other extreme, those who receive four times the minimum wage have access to a small subsidy and to credit at near-market conditions.[2] The higher the income, the smaller the subsidy, and the closer the interest rates are to market levels. Families with incomes higher than four minimum wages rely fully on the market for access to housing.

As elsewhere in Latin America, a low-income housing program of this nature tends to exclude the poorest people. The for-profit private sector that offers housing solutions that take advantage of the subsidy program focuses on the not-so-poor or the lower middle class. Those who are really poor cannot afford to pay for land, infrastructure, and construction, the combined market cost of which exceeds the amount of the subsidy. They also find it difficult to deal on their own with the government bureaucracy to regularize land tenure, obtain building permits, and access the subsidy. FUPROVI's intervention seeks to overcome these constraints.

With the Subsidy, It Is Possible to Manage the Financial Burden

With the SFNV subsidy voucher, FUPROVI's bridge loan can be paid off within two years on average. If the family does not have access to a

---

[2]The minimum wage is a fixed amount which is adjusted every six months.

voucher, FUPROVI establishes a monthly payment, which represents 30 percent of the family's income, so the loan can be paid out over 15 years.

The Mansiones project, which was completed in 1993, demonstrates the significance of this financial burden on families. In those days, the subsidy scheme was working smoothly, and the subsidies paid out at the end of the construction period were sufficient to cover construction of both house and infrastructure.

> WE HAVE SEEN PRIVATE CONSTRUCTION PROJECTS LIKE OURS THAT COST UP TO $30,000 PER HOUSE; THESE HOUSES ARE COSTING US $8,300 APIECE. IN OTHER WORDS, BY WORKING TOGETHER ON THE CONSTRUCTION, WE ARE SAVING A COOL $22,700 EACH.
> —Rose Mary, Villa Maria Project Leader

Ana Alfaro, a leader of this project, explains: "At the end, the cost of each house was $3,057, including the infrastructure, plumbing, and electrical wiring. Adding the debt to IMAS [the National Social Welfare Institute] for the land, the majority owed about $3,343. After they gave us the vouchers, we ended up with debts of around $1,274—an amount the families could handle."

Without the Subsidy, Things Would Be Much More Difficult

A different scenario occurred in the Dina project. Here, the processing of the subsidy voucher was slowed by legal problems related to a neighboring lot. This created a situation in which the project participants had to begin paying back the bridge loan before receiving the subsidy money. A FUPROVI loan recipient at Dina notes, "If this institution is there to help people of scarce resources, they should offer lower interest rates, so we can pay less." The belief expressed here is that if the community puts in its own labor in the project, this should be recognized with a lower financial burden.

One woman at Dina expresses her dissatisfaction: "Each year, the interest is 15 percent, which seems high to me. I always thought that we would not have to pay so much if we were to be putting in so much work. They told us at the beginning that the price was $30, but as the project has taken longer, the interest has gone up. They raised the monthly payments to $94. Many have dropped out because they could not pay. For people here, the lowest salary is $226 and the highest is $471. If the subsidy voucher had come through, the house would almost be free." At the same time, they recognize the value of FUPROVI's work: "They have trained us for the work. We have had a few problems, but not things that we could not fix."

> AS A RESULT OF POLITICIANS' PROMISES, MANY PEOPLE EXPECT
> NOT TO PAY OR TO RECEIVE A FREE VOUCHER. SO WE BEGIN BY
> LOWERING THE LEVEL OF EXPECTATIONS. WE MAKE THEM SEE
> THAT THEY MUST BEGIN WITH WHAT THEY HAVE. WE SUGGEST
> THAT THEY LEARN TO ADMINISTER THESE RESOURCES AND TO
> REALIZE THEIR OWN ABILITY TO COVER THEIR COSTS.
> —Miguel Artavia, FUPROVI Engineer

According to FUPROVI, each house in Dina is worth about $15,000, while the cost to the participants was about $8,750; this is not enough to appease the project participants, however. It is clear that the attitudes of project participants toward the cost of FUPROVI services and the conditions of its bridge loans are determined by the availability of the housing subsidy voucher—the panacea that appears to resolve all problems.

How Can FUPROVI Offer Financing without the Subsidy?

Through three donations of the Swedish International Development Agency, FUPROVI received a total of $14 million, which was used for the institutional development of the foundation and for bridge loans to project participants in a rotating fund mechanism. The institutional development aspect was a key part of the Swedish aid package.

FUPROVI has always tried to follow sound financial management practices and recover cost. As Mario Rodriguez explains, "The goal of FUPROVI is to maintain its resources at $14 million—that is, to maintain the value of the three Swedish grants in hard currency." He notes that the foundation's policy is to divide the funds into three parts: the first is in the hands of the housing associations as bridge loans, the second is securely invested, and the third is kept liquid as a reserve for projects in the early stages of development. FUPROVI finalized negotiations with commercial banks for the establishment of a trust fund arrangement that will allow the banks to take over FUPROVI's cash management chores.

FUPROVI applies near-market interest rates to project participant loans because of its desire to recover all the costs of the services it offers. The organized mutual-help construction methodology lowers the final cost of the operation to below market levels and makes it possible to build the houses with the amount available through the housing subsidy voucher. The system worked well until 1997, when the Costa Rican housing subsidy program began to experience problems. Up to then, FUPROVI projects had followed a predictable pattern. In each project, the beneficiary families were enrolled by FUPROVI in SFNV. While they completed the construction work, FUPROVI assisted them in legalizing the property and getting their subsidy requests processed. With the entry of the subsidy program's donations or soft credit, the state housing finance system would return to the foundation the amount of the bridge loan plus the agreed price of its services. To cover the difference between the subsidy amount and the cost of the houses, the client families would take out a loan from an SNFV-authorized financial institution.

However, when the subsidy model is threatened, the bridge loan becomes a long-term credit option. As a result, two specific problems have arisen. First, for the families, there is the problem of repaying a loan over a 15-year period at interest rates only a little lower than market levels; second, for FUPROVI, there is the serious problem of having its resources tied up in each project for a much longer time than before. As FUPROVI was always repaid through the rapidly authorized state subsidy, its financial cycle was relatively short. This raises the question of how FUPROVI can finance new operations while the participants of previous ones are still paying off their loans.

To this end, and to ensure that loans could be repaid at an interest rate that is affordable to the participants, FUPROVI took several steps in order to preserve the institution and its qualified staff under the new circumstances, and to create new opportunities to reach its target public. One option being pursued is to access soft credit—no longer grant funding—through the Swedish International Development Agency.

> IN ORDER TO SERVE THE NEEDY IN A SUSTAINABLE WAY, THE INSTITUTION MUST ITSELF BE VIABLE. EVERY NICKEL THAT WE INVEST WE HAVE TO RECOVER.
> —*Mario Rodriguez Vargas, FUPROVI Financial Director*

Other options include the following:

- **Reduction of output.** The longer financial cycle has led FUPROVI to lower its output from around 4,000 to around 1,500 units per year, which has also led to the layoff of about 40 percent of the staff.
- **Reduction of unfunded mandates.** The grant-based programs that FUPROVI had launched *inter alia* to promote income generation and assist the elderly have been curtailed.
- **Partnership with Costa Rican banks.** FUPROVI has developed savings and long-term credit products in partnership with Banco Popular and Banco Nacional de Costa Rica, to provide options for families that want to improve existing homes, build homes on existing plots, or buy land for future building. Credit for each of these may be

provided separately so that families may move gradually toward their goal of homeownership.
- **Innovative credit mechanisms.** Innovative credit mechanisms such as *cuota creciente* (increasing montly payment), in which repayment starts out with small installments that increase over time, are being used to enhance affordability and widen the client base.
- **Sale of FUPROVI services, including training, to other organizations.** FUPROVI's institutional experience and the recognized quality of its technical assistance and training services allow it to provide its services to government organizations and other nonprofits.
- **Projects for the lower middle class.** FUPROVI is developing profit-making projects in partnership with private developers for people who earn between four and six times the minimum wage. The profit made on these projects will be invested in FUPROVI's low-income housing programs.
- **Sale of FUPROVI services in other Central American countries.** FUPROVI is looking into the possibility of providing services to international aid organizations active in other Central American countries.
- **Grant funding.** Swedish grant funding is being sought to enable FUPROVI to undertake housing and basic services projects to assist the numerous Nicaraguan immigrants in Costa Rica. Other international aid organizations are being approached for funding for similar projects.
- **Aggressive investment policy.** FUPROVI's investment policy, which had hitherto been very conservative, has been made more aggressive to maximize earnings on resources available for investment.
- **Improvement of credit management services.** Credit analysis and billing and collection services have been improved, and innovations such as the transfer of obligations from housing associations to individual families after construction have been introduced in an attempt to maximize repayment rates.

Actors, Alliances, and Institutional Arrangements

Alliances Are Fundamental

FUPROVI must build strategic alliances with public and private institutions in order to perform its work. FUPROVI does not own any land, and thus alliances with public institutions and other entities are necessary to obtain land for those associations that do not have it and to achieve tenure legalization. The legal aspect of a project sometimes depends on the administrators of these institutions.

One clear example of this need for alliance-building is the group of autonomous public organizations involved in infrastructure and construction to whom the community must apply, with FUPROVI's help, for permits and services. Specifically, FUPROVI must negotiate with the Costa Rican Electricity Institute, the body that regulates and generates electricity on a national level; and with the National Light and Power Company, which is responsible for electricity distribution infrastructure in the greater metropolitan area. It also must obtain a water quota from the Water Supply and Sewerage Institute and road access from the Ministry of Public Works and Transportation. Construction permits, solid waste collection, construction and maintenance of secondary roads, and, in some cases, drinking water supply also must all be arranged for in coordination with the municipality.

Motivation for Partnership: Project Success Is an Important Criterion for Government Credibility

Because public housing for low-income people has been a government priority since 1986, the actors cited above are more than willing to work with FUPROVI: the success of this kind of project is a crucial measure of the government's capacity to deliver on its promises.

Jorge Blanco, an electrical utility official, clarifies. "FUPROVI has always worked closely with us. They are a very committed institution. In most cases, we end up giving away the lines and the posts; the only thing we don't give away are the meters...We are clear that nothing of what we have here in this institution is for ourselves; it belongs to the state. In the end, and over time, when they pay for their electricity, they pay back the investment."

Design and Technology

Urban Design: Tradeoffs in Quality and Standards

The people who participate in FUPROVI projects not only must confront the costs, the legalization of the land, and the effort of obtaining a housing subsidy voucher, but must also obtain the necessary permits. The design must be approved by the various institutions responsible for giving permission for construction. Costa Rican institutions take this quite seriously. There are very strict requirements to fulfill, or else the work may be held up. In practice, this means that FUPROVI is barred from using alternative, and less expensive, technologies for infrastructure. The technology used for drainage, water supply, wastewater collection, and other services is conventional and proven.

Savings are made by focusing on the services that are most important, cutting back on finishings, and using the assisted mutual-help method. Beyond meeting physical planning and housing bylaws and standards and putting the land to maximum use, FUPROVI does not place emphasis on the quality of the urban design of its projects, which look for the most part like traditional public housing. The clients do not seem to mind the rows of identical houses, since the initial and overriding interest of the group is simply to obtain a house. This desire takes priority over interest in design. Especially given that one of the key concerns is to minimize the project's final cost, it is assumed that a more creative or better quality design of free space will require more land than is available or raise the price unnecessarily.

"If there were larger collective open spaces in the settlement, it would have been necessary to relocate a certain number of the families involved...Moreover, if you start talking about parks and large amounts of open space in a public housing project, the people who give the permits begin to get scared," says FUPROVI architect Jorge Rodriguez. This is not to say, however, that there is no a priori design process that takes into consideration basic infrastructural services such as the street network, drinking water supply, electrification, and the management of wastewater. Other services, such as street paving, public transportation, and health and education facilities, are normally not part of the projects. As a result, these have to be addressed by the community itself after each project is completed.

> IN THE END, WHAT WE OFFER IS NOT A TOTALLY FINISHED HOUSE, BUT RATHER A SETTLEMENT WITH BASIC HOUSING: WALLS, A BATHROOM, ROOF, A CEMENT FLOOR, DOORS, WINDOWS AND ELECTRICITY; IN GENERAL, THE CEILING, WALL PAINT, AND INTERNAL DIVISIONS ARE NOT INCLUDED.
> —*Jorge Rodriguez, FUPROVI Architect*

Generally, FUPROVI engineers and architects propose the settlement plan and layout, and are also responsible for infrastructure design. In some cases, the communities already have at their disposal a settlement layout and plan, which is revised by FUPROVI technicians. In all cases, the design is submitted to the housing association for approval, although design parameters are not very flexible (see box 8-3).

> **Box 8-3. Costa Ricans Like Their Houses Set off from the Rest, with a Patio in Back**
>
> The tendency in Costa Rica to build free-standing homes rather than high-density structures puts pressure on design engineers. Jorge Rodriguez corroborates this assertion: "When we talk to the families, the first thing they request is their own plot, with a patio in back; moreover, they don't want to share walls."
>
> When FUPROVI staff propose the possibility of a more efficient use of limited space through the construction of vertical condominiums, they receive responses like that of Lorena Revilla, a social worker. "You could try that possibility with family groups, parents and children, but not with unrelated families. Here we are used to having our own space, our little piece of land, a patio." This cultural pattern causes available space to be used for individual plots rather than public open spaces.
>
> There are a few exceptions. In the Villa Maria project, the houses do share walls, with the goal of reducing the built-up space and expanding the communal areas. FUPROVI made an initial recommendation, and in this case, the housing association accepted it.

New Technological Alternatives for Housing

FUPROVI expresses great interest in construction technology and experimentation in alternatives that reduce costs for its clients without compromising product quality. The ultimate goal is to lower costs and simplify the construction process. This position has led FUPROVI to take advantage of all the construction technology available on the market (see box 8-4).

The variety of technical options for construction favors the versatility of the mutual-help program, at least in relation to the housing itself if not in relation to the infrastructure. The members of the housing association are responsible for 100 percent of the work. They begin to build the houses only after they have 80 percent of the infrastructure in place. FUPROVI has the basic earth-moving machinery and rents it out to the community on a nonprofit basis. Other needed equipment and specialized services are procured from commercial suppliers.

Scale and Sustainability

Sustainability of the Institution

FUPROVI was not established with pilot projects in mind. Rather, its goal is to insert itself competitively into the low-income housing mar-

> **Box 8-4. Use of Appropriate Low-Cost Technologies in Construction**
>
> The most common construction method in Costa Rica is based on the use of concrete blocks. The first public housing built by FUPROVI was made of this material. Later, it began to use prefabricated units, which come in two models: PREFA-PC and ZITRO. The first consists of horizontal panels, and the second of vertical panels. Most of these systems do not allow for the addition of a second floor at a later stage. This limits the use of a strategy that is very common in Latin America, the vertical densification of existing settlements to create space for families that grow, for new generations, for rental, or for the development of a business.

ket, taking on an essentially private sector objective—marketplace survival—in addition to its nonprofit social mission.

FUPROVI recovers its investment by charging a fee for its services. It has also taken advantage of mechanisms the Costa Rican government makes available, both to provide support to its client families and to recover the credits extended to them. Thanks to careful administration, the projects and the institution itself have remained afloat, despite difficulties posed by the country's economic situation. In administering its monies, the foundation has shown itself to be adept at taking account of macroeconomic parameters such as inflation, interest rates, and devaluation, and proficient at methodologies such as cash flow management and handling key financial management concepts.

FUPROVI's financial sustainability has depended on other important factors as well. First, the Swedish International Development Agency's money has allowed the foundation to create a rotating fund that has made bridge loans possible. The terms under which Swedish assistance was granted required FUPROVI to build a solid structure, which has created an internal dynamic capable of dealing effectively with the changing elements of reality. Also, the foundation has had to create its own style of intervention and to develop work methods that are adequate to the realities of poor communities. The institution has adapted itself to the situations it has had to confront.

Second, state subsidies for low-income housing have enabled FUPROVI to achieve a rapid recovery of the bridge loans to ensure that the rotation funds are sustained. We have seen above that the current crisis that plagues the SFNV has forced FUPROVI to reduce its staff and the scale of its operations. Scale and sustainability will both depend on the success of the measures the foundation is taking to cope with the situation.

In its first 10 years of operation, FUPROVI has served about 15,000 families. This figure reflects the total of all FUPROVI projects. In this sense, it may be said that FUPROVI has been successful. "With the resources that we received to take care of 4,000 families, we have helped 15,000," says Mario Rodriguez with pride. FUPROVI clients represent a considerable market share, making up nearly 10 percent of SFNV total housing construction during this time period.

Sustainability of Individual Projects

Two dimensions of the projects are considered in order to determine their sustainability. One is maintenance of project benefits; the other is self-reliance, or the capacity to resolve problems and undertake further development initiatives after the project finishes.

FUPROVI has made inroads along both dimensions. Additionally, in recent years, it has made some progress in terms of the environmental sustainability of its projects. This success has been achieved by including a comprehensive methodology to protect the environment in its urban development activities. Capable professionals have been hired to train, assist, and advise client groups about the importance of sustainable development and how to achieve it.

Regarding maintenance of infrastructure and parks and other public spaces, we noticed that the communities took good care of these in the finished projects we visited (but also see box 8-5). Furthermore, the commitment of project participants is high. The percentage of families that abandon a project during its execution is very low. In Villa Maria, out of 47 families, only 2 dropped out: one because it did not meet its work obligations, and the other because it did not qualify for the subsidy voucher.

Jorge Rodriguez describes the factors that generate a sense of ownership and ultimately the sustainability of these projects: "Early housing projects in the country...failed because they just gave people a finished house, and many families sold out and returned to the squatter settlements since that was where the agencies went to hand out food." With mutual-help construction, which makes housing construction affordable, participation becomes a fundamental requirement for project completion. Participation is a necessity imposed by economic reality. With FUPROVI, housing association members not only build their own houses and the accompanying infrastructure, they also administer the project, and initiate and manage the organization that oversees it.

Surely this is why FUPROVI's mutual-help construction projects have generated other community-based development projects in their aftermath. The ongoing Villa Maria project is one of many such examples. Here, a community made an agreement with two neighboring commu-

> **Box 8-5. "Keeping the Slum in Their Heads": The Atypical San Juan de Pavas Project**
>
> San Juan de Pavas is located west of the capital, in Rincón Grande de Pavas, an area characterized by growing slums. Unique in its history and struggles, this community is made up of extremely poor families from a squatter settlement that was relocated by the National Housing and Urban Development Institute (INVU) and by a large number of illegal Nicaraguan immigrants. INVU had almost finished building the infrastructure through a private contractor, but the project had progressed unevenly. Squatter shacks were juxtaposed with recently finished houses. At this stage, INVU hired FUPROVI to develop and manage the project.
>
> The San Juan project is an exception to the general model of FUPROVI projects. The socioeconomic conditions in San Juan led to the development of a different strategy, which, although it involved the community in construction, did not look to involve the community in administering the process. This was because the community lacked a capacity for self-organization, mainly due to its low socioeconomic status and lower educational levels. Moreover, there were serious problems with crime and substance abuse in the community and authoritarian community leaders—both of which factors made it difficult to introduce participatory decisionmaking processes.
>
> Given this context, it was difficult to generate interest in maintaining the infrastructure. During the final stage of housing construction, when we visited the site, garbage in the streets, foul odors, and unsanitary conditions continued to be a problem throughout the area. FUPROVI's Maria Esther Mejia notes, "It was as if they kept the slum inside their heads, even though the new houses were finished."
>
> All of these factors are reflected in more modest results and a lower level of sustainability here than in other FUPROVI projects. As a result of this situation, of all of FUPROVI's projects, San Juan is the one that most closely resembles the classic urban upgrading model in Latin America—even in the fact that FUPROVI was hired for this project by a public institution rather than by the community.

nities to pave their common access road. A similar example was given by Oscar Mario Garbanzo, a FUPROVI social worker: "In the case of the Oasis project, 27 families paved the road through mutual-help construction, four years after having finished the initial project."

FUPROVI nonetheless feels it must do more to stimulate the continuity of development. Explains FUPROVI executive director Eloisa Ulibarri, "The idea is that the communities are enabled to take steps to obtain other resources. With FUPROVI's limited resources alone, it is very challenging. We need to work more in the last stages of the project to achieve sustainability and local self-management."

According to sociologist José Manuel Valverde, an applied research coordinator working with the UNCHS (Habitat) CERCA initiative, "FUPROVI has been very efficient in delivering the housing solutions it has developed. Other efforts, both governmental and nongovernmental, have been tremendously inefficient. But self-management, understood as the community's capacity to manage a project, is not FUPROVI's principal achievement. If we compare it with initiatives in other Central American countries, FUPROVI can certainly teach them a lesson in efficient delivery and the ability to create solutions. On the other hand, other Central American countries such as Nicaragua and El Salvador could teach FUPROVI something in terms of methods of self-management."

If FUPROVI lacks mechanisms to build community capacity, the impact of the mutual-help construction process on the life of individual participants is nonetheless significant. FUPROVI places great emphasis on teaching families how to manage things and to be responsible for the budget, materials, and waste generated during the construction process. Family members can grow and evolve through the training and practice afforded by the project. Based on the experience of having to adjust construction expenses to available resources, they can cease to live day to day, learn not to spend more than they can afford, and begin to budget for their living expenses. Their new knowledge has an impact on both their own lives and that of their community. For example, the women begin to take on a new role in the family and in the community; all of this contributes to sustainability.

> IF SOMEONE HAD TOLD DOÑA ROSA IN SANTA ANA BEFORE THE PROJECT THAT SHE WOULD BE MANAGING MORE THAN $26,000, SHE WOULD HAVE HAD A HEART ATTACK. NOW THIS IS ROUTINE STUFF FOR HER.
> —*Oscar Mario Garbanzo, FUPROVI Social Worker*

Thus, as people see the home of their dreams take shape, individual and collective change begins. The kind of improvement in urban services brought about by collective action after project completion—such as street paving and the extension of public transport lines—appears to follow a constant pattern, but the process continues. In projects that have been completed for two or three years, one finds not only paved streets and bus lines, but also local businesses, tradespeople, and other community activities.

Conclusions

It could be argued that the FUPROVI experience is so ensconced in the Costa Rican context, which is so different from other South and Central American situations, that it can hardly serve as a model for other areas. One might also argue that because 15,000 homes only represent about a dozen average favelas or barrios, the scope of this experience might speak against its potential for replication in the areas of large concentrations of urban poverty found in most other Latin American countries. However, if one is seeking guidelines rather than a model or template for replication, the FUPROVI project offers much that can be applicable to other areas.

FUPROVI has learned valuable lessons by experimenting with its model of intervention. First, each of its projects has addressed and resolved the problems created by its specific circumstances. Second, in developing these projects, methodologies that were both innovative and appropriate were defined. It is important to understand the mechanisms and conceptual foundations that have shaped FUPROVI's methodology, because it is unique in its context. The following conclusions are an attempt in this direction:

1. Nonprofit private sector involvement has been a fundamental element in defining and developing methodologies appropriate to this work. In recent decades, housing policies similar to the Costa Rican model have met with partial collapse in many developing countries. In various cases—Brazil is perhaps the best known of these—housing policy has not reached the lowest strata of the population. This is due, principally, to methods of intervention that only worked for the middle and lower middle classes and in the context of the formal city. This model is not responsive to the dynamics of low-income and informal sectors. FUPROVI's achievement is to assist the sector of the population that would not have had access to the benefits offered by public policies, using the instruments of those same policies and offering its services on the market as a product. Methodological development is therefore indispensable to the institution, as it represents a benefit for the target population and, at the same time, a clear guideline for housing delivery to the poor that could be adopted by public institutions in general. In other words, in this case, the participation of the private sector, represented by FUPROVI, lends a hand to the state; it represents the meeting point between supply and demand, and it transforms—although not without difficulties and limitations—the participatory process into the principal instrument of its action, taking as its point of departure the expressed demand of the communities involved.

2. Since its initial establishment, FUPROVI has been concerned with its own continuity. It was not designed to manage a specific project with a defined budget and time line, but rather to confront the problem of low-income housing in general terms and over the long term. Therefore, the institution learned how to organize itself so as to best attend to the specific sector of the market represented by housing associations, squatter settlements, and individual families in search of a housing solution. Developing the capacity of its own staff has been an important priority since the beginning. The foundation's current programs are a product of the constant retooling and training of the teams, which have developed new methodologies and approaches to respond to needs as they arise in daily practice. As is typical of the private sector, the foundation considers the elements that might ensure its own continuity to be a necessary (but not sufficient) condition for the sustainability of this process. In this way, a specialized private sector entity comes into being. Specialization arises through the recognition of the diversity and dynamism peculiar to the low-income housing sector. This concept can also be extended to the process of privatization. For example, a private electricity utility company can modify the situation in which many people in low-income communities default on their payments only if it creates new forms of outreach. Also, it is clear that the complexity of the processes of informal settlements imposes the development of strategic alliances with other private sector institutions as well as with the public sector.
3. In FUPROVI's program, the communities control the resources for their project: they directly administer the funds. The process of assisted mutual-help construction represents a necessity for the families. It is the formula that reduces overall cost and makes their homes affordable. Moreover, it serves as a filter, because it enables FUPROVI to focus its program on the poorest communities. The foundation's response to the low-income housing problem is thus based on a realistic point of departure: the realities of the clientele. Experience shows that a project is more efficient when the formulation responds to the actual needs and demands of the population sector involved and when it uses a methodology and workplan that is clear to and shared by the people. In the planning phase, it is necessary to make a considerable effort to formulate project instruments that are appropriate to the characteristics of the beneficiaries. One example of this effort is the training material FUPROVI produces to explain the mechanisms of its intervention, develop an agreement between the parties, and initiate the process of mutual-help construction.

4. The modalities and forms of participation are what define the type and characteristics of a FUPROVI project. The technology applied and the process adopted are consequences of the following factors:
   - Reduction of the time it takes to complete the work, with the goal of limiting the impact of inflation, which might overly reduce the already scarce resources of the participating families
   - The requirement of strong direct community participation in the implementation phase so as to limit construction and development costs
   - Awareness that the project's final product represents only a first stage that the family will improve on over time.

5. The following consequences for sustainability are clear:
   - The level of participation in infrastructure maintenance is high, and the process of home improvement is constant. In all the projects we visited, even though many of them had been completed several years before, we saw no evidence either of lack of maintenance or of vandalism.
   - The process of improvement of the common spaces is very slow. Whoever has participated actively in a FUPROVI project in a position of leadership has lived through significant physical and psychological stress. The families, after many months of intense work, want to finish their own house before dedicating themselves to finding remedies for other problems which—in various ways—the participatory process has made them consider "theirs."
   - In the construction phase, the absence of other actors not directly linked to the housing problem—civil institutions, public institutions, or religious groups that provide social services and represent a support network—slows the onset of the subsequent phase of continuing community development.
   - It is undeniable that the participatory method used in these communities to resolve conflicts as they arise is a key legacy of the mutual-help construction process in terms of both sustainability and the human development of the families.

To generate actions that contribute to a project's sustainability after it has been implemented (i.e., though post-project support) is not sufficient. Continuity, and therefore, human development, is an objective that must be considered from the project's beginning. In this light, structural and physical intervention, as in the case of FUPROVI projects, represents not an end in itself, but rather a fundamental contribution to the ability to meet basic needs.

9

Mexico: Community Upgrading Programs, Tijuana

During the 1990s, significant reforms were introduced by Tijuana's municipal government, including an overhaul of the municipal cadastre, the enhancement of local revenue generation, and the involvement of civil society in the city's strategic planning. Tijuana has pioneered an approach to informal settlement upgrading that couples participatory budgeting, in which the community makes an upfront cash contribution averaging 30 percent of the cost, with community management of small local works projects.

Tijuana's community upgrading programs have successfully performed a significant amount of work over the years and have challenged conventional assumptions about the ability of poor urban communities to participate in development programs. At the same time, the piecemeal approach of these programs, the absence of participatory planning, and the lack of development-oriented community-based organizations has meant that the significant mobilization the programs have generated has not been channeled into a long-term development process for Tijuana's *colonias populares*.[1]

The Tijuana model, which was revised and adapted in 1998 to address the challenges posed by the deficiencies of previous programs as described above, contains many elements relevant to development programs elsewhere.

---

[1] This is the Mexican term for low-income settlements, the majority of which are informal land subdivisions, not chaotic squatter settlements of the kind found in Brazil or Venezuela.

The Importance of the Tijuana Experience

Community upgrading programs in Tijuana are highly innovative, reflecting the Mexican trend toward democratization and decentralization. Although the Tijuana programs have many features peculiar to Mexico—and particularly to its northern border region—they also have features that could be applied outside the country, including the following:

- Citizens have contributed to making decisions and financing the works.
- Organized communities managed all resources, including citizen contributions and government subsidies, and the bidding and contracting of the works.
- Institutional development occurred, including civic participation at the municipal level to define high-priority investments, the decentralization of project management and community coordination to the district and subdistrict levels, the development of appropriate methodologies, and the creation of procedures and administrative routines. Program continuity (since 1992) was instrumental in bringing about these changes.
- The infrastructure programs helped develop low-income communities' capacity for negotiation and structures of representation, and opened a dialogue between communities and government.
- The local municipality drew from Tijuana's autonomous experiences and those of programs elsewhere to develop its own model, based on the intelligent use of its own resources augmented by state and federal funds.

Background

Intense Growth and a Dynamic History

Tijuana is a land of opportunity "where there is a lot of work," says Yadira Guadalupe, community leader of Kiwi Street in the Florido-Mariano district. She came as an immigrant from Culiacán "to the land of the privileged: the border" and has lived through the explosive demographic growth Tijuana has experienced since the 1960s (see box 9-1). It was then that the federal government's border industrialization program made the state an employment-generating center, in addition to being a bridge for migration to the United States.

Tijuana became a magnet for the casualties of Mexico's economic woes. Beginning in 1982, at the time of the international debt crisis which affected many developing countries, the devaluation of the peso and the nationalization of the banks worsened Mexico's economic situation. The

> **Box 9-1. A Snapshot of Tijuana**
>
> Tijuana is the largest city in the state of Baja California Norte, Mexico, occupying the country's extreme northwestern corner. With an area of 1,229 square kilometers Tijuana is adjacent to the U.S. city of San Diego. Bordered on the west by the Pacific Ocean, the city's climate combines the humidity of the sea with the dryness of the desert. Its topography consists of mountains and small valleys, within which abound a great variety of slopes and seasonal streams.
>
> Tijuana has undergone high economic growth and is an attractive location for industry, primarily U.S. and Japanese *maquiladoras* (assembly plants). In 1999, there were 711 maquiladoras—22.6 percent of the national total—employing approximately 147,000 people.
>
> Tijuana's municipal administration is divided geographically into six delegations (La Mesa, La Presa, Mesa de Otay, Playas de Tijuana, San Antonio de los Buenos, and Zona Centro) and eight subdelegations (Sánchez Taboada, Florido-Mariano, Insurgentes, Los Pinos, Miguel Alemán, Francisco Villa, Lomas del Porvenir, and Obrera). The delegations are district offices of neighborhood services and are administered by a director, or delegate. On the next rung down the decentralization ladder, the subdelegations are smaller, decentralized offices within the more populous of the delegations.
>
> In 2000, Tijuana had a population of over 1.2 million. The most intense migratory flow along the northern border of Mexico occurs here. People arriving in Tijuana to improve their standard of living are the principal influence on the city's demographic composition. These immigrants come from many Mexican states, mostly rural areas in central Mexico and on the West Coast, and constitute 52.5 percent of the city's population. Immigrants generally congregate in the colonias populares of Tijuana's Zona Oriente (East Side).

"dollarization" of the economy created difficult conditions for poor families and the middle class, who were tied to wages paid in Mexican pesos. The resilience of Tijuana's economy, both during Mexico's expansion periods and subsequent downturns, made the city an attractive place for those seeking a better life; this was notably evident in the aftermath of the 1994-95 peso crisis.

Tijuana's history has also been affected by important national events. The city was the site of the assassination of Luís Donaldo Colosio[2] in

---

[2]Colosio, a contender for the Institutional Revolutionary Party presidential candidacy in the 1994 elections, was murdered in Tijuana during a political rally in Colonia Lomas Taurinas, an informal settlement area that was a bastion of the opposition.

1994. Earlier, Tijuana and Baja California had a decisive role in the process of Mexico's democratization by electing in 1989 the first municipal and state governments of the National Action Party (PAN), one of the opposition parties to the ruling Institutional Revolutionary Party (PRI). The difficult relationship between the PRI federal government and the PAN local government greatly influenced Tijuana's community upgrading programs.

International migration, the growing presence of large transnational companies, and drug trafficking affect the city's daily life, which is naturally marked by the proximity to California, one of the richest states in the United States. "The line," the immigration "checkpoint," and "the other side" are phrases frequently heard in the conversations of Tijuanans. They live with the tensions, problems, and opportunities generated by their proximity to a country that represents a model and a goal but that is also the "other" in relation to which they affirm their own identity. The relationship with the United States is a difficult and important one for all Latin Americans, but in Tijuana, in full view of the fence marking the border, it becomes almost an obsession.

Government Responses

In Tijuana, rapid growth has meant the rapid expansion of informal settlements, with the attendant deficit of basic infrastructure and services. Additional problems are posed by Tijuana's irregular topography, the great number of inhabited risk areas, and the fact that almost 50 percent of the land area is dedicated to low-density residential use. Over the years, government has implemented a variety of approaches to respond to this web of community upgrading needs (see box 9-2).

The Mexican federal government first introduced participatory community upgrading in Tijuana in 1989 through the nationwide Solidaridad (Solidarity) program. The municipal government of Tijuana began to take part in Solidaridad's implementation the following year; in 1990, 67 neighborhood works committees were formed. By 1991, 194 such committees had been formed. With the assistance of the municipality, the committees developed works such as sidewalks, access ramps, pothole repair, and street paving.

At the municipal level, these community upgrading programs are one of the most visible of the reforms undertaken since 1989 in Tijuana's municipal administration and are a direct product of Mexico's democratization and decentralization process. They were implemented by PAN, and have coupled the enlargement of the city's fiscal base (e.g., by property regularization and a new cadastre system) with restraint in public spending and the participation of civil society in resource allocation and

> **Box 9-2. Events Leading up to Tijuana's Community Upgrading Programs**
>
> - **1970s:** Increased migration leads to the development of many new informal settlements in Tijuana.
> - **1980s:** The federal government begins to dedicate greater portions of state and municipal budgets to providing water and sewerage to low-income and informal settlements.
> - **January 1989:** During the PRI federal administration of Salinas de Gortari (1988–94), the national program Solidaridad (Solidarity), a large social investment fund program, is launched, giving communities a decisionmaking role in resource allocation.
> - **1991:** The Voluntad (Will) program is launched in Baja California by the state government (headed by Ernesto Ruffo Appel of PAN); its objective is to promote civic participation in municipal initiatives.
> - **1992:** The Autogestión (Self-Management) program is launched in Tijuana by Mayor Héctor Osuna Jaime (also from PAN) as part of Tijuana's Municipal Development Plan, to construct infrastructure benefiting low-income residents. This program devolves to the municipal level the development of community upgrading programs which were previously undertaken jointly with the federal Solidaridad program.
> - **Early 1993:** Torrential rains in Tijuana cause the death of more than 30 people, mostly in colonias populares lacking stormwater drainage; this makes the strengthening of the city's urban infrastructure the primary challenge for the new municipal administration (the 14th Ayuntamiento, 1992–95).

strategic planning. The most ambitious of these plans, the Urban Action Program—a citywide referendum on public works that sought business support for urban renewal and infrastructure expansion—was badly hit by the peso crisis of 1994–95. Even with diminished resources, however, the upgrading program has continued and become a key element of the municipality's poverty reduction strategy.

In Tijuana, a range of participatory and organizational options and competing mechanisms have developed in answer to the vast social demand. In addition to the federal Solidaridad program, similar municipal and state programs have been established in low-income settlements. Other entities have participated as well, such as the State Commission for Public Services of Tijuana (CESPT), the Federal Commission on Electricity, and the State Commission for the Regularization of Land Tenure (CORETTE).

The improvements experienced in Tijuana's informal settlements are visible and indicate a corresponding improvement in quality of life.

Manos a la Obra...

In 1994, the 14th Municipal Administration's[3] previous experience in community upgrading resulted in the formulation of the Manos a la Obra (Let's Roll up Our Sleeves) program, which is largely based on the Solidaridad municipal funds formula. There were, however, some departures from this model. One of them was encouraging neighborhood committees to form exclusively for the execution of the works in order to avoid the politically oriented focus and clientelism that have traditionally marred Mexican community organizations.[4] Another difference was a heightened emphasis on technical supervision and quality of the works.

In 1994, the municipality held 16 Forums of Popular Consultation, one per delegation. Later that same year, a Congress of Civic Participation took place, which brought about an inter-institutional agreement between the state and municipal governments to fund the program.

In 1995, which was an election year for the state governor and the mayor, Manos a la Obra was launched. This was the most ambitious effort in infrastructure upgrading that the Tijuana municipal government had initiated in the colonias populares. Undertaken in partnership with the state government of Baja California, Manos a la Obra was the most important of Tijuana's numerous community upgrading programs. The main feature of this program has been to allow poor communities to establish their priorities, manage the resources, and assume partial financial responsibility for infrastructure work.

"We made mistakes, but we did it." This statement describes the inauguration of one of 1,012 works within the Manos a la Obra program in Tijuana's informal settlements and captures the shift from public handouts to community empowerment.

...And Its Successors

The 15th municipal administration (1996–98), maintained the community upgrading programs but without the momentum of Manos a la Obra.

---

[3]This numbering designates successive municipal administrations in Mexico. Tijuana's current municipal administration is the 17th (2001–04).

[4]Although Manos a la Obra neighborhood committees are arguably less clientelistic than their Solidaridad counterparts, this short-term focus has come to be recognized as a problem, since the mobilization achieved during the works is not used for further development initiatives.

During 1996 and 1997, the programs were simply called Obra Social Comunitaria (Social Community Works); in 1998, an election year, Más por Tijuana (More for Tijuana) was launched. Although these were more modest programs, the methodological and institutional development that characterizes participatory urban development initiatives in Tijuana has continued. These programs and their scale are summarized in table 9-1.

The Obra Social Comunitaria programs were designed by a new institutional player, the subcommittees. These were formed in each delegation and subdelegation, with civil society participation, to choose the work that should be carried out each year. Box 9-3 summarizes the steps required to implement these community upgrading projects each year.

In 1998, Forums of Popular Consultation were held in each delegation. Works that had been requested but not undertaken in previous years were ratified and priorities established. That year, decentralization of the management of the community upgrading programs began. The delegations and subdelegations assumed the social support, promotion, and technical control of the works, which had previously been carried out by two central units, the Municipal Administration of Social Development (DESOM) and the Municipal Urbanization Unit (UMU). Social support is provided by community development workers, some of whom are trained social workers, while others come from other backgrounds and are skilled at community work. Technical support and control are provided by civil engineers and architects.

Decentralization has brought the program closer to the people but also has some drawbacks, as discussed below. Development of the Tijuana model will depend on the solutions found to these problems.

Road Paving Projects Predominate

Projects usually arise from the most pressing needs of local residents. In the case of Huejotzingo Street, in the Florido-Mariano district, a stream

Table 9-1. Tijuana's Community Upgrading Programs, 1995–98

Year	Administration	Program name	Works carried out	Total investment (N$)
1995	14th	Manos a la Obra	1,012	80,466,279
1996	15th	Obra Social Comunitaria	488	48,106,041
1997	15th	Obra Social Comunitaria	325	44,447,946
1998	15th	Más por Tijuana	511	75,928,709
Total			2,336	248,948,975

Source: Authors' construction from field study data.

> **Box 9-3. Typical Project Cycle (February to November)**
>
> - **Promotion of the program.** Municipal decentralized offices (delegations and subdelegations) launch each year's program, which is announced by word of mouth and through the mass media. The radio is an effective tool at this stage.
> - **Community preparation of applications.** One or more groups of people in each community prepare requests for needed works. Although their leaders are usually well-known, they do not necessarily act at this stage with a community mandate.
> - **Receipt of applications for projects.** The community delivers its petition to the delegation or subdelegation office or presents it during a consultation forum.
> - **Delegation/subdelegation definition and analysis of projects to be implemented.** The financial ceiling for the year's program and allocations to the delegations and subdelegations are defined at the beginning of each year. Delegation and subdelegation subcommittees then hold meetings to study the project applications received and to decide which priorities to support during the year. The subcommittees also define the contributions that the government and community will be asked to make for each project; these contributions depend on the socioeconomic characteristics of the location and the type of works involved.
> - **Approval of the works lists.** The Tijuana Social Development Council, which has citywide authority, analyzes and approves the lists received from the delegations and subdelegations. Appropriate departments of the municipal government determine the technical feasibility of all works before they are presented to the council.
> - **Social ratification of the project.** Once the project is approved, the municipality's community development workers help organize a community meeting, which at least 80 percent of the residents must attend to express interest in the work and in making a financial contribution.

overflowed during the rainy season. When local people learned about the program, they decided that their highest priority was channeling the stream, in spite of other needs such as paving streets, improving health and education services, and building a footbridge. Now that their most pressing problem has been solved, they may decide to tackle others.

Tijuana's operating manual for community upgrading programs states that funds can be used for street paving, sewers, electricity, storm drain-

- **Election of works committees.** Each community elects a committee to administer the works.
- **Training of works committees.** An informational meeting is held with all the works committees of each delegation or subdelegation to instruct them in their responsibilities, financial management, contract management, and technical supervision.
- **Contractor selection.** The works committee requests budgets from three different contractors, who deliver their bids in sealed envelopes. In a community meeting also attended by the municipality's technicians, the envelopes are opened and the appropriate bid chosen. The community can also use a mutual-help system, in which community members do the work or buy materials and hire independent construction workers, who work under the supervision of the community development workers and delegation technicians. Another option is to rely on a government department to execute the works directly; this is primarily done in the case of footbridge and storm drain construction.
- **Delivery of checks.** Once 30 percent of the expected community contribution is received from the residents, the first check for half the government contribution is given to the committee. The remainder of the money is delivered once the committee spends this amount.
- **Startup of the works.** The works begin once the committee receives the money.
- **Supervision and follow-up.** The municipal government provides social promoters to assist the works committee in dealing with the government, handling conflicts within the community, and helping with community organization. Engineers and architects visit the works regularly to check the quality of the construction process.
- **Inauguration of the works.** Together with the delegation or subdelegation, the works committee inaugurates the work with a small ceremony attended by community members, local officials, and—on occasion—the mayor.

age, earthworks, foot and vehicle bridges, containment walls, perimeter fencing, stairways, ramps, storm catchment basins, sports courts and fields, educational infrastructure, maintenance and restructuring of footpaths, basic health infrastructure, and community centers (municipality of Tijuana, 1998). The delegate of La Presa, Gerardo Cortez, explains that, in spite of all those options, "Half of the works are paving projects. Twenty percent of the petitions are to improve schools, ranging from fixing a classroom to constructing restrooms and sports courts...Where it is not yet possible to pave the streets, they request support for the introduction of electricity, water, sewers, and storm drainage."

In general, throughout Tijuana, community upgrading improvements are undertaken in the following order:

- Land tenure regularization
- Electrification
- Water supply
- Sanitation and storm drainage
- Street paving.

Significant progress has been made in Tijuana in recent years in the first three of these improvement areas. Notably, electrification, which has no limiting factors and thus has always been the easiest service to implement, has a high coverage—95 percent in 1998. Diminished need in these first three areas, combined with several other factors (see box 9-4), has resulted in making street paving the current favorite type of infrastructure in Tijuana's community upgrading programs.

Problems with the Quality of the Works

Gerardo Cortez notes a problem mentioned by many interviewees—difficulties with contractors. The delegate from La Presa explains, "There is an operations manual for the infrastructure works that all the delegations have to follow, but it has flaws such as allowing a contractor's unlimited participation in tenders. There are companies that submit bids for works in all the delegations at the same time. So some small contractors may end up with 15 contracts but are unable to finish them all in time. One decision we have to make is to limit the number of contracts awarded to any one contractor and to monitor the works that a contractor carries out in other delegations to avoid nonfulfillment or delays."

According to officials, the quality of community upgrading works was monitored more thoroughly by the municipal programs, beginning with Manos a la Obra, than by Solidaridad. "Several social development specialists from the municipal and state governments recognized that the positive aspect of Solidaridad was social participation, and what was needed to improve the program, among other things, was a technical surveillance system to ensure that the works resulting from citizen participation would be high quality," observes Luis Bustamante Fernández, DESOM director of the 15th Municipal Administration of Tijuana (1995–98).

> **Box 9-4. Street Paving Answers to Many Needs**
>
> Why are street paving projects such a disproportionate share of the upgrading improvements made in Tijuana? Gerardo Cortez, delegate of La Presa, says that this is because the communities define what is to be done and because more low-income settlements lack paving than lack water supply and sewers. For example, in the low-income settlements of the Florido-Mariano subdelegation, only 30 percent of households lack basic services such as water supply and sanitation, whereas approximately 70 percent lack paving.
>
> Unpaved roads create problems of access in the rainy season and dust in the dry season due to unfavorable soil and terrain conditions (clay soil and steep slopes). Also, paving works are simpler and cheaper than other types of infrastructure, and are a municipal responsibility.
>
> Finally, street paving also has a symbolic value. The status of a paved area improves because it is perceived as part of the "formal" city.

Participatory Process

The commitment and dedication of key residents has been the strongest engine for change in the implementation of Tijuana's community upgrading programs.

An "Antidote" to Solidaridad

Forums for community participation began in earnest with Manos a la Obra. At that time, an initial Forum of Popular Consultation took place in which 6,000 people made requests for 2,451 works. Of those, Manos a la Obra could respond to only 1,012. The format adopted for the forums required that at least 80 percent of the community be present. Such massive participation was evidence of the community's genuine interest in resolving its problems. Another community forum was organized in 1995. There, 1,395 applications were presented for works totaling almost $1.38 million.

In many ways, this scheme was similar to the one Solidaridad had proposed. According to municipal officials, the difference was the emphasis laid by the municipality on nonpartisan resident involvement in the works. The municipality gave the checks directly to the works committees, which improved both the residents' self-esteem and their relationship with the government. (See box 9-5.) The municipality provided incentives for participation, including the promise that better organized communities would more easily receive money for their works and the requirement that a committee already have amassed at least 30 percent

> **Box 9-5. A Positive Change in the Relationship between Government and Community**
>
> Perhaps the most important achievement of the Tijuana programs has been the change in the relationship between the government and the community from one based on traditional paternalism to one of responsibility and transparency. Or, in the words of Lucio Quiñones, "The good thing is that people have the opportunity to manage their tax money themselves."
>
> Residents were asked what it meant to them when the government gave them checks to deposit in accounts they administered themselves. One succinct answer was "responsibility and self-esteem on the part of the residents, trust and honesty on the part of the government." One of the simplest, yet deepest, answers was that "it means that this is a government that believes in its people." By the same token, this new relationship is also fostering people's ability to believe in their government.

of the residents' contribution before beginning to receive the municipal contribution. When the time came to carry out the project, "Everyone agreed; nobody—nobody—said no," says community leader Yadira Guadalupe.

The municipal officials who have participated in Manos a la Obra claim that there are other differences between the new program and Solidaridad, which they saw as a partisan program in the populist tradition. Luis Bustamante points out that "Manos a la Obra was launched as an antidote to Solidaridad...and the antidote worked through democratic participation." Dr. Martín de la Rosa Medellín, director of the Planning Committee for Municipal Development (COPLADEM) of the 15th Municipal Administration of Tijuana, expands on this point. He notes that "Through these participatory forums, many PRI leaders were displaced by new leaders. In other cases, the previous organization in the community was consolidated." As he goes on to explain, however, "This doesn't necessarily mean that the new leaders were more democratic, nor does it mean that all the old ones had been corrupt."

Participation Is Paramount, But Its Intensity Has Varied

Having municipal administrations of the same political party helped guarantee the program's permanency since 1992. Moreover, as one municipal official notes, "The communities have made the programs their own, and the successive administrations don't dare to cancel them." To make it feasible for communities to execute infrastructure programs, the committees are trained to take charge of contracting, financial management, and, at times, execution of the works.

> THE UNDERLYING PRINCIPLE OF MANOS A LA OBRA WAS SOCIAL PARTICIPATION, NOT THE COMMUNITY UPGRADING WORKS. ALTHOUGH THE RESULT WAS INFRASTRUCTURE, THE GOAL WAS ORGANIZED COMMUNITY PARTICIPATION IN DEFINING PRIORITIES AND MANAGING THE WORKS.
> —Luis Bustamante Fernández, Former DESOM Director

After Manos a la Obra, participation became less intense. In Tijuana's community upgrading programs since 1996, officials have recognized that more attention has been given to technical matters than to social ones. In fact, difficulties now exist in communication with the communities. Concerning the changes in the programs after Manos a la Obra, Luis Bustamante observes, "I consider broad-based consultations to be an indispensable mechanism for learning about citizens' needs; however, there are more cautious governments that believe it is risky to ask the people every year what their needs are, since their capacity to respond is limited by the available resources...Changes in the municipal administrations [local elections are held every three years in Mexico] influence the programs' development, independently of whether the mayor and the mayor elect are from the same party. With changes in the government, the intensity of participation has decreased."

Alejandro Chávez, the San Antonio de los Buenos delegate, points out that speed in responding to requests is a key factor in program continuity and in maintaining citizen trust. "On occasion," he says, "We go to a street committee to tell them that their petition has been approved, and then we realize that their problem has already been solved, not always in the best way, and furthermore, that they already have new needs. It happens that, as time goes by and a work is not approved, they gradually lose interest, and it becomes difficult to reorganize them."

Participation and Community Ownership

Another issue affecting the intensity and sustainability of community participation is cost. To make a project possible, a community typically pays an average of 30 percent of the cost of the work. In one example from the Florido-Mariano district, some Kiwi Street residents opposed an upgrading project, but others were convinced that street paving was a necessity that could not be delayed, so they took the lead in promoting the project in their neighborhood. These leaders successfully influenced their neighbors by being 100 percent involved in the construction. Persuasion was their only hope, since they lacked a legal basis to confront residents who did not make their monthly payments.

The key to the success of the Kiwi Street project was that, in the end, the leaders convinced most people to pay, even though a number were very late and some never did pay at all. The Kiwi Street leaders were satisfied with the outcome, however. "We truly deserve recognition because of what we did—seeing the street paved, how everything looks different, and how we did it even though some of the neighbors were hard to convince."

Edgar Palacios, UMU technical coordinator, notes that the sense of community ownership of the works was the primary achievement of Manos a la Obra. "Since it was the community that paid for and watched over the progress of the work, the contractors underestimated the supervision arrangements. They were thinking that they could do whatever they wanted. But the community acted as the supervisor's eyes when he wasn't there."

A New Breed of Community Leaders

One of the historic obstacles for community leaders in Tijuana has been a poor public image of community organizers, since local leaders have been accused of deceiving and taking advantage of communities in the past. In contrast, most of the new generation of leaders who directed Manos a la Obra projects had no links to political parties or any interest in active party politics. Many times, leaders were selected by their neighbors because they were the most well-known people on the street or were the only ones willing to do the work.

> I WAS NOT EVEN THERE THE DAY OF THE ELECTION. I WAS IN THE HOSPITAL, GIVING BIRTH TO MY LITTLE GIRL. SO WHEN I ARRIVED HOME, MY NEIGHBOR FROM ACROSS THE STREET ASKED ME IF I KNEW THAT I HAD BEEN NAMED COMMITTEE SECRETARY. BECAUSE THERE WAS NO WAY TO SAY NO, I JUST GOT INTO IT.
> —*Yolanda Reyes, Secretary, Kiwi Street*

The case of Lucio Quiñones, the Huejotzingo Street leader, was somewhat different. The stream that flooded the street during the rainy season ran right through the middle of Quiñones's property, putting his house at risk. After great deliberation, Quiñones decided that he had invested too much in his house to risk it further. He began to build an underground channel under his property at his own expense, using his previous experience as a mason. It was then that he learned about the community upgrading program and began to convince his neighbors to join him in building the channel all the way to a nearby gully. So, naturally, Quiñones was elected president of the works committee, a function he fulfilled in addition to his direct involvement in the execution of the work.

Legal and Regulatory Framework

A Systematic Plan for Land Tenure Regularization

In Mexico, the problem of land tenure has often prevented the extension of water and sewerage services to many low-income settlements. One difficulty in this regard is that planning regulations are interpreted differently at various levels of government. "Even if we had the Bible here," notes Arturo Carrillo Viveros, subdirector of planning for the 15th Municipal Administration, "We would not be able to apply it because of resource constraints and conflicting policies…So growth has occurred through invasions of private land or subdivisions of *ejido* land,[5] although it is still illegal to rent or sell these plots."

The regularization of land tenure is a precondition to settlement upgrading. Because urban land ownership is a key element of sustainable and equitable urban development, the state government created the State Real Estate Board (INETT), which develops new low-income land subdivisions; and CORETTE, which is in charge of the necessary legal, planning, and surveying work required to issue property titles. The cost of regularization, which is always paid for by the occupant, is approximately $120 for a 200-square-meter plot. To determine the form of payment, CORETTE has a social arm in charge of evaluating its clients' socioeconomic status.

In 1990, Tijuana's backlog was about 100,000 titles; CORETTE delivered about 38,000 between 1990 and 1996. The Tijuana branch of the federal government land tenure regularization program delivered about

---

[5]The ejido, a form of collective rural land holding that is still widespread in Mexico, was one of the key instruments of land reform used by the Mexican Revolution. Many ejidos have since been incorporated into growing cities and have been informally subdivided and sold. The bulk of land tenure regularization in urban informal settlements in Mexico has involved subdivided ejido lands.

10,000 titles in the same period. Table 9-2 shows the type and number of plots regularized between 1990 and 1996.

INETT also provides access to land ownership. It subdivides government properties or consigned private lands and sells plots to buyers who meet the minimum requirements of city residency, employment, income, and number of members in the family. The payment term is from 5 to 10 years, and the average cost is about $2,500 per plot. Explains INETT subdirector of commercialization Gerardo Fajardo, "These subdivisions are of social interest. The prices we offer are below market. The lots are mainly located in the eastern part of the city (La Presa delegation), which is the primary growth area, and where they are already properly surveyed, beaconed, and recorded in the municipal registry." INETT delivered about 24,000 new plots between 1990 and 1996.

Flexibility in the Standards Used for Low-Income Settlements

Informal subdivisions, in addition to lacking infrastructure and space for schools and clinics, often have problems due to patterns of land use and occupation. Settlements built on streambeds expose residents to floods in rainy seasons; settlements built on unstable slopes are prone to landslides. In a semi-arid area such as Tijuana, it is easy to underestimate the destructive potential of water courses, especially those that are seasonal.

When the municipal government authorizes land subdivision, it sets space aside for community equipment and parks and requires a minimum lot size. In cases of land tenure regularization in existing informal subdivisions, however, the municipality has been flexible in enforcing the regulations. Arturo Carrillo Viveros explains, "When an informal

Table 9-2. Land Regularization and Delivery of New Plots in Tijuana, 1990–96

Institution	Affiliation	Type	Number of plots
CORETTE	State of Baja California	Regularization	37,969
INETT	State of Baja California	New plots	24,095
CORET	Federal government	Regularization	10,161
PRODUTSA	Municipal	New plots	10,446
Other organizations	Various	Various	4,694
Total			87,365

Notes: CORET is the Tijuana branch of the federal government land tenure regularization program; PRODUTSA, a company specializing in land development for low-income people is the municipality of Tijuana's equivalent of INETT.

Source: COPLADEM, municipality of Tijuana, 1998.

subdivision is regularized, the CORETTE plan is registered. We ask for changes if there is something too outside the norm, but we rarely need to ask for any major modifications."

In fact, as Manuel Enrique Rivas, the subdirector of CORETTE for Tijuana, explains, "Urban services don't come to an area until after regularization has taken place according to the plans we have developed and recorded in the municipal land registry. That is where agencies providing the services go to see if the settlements meet the requirements for electricity, piped water, or sewers."

According to 1998 data from CESPT, over 95 percent of the city has piped water service, while 60 percent of the population is connected to the sewer system (see table 9-3). Families without piped water number about 30,000, and 65,000 families are without sewers. These data, however, only include regularized and registered low-income settlements. The numbers are probably much greater because many of Tijuana's 1.5 million residents live in informal colonias populares.

Table 9-3. Evolution of Water and Sanitation Coverage in Tijuana, 1989 and 1998

Water (household connections)		Sanitation (household connections)	
1989	1998	1989	1998
109,000 [68%]	285,934 [96.5%]	73,661 [46%]	179,921 [60.7%]

Note: Bracketed figures indicate coverage.
Source: COPLADEM, municipality of Tijuana, 1998.

Institutionalization of Democratic Planning

The community upgrading program was founded on the system of democratic planning, which is based on the 1983 State of Baja California Planning Law, which in turn derives from an earlier federal law. According to these laws, the municipal government should consult citizens to learn about their needs and priorities and then budget their investments in a process known as *participatory budgeting*.

Although critics such as Arturo Carrillo Viveros claim that the mechanisms for participation have not been very effective, an entire participatory planning structure known as COPLADEM has been created in Tijuana's municipal government. COPLADEM organizes systematic consultations with the city's various interest groups.

Resource Mobilization and Financial Sustainability

The Municipality Has Managed Contributions from Different Sources

Tijuana's total investment in community upgrading between 1995 and 1998 was $25 million for a total of 2,336 works (see table 9-1). However, the level of investment changed greatly from year to year, for reasons relating to political and electoral cycles. For example, in 1995, the municipal government of Tijuana and the state government invested in launching the Manos a la Obra program. In a moment of intense political competition, a strong injection of resources was needed to compete with Solidaridad, and resources for community upgrading peaked.

With federal administrative reform and decentralization, federal funds for poverty reduction programs (known as Ramo 33 of the federal budget) were transferred to local governments. Beginning in 1996, Solidaridad was entirely decentralized to the municipalities. In Tijuana, it was incorporated into the local community upgrading programs, after which the programs' resources came from municipal, state, and federal contributions.

Government Contributions Are Distributed According to Need and Community Contributions According to Ability to Pay

Municipal expenditures in the upgrading of low-income settlements are determined annually according to resource availability. The residents' share of construction costs is 30 percent, on average, although the figure varies from 20 to 50 percent according to the community's means. Alejandro Chávez, the delegate of San Antonio de los Buenos, explains that the Más por Tijuana program budget was allocated to five of the six delegations (the downtown Zona Centro is not a participant), which distributed the money among the subdelegations. The level of investment in each area was determined by need, with the neediest areas receiving the highest level of support. The La Presa delegation received 30 percent of the total funds because it is the poorest and fastest growing area in the city, particularly its Florido-Mariano subdelegation.

Administrative problems sometimes delay the delivery of funds and thus the works. The Kiwi Street construction was delayed at the expense of the residents, who had to pay more because of higher cement prices when the work was resumed. The community must also contribute the cost of regularizing land tenure, which is a precondition for any improvement, and part of the cost of water and sewer system construction. The acquisition and regularization of a lot is especially costly, and adds a further burden on poor families. For families with access to subsidized INETT schemes, this burden is somewhat lighter, but it is still there.

Communities thus find it difficult to contribute to community upgrading works until the expenses related to the purchase and regularization of their plots are out of the way. As a result, community upgrading works are carried out only when the community really wants the work and is ready to raise its contribution to the cost of execution.

The Community Perspective

The residents in the Florido-Mariano focus group stated that one of the main problems they encountered in implementing an upgrading program was residents' conflicting views of the government's role in providing urban infrastructure. When asked to make a financial contribution to the project, many residents claimed that it was the government's responsibility to meet those demands based on the taxes it collects.

Other officials and community leaders note that their most prevalent problem is collecting the community's contribution. Gerardo Cortez, delegate of La Presa, explains that there are no legal mechanisms requiring people to pay. The leaders and institutions thus take preventive measures when starting a project: "If there is no social feasibility, we don't begin the work." The most difficult problems occur when this situation is discovered after the work is in progress.

Communities have found creative solutions to these problems. Yadira Guadalupe and Yolanda Reyes, president and secretary, respectively, of the Kiwi Street works committee, note that they had problems locating the owners of several empty lots on their street. "We had obtained their names and telephone numbers from INETT, but many had changed, and we were tired of nobody responding to our calls." To solve the problem, they put "for sale" signs on the empty lots. "Immediately, the owners began to show up—in some cases, more than one owner for the same property."

Initially, it was unclear who would collect payments. Reyes comments, "We requested support from the subdelegation, and they told us that the community development worker would visit the delinquent payers, but he never did. In the meantime, we had opened an account in the bank for people to deposit their share so there wouldn't be any misunderstandings, but almost nobody made a deposit. We had to collect payments house by house. Not everyone wanted to cooperate, and some people didn't receive us very well. Besides, none of us had thought that we would need to play the role of collectors. It was painful."

The community leaders stress that it was left to the committees to solve the problem of delinquency. "It was said that the works committee should decide what to do in this respect. Some of us thought that the street should be left unpaved adjacent to those who were uncooperative, but we didn't want to have unpaved sections in our street."

The Direct Self-Help Program of CESPT

The CESPT program Direct Self-Help assists with the execution of water and sewer systems in colonias populares. Under this program, the community pays 100 percent of the costs. The procedure begins with a socioeconomic survey, after which the works are designed and priced. To get community support for the project, meetings are held within the low-income settlement so that residents know about the work and its projected cost. Once consensus is reached, the users are asked to sign agreements with the utility. Costs can vary between $500 and $1,000, depending on the house's frontage.

CESPT acts as a middleman between the community and the contractor. The management cost incurred by the utility is included in the total cost of the work. CESPT puts out the bids and provides technical supervision. It pays the contractors and recovers the cost from residents in their water bills. The utility acts as project promoter and financing agent. In all CESPT direct self-help projects, the user pays for the work over 12 months, and work begins when CESPT has collected 50 percent of the total costs. At that time, the user has from six to eight months in which to make monthly payments, which are frozen for one year. CESPT is committed to making the final payment to the contractor.

Luís Angel Castro, head of CESPT's Department of Community Promotion, explains: "Part of the utility's resources comes from the government, so it has a financial cushion to allow it to cope with the problems produced by delinquency. Cost recovery is 55 to 60 percent, without problems. The rest must be collected by community development personnel who go to the communities to deliver collection notices. At no time is there intent to instigate legal proceedings, although this has been necessary in some cases. Of these, 10 to 15 percent eventually pay, so the portion not recovered is 30 percent, which is still very high. Most problems are caused by empty lots, people who live on the other side [in the United States], or people who have their houses in another area of the city and rarely come to the project site."

This 30 percent can be considered a nonexplicit subsidy from the government, which does not go to the poorest but to "free riders"—residents who do not pay for one reason or another. In providing a hidden subsidy that does not benefit the poorest, CESPT is following the Latin American populist tradition.

In contrast, in the case of the municipal community upgrading programs, the average subsidy is much higher (70 percent), but the community contribution is clear and explicit. Also, communities usually contribute exactly what they have agreed to contribute.

Actors, Alliances, and Institutional Arrangements

Institutional Architecture of the Programs

Figure 9-1 illustrates the parties that became involved in the community upgrading programs in Tijuana after an agreement was signed between state and municipal governments in 1995 to finance Manos a la Obra. The responsibility for each stage of a project is allocated to a different player. The community identifies the problem, the municipality's technicians design and price the work, and then the community selects and

Figure 9-1. Parties Involved in Tijuana's Community Upgrading Programs

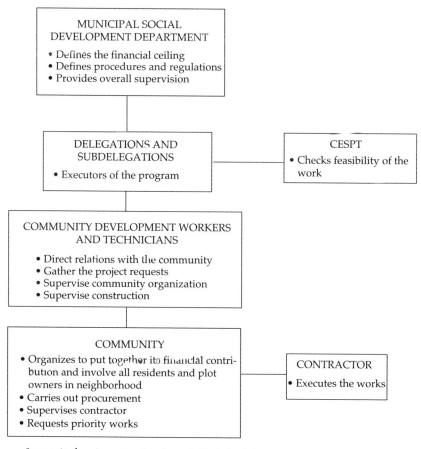

Source: Authors' construction from field study data.

supervises the contractor to execute the work. The municipal government also contributes qualified personnel to supervise the project. Operation and maintenance are in the hands of the community, the delegations, and specific municipal departments. The process begins with a petition from the residents, which, subject to a selection procedure, may be included in the annual work program by the delegation or subdelegation to which they belong. Such work programs can be modified, however, if a community's requests are insistent or if the work is recognized as urgent.

The process of popular consultation used by the first community upgrading programs was developed and improved as the city's system of democratic planning took form.

> WE HAVE SEEN MANY WORKS COMPLETED SINCE 1993. IF WE HAD NOT JOINED FORCES WITH THE GOVERNMENT, THEY WOULD NOT HAVE BEEN POSSIBLE.
> —*Tijuana Resident*

The delegational and subdelegational subcommittees, which were established in 1996, are primarily responsible for selecting works to fund each year. These subcommittees are comprised of the delegate or subdelegate, representatives from municipal social development and other local government offices, and between 5 and 13 elected community representatives, according to the population of the administrative unit concerned.

These subcommittees take the following factors into account when selecting works to fund:

- The poverty level of the population, the degree to which it lacks access to infrastructure and services, and the direct benefits it will derive from the proposed work
- The date of the first request and the date of the settlement's establishment (the oldest requests and oldest settlements have preference)
- The social, financial, and technical feasibility of the request (see box 9-6)
- The number of families that will benefit
- The fact that other city or state departments are not considering funding the same work.

Requests submitted by neighborhood works committees that have the resources for their contribution, or are certain to muster them, have preference.

> **Box 9-6. Feasibility Criteria for Projects**
>
> Three criteria are taken into account in determining the feasibility of a community upgrading project:
>
> - **Social feasibility.** At least 80 percent of the community involved must ratify the need for the work in a general meeting.
> - **Financial feasibility.** Before authorizing the execution of the work and receiving its first check from the government, the works committee has to gather more than 30 percent of the agreed community contribution.
> - **Technical feasibility.** Any work should have a design that meets municipal government specifications. CESPT should evaluate the technical feasibility of street paving to determine if the street already has water and sewerage systems.

New Community Leadership in the Face of Political Rivalry

A new, direct relationship between the municipality and communities has taken shape due to the new system of democratic planning. Although some residents continue to plead for handouts in the old tradition, democratic participation has ushered in a new generation of active community leaders. These new community leaders are different from older leaders who had a clear political affiliation. Instead of requesting support from politicians, the new leaders learned about upgrading programs through the channels of mass communication used by the municipal government. They initially went to DESOM, and, in recent years, they have gone to the delegation or subdelegation of their area to present their request, which is analyzed along with others from the same area.

Before the decentralization of Solidaridad and the state programs to the municipality, it was not uncommon to see community development workers from the municipality, state, and federal Social Development Department in the same area. This caused understandable rivalry and some confusion in the community, which was exposed to contradictory and often conflicting messages. Now, with decentralization, the delegations' community development workers can work without such obstacles.

Private Sector Participation Could Be Increased

Nongovernmental organizations (NGOs) and the private sector do not participate in Tijuana's community upgrading programs. In the private sector, the *maquiladoras* have invested heavily in new plants and equipment in the last few years, but their administrators say that they have not been presented with coordinated, feasible projects in the areas of housing and infrastructure that would address employee turnover and the lack of community attachment. Some argue that they would rather see their tax money used to address these concerns.

Adolfo Nóguez, administrator of the Pacific Industrial Park, where 49 maquiladoras employ 16,000 people, says, "The interest level in the maquiladoras could be raised to support credit programs for housing and for upgrading residential areas, providing educational programs, and developing nurseries, which would contribute to settling people."

Some maquiladoras have supported small-scale NGO projects. Tijuana's numerous NGOs provide social assistance, including education, childcare, health care, care of the elderly, and rehabilitation of substance abusers, but they have done little work in housing and urban development. Their involvement in community upgrading programs has so far been marginal. The municipality supports NGO social work through DESOM, but uses an entirely different channel from the community upgrading one.

The community development workers and community leaders interviewed realize that more participants are needed in the programs. They argue that the community's requirements are numerous and that NGO and private business sector involvement would further both resident and government goals. They believe that the private sector will come in if the government establishes credibility by formulating programs that clearly respond to people's needs rather than to political or personal agendas.

> PLANNING HAS TO BE THE CITY'S AND NOT EXCLUSIVELY THE PUBLIC SECTOR'S. IT IS THE COMMUNITY THAT GUARANTEES CONTINUITY. SO WE ARE PROPOSING THAT POLITICAL DEMOCRACY BE COUPLED WITH SOCIAL DEMOCRACY.
> — *Martín de la Rosa Medellín, Former Director, Planning Committee for Municipal Development*

Organization and Implementation

Decentralization and Its Dilemmas

Starting with Manos a la Obra, the design, approval, and execution of each annual community upgrading program in Tijuana has taken approximately 10 months (February to November; see box 9-3). The decentralization process accelerated the programs by moving decisionmaking closer to the community and leaving assistance to neighborhood committees in the execution of the works in the hands of the delegations and subdelegations. Although Manos a la Obra was still centrally managed, the true participatory spirit with which a significant number of works was speedily carried out under the program may have swayed political sentiment in favor of the government party in the June 1995 elections. PAN kept its position in the state government of Baja California and in Tijuana's municipal government.

Decentralization and other changes that came after Manos a la Obra increased program efficiency but also made them arguably less participatory, because of the reduction in the number of community development workers and technicians dedicated to upgrading. The delegate of La Presa, Gerardo Cortez, explains the new decentralized structure: "Each delegation hires community development workers and technical works supervisors who serve under the delegate's or subdelegate's coordination. Each social worker and technician team supervises between 15 and 20 works...In past years, all social promoters came from DESOM. The UMU also provided technical supervisors, but now everything has been decentralized."

"Decentralization was a good thing, but it was a mistake to do it without developing an appropriate structure at the level of each delegation, in accordance with the population's needs," sums up a community development worker. Workers and technicians also note that communication among colleagues, an important aspect of the previous arrangement, has been lost because promoters and technicians working in different parts of the city never have a chance to meet and compare notes under the new arrangement.

Edgar Palacio, coordinator of works supervision at UMU until 1997, dates this change as occurring in 1998. "All the delegations now have a department of public works that controls the quality, schedule, and cost of the works. With this, the uniform pricing standard that the municipality used to apply to upgrading projects was lost. Now the delegations and subdelegations prepare budgets according to their own criteria."

Another problem is the passing of central-level control responsibilities from technical structures like DESOM and UMU to the municipal comptroller. The delegations and subdelegations feel subjected to an almost police-like control, which is generating many conflicts.

More Community Development Workers Are Needed

A community development worker from the delegation of San Antonio de los Buenos, notes that, "In Manos a la Obra, there used to be more of us. It was a beautiful experience, a fantastic working environment. Now we are far fewer. Each low-income settlement has approximately 200 families, and here in San Antonio a community development worker assists 30 colonias, give or take a few. That's 6,000 families! As you can imagine, the number of workers is insufficient. We focus only on the works. Other activities, such as culture or forestation, are not addressed."

Because socio-technical support is provided only to communities with works projects, other communities are left with no support for their development activities. The developers realize that the change "isn't all bad, because projects have been broken down into simpler units, which allows for improved quality. But they introduced more controls for the contractors, and also for us, and there is too much paperwork for us to do in very little time…This has reduced the quality of the social process even though the communities' interest and motivation are still the same. These bureaucratic requirements take too much time, and we cannot spend time with the community as much as we would like. This is bad, since the projects that had more socio-technical support early on were more successful."

The community development workers see no problem with the external recruitment of social workers and technicians (many current professionals are external personnel with term contracts), but they do not believe that the communities themselves should recruit socio-technical assistance, although this has been done successfully in other cases (e.g., the FUPROVI experience in Costa Rica). Tijuana social promoters generally find that, to carry out their functions effectively, they must somehow represent the municipal government.

Carmen Correa, a promoter from San Antonio de los Buenos, points out that during Manos a la Obra, "There was a great rapport between social promoters from the state and the municipality. From the mayor to the promoters, we all pulled together." Correa notes, however, that this was not true of the relationship with Solidaridad promoters. "Even today, there are conflicts. They block the streets, they create problems in the works…I suppose our actions affected their interests."

Some interviewees believe that these conflicts are actually a good thing, because the community benefits from the competition for votes between PRI and PAN. "When there is plurality, each party wants to do more than the other ones, and this makes the difference," comments Freddy Rubio, a San Antonio de los Buenos community development worker.

Rubio also thinks that many problems could be solved by greater attention to community development work. "Although it would be good if someone came up with a legal mechanism to force free riders to pay, this would not be necessary if social support were adequate. After the work of the last administrations, there are now organizers within the communities who know who to make demands of and who to pressure when necessary. To improve the process, we need to increase the number of community development workers and technicians so that we can address long-term cultural and environmental issues."

Scale and Sustainability

Enhancing Sustainability Requires Increasing the Investment in Socio-Technical Support

In order to learn more about the process of community participation, the municipal government requested that Tijuana's Institute of Social Workers evaluate the Manos a la Obra program; the evaluation was carried out at both the level of the community development workers and technicians and at the community level.

Among the institution's recommendations was the need to dedicate more resources and follow-up to social promotion work. The time frame of each program (February to November of each year) is limited, and a small number of community development workers and technicians must focus exclusively on getting the works completed. Although the programs run for 10 months each year, social promoters and technicians only begin their work around April, after the projects have been approved. Six or seven months is not enough time for capacity-building and raising community awareness, both of which would enhance sustainability and channel the community's energy into a long-term development process.

With the limited socio-technical support provided, it is not possible to engage the community in a participatory planning process. The pressure to complete the year's program is so great that social promoters and technicians tend to focus on works that have an expressed demand and for which community mobilization is easier. The demand for street paving is high, so there is not much need to stimulate requests through social promotion.

The social mobilization generated by paving and other works has not been used to launch a long-term process in each colonia that would guarantee sustainability. In addition, the lack of a participatory information-gathering and planning process means that the opportunity for gathering socioeconomic information for future government planning is foregone.

Since the community upgrading programs began in Tijuana, a group of community development workers, technicians, and community leaders has been formed, which is now able to conduct the process. Current community development workers see their role, however, as a very limited one—providing technical assistance to the management of the works process, advising on fund management, and facilitating the relationship between the government and the community. They and local residents believe that, to increase sustainability and take advantage of the social mobilization generated by the programs, the number of promoters and opportunities for their training should be increased. In addition, year-round socio-technical support should be provided to communities to help with planning and organizational development, rather than limiting assistance to six months and to the specific goal of completing a simple project, as is currently the case.

A Strategy for Sustainability Is Lacking

The social participation that characterized Tijuana's municipal government in the 1990s resulted in democratic election of community representatives, community participation in establishing priorities, community management of resources, and greater attention to the technical quality of the works. But a lack of sustainability, which was one of Solidaridad's weaknesses, is also a problem in the Tijuana programs.

As often happens in projects like these, in the rush to finish the works, less attention is paid to the process of human resource development and training for sustainability than to the project's physical and technical aspects. The Institute of Social Workers' evaluation concurred with this. According to institute director Mario Medina, "In terms of community development, the physical infrastructure can be seen as the indirect benefit of these projects. It is the human development and community dynamics that originate that are most important...In spite of this, the government sees social work as just an expense...So, three months before the elections, they hasten to add it to the budget of the Department of Social Promotion."

The institute evaluation indicated that the primary mistakes undermining sustainability were the reduction of socio-technical support and the abandonment of area-based neighborhood committees broadly focused on development in favor of works committees narrowly dedicated to specific infrastructure projects. Medina notes that the lack of continuity in the methodology developed under Manos a la Obra was a missed opportunity. The evaluation stated that, although the community upgrading programs continued, implementation strategies had cooled off in terms of the amount of participation involved. Tijuana is a good example of a situation in which the *level* of participation—community management— is certainly high, but the *degree of intensity* of participation can be considered low, since its time frame is very limited and its scope very narrow.

The benefits that residents of Tijuana's poor informal settlements have received from the programs have greatly depended on residents' attitude and desire to do better. "In Baja California, people are sensitized, politicized, and have a great need for resources to improve their quality of life. This type of program is viable in Tijuana; the people are ready.

However, contamination by political parties, by religious groups, or by leaders who only look to benefit themselves should be avoided," Medina observes. Yadira Guadalupe, president of the Kiwi Street works committee, concurs: "I only involved myself because it is important to feel useful, and although we are still poor, we used to feel all the more so, with the mire that existed before the street was paved."

Another important issue that is directly affected by the level of the socio-technical support provided is the lack of community involvement in the long-term operation and maintenance of the works. A program of socio-technical support following the completion of the works could build on residents' willingness to participate and contribute, and would in turn enhance sustainability and encourage further development initiatives.

Conditions Seem Favorable to Increase Scale and Sustainability

Tijuana's community upgrading programs have carried out a significant number of works and have generated a critical mass of institutional architecture, technical knowledge, management routines, and qualified personnel. The programs have also demonstrated, through thousands of practical examples, the feasibility of communities contributing to the identification, execution, and funding of works.

> ONE HAS A LOT OF LOVE FOR SOMETHING ONE MAKES WITH ONE'S OWN HANDS.
> —*Lucio Quiñones, President, Huejotzingo Street Works Committee, Florido-Mariano*

Favorable conditions exist to scale up current efforts by:

- Supporting long-term participatory planning for the development process of each settlement
- Improving sustainability by establishing and supporting long-term area-based community organizations
- Stepping up socio-technical support for information gathering, planning, implementation, and follow-up of projects
- Using existing personnel to train additional personnel required by the increased scale and intensity of effort.

A Model for the Continuation of the Community Upgrading Programs

Building on the lessons of Manos a la Obra and its successors, the following model is proposed to enhance the scale and sustainability of community upgrading and household improvement efforts through public-private partnerships. In this model, three parallel but institutionally separate programs would be brought together, as described below:

- **Institute a 100 percent privately funded microfinance institution (MFI) to provide loans under commercial terms to low-income households.** These loans would facilitate payment of connection fees for basic services, land tenure regularization, home improvement, and contributions to community upgrading programs. For formal sector-based borrowers, employers would agree to (1) allow the MFI to collect and disburse its loans automatically through their payroll system, which would significantly decrease MFI operating costs and result in a reduction in the interest rate the MFI would need to charge to cover its costs; (2) permit the MFI to market its financial services and provide borrowers with technical assistance during working hours, thereby increasing the demand for the MFI's financial services and reducing the borrowers' opportunity costs; (3) provide the MFI with background information on employment tenure, wages, and family status to facilitate the rapid identification and screening of applicants for creditworthiness; and (4) match borrower savings to expedite compliance with the MFI's lending requirements, while reducing the borrower's debt service burden.
- **Institute a nonprofit materials cooperative.** The co-op would negotiate bulk purchases of required supplies for home improvement and neighborhood infrastructure works at wholesale prices and pass on part of the cost savings to households within the targeted communities. By lowering the cost of building materials, individual borrower credit needs would be reduced, and the MFI could at the same time serve a lower income client base.[6]
- **Set up a community infrastructure fund (CIF).** The CIF would be managed as a public-private partnership to support common-good services, including access routes, drainage, water supply and sanitation, street lighting, daycare centers, and school improvements, as well as provide socio-technical support to enhance community participation in designing and implementing these works. It would be funded from federal, state, and local government transfers; property and betterment tax revenues; user fees; and business commu-

---

[6]In addition to discounts on materials, the introduction of more flexible technical and service standards for infrastructure services, community self-help construction techniques, and in-kind contributions from borrowers could reduce subproject costs by between 15 and 30 percent compared with the market costs of these goods and services.

nity contributions. The CIF would provide grants to communities, which in turn would pay a minimum share of the costs for an integrated set of services, plus incremental costs for higher technology options. This approach would enable communities to express their demands and priorities across sectors and service levels.

Although these three institutions form an integrated strategy to support community development, they would be managed as independent entities. Separating these operations removes the difficulty in delivering and recovering loans alongside a grant-based program managed by the same institution. Also, market-based programs operated by institutions subject to political intervention or pursuing developmental goals have difficulty operating under commercial principles or reacting to changing borrower demands and market conditions.

Conclusions

The following conclusions relate to the dynamics and organization of community participation and are intended to build on the extraordinary achievements made by Tijuana in democratic planning and community control over decisionmaking and resources. They are based upon recommendations and comments made by Tijuana community members during interviews and focus group discussions (see box 9-7), as well as those by members of the government institutions responsible for managing the community infrastructure programs.

Achievements

- There have been a significant number of completed works.
- The cost of the works is low.
- The methodology for project identification and execution has been strongly decentralized.
- The residents have participated in project identification and execution.
- The community manages all funds (its own contribution as well as that of the government).
- The community manages the procurement process for the works.
- The community contributes, on average, 30 percent of the cost of the works.
- The level of responsibility and self-esteem of the communities involved has increased.
- The relationship between the government and communities has become more productive and transparent.

Box 9-7. Recommendations and Comments Made by Interviewees

- "There is a strong level of participation, and people are accustomed to contributing from their own pockets for the works, which could make it feasible to use this scheme to accomplish different types of works if the demand were stimulated and organized."
- "There are many communication problems among the agents involved in the works. Communication mechanisms should be more efficient to facilitate the process and to make life easier for the neighborhood committees, which often face uncertainty about schedules and procedures."
- "We ought to stop taxing the goodwill of the people by summoning them so often to participate in forums and other events. They find this tiring and begin to distrust the government and its promises."
- "The community, social promoters, delegates, and leaders should participate in annual participatory evaluations. The benefits of this would certainly outweigh the costs."
- "The communities sometimes say 'it takes too much time and paperwork to process the works applications.' The social promoters and technicians concur. This seems to be a setback compared to previous years."
- "The delegations should create their own departments of social communication, because the communication work done by DESOM from city hall is usually not sufficient."
- "The staff of the municipal comptroller do not trust the delegations' management of the works. This has caused unnecessary delays in the execution of the works and, what is more serious, distrust in the community. Political interference should not reach these levels because this discredits the work of the municipal government and shatters the government-community relationship, which is so hard to build."
- "In certain delegations, the rush to complete the works reduced their quality."
- "Decentralization was positive because the delegations now manage the program directly. Thus, the community does not always have to go to city hall. However, it was a mistake to set up this process without strengthening the delegations' administrative capacity and human resources."
- "The peer communication that was possible when all the community development workers were in DESOM and all the technicians in UMU no longer exists."
- "The professionalization of community development workers and the increased social sensibility of the technicians, government officials, and politicians are necessary. If engineers have greater sensitivity and can act as social technicians, their contact with the communities can be put to greater use."

- "A catalogue of unit prices and technical specifications would ensure uniformity of criteria within the municipality."
- "With the transfer of technical supervision to the delegations, no one is in charge of updating and disseminating unit prices and technical specifications. So now the technicians of the municipal comptroller's office lack the criteria to do their job."
- "From an operational standpoint, the work methods and autonomy of each delegation or subdelegation should be respected...there is no point in having strict rules for this, because the delegations know the best way to work with their communities."
- "A program coordination unit should be formed to create a mechanism for coordination, training, and regular meetings for the technicians and social promoters."
- "Unifying criteria are needed to determine the works' relevance and feasibility, so that expensive works are not attempted in areas without sufficient resources. Such works may not get finished, as has sometimes happened."
- "Social promoters and technicians are hired each year in March or April, when the year's program has already started, and are discharged in October or November, just before it is finished."
- "The social energy generated during the works should be used to transform the works committees into permanent neighborhood committees. Otherwise, it is difficult to involve the residents in neighborhood committees because they often don't know their neighbors and don't feel involved...The energy generated by the works should not be wasted."
- "Through participation in works committees, residents spend time together, know each other as never before, and share a sense of achievement. This is very positive for future action."
- "There isn't time for the community workers and technicians to give so many people and works the close attention they need...Providing better logistics such as more vehicles, mobile phones, and computers for the community workers and technicians would allow them to use their time better and be more available to those who need them."
- "More attention should be paid to the image and manners of those responsible for the operation of social policies, including the technical and social support staff of the municipality and, in particular, those responsible for administrative and bureaucratic matters."
- "Social programs should be incorporated into long-term municipal planning, not just brought up at election time. Communities would like to see more of those responsible for social policy, especially the mayor, being more active throughout their term of office. This would help neutralize the perception that politicians are only interested in people's votes and not in the people themselves."

Limitations

- Nonmunicipal services such as water, sewerage, and electricity are subject to a different procedural framework and cannot be extended under the same system, limiting potential synergies.
- Program procedures tend to mask the complexity of social demand and to focus such demand mostly on street paving.
- As a consequence of the above two points, it is difficult to promote works other than street paving.
- Limited understanding of the importance of social support and technical supervision of community activities has resulted in limited funding for these services.
- The programs have been limited in time frame and thematic focus.
- There is no long-term vision of each area's development, and there has been no attempt to build such a vision.
- The potential for social participation is clearly high, but it has not been fully exploited.

Recommendations

- Foster the creation and strengthening of neighborhood committees that have a broad developmental mandate by increasing investment in community development activities such as participatory planning, rather than directing all available resources to street paving.
- Create a program of year-round, low-cost, high-impact community development activities (such as forestation, environmental education, and neighborhood clean-up programs).
- Involve neighborhood committees in preparing integrated area development plans.
- Increase the number of community development workers and technicians to support activities not directly related to the works.
- Increase training opportunities for residents, community development workers, and technicians.
- Limit the potential negative effects of decentralization by creating regular information exchange meetings for community development workers and technicians of different delegations.
- Improve coordination among municipal departments so the government can present a single consistent message to the people rather than several conflicting ones.

10

Peru: The Self-Managed Urban Community of Villa El Salvador, Lima

With a population of close to 350,000, Villa El Salvador (VES) is the largest low-income settlement in the so-called "Southern Cone" of metropolitan Lima; it is also one of the largest such settlements in all of Peru. (See box 10-1.) Founded in 1971 by urban development authorities in Velasco Alvarado's military government, it received approximately 4,000 relocated families that had invaded land close to the city. This was the first of the *bolsón* districts, areas designated and planned by the central government authorities which were settled in an orderly fashion by families needing housing. The lots later had utilities installed and became part of the city.

This chapter focuses on the construction of VES. More than just a project, the construction involved a social process in which neighborhood initiative played a key role. From the beginning, this was manifested in two ways:

- The policy of the highest level political authorities was one of facilitation and compromise in developing this large human settlement and of creating a direct line of communication, which is still in place, between local players and development specialists from Peru and outside the country.
- The vision of the city's development—even given the design imperfections a project originating in Latin America in the 1970s would have—yielded concrete results, which provided a common ground for efficient action.

We interviewed many people in and about Villa El Salvador. Each interview has been a valuable testimony for which we are grateful. The voices transcribed here are representative of the entire community.

> **Box 10-1. Villa El Salvador in the Lima Context**
>
> | District | Area (hectares) | \multicolumn{5}{c}{Population} |
>
> | District | Area (hectares) | 1993 | 1997 | 2000 | 2005 | 2010 |
> |---|---|---|---|---|---|---|
> | VES | 3,343 | 258,239 | 293,710 | 319,105 | 362,272 | 392,390 |
> | Lima | 278,139 | 6,430,309 | 7,048,004 | 7,482,012 | 8,285,814 | 8,822,222 |
>
> The population of Villa El Salvador grew 3.27 percent annually between 1993 and 1998, the highest growth index of the three districts in Lima's Southern Cone. For the 1998–2005 period, the estimated growth rate is 2.57 percent per year; for 2005–15, 1.61 percent. It is estimated that VES will have the highest population in the Southern Cone by 2015. In 1998, the population already exceeded 300,000 inhabitants. The 50,000 new residents added between 1993 and 1998 have increased the population density and the occupation of spaces destined for agriculture and livestock, and even of areas that are not fit for settlement.
>
> Most of the VES population lives in poverty, with 15 percent of residents living in extreme poverty, according to Peru's National Institute of Statistics and Censuses, which counted 38,000 indigent poor in 1995. Apoyo, an influential private marketing survey institute, has determined that 100 percent of VES residents fit into the country's lowest income bracket. This is the kind of information on which large companies base their investment decisions, which discourages private investments in VES.
>
> *Source:* Desco (1998).

The Importance of the VES Experience

As a district, Villa El Salvador conceives of itself as different and successful. VES and its leaders have been acknowledged nationally and internationally. Development professionals believe that Villa El Salvador is a striking case of a successful participatory process taking place in an extensive area with poor natural resources. Much of what is observed in Villa El Salvador may be seen in other informal settlements (the Peruvian phrase for which is *pueblos jovenes,* or young towns) in Lima and Peru. Before the formation of VES, the studies of Peruvian informal settlements by John Turner and William Mangin were already well-known.[1]

---

[1]The well-known books *Freedom to Build: Dweller Control of the Housing Process* (Turner and Fichter 1972) and *Peasants in Cities: Readings in the Anthropology of Urbanization* (Mangin

These studies had a decisive influence on the ideas, first formulated at the United Nations Habitat Conference in Vancouver in 1976, which are now known as "enabling strategies."

What makes VES different from the rest of Peru's pueblos jovenes? Its outstanding feature is the sheer number of initiatives undertaken by organized groups. Even though these initiatives are original in themselves, more significant are the participatory mechanisms they involve, which are varied and generalized. This distinctive feature of VES has to do with the state's support, through a policy of enablement, and with the fact that the settlement had, from the beginning, a negotiated development plan, which constituted a shared vision of development. (See box 10-2 for a summary of the VES initiative.)

A direct relationship between the government and the people and direct intervention of residents in urban matters are central themes in the Northern literature on development and urban management, and North American and European cities are full of interesting mechanisms through which urban democracy is promoted.[2] In Latin America, all this complexity is usually reduced to participation of the poor in projects occurring within their neighborhood. VES goes far beyond that—it is a case of resident involvement in the development process of a *ciudad popular*, or popular city, of 350,000. The participatory mechanisms created in VES are original, and they have endured. These participatory processes do not differ in intent from the principles governing the sophisticated mechanisms of a French municipality or a North American county. The procedures to change construction regulations or zoning requirements or to prevent a resident or company from occupying or developing a public space may be different, but the idea that the collective interest of residents lies behind every city regulation is the same.

Western democracy aspires to establish an egalitarian relationship between authorities and the populace in which differing viewpoints are respected. How is it possible to put such aspirations into practice in countries such as Peru, where institutions are so weak? In the absence of strong institutions, the ability to reach agreements and later keep them is im-

---

1970) are the culmination of a series of articles by these British and North American specialists, respectively. Both researchers came to know the experience of Peruvian informal settlements first-hand due to their professional work, and both were very impressed by the nationwide self-help home-building effort on the part of poor families that migrated to cities from rural areas.

[2]As in the South, however, the social projects of the developed North are not always effective. They are often too expensive, and their success is often due to certain unique features of the local reality. Further, scaling up is often no easier in the North than in the South.

> **Box 10-2. VES Project Synopsis**
>
> **Project name:** Development Program for Villa El Salvador
>
> **Start:** May 1971
>
> **Duration:** 32 years and counting
>
> **Kind of project:** Development of a city by and for its own resident families
>
> **Project scale:** Sub-metropolitan, municipal
>
> **Location:** Urban
>
> **Kind of intervention:** Urban development
>
> **Subjects of the actions:** Residents with low and very low incomes
>
> **Acknowledgments:** International prizes and national acknowledgment; several professional and doctoral degree studies about aspects of the VES development
>
> **Participant entities:** Hundreds of area-based and specific-purpose community organizations, several Peruvian government bodies, the metropolitan municipality of Lima, the VES district municipality, several international and local nongovernmental organizations, international aid organizations, and the Catholic Church
>
> **Resources mobilized:** $330 million (estimated value of the district's real estate, with 55,000 properties at $6,000 each); estimated yearly investment: $10 million
>
> **Population:** 2,507 city blocks; 55,252 lots; 258,239 residents (1993 census); 3,343 occupied hectares

portant. VES families thus place great importance on social organizations. By the same token, the city is proud of its tradition of upholding the opinions and viewpoints of the weakest in a society where social inequality and poverty prevail.

In the case of VES, citizen participation is not reduced to a generic checklist that might apply to any local development project. Rather, what stands out here is a checklist of *processes* which should exist in undertaking strategic decisions in the development of any neighborhood or city. The topic presented here may not be understood without directly relating it to other bibliographies, those that deal with citizenship, governance, governability, democracy, and development. In these bibliographies, the term "participation" is not a buzzword. It's simply a word that appears every time one talks about democracy.

VES is still a poor city, with many difficulties. First of all, the country and its population are poor, and the social and political context is difficult. Second, projects are developed with scarce resources and little high-quality professional support. Some of the tools used in development processes elsewhere have been and are still missing here. The VES process is an inexpensive one, but the lack of resources and project support makes itself felt in its results. In our opinion, VES would need just a little investment in institutional strengthening and project software to become the model of urban development from an initial situation of poverty that the development community seeks.

> VILLA EL SALVADOR IS THE PRODUCT OF SOME CRAZY VISIONARIES WHOSE CRAZINESS MADE THEM LOOK NOT AT THE PRESENT BUT AT THE FUTURE.
> —*Juan Arbuñil, VES Leader*

The following lists key replicable aspects of the Villa El Salvador experience:

- **The crucial role of the state.** As elsewhere in Peru, the state has provided land for low-income urbanization and technical assistance for urban design. What is new here is that, in Villa El Salvador, high-level government officials were in direct communication with the residents. This led to the establishment of a supply structure and clear rules for a gradual development process. This clearly defined process was the result of interaction between the project that external promoters had in mind when they started the activities, and the ideas and priorities of the residents.
- **Building a city, rather than just housing.** VES has been conceived of as a city proper, with a wide range of productive activities, not a "dormitory city." This vision has affected the project's parameters and provided a more complete basis for development than traditional sites and services schemes ever would have. The original proposal for the city was more ideological than current ones. Nevertheless, it was a motivating proposal, emphasizing the notion of a city in progress, rather than focusing on just housing for the poor. From the beginning, the authorities and local residents agreed on an integrated area development plan which became the vision and framework behind the development process.
- **The importance of a plan.** The Peruvian model, especially in the case of VES, indicates that investing in the provision of surveyed lots with an adequate settlement plan and layout, a participatory

area development plan, and socio-technical assistance to the residents, which might be summarized in the formula *lotes con plano y plan*—surveyed and beaconed sites plus a development plan—is a feasible alternative for low-income housing and urban development. In this formula, which seeks to organize and optimize the existing process of informal settlement development, provision of infrastructure and basic services is gradual. The formula could be adapted and institutionalized in other countries where the government is willing to adopt a policy of facilitation and take responsibility for overall coordination and the development plan.
- **Building participation through a structured project.** The VES experience teaches that, while it is true that urban development projects in poor areas do not work without participation, participation also does not work without a project. Projects may be understood as a facilitating environment or supply structure, with resources, technical assistance, and social support—all necessary elements in a participatory process. Projects also must have good design and management. To become sustainable, they must be integrated into the development process. When the desire to participate in an urban area is high, as in VES, investment in community management will usually produce good results. The degree of intensity of participation in VES has always been high, but the level of participation has not always reached forms of community management. The level of participation has depended on the characteristics of different projects in the district's history.
- **Joint population-state decisionmaking and resource management.** The state was an early, strong presence in the VES experience; and local government, nonprofit, and international entities later became supporting parties. The local for-profit private sector (small and microentrepreneurs) was also present, but the formal private sector, comprised of banks and large companies, was largely absent.

Background

In the summer of 1971, more than 4,000 homeless families occupied unsettled lands on the border between the high-income district of Surco and the low-income district of San Juan de Miraflores. The government resolved the political and housing problems created by the "Pamplona invasion," the first organized invasion during General Velasco Alvarado's term as president, by creating Villa El Salvador in the desert south of Lima. (See box 10-3.) The features of the new settlement included:

Box 10-3. The Evolution of Villa El Salvador

1971: Foundation of VES, with strong support from the reformist military government of General Velasco Alvarado.

1971–1975: Families are settled, area-based community organizations are created; the Villa El Salvador Integrated Development Plan is approved. Schools are built, streets are paved, and public and residential electricity is provided.

1976–1980: The pact with the government is broken, and an era of conflict begins under the conservative military government of General Morales Bermúdez. Electrification, school consolidation, and water supply and sanitation are first provided around this time in Lima's Southern Cone. In VES, there is some settlement in areas outside of what was considered in the original plan, but according to the original pattern of residential groups.

1981–1985: Main avenues are paved. The VES district is established, and the municipality created. The Industrial Park Autonomous Authority is also created. Community organizations flourish with the return to democracy, and specific-purpose community organizations begin to acquire importance alongside local area-based community organizations.

1986–1990: An era of economic crisis and terrorist violence begins; Sendero Luminoso applies active pressure. The industrial park and agricultural zone are outfitted and developed.

1991–1995: Terrorism weakens organizations and the local government. Sendero Luminoso stages attempts on the lives of several prominent VES citizens, killing community leader and mayoral candidate Maria Elena Moyano and severely wounding former mayor Michel Azcueta. There is high political instability, with four mayors serving between 1993 and 1995. Consolidation and improvement of housing with durable materials takes place.

1996–present: Recovery process: urban consolidation in housing, infrastructure, and services. Following structural adjustment and the end of the terrorist threat, VES, as a consolidated popular city, emerges as a strong, vibrant, and heterogeneous community. A worrying trend: occupation for housing purposes begins to take place on lands destined for environmental reserves and public equipment, outside the original plan and without respect for the original pattern of residential groups.

1999: A new participatory city development plan is prepared and approved.

- Lotes con tiza (surveyed and beaconed lots), with no services, delivered to people in a desert area that the state decided to devote to a new popular city
- An original settlement design with urban modules called "residential groups" which featured a central plaza to house neighborhood-level urban equipment
- Availability of lots for any family in Lima that needed accommodation
- Promotion and support of the state through its technical departments and mechanisms of social mobilization.

VES did not receive from the government all the resources it needed for its development, but the families did receive more resources than those in nearby neighborhoods, due to their direct dialogue with high-level authorities. VES's model of self-management had the blessing of President Velasco and his highest level group of advisors. The important role this direct relationship played lasted until the political and economic underpinnings of the reformist military regime collapsed, and the conservative General Morales Bermúdez replaced General Velasco as president in the second half of the 1970s.

VES's urban model was in operation from the beginning of the settlement. On the one hand, it reflected the Yugoslav model of self-management that state officials upheld at the time; on the other, it reflected urban planners' previous proposals for satellite cities. The settlement would have three clearly differentiated sectors: a residential zone comprised of more than 100 residential groups of 384 lots, distributed along main avenues; an agricultural zone; and an industrial park.

With the approval of the urban proposal and organizational model at a large convention of community leaders, the VES Integrated Development Plan oriented the activities of both the population and the political authorities at the time. The resulting organization, the Self-Managed Urban Community of Villa El Salvador (CUAVES), was an area-based community organization (ABCO), with the territorial model as its basis. CUAVES had departments in charge of health issues and business development, which was a new idea at that time.

Even though the area lacked resources, the population never abandoned the idea of integrated development, in which productive activities would play a central role. The population always intended, when the time came, to transform part of the unoccupied area in the desert into an agricultural zone, and the other part into an industrial park which would function as a center for manufacturing. Even though the lands that had been set aside were not immediately developed for those purposes, the families did not occupy them for housing—which is what ended up happening in other areas with whose social purposes the population did not identify.

With the arrival of drinking water networks in the late 1970s and early 1980s, the wastewater that was collected was treated and used to water the agricultural zone, thanks to a CUAVES initiative. Subsequently, the home-based small and microentrepreneurs of the newly created district mobilized themselves, with local and national government assistance, to occupy the land that had been reserved for an industrial park and expand their activities.

The idea of satellite cities with all needed services is not a new one. In the 1960s, projects of this kind were carried out in Latin American cities with U.S. Agency for International Development support. What is different about this case is that the authorities made an initial commitment, and the population mobilized to see it through over the long term. The initial and subsequent stages of VES development indicate that the residents were thinking of creating a city, not another low-income neighborhood, from the very beginning. This essential ingredient of the VES experience contradicts a tenet of many projects, namely that low-income housing is just about housing, while it is actually about city development.

Participatory Process

Contributory Factors

The population that settled in Villa El Salvador was similar to other low-income groups. Not everyone had a tradition of organization, and public authorities played an important role in supporting community organization. (See box 10-4.) This had an important impact, since community organization, which is normally a spontaneous and gradual process, was helped along in VES, and was thus established better and more quickly than in conventional cases.

Other factors that had an impact on participation included the following:

- The Peruvian population's average standard of living in 1973 and 1974 was the highest in the last 30 years.
- Many young families that came to the settlement were infected by the optimistic climate created by the reformist military government.
- There was a group of leaders with political experience who moved into this new settlement, which allowed them to fulfill a natural role as organizers.

Box 10-4. Roots of the Participatory Process and Local Organization in VES

Several residents and leaders explained how community participation and organization took rapid root in Villa El Salvador. Oscar Balbuena, the director of a Lima NGO, says, "At the start, CUAVES had a direct relationship with the government, with no intermediaries. There were high-ranking people in the state apparatus who were willing to establish a close relationship and move things forward."

Juan Arbañil, longtime VES leader and currently in charge of one of the VES decentralized municipal offices, points out, "At the beginning, the residents weren't organized. Each would go to the authorities individually and ask for a plot. There were people in the area of every background who hardly knew one another. The government, which wanted to resolve this problem because it was a major headache, created the National Office for the Development of Shantytowns, a government institution that developed training for community delegates."

Schoolteacher and community leader Gregoria Brito adds her impression. "We were privileged to have a deal with the government during the Velasco period. We had more support than other neighborhoods, but everything came to us because of the vitality the people had. We were young, we wanted the best, a better life. We all became infected with the same idea, and we worked hard. We had nothing when we started out, and participation was massive."

Juan Arbañil expands on the point. "The organization became stronger with the need to get water. Water trucks and cars could not get in because of the large expanse of sand. There were no stones, no gravel, no solid materials, so cars would get stuck and residents had to push them out. That gave rise to the pro-water committees. Groups of women would go to Curva de la Tablada to stop each water truck and bring it here by force. That's why groups of ladies would come in sitting atop a water tank. They would sit on the tank, delighted to have hijacked a water truck. This was the first organized effort here. Afterwards, the need for schools arose."

A Horizontal Relationship with the Authorities

The frequent visits of President Velasco to VES were the most visible example of a horizontal dialogue between state authorities and community leaders. Anecdotes about what happened to his successor, General Morales Bermúdez, indicate that the population sought to keep an egalitarian relationship with the authorities, even when the pact between highest level authorities and the population had been broken (see box 10-5). The population maintained an attitude of respect for its own organiza-

> **Box 10-5. Challenging the General-President**
>
> "In 1976, we organized a big march because we wanted the government to assume its responsibilities: construction of passable roads for buses, water, sewerage, all that. We had our march, and the police intervened on the Atocongo Bridge, off the VES border. Despite that confrontation—they had water hoses, we got wet, they even threw their armored police cars against us—we got to the presidential palace in Lima. We sang the national anthem, and a commission communicated our requests. Later, we invited Morales Bermúdez to make a commitment to the people for the VES anniversary. He came with all his ministers and their wives, but it was not as in previous years, with a warm reception and food. We couldn't afford that.
>
> "The people came, not in support, but in protest, with posters to make him see all the needs they had. They offered to sign the water and drainage agreement at 10,000 soles of the time, payable in 10 years. The housing minister later gave us a figure of 30,000 soles. We didn't accept it. We informed the residents, who didn't accept it either. When we went back, General Gerónimo Cafferata wouldn't receive us. He said, 'What do you people from the provinces want in Lima?' We had such a serious argument that we almost didn't sign the water contract. It was signed, but at 30,000 soles down payment and 50,000 soles in installments. We fought to keep the earlier price, but it was impossible because he was very stubborn. In July, after the national strike of 1976, we couldn't hold any more meetings because of the curfew and suspension of constitutional guarantees."
>
> —Gregoria Brito

tion, the municipality, and the organized sectors of the district. The authorities, on the other hand, vacillated between respect for and open repression of CUAVES.

Legal and Regulatory Framework

The central government created VES by subdividing desert land in 1971. The lots were laid out with a piece of chalk and then given to more than 4,000 families. The delivery certificate of these lots, within the framework of Law 13517, the Ley de Barriadas, or Law of Informal Settlements, ensured the legality of the land tenure until the beginning of the 1980s. This 1961 law is an indication of the Peruvian state's innovative attitude toward spontaneous urbanization.[3] It established ad hoc mecha-

---

[3]The Peruvian process of massive *barriada* development and self-help housing construction gave rise to influential thinking. Turner and Fichter's previously cited *Freedom*

nisms to regulate the initial settlement and gradual improvement of informal neighborhoods. Due to this law, the illegal developers known as "pirates" that are so common in Latin America disappeared from Peru's cities for almost 40 years.

The law also requires public authorities to intervene directly in neighborhood improvement after irregular or illegal occupation occurs. In the 1980s, the city of Lima delivered ownership titles to VES families. In the 1990s, by means of a new institution, the Commission for the Formalization of Informal Property (COFOPRI), the validity of these titles was confirmed, and they were recorded in the recently created Urban Real Estate Registry. The delivery of ownership title deeds to some areas of recent settlement in the VES district is still pending.

Importance of Integrated Development Plans

The dialogue with local organizations has been important for the development process because it has generated learning opportunities and the self-confidence that is still present in the population. In 1975, the first VES Integrated Development Plan was completed; this was partially modified in 1985. In 1999, the municipality promoted an ample participatory process that had as its target a new plan for Villa El Salvador. Due to its conceptual nature and features, the plan has become a more important development tool than any conventional legislative framework.

The population has always had a good idea of what it wants, and the development of Peruvian informal settlements follows unwritten but inexorable rules. First, the plans must be approved and the lots surveyed and assigned, which gives security to the holding. Second, a school must be built for the small children who cannot leave the neighborhood to study. Third, infrastructure works are developed. On the dry coastal areas of Peru, electricity comes first, then water and sanitation, which are more expensive and time-consuming. Lastly, the roads are paved: first

---

to Build: Dweller Control of the Housing Process (1972), a theory of self-help construction, shaped much of the international debate on low-income housing in the 1970s and 1980s. Hernando de Soto's *The Other Path: The Invisible Revolution in the Third World* (1989), published during Peru's dark years of terrorism and economic crisis, showed that the informal city is not just about housing. De Soto sees it as a hub of economic activity whose vitality needs to be freed from the constraints of an unjust and outdated legal and regulatory system, and brought into the mainstream. *The Other Path* has been, and remains, highly influential in shaping the debate about legal reform in developing countries, and was partly responsible for Peru's legal and procedural reform of its land registration system, which has allowed the regularization of tenure of 1.2 million urban plots through the COFOPRI scheme.

the access and main roads and then, if possible, secondary roads and sidewalks.

One difficulty planners and people in charge of urban upgrading projects often have is that they propose a project without realizing that the community already has its own. From the inception of VES, authorities and residents agreed on an integrated project, which then constituted the regulating framework of the development process. To summarize:

- The project was called CUAVES.
- The project document is the certificate that recognizes CUAVES. There were no other official documents establishing the relationship between the authorities and the residents.
- Much later, CUAVES was legally recorded in the public registries as a civil association.
- No written agreement between the residents and the state ever existed. The agreement was by nature, and from the start, a *social pact*.
- The agreement lasted only until 1976, but its heritage is still evident in the community.

The New Integrated Development Plan

The 1970s VES development plan has become obsolete, but it still epitomizes the collective spirit necessary to build a city. In 1985, the municipality, headed by the charismatic schoolteacher Michel Azcueta, proposed that the people update the plan, with partially successful results. Today, the need to reorient district development and the tradition of working with participatory development plans go hand in hand. In 1997, the process began afresh, and a new vision for the district arose, which was shared with all the residents: "Villa El Salvador must be a productive district, a healthy city, and a community of solidarity." In 1999, the impulse became even greater when the new administration took office. During the first half of 1999, the young new mayor, Martín Pumar, 28, organized more than 200 meetings in 10 different sectors of the district. The citizen consultation for formal approval of the new plan was held November 14, 1999. Close to 3,000 youngsters collected the votes of 48,119 residents aged over 16, equivalent to 30 percent of the district's over-16 population.

The new plan took shape in a context different from that of the previous plan (see box 10-6). As Néstor Ríos, the municipal official in charge of the Integrated Development Plan stated, "This plan takes place in the middle of a crisis. When doing the SWOT [Strengths, Weaknesses, Opportunities, and Threats] analysis and assessing trends, we found that,

> **Box 10-6. A Young Mayor's Vision**
>
> "The development plan is a policy of this administration which is based on the municipality and community working together. The plan is our main instrument for development. We believe that the easiest thing to do would have been to hire a specific institution or technical group to prepare the plan…The other possibility was to make a participatory plan in which neighbors participate, give opinions, and make suggestions. This delayed the process, but we chose the second option because we wanted people to feel part of the project. It's not just about making the place nice; it's about the people feeling it's theirs.
>
> "We propose what we want as a municipality based on our vision of the future. Likewise, residents give their vision as popular organizations, as leaders, neighbors, and citizens. As a result, we develop a complete proposal. We have programmed 200 public events to shape our vision for the future of Villa El Salvador.
>
> "We want residents to take an active part in the community. We want to build a cooperative space where each resident feels part of local government. If we can complain or make demands, then we must also be ready to govern. A resident in a residential group of 384 families will no longer just complain about things, but will be able to promote his own views for urban development. We don't want spectators, but responsible participants. Some of them will be the public officials, who have a mandate to represent the government institutions. Others will represent themselves, their families, their associations, but we're all part of development.
>
> "This will build Villa El Salvador's identity…This process is not only about having a planning document; it's about the neighbors who vote to say 'I agree with this development plan.' If they don't agree, we have to go back and discuss it again. If people approve the development plan, then the budget for the year 2000 must be a participatory budget. The starting point is not what we think about the municipal council, but what action we can take with the budget. Rather than the municipality, nongovernmental organizations, and ministries working separately, each with their budget, we can come together, join forces, and do a bigger project. We want the development plan be a tool to address these projects, advancing them cooperatively and efficiently."
>
> —*Mayor Martín Pumar*

three years ago, people thought Peru would be better off, but now people feel the situation has not improved."

Resource Mobilization and Financial Sustainability

There have been many approaches over the past several decades to project development. During the 1970s, all Latin American countries had many state companies. Every public work of importance had hidden subsidies and more or less open corruption. In the 1980s, with an emerging consciousness of the importance of cost recovery, it was impossible to hide the failure of most housing and infrastructure projects for low-income families. In the 1990s, privatization of public services gained acceptance. The development projects that took place in VES were not immune to this changing national and international context.

Because development projects in VES have always belonged to the community rather than the state, the public has wanted to know the costs they would pay. Thus, many residents know precisely how and by whom various community projects began and are operated. Efraín Sánchez, a local leader, knows that the sports courts in his residential group are the result of an agreement between the Peruvian Sports Institute and the German government. Pio Bailén, president of the credit committee of a home improvement project, notes that the pilot project had a guarantee fund that was granted by the city of Rezé, France. Committee leaders of the Glass of Milk nongovernmental organization (NGO) are proud of the fact that the money for their program was obtained from the central government after a mobilization staged in 1997 by their committees and the metropolitan municipality.[4]

Eduardo Zevallos, who worked in Villa El Salvador as a government official at the beginning of the project, describes the prevailing attitude at the time. "We had a very important funding package, but it wasn't enough. What did we do? We took advantage of the organization and held meetings with the leaders. We told them, 'Gentlemen, the cost of water and sanitation in this neighborhood is this much; in this other neighborhood, it is that much, etc.' They knew all the costs and had to decide where to make improvements. It was cheaper in some towns; in others more expensive. We had to decide where to do it, because if we didn't, we would have to give the money back. We gave people the technical specifications and the costs. The first meeting was chaotic. I thought, 'This will never work.' During the second meeting, I began to have some faith, and later we had some incredible situations. People from one area, for instance, would vote to postpone their service to give it first to those

---

[4]Glass of Milk (Vaso de Leche) is a basic nutrition program for children implemented through a partnership between the central government, which provides the resources, and local organized groups—mostly women's groups—which deliver the assistance.

in a more disadvantaged area. I saw that with my own eyes...The result was recognized by everyone— an agreed budget for water, sanitation, electricity, community centers, and sports courts."

It must not be forgotten, moreover, that the settlers usually made their contribution before demanding that others make theirs.

Gregoria Brito says, "So the people had to build classrooms; each residential group wanted a school made of durable material. While waiting for the durable material, some straw matting classrooms were built in each residential group. The agreement was that every resident, whether or not he or she had children, had to pay 100 soles of the time to get the durable materials." Juan Arbañil notes an additional result. "The teachers became more involved with the communities. They adopted the role of encouraging and helping the parents with the construction and created organizations to support the schools." (See box 10-7.)

Box 10-7. The Peru-BIRF Project

In curious ways, VES residents have taken ownership of official agreements, such as the one Peru had with the World Bank (abbreviated BIRF in Spanish) in the 1970s for school construction. The Colégio Técnico República de Bolivia was the result of lobbying by VES residents, after they found out that Peru had signed an agreement with the World Bank to build several such technical training institutions in Lima. Juan Arbañil notes, "The agreement involved several countries: Ecuador, Chile, Bolivia, Peru, and others. This school is currently known as Colegio República de Bolivia, or simply "Peru-BIRF." In 1976, it was originally a temporary structure, built with straw mats, which accommodated approximately 50 or 60 children. The school was located on top of the hill in Residential Group 13, on a huge expanse of sand. The large number of students was worrisome...We had marched to the Palacio de Gobierno to show the military government of Morales Bermúdez that Villa El Salvador's needs were real and pressing ones. Because of the marches, the movement, and the protests, Morales Bermúdez came to Villa. José Yataco, the school director at that time, the Education Council, and the CUAVES Executive Council had been fighting for this project. We had already sent a letter asking that Villa El Salvador have one of the Peru-BIRF schools. Morales Bermúdez visited the school with his wife. They saw the bent matting and the children sitting on the sand with their notebooks on their laps. He immediately gave his consent to build a school there, since the location of the Peru-BIRF project school had not been decided yet."

Mobilizing Resources and Reporting on Expenditure

The per capita municipal budget of VES is very limited. In 1999, the figure for new investments was about $7.25 per inhabitant, from the Municipal Works Fund. Total municipal revenue collection was estimated at about $6.35 per inhabitant in 1999. Therefore, there has been a transition to making the community pay for certain services. However, obtaining regular payments from families for services is difficult. In the words of José Pisconte, the city's financial director, the main problem is that the population does not yet have a "payment culture." To address the situation, the municipality has tried to improve collection systems and enhance transparency in public spending. Mayor Martín Pumar says, "We have programmed four reports on municipal spending. Later today, I have an event in Sector 1. There, they're the most difficult ones, so we have to report to them often, so that they realize we're serious. The idea is not to have our supporters come to the reporting sessions, but the neighbors who disagree with us. We want to convince them about the importance of a plan, the importance of knowing what happens to your investments. The community will receive a chart from the city's internal audit, which reports income from service fees, real estate taxes, government transfers, and total income and expenses. It also shows the general accounts, how much is spent on staff, and how much is paid to the mayor and each town councilor. The idea is to be transparent so that residents will participate in internal management processes. True participation and democracy demand transparency."

An Example: Paving Streets in the Residential Groups

By the 1990s, a lot of progress had been made in basic infrastructure, and residents wanted the local streets within their residential group paved. José Pisconte describes the mobilization of resources for the initiative. "In the middle of the electoral campaign, the central government began to work on the residential group adjacent to the mayor's residence, promising to pave 60 or 70 residential groups if their candidate won. The army completed the paving,[5] which represented a large investment of approximately 700,000 or 800,000 soles for each residential group."

This was more electoral ploy than sensible policy, since, for the same cost, two kilometers of a central avenue could be paved, which would meet the needs of the entire district. A different strategy was needed.

---

[5]There is a long tradition in Peru of the army executing public works.

Pisconte continues. "To establish a process that would build on everyone's resources, we issued an ordinance that gave birth to the local works committees. This ordinance gives the local works initiative due recognition, but it also tries to prevent the creation of pro-sidewalks committees, pro-highways committees, or pro-streets committees that compete with one another. The ordinance states that the works committee has to be comprised of at least half the residential group population. That is, out of 384 families, it needs to have the signature of half of those families plus one. They can elect a coordinator, a secretary, or take any organizational form they want." The municipality then signs agreements with these neighborhood groups.

"Under this co-management agreement," Pisconte explains, "the municipality has to review and approve the designs that are submitted by the community groups. In addition to preparing their own technical files, the committees are supposed to finance 20 to 30 percent of the total cost of the work. The residents are also supposed to clear the way for the works by removing debris and construction materials, which are often stored by the roadside. If any trees are in the way, the residents are supposed to remove and replant them. The residents also pay for other things, such as the booth for the guards, and the meetings to be held at the block and residential group levels. Some groups finance their technical files and other costs with barbecue parties, charity fairs, or bingo. The rest is financed through payments collected house by house. The works committees are asked to open an account in the bank of their choice to manage the resources they generate."

This process generates competition among residential groups, since the municipality uses selection criteria. José Pisconte states, "One of the requirements for starting the work was to have the technical file approved. Another element is the revision of fiscal debt with respect to the municipality. If a residential group that requests paving owes too much money, then another group may be selected in its stead…The dynamism of the works committee was assessed by the number of meetings held. The residents analyzed and signed the minutes, and a town councilor attended the meetings. All of this strengthened the decisionmaking process."

Leveraging Resources for Street Paving

José Pisconte states, "We realized that not only the municipality and the residents are supposed to pay for the paving, but that we can also draw on INVERMET, the Metropolitan Investment Fund. Thus, if we are to spend 500,000 soles on a residential group, we can split it 50-50 by signing an agreement with INVERMET. We then have enough money to do another residential group. Because of this, we have been able to pave more residential groups than we initially thought possible. When the work is finished, we sign a delivery certificate for the work to the works committee, entrusting them with the custody and responsibility of the new streets."

Pisconte summarizes. "This means that the population feels that the paved road belongs to them. I believe that this has improved the care of the roads. For example, when neighbors or the water company break the asphalt to repair pipes, the committee is responsible for making sure that the road is repaired afterward."

Improving Municipal Revenue Collection

José Pisconte analyzes municipal revenue collection and the efforts made by the municipality to increase the resources available for development. "The municipality has approximately 21 to 23 million soles for 1999 [equivalent to $6.3 to 6.9 million]. Of this total, approximately 7 million soles come from the municipal compensation fund, which is transferred from the central government. Another 6 or 7 million comes from the Glass of Milk program, which is funded by the central government; and the remaining 6 or 7 million is our own revenue from municipal fees, real estate taxes, the cleaning levy, etc. These resources are used to leverage other resources for district development."

Municipal revenue collection has been enhanced by:

- Improving the scheduling of payments so that families do not all have to go to the municipality the same day
- Rewarding residents who are up to date on their payments by giving preference in infrastructure and service works to the residential groups that are most current[6]
- Reporting regularly to sectors of the district about municipal spending
- Allowing low-income residents to provide labor in exchange for debt; this system only applies to male heads of households, so as not to overburden women
- Collecting payments door-to-door through ad hoc teams, and adopting social marketing strategies (see box 10-8).

---

[6]As part of the program to improve collection, the municipality has held raffles—the prize being a vehicle that can be used as a taxicab—for taxpayers who are up to date on their payments.

> **Box 10-8. Door-to-Door Collection**
>
> José Pisconte reports that the collection system residents use for garbage removal fees works well, and the VES municipality is considering applying it to local taxes, but that there is some resistance. In this experimental model of collection, local teams (generally made up of women) collect payments for the work of four small garbage collection companies. Residents pay their fees to these women, who are well known in the community and receive a small percentage of the amount collected for their efforts. They are known in Sector 1 of Villa El Salvador as the "tigresses" for their ability to get residents to pay their debts.
>
> This collection method combines participatory measures with community traditions. As Pisconte notes, "We need to look closely at what happens in the residents' daily life. We only regulate what custom has begun to shape. In the end, the law only recognizes what's already alive in society."

Actors, Alliances, and Institutional Arrangements

No entity has exclusive responsibility for city development. In the case of VES, popular institutions have always worked in conjunction with state, national, and international institutions. Since the creation of the VES district municipality in 1983, the municipality has played an important role in linking institutions together.

> I THINK WE'RE VERY SKILLFUL IN GETTING OUTSIDE PEOPLE WITH RESOURCES, INCLUDING TECHNICIANS, TO PARTICIPATE IN OUR COMMUNITY AND LEND US A HAND...WE WILL SAY, "RETURN WHAT YOU'VE TAKEN FROM THE PEOPLE OR LEARNED FOR FREE AT PUBLIC UNIVERSITIES"...THUS, SOME INSTITUTIONS ARE VERY COMMITTED TO US.
> —*Juan Arbañil, VES Leader*

Actors and Alliances in Action: The VES Industrial Park

When Villa El Salvador was founded, it was intended that the city would not only have an agricultural and livestock zone, but also an industrial park, and an area was assigned for that purpose. However, there was no water for the zone, and large industrial companies did not want to locate in this area of extreme poverty far from roads and service centers.

Thus, land parcels of more than 10,000 square meters awaited industry that never arrived. In VES's original plan, large companies were to locate there,[7] but only a few did, and gradually there was a crisis. Nevertheless, the residents kept their hopes up, as demonstrated by their rejection of seven proposals to infiltrate the zone for residential purposes. They did not want the zone to become a dormitory city, but a center of production.

As former mayor Michel Azcueta notes, "Education is essential to strengthening a joint, integrated vision…particularly for metropolitan and regional projects that will bring about benefits that people don't perceive initially. One example is the industrial park, which does not benefit all community members directly. Nevertheless, people have known for years that an industrial park would be good for VES. Because of this, an incursion into the area set aside for the industrial park to use the land for housing was never allowed by the residents' organizations. It was the state that eventually 'invaded' part of the land to develop the Pachacamac sites and services project."

As VES Consolidated, the Park Could Be Developed. In 1983, the district municipality was created, and informal economic activities within the housing zone were developed. The concept of an industrial park to develop small and microenterprises became a reality. Today, the industrial park places VES on the map as a productive district, and important Lima businesses seek to establish themselves there. It is a significant source of furniture, footwear, and mechanical parts for consumers in all of Lima, and a model for the promotion of business. It offers 15,000 direct jobs and features eight productive sectors: handicrafts, food, furniture, clothing, textiles, metal mechanics, footwear, and services.

The development of the industrial park was based on numerous initiatives. Small businessmen and the district municipality are the most well-known actors, but not the only ones (see box 10-9). Ivan Mifflin heads the Special Support Program for Microenterprise, which is supported by the Peruvian Ministry of Industries. VES's experience was very important for the development of this program. Mifflin explains that many mayors had industrial park projects that never worked out: "In Sullana, in the north of Peru, the park was abandoned. In Trujillo,

---

[7]The Yugoslav model of self-management adopted by VES founders was predicated on the involvement of large, collectively owned production companies in various sectors of economic activity. Some of the companies initially envisaged for VES, such as a bakery and one specializing in construction materials, were actually established and functioned for several years but eventually closed their doors.

> **Box 10-9. Actors in the Creation and Development of the Industrial Park**
>
> No initiative of the scale and scope of the VES industrial park can be carried out by one or two isolated actors. Those involved in the creation and development of the park thus included several groups of producers, most of them informal, from each sector in Villa El Salvador (these joined together to form APEMIVES); the district municipality; CUAVES; the Spanish Development Cooperation; the United Nations Industrial Development Organization; the United Nations Development Programme; the National Planning Institute; the Finance Development Corporation; several NGOs; the National Compensation and Social Development Fund; the Ministry of Industries; and the Vice Presidency of the Republic.
>
> The key to developing the industrial park was the establishment of an Autonomous Authority in which all the actors were represented. The presidency of the authority was given to local government. This was an unusual move in Latin America, where local governments usually lack the needed operational capacity. The VES local government had the necessary vision to adapt the original proposals for the industrial park, using an innovative formula that made informal entrepreneurs—who are usually left out of economic development programs—the key actors in a park for micro- and small enterprises.
>
> Interestingly, banks have not participated in the industrial park. It is striking indeed that the park has been successful in a near-total credit vacuum. Currently, none of the large Peruvian banks has a branch in the district. In the industrial park, there is only a branch of a bank that grants expensive credit, with annual rates above 40 percent in dollars. Microentrepreneurs criticize Mibanco, a new financial institution whose declared aim is to offer loans to microenterprises, for giving credit to merchants but not to producers.
>
> Notwithstanding this one deficiency, the park's success has already been proven and appears sustainable. It was created thanks to a unique cooperative effort supported by a national and local policy framework. The key features of this effort could be replicated elsewhere and mainstreamed into official policy.

there is an official park, with 1,700 hectares of vacant land. Meanwhile, in the El Porvenir district, there is a spontaneous industrial park with more than 3,500 footwear manufacturers."

Mifflin continues, "The real industrial park generated by the market is often established outside the planned parks. What happened differently in VES? What conditions benefited the creation of an industrial park in the area set aside by the original plan? There was strong coordination between the municipality, small industrial organizations, and central government bodies, which for some time had provided significant financial support to the initiative.

"The institutionalization of the industrial park was marked by the Autonomous Authority, which managed the park from 1987 to 1995. The formation of the Autonomous Authority reflects the complexity of the cooperative process, which involved three local actors: the town council, which presided over the park; APEMIVES, [the Small and Medium-Sized Industry Association of Villa El Salvador]; and CUAVES, the neighborhood organization of the district. There were also three central government institutions: the former National Planning Institute, which disappeared in 1991; the Finance Development Corporation; and the Ministry of Industries.

"This composition reflected an equilibrium between the central government and local interests, which helped in managing conflicts among different interests. There were radical groups that confronted local economic development interests. The municipality was a link and a mediator. In many cases, the town council got support from the central government to confront the radicals; in other cases, it got support from the social organizations when it needed to confront a bossy central government. External support has consisted of technical assistance, which has served to lure international corporations, particularly those from Spain.

"For years before the park's formation, there were a large number of fragmented business initiatives that were organized not on common business interests, but on very specific, aggressive interests. There were many business groups in VES; in each group, there were carpenters, clothiers, metalworkers, even retailers. The need for a strong channel of representation helped create a single group representing all sectors, APEMIVES. Afterwards, sectoral groups began to emerge."

An important actor has been the central government, which implemented massive purchasing programs. The National Compensation and Social Development Fund has purchased 2 million pairs of school footwear in the last two years. This has required thousands of businessmen to come together to cover those orders. In VES, the groups had productive leaders that used spaces destined for industrial incubators and service centers to achieve economies of scale in order to meet this challenge.

Mifflin states, "The park is a kind of laboratory, offering a set of different types of services and experiences in different fields—in commerce, finance, and technical assistance—which has had repercussions in other fields. In the beginning, the land was set aside and businessmen claimed it, but what became most important in the long run was business development, the expansion of productive capacity, and so on."

Local Businesses' Demand Drove the Industrial Park to Fruition. Ivan Mifflin observes that, "People moved to the industrial zone from their home-based workshops around Villa El Salvador. Families, workshops, and production used to share space in their homes. There were pollution problems and of course severe space limitations, all of which pushed them to move."

Julio Rivas, a VES footwear manufacturer, says, "In the 1980s, trade associations were formed, encouraged by government-sponsored production programs. A group of entrepreneurs in each sector of industry was created through this process, so that when the time came, they were able to take over the park by fulfilling the series of requisites that had been established. Some were businessmen who were already producing; others were newcomers, people for example who had been fired from their jobs because of taking part in national strikes. Large companies fired them because in some cases they were the leaders of those strikes. Unemployment compelled them to work in their own homes; almost 90 percent of the people who came to the park were doing something at home. My case was the same. I was self-employed under Fujimori's government. The economic situation became asphyxiating; I could no longer make ends meet. I had to learn how to do something. Almost by chance, I chose footwear."

The industrial park was not originally designed to accommodate small businesses. Mifflin notes, "The original idea that came from the Velasco government involved large enterprises, not small or microenterprises. They were thinking of community-owned and -operated firms, following the Yugoslav model, and large private firms. This resulted in the park's initial failure, because what was really happening in VES were small private companies that had emerged in the new urban area. So we saw a shift from the old perception of the large company to a notion based on the small and microenterprise.

"The park had to be adapted to the needs of small firms, because the infrastructure that was originally planned did not take this phenomenon into account. A series of investments were required for urban equipment and the subdivision of the original large lots into smaller ones. The original lots had 10,000 square meters, and 44 of them were allocated. But only 12 companies had established themselves, and they did not occupy all the area. The 200-hectare park had to be re-subdivided to open it up to small companies. A totally new use of space and infrastructure was envisioned in the park's redesign. Service centers for microentrepreneurs and industrial incubator centers were created, with machinery and tools, as well as some exhibition areas, that have proven to be actually insufficient to the need."

A Special Kind of Infrastructure for Microentrepreneurs: The Machicenters. Mifflin continues, "Another feature of the design was that all the areas had a space for a common machinery center. The notion of 'machicenters,' which has been touted lately, arose in the VES industrial park. The machinery center would supply machines that could not be purchased by a single business. As it turned out, the machicenter idea was evidence that the participatory process has its limitations: the center belonged to everyone and to no one. The responsibility for managing these spaces was not clearly defined. The machines were not in optimal condition, so they were no help in achieving proper industry standards. We underestimated the businessmen; we thought they could use secondhand machines.

"These communal spaces ended up having another function. More than 10 or 20 companies joined forces and organized production lines in these spaces to fill large orders from state purchasing programs—footwear, jogging suits, or sweatshirts, for example. There were orders for 1 million jogging suits, 1 million shoes, 1 million notebooks. These groups had collective technical assistance provided in these common spaces."

The Purpose Has Evolved over Time. Sigisfredo Velásquez, the municipal official responsible for the industrial park, says that the park has changed from one used exclusively by producers to one that boasts showrooms and a lot of sales activity. "One and a half years ago, there were only three shoe stores: Julio Turbo, Primitivo, and Estefani. Now, there must be 48 or 50 sales outlets alongside the production sites."

Local Business People Have a Vision of the Future. Julio Rivas told us about the business strategy of the industrial park's micro- and small footwear businesses. "First, there will be EXPOPYME, a small and medium-sized enterprise exhibition,[8] at which we will launch our new fashions. This event will be held in the industrial park and will be similar to events held in Lima by the large footwear manufacturers. To do this, though, we will need the help of the local government. If it does not help us, we will have to go to the central government, but that's a lot more difficult."

---

[8] As it turned out, EXPOPYME was quite successful. Francisco Rozas from the Organization Commission reports that, "The results of the Second National Fair of Small and Medium-Sized Businesses at VES—EXPOPYME 99—could not have been better. Sales came to $1.5 million. Initially, the fair was to occupy three areas, but more space had to be annexed." At the close of the event, awards were given to a PYME [Small or Medium-Sized Business] businessman of the year, a young business creator, the most entrepreneurial woman, as well as the first PYME to go into the export market.

"Second, we will create a wholesale complex in Villa El Salvador. Trujillo [an important city in northern Peru] is the mecca of footwear production in Peru. Also, the North Cone in Lima has a large market where all shoe models are sold wholesale…These markets have quantity, but not quality—they sell cheap synthetic footwear. We want to make quality footwear and lower our production costs so as to attract the public. Since synthetic shoes are not made here, everyone who comes to VES to buy shoes is looking for leather footwear. That needs to be our distinctive mark and selling point."

State Help Is Still Needed. Julio Rivas notes that help is still needed in terms of technical support and logistics. Also, as he and Sigisfredo Velásquez explain, a manufacturer's certificate of origin for products made and sold in VES would be very useful. Such a certificate would reassure potential customers, as Rivas points out: "Why is this key? Because we are visited daily by approximately 200 buyers for footwear alone. We have to offer clients a good quality product so they will come back for more. If a merchant sells a buyer a poor quality product, he may never come back. We don't want this to happen, so here the municipality must play an important role." In this scheme, the municipality's role would be to grant a license to merchants with the prior approval of the sector's trade association, which would ensure that certain quality standards are met by the business seeking the license. Only businesses holding such a license would be entitled to issue a manufacturer's certificate of origin for their products.

Institutional Agreements in a Smaller Park

The maintenance of a residential group's central park is a good indicator of the level of organization in each neighborhood. Parks in adjacent residential groups may have very different levels of maintenance: a public space that lacks maintenance denotes a community with little organization.

Maintaining a park is a community effort involving many actors. The park of Residential Group 20 in Sector 3 is better equipped than others in VES. It has a UNICEF-supported preschool; a sports court built under the temporary employment program of the Alan García administration; and another sports facility, on which we will focus in more detail.

Efraín Sánchez, the general secretary of Group 20, told us about the institutional coordination and lobbying that made the sports facility possible. "This sports facility was part of the Peruvian-German sports agreement, which was signed when Orrego was metropolitan mayor of Lima [1981–83]. Back then, there was an agreement between the Federal

Republic of Germany and the Lima municipality to build sports facilities. In Lima, about 20 multi-use sports courts were built. Some were also built in Arequipa, Huancayo, and other provinces. This agreement stated that facilities would be built with materials purchased with German aid and labor provided by the community. Germany also trained sports promoters and coaches, because the goal was really to put these sports facilities to use. In each sports facility built, a competition was held for resident youngsters to select people to train as sports promoters. Two promoters were required for each facility. I was one of the promoters for our facility."

The use of floodlights for nighttime activities allows sports teams, and not teenage gangs, to enjoy this space at night. Sánchez notes, "We have achieved this by getting our sports events sponsored by the municipality, NGOs, and other institutions. Before organizing an event, we approach companies for support, in exchange for an endorsement. Last year, for example, the newspaper *Todo Sport* sponsored us; this year, the newspaper *La República* decided to do the same. Our sponsors were able to help us get reflectors and lampposts, and we make arrangements to get the energy from Luz del Sur." The lighting of this sports facility is the outcome of an agreement between residents, the electricity company, and the municipality. The cost of the electricity consumed is billed to all residents, in the public lighting bill.

Various actors have intervened in developing this park. They are not the same actors that have intervened in the more than 150 parks of VES, but one actor is always the same—the local population, which collectively appropriates the public space. As in the case of Residential Group 20, the external supporting actors do not just provide funds for the development of community activities. They are also parties to activities and institutional agreements such as the following:

- The construction of the sports facility, through an agreement between the German government and its Peruvian counterpart institutions
- The organization of sporting activities at the neighborhood and district level
- Getting their sports festivals sponsored, through agreements with newspapers such as *La República* and *Todo Sport*
- Using sponsorship funds to buy posts and floodlights for the sports court, through an agreement with the municipality and local ABCO
- Connecting the floodlights to the electricity grid and metering and billing their electricity consumption, through an agreement with the Luz del Sur electricity company.

Anyone who has organized a social or sporting activity knows that even the simplest agreements with neighbors, companies, and institutions require much work and experience. What we find in VES is a culture of agreements among different social actors.

Actors—and Actresses

Municipal official Néstor Ríos says, "When we refer to social actors in Villa El Salvador, we cannot forget to talk about the women. The Fujishock brought about very hard times. [See box 10-10.] Women such as those in the Women's Federation of Villa El Salvador (FEPOMUVES) took the initiative in feeding the population. Even the women who did not belong to organizations, such as my mother, had to be very creative in order to save their families from hunger. Potatoes are our staple, but they were scarce, so cassava was used instead. New dishes were invented, such as fish cau cau."

Ríos's remark is equally valid for all the difficult times faced in VES. Women are always on the frontlines. Women of the federation and residential group organizations took the lead in the confrontations with the government during the struggle for water in the 1970s and with security forces and Sendero Luminoso during the difficult period of terrorist activity in the second half of the 1980s and first half of the 1990s.

Design and Technology

Urban Design

Two characteristics of VES urban design encouraged residents' participation:

1. As in most of the pueblos jovenes formed since 1961, an urbanization plan has been in place since the beginning of land occupation. Residents know the hierarchy and the width of the roads, neighborhood zoning requirements, and what lands are reserved for future urban development. Individual plots are surveyed and beaconed, and public and private spaces are clearly demarcated. VES was no exception to this rule.
2. The plan of Villa El Salvador defined a neighborhood, the residential group, that lies somewhere between a typical city block and a large-scale residential development. Each of the more than 100 residential groups was conceived on a scale that allowed families to appropriate this space: 384 families were distributed in 16 blocks. A health center, preschool, and sports area are in the middle of each residential group, in a central park. Each residential group occu-

Box 10-10. Confronting Crisis

VES's tradition of participation is well known. It was put to the test in the early 1990s, when Villa El Salvador suffered attacks of terrorist violence and Peru went through the Fujimori administration's structural economic adjustment, known as "Fujishock." This period of crisis strengthened, and tested, alliances as people faced fear and adversity.

Economic Crisis

Former town councilor Genaro Soto observes, "Everyone remembered the rise in prices under the Belaúnde government in the early 1980s, but this time it was worse: people went to the market and came back crying because they didn't have enough money to buy food. María Elena Moyano and I were selling sugar here in the plaza. There was a line two or three blocks long. An entrepreneur had bought sugar because he knew it was going to be three or four times more expensive after the economic shock plan was announced. Suddenly, people had no money and nothing to eat."

Enriqueta Mesías, schoolteacher and communicator, says, "We realized that with what we had we could not even buy a kilo of potatoes. The people immediately formed a close relationship with the municipality and created a soup kitchen for each residential group. CUAVES requested food from the government, which helped, but everything was channeled through a mixed commission with CUAVES and municipal representatives. The church also played an important role. The commissions in the residential groups were made up of representatives from the municipality, CUAVES, the church, and FEPOMUVES. We had to create or improve many community soup kitchens, since the existing dining rooms could not meet the needs of 360 families. Everybody would show up to cook; the neighbors would bring firewood and chop potatoes."

Violence

Former mayor Yoni Rodríguez notes, "Villa El Salvador was one of the places chosen by the Sendero Luminoso to carry out its activity. Its objective was to get rid of community leaders considered anti-revolutionary. This caused a wave of violence without precedent. Some of their crimes had national resonance, such as the murder of district lieutenant-mayor María Elena Moyano, and the attempt on the life of Michel Azcueta, probably the most well-known district leader. They killed police officers, María Elena Moyano, her successor, and the Parents' Association president."

Former leader Alfonso Cotera adds, "In Villa, the population and leaders were between two fires, the Sendero killers and the military, who would put people in jail or accuse them of subversion. So, people lived in fear."

Rodríguez agrees. "Those two years were very difficult. We had to go wherever the Sendero Luminoso appeared to keep people from being afraid, to tell them, 'Look, we're here, we're not afraid.'"

pies an area of 8.4 hectares. The local ABCO has taken the residential group as its basis. Elsewhere in Peru, local organization is by city block or at the level of the whole settlement, with no intermediate organizational levels. The neighborhood scale is missing. In VES, on the contrary, the neighborhood scale is very much present, through the residential group. This has permitted VES to combine the hierarchy of space with the organizational hierarchy of participation, which has proven to be a very important factor in generalizing participation in development (see Riofrío 1996).

It was not enough to create an intermediate residential module between the city as a whole and the block. Such a module must be carefully designed so as to fulfill the dual purpose of encouraging the participatory appropriation of space and constituting a clearly defined level in the urban hierarchy. In Huayacán, another important area of low-income urbanization in Lima, the residential module is for 60 families rather than VES's 384, but it has achieved the same results. In the Pachacamac settlement—part of the VES district—and in Canto Grande, east of Lima, the results were different. In these cases, the urban design sought to increase the density of occupation through the use of footpaths and small lots. This did indeed increase the initial density with horizontal occupation, but it is a model that precludes further densification without crowding. In Pachacamac, the development of nonresidential activities such as markets, which was not taken into consideration by the initial design, has already congested the narrow streets. The urban design of VES, based on universal vehicle access, wide streets, and relatively large lots, will allow a much higher final density of occupation—with much better quality of life.

Small Solid Waste Collection Companies

The story of the Pachacamac sector, where one-fifth of VES residents live, is a revealing example of residents' participation in service provision. Four small garbage collection companies have done business in the Pachamac sector since 1990. The municipality has now decided to expand collection services using this model, due to the many advantages it has. The cleaning companies use nonmotorized tricycles, an efficient and cost-effective option for the collection of domestic solid wastes in areas with low waste density and difficult road access. From the selection and training of staff to the final disposal of waste, the logistics of organizing this service involved all the problems of setting up any economic operation. The key lesson of this activity is that these service providers continued to operate, even under adverse conditions, when the municipality decided not to pay them. The system survived, even if just barely, by charging residents directly for garbage collection.

Toward 1990, four local microenterprises were organized with support from the local NGO IPES and obtained service contracts from the municipality. (See box 10-11.) The training the entrepreneurs—mostly women—received was brief, but what they learned in operating these businesses for over 10 years is of immense value to professionals in this field.

When the NGO project ended, just a year later, and the municipality lost interest in garbage collection in the area, the four microenterprises continued on their own. They were successful in a number of ways:

- For several years, they collected garbage in a significant part of the Pachamac sector, with no other municipal support than the authorization to do so.
- They educated families about waste disposal. Families are now used to deliver their domestic wastes properly packed, and they take out their wastes at specific times.
- They developed original ways to bill and collect payment for collection services, while hardly anyone in VES paid for conventional waste collection service, even in those areas where it worked.
- They made efforts to ensure an appropriate final disposal of waste, by concentrating it in one point and renting a truck to take it to the metropolitan landfill.
- They opened up the market so that the municipality could develop it.
- They had enough income to remain in the market on their own for six long years.

When the municipality, six years down the road, realized that the system was working well and sought to develop and extend garbage collection services using the microenterprises as a model, the partners:

- Helped the technicians establish collection routes and other operational details
- Showed infinite patience vis-à-vis officials and technicians who believed they knew what they were doing
- Provided unpaid labor-hours to organize things so that services would be extended.

New Services for the New City: An Internet Café

Villa El Salvador is not only a neighborhood; it is a city. Its urban characteristics—those of a planned *ciudad popular*—have generated partici-

Box 10-11. Lessons in Organization

We had an enlightening conversation with some of the partners of Virgen del Chapi and Nuevo Amanecer, two garbage collection microenterprises.

Partner 1: At the beginning of the project, in 1990, we enrolled because of the advertisements placed by the municipality, [the NGO] IPES, and the church. And then we took the training, which lasted about a week if I recall correctly…There was an evaluation and we qualified to enter the service. Then we began to work directly with the municipality, hired as a company.

At the beginning, the municipality kept its end of the bargain, issuing the bills, collecting payments from users and paying the microenterprises. After a while, though, the municipality lost interest in the scheme and stopped paying the concessionaires, which produced a crisis. The most entrepreneurial of the microenterprises decided to continue providing services and charge for them on their own.

Partner 2: We worked for eight months with the municipality; at the beginning it worked well, but then there was a decline. There was no money, so we could not work anymore.

Partner 3: What were we going to do in this situation? We had to fight back and look for areas that agreed to pay for our services. We had to enter new areas. We needed to raise cash to be able to rent a truck for the final disposal.

Partner 2: There was quite a variation in our earnings because we needed to cover the cost of the truck and our salary, and there were months when we couldn't cover it. We ended up earning just 40 soles a month. Most of us wanted to leave the business.

Partner 1: We were going to return the tricycles, but I said, "This can't be, we have to fight. If we return the tricycles, it means that the business is taken away from us. So, I'm going to keep the four tricycles."

Partner 2: In Pachacamac, there was no public solid waste collection service, so we requested a concession. An agreement with the mayor was what let us work in the area.

Their independent activity lasted until 1997, the year the municipality decided to resume its support and expand the concession system so that the microenterprises could render services to all Pachacamac. Supervisión y Servicios, a formal sector management services company, has been hired to take charge of administration because the municipality believed that the microenterprises did not have the necessary capacity. Since then, the municipality has taken a more active role, because it understands that an active partnership between the municipal authority and microenterprises in the private sector may be a good way to provide this service. However, not all problems have been solved. Collection has increased quickly, and management capacity has not improved at the same pace. Nevertheless, the dialogue between the municipality and the microenterprises continues. The latter are glad that the authorities have decided to expand services based on their model to other low-density areas in the district. The relationship between authorities and local enterprises is egalitarian, as the following dialogue shows.

Question: What are the advantages and disadvantages of working with an outside company such as Supervisión y Servicios? What function does this company currently have?

Municipal official: It is involved in administration, management, and operations. In terms of operation, they have a lot of experience.

Partner 2: Actually, we do everything. We are the ones involved in operations.

Municipal official: But not the zone design…

All: We have done the zone design.

Municipal official: But with them, isn't it true?

Partner 1: No. We are the ones who know the field. They know the field by doing drawings, but you can't really work like that.

Question: Would it be difficult for you to assume the administrative functions? Would you have to hire somebody?

Partner 2: Yes, we would have to hire someone, a professional.

Municipal official: We hired Supervisión y Servicios because the microenterprises were not properly incorporated as companies; they could not issue any official receipts. They were incorporated at the start, but, as you heard, for six years they had been working informally.

Partner 3: We went into informality because the attitude that the municipality now has did not exist before. That's why, the municipality was totally irresponsible. It was their fault.

Partner 1: Oh, yes. But we're still here. We held out on our own, and the four microenterprises didn't disappear.

patory development approaches and appropriate technologies that give the lie to those who doubt the urban poor's capacity for development. And a key characteristic of VES's population is that it does not fear innovation.

CECOPRODE-VES, or El Centro (the Center for Popular Communication of Villa El Salvador), has a radio and UHF TV channel that transmits even beyond the district border. In 1999, it launched an Internet café which is now in operation from 9 a.m. until 11 p.m. everyday, including Sundays and holidays. One morning during the week, we found 5 boys and 14 girls navigating the Internet.

Francisco Ticona, who is in charge of this activity, notes, "In the afternoons, from 3 p.m. until 10 p.m., the cabin is full. It's a good way to use spare time, which we want to promote, at a time when gangs are multiplying in Lima…The demand is bigger than the supply. We're now seeking donations of computers because we can't afford to take out a loan in dollars. We also assist users who don't know how to navigate or how to open a Hotmail account."

The new service is called Tinkuy Internet Café. Ticona continues. "*Tinkuy* is a Quechua word that means encounter. We decided to link VES to the world with the use of this new technology. We want to democratize Internet access for all teenagers and youngsters. Another objective is to use the Internet as a tool in the citizen's participatory process, with the city government, for instance."

The Internet café opened in 1999 with the support of Telefónica del Perú and the newspaper *El Comercio*. Ticona notes that "On February 2, at 6 p.m., we had the first trial connection…Then we gave 10 free days of Internet access to the population. At that time, we had between 900 and 950 users, mostly children, teenagers and youngsters. As of March, we have started to generate income that will gradually cover expenses. We have observed that incomes have gradually increased, and we have lowered our costs. We were charging 3.50 soles[9] an hour; now we're charging 3.00. That has allowed us to extend access and increase users. The people who visit most frequently are 14 to 26 years old. Most are women. There are more women than men, which we didn't think would be the case when we started.

"This is a kind of communal Internet café. We offer three basic services: navigation, which is basically research, locating topics of interest; e-mail accounts; and real-time communication such as chat rooms, which is a coveted service." About similar services in Lima, Ticona explains, "The Internet cafés in downtown Lima are more comfortable and pri-

---

[9]The prevailing exchange rate was 3.30 soles to US$1.

vate; ours is more communal and basic. But we try to compensate by offering quality attention."

Although CECOPRODE still needs external support to run Tinkuy, the service has been thought out in an entrepreneurial manner. The estimates for the number of machines and working hours needed to make this Internet café a profitable business have already been made. Ticona says, "With now have nine computers. With 10 computers, we can self-finance our service; with 20 computers, it would be profitable, and the demand is there. However, it's difficult to obtain machines with our own resources. We have to look outside for donations of used computers. We want to propose a project to see if someone would be interested in supporting it. However, I have the impression that development aid institutions and foundations give more support to projects linked to extreme poverty and health, not to education and learning." Ticona continues, "CECOPRODE has always been interested in using information technology in development. In 1997, the first automatic bibliographic search service was inaugurated through Micro Isis, which was donated by UNESCO in cooperation with the Ricardo Palma library of the municipality of Miraflores [a wealthy district of Lima]. We also partnered with the Population Council in an Internet-based information project on reproductive health for youngsters."

The demand for Internet access in VES is also driven by other factors besides education and the desire youths have to be connected to the global village. Many local residents have family members who have left Peru as immigrants, mostly to Europe and the United States. Ticona says, "Ninety percent of our users use e-mail. Many people with relatives in the United States use the service every other day because it's so economical."

Telefónica del Perú estimates that there are approximately 400,000 low-income Internet users in the country, a figure that will continue to grow.

Home Improvement Efforts

The Center for Development Studies and Promotion (Desco), a Peruvian NGO that has provided support to the community and the municipality in VES for many years, had a project that provided technical and financial support for families to build one or more rooms, adding new floors to existing houses. This residential densification project allowed those who build in stages to obtain microcredit through a conventional bank. Even though the project established a proven system and delinquency in the portfolio was minimal, the private bank who had partnered with Desco eventually withdrew from the scheme, probably due to a lack of interest in this low-income clientele, thus affecting those who needed credit the most.

Credit is not the only difficulty. Low-income people's homes usually need repairs and structural strengthening before additional rooms can be added. However, there are no technical support systems for those working on improving their own homes, and many municipalities do not issue construction permits in popular districts or pueblos jovenes. The municipality of VES and Desco have begun to establish a municipal service for housing permits and building regularization. Families that want regularization can have plans of existing structures recorded in the Urban Real Estate Registry. In addition to the registry document, the municipality will issue to families a "quality assurance document" with recommendations for resolving structural and design problems before expanding the house.

Scale and Sustainability

Villa El Salvador has the same characteristics as any other Peruvian ciudad popular. Its population is basically the same as that in the rest of Lima and Peru, except that its people are a little poorer. Nor is VES insulated from the country's political and economic situation. What does make VES different are the goals proposed at its inception. VES is about building a *city*, not just another low-income neighborhood. It is about generating a *process*, not just another project. VES families were part of this process from the beginning. The scale of the process and the mechanisms used for sustainability were also present since the beginning.

Three main factors ensure the scale and sustainability of the VES process. The first of these is a sense of the future, a sense was expressed in all the interviews we conducted. As former mayor Michel Azcueta explains (see box 10-12), "I have always said that we have to incorporate in all our work what we in pedagogy call the 'element of the future.' I believe that every plan is linked to the future because that is what a plan is. People must be convinced that there is a future for them…We have to find out what elements of the future people bring within themselves, what their idea of progress is…I believe that this is what motivates the people of VES. This is a town that jumps into the future. Even the poorest people here believe that there are opportunities for progress and that Villa El Salvador and the community have a future. We have to start from that concrete feeling, which is not limited to their most urgent needs, but encompasses all they want to accomplish and are convinced they will accomplish. In VES's 30 years of existence, there have been more triumphs than failures. Psychologically, this has great importance. I believe it's the small triumphs that make people believe they can accomplish greater things."

> **Box 10-12. "El Profesor" Michel Azcueta**
>
> VES's first district mayor, Michel Azcueta (who served a later additional term in 1996–98 after an attempt on his life by the Sendero Luminoso), had much to do with the development of Villa El Salvador's particular style of governance. Azcueta, known in Lima simply as "Michel," was a professor in the Fe y Alegría high school from its foundation until attempts on his life put the lives of his students in danger. His personality and graduate studies abroad have made him an excellent spokesperson for his community.
>
> Azcueta says, "We have always clearly proposed our objectives to the many central governments we have had. Our trick is to stay ahead of government proposals. For example, the military will pave roads anywhere they want to. We told the general that he could pave Avenida María Reiche and the road down to the beach, which is our priority. We told him: 'You are welcome, but you do what we want.' So we stay ahead of the game. At the political level, it is important that everyone benefits from a proposal—so we try to make sure that politicians do get their political dividends, but only by supporting things that are really useful to the community and respond to real demand."

The second element is the local population itself and its willingness to participate. The user, resident, or customer is a key actor in the development process. If there is no participation, there is no sustainability to development; there is no way to imagine a sustainable project that is not embedded in the social process. Sustainability is impossible without the initiative of those who remain after the project's implementation. It is important to remember that once a project ends, only two actors remain in the area: the population and the local government.

> LAST NIGHT, I WAS TALKING TO SOME OF THE FOUNDERS OF VES. THEY FEEL THAT THE MOST IMPORTANT THING IS THAT THE TOWNSPEOPLE MAY DECIDE WHAT TO DO. IT DOESN'T MATTER IF THEY MAKE MISTAKES. EVEN IF THEY DO, THEY WILL LEARN FROM THEIR MISTAKES.
> —*Juan Arbañil, VES Leader*

VES's third defining element was the direct participation of high-level Peruvian authorities at the time of the city's establishment. Even though the concept of enabling strategies had not yet been developed, there was a sense that VES development would rely on a different kind of relationship between the authorities and the population. There was a collective enthusiasm and sense of purpose that were part of the revolutionary political project of the then-ascendant military regime. Federico Velarde, a former member of the Velasco Alvarado military government, explains the government's attitude toward VES: "There is an old tradition of direct execution of infrastructure by the military in Peru which made them roll up their sleeves and go for it."

Even now, over 30 years later, the population of VES treasures the memory of their special relationship with President Velasco, and the town's main avenue is proudly named after him. This connection was immeasurably important, but even so, it is now possible, in a less ideological age, to identify many components of the VES experience that depended more on common sense and willpower than ideology, and hold promise for the future.

This experience did not happen in other urban areas. VES is also special in that it always had enough space, and, because that space was not immediately developed, residents had the time and opportunity to envision their city's future. In developments for low-income people in cities where space is at a premium, as in most big cities in Latin America, minimum standards are used for space and infrastructure, and this may eventually translate into crowding and become a limitation for development.

Conclusions

The residents' efforts in Villa El Salvador have produced striking results, but there is still much to do and no guarantee that these results will last. Many local initiatives in VES have been hampered by the lack of urban planners and other badly needed professionals. The VES process has lacked a core of professional people—not working as volunteers, but as paid development professionals. Every strictly voluntary effort has a touch of amateurism which often causes even the best ideas to flounder, and VES is no exception to this rule. With first-class training and full-time professionals, the efforts of the residents could have been channeled into a much more efficient and effective process.

Both Peru in general and VES in particular are examples of the Latin American paradigm of societies whose populations have had, as in Turner's phrase, "the freedom to build." It has been, however, the freedom of one left to one's own devices, lacking the support and protection of a financial, administrative, and technical structure. Other than the initial support of the military and the respect that the current municipal government has for the population's initiatives, no real systems are in place that could transform local effort into long-term policy. What if there were appropriate financial mechanisms for the development of microenterprises for housing construction? What if there were technicians and professionals of sufficient quantity and quality to ensure technically sound support to the population? What if official policies for the city of Lima—with more than 7 million habitants, 50 percent of them living in poor neighborhoods—took into account what has been learned at VES?

The VES experience suggests some elements to guide policy in urban upgrading initiatives, as follows:

1. **An enabling authority that supports the private initiatives of families and does not abandon its responsibilities during the development process is crucial.** The significance of government's facilitating role can be seen in VES's history. At the beginning, the central government authorities created appropriate conditions for the participatory process. Even when the political winds shifted, that process continued, albeit with much difficulty. During the 1980s, it was the municipality that inherited the tradition of working with the community, but its capacity for mobilizing resources and creating a favorable environment for development was limited and only reached the district level. Moreover, there were no metropolitan or national authorities taking an interest or exercising influence on local affairs. This lack of interest and support from the authorities explains many of the current weaknesses in the VES process.

    Facilitation is an active, not a passive, role. The Villa El Salvador experience demonstrates this, revealing the limitations of processes in which, although the participation of the population in the development of the city is exemplary, true development has not been achieved. VES has generated a kind of social participation that has not always happened in other cities, but has lacked the appropriate support and enabling environment for its projects, and appropriate technical management. The efficiency and effectiveness of the process would have been better with a real facilitating environment, and not just piecemeal and erratic support. Private efforts—and that is what the efforts of the community are—are not sufficient to ensure the success of this kind of enterprise.

2. **The desire to innovate is more important than any specific innovative plan.** The important thing about VES is not really the content of the numerous innovative initiatives that can be observed there. For one thing, some of these proposals are only applicable to the Peruvian reality or to a specific geographic or social environment. But all of these initiatives, from the collection of municipal revenues by local residents to the establishment of an Internet café, have as their point of origin a quest for solutions that are appropriate to the local reality and its resource constraints.

The remarkable thing about VES is that it continues to generate innovation and appropriate proposals. This innovative mentality is a result of a participatory process in urban development, in which a great number of social actors share a vision or development plan. The most critical social agreement in VES was its founding one, the determination to build this town. The term "urban poverty" is often resented by VES residents, who do not want to be seen only as "the poor." For them, as it should be for development professionals, it is useful to consider poverty a temporary situation which they are determined to overcome.

Appendix A
Sample Strategic Plan Outline

Chapter 1. General Framework
A. Historical Background and General Diagnosis
    1. Background: Migration and Urban Marginalization
        a. Immigration and Population Growth
        b. Informal Settlements as an Alternative
    2. General Diagnosis
    3. Poverty Maps and Indicators
    4. Life in West Juárez
        a. Population, Housing and Environmental Features
            (1) Population
            (2) Housing
            (3) The Local Environment
        b. Levels of Income and Types of Employment
        c. Coverage of Public Services
            (1) Water Supply and Sewerage
            (2) Light and Power
            (3) Natural Gas
            (4) Road System
        d. Current Cost Recovery Strategies and Levels of Willingness and Ability to Pay for Public Services
        e. State Presence and Urban Equipment
            (1) Education
            (2) Health

Note: This material is taken from the strategic plan developed for the proposed upgrading program in Ciudad Juárez, Mexico.

            (3) Recreation and Sports
            (4) Other Services
        f. Schools in the Area
        g. Gender Issues
    5. Strategic Context
        a. Government Actions in West Ciudad Juárez
        b. A New Perspective for Municipal and State Government
        c. A Sector Strategy for the Western Zone
        d. The Necessity of an Integrated Program
B. Conceptual Summary of the Program
    1. Development Objectives
    2. Specific Objectives
    3. General Program Description
    4. Program Components
        a. Focus Area
        b. Criteria for Beneficiary Eligibility
        c. Types of Eligible Projects
        d. General Criteria for Eligibility of Projects
        e. Co-Financing
        f. Social Evaluation
C. Available Experience
    1. Present Experiences with Community Participation in Ciudad Juárez
        a. Social Infrastructure
        b. Economic Infrastructure
        c. Water, Sanitation and Environmental Infrastructure
    2. The Role of Government, Communities and Private Sector
        a. Municipal Government
        b. Communities
        c. Private Sector
    3. Evaluation of Community Participation Experiences
    4. Existing Demand for Participatory Upgrading Projects
    5. Existing Participatory Upgrading Programs and Projects and Their Potential Relationship with Proposed Program
D. Program Rationale
    1. Program Contributions to Communities
    2. Lessons Learned and their Incorporation to the Program
        a. A Special Focus on Marginalized Areas
        b. A Decentralized and Autonomous Program
        c. A Highly Participatory Program That Is Responsive to Needs
        d. A Special Focus on the Needs and Participation of Women
        e. A Special Focus on the Local Living Environment of the Poor
        f. Reduction of the Need for Resettlement
        g. Reduction of the Cost of Service Extension

3. Program Added Value
E. Description of Main Risks and Critical Assumptions of the Program
   1. Social Aspects
   2. Environmental Aspects
   3. Technical Aspects
   4. Financial Aspects
   5. Economical Aspects
   6. Political Aspects
   7. Need for Resettlement and Resettlement Strategy
   8. Cost Recovery and Other Factors for Ensuring the Maintenance of Program Benefits

Chapter 2. Institutional, Legal, and Financial Arrangements
A. Institutional and Financial Arrangements
   1. A Trust Fund for the Management of Program Resources
   2. A Civil Association for Channeling Resources to Communities
B. Description of Organizations Responsible for Program Implementation, Their Functions and Responsibilities
C. Program Implementation Process
   1. Design and Preparation
   2. Coordination
   3. Implementation
   4. Supervision
   5. Monitoring and Evaluation
D. Legal Framework
   1. Interinstitutional Arrangements
   2. Legal Structure for Trust Fund Operations
   3. Required Agreements Between and Among Participating Organizations

Chapter 3. Activities and Operational Procedures of the Program
A. Evaluation of Organizational Capacity at the Local Level
B. Social Intermediation and Social Communication
   1. Intermediation and Communication Strategy
   2. Developing Indicators and Monitoring Dissemination and Communication
   3. Evaluation of Dissemination and Communication Campaign
   4. Supporting Project Identification by Communities and Their Participation in Implementation
C. Capacity Building Inside the Program
   1. Capacity Building Strategy
   2. Capacity Building Organizations
   3. Some Aspects to be Considered in Capacity Building
   4. Monitoring and Evaluating Capacity Building

D. Project Formulation and Approval Process
   E. Program Implementation Control and Evaluation Plan
   F. Criteria and Procedures for Allocation of Funds to Projects
   G. Selecting and Contracting Project Implementation; External Supervision
      1. Selection Policies and Contracting
      2. Activities of the Selection and Contracting Process
      3. Implementation Norms and Procedures According to Project Type
   H. Project Implementation and Monitoring
   I. Operation and Maintenance Following a Project
      1. Economic Characteristics of Operation and Maintenance
      2. Management Requirements of Operation and Maintenance
      3. Monitoring and Evaluating Operation and Maintenance
   J. Ex-Post Project Evaluation
   K. Administrative and Financial Aspects
      1. Annual Work Plan and Budget
      2. Procurement Procedures
      3. Disbursement Procedures
      4. Accounting and Auditing Procedures
      5. Personnel Management Procedures
      6. Operational Support Systems (e.g., Management Information Systems)

Chapter 4. General Aspects
   A. Goals to Be Reached
      1. Number of Communities and Beneficiaries to Be Reached
      2. Number and Type of Investments to Be Made and Estimated Average Project Cost
   B. Procurement and Contracts
      1. Description of Methods of Selection and Their Applicability
      2. Number of Expected Selections by Method With Their Estimated Cost
   C. General Program Timetable
   D. Program Uses and Sources of Funding
   E. A Vision of the Future of the Program: Perspectives for Long-Term Development

Appendix B
Sample Operating Manual Outline

Prologue
Glossary of Terms
Part A. General Aspects
    Chapter 1.   Goals, Components, and Main Actors Participating in CIF
        1.1   Objectives
        1.2   Project Components
        1.3   Main Actors Participating in CIF
    Chapter 2.   Project Conditions
        2.1   Target Areas
        2.2   Criteria for Eligibility of Beneficiaries
        2.3   Types of Eligible Projects
        2.4   General Criteria for Eligibility of Projects
        2.5   Co-financing
    Chapter 3.   Organic and Functional Characteristics of the Program Management Unit (UCP)
        3.1   Organic Structure
        3.2   Functions of the Different Sections
        3.3   Interinstitutional Relationships
    Chapter 4.   Participatory Methodology of the Program
Part B. Project Activities and Operational Procedures
    Chapter 1.   Evaluation of the Capacity of Organizations at the Local Level
    Chapter 2.   Social Intermediation and Communication

Note: This material is taken from the operating manual developed for the proposed community infrastructure fund in Ciudad Juárez, Mexico.

- 2.1 Introduction
- 2.2 Objectives of Social Intermediation
- 2.3 Social Intermediation and Communication Strategy
- 2.4 Stages of Social Intermediation
- 2.5 Results to be Achieved from Above Activities
- 2.6 Presentation of CIF to Municipal Government and to Public and Private Institutions
- 2.7 Interinstitutional Communications Flows
- 2.8 Project Identification by Communities

Chapter 3. Capacity Building Within the Project
- 3.1 Capacity Building Strategy
- 3.2 Institutional Coverage
- 3.3 Coverage of the Project Cycle
- 3.4 Strategy for Replication

Chapter 4. The Project Cycle
- 4.1 Introduction
- 4.2 Studies of Local Reality and Identification of Priority Problems
- 4.2.1 Diagnosis of Present Reality
- 4.2.2 Analysis of Information From the Diagnosis
- 4.2.3 Two Methods for Identifying and Quantifying Our Main Problems
- 4.2.4 Analysis of Causal Factors and Their Interrelationship
- 4.2.5 Identification of Possible Alternatives
- 4.2.6 Selection of Project Ideas by Priority
- 4.2.7 Synthesis of the Work Done
- 4.3 Proposal Definition and Formulation
- 4.3.1 Development Objectives
- 4.3.2 Specific or Immediate Objectives
- 4.3.3 Expected Project Results
- 4.3.4 Project Activities
- 4.3.5 Project Resource and Input Needs
- 4.3.6 Project Matrix
- 4.3.7 Guide for Presentation of Project Proposals to UCP
- 4.3.8 Complementary Documentation
- 4.4 Evaluation of Project Proposals by UCP
- 4.4.1 Introduction
- 4.4.2 General Operational Process for Proposal Evaluation
- 4.4.3 Meaning of Proposal Evaluation
- 4.5 Criteria for Project Selection
- 4.5.1 Social Criteria
- 4.5.2 Gender Criteria
- 4.5.3 Technical Criteria

- 4.5.4 Environmental Criteria
- 4.5.5 Economic Criteria
- 4.5.6 Community Contributions
- 4.5.7 Payment Mechanism for Community Contributions
- 4.6 Selection and Contracting of Project Implementation and Technical Assistance
- 4.6.1 Selection and Contracting Policies
- 4.6.2 Activities for Selection and Contracting
- 4.6.3 Norms and Procedures for Direct Selection and Contracting
- 4.6.4 Norms and Procedures for Selection and Contracting Through an Invitation to Bid (Closed Bidding Process)
- 4.6.5 Norms and Procedures for Selection and Contracting Through an Open Bidding Process
- 4.6.6 Norms and Procedures for Implementation of the World Bank Learning and Innovation Loan (LIL) Modality
- 4.6.7 Norms and Procedures for Selecting and Contracting Consultants
- 4.7 Project Implementation and Monitoring
- 4.7.1 Norms and Procedures for Project Implementation and Monitoring
- 4.7.2 Methodology for Project Implementation and Monitoring
- 4.8 Operation and Maintenance Following a Project
- 4.8.1 Economic Characteristics of Operation and Maintenance
- 4.8.2.1 Management Requirements of Operation and Maintenance
- 4.8.3 Monitoring and Evaluating Operation and Maintenance
- 4.9 Ex-Post Project Evaluation
- 4.9.1 Introduction
- 4.9.2 Some Practical Applications of Ex-Post Evaluation
- 4.9.3 Types of Ex-Post Evaluation
- 4.9.4 Methodological Steps

Part C. Administrative and Financial Aspects
- Chapter 1. Annual Program Work Plan and Budget
  - 1.1 Preparation of Quarterly and Annual Program Work Plans and Budgets
  - 1.2 Institutional Responsibilities and Applicable Formats
  - 1.3 Procedures for Approval by the Trust Fund's Steering Committee
  - 1.4 Procedures for Revision and Correction of Work Plans
- Chapter 2. Program Procurement and Purchases
  - 2.1 Basic UCP Purchase Goals
  - 2.2 Arrangements and Procedures for Project Procurement and Purchases

2.3   Purchase of Goods and Services
2.4   Contracting Consultancy Services
2.5   Revision of Purchases by the World Bank
2.6   Methodology for Procurement and Purchases
2.7   Process of Tender Selection
2.8   Acquisition of Technical Assistance and Rules for Contracting Consultants

Chapter 3. Disbursement
3.1   UCP Bank Account
3.2   Transfer of Funds From Account at Central Bank to Community Accounts
3.3   Payments of Funds from Community Accounts to Project Contractors and/or Building Materials and Equipment Suppliers
3.4   Payment Methods
3.5   Justification and Documentation Required for Payments

Chapter 4. Accounting and Auditing
4.1   Responsabilities of the UCP Accounting Unit
4.2   Reporting Obligations
4.3   Accounting System
4.4   Auditing System

Chapter 5. Administrative Procedures
5.1   Procedures for Hiring Staff
5.2   Contract and Employment Terms
5.3   Administrative Rules for Staff

Chapter 6. Operational Support Systems
6.1   Management Information System

Annex 1.   Percentage of Co-Financing per Sector or Category of Investment
Annex 2.   Level of Poverty and Marginalization by Sub-Zone
Annex 3.   UCP Organizational Chart
Annex 4.   UCP Functions, Job Descriptions of the Main Posts and Operating Budget
Annex 5.   Flowchart of Program Operations
Annex 6.   Community Diagnosis Checklist
Annex 7.   Contract Template
Annex 8.   Interinstitutional Agreement Template
Annex 9.   Capacity Building Modules
Annex 10. Report Template
Annex 11. Flowchart and Description of the Project Cycle
Annex 12. Applicable Technical Standards

References

Abbott, John. 1996. *Sharing the City: Community Participation in Urban Management.* London: Earthscan.
———. 1997. "Governance and Participation." Paper presented at the International Conference on Urban Poverty, Governance and Participation: Practical Approaches to Urban Poverty Reduction—Towards Cities for the New Generations, United Nations Centre for Human Settlements (Habitat), Florence, Italy, November 9–13.
Acioly, Claudio C., Jr. 1992. "Settlement Planning and Assisted Self-Help Housing: An Approach to Neighborhood Upgrading in a Sub-Saharan African City." Delft, Netherlands: Delft University of Technology.
Aina, Tade Akin. 1997. "Governance and Urban Poverty in Africa: Challenges for Policy and Action." Paper presented at the International Conference on Urban Poverty, Governance and Participation: Practical Approaches to Urban Poverty Reduction—Towards Cities for the New Generations, United Nations Centre for Human Settlements (Habitat), Florence, Italy, November 9–13.
Alberdi, Baralides. 1999. "La Financiación a la Vivienda en América Latina. Taller de Mejoramiento Urbano en América Latina." Paper presented at the World Bank Scaling up Urban Upgrading in Latin America Workshop, Washington, DC, September 13–17.
Altaf, Mir Anjum, Haroon Jamal, and Dale Whittington. 1992. *Willingness to Pay for Water in Rural Punjab, Pakistan.* Water and Sanitation Report No. 4. Washington, DC: UNDP–World Bank Water and Sanitation Program.
Angel, Shlomo. 1998. "A Housing Policy and Institutional Development Program for Nicaragua." Research paper. Washington, DC: Inter-American Development Bank.
———. 1999. "Upgrading Indicators: Measuring the Performance of National Urban Upgrading Programs." Paper presented at the World Bank Scaling up Urban Upgrading in Latin America Workshop, Washington, DC, September 13–17.

Angel, Shlomo, and Stephen K. Mayo. 1993. *Housing: Enabling Markets to Work.* World Bank policy paper with technical supplements. Washington, DC: World Bank.

Ardila, Sergio, Ricardo Quiroga, and William J. Vaughan. 1998. "A Review of the Use of Contingent Valuation Methods in Project Analysis at the Inter-American Development Bank." Research paper. Washington, DC: Inter-American Development Bank.

Asian Development Bank. 1993. *Managing Water Resources to Meet Megacity Needs: Proceedings of Regional Consultation.* Manila.

Associazione Volontari per il Servizio Internazionale (AVSI). 1992. "Il Processo di Legalizzazione della Proprietà Della Terra Come Risorsa: Progetto AVSI a Belo Horizonte – Minas Gerais." Research paper. Cesena, Italy.

Auriault, Anne, and Mina Asïdi-Sharouz. n.d. *Assainissement et Développement Urbain: Quartiers d'Afrique Noire, Burkina Faso, Côte d'Ivoire.* Paris: Ministère de la Cooperation and Association Française des Volontaires du Progrès.

Ayala, Josefina Baldó, and Federico Villanueva Brandt. 1996. "Los Barrios Caraqueños: Problemas y Soluciones." Paper presented at Habitat II, the Second United Nations Conference on Human Settlements, Istanbul.

Azcueta, Michel. 1999. "La Dinamica Urbana. El Caso Peruano y los Aportes desde Villa Salvador." Paper presented at the World Bank, Washington, DC.

Barros, M. C. Mendonça de. 1997. "Un Processo di Stabilizzazione Non Lineare." *America Latina* 4(8).

Berghäll, Pii Elina. 1995. *Habitat II and the Urban Economy: A Review of Recent Developments and Literature.* Research paper. Helsinki: United Nations University, World Institute for Development Economics Research.

Bird, R. M. 1997. *Financing Local Services: Patterns, Problems and Possibilities.* Major Report No. 31. Toronto: University of Toronto, Centre for Urban and Community Studies.

Bolaffi, Gabriel. 1975. "Habitação e Urbanismo: o Problema e o Falso Problema." Paper presented to the Housing Symposium at the 27th annual meeting of the Sociedade Brasileira para o Progresso da Ciência, São Paulo.

Brandt, Federico Villanueva, and Josefina Baldó Ayala. 1996. "Local Agency of Urban Development. Community Self-Reliance in Catuche, Caracas." Paper presented at Habitat II, the Second United Nations Conference on Human Settlements, Istanbul.

Bravo, M. A., et al. 1997. "El Programa de Urbanización de El Mezquital, PROUME. Una experiencia de coordinación comunitaria e institucional, y modelo autogestionario para vivir mejor." Evaluation report. Guatemala: COINAP-UNICEF.

Breslin, Edward D. 1999. "Lessons from the Field: Rethinking Community Management for Sustainability." Paper presented at Rural and Peri-Urban Water Supply and Sanitation in South Africa: Appropriate Practice Conference, East London, March 14–17.

Caixa Econômica Federal. 1989. *Manual de Orientação para Execução Racionalizada de Instalações em Intervenções por Ajuda-mútua: Instalações Hidráulico-Sanitárias.* São Paulo: Instituto de Pesquisas Tecnológicas do Estado de São Paulo S.A., Departamento Central de Pesquisas e Extensão Tecnológica.

Campbell, Tim, with Travis Katz. 1996. *The Politics of Participation in Tijuana, Mexico: Inventing a New Style of Governance.* Washington, DC: World Bank.
CERFE. 1995. "Review of Current Global Trends in Economic and Social Development." Report of a research project carried out for the United Nations Centre for Human Settlements (Habitat) in preparation for the Habitat II Conference. Rome.
———. 1998. "Politiche Urbane Brasile: Dossier degli studi preparatory." Research report. Rome.
Chavez, Roberto, Dean Cira, Ivo Imparato, and Teresa Serra. 1999. "Taller de Mejoramiento Urbano en America Latina. Mejoramiento Urbano: Como Pasar a Escala?" Paper presented at the World Bank Scaling up Urban Upgrading in Latin America Workshop, Washington, DC, September 13–17.
Cities Alliance. 1999. *Cities Alliance for Cities without Slums: Action Plan for Moving Slum Upgrading to Scale.* Washington, DC: World Bank/United Nations Centre for Human Settlements (Habitat).
Clarke, Giles. 1994. "Reappraising Urban Planning Process as an Instrument for Sustainable Urban Development and Management." Working paper. Nairobi: Urban Management Programme
Cofino, Roberto Gonzales. 1995. *A Successful Approach to Participation: The World Bank's Relationship with South Africa.* Human Capital Development and Operations Policy Working Papers. Washington, DC: World Bank.
Companhia de Desenvolvimento da Região Metropolitana de Salvador (CONDER). 1998. *Projeto Metropolitano: Investimentos Urbanos na Região Metropolitana de Salvador.* Salvador, Brazil.
Consejo Nacional de la Vivienda. n.d. *Preparación de Planes para Proyectos de Mejoramiento de Desarrollos no Controlados.* Caracas.
Cooperazione Italiana. n.d. *La Struttura e il Modello Operativo di PRODERE. Le Strategie, i Metodi ed i Risultati di un Programma per lo Sviluppo Umano, la Pace e la Democrazia in America Centrale.* Rome.
Cotton, A. P., M. Sohail, and W. K. Tayler. 1998. *Community Initiatives in Urban Infrastructure.* Leicestershire, UK: Loughborough University, Water, Engineering and Development Centre.
de Soto, Hernando. 1989. *The Other Path: The Invisible Revolution in the Third World.* New York: HarperCollins.
Desco. 1998. "Materiales para el Presupuesto Participativo." Study reports for preparation of Villa El Salvador participatory planning. Lima.
Dillinger, William. 1993. *Decentralization and Its Implications for Urban Service Delivery.* Urban Management and Infrastructure Series No. 16. Washington, DC: World Bank.
Duebel, Achim. 1999. "Lowering the Barrier to Formal Housing Finance in Latin America: Policy Issues and Strategy Elements." Paper presented at the World Bank Scaling up Urban Upgrading in Latin America Workshop, Washington, DC, September 13–17.
Economic Commission for Latin America and the Caribbean (ECLAC). 1998. *Statistical Yearbook for Latin America and the Caribbean.* Santiago.
———. 2001. *Statistical Yearbook for Latin America and the Caribbean.* Santiago.

Edwards, Daniel B., and John J. Pettit. 1988. *Facilitator Guide for Conducting a Project Start-up Workshop.* WASH Technical Report No. 41. http://www.dec.org/pdf_docs/pnaaz424.pdf.

Environmental Health Project. 1998. *Building Community Partnerships for Change: The CIMEP Approach.* Special Brochure 1. Washington, DC: U.S. Agency for International Development.

Estache, Antonio. 1995. *Decentralizing Infrastructure: Advantages and Limitations.* Discussion Paper No. 290. Washington, DC: World Bank.

Estache, Antonio, and Sarbajit Sinha. 1995. *Does Decentralization Increase Spending on Public Infrastructure?* Policy Research Working Paper No. 1457. Washington, DC: World Bank.

Federative Republic of Brazil. 1996. "Brazilian National Report." Paper presented at Habitat II, the Second United Nations Conference on Human Settlements, Istanbul.

Fox, William F. 1994. *Strategic Options for Urban Infrastructure Management.* Urban Management and Infrastructure Series No. 17. Washington, DC: World Bank.

FUNDASAL. 1996. "Argoz: An Example of a Large-Scale Private Developer Process." Paper presented at the World Bank Round Table for the Provision of Services for the Urban Poor in Latin America and the Caribbean, El Salvador, December 11–13.

Gilbert, Richard, Don Stevenson, Herbert Girardet, and Richard Stren. 1996. *Making Cities Work: The Role of Local Authorities in the Urban Environment.* London: Earthscan.

Goethert, Reinhard. 1998. Presentation notes to Thematic Group for Services to the Urban Poor, World Bank. Prepared by Special Interest Group in Urban Settlement, School of Architecture and Planning, Massachusetts Institute of Technology.

———. 1999. "Upgrading Urban Communities: A Resource Framework." Paper presented at the World Bank Scaling up Urban Upgrading in Latin America Workshop, Washington, DC, September 13–17.

Goldmark, Lara. 1996. *Servicios de Desarrollo Empresarial: Un Esquema de Análisis.* Washington DC: Inter-American Development Bank. http://www.iadb.org/sds/doc/mic%2D101s.pdf.

Gopal, Gita. 1995. *Bank-Financed Projects with Community Participation: A Manual for Designing Procurement and Disbursement Mechanisms.* Washington, DC: World Bank.

Government of Bolivia, Human Development Ministry, People's Participation Secretariat. 1996a. *Procedure Manual for Surveillance Committees.* La Paz.

———. 1996b. "Notes for District Workshops." La Paz.

Government of the Republic of Italy, Ministry of Foreign Affairs. 1990. *Supporting Primary Environmental Care.* Report of the PEC Workshop, Certosa di Pontignano, Siena, January 29–February 2. Rome: Directorate General for Development Cooperation.

———. 1991. *Primary Environmental Care: Proposte Operative per la Cooperazione Italiana.* Preparatory document for the Second PEC Workshop. Rome: Directorate General for Development Cooperation.

———. 1992. *Primary Environmental Care: Esperienze e Proposte della Cooperazione Italiana*. Report of the Second PEC Workshop, Certosa di Pontignano, Siena, December 1–7, 1991. Rome: Directorate General for Development Cooperation.

Government of the Republic of Zambia. n.d. *Project Implementation Manual*. Lusaka: National Commission for Development Planning, Microprojects Unit.

Gunyon, William. 1998. *India: Making Government Funding Work Harder*. London: WaterAid.

Habitat II. 1996. *Urban Poverty, a World Challenge*. The Recife Declaration. International Meeting on Urban Poverty, Recife, Brazil, March 17–21.

Habitat International Coalition. 1997. *Lecciones & Propuestas: Aprender de los Procesos de Colaboración*. Mexico City.

Hamdi, Nabeel. 1995. *Housing without Houses: Participation, Flexibility, and Enablement*. Exeter, UK: Intermediate Technology Publications.

Hasan, Arif. 1992. *Manual for Rehabilitation Programmes for Informal Settlements Based on the Orangi Pilot Project Model*. Karachi, Pakistan: Orangi Pilot Project Research and Training Institute.

———. 1994. "Options for Urban Poverty Alleviation Actions at Municipal Level for Sukkur (Pakistan)." Report prepared for the Urban Management Programme/United Nations Development Programme Malaysia.

Hentschel, Jesko. 1994. *Does Participation Cost the World Bank More? Emerging Evidence*. Human Resources Development and Operations Policy Working Paper 31. Washington, DC: World Bank.

Huchzermeyer, Marie. 1997. *Towards a New Understanding of the Informal Settlement Phenomenon: Essential Insights of the Search for Successful Intervention and the Transfer of Experience across Developing Countries*. Cape Town: University of Cape Town, Department of Civil Engineering.

Instituto Brasileiro de Geografia e Estatística (IBGE). 1990. *Pesquisa Nactional por Amostra de Domicílios*. Brasília.

———. 1994. *Pesquisa Nactional por Amostra de Domicílios*. Brasília.

———. 1996. *Pesquisa Nactional por Amostra de Domicílios*. Brasília.

Inter-American Development Bank (IDB). 1996. *Involuntary Settlement in IDB Projects*. Washington, DC.

———. 1997a. *IDB Extra 1997: Urban Renaissance in Rio de Janeiro*. Washington, DC.

———. 1997b. *Resource Book on Participation*. Washington, DC.

———. 1998. *Facing up to Inequality in Latin America: Economic and Social Progress*. Washington, DC.

International Forum on Urban Poverty, Special Committee on Children and Youth. 1997 "Proposal on Children and Urban Poverty." Paper presented at the International Conference on Urban Poverty, Governance and Participation: Practical Approaches to Urban Poverty Reduction—Towards Cities for the New Generations, United Nations Centre for Human Settlements (Habitat), Florence, Italy, November 9–13.

IPLANRIO. 1996. *Favela-Bairro: Integrating Slums in Rio de Janeiro*. 3rd ed. Rio de Janeiro.

Isham, Jonathan, Deepa Narayan, and Lant Pritchett. 1994. *Does Participation Improve Project Performance? Establishing Causality with Subjective Data*. Policy Research Working Paper No. 1357. Washington, DC: World Bank.

Jordan, Ricardo. 1997. "Urban Management in Selected Medium-Sized Cities of Latin America and the Caribbean: Proposal for Intervention in Ouro Preto Peripheral Area." Paper presented at the International Conference on Urban Poverty, Governance and Participation: Practical Approaches to Urban Poverty Reduction—Towards Cities for the New Generations, United Nations Centre for Human Settlements (Habitat), Florence, Italy, November 9–13.

Kessides, C. 1997. "World Bank Experience with the Provision of Infrastructure Services for the Urban Poor: Preliminary Identification and Review of Best Practices." Research paper. Washington, DC: World Bank.

Kim, K. H. 1997. "Improving Local Government Finance in a Changing Environment." *Habitat International* 21(1).

Komives, Kristin. 1999. "Water and Sewer Concessions and the Urban Poor: The Aguas del Ilimani Concession in Bolivia." Study report. Washington, DC: World Bank.

Kumar, Krishna. 1993. *Rapid Appraisal Methods*. Washington, DC: World Bank.

Lall, Vinay D., and Stuti Lall. "Shelter and Employment in Informal Cities: Indian Experience." Paper presented at the International Conference on Urban Poverty, Governance and Participation: Practical Approaches to Urban Poverty Reduction—Towards Cities for the New Generations, United Nations Centre for Human Settlements (Habitat), Florence, Italy, November 9–13.

Lee, Kyu Sik, and Roy Gilbert. 1999. *Developing Towns and Cities: Lessons from Brazil and the Philippines*. Washington, DC: World Bank.

León, Shirley Elizabeth Quiñones de. 1998. *Metodología para la Elaboración de Diagnósticos Comunitarios*. Guatemala: World Bank.

Loach, P. W., and M. V. Serra. 1998. *Guatemala Municipal Development Report*. Implementation Completion Report Loan 2972-GU. Washington, DC: World Bank.

Lopes, Juarez Rubens Brandão. 1996. "A Reestruturação Econômica e os Novos Focos da Política Social Urbana." Research paper. Campinas, Brazil: State University of Campinas.

Lungo, Mario, Ninette Morales, Mariam Pérez, Lily Caballero, and Juan Serrarols. 1996. *Centroamerica en Estambul: Los Planes Nacionales de Accion*. San Salvador: Cyted Network, Science and Technology for Development Program.

Lungo, Mario, Martin Rieger, and Roberto Chinchilla. 1997. *Programa de Renovación Urbana Integral – Una Propuesta de Gestion Urbana*. San Salvador: Central American University José Simeón Cañas.

MacDonald, Charles L. 1998. "Economic Analysis: Greater Guatemala City Low-Income Barrios Improvement Project." Study report. Arlington, VA: Development Ideas, Inc.

Magalhães, Sérgio Ferraz. 1999. "The Favela-Bairro Program in the Context of Rio de Janeiro's Housing Policy." Paper presented at the World Bank Scaling up Urban Upgrading in Latin America Workshop, Washington, DC, September 13–17.

Mangin, William, ed. 1970. *Peasants in Cities: Readings in the Anthropology of Urbanization*. Boston: Houghton-Mifflin.

Marcuse, Peter. 1998. "Sustainability Is Not Enough." *Environment and Urbanization* 10(2):103–11.
Mathäus, Horst. 1997. "PRORENDA Slum Upgrading, Rio Grande do Sul: From the Provision of Infrastructure to Strengthening the Self-Management Capacity of the Poor." Paper prepared for meeting of the Latin American Studies Association, Guadalajara, April 17–19.
———. 1998. *Alleviation of Urban Poverty.* Rev. ed. Recife, Brazil: Network of GTZ Consultants on Municipal and Urban Development.
———. 1999. "PRORENDA Upgrading Program: Technical Cooperation Brazil-Germany." Paper presented at the World Bank Scaling up Urban Upgrading in Latin America Workshop, Washington, DC, September 13–17.
MBIA/Capital Advisors, Ltd. 1998. "Demand for Market-Based Financial Services for Progressive Housing and Microenterprise Development on Mexico's Northern Border: Results of a Comprehensive Survey of Low-Income Households in Tijuana, Juárez, and Matamoros." Study report. Washington, DC.
McCommon, Carolyn, Eduardo A. Perez, and Fred Rosensweig. 1998. *Providing Urban Environmental Services for the Poor: Lessons Learned from Three Pilot Projects.* Environmental Health Project, Applied Study No. 7. Washington, DC: U.S. Agency for International Development.
McGranahan, Gordon, Josef Leitmann, and Charles Surjadi. 1997. *Understanding Environmental Problems in Disadvantaged Neighborhoods: Broad Spectrum Surveys, Participatory Appraisal, and Contingent Valuation.* Stockholm: Stockholm Environment Institute. http://www.sei.se/dload/1997/urbanenv3.pdf.
Medellín Municipality. n.d. "PRIMED Fase II." Evaluation report of the PRIMED Program. Medellín, Colombia.
Michelini, Anna. 1997. "Training of Technicians of Local Institutions and Community Employment for the Management of Interventions and of Needs in Informal Settlements." Paper presented at the International Conference on Urban Poverty, Governance and Participation: Practical Approaches to Urban Poverty Reduction—Towards Cities for the New Generations, United Nations Centre for Human Settlements (Habitat), Florence, Italy, November 9–13.
Morley, Samuel. 2001. *The Income Distribution Problem in Latin America and the Caribbean.* Santiago: Economic Commission for Latin American and the Caribbean.
Moser, C. 1996. *Confronting Crisis: Household Responses to Poverty and Vulnerability in Commonwealth, Philippines.* Washington, DC: World Bank.
Mostajo Deheza, René. 1998. "Preface." In Ministry of Sustainable Development and Planning, *Participación Popular, Una Evaluación-Aprendizaje de la Ley, 1994-97.* La Paz: Vice Ministry for People's Participation and Municipal Strengthening.
Murguettio, José. 1997. *Cómo Evaluar la Capacitación y la Asistencia Técnica? Manual Para la Gerencia de Programas de Capacitación y Asistencia Técnica.* Minga Project. Quito: IULA-CELCADEL.
Narayan, Deepa.1993. *Participatory Evaluation: Tools for Managing Change in Water and Sanitation.* Technical Paper No. 207. Washington, DC: World Bank.

Novara, Enrico. 1996. "Providing Services in Brazilian *Favelas*: The AVSI Experience." Paper presented at the World Bank Round Table for the Provision of Services for the Urban Poor in Latin America and the Caribbean, El Salvador, December 11–13.

Oakley, Peter. 1994. "People's Participation in Development: Reviewing the Balance Sheet." Save the Children Working Paper. London.

Ostrom, Elinor. 1996. "Crossing the Great Divide: Coproduction, Synergy, and Development." *World Development* 24(6):1073–87.

Patel, Sheela, and Kalpana Sharma. 1997. "One David and Three Goliaths: A Mumbai Transport Case Study." Paper presented at the International Conference on Urban Poverty, Governance and Participation: Practical Approaches to Urban Poverty Reduction—Towards Cities for the New Generations, United Nations Centre for Human Settlements (Habitat), Florence, Italy, November 9–13.

Paul, Samuel. 1987. *Community Participation in Development Projects: The World Bank Experience*. Discussion Paper No. 6. Washington: World Bank.

Peltenburg, Monique, Forbes Davidson, Hans Teerlink, and Patrick Wakely. 1996. *Building Capacity for Better Cities: Concepts and Strategies*. Rotterdam: Institute for Housing and Urban Development Studies.

Pendakur, V. Setty. 1997. "Urban Poor and Urban Transport: Their Mobility and Access to Transport Services." Paper presented at the International Conference on Urban Poverty, Governance and Participation: Practical Approaches to Urban Poverty Reduction—Towards Cities for the New Generations, United Nations Centre for Human Settlements (Habitat), Florence, Italy, November 9–13.

Pereira, L. C. Bresser. 1997. "Managerial Reform in Brazil's Public Administration." Paper presented at the Political Economy of Administrative Reform in Developing Countries Conference, Northwestern University, Chicago, May 29.

Pérez Coscio, Luis. n.d. *Mejoramiento Habitacional en Argentina: Estrategias de Crédito y Asistencia Técnica para Sectores Populares*. Buenos Aires: El Instituto Internacional de Medio Ambiente y Desarrollo- América Latina, El Programa de fortalecimiento Institucional y Capacitación de Organizaciones No Gubernamentales.

Peterson, George, G. Thomas Kingsley, and Jeffrey P. Telgarsky. 1994. *Multi Sectorial Investment Planning*. UMP Working Paper Series 3. Nairobi: Urban Management Programme.

Prates Coelho, M. 1996. "Urban Governance in Brazil." In Patricia L. McCarney, *Cities and Governance: New Directions in Latin America, Asia, and Africa*. Toronto: University of Toronto, Centre for Urban and Community Studies.

Prefeitura do Município de São Paulo (PMSP). 1992. *Censo das Favelas do Município de São Paulo*. São Paulo.

Prefeitura do Município de São Paulo, Secretaria de Habitação e Desenvolvimento Urbano. 1994. *Fundo Municipal de Habitação e Conselho Municipal de Habitação*. São Paulo.

———. 1995. *A Política Setorial do Governo Municipal para a Habitação*. São Paulo.

Prefeitura do Município de São Paulo e Diagonal Urbana Consultants Inc. 1998. *Monitoramento Pesquisa Sócio-Econômica – Relatório Executivo*. Secretaria da Habitação e Desenvolvimento Urbano. Cingapura Project. São Paulo.

Programa de Desarrollo Local (PRODEL). 1996. "Decentralization and Urban Poverty Reduction in Nicaragua: The Experience of the Local Development Program." Paper presented at the World Bank Round Table for the Provision of Services for the Urban Poor in Latin America and the Caribbean, El Salvador, December 11–13.

Ravallion, Martin, and Quentin Wodon. 1998. *Poor Areas, or Only Poor People?* Washington, DC: World Bank.

Reitbergen-McCracken, J., ed. 1996. *Participation in Practice: The Experience of the World Bank and Other Stakeholders.* Discussion Paper No. 333. Washington, DC: World Bank.

Riofrío, Gustavo. 1996. *Urban Upgrading with Popular Participation.* Eischborn, Germany: Gesellschaft für Technische Zusammenarbeit.

Riofrío, Gustavo, and J. C. Driant. 1987. *Que Vivienda Han Construido? Nuevos Problemas en Viejas Barriadas.* Lima: Cidap and Tarea.

Rodriguez, A., and L. Winchester. 1996. "The Challenges for Urban Governance in Latin America: Reinventing the Government of Cities." In Patricia L. McCarney, *Cities and Governance: New Directions in Latin America, Asia, and Africa.* Toronto: University of Toronto, Centre for Urban and Community Studies.

Rodríguez, Alfredo, and Velázquez, Fabio. 1994. *Municipio y Servicios Publicos: Gobernos locales en ciudades intermedias de América Latina.* Santiago: Ediciones SUR.

Rolnik, Raquel. 1999. *Territorial Exclusion and Violence: The Case of São Paulo, Brazil.* Comparative Urban Studies Occasional Papers No. 26. Washington, DC: Woodrow Wilson International Center for Scholars.

Rosell, Patrick, Ousmane Blondin Diop, Martine Blatin, and Marie-France Fabre. 1996. *Évaluation du Projet D'Appui a la Décentralisation et au Développement Urbain au Sénégal (PADDUS).* Paris: Ministère de la Coopération.

Salmen, Lawrence F. 1993. *Beneficiary Assessment: An Approach Described.* Environmentally Sustainable Development Paper No. 023. Washington, DC: World Bank.

Schmidt, Mary. 1996. "Popular Participation and the World Bank: Lessons from Forty-Eight Case Studies." In J. Rietbergen-McCracken, ed., *Participation in Practice: The Experience of the World Bank and Other Stakeholders*, pp. 21–25. Discussion Paper No. 333. Washington, DC: World Bank.

Schuebeler, Peter. 1996. *Participation and Partnership in Urban Infrastructure Management.* Washington, DC: World Bank.

Schulte-Sasse, Josef. 1998. *Poverty Alleviation Strategies – Service Provision to the Poor. Water, Sanitation and Shelter.* Mexico City: Operational Center for Housing and Urban Settlements.

Secretaria Municipal de Habitação. 1999. *Cidade Inteira: A Política Habitacional da Cidade do Rio de Janeiro.* Rio de Janeiro: Prefeitura da Cidade do Rio de Janeiro.

Sekles, Flávia. 2000. "From Favelados to Citizens." *Urban Age* Winter:34–36.

Serageldin, Ismail. 1994. *Water Supply, Sanitation, and Environmental Sustainability: The Financing Challenge.* Washington, DC: World Bank.

Serra, Teresa. 1999. "El Reacomodo de Poblaciones en Proyectos de Mejoramiento de Barrios." Paper presented at the World Bank Scaling up Urban Upgrading in Latin America Workshop, Washington, DC, September 13–17.

Silva, Ricardo Toledo, Nelson Luiz Rodrigues Nucci, and Alex Kenya Abiko. 1995. "Latin America: The Situation in Brazil and the Impact of Peri-Urban Development Technically, Financially, and Socially." Paper presented at the 20th International Water Supply Congress, Water Supply: The Essential Service—Working for Excellence, Durban, September 13.

Skinner, Reinhard J., John L. Taylor, and Emiel A. Wegelin. 1987. *Shelter Upgrading for the Urban Poor: Evaluation of Third World Experience*. Manila: Island Publishing House, Inc.

Sola, L. 1997. "Riforme Politiche, Rielezione e Riforme Economiche." *America Latina* 4(8).

Solo, Tova Maria. 1999. "Small-Scale Entrepreneurs in the Urban Water and Sanitation Market." *Environment and Urbanization* 11(1):117–32.

Solo, Tova Maria, with Carmen Arevalo, Luis Brusco, Peter Loach, Juan Nunura, and Fernando Troyano. 1998. "The Other Private Participation in Water and Sanitation: Tales of Small Independent Providers in Latin American Cities." Research report. Washington, DC: World Bank.

Sow, Seydou Nourou. 1997. "Local Initiatives, Community Development, and the Struggle against Poverty in the Urban Milieu: The Yeumbeul Example (Senegal)." Paper presented at the International Conference on Urban Poverty, Governance and Participation: Practical Approaches to Urban Poverty Reduction—Towards Cities for the New Generations, United Nations Centre for Human Settlements (Habitat), Florence, Italy, November 9–13.

Tayler, Kevin. 1998. *Infrastructure Upgrading in Pakistan: Lessons from Experience and Directions for the Future*. London: GHK Research and Training. http://www.ghkint.com/pub_pub7.htm.

Tipple, Graham A. 1997. "Housing Is Good for Employment." Paper presented at the International Conference on Urban Poverty, Governance and Participation: Practical Approaches to Urban Poverty Reduction—Towards Cities for the New Generations, United Nations Centre for Human Settlements (Habitat), Florence, Italy, November 9–13.

Turner, John F.C., and R. Fichter. 1972. *Freedom to Build: Dweller Control of the Housing Process*. New York: Macmillan.

United Nations Centre for Human Settlements (Habitat). 1996a. *Centroamérica Construyendo las ciudades de Cara al Siglo XXI*. San José: Resource Center for Sustainable Development of Human Settlements in Central America.

———. 1996b. "Squatter-Free Urban Development?" Report of a panel discussion on the possibility and sustainability of squatter-free urban development, Habitat II, the Second United Nations Conference on Human Settlements, Istanbul.

United Nations Centre for Human Settlements (Habitat) and Together Foundation. 2002. "Best Practices for Human Settlements." http://www.bestpractices.org/.

United Nations Development Programme (UNDP). 2000. *Human Development Report*. New York.

———. 2002. *Human Development Report*. New York

"Urban Entrepreneurs and the 'Real Economy.'" *Urban Age* 1(2).

Urban Management Programme (UMP). 1994. "Options for Urban Poverty Alleviation Actions at Municipal Level." Draft research report. Nairobi.

Urban Partnership and the TWU Urban Division. 1998. *The Urban Dialogues: Learning Events Summary Notes*. Washington, DC: World Bank.

Wegelin, Emiel A. 1996. "Options for Municipal Interventions in Urban Poverty Reduction." *Habitat Debate* 2(2).

Werna, Edmundo. 1997. "Shelter, Employment and the Informal City in the Context of the Present Economic Scene: Implications for Participatory Governance." Paper presented at the International Conference on Urban Poverty, Governance and Participation: Practical Approaches to Urban Poverty Reduction—Towards Cities for the New Generations, United Nations Centre for Human Settlements (Habitat), Florence, Italy, November 9–13.

World Bank. 1994. *The World Bank and Participation*. Washington, DC.

———. 1996. *The World Bank Participation Sourcebook*. Washington, DC.

———. 1997a. *Brazil – Bahia Municipal Infrastructure Development and Management Project*. Staff Appraisal Report No. 16258. Washington, DC.

———. 1997b. *Toolkit 1: Selecting an Option for Private Sector Participation*. Toolkits for Private Participation in Water and Sanitation. http://www.worldbank.org/html/fpd/water/wstoolkits/Kit1/frame.html

———. 1999. "Serving the Poor: How Can Partnerships Increase Access and Improve Efficiency?" Paper presented at the Water Supply and Sanitation Forum, Washington, DC, April 8–9.

———. 2002. *World Development Report – World Development Indicators*. Washington, DC.

———. n.d. *Autoconstruccion de Obras de Infraestructura de Servicios Publicos con Entrega de Materials: AOISPEM*. Case study prepared by the Universidad del Valle for the World Bank Group Partnerships for Poverty Reduction. Cali, Colombia. http://www1.worldbank.org/ppr/profiles/CaseStudies/69-en.html.

World Bank, Learning and Leadership Center and Operations Policy Department. 1996. *Handbook on Economic Analysis of Investment Operations*. Washington, DC: World Bank.

World Bank and Municipality of La Paz. n.d. "Proyecto de Fortalecimiento Municipal. Plan Participativo del Distrito 4 – San Antonio." Technical report of the Municipal Strengthening Project. La Paz: Instituto de Investigación y Planificación Municipal.

Zolezzi, Mario, and Julio Calderón. 1987. *Vivienda Popular: Autoconstrucción y Lucha por el Agua*. Lima: Desco.